Internship Training
in Professional Psychology

THE SERIES IN CLINICAL AND COMMUNITY PSYCHOLOGY

CONSULTING EDITORS

Charles D. Spielberger and Irwin G. Sarason

IN PREPARATION

Contents

PART TWO: SELECTED READINGS

Preface

This book is about training in professional psychology, including the areas of clinical, counseling, school, clinical child, and health psychology, and emphasizing the internship experience. A panorama is provided on training that is historical, contemporary, and future oriented.

Training in professional psychology has evolved from recommendations and plans developed in a series of conferences, beginning in 1949 and continuing into the July 1987 Graduate Education in Psychology Conference. While the contents of these conferences have been separately addressed and briefly summarized in textbooks, there has been no single reference on training. The training that occurs during internship has been even less well chronicled in the literature and has been reported primarily in journal articles.

This book contains a description of the major academic models and includes the entire process of internship from program selection and application procedures to the specific ingredients of training and future agendas for cost-effective and responsible professional training. In addition, the major published papers relevant to this discussion are reprinted in order to provide a comprehensive information resource. The potential readers of this volume are undergraduate students anticipating careers in professional psychology and graduate students seeking palliatives for anxiety in the form of information that is specific to their task of program selection and application for internship. Moreover, mentors, advisors, department chairs, and program directors of these students will find a desk reference and general referral source providing background information that will be useful in considering specific questions concerning specific internship programs.

We are now at several crossroads in graduate education that pertain to professional identity and modes of practice for the immediate future. This book addresses issues of service delivery and specialization. There are clinicians who equate service delivery with research and clinicians who value practice as an end in itself. Scenarios for training during internship can affect the professional service delivery stance as well as the quality of service. There is an increasing coalescence of clinical and counseling psychology. School psychology is in flux while health and clinical child specialty areas are in the process of establishing separate identities.

In the immediate future there will be more attention to evaluation of training in the form of accreditation mechanisms and intern productivity as well. Cost-effectiveness and funding are present issues that shape a future in which training will become increasingly relevant to professional work. Similarly, a new emphasis on competence is part of an accountability to psychological services consumers. This book is a resource for consideration of mechanisms whereby internships can facilitate competence and foster increased social responsibility and credibility for professional psychology.

Richard H. Dana
W. Theodore May

Acknowledgments

In most publishing ventures, a variety of serendipitous events, persons, and communication networks have facilitative (and sometimes hindering) functions. We can attest to this observation as a result of writing and collating the present volume. This volume would, of course, not have been possible in this form had we not received almost completely painless permission from the authors of articles (previously published or not), which have been reprinted herein.

Appreciation needs to be expressed to some officers and staff of the American Psychological Association—particularly to Ray Fowler, Gary VandenBos, and Adele Schaefer who worked cooperatively in red-tape cutting of financial, legal, and technical aspects concerning the utilization of the reprinted articles originally appearing in APA journals.

The present writers have no special expertise in the areas of education and training of counseling psychologists, school psychologists, and clinical child psychologists. Tom Fagan (School Psychology, Memphis State University) and Burl Gilliland (Counseling Psychology at Memphis State University) read and commented on the developmental history of training and education in their respective fields as well as provided references and background material not previously available to the authors. Honore Hughes (University of Arkansas) graciously examined the section on Clinical Child Psychology. Their contribution has enhanced these respective sections.

There are equally supportive persons, associated with the publishers, who may have taken some chances in the earlier days of the project. Special thanks go to Brenda Brienza and Kate Roach for guiding the project through the pathways of the publication process. The contribution of anonymous reviewers is herewith acknowledged. The changes that were made in response to their early reviews have made this a more comprehensive and better-balanced book. We also express appreciation to Charles Spielberger for his support.

The support of the respective academic departments of the editors must be mentioned as being more than ample as personnel and support services were made available without question. We especially want to acknowledge the typing skills and careful attention to details of style and format on the part of Kim Held and Vona Skaggs. Tom Hoffmann carefully examined the final product from the vantage of a prospective intern and his comments were helpful and appreciated. Lastly, a word of appreciation to the wife of the junior author for often providing conducive contexts for productive work.

Richard H. Dana
W. Theodore May

Part One

Introduction

Chapter 1

Overview

Richard H. Dana
W. Theodore May

INTRODUCTION

As professional psychologists continue to examine their services to society and to envision new roles, responsibilities, and domains for themselves, it is helpful to consider an important segment of professional education in psychology—internship training. Although we have distanced ourselves from Boulder model origins by a proliferation of professional programs, we continue to struggle with the scientist-professional image. We recognize its uniqueness and power as progenitor of an autonomous profession. Simultaneously, it can be acknowledged that some limitations and flawed implementations continue to stimulate controversy as well as to encourage the emergence of new training models.

The internship follows the relative narrowness of the academic years with their emphasis on cognitive learning and knowledge as a panacea for human problems. Interns, however, are not misled when they perceive internship as the significant hands-on experience in their training. In Schneider's (1985) words, the internship is "the genuine article." During this year there is opportunity for transition experiences in a protected and nurturant setting with practitioner role models and clients who engage them in service settings. This is

While this book was in press, a variety of major training conferences were in process that will affect the immediate future of prospective interns and internships, including the National Council of Schools of Professional Psychology described in "Note added in proofs" (page 73), The National Conference on Internship Traning in Psychology, and the National Training Conference on Issues of Graduate Education.

the time for making sense out of the knowledge-skills base as it impacts on the student's own developmental process. The skills become internalized, or second-nature, and a self-confidence emerges that is both personal and psychological. For the first time the student can say, "I am a professional psychologist." Identity-formation is consolidated within a professionalization experience in which ethics are endowed with tangible meaning and interprofessional relationships are formed for the purpose of more effective service-delivery. For these reasons the internship may be considered to be the essential process in the making of a professional psychologist.

This book will describe the entire training process, including both academic and internship experiences as preparation for the world of professional psychology. Our orientation is both scholarly and hortatory. While it is vital to present the descriptive content and historical antecedents of professional psychology in an orderly and organized fashion, it is also of equal cogency to include some of the passion and commitment that characterize the profession.

The descriptive content will include the clinical psychology models of training—Boulder, Vail, and Health—as well as Counseling Psychology, School Psychology, and Clinical Child Psychology as all contribute to an emerging professional psychology or human services psychology. Academic training provides not only a knowledge base and a skills repertoire but implicitly focuses student attention upon attitudes that shape the process of service delivery and identify the recipients of services. Moreover, the opportunity is provided to impart a distinctly psychological orientation, a unique way of thinking about human beings and their problems. This selectively in requirements and experiences typically occurs at a time when personal identity is being developed.

Although the internship training materials are organized around a description of the variety of training settings, details of the selection process and experience from the standpoint of internship settings and prospective interns are also provided. In addition to descriptive information, these materials should contribute to the student decision-making process in applications for internship and subsequent acceptance of an internship.

Supervision models are described in some detail because supervision helps to determine the kind of professional person who will emerge from internship. This learning in supervision, contacts with clients, and from other interns is directly relevant to personal and professional growth. An appreciation of who one is constitutes the self-documentation that permits the intern to become an instrument for effective intervention. Evaluation of internship includes retrospective commentary and criticism by interns of training settings they have experienced and their day-to-day encounters with clients, supervisors, and settings.

A third section presents several issues of professional accountability that are salient now and which will shape the future of training in internship settings. These issues include financing, academia-internship interface, patterns of training, and training models. The design of training settings, quality of training, and attendant costs and benefits for all participants are some future issues which emerge from this discussion.

Internship programs and the professional phenomenon of internship have dimensions of accountability to the profession and to society. These patterns of professional and public accountability will be emphasized. Moreover, the entire training process as evidenced by the models used to design the content of academic programs and the greater permeability of internship programs to social and economic conditions will be discussed.

A unique feature of this book is the blend of introductory materials described above with a selection of readings. These readings provide much of the data and background detail for the text. They suggest the excitement and complexity of preparation in graduate school academic programs, some of the flavor and ingredients of the internship process, and some consequences of the internship experience. These readings describe the academic preparation, the selection process as experienced and carried out by interns and internships, the kinds of experiences and supervision quality provided by internships, the evaluation of internship training, and some future directions. The blend of readings and text materials will provide a contemporary overview of internship training per se as well as some of the larger professional and societal contexts that will continue to shape the decisions of specific training programs and the content of their training procedures.

Numerous books and chapters on graduate education in professional psychology are available. However, any comparable comprehensive literature for internship training has been neglected. While relevant areas of knowledge and concern have been well documented in the existing literature (e.g., supervision), and more has been written about internship training in recent years (e.g., such journals as *Professional Psychology: Research and Practice*), no published work integrating the various aspects of the internship experience with one another as well as with the academic preparation prior to that training period presently exists. It is the purpose of this book to address that need.

This book speaks to several sets of contiguous audiences. The content and the readings should be of value to prospective graduate students (who may presently still be undergraduates), to graduate students planning for their internships and/or postdoctoral training, to graduate psychology faculty, to clinical supervisors and administrators of internship programs, and to nonprofessional psychologists in need of perspective on their own training endeavors.

ACADEMIC TRAINING

Training for professional psychology has undergone a transformation in the decades since the Shakow report (APA, 1947) formulated training recommendations for clinical psychology. This transformation has included the emergence of several distinct specializations each with a unique academic history. Clinical psychology has a dual identification with a Boulder model scientist-professional (Raimy, 1950) as well as with a Vail model practitioner (Korman, 1976). Counseling and school psychology have also developed separate professional identities that formalize their unique foci of interest but also overlap considerably with clinical psychology, especially in shared skills and common internships experiences (Goldschmitt, Tipton, & Wiggins, 1981; Rosenfeld, Shimberg, & Thornton, 1983). Health psychology is currently in process of forging an identity and developing guidelines for training programs (Matarazzo, 1983). Clinical child psychology has even more recently entered the professional arena (Tuma, 1986).

The nature of the training process has altered from provision for generic skills to an accumulation of specific skills in both assessment and intervention. A didactic knowledge base is gradually being supplemented by a training criterion of competence in specific skills. The variety of services in the community have changed over time as a result of *new* problems, *new* populations, and *new* service-delivery settings. New problems are reflected in the DSM-III and DSM-III-R nomenclature changes that differentiate more fully among psychotic processes, denote higher frequencies of personality disorders, fewer neurotic conditions, and more reactions to environmental stressors. Client populations served now include more minorities and poor persons as well as medical patients and some of the general public who present nonpsychiatric problems. Service delivery settings have expanded from psychiatric institutions and psychological clinics to include community mental health centers, general medical hospitals, community agencies, and a variety of private practice models.

Such major alterations in academic preparation, demands for specific services, and enlargement of the populations served require complex and continuous accommodation by internship settings. Historically, there has been an uneasy progression from academia to internship characterized by a relatively poor fit between the skill ingredients of the prospective intern and the prevailing conception of clinical practice (Dana, Gilliam, & Dana, 1976; Rice & Gurman, 1973; Shemberg & Leventhal, 1981). The internship is responsive to service needs in the variety of potential patient populations and service-delivery settings.

University-based training will be examined at the onset including training models and the separate professional areas of clinical, clinical child, counseling, school, and health psychology as they provide preparation for a professional internship.

Clinical Psychology

Boulder Model While scattered training facilities for clinical psychology had existed prior to 1946, the formal origins of clinical psychology are dated from the period 1947-1949. Social pressures for increased human services followed World War II, particularly within the Veterans Administration hospital system. These hospitals were responsible for treating the personal anguish called psychopathology that coincided with dislocation, prolonged separation, and stress of war. Simultaneously, psychology departments began to offer training in clinical psychology. A committee on training of the American Psychological Association produced a recommended graduate training program in clinical psychology, the Shakow report (APA, 1947). A 1949 conference on graduate education included the Shakow report, but consolidated and amplified these original recommendations into the document that became known as the Boulder Conference Report (Raimy, 1950).

The Boulder model was an educational experiment designed to blend the theoretical, applied, and research aspects of clinical psychology into a single training program. The training goal was a scientist-professional with "the combination of the skilled acquisition of reality-based psychological under-standing and the attitude of constant inquiry toward this knowledge" (Shakow, 1976, p. 554). Clinical psychology was the only profession that purported to combine research and applied aspects of training.

The 1947 Shakow report began with the following list of personal qualities for potential clinical psychologists that was incorporated into the Boulder model:

1 Superior intellectual ability and judgment.
2 Originality, resourcefulness, and versatility.
3 "Fresh and insatiable" curiosity; "self-learner."
4 Interest in persons as individuals rather than as material for manipulation—a regard for the integrity of the other person.
5 Insight into own personality characteristics; sense of humor.
6 Sensitivity to the complexities of motivation.
7 Tolerance; "unarrogance."
8 Ability to adopt a "therapeutic" attitude; ability to establish warm and effective relationships with others.
9 Industry; methodical work habits; ability to tolerate pressure.
10 Acceptance of responsibility.
11 Tact and cooperativeness.
12 Integrity, self-control, and stability.
13 Discriminating sense of ethical values.
14 Breadth of cultural background—"educated man."
15 Deep interest in psychology, especially in its clinical aspects (Raimy, 1950, p. 212-213).

A clinical psychologist was defined as a person with a Ph.D. resulting from a four-year combination of academic and clinical training plus an internship. The concern was to train a psychologist first and practicing clinician second by an integration of theory and practice. Basic principles and core courses taken by all psychology students were stressed. Continuous contact with psychopathological content as well as experience with normal or nonpsychopathological content was specified. A shared training experience with related disciplines was envisioned. Research implications were foreseen as a mandatory component of training.

Graduate education was to include general psychology (systematic, experimental, social psychology), clinical psychology, (theory, method, technique), field work (variety in problems and levels of responsibility), and research. Research was emphasized as a basis for understanding human behavior, improving diagnostic techniques, developing treatment methods, and ultimately focusing upon prevention or mental hygiene. Twelve areas of clinical core content were proposed: human physiology; personality theory; developmental psychology (biological, social, cultural determinants); social relations (social psychology, sociology, economics, anthropology); psychopathology; personality appraisal; clinical medicine and clinical psychiatry (medical model); psychotherapy and remedial procedures; clinical research methodology; professional and interprofessional relationships; community resources and organizations; practicum and internship experiences.

Training in clinical methods was to be exclusively for graduate students. General knowledge was needed in order to permit critical selectiveness among methods and for demonstrable proficiency within each of the following general clinical method categories:

1 observation (participant observation).
2 interviewing (standardized and unstructured approaches).
3 administration and interpretation of objective diagnostic tests (ability, achievement, interest, special function, deficit).
4 projective techniques.
5 methods of case integration for treatment and research.
6 therapeutic and remedial procedures.
7 research techniques (for data from clinical procedures).

Research training emphasized the completion of a Ph.D. dissertation. Specific clinical psychology research skills should include analysis of clinical phenomena in order to generate useful concepts, careful definition of concepts for use in staff meetings and clinical reports, formulation of research problems and design of investigations for personality and clinical issues, competence in statistical analysis of data, and presentations of written research findings.

While psychotherapy training was to be largely postdoctoral, general training in theory and practice was envisioned for all clinical students. It was necessary to have qualified psychotherapy supervisors who were also capable of teaching academic courses at the graduate level. Personal (didactic) psychotherapy was recognized as desirable. Moreover, the training mandate was for self-evaluation throughout the entire graduate experience. A monitoring of the development of psychotherapy skills was required for student self-awareness and recognition of limitations. Collaboration with other professionals in the form of referral and consultation (now known as peer review) was required. Unsupervised psychotherapy practice was not to be permitted. All psychotherapy practice would be done in accord with ethical codes. Research would be conducted on the practices and training procedures themselves.

Field training or practicum experience was recognized at three levels: laboratory experience, clerkships (practica) either on campus or in a community setting, and internships, which were generally further away from campus. The laboratory focus was upon development of skills, or prefield work in order to acquire a "clinical attitude." Integration of academic and clinical content was to be accomplished using a practicum setting in a departmental clinic, with departmental affiliation for field supervisors, using syllabi created for this purpose, and by keeping records of student diagnostic and therapy experience.

The clerkship experiences had several explicit purposes and usually occurred in off-campus settings:

1 Developing a feeling of responsibility for the client and a sensitivity to the clinician-client relationship.

2 Developing of minimal competence in the use of psychological techniques in a clinical setting.

3 Familarization of students with a wider range of techniques.

4 Teaching of the nature and meaning of service.

5 Beginning of integration of university course content with the clinical viewpoint and with procedures in a service setting.

6 Introducing the interdisciplinary approach to clinical problems; learning to cooperate with colleagues of other disciplines.

7 Applying professional ethics.

8 Learning to communicate by the writing of case reports for clinical use.

9 Providing a wide range of clinical contacts at a relatively superficial level through a variety of clerkships (Raimy, 1950, p. 105).

The internship was distinguished from the clerkship by:

1 Supplying *intensive* and long-term clinical experience.

2 Developing a degree of professional competence at a level comparable to that of junior staff members.

3 Providing intimate contact with clinical problems in which the intern's activities have a bearing on the handling and disposition of a case.

4 Developing a responsibility for the management of a case through semiindependent handling of a psychological examination and treatment.

5 Developing confidence in operating in a service setting, particularly in the manner of assuming responsibility.

6 Establishing close working relationships with trainees and staff members of other professions by working intensively as a member of a clinical team; actual practice in the appreciation of the interdisciplinary approach to clinical problems.

7 Intensive training in the techniques of communicating clinical information to colleagues on the clinical team.

8 Imbuing the student with the spirit and values of the field institution.

9 A primary purpose of the internship is to provide a learning experience for the intern in a setting in which he contributes to service because competent and essential provision of service is one of the best contexts in which to learn (Raimy, 1950, pp. 105–106).

Specialization (e.g., age group, psychotherapy) was not recommended, but reserved for the future. There was no specified locus for specialized training—postdoctoral vs. within the doctoral program. Private practice as a professional goal was not encouraged at that time due to the absence of licensing statutes. Subdoctoral training was not specifically considered. Postdoctoral training was envisioned, particularly for psychotherapy but was not then available. A reading knowledge of two foreign languages was originally required.

Table 1 summarizes characteristics of the Boulder model. This table includes admission requirements, length of program, general psychology content, clinical core, organization of training, mode of integrating academic and clinical materials, research tools, and training goals.

The organization of a Boulder model program is predicated on a formal sequence of courses and clinical experiences, beginning with theoretical content and laboratory experience with normal persons and then providing continuous, supervised, and progressively more autonomous experience with emotionally disturbed persons. The integration, or manner of relevantly juxtaposing and interpenetrating didactic and clinical activities, was to employ the training media of a psychological clinic. Field supervisors with departmental appointments would serve to infuse clinical contents and experience in nonuniversity settings with the program. Finally, a formal document, or syllabus describing the fusion of academic content and clinical skill training was to be available. Such a document delineating an ideal fusion could then be compared with each student's record of clinical and academic experiences.

The scientist component of the Boulder model was to be represented by training in statistics (and more recently by computer programming skills) with an emphasis on methodology to describe clinical contents. A thesis (master's degree) and dissertation (doctoral degree) provided vehicles for applying the training in statistics and methodology to clinical problems.

Standards for graduate programs, clerkships, and internship agencies needed

Table 1   1949 Boulder Model Characteristics

Admission	GPA and GRE scores primarily: Academically competitive.
Time	Four academic years.
General psychology	(a) Systematic; (b) experimental; (c) social.
Clinical core	(a) Physiology; (b) personality; (c) developmental; (d) social relations (sociology, economics, anthropology); (e) psychopathology; (f) personality appraisal (participant observation; interviewing, objective and projective tests; case integration); (g) clinical medicine and psychiatry; (h) introductory psychotherapy; (i) clinical research methodology; (j) professional relationships; (k) knowledge of community resources; (l) practicum/internship.
Specialization	Not recommended.
Organization	(a) Continuous contact with psychopathological content; (b) nonpsychopathological content first; (c) supervision with progressively greater responsibility and autonomy.
Integration	(a) Via departmental clinic; (b) via departmental affiliation of field supervisors; (c) via syllabi to describe the manner of integrating academic and clinical content; (d) via records of students' clinical experience.
Research	Statistics. Descriptive emphasis-clinical content.
Training goal	Scientist-professional.

to be established and were provided subsequently by the development of evaluation standards. Site visit procedures leading to possible accreditation by the American Psychological Association resulted in scrutiny of 43 programs in 41 schools and full approval for 20 of these clinical programs (APA, 1949). However, there were 74 approved clinical psychology programs by 1968 (APA, 1968) and 130 approved programs by 1984 (APA, 1984a; APA, 1984b).

Subsequent conferences have evaluated and modified the Boulder model legacy. Wolff (1972) has described the major training models delineated by the various conferences. A progression from orthogonal practice and research components to the Boulder model synthesis was followed by parallel exposure to separate training components. Wolff foresaw a future shift toward reintegration of the research and practice components in more pragmatic terms allowing for greater flexibility in order to make use of specific training settings.

As an example, the impact of the 1965 Chicago conference was investigated by survey comparisons between 1964-1965 and 1968-1969 program activities (Simmons, 1971). Enthusiasm for core courses had diminished, clinical faculty members were more numerous, behavior therapy and community psychology content was available in most programs, and training in psychotherapy was more frequent during the first year. By 1974, Merenda could report an increasing number of programs offering clinical specializations.

Nonetheless, by 1966 Sol Garfield believed that the Boulder model educational experiment had failed to integrate research and practice. Students experienced a split because neither pole was responsibly represented in their training, professors were not good practitioner role models, and much of the required research training was not relevant to clinical or social problems. There were problems of identity and doubts regarding professional self-worth.

A national survey of graduate students and faculty in 1970–1971 (Lipsey, 1974) documented concerns about student dissatisfaction with training. Nearly half of these clinical graduate students were distressed by preoccupation with method in their training. The social concerns leading them to clinical psychology were not being fostered by graduate experience. Psychology appeared to be deficient in relevance to the human condition. Arthur (1972) felt that this dissatisfaction existed because Boulder model programs purveyed an excessively theoretical science with an experimental paradigm unsuited to solution of everyday problems. Strupp (1976) saw a devaluation of clinical experiences and relegation of students to postures of passivity, rote memorization, and eventual professional mediocrity. Frank (1984) argued that insufficient attention to learning research skills, faculty preferences for basic research, clinical supervisors who were poor research role models, and postgraduate expectations for service were responsible for the minimal research activity among clinical psychologists.

Boulder model programs, however, have been responsive to criticisms (Perry, 1979). Clinical and research training are now typically coextensive, all accredited programs have a psychological service center or clinic staffed by faculty members, and the scientist-professional dichotomy has been moderated by program emphasis on either the scientist or professional pole. Clinical psychologists, especially behaviorally-oriented professionals, are increasingly active in research, regardless of the settings in which they practice (Bornstein & Wallersheim, 1978).

David Shakow articulately defended the model that he exercised so much responsibility for creating while George Albee passionately enunciates its obsolescence. Shakow (1976) reiterated training goals of responsibility and resourcefulness. He recognized that these goals are implemented by competent and humane role models as well as by an educational environment that respects student initiative. The Boulder model can function to integrate theory and practice by fostering a progression from personality study to applications in life situations and clinical settings. Method is both research methodology and observation that is objective, subjective, participant, and self-directed. The professional product is a generalist who can sustain lifelong self-education and can practice the profession objectively and the science humanistically. The idealism of these objectives is in contrast to a belief in professional reactivity to "convulsive changes" (Wertheimer et al. 1978).

George Albee (1970) does not believe that the Boulder model has been effective for training clinical psychologists. Incompatibilities between clinical psychology and psychology and between clinical psychology and psychiatry are responsible. Clinical psychology adopted inappropriate models of science and sickness. A setting-specific narrowness with predominantly middle-class values resulted in pathologization of clients and a studied ignorance of the major psychological problems that plague society—racism, sexism, and economic manipulation/exploitation. Moreover, fundamental differences between scientist and professional were seen as vitiating Boulder model ideology by forcing a poor fit in both directions for students. These differences include openness, mutual criticism versus privacy, the coerced role play of the science game with its attendant self-criticism, available and germane research methods which are vulnerable to deprecation, and advocacy for lobbying and social action. Students, therefore, found that their values were violated by graduate education with the result that commitment to both research and practice components in training are diluted and replaced by faithful but uncritical task orientations. Albee indicated that the seriousness of these differences required separation between the science and the profession of psychology and establishment of two American Psychological Associations.

Several future paths were envisioned as available for clinical psychology. The science-professional model could continue to be a traditional training pattern, although Albee did not believe that this training model would survive. Separate professional programs/schools constituted a second avenue. It would be possible to train more persons and employ community professionals motivated toward service careers as supervisors and instructors. A new major alliance with another profession that owns training facilities was a third option. Medicine, social work, and education become potential homes for professional training programs. In fact, only the alliance with medicine has persevered, first in behavioral medicine and more recently in health psychology, clinical child psychology and pediatric psychology. A fourth possibility involved abandonment of clinical psychology as a separate area. Psychology could then have become a basic science for other professions. In this paper, George Albee predicted some of the changes that actually would occur in the structure of professional psychology training and practice.

By 1982, Albee believed that recent clinical psychology practice had narrowed and become equated with psychotherapy. Training a large number of psychologist-psychotherapist practitioners will not improve the level of mental health of the public. A practice model of one-to-one service reinforces the health-illness model used to explain psychopathology. The growing shortage of psychiatrists and increasing third party psychotherapy reimbursement eligibility for psychologists working with personal problems of an educated middle-class have been responsible for this narrowing of practice. The flow of human resources towards psychotherapeutic practice has also encouraged the development of professional schools of psychology.

According to Albee, the future holds professionalism and self-interest guild orientations among practitioners. An individual therapy model will leave unserved those who are most seriously in need. The poor, elderly, minority groups, children, adolescents, and unemployed, may have high rates of emotional distress, but these populations do not generally seek or receive psychotherapy. By accepting a medical model, psychology has identified with a traditional illness model and runs the risk of forgetting or ignoring primary prevention of psychopathology. Albee (1986) has continued to assert that prevention means social change and political action leading to a more equitable and just society. Although presently quite limited in scope and number and not necessarily in agreement with the goals and values of Albee's position, internships with a community/prevention orientation could offer a future alternative to medical model oriented clinical psychology internships.

Vail Model   For all of the strengths of the Boulder model, implementation within traditional psychology departments meant that the needs and interests of experimental faculty who typically controlled departmental politics and policies were given priority. The scientist side of the scientist-professional training ideal received disproportionate attention. Increasing dissatisfaction from students, clinical psychologists, minority group persons, and women who felt that their needs and society's needs were not being served adequately culminated in the 1973 Vail Conference. The overriding concern of this conference was:

> that psychology with its keen research tradition and vaunted sense of social responsibility has consistently avoided setting in motion a definitive analysis of the *training/competency/task/delivery* paradigm as it related to psychological services. . . (Korman, 1976, p. vii).

More specifically, Korman documented four interrelated components of this refusal to analyze what was available and what was needed in the arenas of training and services. First, there had been meager research products from Boulder model research training. Since 10% of psychologists had generated the major portion of scientific information with the modal number of publications from clinical psychologists being zero, an exclusive scientist-professional training model was ill-advised. The majority of persons who had experienced Boulder model training were not doing research.

Second, there was an absence of recognition or status for subdoctoral persons and hence of adequate training at the subdoctoral level. Persons with master's degrees were accorded second-class professional status, while continuing to provide the larger part of psychological services. For example, there were 20,000 students completing graduate work in clinical psychology between 1957 and 1966. Of these students 60% obtained master's degrees and subsequently performed professional psychological work. In addition, the number of doctoral degrees relative to master's degrees had been steadily declining over time. The issue of the place of master's level training was evaded. In Schofield's words: "Respectability is being valued over responsibility" (1969, p. 579). The implication was that identification as a professional by means of the Ph.D. degree and the title "Doctor" had displaced concerns with quality and extent of service delivery in a democratic society.

Third, curricular revision within academic psychology was generally the outcome of administrative-political compromise rather than genuine response to altered social conditions calling for new services, the availability of more satisfactory technologies, or novel service delivery. Korman expresses this matter cogently (1976):

> ... there is no science of curriculum making that will help psychology... We have insufficient knowledge of our means-end relations in the learning process; we have insufficient control of the relevant variables in the classroom or in the curriculum; we have insufficient understanding of the complex interaction effects among student characteristics, teacher characteristics, and the subject-matter content (p. 8).

Finally, there is the "professionalism" necessary for professional identity and survival of the profession. Professionalism is a set of characteristics that compose a profession including the need for special services, an organized body of knowledge, an organization of persons with that knowledge and dedicated to using it, control of recruits, ethical codes, subspecialties, and legal recognition (Moore, 1970). Every profession provides indoctrination by standardized training procedures, peer sanctions, and career continuity in order to substantiate the professional image and to perpetuate a unique identity. Clinical psychology has experienced some discomfort in becoming a profession as a result of excluding subdoctoral professional persons, by retaining ties to a training model of unproved adequacy for *all* training purposes, and lacking sufficient motivation or interest to evaluate that model.

Ten areas of relevance composed the format for the Vail Conference and were discussed by task groups of psychologists who were *not* representative of the establishment, especially minority group members, and women, as well as other interested persons. These areas included the contents of training programs at different levels (bachelor and below, master's, doctoral, postdoctoral, and continuing education), human resources (including the training of women and minority groups), the training settings themselves, evaluation of training as well as service delivery models, and legal-administrative issues.

Table 2 organizes the major contents of the Vail model as abstracted from the recommendations of the conference task groups (Korman, 1976). This table includes admission requirements, general psychology and other course areas, clinical core, specialization, organization, integration via interface of academic and applied settings, research, and training goals.

A major result of the Vail Conference was to focus attention on the institu-

Table 2   1973 Vail Model Characteristics

Admission	Central application procedure, encourage part-time students; provision for career lattice. Concern with personal history of helping skills; employment, and volunteer activities as well as more formal academic criteria.
Time	Separate but coordinated AA, BA, master's doctoral (PsyD) and continuing education for professional development.
General psychology	Development and child
Other course areas	Contemporary social problems. Multicultural and ethnic perspective: Values and lifestyles of culturally diverse groups, including women, children, elderly, minorities.
Clinical core	Basic skills plus program development, administration, evaluation. Field research. Design and evaluation of new service delivery system. Supervision and training. Training in accountability to recipients of services, employers, peers, other professions, and the public. Formal and field education in nature of systems, how systems affect individuals, and how to produce system change.
Specialization	Required.
Organization	Student participation in design of own program. More practicum experience in diverse/novel settings, particularly those without psychiatrists, and with underserved populations. Exchange of faculty/staff across training and service settings. Utilization of non-university persons and faculty from other universities as experts in dissertation area.
Integration	Faculty include more persons with diverse origins and professionals in applied settings. Continuous self-study of program (as well as independent evaluation for accreditation). Evaluation of graduates during their professional careers. Feedback of all evaluation materials to program. Advocacy roles.
Research	Dissertation relevant to professional role or evaluation of professional interventions.
Training goal	Professional person with specialized skills, responsive to social issues and serving broad population base. Participation in Human Services Center.

tionalization of clinical psychology training within academic settings. A single focus for training renders it difficult to envision and implement different kinds of training for a variety of students in a wide spectrum of services for particular populations. It was concluded that professional programs should be developed in many different settings including medical schools, colleges of education, free-standing schools of professional psychology, and autonomous professional schools in academic settings. Issues of training continuity, competence evaluation, and representation of cultural diversity in selection, training, and services continued to be argued.

Admission requirements and practices would be altered away from exclusive preoccupation with doctoral training. Training would encompass a career lattice beginning with an Associate of Arts (AA), two-year college or junior college degree and extending through the master's (MS or MA) and doctoral degrees (Ph.D. or Psy.D.). A lattice refers not only to increasing competence in skills with more training but to an increasing diversity of professional skills as well. Admission for any level of desired training would be determined by both academic and nonacademic qualifications. Nonacademic qualifications would include "socially relevant experiences" to enable admission of a greater number of "nontraditional" students, especially those from culturally diverse backgrounds who had been historically underrepresented.

While a background in psychology courses is necessary, the Vail model does not specify courses except for Child or Developmental. Instead, there should be background in social problems and cultural matters pertaining to the identity and lifestyles of nonwhite, nonmiddle-class persons. Sociology and anthropology training are thus desirable. Finally, investment in values that result in an advocacy position suggests a role for commitment and personal involvement in matters of public concern.

The Vail model recognizes that traditional clinical skills are prerequisite to specialty training. Specialized skills include an understanding of the workings of programs and clinical or field research. Training and/or supervising others is also a necessary skill component of a lattice system. Accountability requires that whatever the professional person does is open to scrutiny by peers, clients, and ultimately the general public. Training in accountability as a clinical skill implies an openness in the training setting to observation of faculty clinical skills and to sharing of clinical activities by faculty and students. Thus, "being accountable" is an attitude about oneself and requires a clear-eyed stance regarding one's own abilities and limitations. Being accountable, however, goes beyond responsibility for one's own professional activities and implies responsivity to the larger society. Understanding of the nature of social systems, their differential impact on persons, and the technology of intervention and change in social systems thus becomes a clinical skill. Social system intervention is the skill component of the advocacy role.

The organization of a Vail model professional program reflects an extended range of skills and variety of clients served. In order to provide such services there is need for greater student self-determination (i.e., increased responsibility for their own programs, earlier professional accountability, participation in program evaluation) and more practical experience in novel settings with other professionals and nonprofessionals. The proposed professional program mirrors the demands of the professional world more closely than typical Boulder model programs. For this reason it has been easier for Vail-type programs to develop in settings that are either autonomous, or at least physically and fiscally separate from the academic politics of colleges of Arts and Sciences.

While "integration" in describing the Boulder model (Table 1) referred to an integration of scientist and practitioner training, within the Vail model it suggests that greater interpenetration between training and practice can be achieved. Organization and integration in a Vail model program may be two sides of the same coin—a training program that is faithful to the changing needs of society in the skills offered and the settings in which training occurs. The emphasis on self-directed change and development of the training program parallels what is expected of the individual student.

The Vail Conference provided consensual endorsement for proposed changes in professional training while the subsequent Virginia Beach conference provided details for implementation of this practitioner model (Caddy, 1982). Entrance requirements, performance assessment, curriculum development, practicum programming, and institutional locus were included topics (Watson, Caddy, Johnson, & Rimm, 1981). Following the Virginia Beach conference, the increase in professional training was justified by reference to national mental health care needs, primary health care needs, and interest by students and professionals in practitioner training (Marwit, 1982). By 1982 there were 4,992 students enrolled in 44 practitioner programs (Caddy & LaPointe, 1986). Thirty-six of these programs graduated 320 persons in 1979 (Caddy, 1981), and only 14 of these programs had APA approval status (APA, 1983; APA, 1984a). However, these programs have enrolled 50% of those pursuing doctoral degrees in clinical psychology (Fox, Kovacs & Graham, 1985). The proliferation of professional programs—29 in California alone (California State Psychologist, 1984)—produced an invited interaction between concerned psychologists and proponents of a practitioner training model (Polansky et al., 1979) as well as recent explication of the Vail Model (McConnell, 1984).

Health Model Matarazzo (1982) has provided a consensual definition of health psychology:

> Health psychology is the aggregate of the specific education, scientific, and professional contributions of the discipline of psychology to the promotion and maintenance of health, the prevention and treatment of illness, the identification of etiologic and diagnostic correlates of health, illness, and related dysfunction, and to the analysis and improvement of the health care system and health policy information (p. 4).

Health psychology is a new emergent that employs the empirical research basis of medical psychology and behavioral medicine. The locus of practice is with medical patients, but it is anticipated that interventions for ineffective lifestyles and "bad" habits will extend this locus to the general population.

There are four striking similarities between the climate of readiness for a new (renewed) profession during the late 1940s and the middle 1980s. Some common ingredients are demonstrated need, an available support base, the presence of a few academic training programs, and a national conference.

After World War II there was a need to provide psychiatric services for veterans who were making the transition to civilian life. Now there is need for an extended range of health care services for medical patients and ultimately for prevention of illness in the general population. As a result of the shift in thinking away from single-cause, single-effect (medical model) toward multicategory, multicause, multieffect (biopsychosocial model) explanations, the complexity of the service delivery paradigm has altered dramatically.

In addition to intervention for psychiatric symptoms which complicate medical care, it is recognized that medical patients need adequate motivation for treatment and self-care. Reduction of anxiety/tension may be accomplished using contingency programs or cognitive therapy. Compliance by patients with medical regimens often requires help in the form of structure, support, and encouragement. Alleviation of stress and enhancement of coping behaviors is relevant to pain management and reduction of post operative shock. Moderator variables that inhibit specific physical illnesses require identification as well as training programs to maximize lifestyles that foster such intervening conditions between stress and illness. Promotion of health-maintenance behaviors to permit weight control and reduce reliance on tobacco, alcohol, and drugs also contributes to prevention of physical illnesses and mortality. These new services by professional psychologies to medical patients are part of a biopsychosocial orientation to physical illness. Moreover, the need for prevention of illness within the general population has created a legion of research-based interventions.

Belar, Wilson, and Hughes (1982) have surveyed all 1980–1981 graduate psychology programs and located 38 institutions that offer some training in health psychology. Six institutions had programs with a major focus on health psychology. Matarazzo (1983) has described these programs in detail. By 1984, however, Altmaier reported that approximately 40% of counseling psychology training programs were also offering relevant course work and nearly 60% had practicum experience, internship, or employment in health-service settings.

In the late 1940s federal support was made available for training programs. The Veterans Administration Training Program in Clinical Psychology was responsible for funding the first generation of students in Boulder model programs. The support base is now more local although federal funds for research conducted in medical schools on psychological aspects of physical illnesses continue to be available and will be used for student research stipends and assistantships. The National Working Conference on Education and Training for Health Psychology was held in May 1983 (Weiss, 1983). Conference summaries have appeared in *Health Psychology* (Stone, 1983) and in the *American Psychologist* (Olbrisch, Weiss, Stone, & Schwartz, 1985). The format is thus similar to the earlier Boulder and Vail conferences.

This conference considered the doctoral degree to be the entry level for professional health psychology practice. Core training in psychology was recognized as essential with practicum/clerkship experience and a one-year internship in a professional health psychology setting. A model of apprenticeship opportunities in all training settings was advocated. Research training and professional training at the postdoctoral level was endorsed. A two-year post-doctoral residency for health service providers would follow completion of the health psychology doctoral program. Specialized training in health policy and the health care system would include public health, epidemiology, prevention, biostatistics, and ethical and legal issues in health policy. Continuing education and competency-based approaches to evaluation under the aegis of the American Psychological Association were deemed mandatory. The Health Psychology Division of the American Psychological Association (Division 38) will assume responsibility for implementation and there is a Council of Directors of Health Psychology Training Programs and an American Board of Health Psychology that plans to develop procedures leading to a recognized diplomate in health psychology. These plans indicate the belief of the working conference partici-pants that health psychology has achieved an independent professional status.

As one avenue toward implementation of a health psychology model, Fox (1982) describes an emerging need for services to new consumers who wish to alter personal health habits and/or lifestyles. However, a majority of the approximately 35,000 licensed health care providers in psychology are still providing services only to the mentally ill. In order to remedy this dilemma, Fox proposes that professional education contain training and inter-actions with a variety of health specialists leading eventually to group practices. Role modeling for these new services is mandatory, although not generally available because psychologists do not often have autonomy in hospital settings. Finally, the development of new services for new consumers and new services for old consumers such as hospital-community transitions is also necessary.

Central to the need for new services is a locus for the delivery of these indigenous psychological services. A comprehensive psychological service center would be able to provide in-house residential care, certain transition services, crisis care, substance misuse programs, and psychosocial approaches to pain and treatment-compliance. Faculty private practice groups can combine service and training within one setting that provides brief, effective intervention for problems thoughout the lifespan.

Counseling Psychology

Norman Kagan (1977) has described counseling psychology as without viable history or clear cut lineage but presenting a *potpourri* of interests. Vocational guidance began as a philanthropic movement and social agencies provided information and orientation services. Psychometricians soon began to argue for a test-based practice (e.g., Hull, 1928). The depression of the 1930s emphasized job-placement while the beginnings of Rogerian psychotherapy and the study of personality development provided additional impetus for a counseling profession. However, the job title—counseling psychologist—did not emerge until 1951 (Super, 1955). Counseling psychologists have always been distinguished by a professional focus on normal behavior in a variety of work settings.

The 1964 Greyston Conference conducted by representatives of most of the APA-approved counseling programs envisioned two levels of training within psychology departments, a two-year master's program and a professional doctoral degree that encompassed research, practice, and service. Brayfield had reported a 1963 consensus in training areas for professional practice with normal persons that included life span, strengths/assets, cognitive activities/ decision-making, and situational factors/environmental modification. In 1968, three primary roles for counseling psychology were delineated: remedial/rehabilitative, preventive, and education/developmental (Jordaan, Myers, Layton, & Morgan, 1968). While these roles were still evident in 1976, Ivy believed that the educational/developmental role was salient although this role was no longer counseling per se but psychoeducation! However, in spite of some unique counseling areas—personnel psychology, vocational/occupational psychology, occupational counseling, and human engineering psychology—by 1960 there was little differentiation from clinical programs (Patterson & Lofquist, 1960) and a substantial minority of the APA Divison of Counseling Psychology (Division 17) members were identified with clinical psychology. As recent evidence for this overlap, counseling psychology interns have been evaluated favorably by internships across a broad range of professional activities with the exception of neurological assessment and projective assessment (Tipton, 1983a).

Kagan (1977) reports that doctoral level APA-approved training in counseling psychology now includes a general psychology core (i.e., biological, cognitive/affective, and social bases of behavior, individual differences), method (i.e., statistics, psychometrics), supervised practicum, internship, field/laboratory training, plus specialization. Counseling psychologists are seen as "mental health primary care workers."

While internships for clinical and counseling psychology are not separated in the Association of Psychology Internships Centers (APIC) and American Psychologist annual listings, it is generally accepted practice that programs training both specialties should have appropriate experiences and role models for both specialties. As of the end of 1984, there were 256 fully approved internships, 19 on provisional status, 2 on probation (APA, 1984d), and 105 listed, nonapproved (APIC, 1985-86). There were 209 listed, APA-approved and 83 nonapproved internships that will consider applicants from approved counseling psychology programs and 81 approved and 70 nonapproved internships that will consider applicants from nonapproved counseling programs (APIC, 1985). Currently, there are 41 counseling programs that have approved or provisionally approved status (APA, 1984d). By extrapolation from 1980 data (APA, 1981a), there were 275 doctoral degrees from approved counseling programs for that year. Presumably these students could have occupied approximately 14 percent of the estimated 1700 available internships.

Counseling psychologists originally practiced with normal, school-aged persons. However, between 1964 and 1980 the percentages of counseling psychologists working with this population in educational settings declined from 64 percent to 38 percent while health care services, primarily in community mental health centers, claimed another 38 percent by 1980 (Banikotes, 1980; Stapp et al., 1981). The cornucopia of intervention modes and the ever-widening potential audiences for these services have transformed counseling psychologists into specialists with segmented identities (Aubrey, 1977). However, the Council of Counseling Psychology Training Programs (CCTP) has recently adopted the stricter APA policy statement regarding criteria for designating psychology training programs. This has led to a reduction of CCTP membership from 75 to 53 between 1980 and 1982. A 1982 survey of these 53 programs yielded a 74 percent response rate. Fifty-nine percent of the respondents presently require a full year internship as opposed to 9 months or less, with 65.4 percent of APA-approved programs and 46.2 percent of non-approved programs maintaining the full year requirement (Alcorn & Nichols, 1983).

Recent authors emphasize identity confusion (Cleveland, 1980; Domke, 1982; Watkins, 1983) as exposed in an entire 1977 issue of *The Counseling Psychologist.* APA no longer distinguishes between clinical and counseling psychology internships listings and now includes a professional psychology designation. Doctoral students view their 23 APA counseling programs as eclectic in theory, experiential in orientation, and dissimilar in emphasis on research, practical applications, or personal growth (Halpin & Adams, 1978). While counselor licensure is available in six states, another dozen states have legislation pending (Johnston, 1982).

In spite of these portents, Division 17 (Counseling Psychology) members share common interests in counseling activities that are of relatively short duration, didactic, and directed toward problem-solving or behavior change regardless of their identification as counseling or clinical psychologists (Goldschmitt, Tipton, & Wiggins, 1981). When clinical and counseling psychology faculty and supervisors in APA-approved academic and internship settings rated 50 professional activities for counseling psychologists (Tipton, 1983b), the counseling psychologists preferred preventive treatment, consultation, development of outreach programs, vocational counseling, and therapy of less than 15 sessions with persons who were mildly or moderately disturbed. Clinical and counseling psychologists shared similar perceptions of the activities of counseling psychologists. Counseling psychologists have also expressed disappointment that their profession lacks sustained, collective efforts, has no explicit professional purpose, and limited research methodologies (Fretz,

1980). An occupational analysis of counseling psychology (Fitzgerald & Osipow, 1986) suggests a practice orientation with emphasis on psychotherapy. Empirical comparisons between national surveys of counseling and clinical psychologists (Watkins, Lopez, Campbell, & Himmell, 1986) reinforce this emphasis on psychotherapy for both specializations but suggest that changes in training for future practitioners are needed. While another possible training and education conference is envisioned as a sidestep toward resolution of identity issues, this current stasis augurs for more umbrella-type programs with training in a variety of specialties leading to the occupational title of "professional psychologist."

School Psychology

School psychology has origins somewhat similar to those of clinical psychology in public schools, special education for the mentally retarded, and university psychoeducational clinics as early as the 1890s (French, 1984). The earliest specifically titled school psychology training program appears to have been at New York University in the late 1920s which included undergraduate, master's and doctoral degrees. Although several nondoctoral programs existed at the time, the program established by T. Ernest Newland at the University of Illinois in 1951 has been recognized as the first well organized curriculum and independent program at the doctoral level for school psychologists. The New York State Department of Education certification of school psychologists in 1935 probably represents the initial form of official credentialing in professional psychology. At present all states and the District of Columbia provide some form of educational certification while at least 8 states have licensure for school psychologists (Brown, Horn & Lindstrom, 1981). There are now approximately 14,000 professional school psychologists (at least MA level) (Alpert, 1985) with over 2,000 new graduates per year from over 200 programs.

As of 1983 there were three levels of professional training including the master's degree with 1,174 enrolled students in 80 programs, a sixth year or specialist degree of at least 60 hours with 2,526 students in 174 programs, and the doctoral level with 79 programs and 2,301 students (Brown, 1984). Training has been provided by both psychology and education departments.

A 1975 survey of doctoral programs curricula (Goh, 1977) isolated nine factors that accounted for 73 percent of the total variance in the returns. School-based consultation, educational assessment and remediation, behavior modification technology, psychological evaluation, psychotherapeutic procedures, quantitative methods, community involvement and consultation, professional roles and issues, and psychological foundations constituted common core elements of the 97 graduate programs that completed the survey.

Both the National Council for Accreditation of Teacher Evaluation (NCATE) and APA have provided accreditation standards, although there is no comprehensive set of training standards for school psychology. NCATE accreditation for doctoral students requires a minimum of one academic year, or 1,200 clock hours of supervised internship, with at least 600 hours in a school setting in addition to practicum hours (Knoff & Batsche, 1985). APA accreditation requires a full-time internship experience for at least an academic year (1200 hours), although there are no APA approval mechanisms exclusively for school psychology internships. Fagan (1985) believes that by 1995 school psychology accreditation will include specialist (NCATE) and doctoral (NCATE and/or APA) levels, and has provided historical and contemporary context (Fagan, 1986).

The 1954 Thayer Conference (Cutts, 1955) had recommended guidelines for practice that included a two-year program and a six-month internship. In 1980 the Spring Hill Symposium described the status of psychoeducational research, applications to social needs, and general/special education issues in order to plan for the Olympia Conference the following year (Ysseldyke & Weinberg, 1981). The Olympia Conference developed alternate scenarios for the future of school psychology and identified six salient areas (Cardon, 1982): (a) impact of high technology; (b) proliferation of private and home-based schools; (c) increasing percentages of minorities and handicapped children; (d) merger of regular and special education; (e) lifelong education; (f) changed education roles and new professionals. The futuristic concerns occurred in a context of changing societal values and political institutions, racial discrimination in a pluralistic society, economic considerations, legislation and litigation—all in an age of "accountability" (Ysseldyke, 1982). Both the Spring Hill Symposium on the Future of Psychology in the Schools (Ysseldyke & Weinberg, 1981; Ysseldyke, 1982) and the subsequent Olympia Conference (Brown, Cardon, Coulter, & Meyers, 1982) were developed largely as a result of socio-political, economic, legal, and societal issues, although there were (and still are) a number of unresolved professional issues.

These professional issues include the entry level for practice, relationships with clinical psychology, and the training and internship ingredients essential for competence and accreditation. The Spring Hill Symposium had highlighted these issues (Peterson, 1981) which remain unresolved and have been discussed by Bardon (1982), Kratochwill (1982), Trachtman (1981), and Ysseldyke and Schakel (1983).

Within an education and training context, the models of training are most cogent. There are many loci of training including departments of psychology, departments of educational psychology in schools of education, departments of education, departments of counselor education, schools of professional psychology, departments of school psychology, and special education departments. This range of educational sponsorship clearly suggests the multiplicity of origins for the field—particularly various aspects of education, generic psychology, and clinical/counseling psychology.

Gilmore (1974) has identified five models for school psychology activities that include clinical, psychoeducational, educational programming, system level problem solving, and preventive measures in mental health. These functional roles imply different kinds of training with the basic emphasis in graduate education either on helping the K-12 student become a more effective learner (primary prevention), or focusing on the mental health of the student (i.e., rehabilitation, or what is perhaps incorrectly called tertiary prevention). Although there are some overlapping functions between school and clinical psychology in mental health centers, hospitals, pediatric and clinical child settings, private practice, and school consultation, there remain clear distinctions with regard to prevention and intervention for school-related learning and behavior problems that continue to be reflected in training and internship.

A perusal of professional specialty guidelines (APA, 1981b) suggests increasing overlap of professional activities between school psychology and clinical psychology. Two recent surveys of graduate education in school psychology (Goh, 1977; Pfeiffer & Marmo, 1981) found not only a recent rapid growth of school psychology graduate programs but also a broadening of the professional base of graduate programs with an emerging emphasis on program planning, evaluation, research, and child-related intervention besides the more-or-less traditional triad of psychodiagnostic assessment, consultation, and psycheducation/behavioral intervention. Furthermore, a recent factor analytic study of job responsibilities indicated a high degree of comparability among clinical and school psychologists (Rosenfeld, Shimberg, & Thornton, 1983).

Although APA has for some time now held the doctoral degree as the professional entry degree, the field of school psychology (including its national organization—NASP) is by no means in agreement. The general consensus among that group and most doctoral level academic school psychologists, is that the Specialist degree level or its equivalent (approximately 60 semester hours) is more realistically the relevant and appropriate degree. However, as professionalization of the field matures (e.g., licensing, private practice, third party reimbursements, etc.) and opportunities in schools decrease from a numerical standpoint, the doctoral degree should increasingly become the relevant degree. School psychology is still primarily a nondoctoral field with approximately 80 percent being nondoctoral practitioners. The majority of those practitioners have completed 1,000 hour internships as regulated by state guidelines. The six-year certificate requirement may become an intermediate step between the master's and doctoral degree levels (Goh, 1977; Trachtman, 1981). There seems to be an end in the forseeable future to the lack of nonuniform internship requirements within doctoral graduate school psychology programs noted by Pfeiffer and Marmo (1981).

While there are probably several hundred unlisted internships available in public school systems exclusively for school psychologists, there are estimated to be only 33 (12 percent) of 278 APA-approved internships listed (APIC, 1985) which would consider applicants from school psychology programs. Most of these internships gave preference to clinical psychology students and/or would give preferential consideration to applicants from APA-approved programs. In addition, there were 32 non-APA-approved internships which would accept APA-approved school psychology program applicants and 29 non-APA-approved programs open to non-APA-approved school program students. It is likely that when "school psychology continues to demand higher standards for its programs, additional opportunities for clinical training will be made available" within the format and using settings that have been approved by APA (Cook, 1983, p. 6). However, the issues of training and internship for school psychologists are complex with both state and APA approval guidelines and mechanisms which are qualifying for state licensure.

Clinical Child Psychology

For at least 10 years there has been awareness that in spite of increasing demand for clinical child services, existing doctoral programs have been able to train only a fraction of the needed numbers of service providers. Alpert (1985) reports that 63.4 million persons are under 18 years of age and 3.2 million of these children and adolescents are in need of mental health services. However, only about 10 percent are being served by 1 percent of psychological service providers. In addition, there has been no historical consensus on definition of the area of clinical child psychology or the required training content (Mannarino & Fischer, 1982). While 10 percent of programs have offered a specialty degree and 15 percent have a clinical child psychology track (Tuma & Pratt, 1982), variability of training has been the rule. Hughes (1985) suggests that all clinical psychology programs require a survey course including legal/ethical issues, psychopathology, objective and projective measurement, and diverse treatment approaches plus practica experience.

These issues led to the National Conference on Training Clinical Child Psychologists at Hilton Head Island, May 1985, which was sponsored by Division 12 (Clinical Psychology), Section 1 (Clinical Child Psychology) of the American Psychological Association. The conference addressed issues concerning differences from other child professionals, or definition, the training model, specialty training per se in all clinical psychology programs, and specific curriculum issues for specialty programs. The material that follows is from conference reports (Ollendick, 1985; Tuma, 1985, 1986).

All clinical psychology programs should incorporate a course emphasizing the developmental bases of normal behavior over the life span. Experiences with nondisturbed children in everyday settings would be required. Minimal competencies in assessment, psychopathology, and intervention with children, youth, and families would be demonstrated by course work and practica. This knowledge base and experience would be applied to children from various minority backgrounds in addition to representative mainstream children.

Clinical child programs would endorse the Boulder scientist-practitioner model and Division 37 (Child, Youth and Family Services) training guidelines (Roberts, Erickson & Tuma, 1985). The knowledge base and experiences would be similar to clinical child requirements for all graduate programs with a more intensive appreciation of developmental contexts and service settings. Each program must have at least one clinical child psychology faculty member and APA site visit teams would include one member with appropriate expertise.

Clinical child psychology internship programs would provide broad based experiences with populations and theoretical orientations, including adults and children diverse in ages, gender, SES background, ethnic origins, and presenting problems. Training would be both didactic and supervised in assessment, interventions, case management, and consultation. Child-oriented internships would offer two-thirds of their training in child-related activities. Research time and appropriate research role models would be provided by each internship setting. An augmented collaboration with the student's graduate program would include individualized plans for each intern at the onset of internship. A standing committee of Division 37 on internship training would be established. A recommendation for continuing education was made and included provision for programmatic postdoctoral training. A Section 1 task force would be responsible for continuing education criteria, for identification of specific programs by survey, and for the development of appropriate guidelines for these programs. A directory (Tuma, 1985–1986) lists 42 predoctoral internship programs with positions for 78 interns in 23 APA-approved programs and for 49 interns in 19 nonapproved programs while 22 postdoctoral programs have 44 positions.

Professional Psychology

Professional psychology constitutes an amalgam of previously separate competency areas—clinical, counseling, school, health, clinical child, clinical neuropsychology, etc. Professional psychology grew out of the success of practitioners in the community and the demand for these practitioners has increased over time. A large part of this success story was due to the emphasis on providing direct care, especially psychotherapy, and the development of other new areas.

Professional psychology also developed as a result of dissatisfaction with academic (Boulder model) training which provided impetus for professional schools in which practitioners, or service-providers, were trained. Dissatisfaction with the traditional academic experience was initially stimulated by a research process that was alien to practice and became identified by students as being socially irrelevant. However, over time and with shaping by admissions committees and events in the larger culture, students have become less concerned with social relevance. Instead, an increasing anxiety about personal economic security in a climate of scarcity signaled a narrowing of perspective and the task orientation required for learning a multitude of specific skills. Graduate academic education began to deemphasize hands-on experience within a service-delivery context in favor of empirical practices (skills) which could be conducted with attempted laboratory precision in a medical model health care service delivery format. Within clinical psychology a bifurcation in training was occurring. On the other hand, narrow gauge specialists such as oncological and cardiological psychologists were emerging from the health psychology academic training. Simultaneously, an even larger number of practitioners were being trained in professional schools to be psychotherapists (Peterson, 1985). Two populations—medical patients and psychiatric patients—were being served by professional psychologists from different training models that selected students whose values and ambitions conformed to the scientist-professional or practitioner model.

It is is understandable that Fox, Barclay, and Rodgers (1982) underscore the lack of consensus on how to define the profession of psychology. This problem affects education by hampering both the establishment of uniform training procedures and unambiguous credentialing. The sections on clinical psychology—Boulder, Vail, and Health models—plus counseling, school and clinical child psychology indicate that while we have clearly defined practitioner specialists, the field lacks any generic definition to encompass these separate areas. Fox et al. propose a definition:

> Professional psychology is that profession which is concerned with enhancing the effectiveness of human functioning. Therefore, a professional psychologist is one who has expertise in the development of quality services to the public in a controlled, organized, ethical manner; based upon psychological knowledge, attitudes, and skills, in order to enhance the effectiveness of human functioning (1982, p. 307).

Since there is responsibility to consumers of psychological services, Fox et al. suggest using the Ph.D. for a research-oriented degree while the Psy.D. becomes the practitioner degree. Their argument rests on the fact that at least 35 different degrees have been submitted by licensed psychologists as professional credentials in the past. This suggestion has merit, although whether or not a practitioner degree is a Ph.D. or Psy.D. has been often an accidental event in the development of specific programs.

The evolution of psychology through the Boulder, Vail, and Health models and the emergence of counseling, school, clinical child, and industrial specialties in addition to clinical psychology suggests that applied psychologists now require a more cohesive professional image and self-presentation to the public. Professional psychology does provide a possible rubric, or generic label, to encompass both presently constituted and future specialty areas.

Just as there have been identity crises in clinical psychology in the past,

Schneider (1985) and Levy (1984) discern a contemporary identity problem. Schneider sees a demise of generic educational preparation in favor of training for credentialing in both scientist-professional and practitioner programs. The locus of research shifts away from academia and an increasing societal pluralism is ignored by scientist-professional programs. Practitioners programs attenuate their ties to a scientific basis for practice that has origins in the larger academic psychology community. Practitioners become identified with specialty areas, each proclaiming to provide unique professional identity. Simultaneously, however, there has been a blurring of the boundaries between these specialties as well as between professional psychologists and a host of other service providers. As Levy correctly indicates, the Boulder model provided clear boundaries for the profession as a result of specific knowledge or skills while practice was conceptualized within a psychological framework. Health psychology specialization, in particular, diluted the indigenous psychological perspective with medical model thinking and a legitimization that was more appropriate to medicine. Such identification with medicine may minimize the possibility that psychology can contribute to improved health services as a result of a unique professional perspective (Elfant, 1985; Riska & Vinten-Johansen, 1981).

Schneider (1985) proposes a new integrative model in which schools of psychology are independent at the graduate level, with greater interface with the community, and a life-span development theoretical focus. In order for the school of psychology to have an effect on the community, direct and indirect services would be expanded, especially preventive activities. Applied, policy, and evaluation research, consultant services, and active dissemination of research findings would occur in community contexts. Continuing education for professional psychologists and a variety of programs providing information to the general public would be available.

Levy (1984) proposes an integrative model that also presupposes generic training in order to understand and deal with human problems. A human services psychology rubric would define a professional psychologist rather than any identification by specialization. A biopsychosocial approach calls for careful interdisciplinary training that is described by a matrix for integration of content, levels of intervention, and modes of intervention.

Professional psychology has gone through a developmental process that began with integration (Boulder model), proceeded to differentiation (specialization), and now seems to be focused on a more complex integration (human services psychology). The future seems to hold generic graduate training programs from a human science aegis leading to a 2-year specialty internship/residency. It is possible to forsee a merger of values, a psychological orientation, and a unique human service delivery process that will contribute to an enhanced identity as a professional psychologist.

INTERNSHIP TRAINING

Selection

Professional psychology graduate students who apply for internship have already experienced an application process for graduate school that was cumbersome, time-consuming, and costly. After an additional investment of 3 to 5 years in graduate school, they face the prospect of an application process for internship that may be even more anxiety-producing. While there are clear procedures for application (APIC, 1985) with an undergirding of APA ethical codes, and a strict time schedule, the process for matching 1700+ students with 400+ internships has never been efficient.

An early survey of this matching process was completed for 1971-1976 with projections through 1979 (Tuma & Cerny, 1976). Information was obtained from graduate programs and predoctoral internship settings. While the data from this study are only of historic interest, many of the major issues are still germane. Tuma and Cerny found that the numbers of prospective interns exceeded the number of available placements, placement rates for students from APA-approved programs and nonapproved programs favored those from approved programs, and the financial support base was largely from federal and state sources.

In selecting from an increasing pool of applicants, internship directors look closely at clinical skills (Drummond, Rodolfa, & Smith, 1981; Petzel & Berndt, 1980; Spitzform & Hamilton, 1976; Tedesco, 1979), especially the amount and kind of practical experience in psychodiagnosis and psychotherapy. The quality of these experiences is evaluated primarily by letters of recommendation, particularly for students from approved programs. It should be noted that the standards recommended by a committee of the Association of Psychology Internships Centers (1981) include 400-500 hours of practicum with 250 hours of direct services to clients and at least 100 hours of supervision.

Although directors of internships programs have never been impressed by the relevance of academic training for internship (Dana, Gilliam, & Dana, 1976), they still endorse Boulder model training (Shemberg & Leventhal, 1981). As a result they continue to examine applications carefully for evidence of clinical skill while academic credentials may be linked to their global ratings in a less direct manner (Stedman et al., 1981). A recent estimate suggests that the numbers of internship positions may exceed applications by about 10 percent (Barnes, 1982). A review of the Association of Psychology Internship Centers Clearinghouse data substantiates this estimate since applicants find internships readily (Laughlin, Hutzell, Schut, Langmade & Straight, 1984). Moreover, 90 percent of internship positions are still being funded with an average 1984-1985 stipend of $9,985 for APA-approved programs ($9600 is 1986-1987 median) and $9,638 for nonoapproved programs (Laughlin, 1985).

Students often do not have sufficient information in order to make informed applications or decisions. Academic programs vary in amount of information, encouragement, support and direction provided for the application process. More detailed information should be obtained from the yearly *Directory of Internship Programs in Clinical Psychology* (APIC, 1986-87), materials sent out by internships, and advice from academic faculty and/or program director. Accreditation procedures have required "truth in advertising" from internships and APA site visitors routinely scrutinize descriptive program materials. However, data from previous interns concerning supervision, training experiences, patient population, and satisfaction are usually omitted from descriptive materials (Barnes, 1982). To our knowledge information concerning satisfaction experienced *during* the internship is potentially available from only one setting (Dana & Brookings, 1980). However, students generally prefer APA-approved programs that are large, provide interdisciplinary stimulation, varied patient populations, and are congenial workplaces (Burstein, Schoenfeld, Loucks, Stedman & Costello, 1981; Tedesco, 1979).

Part of the inefficiency in the application process occurs in the many redundant applications by each student. Tedesco (1979) reported an average number that exceeded 13 per student! The Georgia State program has devised a procedure for making accurate and detailed information available on internships that had previously accepted their students and subsequently limited each student to 3 or 4 applications (Craddick, Cole, Dane, Brill, & Wilson, 1980). There are several descriptions of how to manage the application process from the standpoint of students in order to reduce anxiety and maximize the possibility of acceptance in a desirable program (Belar & Orgel, 1980; Brill, Wolkin, & McKeel, 1985; Grace, 1985; Hersh & Poey, 1984). One source of anxiety has been the uniform notification date system. APIC has accepted a proposal to retain this uniform notification date and to allow student initiative for early acceptance as well (APIC, 1986).

Training Settings

Most of the literature on internship training describes the various training settings. Medical settings provide the largest numbers of internship programs, many of these housed in Departments of Psychiatry. Psychiatric settings present unique problems of adaptation for clinical psychology students (Burstein, Barnes, & Quesada, 1976; Shows, 1976). A 1976 survey (Lubin, Nathan, & Matarazzo, 1978) indicated that 2,336 professional psychologists had academic appointments in medical schools with a mean number of 29 per school. At present there are over 2500 faculty psychologists in medical schools (Matarazzo, Carmody, & Gentry, 1981).

Within these medical settings there is training in traditional clinical/counseling psychology as well as medical psychology, behavioral medicine, behavior modification, and more recently in health psychology, although health psychology internships are primarily postdoctoral. One survey (Gentry, Street, Masur, & Asken, 1981) reported that approximately three-fourths of responding internship programs had formal training experiences in medical psychology. Included were consultation-liaison services, biofeedback, and services on pediatric and neuropsychological wards. Such training was required in about two-fifths of these programs. The opportunities for interns in behavioral medicine that have been described (Belar, 1980) are largely with nonpsychiatric, medical patient populations. This area is now coextensive with Health Psychology. Behavior modification experiences and training—part of the technique basis for these area—was well represented in internship programs as early as 1972 (Johnson & Bornstein, 1974).

At present there is a rich literature describing internship settings which include behavioral medicine, community mental health centers, gerontology, medical psychology, neuropsychology, physical rehabilitation, and the U. S. Armed Forces. Within these internship settings there are reported opportunities for specialty training in administration, consultation, crisis intervention, forensics, hypnosis, group treatment, and program evaluation. Didactic training has been reported to be available in the form of orientation and seminars. Table 3 identifies this literature.

Supervision

The numbers of education and mental health personnel dramatically expanded following the end of WW II and should continue to increase even beyond any necessity for replacements. Learning/teaching situations which include classroom settings, and reading, writing, or attitudinal learning provide opportunities for feedback to the student/learner by the teacher. Supervisory support and treatment planning has been documented to be of equal importance at several different levels of training (Rabinowitz, Heppner, & Roehlke, 1986). The clinical supervisory process provides the most significant learning of techniques and applications of theoretical material as well as for internalization of professional attitudes and behaviors. The supervisory process has been scrutinized by all mental health professions in recent publications (Bruch, 1974; Ekstein & Wallerstein, 1972; Fleming & Benedict, 1966; Goin, 1982; Hess, 1980; Langs, 1979; Mueller & Kell, 1972; Munson, 1979; Peake & Archer, 1984) and journals solely devoted to the area (e.g., *The Clinical Supervisor; Counselor Education and Supervision*). Literature reviews may be found in Hess (1980), Cohen and DeBetz (1977), and McElfresh (1983). These published materials are primarily concerned with psychotherapy supervision, although psychological assessment supervision has received some attention (Blatt, 1973; Smith & Harty, 1981).

Hess (1980) has tentatively defined this complex process as "a relationship where one or more person(s) in conducting psychotherapy or mental health services are intentionally and potentially enhanced by the interaction with

Table 3 Descriptive Literature on Internship Settings, Specializations, and Didactic Training Content

Setting	Specialization	Didactic training

Behavior medicine
  Swan et al. (1980)
	Administration
	  Edwards & Wyrick (1977)
		Ethics
		  Baldick (1980)
		  Newmark & Hutchins (1981)

Community mental health centers
  Pinkerton et al. (1972)
  Zolik (1983)
	Consultation
	  Murphy (1984)
	Crisis intervention
	  Barlow (1974)
		Orientation
		  Malouf et al. (1983)
		Seminars
		  Monti et al. (1983)

Gerontology
  Siegler et al. (1979)
	Lamb et al. (1983)
	  Zimet & Weissberg (1979)	

Medical psychology Gentry et al. (1981)	Forensics	

Neuropsychology
  Goldberg & McNamara (1984)
  Golden & Kuperman (1980)
  Lubin & Sokoloff (1983)
	Levine et al. (1980)
	  Lawlor et al. (1981)
	Group treatment
	  Carmody & Zohn (1980)	

Physical rehabilitation
  Gold et al. (1982)
	Hypnosis
	  Rodolfa et al. (1982)
	Program evaluation	

U. S. Army Scott (1975)	Korn et al. (1982)	

another person" (p. 528). The goal is thus to foster competent psychotherapists. Hess suggests that there are at least five components to this definition: supervisee, supervisor, what was learned, how this was done, and the distinction between this process and generic relationships such as teaching, consultation, and administration.

The history of the supervisory process in psychotherapy has separate but parallel developmental paths in the mental health disciplines. Psychiatry and psychoanalysis had the earliest supervision while social work and professional psychology were influenced heavily by psychoanalytic practices. Rogers (1956) emphasized the role of supervision in learning facilitative skills and in developing human qualities for psychotherapy. Nonpsychoanalytic references to supervision have grown steadily since then.

There are several reasons for the present interest in psychotherapy supervision in addition to what might be expected from the increasing numbers/types of persons being trained to provide psychotherapeutic services. These factors include a need for imposition of quality control and accountability on human services and on health and mental health services in particular. Knowledge is now available concerning the efficacy of psychotherapy, and more specifically there is understanding of matching type of therapy and/or therapist with client problems. It is clear that the presence of a general therapeutic attitude of genuineness, empathy, and warmth may be still basic (Patterson, 1984). Robiner (1982) has indicated that it is the resourcefulness and integrity of the supervisor which provides a model for personal style and professional identity. There is need for competent, knowledgeable, ethical supervisors committed to the professional development of their supervisees without any neglect of client rights/needs.

Minimum credentials are now required for professional recognition. Reimbursement by third party insurance companies often requires supervision for those with less than terminal degrees. Many states as well as the National Register for Health Care Providers require a second year (in addition to the internship year) of supervised experience for license eligibility. Some states already require participation in continuing education (which may include supervision) for license maintenance. Finally, a therapist may benefit from peer supervision in order to break away from isolated clinical functioning, enhance skills and self-development, and solve specific clinical problems (e.g., transference and counter-transference).

A number of models of psychotherapy supervision may be found in the existing literature and several will be described here. Hess (1980) proposed possible models of lecturer, teacher, case reviewer, collegial peer, monitor, and therapist. Each model has goals, a degree of supervisee choice, and specified supervisor-supervisee relationship (Table 4). Robiner (1982) proposes a somewhat similar set of possible models and suggests problems associated with conflict of roles played by the supervisor either simultaneously or sequentially.

Curtis and Yager (1981) present a systems analysis of supervision in school psychological services (both in training and service delivery) which is unique. Collaborative development, a time perspective for supervisory-supervisee interactions, and attention to interpersonal/intrapersonal dynamics of the supervisee as well as the environmental context of the process are emphasized by this format.

McElfresh (1983) has developed a comprehensive, multidimensional, or "professional model," which also has a systematic evaluation component. Three dimensions address student needs (conceptual, process, and personal), supervisory roles (teacher, therapist, consultant, administrator), and supervisory process (client intrapsychic and interpersonal activities, therapeutic relationship with client, and learning relationship with supervisor). Student needs constitute the primary dimension with supervisor style/function and focus of interaction appropriately integrated. In this model, supervisor and supervisee jointly develop a systematic evaluation of strength, weakness, interest, etc., that results in an individualized training plan (ISP) with clearly delineated goals and objectives.

Friedlander, Dye, Costello, and Kobos (1984) posit a developmental crisis/learning model which highlights the cardinal importance of those growth-enhancing interactions which supersede models, facts and techniques in their lasting impact on trainees. Several reasons were cited for the complexity of supervision. First, supervisor commitment is divided between supervisee learning and welfare of the supervisee's client. Second, the process involves communication between two people about a relationship that one of them has with a third person. Third, the supervisory process has much in common with psychotherapy (parallel processes) and must be handled with tact and subtlety. Lastly, supervision needs to be adapted to supervisees with varying degrees of training/background and personal proclivity for psychotherapy.

Friedlander et al. also describe the supervisee's developmental stages/crises. The first involves a demand for tolerance of ambiguity while the second is an encounter with the limits of the learner's capacity to offer therapeutic conditions. The third crisis deals with understanding of therapy as deepest communication, well beyond administration of a technique. The final crisis confronts the trainee with the development of conceptual attitudes in which various models of interventions are seen as tasks in a goodness-of-fit match with needs of the client. Modeling by the supervisor is a crucial component of learning in a growth-crisis-orientation framework.

Various other authors (Curtis & Yager, 1981; Grater, 1985; Grotjahn, 1955; Hess, 1984; Weiner & Kaplan, 1980) describe the process of learning psychotherapy. While they agree that there are at least three major stages in the learning of the process, Hess (1984) has summarized these stages. Demythologizing psychotherapy (stage one) focuses on the student need to form an identity and deal with feelings of adequacy versus inadequacy. Beginning therapists have to learn that no single intervention is sufficiently powerful to destroy the client but

Table 4 Models of Psychotherapy Supervision

Model	Goal	Choice	Relationship
Lecturer	Convey global conceptual schemes and technique. Generate enthusiasm	High	One to mass audience
Teacher	Teach specified content and skills within programmatic scheme.	Moderate	Subordinate to
Case review	Explore ways of thinking and relating to cases.	Low	Elder to younger
Collegial-peer	Support and gaining a different, unforced view.	High	Equals in shared intimacy
Monitor	Maintain at least minimally acceptable levels of service.	Low	External censor, evaluator
Therapist	Help psychotherapist grow and reach new levels of adaptiveness with self and clients.	Moderate to high	Benign supervisor, trusted model

they do require support from the supervisor at the same time. The end point is gaining confidence and reducing apprehension about entering the therapeutic process.

The second stage (specific skill learning) is generally seen as the core of learning psychotherapy. These skills include the development of good listening, appropriate reflection, specific behavioral techniques, and collecting information for conceptualization and tentative interpretation. Here, basic learning is along an independence versus dependence dimension.

The last stage (professional identity) is best described as a collegial or mentor-type of supervisory relationship with conditional dependence versus individuation as the theme. The major focus is the impact of therapist personality on the client. At times, however, without the supervisory relationship becoming one of psychotherapy itself, the supervisor's intervention may be therapeutic.

Perceptions of supervisors and supervisees have also been examined. Supervisors may be viewed by students along dimensions of defensiveness, professionalism, experience as a clinician, theoretical base, experience as a teacher, appropriateness of interest in student's life, likeability, and motivating ability (Aldrich, 1982, cited in Hess, 1984). Moreover, supervisors see supervisees along dimensions of interest in client and client welfare, preparation for supervision, knowledge, self-exploration and self-awareness, openness to suggestion, interpersonal and clinical skills, competence, boundary management and decision-making ability (Swain, 1982, cited in Hess, 1984).

In describing the developmental process that interns experience during the internship year, it is important to note that this development interfaces with the career stages of supervisors and program directors. Now that there are over 400 predoctoral internship settings, attention is being given to the career stages of internship directors (Lamb, Anderson, Rapp, Rathnow, & Sesan, 1986; Lamb, Roehlke, & Butler, 1986). Stages of entry, identity, doubt, reimmersion, and exit have been identified. These developmental transitions influence the performance of internship directors and may have direct impact on individual interns.

Evaluation

In 1977 an Association of Psychology Internships Centers Standards Committee began to develop goals for evaluation of intern competency and specialties in clinical, counseling and school psychology (APIC, 1981). Entry level skills were to be evaluated and compared with exit skills. The outcome was to achieve a reliable process which would permit comparisons (across interns, among interns, and over time) of competence with relevant patient populations. A sample of skill areas had been previously suggested by the American Board of Professional Psychology, including rapport, oral fact finding, observation, empathy, warmth, clinical inference, intervention techniques, flexibility, ability to deal with manipulative behaviors, stress resistance, writing skills, evaluation and conceptualization, objectivity in professional relationships, circumspection, scientific knowledge, self-awareness, maturity, etc. In addition, different specialty skills for clinical, counseling, and school psychologists were outlined by this APIC committee. Clinical psychologists would demonstrate competence in multiple assessment techniques, group and individual, long- and short-term psychotherapy, crisis intervention, and consultation. Counseling psychologists were to be competent in primary prevention, crisis intervention, short-term treatment, vocational assessment, career planning/development, and consultation. School psychologists were to be evaluated for psychological/ psychoeducational evaluation, assessment of school functioning, consultation, and program development/evaluation.

These APIC recommendations define ideal competence standards toward which each internship should direct evaluation efforts and program evaluation. However, Miller (1977) had completed a relevant survey of internship evaluation practices prior to the development of these APIC standards. While the 30 percent return rate suggested that only a minority of programs were willing to be seriously engaged by evaluation issues, these respondents taught and evaluated clinical intervention skills, assessment or behavioral analysis, inter- personal relationships, and consultation. Most of these programs used evaluation reports twice yearly (29%), thrice yearly (13%), or quarterly (16%). Informal qualitative procedures were typical of evaluation in 179 accredited internships (Norcross, Stevenson, & Nash, 1968).

Evaluation is also provided by successful completion of internship. Most persons who are not academically or personally suited for professional psy- chological practice have already been eliminated prior to application for internship. However, a small percentage of trainees may run into difficulties during the internship year (Rangel & Boxley, 1984; Tedesco, 1982). These difficulties range from stress-related issues (e.g., change of roles and lifestyles) to levels of impairment necessitating premature termination by the internship setting.

Interns, and former interns, however, have been more vocal in addressing evaluation issues. For example, Johnson (1978) and Pleck (1976) report and critique their own personal experiences. Lamb, Baker, Jennings, and Yarris (1982) identify five distinct chronological passages of internship. These passages articulate identity formation, first as intern and subsequently as professional psychologist. This is a careful model of the process and is stated with sufficient generality to be applicable to most interns. The model was created by current and former interns as well as agency training staff (also former interns) and evaluated by independent interns and directors of training. Solway (1985) elaborates on the Lamb et al. internship passage years by focusing on the transition into the internship year. He suggests that this change from graduate school to the real world of practice has not been adequately recognized as being uniquely stressful. The author points to clinical stresses (e.g., intense supervisory relationships and the learning of new skills), institutional stresses (e.g., the change of status by the intern, confronting issues of authority within a new bureaucracy, etc.), and personal stresses (e.g., issues of separation and loss, the necessity of developing a new social network, etc.) as constituting areas to which all concerned need to be sensitive. Suggestions to the faculty of the graduate program, incoming intern, and internship setting staff could, if implemented, make the transition as comfortable as possible. Kaslow and Rice (1985) also describe major stresses that include program adjustment, development of trust, questioning one's competence, risk taking to learn new skills, accurate self-assessment, and planning for professional life after internship. These authors see the internship year as a separation-individuation process that is similar to a description provided by the psychoanalyst Mahler.

The more substantive literature, however, comes from 7 surveys (Table 5) in which current and former interns report time allocations on internship as well as the relevance and quality of internship experiences to current professional activities. While these studies certainly provide data, their results are limited to the sampling of internship settings (5 studies survey former interns from only *one* internship), and to the time periods in which the interns received training. These findings are illustrative and demonstrate a need for continuous, method consistent evaluation across training settings with annual updating. It seems reasonable to expect internships to report annually on time allocations by interns as well as intern satisfaction with these activities (e.g., Dana & Brookings, 1980) and to have some follow-up on former interns (perhaps by APIC) in order to monitor the relevance of training experiences for subsequent training activities.

PROFESSIONAL ACCOUNTABILITY

Historical Context

Professional psychology has grown rapidly during the approximately 40 years of institutionalized existence in this country. There has been remarkable growth in development of human resources with an increase in clinical doctorates from 241 in 1960 to 1,256 in 1981, with figures for both dates representing approximately 30 percent of all psychology doctorates. Equally or more rapidly increasing numbers are found in the counseling and school psychology fields for the same time period—66 to 351 doctorates in counseling and 7 to 133 in school psychology (Syverson, 1982). Similarly, there are presently over 400 listed internship programs with more than 275 of these approved by the American Psychological Association (APA) as compared to 72 such approved programs in 1960 (APA, 1961).

New patterns of training (e.g., professional schools, professional programs,

Table 5 Surveys of Interns and Former Interns

Survey	Interns	Settings	Data
Cole et al. (1981)	60 (former)	35 (15 states).	Time allocations on internship. Quality of experience.
Hays (1976)	56 (former)	Texas Research Institute of Mental Sciences	Current professional activities. Relevance of internship.
Khol et al. (1972)	146 (current)	73	10 questions regarding experience.
Rosenkrantz & Holmes (1974)	8 (current)	Wm. S. Hall Psychiatric Institute	12 skill areas. Personal growth.
Steinhelber & Gaynor (1981)	82 (1968) 91 (1977) (former)	Langley Porter Psychiatric Institute	Current professional activities. Satisfaction.
Stout et al. (1977)	25 (former)	Wm. S. Hall Psychiatric Institute	Current professional activities. Relevance of internship.
Weiss (1975)	18 (former)	Oklahoma UHSC	Current professional activities. Relevance of internship.

combined programs), expansion of psychology into health care areas, development of subspecialties such as clinical child and applied neuropsychology, have been accompanied by a pervasive impact of accountability on the educational and training establishment. With federal funding for professional training drying up, other patterns of programmatic support must be found. The trainees will have to make tangible contributions to the agency in which the internship training program is housed.

Historically, the Veterans Administration (VA), and the National Institute of Mental Health (NIMH) have been in the foreground of providing financial support for professional psychology students in academic settings and for internships. However, cutbacks (particularly NIMH stipends and practicum support by the VA), increased service requirements for funded interns (e.g., payback requirements by NIMH, and reallocation of priorities to training programs targeting underserved populations) make for increasing numbers of unfunded internships (about 12% of all listed internship positions) and/or cost-effective oriented local funding.

Despite the increasing financial constraints on student support, the number of graduate professional programs and internships continued to grow during the late 1970s and early 1980s. The decline of the postwar baby boom will impact numerically in the late 1980s. The Association of Psychology Internship Centers (APIC) Clearinghouse Program was established in 1977 to enable communication between prospective interns and agencies offering unfilled internships subsequent to the early/mid February offer/acceptance period. It has already been noted that an adequate number of internship positions are reported to be available for persons seeking placements subsequent to notification dates.

It cannot be predicted how long this unmanaged pattern of approximate numerical equity between the 1,700 plus prospective yearly interns and available training positions will continue. The uncertainty of the situation is increased by lack of public listing of some internship programs, including an unknown number of non-APA-approved ones (e.g., in school psychology) and those in "captive" agencies. An increased demand for internships due to rapidly expanding numbers of students in professional schools is likely (Caddy, 1981; Fox, Kovacs, & Graham, 1985; McConnell, 1984).

At the present time, the American Psychological Association does not take any direct responsibility—and perhaps should not—except indirectly through the accreditation mechanism, for exerting influence on what appears to be a classical laissez-faire market situation. However, the recent Graduate Medical Education National Advisory Committee Report (1980) suggests that more centralized control over production of health care human resources—in this case medical specialties including psychiatry—may well be in the offing.

Financing

While the average APIC Directory listed, APA-approved internship stipend was reported to be $9,985 for the 1984-1985 internship year ($9,638 for nonapproved programs), it is noteworthy that the range was from zero to $26,400, with the latter being offered by the US Armed Forces, in which a service commitment is required (Laughlin, 1985). However, the distribution of these stipends is skewed. V.A. funded stipends (350 general and 38 for geriatrics training) are for $10,000 each and account for more than 25 percent of the total number of funded internships during recent years. There are forces pulling stipend amounts in both directions. Some desirable internships sites offer unfunded positions (Carlin, 1983) to accommodate demands while others (Wiens & Dresdale, 1984) assert that, in medical settings at least, clinical psychology interns should receive the same stipend as first year medical interns in order to attain similar status and privileges as physician-trainee colleagues. Another proposal for obtaining status/privilege equality in medical centers has been advocated by calling students on internship "residents" similar to medical education patterns (Sheridan, 1981).

Since internships are *not* exclusively in medical settings it is important to consider trainee needs. The potential graduate student now has to rely more on private or borrowed funds for financing education which leads to greater indebtedness and less likelihood of recruiting appropriate numbers of minority students. For the above reasons, as well as for adequate self-perception and minimal distraction from learning, it may be argued that stipends are a desirable and necessary component of the internship year. Moreover, interns who accept nonfunded slots for the sake of convenience may have a financially supporting mate, and/or may make a financial trade-off in order to obtain a desirable internship placement. The APA Committee on Accreditation has recently taken the position of supporting funded internships, but will consider unfunded slots in special programs and individual circumstances in quality settings. However, "the burden of evidence" lies with the program to show that absence of funding has no negative effect on morale or training quality (APA, 1984b).

In the recent past, health care costs have taken an increasingly larger share of the national economy. As part of a national policy, a variety of recent cost-containment and/or reduction measures have been introduced in voluntary, negotiated, administrative, or legislative patterns and will certainly continue and probably increase. Professional psychology has been eminently successful since the second world war (i.e., state licensing laws, freedom-of-choice laws, burgeoning private practice, development of professional schools, inclusion in much federal legislation, attainment of important administrative and political positions, greater access to practice in hospitals, development of scientific data on efficiency and effectiveness of services, innovations in service delivery approaches and systems, etc.). As a result, it is not surprising that the profession is being scrutinized for accountability as are all health care professions and their educational and training institutions. This process is part of a larger context of public policy and other societal forces working their often contradictory wills on health care structures and systems. It is in this context that the issue of cost-effectiveness of internship training may be raised.

Loucks, Burstein, Schoenfeld, and Stedman (1980), as well as Wiens and Dresdale (1984) have shown that clinical psychology interns are cost-effective in medical settings as Weiskopf and Newman (1982) have done for a mental health center. These studies do not even include more subtle benefits of providing internship training that are less translatable into dollars and cents. For example, participation in internship training may increase staff morale, provide professional stimulation, and opportunity to observe a potential staff or faculty member first hand over a period of time, thus offering an inexpensive and more reliable manner of staff recruitment.

Several suggestions for cutting costs of the present uniform notification system have recently been made. A national computer matching program in the past has not received any serious attention from graduate programs and APIC found it financially infeasible, although it is being suggested again (Briggs, 1984). APIC is considering other options at the present time and will probably implement some changes in the selection process within a few years. Another possibility (May, 1975) is to make better use of available facilities on a contractual basis within geographic regions. Internship agencies in several regions of the country already coordinate their recruitment and selection efforts.

Academia-Internship Interface

A slightly different approach is emerging from some well-known, APA-approved graduate programs that is similar to May's suggestion and the "captive agency" model from the years prior to V.A. programs receiving training monies directly from the V.A. Central Office in the mid-1970s. When the graduate program received V.A. monies directly, these programs usually had "arrangements" for sending their trainees to predetermined settings. This training pattern still exists in some school systems and university counseling centers that have arrangements with school and counseling psychology programs. The proposal suggests that internships settings agree to accept one or two students from one or more universities every year or second year (Burstein, 1983; Craddick, 1984). There is no doubt that adoption of this proposal would result in considerable savings (e.g., money, time, effort) in the costly application-selection process. Proponents of this suggestion prefer to conceptualize it as a "placement" and an alternative to the present APIC-sponsored system, rather than a substitute. However, the APIC membership consensus at this time seems to be opposed to this notion, although it may be argued that unwritten understandings already exist between some graduate programs and some internship settings. APA has recently accredited on a posthoc basis some earlier and current captive internship settings (APA, 1985).

One approach for cutting costs in money, materiel, and human resources is a less drastic but monitored system for internship placement used by at least one university (Craddick et al., 1980). With cooperative screening and negotiating, this graduate program requires prospective interns to limit their number of applications to 3 or 4 acceptable internships while no 2 students may apply to the same setting. A disadvantage for prospective interns is that the internship, knowing the applicants' first choice, may put students "on hold" and deprive them of this first choice as a result. Despite possible drawbacks other graduate programs are also adopting the Georgia State approach.

As mentioned earlier, restrictions have already developed in the V.A. as these settings have been able to accept counseling and clinical trainees only from APA-approved schools since 1982 *and* recruit only potential staff members who have completed both an APA-approved graduate program and internship. As a consequence a double standard in professional psychology may be developing with non-APA-approved training and internship programs. Some professional psychologists also become ineligible for certain positions (e.g., VA's). Graduate programs are attempting to regain autonomy by beginning to control some of their own internships—e.g., Fuller, Wright State, Virginia Consortium, etc. The question may be asked whether or not this pattern will become a subtle way of monitoring the production of professional psychology human resources. More importantly, however, this approach provides the possibility for doctoral programs to develop their own service delivery system and thus act in more responsible ways for the total education and training of their students (e.g., Fuller, St. Louis University).

Evidence has accrued over the past 15–20 years that considerable disparity exists between academic education and realities of the professional practice world—as first clearly discernable in the internship (Dana, Gilliam, & Dana, 1976; Shemberg & Leventhal, 1981). In part, the development of professional schools was in response to this discrepancy. There are vast differences between APA-approved programs within the same specialty. These differences occur both between and within the APA specialty categories in terms of the appropriateness of academic/practice background and experience that is provided to the graduate student. Boulder and Vail model programs will probably continue to diverge with Boulder model programs graduating research clinicians and Vail model programs training practitioners. Counseling and school psychology may focus more on primary or secondary preventive aspects of mental health care.

The concern with excellence (Strupp, 1976), and the adequacy of preparation for internship (Dana, Gilliam, & Dana, 1976; Shemberg & Leventhal, 1981) may presage generic graduate professional training for subsequent differentiation/specialization as a result of internship. There has been reluctant awareness that the Boulder model may be unattainable in clinical psychology

(Frank, 1984), that a clear definition and identity for counseling psychology is lacking (King & Seymour, 1982; Tipton, 1983b; Watkins, 1984), and that there are direct service delivery vs. consulting and generalized vs. specialized educational role model dichotomies in school psychology (Abramowitz, 1981; Phillips, 1981a).

Patterns of Training

Clinical psychology education and training programs probably tend to agree more on what pattern of training constitutes an internship than counseling and school psychology. Standardization of practicum experience and internship diminishes somewhat in school psychology (Phillips, 1981b; Pfeiffer & Marmo, 1981), as exemplified by captive internships. In some clinical programs (including some professional schools) the shift from practicum to internship is not clear-cut or the program may require a given number of practicum hours without specifically designating the number of internship hours or vice versa.

At present, APA and its constituent subgroups seems to be moving toward adoption of a generally acceptable definition of an internship. Originally proposed as standards for evaluation for National Register eligibility, APIC has suggested adoption of very similar definitions as criteria for internship (APIC, 1983) and developed more comprehensive standards for evaluation and training for all professional psychology internships (APIC Newsletter, 1981). Most recently, the APA Accreditation Committee has indicated that the student's specialty (e.g., clinical, counseling, school) is primarily determined by the degree-conferring program with both academic and internship programs being responsible for appropriate matching. Furthermore, the guidelines suggest that the presence of appropriate role models in the internship is of primary importance in specialty designation (APA, 1984b). Despite these general criteria, standardization and evaluation of knowledge, attitudes, skills, etc., of professional psychology students has yet to be fully attained (Miller, 1977; Peterson & Bry, 1980; Stevenson, Norcross, King, & Tobin, 1984).

Historically, there was very little communication between internship settings and graduate programs concerning issues of mutual interest. There are, of course, the application materials, recommendation and feedback letters, and occasional phone calls. Although less true today than in the past, grants and departmental or program funding allow graduate faculty to visit interns regularly or have the internship staff meet with other similar staffs at the parent program setting. With funding cutbacks, however, these face-to-face interactions patterns are disappearing and the gulf between graduate programs and most internship settings increases.

Prior to the late 1960s, the usual date of agreement for acceptance between internship setting and applicant was around April 15. With increasing numbers of students and training agencies, competition led to a decline in the consistency of this pattern. The situation became chaotic and often bordered on the unethical, with more pressure being put on students for earlier and earlier acceptance of offers—sometimes as much as 9-10 months prior to the starting date.

With the institution of uniform acceptance procedures by APIC members, the situation has been largely rectified. The pattern first agreed upon in the late 1970s by APIC (consisting of almost all APA-approved programs and others) presently allows 1½ days for offer-acceptance times from the morning of the second Monday in February. This procedure has been generally successful, although there are still some reported violations of the agreed-upon rules and almost yearly reconsideration for the possible modification of the procedure by APIC at the annual APA meeting.

There is, however, no uniformity among internship centers concerning expectations regarding dissertations (if required by graduate programs). Some centers want the applicant to be finished with the dissertation before internship as do some graduate schools. The more typical pattern is for the graduate program to require that all course work for the degree, including a dissertation proposal, be completed before starting internship. In this pattern, the intern usually works on the dissertation during the internship period. The least desirable pattern for dissertation requirements (from the intern's point of view) is to have to return to the parent program to finish the dissertation. The post-internship student who has gone through a profound professionalization process (Lamb, Baker, Jennings, & Yarris, 1982) finds it difficult to return to the role of a student from that of a peer!

There is much variability among internship settings concerning the amount of "official" time (not counting evenings/weekends) which may be devoted to dissertation work—from none to a day a week for the entire year. It might be worthwhile to encourage or even require students to be finished with the data collection phase (and possible data analysis as well) before going on internship in order to interfere minimally with a full-time commitment to professional experience. Expectations and commitments regarding allotted hours and research support (e.g., availability of potential subjects, requirements for research protocol procedures, availability of support by facilities and staff, staff consulting competence, etc.) should be agreed upon prior to the time of offer/acceptance.

There is considerable variation among internship settings regarding the number and kind of rotations with which an intern is expected to be affiliated during the training year. A variety of rotations is typical, particularly in comprehensive hospitals (e.g., V.A. General Medical and Surgical), medical centers and consortia. One usual pattern may consist of 4-12 or 3-16 week (approximately) rotations in different settings during the year plus possibly minor rotations. The availability of supervising staff, specialty program emphasis, and rotation requirements necessary for funding support, are all factors which influence the pattern. In all likelihood, the above factors may be more basic in determining the rotational pattern than any philosophy of training to which the internship center staff might want to adhere. On the other hand, Langston (1979) has argued for a single rotation.

As more and more intervention techniques and skills become proven for cost-effectiveness, and as new areas of activity are developed, there is demand for greater diversification of practical experience in education/training. The development of a professional degree emphasizing hands-on experience is partially a response to frustration felt by practitioners, employees, and students that results from mismatch between training and job requirements (Kelly, Goldberg, Fiske, & Kilkowsky, 1978; Steinhelber & Maynor, 1981).

Another suggestion is for a second year of internship training which could be postdoctoral, but few schools have adopted this as a requirement. While students often decry the absence of a second year upon completion of their internship year, only a minority go on for a postdoctoral year. This additional training year is usually a specialization year (e.g., clinical child, neuropsychology, health psychology, etc.) and, incidentally, could provide the second year of supervised experience required for licensure in many states and the National Registry of Health Care Providers. For the 1986–1987 internship year, less than 130 funded postdoctoral adult clinical slots were listed in the 1985–86 APIC Directory. However, in the rapidly expanding Health Psychology field, for example, 43 predoctoral internship programs were listed in 1984 alone as a result of a Health Psychology Division survey. There is no system for accreditation of this level of training, but there are a number of other postdoctoral training positions available and postdoctoral training program criteria have recently been adopted by APIC (APIC, 1986).

Another atypical internship training issue concerns so-called respecialization or doctoral level psychologists with an area of competency other than clinical, counseling, or school who wish to respecialize in one of the above professional areas. APA has promulgated guidelines for the whole profession to facilitate and standardize this process (Conger, 1976). While internship centers tend to follow these guidelines, the individuals involved often present unusual issues to training programs such as age differences from other interns, or considerable ability/experience in nonprofessional aspects of psychology giving the appearance of competence. Evaluating applicant credentials for internship eligibility is also problematic since there are a small number of graduate programs which readily accommodate persons desiring respecialization (Stricker, Hull, & Woodring, 1984) and most frequently do so on an *ad hoc* basis. It can be anticipated that the demand for respecialization training will continue to increase (though no hard data seems readily available) as academic and research areas continue to be oversupplied with personnel.

The APA governance structure is now looking at the possibility of permitting developmental psychologists to be eligible for APA-approved clinical internships possibly without the respecialization preparations. It may be anticipated that the predictable burgeoning of Health Psychology training programs will probably increase the demand for health care clinical and/or postdoctoral respecialization internships. This phenomenon may arise from research-trained doctoral level psychologists who develop interest in health care as a result of research contact with the physically ill.

Training Models

Most internship programs train generalists, although the nature of the setting provides the limits and foci of training experiences. While interns may be trained in specific competency areas (neuropsychology, health psychology, hypnosis, mental health consultation, etc.), it is mostly in the clinical child competency area that established, full-time training is available in some internships—either in programs teaching clinical or school psychology interns. A pattern of labeling internship agencies as "general" or "specific" was utilized by APA in its accreditation designations for some years in the 1960s. This occurred prior to the development of community mental health centers, other more comprehensive service delivery systems, and increasing numbers of doctoral programs. The proliferation of competency areas in professional psychology, the development of consortia, "captive" or "wholly owned" internships, etc., may again lead to possible differentiations in internship program designations.

As budgets for internship training, including stipends, become tighter and training is more encumbered with some kind of service requirement, many present and future settings will be forced to look for training patterns that encourage better resource utilization. Consortia constitute one such emerging pattern. These are the most rapidly developing type of internship training arrangement. Each member of a consortium may not be strong enough in terms of staff, funding, and available experiences to provide appropriate training. As a group, however, consortia are likely to be able to provide more diversity of role models and experiences for more interns than the average of most single setting internship agencies.

APA recognized consortia are a viable new training structure, as indicated by the recently added evaluation criteria enumerated in the Accreditation Handbook (APA, 1983). Central administration, uniformity of policies, standards of intern admission and evaluation, quality control of training, and balance between flexibility and cohesiveness of training are of crucial importance for successful operation of such programs. Some consortia consist of 3-4 agencies, while some complex ones include a dozen or so participating training settings (Kurz & Wellner, 1983).

PUBLIC ACCOUNTABILITY

Professional psychology internships are accountable to national organizations, state license boards and other credentialing bodies, and to local institutions

Internship Training in Professional Psychology

Richard H. Dana

University of Arkansas, Fayettevile

W. Theodore May

University of Tennessee, Memphis

Tennessee Tech. Library
Cookeville, Tenn

HEMISPHERE PUBLISHING CORPORATION, Washington
A subsidiary of Harper & Row, Publishers, Inc.

Cambridge   New York   Philadelphia   San Francisco
London   Mexico City   São Paulo   Singapore   Sydney

and agencies responsible for funding. These various loci of responsibility can be described by designation of what constitutes an internship, approval mechanisms, and maintenance strategisms.

An internship is designated as an internship by credentialing, or approval, provided by the accreditation process of the American Psychological Association. In addition, however, the state license boards monitor the qualifications of individual interns while the profession exercises less direct control by means of guidelines for service providers in specialty areas. The internship provides opportunities for training that dovetail with these guidelines. There are also directories of designated service providers such as the National Register.

The accreditation procedures provided by the Education and Training Board of the American Psychological Association have evolved a pattern of requiring substantial documentation. A fairly standardized set of procedures has been promulgated in the present Accreditation Handbook (APA, 1983). As a result, the site visit, documentation requirements, reporting and review procedures are relatively independent of the two individuals who compose the site visit team. Even appeal processes within the American Psychological Association are clearly stated with procedures of demonstrated efficacy. Assessment criteria for internship accreditation are at the same level as those procedures for accreditation of graduate programs.

The importance of completing an APA-approved internship (and graduate training program) is gradually being recognized by prospective employers. For example, the Veterans Administration only hires staff psychologists who are from APA-approved programs and internships. The VA internship programs have been subject to these APA approval mechanisms since 1980. Prior to that date, it was tacitly assumed that blanket approval for all VA internships existed, although the first VA internship programs obtained APA-approval on a voluntary basis in the mid 1970s.

The Association of Professional Internship Centers (APIC) exercises nominal control over the selection process by a clearinghouse to put prospective interns and internship settings together after the usual selection process. In addition, APIC suggests exit criteria for internships. However, the American Psychological Association has been unwilling to provide money for computer matching of students with internships. Without such procedures the selection processes are characterized by undue pressures on students. The kind and extent of external monitoring which should be provided over the selection process is an open question. While the American Psychological Association has professional responsibility for human resource management, it is not clear whether this mandate extends to internship. It is evident, however, that present selection processes are anxiety-producing for the students who are prospective interns. The system is cumbersome, inefficient, uneconomical, and unnecessarily stressful for everyone (Stedman, 1983).

The critical issue for the immediate future pertains to scarce federal funding, or how to maintain and continue a sufficient number of internships to satisfy applicants from approved training programs. More persons are now going on internships as a result of the proliferation of professional schools and the higher student enrollments in these programs. In addition, there are counseling and school psychology interns in increasing numbers. Indeed, counseling psychology programs often use their own counseling centers while school psychology programs use placements that are not publicly listed, contractual, or even necessarily labeled as internships in school systems. There are even funded internship slots for particular intern applicants which further reduces the pool of competitively available internships.

Moreover, since increasing numbers of professionals in service delivery settings must show cost-effectiveness, psychology interns also have to generate income by providing services (Rosenberg, Bernstein, & Murray, 1985; Weiskopf & Newman, 1982; Wiens & Dresdale, 1984). This pressure for income as a result of intern services may reorder the internship priorities, and even make licensure before internship mandatory as in medicine. At the very least, there is potential conflict between service and training functions of internship. Such conflicts involve the university training programs which require assurance that training of their students is the primary concern of the internship setting. As a result of these issues internships in the future may include a larger number of private practice for profit settings.

As a result of these pressures, some students are forced to take internships that are not desired, or even among their top choices. A few programs protect their students by linkages with competent internships so that their students will not have to compete among themselves for these slots. Finally, professional schools are making the argument for captive internships and providing demonstrations of their effectiveness. Wright State, the Virginia Consortium, and Fuller have already turned in this direction. Whenever graduate programs have their own internships, they also must have their own model of training which incorporates a viable service delivery system. At the opposite extreme are about 15 internships that combine the resources of several independent settings into a consortium. As a result an extended array of training opportunities across varied patient populations for larger number of interns becomes available.

In the future there will be demand for additional resources, better use of resources, and increased cost-effectiveness in order to train more students. The American Psychological Association will have to provide overall aegis with systematic exploration of the utilities of many of the procedures already mentioned. Computerized selection, regionalized consortia, internship-training program specificity, internships that are captive within a single training program, and specialty internships constitute some of the alternative structures for more efficient, goodness-of-fit between student and internship. In addition, each of these alternatives contributes to rapprochement between training programs and internships because they all demand cooperative relationships. Finally, there is impact from each of these alternatives upon students, service delivery systems, and anticipated needs for services.

EVALUATION AND PROSPECTS FOR PROFESSIONAL PSYCHOLOGY TRAINING

Boulder Model

While there is still debate among professional psychologists concerning the adequacy of the traditional training model, clinical research has had little or no impact on practice (Barlow, 1981), and professional psychology has been unable to make a responsible contribution to society (Sarason, 1981). Our theories have been indicted as "scientifically unimpressive and technologically worthless" (Meehl, 1978, p. 806), and we have been accused of "ameaningful thinking," or fabricating knowledge as a result of methodology (Koch, 1981). Practitioners not only eschew research, but have little interest in examining journals that contain reports of empirical studies.

When the Boulder model was first described, psychology was an experimental science aping physics and biology. The values of that science included objectivity, operationism as method, the establishment of meaning by experimental procedure, and the use of analogues from lower animals. Instead of focus upon the study of one person, or differences among persons in various settings, the accepted and only legitimate research approach was to look for differences among experimental conditions. The subjects for research and experimentation were almost exclusively college students and for generations they were manipulated and/or deceived.

This heritage from Newtonian classical physics defined nature as independent of human beings, and therefore, objectively observable. As a result there were false dichotomies of person-nature, inner-outer, and observer-observed. Wyatt (1967) has emphasized the role of objectivity in creating these dichotomies. He described an "unsteadiness of facts," a changing array of data over time, coupled with a selectivity provided by the method or preconceptions of the observer, that made the demand for rigor gratuitous. By extrapolating somewhat from Wyatt's argument, the demand for objectivity can be conceived as a barrier, a set of limiting constraints between oneself and everything else. Objectivity is distance from primary data, an intellectualized detachment that results in distrust of sensory experience. Trust is placed in intellect so that ultimately the environment and other persons exist separately from ourselves. This subject-object split has been a central concern of existential writers (R. May, 1967).

Psychology has been reluctant to heed the new philosophy of science (Manicas & Secord, 1983) or to recognize that a new paradigm is required for a human science. Nonetheless, current popular writings offer the beginnings of a new paradigm that embraces all sciences (Capra, 1983). Kenneth Gergen (1982) has provided a sociorationalist metatheory that defines knowledge as a communal creation in which interpersonal colloquy can determine "the nature of things." It is sufficient to suggest here that the failure of the Boulder model was a failure of the prevailing model of science to be applicable to human beings. In a larger context, as a direct result of having implemented our traditional model of science to the limits of its effectiveness, we have societal problems which are apparently unsolvable, at least with our present technologies.

Training During Rapid Culture Change

Our culture has now entered an era in which new values and behaviors may be prerequisite to survival on this planet. We have an information, service, and consumer-oriented society with approximately four times as many service-producing workers as in 1947 when there were equal numbers of service- and goods-producing workers. A service society caters to consumers and offers a technical-managerial approach to human problem-solving. An information society encourages more critical and demanding consumers who can potentially provide themselves with a significant portion of existing professional services.

Professional training in psychology is complicated by interpenetrating issues that include the magnitude of our current social problems and an experienced sense of despair and inability to respond constructively to these problems. The changing population demographics both complicate these problems and provide new resources for problem-solving. A shift in values has increased our sensitivity to social and individual dilemmas. This section will focus on the implications of the shift in values and the issue of stability versus change in the design and operation of professional psychology training programs.

Values Although there has been a recent trend toward conservatism, the values that now undergird our society are essentially humanistic. These values were fostered during the 1960s by Vietnam, counter cultures, and a new consciousness that emerged with the increasing numbers of college educated service-producing workers, particularly women and minority persons. Gartner and Reissman (1974) have described these values as consonant with extended human rights coupled with emergent liberation- personal identity themes that reflect an emphasis on group oriented interpersonal relations or communion. Communion is wholeness producing by contact, openness, and noncontractual cooperation, or being at one with others (Bakan, 1966). Explicit in this definition is a shared, cooperative basis for livelihood and experiences that emphasizes societal survival, well-being, and commitment beyond the self (Bellah, Madsen, Sullivan, Swidler, & Tipton, 1985).

Historically, however, it was individualism that described the pioneer spirit of the Horatio Alger myth that will power, determination, capacity for delayed gratification, and intense personal industry inevitably resulted in success. Individualism embodied the culturally-defined masculine virtues that were believed to be necessary for survival on the frontier in a primarily agricultural society and later in the competitive marketplace of industrial capitalism.

The augmented status of minorities, especially Blacks and Hispanics, has resulted in a demand that society be responsive to their values in addition to their needs. Two such values are communion/cooperativeness—the recognition that the larger social reality must be considered in all transactions—and a prioritization of persons which results in a more relaxed pace and recognition that there must be time to relate sensitively to individuals in order to acknowledge their presence and primacy in a high technology, task-oriented society which provides evaluation on the basis of performances.

The status of women—as embodied in the sexism of sex-role sterotypy—also emerged from the rubric of an individualistic and paternalistic society. In the past, sharing, cooperation, and sensitivity to the needs of others were considered to be signs of weakness in males and only acceptable as female traits which were undesirable in themselves. Sex-role stereotypy—the ascription of negatively toned traits to normal women—relegated women to the status of second class citizens whose power came from discreet and manipulative associations with men. Knowledge of sex-role stereotypy began with the discovery that mental health professionals equated male characteristics with healthy traits (Broverman, Broverman, Clarkson, Rosencrantz, & Vogel, 1970).

In spite of a woman vice-presidential candidate in 1984, the Equal Rights Amendment is still in limbo. Male professional psychologists still derogate women clients (Bowman, 1982; Steuer, 1982) and the frequently capricious and sexualized supervision of women interns and graduate students (Dana, 1987; Pleck, 1976; Rozsnafszky, 1979) is testimony to bias in professional training. Cross-sex professional gambits in training involving power, sexuality, and prejudice (Gallessich, Gilbert, & Holahan, 1980) have not been addressed in any formal manner by training programs. That these gambits occur is certainly related to the fact that nourishment of intimate relationships is the most difficult life task in this culture.

Slater (1974) and Hogan (1975) have argued that individualism while historically necessary for the development of this society may now be antithetical to survival. Both individualism and communion are represented in professional psychology training and activity in the form of health psychology and community psychology as well as by Alpha and Beta students, respectively. Alpha students conform to objective reality and social responsibility ethics while Beta students perceive reality subjectively and abide by personal conscience ethics (Dana, 1982). At the present time, individualism also appears in the form of practicing relevant specialties in the private sector. Private practitioners in psychology have become akin to physicians and lawyers—a successful elite with status, affluence, and power. This success story which will continue in the next decade has occurred because professional psychology combines aspects of religion, medicine, and science into an expectation for knowledge, healing, and salvation in the form of sustained health and psychological well being. The expression of individualism in professional psychology should prevail for the immediate future while communion may diminish as community psychology continues to be disenfranchised by political and economic changes in society.

Within professional psychology we have become aware of a penchant for blaming persons for their emotional problems (Beit-Hallahmi, 1974). There are clear societal consequences that have been described by Caplan and Nelson (1973): (a) cultural institutions are exonerated from blame for the creation of personal problems; (b) simultaneously institutions are not obligated to ameliorate social conditions; (c) person-change thus becomes mandatory in order to control troublesome groups or discredit system-oriented critique; (d) the mental health machinery placates by providing occupation for those professionals who could potentially change the system; and (e) finally the social myth that persons control their own fate is reinforced, at least for those with positions of power and prestige, especially professional persons. By focusing professional acts upon situationally-relevant behaviors as well as person-emanating behaviors, matters of social policy that ultimately affect the welfare of all persons may be minimized or disregarded.

The effect of shifts in values (communion vs. individualism) and rapid social change permits a focus upon the use of skills and knowledge for prevention of human distress as well as for social system intervention (Sarason, 1986). Schneider (1971) has called the new professional psychologist a "passionate social advocate" and this description is appropriate for a consumer-oriented society. Accountability for professional services and the rights of consumers of these services are major issues that are consonant with a human science ideology.

Hogan (1970) argued for a distinction between professional acts based upon personal conscience and those acts that stem from social responsibility. These two dimensions reflect underlying personality structures that contribute substantially to the justification of moral judgments and decisions. Persons who act in terms of personal conscience have intuitive notions of right and wrong based on higher laws which may be unrelated to prevailing human legislation. They are quick to transcend the dictates of custom and law, unconventional, independent, liberal, progressive, and sometimes even capricious or undependable. Believing that the locus of importance resides in individuals, they can be advocates of system change or system evolution. These persons are Dana's (1982) Beta students and Lipsey's (1974) social activists who perceive reality by intuition that is based on a humanistic ideology.

The major direction of practice based on personal conscience ethics was community psychology in its broadest sense. First, cultural amplification is derived from a deliberate search for community sources of strength and their development. By maximizing ignored but existing community resources, the disadvantaged discover collective power and desirable differences between groups are identified and sustained. Professionals act as partners who facilitate the expertise of their clients in new areas. This constitutes a grassroots approach to system-change by the creation of local, alternative settings, whose function helps to prevent community problems in ways that are personally and socially relevant and meaningful (Felner, Jason, Moritsugu, & Farber, 1983; Rappaport, Davidson, Wilson & Mitchell, 1975).

Second, personal conscience ethics may be demonstrated by political investment in creation of social policy per se or an implementation of existing policy. Such primary prevention is conducted in concert with members of other professions—city planners, architects, engineers, agricultural specialists, etc. Finally, there may be an involvement in the development and use of objective description of the quality of life. Such indices can eventually monitor the "good life" for all citizens by reflecting changes in education, health, economic conditions, crime, politics, and population changes. In addition, life experience measures including well-being, happiness, or satisfaction, general affect, and perceived stress can provide a mirror for the quality of life. Thus, there are three levels of focus on institutions and a role as change agent that may be labeled as political, cooperative-interprofessional, and quality of life monitoring.

Professional psychology carefully elaborated the ethics of personal conscience in the Vail model, practitioner programs, and nourished those students whose values coincided with practice/research that was socially relevant. However, the pendulum shifted and the world these students desired was not to be immediately forthcoming. Students who function under a social responsibility ethic and abide by rational considerations were increasingly selected and rewarded in training programs that emphasized an indigenous behavioral-learning basis for professional practice. These students seek structure and order and tend to be thoughtful, considerate, honest, conventional, and overly conforming. They strongly distrust personal, intuitive conceptions of morality and they prize stability and order. They are Dana's Alpha students and Lipsey's (1974) social engineers, objective in their vision of reality and normative in their personal ideology. They are the professional psychologists of this generation who are focused on service delivery to individuals—the inheritors of individual and group psychotherapy roles. These persons are more likely to be trained in Boulder model programs because what they do professionally is ultimately based on the acquisition of traditional skills, especially those skills that depend upon behavioral technology.

Professional psychology practice that is motivated by a social responsibility ethic will be creative in using a variety of techniques and skills since there are many avenues to internal scanning and greater voluntary controls over our bodies, our heads, and ultimately our lives. While this area defines a practice that ideally may become growth-inducing and preventive of personal and social distress, it is more likely to provide only situationally limited but increasingly effective tertiary interventions.

It would be desirable if professional psychologists of the immediate future could combine individualism and communion in order to fuse responsible actions with more genuine caring and commitment. The fostering of human service professions that encourage a lifetime of professional investment in other persons involving shared skills, feelings, responsibility, and intimate relationship is one antidote for the social crises of the present time. While the personal value of such services for the service provider has been only infrequently described (Dana, 1974, Sarason, 1985), an honest motive for human service is nourishment of the humanity of the service provider.

Stability Versus Change Professional psychologists and training programs for these psychologists are affected by rapid social change. As individuals and programs they must be able to monitor their practices in order to be able to react to demands for specialized services without losing contact with their psychology origins. In the past, however, psychologists and psychology programs were reluctant to be scrutinized. For example, psychotherapists have been conspicuously unwilling to have their therapy transactions closely examined (Bednar & Shapiro, 1970) and there are few case studies of institutional function as it impinges upon persons (e.g., Dana, 1964; Sarason, 1972; Stotland & Kobler, 1965).

Notable exceptions to this statement have been the clinical psychology programs at the University of Kansas and the University of Alabama. These programs permitted and encouraged a careful examination of the goodness-of-fit between their stated training values and practica, courses, and program governance (Dana, 1978). The Kansas department engaged in routine monitoring of all training/services performed by staff/students in the Psychological Clinic while some other departments have also completed follow-up studies of their graduate students in order to have a responsible awareness of program effectiveness (e.g., Barry, 1978; Rickard & Siegel, 1976). Psychologists as service-providers, and graduate programs or internships as purveyors of the culture of professional psychology, should engage in constant self-study and monitoring of their functions in order to have a data base for use in implementing change in response to external pressures.

However, we have not developed any generic prospectus for training during this period of rapid social change. The rapid social change and our increasing inability to cope on a worldwide basis are symptoms of a need for a new scientific paradigm upon which to base our understanding and our actions. As the magnitude of social problems increases, humanistic values will make awareness of these social problems more poignant and unsettling for more persons. For example, Peter Nathan, Alan Ross, Nichols Cummings, and Donald

Peterson provided scenarios which illustrate such awareness (Strupp & Schacht, 1984). Consumers of the services of health providers are largely invisible to professional psychologists and are disadvantaged in communication with us. As we have unwittingly repeated the tragedy of the commons—depredation of our communal professional resources—we accelerate the demise of a Golden Era in clinical psychology. However, there are a variety of harbingers of more socially and professionally beneficial outcomes for this present period of reassessment: (a) some proposals for generic training programs in which salient issues are selection of students, curricula, and proposed resolutions of the scientist-professional interface within professional education contexts; (b) some proposals for preparation and regulation of professional psychologists (Fox, Kovacs, & Graham, 1985); (c) the Morgantown Planning Conference on Issues in University-based Graduate Education (Bickman, 1985); (d) a 1986 national training conference on internships proposed at the Executive Business Meeting of the Association of Psychology Internship Centers (APIC Newsletter, 1985) and conducted early in 1987; (e) a national conference on the future of graduate education and training held in San Diego in December 1986 by the National Council of Schools of Professional Psychology (NCSPP).

Recently, generic training programs have been proposed by Dana (1984), Levy (1984), and Schneider (1985) on the premise of rapid social change and the sense of an emerging, new paradigm. Dana's program focuses on selection of Beta students who would be trained to practice and to do research within a human science rubric. The goodness-of-fit between student and program would be dramatically increased as well as the relevance of the training ingredients to current social problems and amelioration of quality of life by primary and secondary interventions. While the scope and contents of this proposed academic training program are beyond the purview of this book, internships would be increasingly within captive settings and there would be an even greater intermeshing of academic and practice settings and contents than is currently available. Moreover, the basic training in psychology would reflect the human science approach and thus be congruent with the values and consciousness of more students.

Comprehensive overhaul of the entire educational system for professional psychology has been suggested (Fox, Kovacs, & Graham, 1985). Twenty proposals were offered as a stimulus to debate. These proposals pertain to education for professional practice, licensure for professional practice, and professional practice specialties. Educational proposals include a preprofessional psychology major, a bona fide degree of master of psychology (MPsy), and restriction of training to schools of psychology affiliated with accredited universities. Doctoral level education should be generic, require four years in accord with a practitioner-scholar model, result in a doctor of psychology (PsyD) degree from programs that are organized to provide easy access for part-time and master's degree students. Functional specialization as the result of a two year full-time experience in an accredited comprehensive psychological service center is recommended. Professional practice proposals include a generic license to permit practice by persons with PsyD degrees from approved schools of professional psychology with 3000 hours of appropriately supervised professional experience. This licensing examination should assess competency for practice and specify specialty titles in addition to the title "psychologist." These license boards would regulate the practice of limited practitioners. Specialty diplomas would be issued by the American Board of Professional Practice, or similar entities, to licensed professional psychologists on the basis of knowledge of the specialty, legal and ethical issues in specialty practice, and demonstrated competence in specialty practice.

The Morgantown planning conference (Bickman, 1985) included 20 distinguished participants and 10 observers representing groups and organizations. Twelve papers on issue areas were contained in a report resulting from this conference which was widely circulated with a call for commentary. A National Training Conference on Issues of Graduate Education in Psychology is being scheduled for 1987. This conference report is distinguished from the Fox et al. (1985) proposals by delineation of problems and problem areas rather than any suggestion of specific remediations. The balance between professional practice and research, or Boulder scientist-practitioner model, has evolved into scholar-practitioner and practitioner-researcher models. Curriculum issues—core versus individualized and breadth versus depth—were recognized as well as a need for identification of contents appropriate for various levels of education. A necessity for application of what we have already developed as a psychology profession to graduate education was emphasized. The complexity of training settings and their organizational structures was acknowledged. Issues of application included technology transfer—"systematic organization of applied psychology to meet the needs of society." Program quality control, or evaluation of training effectiveness, are issues for the immediate future in a society where costs and benefits of training are constantly being reexamined. The directions and areas for future growth raised issues regarding the use of knowledge from basic sciences, the importance of common interests among psychologists, and planning for transitions from research to practice. Finally, student issues that are pertinent to the themes of this book—recruitment, retention, and socialization—were examined with particular reference to ethnic minorities and the provision of training for cross-cultural service-delivery. Norcross (1984) has also indicated that we must reconcile discrepancies between training and practice. For example, 50 percent of professional psychologists see racial minority clients while only one-fifth of programs provided any relevant training for these services.

The proposed 1986 national training conference on internships has been antedated by visits from a steering committee member, Kent Poey, to 12 internship programs (Poey, 1985). In addition to descriptive information, Poey portrayed interns' working conditions and stress, examined recruitment and notification procedures, including minority recruitment. Evaluation of interns and interns' evaluations of program/staff/training were examined, including the disposition of impaired interns. Stress management mechanisms were absent in most programs. Programs emphasized one theoretical model for supervision, specifically either psychodynamic, behavioral-cognitive, eclectic, or family. Interns' training and research practices, including health psychology activities, and innovative training were listed as behavioral medicine, short-term therapy, supervision techniques, and mental health administration. These recent issues discussed by Kent Poey include the range of content in this book.

REFERENCES

Abramowitz, E. A. (1981). School psychology: A historical perspective. *School Psychology Review, 10,* 121–126.

Albee, G. W. (1970). The uncertain future of clinical psychology. *American Psychologist, 25,* 1071–1080.

Albee, G. W. (1982) The uncertain direction of clinical psychology. In J. R. McNamara and A. G. Barclay (Eds.), *Critical issues, developments, and trends in professional psychology* (pp. 295–312). New York: Praeger.

Albee, G. W. (1986). Toward a just society: Lessons from observations on the primary prevention of psychopathology. *American Psychologist, 41,* 891–898.

Alcorn, J. D., & Nicholas, D. (1983). Training in counseling psychology: Data and trends. *The Counseling Psychologist, 11*(4), 93–94.

Aldrich, L. C. (1982). *Construction of mixed standard scales for the rating of psychotherapy supervisors.* Unpublished master's thesis, Auburn University, Auburn, AL.

Alpert, J. L. (1985). Change within a profession: Change, future, prevention and school psychology. *American Psychologist, 40,* 1112–1121.

Altmaier, E. M. (1984, August). Survey of health psychology training among counseling psychology programs. In G. Howard (Chair), *Counseling psychology and health behavior: Current status and future possibilities.* Symposium conducted at the meeting of the American Psychological Association, Toronto.

American Psychological Association. (1947). Committee on Training in Clinical Psychology. Recommended graduate training program in clinical psychology. *American Psychologist, 2,* 539–558.

American Psychological Association. (1949). Committee on Training in Clinical Psychology. Doctoral training programs in clinical psychology. *American Psychologist, 3,* 331–341.

American Psychological Association. (1961). Internships for doctoral training in clinical psychology approved by the American Psychological Association, *American Psychologist, 16,* 25–29.

American Psychological Association. (1968). APA-approved doctoral programs in clinical and in counseling psychology: 1968. *American Psychologist, 23,* 752–753.

American Psychological Association. (1980). *Accreditation handbook*. Washington, DC: Author (Revised March, 1983).

American Psychological Association. (1981a). *Graduate study in psychology: 1982-1983* (15th Ed.). Washington, DC: Author.

American Psychological Association. (1981b). Specialty guidelines for delivery of services by school psychologists. *American Psychologist, 36*(6), 670-681.

American Psychological Association. (1982). Approved doctoral programs in clinical, counseling, and school psychology: 1982. *American Psychologist, 37*, 1374-1376.

American Psychological Association. (1982a). APA-approved predoctoral internships for doctoral training in clinical and counseling psychology: 1982. *American Psychologist, 37*(12), 1369-1373.

American Psychological Association. (1982b). APA-approved doctoral programs in clinical, counseling, and school psychology: 1982. *American Psychologist, 37*(12), 1374-1376.

American Psychological Association. (1984a). APA-accredited doctoral programs in professional psychology: 1984. *American Psychologist, 39*, 1466-1472.

American Psychological Association. (1984b). Supplement to listing of APA-accredited doctoral and internship training programs. *American Psychologist, 39*, 690.

American Psychological Association. (1984c). Capsule, *1*(1), 3.

American Psychological Association. (1984d). APA-accredited predoctoral internships for doctoral training in psychology: 1984. *American Psychologist, 39*, 1455-1465.

American Psychological Association. (1985). Accredited captive internships listed. *Monitor, 16*(5), 39.

Arthur, A. (1972). Which is the relevant science for the scientist-professional? *Professional Psychology, 3*, 327-330.

Association of Psychology Internship Centers. (1985). Minutes of the Executive Business Meeting, *11*(1), 6-11.

Association of Psychology Internship Centers. (1985-86). *Directory: Internship programs in professional psychology, including post-doctoral training programs.* Author.

Association of Psychology Internship Centers. (1986). *Newsletter, 11*(2).

Association of Psychology Internship Centers Directory. (1983. Proposed guidelines for defining internships in Psychology, *12*, 26-27.

Association of Psychology Internship Centers Newsletter. (1981). Standards for evaluation and training, *8*(1), 20-25.

Aubrey, R. F. (1977). Historical developments of guidance and counseling and implications for the future. *The Personnel and Guidance Journal, 55*, 288-295.

Bakan, D. (1966). *The duality of human existence.* Chicago: Rand McNally.

Baldick, T. L. (1980). Ethical discrimination ability of intern psychologists: A function of training in ethics. *Professional Psychology, 11*, 276-282.

Banikotes, P. G. (1980). Counseling psychology training: Data and implications. *The Counseling Psychologist, 8*(4), 73-74.

Bardon, J. I. (1982). School psychology's dilemma: A proposal for its resolution. *Professional Psychology, 13*(6), 955-968.

Barlow, D. H. (1974). Psychologists in the emergency room. *Professional Psychology, 4,* 251-256.

Barlow, D. H. (1981). On the relation of clinical research to clinical practice: Current issues, new directions. *Journal of Consulting and Clinical Psychology, 49,* 147-155.

Barnes, B. (1982). Do intern applicants really need a survival guide? *Professional Psychology, 13,* 342-344.

Barry, J. R. (1978). A survey of Ph.D. graduates from the Department of Psychology of the University of Georgia. *Professional Psychology, 9,* 665-671.

Bednar, R., & Shapiro, J. (1970). Professional research commitment: A symptom or a syndrome. *Journal of Consulting and Clinical Psychology, 34,* 323-326.

Beit-Hallahmi, B. (1974). Salvation and its vicissitudes. Clinical psychology and political values. *American Psychologist, 29,* 124-129.

Belar. C. D., & Orgel, S. A. (1980). Survival guide for intern applicants. *Professional Psychology, 11,* 672-675.

Belar, C. D., Wilson, E., & Hughes, H. (1982). Health psychology training in doctoral psychology programs. *Health Psychology, 1,* 289-299.

Bellah, R. N., Madsen, R., Sullivan, W. M., Swidler, A., & Tipton, S. M. (1985). *Habits of the heart: Individualism and commitment in American life.* Berkeley, CA: University of California Press.

Berkman, A. S., & Berkman, C. F. (1984). The supervision of cotherapist teams in family therapy. *Psychotherapy, 21,* 197-205.

Bickman, L. B. (Ed.). (1985). *Issues and origins: Graduate education in psychology.* Washington, DC: American Psychological Association.

Blatt, S. J. (1963). The objective and subjective modes: Some considerations in the teaching of clinical skills. *Journal of Projective Techniques, 27,* 151-157.

Bornstein, P. H., & Wollersheim, J. P. (1978). Scientist-practitioner activities among psychologists of behavioral and nonbehavioral orientations. *Professional Psychology, 9,* 659-664.

Bowman, P. R. (1982). An analog study with beginning therapists suggesting bias against "activity" in women. *Psychotherapy: Training, Research and Practice, 19,* 318-324.

Brayfield, A. H. (1963). Counseling psychology. *Annual Review of Psychology, 14,* 319-350.

Briggs, D. W. (1984). Proposal for a centralized computer internship matching system. *APIC Newsletter, 9,* 4-16.

Brill, R., Wolkin, J., McKeel, N. (1985). Strategies for selecting and securing the predoctoral clinical internship of choice. *Professional Psychology: Research and Practice, 16,* 3-6.

Broverman, K., Broverman, D., Clarkson, F., Rosencrantz, P., & Vogel, S. (1970). Sex role stereotypes and clinical judgments of mental health. *Journal of Consulting and Clinical Psychology, 34,* 1-7.

Brown, D. T., & Minke, K. M. (1984). *Directory of School Psychology Training Programs.* Washington, DC: National Association of School Psychologists.

Brown, D. T., Horne, A. J., & Lindstrom, J. P. (1981). *Handbook of certification/licensure requirements for school psychologists* (3rd ed.). Washington, DC: NASP

Brown, D. T., Cardon, B. W., Coulter, W. A., & Meyers, J. (Eds.). (1982). The Olympia proceedings. Section I: Introduction and background. *School Psychology Review, 11*(2), 107–111.

Bruch, H. (1974). *Learning psychotherapy: Rationale and ground rules.* Cambridge, MA: Harvard University Press.

Burstein, A. G. (1983). A new look at internship placement procedures. *APIC Newsletter, 9,* 15–16.

Burstein, A. G., Barnes, R. H., & Quesada, G. M. (1976). Training clinical psychologists in medical settings: Ideological and practical considerations. *Professional Psychology, 7,* 396–402.

Burstein, A. G., Schoenfeld, L. S., Loucks, S., Stedman, J. M., & Costello, R. M. (1981). Selection of internship site: Basis of choice by desirable candidates. *Professional Psychology, 12,* 596–598.

Caddy, G. R. (1981). The development and current status of professional psychology. *Professional Psychology, 12,* 377–384.

Caddy, G. R. (1982). The emergence of professional psychology: Background to the Virginia Beach Conference and beyond. In D. R. Peterson (Ed.), *Educating professional psychologists* (pp. 3–16). New Brunswick, NJ: Transaction Books.

Caddy, G. R., & LaPointe, L. L. (1986). The training of professional psychologists: Historical developments and present trends. In G. S. Tryon (Ed.), *Professional practice of psychology* (pp. 3–49). Norwood, NJ: Ablex.

California State Psychologist. (1984, April). *California accredited and approved programs in psychology, 19*(4), 6.

Caplan, N., & Nelson, S. (1973). On being useful: The nature and consequences of psychological research on social problems. *American Psychologist, 28,* 199–211.

Capra, F. (1983). *The turning point.* New York: Bantam.

Cardon, B. W. (1982). Synthesis of the scenarios. The future: A context for present planning. *School Psychology Review 11*(2), 151–160.

Carlin, A. S. (1982). *Is there a free lunch? Experiences with unfunded interns.* Paper presented at the Association of Psychology Internship Centers Annual Meeting, Washington, DC.

Carmody, T. P., & Zohn, J. (1980). APA-approved group treatment internship training opportunities: Present status and future directions. *Professional Psychology, 11,* 213–219.

Cleveland, S. E. (1980). Counseling psychology: An endangered species. *Professional Psychology, 11,* 314–323.

Cohen, R. J., & DeBetz, B. (1977). Responsive supervision of the psychiatric resident and clinical psychology intern. *American Journal of Psychoanalysis, 37,* 51–64.

Cole, M. A., Kolko, D. J., & Craddick, R. A. (1981). The quality and process of the internship experience. *Professional Psychology, 12,* 570–577.

Conger, J. J. (1976). Proceedings of the American Psychological Association, Incorporated. for the year 1975: Minutes of the annual meeting of the Council of Representatives. *American Psychologist, 31,* 406–434.

Cook, V. J. (1983). *Clinical internships for school psychologists: The view from academe.* Paper presented at the annual meeting of the National Association of School Psychologists, Detroit.

Craddick, R. (1984). A suggestion for making a cumbersome procedure more efficient in the internship placement process. *APIC Newsletter, 9,* 7–9.

Craddick, R. A., Cole, M. A., Dane, J., Brill, R., & Wilson, J. A. (1980). The process of selecting predoctoral internship training sites. *Professional Psychology, 11,* 548–549.

Curtis, M. J., & Yager, G. G. (1981). A systems model for the supervision of school psychological services. *School Psychology Review, 10,* 425–433.

Cutts, N. (Ed.). (1955). *School psychologists at mid-century.* Washington, DC: American Psychological Association.

Dana, R. H. (1964). The impact of fantasy on a residential treatment program. *Corrective Psychiatry and Journal of Social Therapy, 10,* 202–212.

Dana, R. H. (1974). Psychotherapist into person: Transformation, identity, and practices. *Journal of Individual Psychology, 30,* 81–91.

Dana, R. H. (1978). Comparisons of competence training in two successful programs. *Psychological Reports, 42,* 919–926.

Dana, R. H. (1982). *A human science model for personality assessment with projective techniques.* Springfield, IL: Thomas.

Dana, R. H. (1984). Megatrends in personality assessment: Toward a human science professional psychology. *Journal of Personality Assessment, 48,* 463–579.

Dana, R. H. (1987). Training for professional psychology: Science, practice and identity. *Professional Psychology: Research and Practice, 18,* 9–16.

Dana, R. H., & Brookings, J. B. (1980). *Program evaluation: An evolving methodology for an internship.* Unpublished paper, University of Arkansas.

Dana, R. H., Gilliam, M., & Dana, J. (1976). Adequacy of academic-clinical preparation for internship. *Professional Psychology, 7,* 112–116.

Domke, J. A. (1982). Current issues in counseling psychology: Entitlement, education, and identity confusion. *Professional Psychology, 13*(6), 859–870.

Drummond, F. E., Rodolfa, E., & Smith, D. (1981). A survey of APA- and non-APA-approved internship programs. *American Psychologist, 36,* 411–414.

Edwards, D., & Wyrick, L. C. (1977). An administrative rotation in the clinical psychology internship: The chief intern at Duke Medical Center. *Professional Psychology, 8,* 253–255.

Ekstein, R., & Wallerstein, R. S. (1972). *Teaching and learning of psychotherapy.* New York: International University Press.

Elfant, A. B. (1985). Psychotherapy and assessment in hospital settings: Ideological and professional conflicts. *Professional Psychology: Research and Practice, 16,* 55–63.

Fagan, T. K. (1985). Further on the development of school psychology. *American Psychologist, 40,* 1262–1264.

Fagan, T. K. (1986). School psychology's dilemma: Reappraising solutions and directing attention to the future. *American Psychologist, 41,* 851–861.

Felner, R. D., Jason, L. A., Moritsugu, J. N., & Farber, S. S. (Eds.). (1983). *Preventive psychology: Theory, research and practice.* New York: Pergamon.

Fitzgerald, L. F., & Osipow, S. H. (1986). An occupational analysis of counseling psychology. *American Psychologist, 41,* 535–544.

Fleming, J., & Benedek, T. (Eds.). (1966). *Psychotherapy supervision.* New York: Grune & Stratton.

Fox, R. E. (1982). The need for a reorientation of clinical psychology. *American Psychologist, 37,* 1051–1057.

Fox, R. E., Barclay, A. G., & Rogers, D. A. (1982). The foundations of professional psychology. *American Psychologist, 37,* 306–312.

Fox, R. E., Kovacs, A. L., & Graham, S. R. (1985). Proposal for a revolution in the preparation and regulation of professional psychologists. *American Psychologist, 40,* 1042–1050.

Frank. G. (1984). The Boulder Model: History, rationale, and critique. *Professional Psychology: Research and Practice, 15,* 417–435.

French, J. L. (1984). On the conception, birth, and early development of school psychology with special reference to Pennsylvania. *American Psychologist, 39,* 976–987.

Fretz, B. R. (1980). Counseling psychology: 2001. In J. M. Witely and B. R. Fretz (Eds.)., *The present and future of counseling psychology.* Monterey, CA: Brooks/Cole.

Friedlander, S. R., Dye, N. W., Costello, R. M., & Kobos, J. C. (1984). A developmental model for teaching and learning in psychotherapy supervision. *Psychotherapy, 21,* 189–196.

Gallessich, J. M., Gilbert, L., & Holahan, C. (1980). A training model to facilitate professional effectiveness in power-salient and sex-salient situations. *Professional Psychology, 11,* 15–23.

Garfield, S. (1966). Clinical psychology and the search for identity. *American Psychologist, 21,* 353–362.

Gartner, A., & Reissman, F. (1974). *The service society and the consumer vanguard.* New York: Harper & Row.

Gentry, W. D., Street, W. J., Masur, F. T., & Asken, M. J. (1981). Training in medical psychology: A survey of graduate and internship training programs. *Professional Psychology, 12,* 224–228.

Gergen, K. J. (1982). *Toward transformation in social knowledge.* New York: Springer-Verlag.

Gilmore, G. E. (1974). Models for school psychology: Dimensions, barriers, and implications. *Journal of School Psychology, 12,* 95–101.

Goh, D. S. (1977). Graduate training in school psychology. *Journal of School Psychology, 15*(3), 207–218.

Goin, M. (1982). The basic principles of psychotherapy supervision. In *The art of psychotherapy: Highlights of the third annual Vail Conference of the Menninger Foundation*. Philadelphia: Smithkline.

Gold, J. R., Meltzer, R. H., & Sherr, R. L. (1982). Professional transition: Psychology internships in rehabilitation settings. *Professional Psychology, 13*, 397–402.

Goldberg, A. L., & McNamara, K. M. (1984). Internship training in clinical neuropsychology. *Professional Psychology: Research and Practice, 15*, 509–514.

Golden, C. J., & Kuperman, S. K. (1980). Training opportunities in neuropsychology at APA-approved internship settings. *Professional Psychology, 11*, 907–918.

Goldschmitt, M., Tipton, R. M., & Wiggins, R. C. (1981). Professional identity of counseling psychologists. *Journal of Counseling Psychology, 28*(2), 158–167.

Grace, W. C. (1985). Evaluating a prospective clinical internship: Tips for the applicant. *Professional Psychology: Research and Practice, 16*, 475–480.

Graduate Medical Education National Advisory Committee. (1980). Report to the Secretary, U.S. Department of Health and Human Services publications (HRA) 81-651-657. Hyattsville, MD., Health Resources Administration, Office of Graduate Medical Education, Vols. 1–7.

Grater, H. A. (1985). Stages in psychotherapy supervision: From therapy skills to skilled therapist. *Professional Psychology: Research and Practice, 16*, 605–610.

Grotjahn, M. (1955). Problems and techniques of supervision. *Psychiatry, 18*, 9–15.

Halpin, R. J., & Adams, J. F. (1978). Doctoral students view their APA counseling psychology programs. *Professional Psychology, 9*, 650–658.

Hays, J. R. (1976). Study of former interns of the Texas Research Institute. *Psychological Reports, 38*, 835–838.

Hersh, J. B., & Poey, K. (1984). A proposed interviewing guide for intern applicants. *Professional Psychology: Research and Practice, 15*, 3–5.

Hess, A. K. (1980). *Psychotherapy supervision: Theory, research and practice*. New York: John Wiley & Sons.

Hess, A. K. (1984). *Learning counseling and psychotherapy skills: A challenge in personal and professional identity*. Paper presented at the meeting of the Southeastern Psychological Association, New Orleans.

Hess, A. K., & Hess, K. A. (1983). Psychotherapy supervision: A survey of internship training practices. *Professional Psychology: Research and Practice, 14*, 504–513.

Hogan, R. (1970). A dimension of moral judgment. *Journal of Consulting and Clinical Psychology, 35*, 205–213.

Hogan, R. (1975). Theoretical egocentrism and the problem of compliance. *American Psychologist, 30*, 533–540.

Hughes, H. M. (1985). The need for more child-oriented training for clinical psychologists. *Journal of Clinical Child Psychology, 14*, 165–166.

Hull, C. L. (1928). *Aptitude testing*. Yonkers: World Book.

Ivey, A. E. (1976). Counseling psychology: The psychoeducator model and the future. *The Counseling Psychologist, 6*(3), 72–75.

Johnson, J. H., & Bornstein, P. H. (1974). A survey of behavior modification training opportunities in APA-approved internship facilities. *American Psychologist, 29,* 342–348.

Johnson, J. W. (1978, April). *The hazards of effective training.* Paper presented at the meeting of the Southwestern Psychological Association, New Orleans.

Johnston, J. (1982). Licensure laws sought. *Guidepost* (Newsletter of the American Personnel and Guidance Association), *24*(13), 1–6.

Jordaan, J. P., Myers, R. A., Layton, W. L., & Morgan, H. H. ((Eds.). (1968). *The Counseling Psychologist.* New York: Teachers College Press, Columbia University.

Kagan, N. (1977). Presidential address, Division 17. *The Counseling Psychologist, 7*(2), 4–9.

Kaslow, N. J., & Rice, D. G. (1985). Developmental stresses of psychology internship training: What training staff can do to help. *Professional Psychology: Research and Practice, 16,* 253–261.

Kelly, E. L., Goldberg, L. R., Fiske, D. W., & Kilkowski, J. M. (1978). Twenty-five years later: A follow-up study of the graduate students in clinical psychology assessed in the VA selection research project. *American Psychologist, 33,* 746–755.

Khol, T., Matefy, R., & Turner, J. (1972). Evaluation of APA internship programs: A survey of clinical psychology interns. *Journal of Clinical Psychology, 28,* 562–569.

King, P. T., & Seymour, W. R. (1982). Education and training in counseling psychology. *Professional Psychology, 13,* 834–842.

Knoff, H., & Batsche, G. (1985). *Standards for the credentialing of school psychologists.* NASP Executive Board/Delegate Assembly.

Koch, S. (1981). The nature and limits of psychological knowledge: Lessons of a century qua "science". *American Psychologist, 36,* 257–269.

Korman, M. (Ed.). (1976). *Levels and patterns of professional training in psychology.* Washington, DC: American Psychological Association.

Korn, J. H., Keiser, K. W., & Stevenson, J. F. (1982). Practicum and internship training in program evaluation. *Professional Psychology, 13,* 462–469.

Kratochwill, T. R. (1982). School psychology: Dimensions of its dilemma and future directions. *Professional Psychology, 13*(6), 977–989.

Kurz, R. B., Fuchs, M., Dabek, R. F., Kurtz, S. M. S., & Helfrich, W. T. (1982). Characteristics of predoctoral internships in professional psychology. *American Psychologist, 37,* 1213–1220.

Kurz, R.B., & Wellner, A. M. (1983). Accreditation of professional training programs in psychology. B. D. Sales (Ed.), *The professional psychologist's handbook* (pp. 203–221). New York: Plenum Press.

Lamb, D. H., Anderson, S., Rapp, D., Rathnow, S., & Sesan, R. (1986). Perspectives on an internship: The passages of training directors during the internship year. *Professional Psychology: Research and Practice, 17,* 100–105.

Lamb, D., Boniello, D., Bown, D., Isabelli, K., & McCormack, S. (1983). Crisis intervention training at a predoctoral internship in professional psychology. *Professional Psychology: Research and Practice, 14,* 714–717.

Lamb, D. H., Roehlke, H., & Butler, A. (1986). Passages of psychologists: Career stages of internship directors. *Professional Psychology: Research and Practice, 17,* 158–160.

Langs, R. (1979). *The supervisory experience.* New York: Aronson.

Langston, R. D. (1979). A case for the non-rotational internship. *Professional Psychology, 10*(5), 666–669.

Laughlin, P. (1985). Positions and funding levels by types of facilities: 1984–1985. *APIC Newsletter, 10*(2), 22.

Laughlin, P. R., Hutzell, R. R., Schut, B. H., Langmade, C. J., & Straight, R. A. (1984). More on the Psychology Internship program application process. *Professional Psychology: Research and Practice, 15,* 7–8.

Lawlor, R. J., Siskind, G., & Brooks, J. (1981). Forensic training at internships: Update and criticism of current unspecified training models. *Professional Psychology, 12,* 400–405.

Levine, D., Wilson, K., & Sales, B. D. (1982). An exploratory assessment of APA internships with legal/forensic experiences. *Professional Psychology, 11,* 64–71.

Levy, L. H. (1984). The metamorphosis of clinical psychology: Toward a new charter as human services psychology. *American Psychologist, 39,* 486–494.

Lipsey, M. (1974). Research and relevance: A survey of graduate students and faculty in psychology. *American Psychologist, 29,* 541–555.

Loucks, S., Burstein, A. G., Schoenfeld, L. S., Stedman, J. (1980). The real cost of psychology interns services: Are they a good buy? *Professional Psychology, 11,* 898–900.

Lubin, B., & Sokoloff, R. M. (1983). An update of the survey of training and internships programs in clinical neuropsychology. *Journal of Clinical Psychology, 39,* 149–152.

Lubin, B., Nathan, R. G., & Matarazzo, J. D. (1978). Psychologists in medical education: 1976. *American Psychologist, 3,* 339–343.

Malouf, J. L., Haas, L. J., & Farah, M. J. (1983). Issues in the preparation of interns: Views of trainers and trainees. *Professional Psychology: Research and Practice, 14,* 624–631.

Manicas, P. T., & Secord, P. F. (1983). Implications for psychology of the new philosophy of science. *American Psychologist, 38,* 399–413.

Mannarino, A. P., & Fischer, C. (1982). Survey of graduate training in clinical child psychology. *Journal of Clinical Child Psychology, 11,* 22–26.

Marwit, S. J. (1982). In support of university-affiliated schools of professional psychology. *Professional Psychology, 13,* 181–190.

Mararazzo, J. D. (1982). Behavioral health's challenge to academic, scientific, and professional psychology. *American Psychologist, 37,* 1–14.

Matarazzo, J. D. (1983). Education and training in health psychology: Boulder or bolder. *Health Psychology, 2,* 73–113.

Matarazzo, J. D., Carmody, T. P., & Gentry, W. D. (1981). Psychologists on the faculties of United States schools of medicine: Past, present and possible future. *Clinical Psychology Review, 1,* 293–317.

May, R. (1967). *Psychology and the human dilemma.* Princeton, NJ: Van Nostrand.

May, W. T. (1975). On regionalizing clinical psychology internships. *Professional Psychology, 6,* 228–233.

McConnell, S. C. (1984). Doctor of psychology degree: From hibernation to reality. *Professional Psychology: Research and Practice, 15,* 362–370.

McElfresh, T. (1983). *A professional model of psychotherapy supervision.* Unpublished paper, Wright State University.

Meehl, P. E. (1978). Theoretical risks and tabular asterisks: Sir Karl, Sir Ronald, and the slow progress of soft psychology. *Journal of Consulting and Clinical Psychology, 46,* 806–834.

Merenda, P. (1974). Current status of graduate education in psychology. *American Psychologist, 29,* 627–631.

Miller, P. M. (1977). Evaluation of trainee performance in psychology internship programs. *The Clinical Psychologist, 30,* 2–5.

Monti, P. M., Wallander, L. J., & Delancey, A. L. (1983). Seminar training in APA-approved internship programs: Is there a core curriculum? *Professional Psychology: Research and Practice, 14,* 490–496.

Moore, W. (1970). *The professions. Roles and rules.* New York: Russell Sage Foundation.

Mueller, W., & Kell, B. (1972). *Coping with conflict: Supervising counselors and psychotherapist.* New York; Appleton-Century-Crofts.

Munson, C. E. (Ed.). (1979). *Social work supervision: Classic statements and critical issues.* New York: Free Press.

Murphy, J. K. (1984). A psychology intern on a psychiatric consultation team: An intern's perspective. *Professional Psychology: Research and Practice, 15,* 467–470.

Newmark, C. S., & Hutchins, T. C. (1981). Survey of professional education in ethics in clinical psychology internship programs. *Journal of Clinical Psychology, 37,* 681–683.

Norcross, J. C. (1984). Some training predictions and recommendations. *The Clinical Psychologist, 37*(1), 23–24.

Norcross, J. C., Stevenson, J. F., & Nash, J. M. (1986). Evaluation of internship training: Practices, problems, and prospects. *Professional Psychology: Research and Practice, 17,* 280–282.

Olbrisch, M. E., Weiss, S. M., Stone, G. C., & Schwartz, G. E. (1985). Report of the National Working Conference on Education and Training in Health Psychology. *American Psychologist, 40,* 1038–1041.

Ollendick, T. H. (1985). Summary report on the National Conference on the Training of Clinical Child Psychologists. *Journal of Child and Adolescent Psychotherapy, 2,* 311–312.

Patterson, C. H. (1984). Empathy, warmth, and genuineness in psychotherapy: A review of reviews. *Psychotherapy, 21,* 431–438.

Patterson, D. G., & Lofquist, L. H. (1960). A note on the training of clinical and counseling psychologist. *American Psychologist, 15,* 365–366.

Peake, T. H., & Archer, R. P. (Eds.), Clinical training in psychotherapy. *The Clinical Supervisor, 2*(4), 1–125.

Perry, N. W., Jr. (1979). Why clinical psychology does not need alternative training models. *American Psychologist, 34,* 603-611.

Peterson, D. R. (1981). Overall synthesis of the Spring Hill symposium on the future of psychology in the schools. *School Psychology Review, 10*(2), 307-314.

Peterson, D. R. (1985). Twenty years of practitioner training in psychology. *American Psychologist, 40,* 441-451.

Peterson, D. R., & Bry, B. H. (1980). Dimensions of perceived competence in professional psychology. *Professional Psychology, Research and Practice, 11,* 965-971.

Petzel, T. P., & Berndt, D. J. (1980). APA internship selection criteria: Relative importance of academic and clinical preparation. *Professional Psychology, 11,* 792-796.

Pfeiffer, S. I., & Marmo, P. (1981). The status of training in school psychology and trends toward the future. *Journal of School Psychology, 19*(3), 211-216.

Phillips, B. N. (1981a). Characteristics of internships for school psychology students in psychology internship centers. *APIC Newsletter, 6*(2), 15-19.

Phillips, B. N. (1981b). Experiences of school psychology interns in psychology internship centers. *Journal of School Psychology, 19,* 217-221.

Pinkerton, R. S., Miller, F. T., & Edgerton, J. W. (1972). The community mental health center and psychology internship training. *Professional Psychology, 3,* 57-62.

Pleck, J. H. (1976). Sex role issues in clinical training. *Psychotherapy: Theory, Research and Practice, 13,* 17-19.

Poey, K. (1985). *Letter to twelve internship programs.* Amherst: University Health Services.

Polonsky, I., Fox, R. E., Wiens, A. N., Dixon, T. R., Freedman, M. B., & Shapiro, D. H., Jr. (1979). Models, modes, and standards of professional training. *American Psychologist, 34,* 339-349.

Rabinowitz, F. E., Heppner, E. P., & Roehlke, H. J. (1986). Descriptive study of process and outcome variables of supervision over time. *Journal of Counseling Psychology, 33,* 292-300.

Raimy, V. (Ed.). (1950). *Training in clinical psychology.* New York: Prentice-Hall.

Rangel, D. M., & Boxley, R. (1985). Clinical trainee impairment in APA-approved internship programs. *APIC Newsletter, 10*(2), 18-21.

Rappaport, J., Davidson, W., Wilson, M., & Mitchell, A. (1975). Alternatives to blaming the victim or the environment. *American Psychologist, 30,* 525-528.

Rice, D. G., & Gurman, A. S. (1973). Unresolved issues in the clinical psychology internship. *Professional Psychology, 4,* 403-408.

Rickard, H. C., & Siegel, P. S. (1976). Research-apprenticeship training for clinical psychologists: A follow-up study. *Professional Psychology, 7,* 359-363.

Riska, E., & Vinten-Johansen, P. (1981). The involvement of the behavioral sciences in American medicine: A historical perspective. *International Journal of Health Services, 11,* 583-596.

Roberts, M. C., Erickson, M. T., & Tuma, J. M. (1985). Addressing the needs: Guidelines for training psychologists to work with children, youth, and families. *Journal of Clinical Child Psychology, 14,* 70–79.

Robiner, W. N. (1982). Role diffusion in the supervisory relationship. *Professional Psychology, 13,* 258–266.

Rodolfa, E. R., Kraft, W. A., Reilly, R. R., & Blackmore, S. (1982). Psychology internships offering hypnosis training. *Association of Psychology Internship Centers Newsletter, 7,* 14–17.

Rogers, C. R. (1956). Training individuals to engage in the therapeutic process. In C. R. Strothers (Ed.), *Psychology and mental health* (pp. 76–92). Washington, DC: American Psychological Association.

Rosenberg, H., Bernstein, A., & Murray, L. (1985). Cost-efficiency of psychology internship programs: Another look at the monetary and nonmonetary considerations. *Professional Psychology: Research and Practice, 16,* 17–21.

Rosenfeld, M., Shimberg, B., & Thornton, R. F. (1983, December). *Job analysis of licensed psychologists in the United States and Canada: A study of responsibilities and requirements.* Princeton, NJ: Educational Testing Service.

Rosenkrantz, A. L., & Holmes, G. R. (1974). A pilot study of clinical internship training at the William S. Hall Psychiatric Institute. *Journal of Clinical Psychology, 30,* 417–419.

Rozsnafszky, J. (1979). Beyond schools of psychotherapy: Integrity and maturity in therapy and supervision. *Psychotherapy: Theory, Research and Practice, 16,* 190–198.

Sarason, S. (1972). *The creation of settings and the future of societies.* San Francisco: Jossey-Bass.

Sarason, S. (1981). *Psychology misdirected.* New York: Free Press.

Sarason, S. (1985). *Caring and compassion in clinical practice.* San Francisco: Jossey-Bass.

Sarason, S. B. (1986). And what is the public interest? *American Psychologist, 41,* 899–905.

Schneider, S. F. (1971). Reply to Albee's "the uncertain future of clinical psychology." *American Psychologist, 26,* 1058–1070.

Schneider, S. F. (1985, March). *Psychology in the '80s: More issues than answers.* Paper presented at the meeting of the Society for Personality Assessment, Berkeley, CA.

Schofield, W. (1969). The role of psychology in the delivery of the health services. *American Psychologist, 24,* 565–584.

Scott, C. R. (1975, September). *Can a psychology intern find happiness in the military?* Presented at the meeting of the American Psychological Association, Chicago.

Shakow, D. (1976). What is clinical psychology? *American Psychologist, 31,* 553–560.

Shemberg, K. M., & Leventhal, D. B. (1981). Attitudes of internship directors toward preinternship training and clinical training models. *Professional Psychology, 12,* 639–646.

Sheridan, E. P. (1981). Advantages of a clinical psychology residency program in a medical center. *Professional Psychology, 2,* 456–460.

Shows, W. D. (1976). Problems of training psychology interns in medical schools : A case of trying to change the leopard's spots. *Professional Psychology, 7,* 393–402.

Siegler, I. C., Gentry, W. D., & Edwards, C. D. (1979). Training in geropsychology: A survey of graduate and internship training programs. *Professional Psychology, 10,* 390–395.

Simmons, W. (1971). Clinical training programs, 1965–1966 and 1968–1969: A characterization and comparison. *American Psychologist, 26,* 717–721.

Slater, P. (1974). *Earthwalk.* New York: Anchor.

Smith, W. H., & Harty, M. K. (1981). Issues in the supervision of diagnostic testing. *Bulletin of the Menninger Clinic, 45*(1), 55–61.

Solway, K. S. (1985). Transition from graduate school to internship: A potential crisis. *Professional Psychology: Research and Practice, 16,* 50–54.

Spitzform, M., & Hamilton, S. (1976). A survey of directors from APA-approved internship programs on intern selection. *Professional Psychology, 7,* 406–410.

Stapp, J., Fulcher, R., Nelson, S. D., Pallak, M. S., & Wicherski, M. (1981). The employment of recent doctorate recipients in psychology: 1975 through 1978. *American Psychologist, 36,* 1211–1254.

Stedman, J. M. (1983, March). Fear and loathing on intern selection day. *Monitor, 14*(3), 5.

Stedman, J. M., Costello, R. M., Gaines, Jr., T., Schoenfeld, L. S., Loucks, S., & Burstein, A. G. (1981). How clinical psychology interns are selected: A study of decision-making processes. *Professional Psychology, 12,* 415–419.

Steinhelber, J., & Gaynor, J. (1981). Attitudes, satisfaction, and training recommendations of former clinical psychology interns: 1968 and 1977. *Professional Psychology, 12,* 253–260.

Steuer, J. L. (1982). Psychotherapy with older women: Ageism and sexism in traditional practice. *Psychotherapy: Training, Research and Practice, 15,* 49–55.

Stevenson, J. F., Norcross, J. C., King, J. T., & Tobin, K. G. (1984). Evaluating clinical training programs : A formative effort. *Professional Psychology: Research and Practice, 15,* 218–229.

Stone, G. C. (1983). Proceedings of the National Working Conference on Education and Training in Health Psychology. *Health Psychology, 2*(5), Supplement.

Stotland, E., & Kobler, A. (1965). *Life and death of a mental hospital.* Seattle: University of Washington Press.

Stout, A. L., Holmes, G. R., & Rothstein, W. (1977). Responses by graduates to memory of their internship in clinical psychology. *Perceptual and Motor Skills, 45,* 863–870.

Stricker, G., Hull, J. W., & Woodring, J. (1984). Respecialization in clinical psychology. *Professional Psychology: Research and Practice, 15,* 210–217.

Strupp, H. (1976). Clinical psychology, irrationalism, and the erosion of excellence. *American Psychologist, 31,* 561-571.

Strupp, H., & Schacht, T. (Eds.). (1984). The training of clinical psychologists. *The Clinical Psychologist, 37*(1), 19-35.

Sturgis, D. K., Verstegen, J. P., Randolph, D. L., & Garvin, R. B. (1980). Professional psychology internships. *Professional Psychology, 11,* 567-573.

Super, D. E. (1955). Transition: From vocational guidance to counseling psychology. *Journal of Counseling Psychology, 2*(1), 3-9.

Swain, D. (1981). *Behaviorally anchored rating scale for recipients of psychotherapy supervision: Instrument construction.* Unpublished master's thesis, Auburn University, Auburn, AL.

Swan, G. E., Piccione, G., & Anderson, D. C. (1980). Internship training in behavioral medicine: Program description, issues, and guidelines. *Professional Psychology, 11,* 339-346.

Syverson, P. D. (1982). Two decades of doctorates in psychology: A comparison with national trends. *American Psychologist, 37,* 1203-1212.

Tedesco, J. F. (1979). Factors involved in the selection of doctoral internships in clinical psychology. *Professional Psychology, 10,* 852-858.

Tedesco, J. F. (1982). Premature termination of psychology interns. *Professional Psychology, 13,* 695-698.

Tipton, R. M. (1983a). Evaluation of counseling psychology interns: A survey. *Association of Psychology Internship Centers Newsletter. 8*(2), 8-11.

Tipton, R. M. (1983b). Clinical and counseling psychology: A study of roles and functions. *Professional Psychology: Research and Practice, 14,* 837-846.

Trachtman, G. M. (1981). On such a full sea. *School Psychology Review, 10*(2), 138-181.

Tuma, J. M. (Ed.). (1985). *Proceedings. Conference on Training Clinical Child Psychologists.* Washington, DC: American Psychological Association.

Tuma, J. M. (1986). Clinical-child psychology training: Report on the Hilton Head Conference. *Journal of Clinical Child Psychology, 15.*

Tuma, J. M., & Pratt, J. M. (1982). Clinical child psychology practice and training: A survey. *Journal of Clinical Child Psychology, 11,* 22-26.

Tuma, J. M. (Ed.). (1985-1986). *Directory of internship programs in clinical child and pediatric psychology* (5th ed.). Author.

Tuma, J. M., & Cerny, J. A. (1976). The internship marketplace: The new depression? *American Psychologist, 31,* 664-670.

Watkins, C. E., Jr. (1983). Counseling psychology versus clinical psychology: Further explorations on a theme or once more around the "identity" maypole with gusto. *The Counseling Psychologist, 11*(4), 76-92.

Watkins, C. E., Jr., Lopez, F. G., Campbell, V. L., & Himmell, C. D. (1986). Counseling psychology and clinical psychology: Some preliminary comparative data. *American Psychologist, 41,* 581-582.

Watson, N., Caddy, G. R., Johnson, J. H., & Rimm, D.C. (1981). Standards in the education of professional psychologists: The resolutions of the conference at Virginia Beach. *American Psychologist, 36,* 514-519.

Weiner, I. B., & Kaplan, R. G. (1980). From classroom to clinic: Supervising the first psychotherapy client. In A. K. Hess (Ed.), *Psychotherapy supervision: Theory, research and practice* (pp. 41–50). New York: John Wiley & Sons.

Weiskopf, R., & Newman, J. P. (1982). Redesigning internship training programs: A cost-efficient point of view. *Professional Psychology, 13,* 571–576.

Wiens, A. N., & Dresdale, L. E. (1984). *Maintaining quality internship training in the face of increasing financial and service pressures.* Unpublished manuscript.

Weiss, S. L. (1975). The clinical psychology intern evaluates the training experience. *Professional Psychology, 6,* 435–441.

Weiss, S. M. (1983). The training conference: A progress report. *The Health Psychologist, 5*(1), 1–2.

Wertheimer, M., Barclay, A. G., Cook, S. W., Kiesler, C. A., Koch, S., Riegel, K. R., Rorer, L. G., Senders, V. L., Smith, M. B., & Sperling, S. E. (1978). Psychology and the future. *American Psychologist, 33,* 631–647.

Wolff, W. M. (1972). Training models trends in psychology. *Professional Psychology, 3,* 343–350.

Wyatt, F. (1967). How objective is objectivity? *Journal of Projective Techniques and Personality Assessment, 31,* 3–19.

Ysseldyke, J. E. (1982). The Spring Hill Symposium on the future psychology in the schools. *American Psychologist, 37*(5), 547–552.

Ysseldyke, J. E., & Schakel, J. A. (1983). Directions in school psychology. In G. W. Hynd (Ed.), *The school psychologist: An introduction* (pp. 3–26). Syracuse, NY: Syracuse University Press.

Ysseldyke, J. E., & Weinberg, R. A. (Eds.). (1981). The future of psychology in the schools: Proceedings of the Spring Hill Symposium. *School Psychology Review, 10*(2), 1–318.

Zimet, C. N., & Weissberg, M. P. (1979). The emergency service: A setting for internship training. *Psychotherapy: Theory, Research and Practice, 16,* 334–336.

Zolik, E. S., Bogat, G. A., & Jason, L. A. (1983). Training of interns and practicum students at community mental health centers. *American Journal of Community Psychology, 11,* 673–686.

NOTE ADDED IN PROOFS

The National Conference on Internship Training in Psychology was held in Gainesville, Florida from February 28 to March 3, 1987. Task groups addressed 7 major questions: Purpose and product of internship training; time period in graduate education for internship; specific psychology career appropriateness of internship; entrance and exit criteria; necessary processes and structures; core content and specialization; current state and anticipated future of financial and administrative issues.

The 1986 NCSPP conference included representatives from 27 member schools and 7 invited speakers and/or participant observers. Curriculum and evaluation subgroups examined the areas of knowledge, skills, and attitude.

Three general resolutions included a reaffirmation of the commitment to practitioner training and the continuing development of an interdisciplinary knowledge base. It was also proposed to initiate a recruitment strategy for increasing the numbers of ethnic minority students and faculty. Curriculum would be provided for preparation of all students for delivery of human services and health care to ethnic minority groups and underserved populations. A committee structure was proposed to implement these resolutions. These recommendations are designed to insure quality and competence in professional psychology education. The published proceedings of this NCSPP conference will provide a resource for the 1987 National Conference on Issues of Graduate Education in Psychology.

Part Two

Selected Readings

Chapter 2

Academic Training

David Shakow (1976) reaffirms the validity of the scientist-professional model which embodies motivation for professional psychology. A scientific attitude permits the acquisition of a knowledge base and a continual questioning of content and method that results in expansion of this base. The professional attitude requires sensitive, caring resonance to the problems of persons and societies. Since psychology is an interface between science and the humanities, the model is appropriate. Teaching/training should include real life settings, emphasis on general attitudes, group and individualized learning experiences, constant environmental pressure, and relevant role models. Integration of theory and practice would occur as a result of communication with practicum agencies and between the academic disiciplines. University training should include the three substantive areas—personality principles, real personal life situations, and real clinical situations. A methodology area should include observational training (objective, participant, subjective, and self) and a postinternship dissertation provides the most compelling evidence of intellectual and research talent.

Shakow defines clinical psychology as knowledge emerging from correlational and experimental methods which reflect the underlying genetic, cryptic, dynamic, psychobiological, and psychosocial principles. Clinical psychology training programs are queried for the extent to which generalists are being trained, for adequacy of organization to enable practice of a profession objectively and a science humanistically, and for their capacity to develop self-teachers. Specialization is not seen as the function of doctoral training and while *clinical psychology* is used as a generic term to encompass counseling, school, rehabilitation, and community psychologies as well as psychotherapy, *professional psychology* would now be the preferred label.

Peterson (1985) describes a history of overemphasis on science and disparagement of practice that resulted in discrepancies between available manpower and societal demands for services. In 1964 there was only one practitioner program whereas there were 44 programs with nearly 5000 students in 1982. The period of rapid increase in practitioner programs has probably ended, at least for major research universities. Education for future practitioners will occur in professional schools and small departments leading to either the Psy.D. or Ph.D. degree.

There now appear to be few demonstrable differences in practitioner competence as a result of training in either scientist-practitioner or practitioner programs. Nor are curricula different between programs since both are influenced by accreditation criteria of the American Psychological Association. However, practitioner programs may include more hours of supervised preinternship experience while there may be greater emphasis on research in scientist-practitioner programs. Scientist-professional programs may also encourage greater specialization.

There are, however, genuine differences in attitudes, interest, and values between scientist-professional and practitioner programs. Students and faculty converge in these areas in order to create a culture of practice or research. While it is feasible for these usually separate cultures to coalesce by "liberalization of methodological constraint," there is also argument for an integrated applied research model or use of the disciplined knowledge in many forms of scholarly activity.

Professional practices now include a preponderance of psychotherapy and enlarged arenas for assessment service. Education for practice requires a broader range of knowledge than does education for research. A distinction among loci for education—logocentric, democentric, and practicentric—suggests that the development of practitioner skills or practicentric education is essential.

Watkins (1983) uses a provocative title to explore not only the identity but the history, roles and functions, training conferences plus training/internship experiences, work settings, and future counseling psychology. In order to focus on identity issues, contrasts are made between counseling and clinical psychology on these themes.

Historically, counseling psychology had roots in the vocational guidance movement, the psychometric trend, and the psychotherapy tradition. The vocational guidance origins which provide for person-job matching include interest and aptitude evaluation as unique identity components. Counseling psychology differs from clinical psychology in the relative emphasis on a normal population with developmental problems (ego maturity) but who are in substantial control of their own lives. Counseling psychologists prefer objective assessment primarily because the unconscous is not their focus of interest.

Intervention roles are educational/developmental (primary and secondary prevention) rather than essentially remedial. Training in counseling psychology has substantial overlap with clinical psychology but differs in providing less emphasis on general psychology and more emphasis on vocational psychology.

Counseling psychologists do share many work places and professional activities with clinical psychologists. In the future, the trend toward blurring of boundaries between psychological specialty areas should continue. Counseling psychologists will continue to practice in the area of health psychology employing the psychoeducator model: client dissatisfaction—goal setting—skill teaching—goal achievement. Counseling psychologists will also increasingly practice an eclectic psychotherapy while eschewing vocational assessment/ counseling and thus provide more remediation services.

Abramowitz (1981) provides an historical context for school psychology in order to examine prospects for the future. School psychochology has two major organizations—Division 16 of APA for doctoral level persons and the National Association of School Psychologists primarily for master's degree persons. Two sets of guidelines for licensure/certification reflect a competitive stance by the major organizations with a result that independent practice has been restricted to doctoral level school psychologists. Similarly, accreditation by APA is for programs housed in psychology departments while the National Association of Accreditation of Teacher Education sanctions programs located in education colleges. Recent federal legislation has affected school psychologists by providing funds for new jobs but limited their professional activities to assessment. As a result a definition was legislated that did not include the desired role of mental health consultation. Litigation has also directly affected school psychologists in areas of intelligence testing. The roles of school psychologists were changed to reflect membership on interdisciplinary child-study teams and "new" testing instruments were demanded. School psychology also had neglected responsibilities for shaping public issues, making educational policy decision, and being concerned with major social events.

Fox, Barclay, and Rodgers (1982) argue for a single, agreed-upon definition of the profession, uniform educational process that leads to public expectations for competence, and unambiguous identification by credentialing. Psychology specialties for practitioners have been defined by APA—clinical, counseling, school, industrial. Training should be generic or comprehensive across sub-specialties first, with specialization occurring at a later time. A definition for professional psychology focuses on enhancing the effectiveness of human functioning. All practitioners would be identified by the field of need that they service. Current education and practicum training now occurs in settings controlled by others while education and degree credentialing is not differen-tiated from nonpractitioner psychologists. The varied organizational settings for professional psychology training contribute to confusion with regard to qualifying preparation and identity. Practicum training in a service delivery system that is owned by professional psychology would demonstrate profession-appropriate ethics, organization, competencies, and conceptualizations. Unequivocal differentiation of practitioners from other psychologists would become possible by a standardized degree—the Psy.D.—that would attest to uniformity of training.

Levy (1984) argues that clinical psychology is at the threshold of an identity change. The Boulder model provided clear boundaries for practice as a clinical psychologist as a result of specified knowledge and skills. Practice was conceptualized within a psychodynamic orientation or psychological framework. At present these boundaries are blurred and skills are shared with other professions and with lay practitioners. There are new foci for practice—behavioral, cognitive, clinical-community, etc.—and a new pluralism that provides new professional identities as Health Psychologists, Rehabilitation Psychologists, and Clinical Neuropsychologists among others.

There are also external change agents in the form of sociopolitical forces. A neopopulism finds authority and tradition to be suspect and demands greater accountability by professions as well as an augmented patient participation in services. Moreover, the increased political power of minority groups, the poor, and the aged raise issues of equity and redress. Federal funding continues to provide guidelines for inclusion of primary prevention and health care as well as for services to underserved populations.

As a result, Levy proposes a new charter or integrative model—an inclusive human services psychology—that recognizes the generic nature of problems and the means of dealing with these problems. In such a model there would be accreditation for human service psychology programs but not for their identified components or specializations. These programs would interface with other disciplines to permit operation of a biopsychosocial approach to human services. A matrix is provided for integration of content, levels of intervention, and modes of intervention. Cells in this matrix could be precisely identified with specialty areas within a human services psychology.

Reading 1

What *Is* Clinical Psychology?

David Shakow
National Institute of Mental Health, Bethesda, Maryland

I last addressed the Division of Clinical Psychology in 1948 in Boston when I was required to give a presidential address. By that time I had lived over a quarter of a century on the exhilarating but "perilous" professional borders surrounding clinical psychology. At different periods in that career I had been directly concerned with teaching, field training, diagnosis, therapy, research, and administration. Such activities involved not only the field of clinical psychology but also the other "helping" professions of psychiatry, social work, nursing, and medicine. These professional preoccupations naturally afforded many opportunities for formulating principles of conduct, testing out methods and techniques, and expressing opinions on the issues involved. From this experience developed a consistent philosophy, a *bias,* some might say, which derived fundamentally from William James and to some extent from Sigmund Freud, but more directly from a number of my teachers—particularly Fred Wells, William McDougall, Grace Kent, and Edwin Boring.

My theme at the Boston meeting was "Psychology and Psychiatry: A Dialogue" (Shakow, 1949). I had selected that topic because I believed that a fair and open exchange of the views and attitudes of forthright proponents of these two professions could lay out the issues relating to philosophy, educa-tion, practice, and research embraced by mental health activities not only for their own but for all professions involved.[1]

Today, however, I come as an *invited* guest at the urging of Hans Strupp. On my own, I would not have come, for I have long held to the principle that members of a profession have an obligation to involve themselves heavily for a limited time in professional policy matters, and then to get out completely in favor of younger persons who would carry on. Otherwise, how can progress come about? I must admit that with respect to this area of professional policy making, I have slipped in the intervening years, but not seriously (Shakow, 1965, 1968a, 1968b).

If I were doing today's job properly, my contribution might be another "dialogue." This time, however, the dialogue would be held between two proponents from *within* the profession: one long established in clinical psy-chology and one just establishing himself professionally. The discourse might

---

Reprinted from American Psychologist, August, 1976, 553–560. Preparation of this article was in part aided by a grant from the Benevolent Foundation of Scottish Rite Free-masonry, Northern Jurisdiction, United States of America.

[1] The success of the Dialogue was perhaps best indicated by the comment of a leader in psychiatry who admitted to being "shamed" by my contribution.

very well be entitled "What *Is* Clinical Psychology?: A Dialogue Between a Novice and a Veteran Clinical Psychologist," However, even if I do not go through with this task, I trust that you will at least permit me to present some of the major issues that would be central to such a discussion from the viewpoint of a great-grandfather or, at least, a grandfather. But let me stress, these are the views of an elder who still, rightly or wrongly, has a suspicion that he is ahead of his time. If you will permit me, I'll postpone defining clinical psychology until later. In any case, I think its definition will be clear from the nature of the preparation that I recommend for the practice of clinical psychology.

I believe that many of the issues current today in the field can be addressed by discussing the question of training. I wish to warn you that the model I want to present to you for training—and I repeat, *training*—is the *scientist-professional* model. Why stick to this model, which some of our colleagues consider outmoded? I believe that the viability of this model has many bases but derives fundamentally from the recognition by clinical psychologists that in the scientist-professional they have captured most adequately the underlying motivation that led them to select psychology as a lifework, which is other-understanding through self-understanding by way of science. They see in the scientist-professional a person who, on the basis of systematic knowledge about persons obtained primarily in real-life situations, has integrated this knowledge with psychological theory, and has then consistently regarded it with the questioning attitude of the scientist. In this image, clinical psychologists see themselves combining the idiographic and nomothetic approaches, both of which appear to them significant.

A clearer definition of the scientist-professional perhaps comes from a deeper examination of the value systems that characterize such a person. The value systems include a self-image of a psychologist identified with both his or her field and its history, and beyond that with science, whose major value Bronowski calls the "habit of truth." This habit is manifested in the constant effort to guide one's actions through inquiry into what is fact and verifiable, rather than to act on the basis of faith, wish, or precipitateness. Underlying and combined with this "hardheadedness" lies a sensitive, humanistic approach to the problems of persons and their societies. The scientist-professional recognizes, in the context of our overwhelming ignorance, the primacy of the need to build for the future well-being of persons and groups on a solid base of knowledge. Thus, integral to this attitude is an implicit modesty, the acceptance of the need for experiment, and the long-term view. The scientist-professional emphasizes principles, not techniques, ends rather than means; he keeps as close as possible to real situations, while approaching their study with as much rigor as possible. Although he recognizes the legitimacy of the psychonomist's approach to psychological problems through the use of more segmental and more controllable laboratory approaches, for his own area of interest, he, with dignity, insists on the importance of his own more molar approach. He also raises questions about the narrow and rigid boundaries within which the psychonomist attempts to confine psychology. In this molar approach, the scientist-professional exercises the utmost rigor compatible with maintaining the integrity of the situations faced. Thus, what defines the "scientist-professional" is the combination of the skilled acquisition of reality-based psychological under-standing and the atitude of constant inquiry toward this knowledge.

Essentially, what we want is the "Faith of the Humanist," as stated so aptly by Bertrand Russell (1947/1961): "When I try to discover what are the original sources of my opinions, both practical and theoretical, I find that most of them spring ultimately from admiration for two qualities—kindly feeling and veracity (p. 144).

With regard to training under the scientist-professional model, let me start with the proposition that, as in the other helping professions, two features are essential for the practice of clinical psychology: acquisition of *knowledge* and the acquisition of an *attitude* appropriate to the dispensing of that knowledge. Both require training, but of different kinds. From the first kind of training comes the limited security that grows with knowledge. From the second comes the humility that arises from self-knowledge. (And I'm old-fashioned enough to believe that this self-knowledge should come from some form of fairly extended analysis under guidance, rather than from mere "self-exposure" therapy. But be that as it may!)

Of course, some people would seem to be "god analyzed" and in need of little additional training in the second area, but fortunately we don't have to plan on such rare persons. However, the rest of us need to put ourselves through some form of self-evaluation under guidance, to clarify our motivations, because good will alone, as we know, is not enough. If I had my way, I would emblazon at the entrance to all schools for clinical psychologists the quotation from Browning's "Light Woman":

'Tis an awkward thing to play with souls
And matter enough to save one's own.

But knowing the human propensity for habituation, I would have it pop up in unexpected places and at unexpected moments so as to keep it fresh and attempt to foil this tendency.

What we want finally are persons with a distinct ethical code of their own, but who make no judgments about the ethical codes of their clients or patients. We want persons who do not use their prestige to practice beyond their competence, as Crothers (1932, p. 24) has put it. We want persons who recog-nize the responsibility which they undertake in working with a human being and who are aware of the danger of solving their own problems through the other person. (The safeguards around the process menioned by Wampler and Strupp [1976] are to be recommended heartily! But it is too bad that we have not grown up enough to dispense with these.)

Recognition of how little is known in comparison to our ignorance would strengthen this trend toward humility. Even the most expert of us, with all the good will in the world, know little more than the ignorant, and we must depend on this knowledge for our expertness. Humility is the *sine qua non* of practice at whatever level—the bachelor's, the master's, or the doctoral. We can let bright, young, enthusiastic college students blessed with this quality practice within limited spheres knowing that they will not practice beyond their competence. But how to harness their enthusiasm, balancing it with the proper amount of modesty, is the problem. We must capture the enthusiasm, for it provides the motivation that lies at the root of clinical psychology as well as other professions. Self-knowledge obtained under guidance is not a panacea, for the rationalizations of humans are insidious. But it is by far the best device we have for attaining this state of self-knowledge which is fundamental to the understanding of others.

The scientist-professional model's strength lies in its basic appropriateness for a field such as psychology which is at an interface between science and the humanities. (Its values in this respect are shared by psychiatry, a point which was emphasized by John Spiegel, 1975.) The model's strength also lies in its remarkable flexibility, because the value systems on which it is based can tolerate great diversity within their legitimate limits. In some respects, too, it offers an ideal opportunity for combining the values of the scientist and the values of the humanist in actual practice. Such a combination is important for most branches of psychology. However, some specialties in psychology can achieve it by developing persons who only *in parallel* can be both good psychologists and good citizens. It is from this general level of preparation that one can go on to practice as professional, as researcher, or as any mixture of the two. And it is from the doctoral program that one can go on to post-doctoral specialization.

MAJOR PRINCIPLES OF CONTEXT

Thus far I have been discussing goals of the program, and the personal requirements of the practitioner. Teaching, however, must be carried out in a concrete context with certain methods and procedures. Six major principles of context appear to be involved: (a) real-life settings to complement the more didactically presented aspects of the program; (b) establishment of general attitudes; (c) group participation in learning; (d) individualized techniques in learning; (e) unremitting environmental pressures; and finally, and perhaps most important, (f) appropriate role models. Let us consider some aspects of each of these principles separately, together with a few suggestions for their execution.

From the earliest days of the program and whenever possible throughout the program, serious consideration should be given to teaching concretely and in field situations—*in real-life settings*. Although it may occasionally be necessary to set up simulated situations, as in some aspects of training in observation, these situations should at least have the advantage of being concrete. And whenever possible, the student should be an active participant. Again, I would urge emphasis on learning by doing, rather than on learning by listening; there is little question about which is the more effective.

Foremost among the characteristics of the psychologist is the recognition of the importance of *attitudes,* generalized sets, in interpersonal relationships—both those of the client and those of the psychologist himself. Sympathetic entry into the personal processes of another, as Gardner Murphy has put it, needs little more than the mentioning.

Group participation, both within one's own profession and across professions, is one of the most effective learning devices we have. How else can one capture the satisfactions that come from common learning and being part of a group striving toward a common social goal?—especially the satisfaction that springs from overcoming the differences in status and backgrounds of the participants, and making whatever is at hand the conjoint project of all.

Common learning and identification have their place in the educational program, but the importance of the student's *individuality* in the educational process should constantly be kept in mind. Individualized techniques are needed as well. In many ways, the issue revolves around the dangers that any common educational program holds for the development of educational stereotypy—what I have come to call the "fleeting fledgling" phenomenon. Any prolonged common course of training tends to develop in students a sameness, even a jadedness, that is in sharp contrast with their original variety, spontaneity, and potentiality. Despite obvious benefits, our conventional education, at whatever level, apparently effects changes in our students which good teachers don't like. It seems to reinforce stereotyped patterns and conventionalization, and to extinguish originality, flexibility, and creativity. The problem—one rarely solved by educators—is how to educate, yet preserve essential creative qualities.

Integral to this problem and even more important is the possible loss of individuality. In my writings I have frequently referred to the Kluckhohn-Mowrer-Murray felicitous delineation of an individual's personality as comprising three kinds of characteristics: some like *all* other persons', some like *some* other persons', and some like *no* other persons'. The last of these is of concern to me here. So many forces in our culture, in their apparent efforts to reduce the complexities of life, work toward constricting both the boundaries of privacy and the importance of individuality. And in speaking of individuality, I am not, of course, referring to idiosyncracy. In his discussion of the meaning of evolution, Simpson indicates, from a biologist's view, how important for this process is the maintenance of man's evolved individuality. If we are to save the best aspects of our civilization, must we not labor ceaselessly to foster nature's gift of individual differences?

The problem centers in part around the continuing development in the professional situation of the responsibility and resourcefulness that should have begun in early childhood. Settings should be designed in which students become involved in the situation and develop a sense of responsibility toward the patients, the students themselves carrying as much of the burden as is feasible. That cardinal pedagogical principle of stretching students just a little beyond their capacities is a good guide. Most teachers tend to underestimate their students, and consequently fail to take advantage of their potentialities. An atmosphere of warm concern for the client should, of course, characterize the setting, yet the student must have an opportunity to make errors and to correct them. This universal educational paradox of the helping professions can be partly reconciled by providing the student with situations carrying the least hazards for the patient.

Unremitting *environmental pressures* are another necessary part of the educational program. I have, in discussing the problem of individual development, emphasized the need for stretching the individual. But this need must be broadened to include the whole program, because it works in groups as well as in individuals. Its relationship to the Jamesian tenet of tapping the "energies of men" is obvious.

I now come to the last of the contextual principles—the part played by *role models.* I venture to suggest that the most important factor for developing the kinds of workers we hope for lies in the caliber of the teachers we provide— the exemplars we set before students. It is unfortunate, therefore, that so relatively few of our teachers provide role models worthy of emulation. Models seem crucial, not only in general but also for the ethical principles students adopt, the humility they develop in the face of the complex problems they have to deal with, and the freedom they achieve from too much dependence on orthodoxy.

PROGRAM OF PREPARATION

Having described the values of the scientist-professional model, the program of preparation itself should be considered. For the present purposes, I wish to take up a suggestion that I made 20 years ago (Shakow, 1956), which I don't believe has received enough recognition. It bears repeating. My suggestion is that the university (or professional school) and the field-center training activities be as completely integrated as possible. *Integration* does not mean *sameness,* which results in a loss of vigor that comes with having the same point of view. Various points of view should be represented, but communication between these agencies is essential. It goes without saying that there should be integration within the university as well. The fundamental principle of the plan is that theory and practicum must be constantly associated and tied together whether in the university or in the field station, and that both types of activity—theory and practicum—start with the very beginning of the program. I would suggest as axiomatic: *The greater the degree of integration between theory and practice, and between university and field center, the more effective the program.*

What I am saying is that we must get away from the *layer*-cake principle on which most of our programs are based. I even believe that we must go beyond the *marble*-cake principle on which perhaps the most advanced among us base our programs. We must work toward achieving that ultimate level represented by a cake whose ingredients cannot be distinguished either in appearance or in taste, the one in which true fusion has been achieved.

Each year would have both its theory and practicum—provided either by the university or by the field center, but usually by both. In the first year, major emphasis would be on theoretical courses at the university, and at the same time the university would provide laboratory practice in observation and tests, and laboratory work in experimental psychodynamics or similar courses. The practicum agency would provide introductory experiences in normal situations. In the second year, the university would provide additional advanced theory, and the field would provide the clerkship with its associated theory. In the third year, the first internship year, the field station would be required to provide theory related to the fieldwork as well as the fieldwork itself. I recommend that the fourth year become a second internship year during which the dissertation work is done at the field center. During this year, both the university and the field station take the responsibility for the theoretical work connected with the dissertation and any other aspects of the training. Although during each year one of these agencies would carry a major responsibility, it is my thought that the other agency would also carry some degree of responsibility for the program. If I seem to have stressed insufficiently the place of theoretical training in basic psychology at the university, it is because I take it for granted.

In the *substantive* area, I would include three kinds of training: in personality principles, in real-life situations, and in real clinical situations. In the *methodological* area, I would include two kinds of training: in observation and in specific research methodology.

The programs on the nature and development of personality, whenever possible in the context of actual life situations and concrete case material, would aim at producing an apperceptive mass in the student incorporating the five principles basic to the understanding of personality: the genetic, the cryptic, the dynamic, the psychobiologic, and the psychosocial. The *genetic* principle acknowledges the role of continuity in the development of the individual's personality characteristics—the significance of earlier influences on present manifestations of one's personality. The *cryptic* principle recognizes that unconscious and preconscious factors act as crucial determiners of behavior, that behavior has, besides the obvious conscious motivations, further motivations that are not conscious. The *dynamic* principle states that behavior is drive-determined, that behind behavior lie certain innate or acquired impelling forces. The *psychobiological* principle holds that the personality is integral and indivisible, that there is a pervasive interrelationship between psyche and soma. This involves the acceptance of an organismic concept of total, rather than segmental, personality. The *psychosocial* principle recognizes the integration of the person and his or her social environment as a unit. It states that behavior is expressed as individual response within a social context, and that both the individual and his or her environment are important in the determination of personality and conduct.

The second substantive area would involve the student in as many normal settings, both adequate and deprived, as possible—in home, community, school, playground, etc.—so that experience may be acquired with a broad range of normal individual and social behavior.

The third substantive area would involve the student in experience with varieties of clinical situations, from the minor aberrations of personality through the most complex of the psychoses.

Although I shall now now enter into a detailed explication of this aspect of the program, I cannot emphasize strongly enough the importance of both of these kinds of fieldwork for developing the psychologist we seek. In many ways I consider the extensive "clinical" experience—with human beings in a diversity of human settings—as the very foundation of a sound program of education.

On the *methodological* side, two major areas of training are indicated. The first would provide varied experience with the different types of observation; the second, experience with more specific research methodology, in part based on the training in observation. Let me first consider the *nature* of the different kinds of observation. I distinguish four major types of observation: objective, participant, subjective, and self.

Objective observation involves the careful description of the impact on the observed of those impinging internal and external forces—physical, psychological, and social—that lead to the observed behaving the way he or she does. Such observations are those of the naturalist; they are made from a point outside the subject and the situation. Here it is particularly important for the observer to become sensitive to the more transient, non-verbal behavioral aspects, such as body movement and facial expression. Objective observation plays a significant role as well in the process of building up the "computer" capability of the student. (We must, nevertheless, keep in mind that objective observation is a misnomer, the Heisenberg Principle being involved; cf. Wheeler, 1974. It is an ideal.)

The second kind of observation, *participant observation,* implies a distinctly more intimate relationship between the observer and the observed, for in this situation both are interacting within a group. To the observer falls the difficult task not only of making objective observations but also of determining how his role as a participant in the group modifies the situation. He needs, as well, to evaluate, even more than in naturalistic observation, the effect that the very act of observing has on the observed and the observation.

The third kind of observation, *subjective observation,* is a particularly important one for psychologists. It involves the observer's attempt to empathize with the patient, to try to understand how he feels about himself, his family, and his illness. Whether these feelings be realistic or unrealistic, they are essential toward understanding the patient's difficulties.

The fourth kind of observation is *self-observation,* which comes about through a process of self-examination under guidance. It is the student's effort to understand personal feelings and attitudes. Here he asks himself why he behaves the way he does—why, for instance, he is so anxious with one patient and so calm with another. This important quality in the person who undertakes clinical work has already been singled out for special consideration.

Clearly, in this discussion of observation methods, I am emphasizing techniques for learning by experiencing, as opposed to learning by listening. Real-life learning techniques, however, carry with them certain hazards. On the one hand, they may disturb the validity of the observations, and, on the other, they may develop self-consciousness or exaggerated introspectiveness. Such hazards call for caution on the part of the preceptors and their students, and for careful consideration of ways of reducing these negative aspects.

The second area of methodological training, though based fundamentally on the training in observation, is that area more directly related to research methodology. Obviously the range here is great. The general principles common to all researchers, such as accuracy and reliability of report, would presumably have been acquired largely through the training in observation. The specifics of the particular disciplinary techniques set up to yield dependable data, the experimental and statistical controls necessary to support them, and other substantive and methodological details, remain the concrete problem of the educators in each of the disciplines—from the biological through the social.

Some of the issues come to a focus most clearly in relation to the dissertation. A portion of what I have to say has relevance not only for the clinical student but for graduate students in psychology generally. However, I shall limit myself to the discussion of the problem as it relates to the clinical student.

There was some thought at one time that it might be possible for students to get at least part of their dissertation work done during the internship. This (with rare exceptions) turned out to be impossible to achieve because of the amount of ground to be covered during the internship. Under the circumstances, what has generally happened is that the students go back to the university after their internship and do their dissertation work during that year. In order to be sure of getting through in time, they generally pick "safe" dissertations, frequently nonclinical ones (because they are usually more easily packageable), and not too infrequently a problem handed to them by one of their instructors. How does this compare with what should ideally happen?

Of all the opportunities the PhD program affords to test out a student, the dissertation is the best single device for indicating what kind of person he or she is intellectually and in research ability. Isn't it therefore important to watch students through the various steps in the process of becoming investigators?—see them intrigued by a phenomenon, watch them learning how to put the proper question to nature, and then observe how they go through the process of trying to get an answer to the question.

For the clinical student, is it not important, too, that this question should be asked in the place where he has most likely become intrigued with a problem, about the area in which his primary work lies? This area is full of unanswered questions that have to be faced daily, an area where the difficulties of research and the need for more research are great.

By having the students go back to the universities for their dissertations, what kind of attitudes are we encouraging? Aren't we in a sense saying that research is not something to associate with the field setting: the *field setting* is the place where service functions are carried out; the *university* is the place for theory and research. What does this do to hinder our efforts to build up this research area and the field stations as research centers? By going even further, and having the clinical students do their dissertations on topics only remotely related to their areas, what are we doing? Aren't we by implication discouraging the development of an attitude that the problems in this area are researchable problems, and even more than in the previous case associating not only clinical *settings* but the clinical *area* with service and nonresearch? But when we go even still further, and we have a clinical student do a nonclinical dissertation on a question which has never troubled *him* but which instead came out of the file drawer of a professor who had some minor question which needed answering as part of a larger problem troubling *him,* what effect on the development of the investigative attitude of the student do we achieve? (Happily, this situation is becoming rarer.)

What I am saying is: Don't we have very definite responsibilities to our clinical graduate students? Should we divert them or make research assistants out of them in connection with their dissertations? Can't they do their research assisting, if that is necessary for earning, or even learning, on the side? As "dissertationers," should they not work in the area of their major interest and be independent through the *various* steps of the process, with only the most necessary guidance and help to which they are entitled?

The professional relationships betweeen the two institutions must become much closer than has until now generally been the case. The two institutions must become almost as one professionally, with the *major responsibility falling upon the university to achieve the unity because it is the degree-granting agency.* Program planning must from the beginning be carried out in close association. It is important that the university people have free access to and whenever possible appointments at the internship center. The reverse must be true for the personnel from the clinical center. Their staff must be raised to the level of acceptance by the university. For program purposes, the staffs of the two institutions should be thought of as much as possible as one. This is a most difficult goal to reach, but an essential one if we are to achieve a unified program. I want to assure you it can be done.

The program places so much emphasis on theory—whenever possible in the context of practice—because of a fundamental principle which is implicit in my whole discussion. This is the principle that our training programs at the doctoral level must be programs directed toward providing a *general* kind of professional psychological education, the only kind of foundation on which later specialization can soundly be built.

DEFINITION OF CLINICAL PSYCHOLOGY

Earlier in this article, I promised you a definition of clinical psychology. Cronbach (1957, 1975) has discussed persuasively two different kinds of methods in psychology: correlational and manipulative. In the first, "nature the old nurse" takes one on its knee and unfolds the storybook, that Longfellow had conjectured Agassiz as experiencing. In this case, *nature* determines the variances, and the correlator finds his or her data in the observations of already *existing* variations between individuals, between groups, and between species. In the manipulative or experimental, on the other hand, the *experimenter* is the manipulator, who *changes* conditions in order to observe their consequences and variances. Clinical psychology has been substantially a correlational psychology from its beginnings. But in recent years there has been a distinct trend toward the experimental and I now see a happy marriage of the two, if each recognizes its proper role. It is true that the clinician will tend to emphasize those aspects of "hierarchic transformations" that will permit adequate handling of field problems taken into the laboratory. But the trend will grow, without interfering with the continuation of the correlational approach.

So the definition which I give holds that clinical psychology, a branch of psychology, is a body of knowledge growing out of both correlational and experimental techniques which are based on genetic, cryptic, dynamic, psychobiological, and psychosocial principles. The skills of assessment and therapy which derive from this knowledge can be used to help persons with behavior disabilities or mental disorders to achieve better adjustment and self-expression. To practice these skills it is most often necessary to go through some course of self-evaluation under guidance.

SUMMARY

Now, let me try to sum up what I have been trying to say. It appears to me that psychology must now ask itself searchingly several questions about its programs in clinical psychology. These are:

1. How *broadly conceived* are these programs? How well are they training *generalists* well-grounded in practice that is oriented to theory? How well are the programs providing a generalized training which is adaptable and on which later, postdoctoral, specialization can best be based?

2. *How well are the programs organized to achieve the double goal of developing persons to practice either or both a profession objectively and a science humanistically?* First, how fully do they recognize their responsibility to aid in self-evaluation? How well do they develop practitioners who can carry responsibility in relation to persons who come to them for help? How well do they develop practitioners who can deal with these persons sympathetically and with understanding? Second, how well do the programs develop persons who can examine evidence critically, who are concerned with the advancement of knowledge, and who, if necessary, can carry on activities directed at the acquisition of this knowledge?

3. *How well do they develop self-teachers,* persons who will continue the education which has at least begun with the program?

I have presented some of the issues which I think must be dealt with in trying to answer these questions. I have also presented a tentative program which I believe has possibilities for advancing us further toward the goals that are implied by these questions. The program I have sketched is obviously not intended to prepare persons to be narrow specialists. It is not even intended to train medical psychologists or counseling psychologists or school psychologists or rehabilitation psychologists. It *is* intended to train *psychologists* (*clinical*), which all of these are. We might even make this parenthetical compromise with elegance to get the point across. I don't, however, think that this compromise is necessary if counseling psychology, school psychology, rehabilitation psychology, community psychology, and psychotherapy recognize their relationship to a clinical psychology of this broadened scope. Is it not desirable to use the most available (probably the *only* available) common term—*clinical* psychology— generically for all these areas of psychology concerned with the emphasis on the individual and his or her problems? I think it is a shame to get hung up on semantic differences. The term is used properly, and the proprietary owners—if there are any—will gladly allow the change. Usage will, in any event, I am sure, result before long in recognition of the broadened meaning intended.

The greatest concession that such a program might make to specialization would be in permitting students who have clear-cut interests to have their clerkships or even their internships in those *good* institutions which come closest to the area of their interest—school or hospital or counseling center. This would permit them to obtain on the side, but only as a by-product, skills in dealing with these types of problems and techniques. The institution's *training* program itself would be directed primarily at the more general aspects of clinical psychology, leaving for the postdoctoral period (or the employment period) the specialization.

We are, of course, not quite ready to carry out effectively programs of this kind. But now, after our periods of very serious efforts in different directions, aren't the signs fairly clear that this is the direction in which to turn our eyes and our efforts?

REFERENCES

Cronbach, L. J. The two disciplines of scientific psychology. *American Psychologist*, 1957, *12*, 671–684.

Cronbach, L. J. Beyond the two disciplines of scientific psychology. *American Psychologist*, 1975, *30*, 116–127.

Crothers, B. (Chair). Psychology and psychiatry in pediatrics: The problem. Report of the Subcommittee on Psychology and Psychiatry. In *White House Conference on Child Health and Protection*. New York; Century, 1932.

Russell, B. The faith of the humanist. From "The faith of the rationalist" (talk broadcast in 1947). In M. Knight (Ed.), *Humanist anthology*. London: Barrie & Rockliff, 1961.

Shakow, D. Psychology and psychiatry: A dialogue (Parts I and II). *American Journal of Orthopsychiatry*, 1949, *19*, 191–208; 381–396.

Shakow, D. The improvement of practicum training and facilities. In C. L. Strother (Ed.), *Psychology and mental health*. Washington, D.C.: American Psychological Association, 1956.

Shakow, D. Seventeen years later: Clinical psychology in the light of the 1947 Committee on Training in Clinical Psychology report. *American Psychologist*, 1965, *20*, 353–362.

Shakow, D. Some thoughts on training in clinical psychology. *Clinical Psychologist*, 1968, *21*(4), 167–171. (a)

Shakow, D. Troubled clinical waters (*Homo scientius et homo professionalis–sempervirens?*). Review of E. Hoch, A. O. Ross, & C. L. Winder (Eds.), *Professional preparation of clinical psychologists*. *Contemporary Psychology*, 1968, *13*, 225–229. (b)

Spiegel, J. P. Presidential address: Psychiatry—a high-risk profession. *American Journal of Psychiatry*, 1975, *132*, 693–697.

Wampler, L. D., & Strupp, H. H. Personal therapy for students in clinical psychology: A matter of faith? *Professional Psychology*, 1976, *7*, 195–201.

Wheeler, J. A. The universe as home for man. *American Scientist*, 1974, *62*, 683–691.

Reading 2
Twenty Years of Practitioner Training in Psychology

Donald R. Peterson
Rutgers University, New Brunswick, New Jersey

Twenty years ago, Adrien Pinard, president of the Canadian Psychological Association, concluded his address to the Association as follows:

> I shall limit myself to summarizing in three propositions the tissue of commonplaces which make up the thread of my address. In the first place, I have called attention to the paradox that arises from the fact that the very large majority of psychologists are practitioners, while the model generally applied to the training of these practitioners is the scientist-professional model, a model essentially centered on scientific research. In the second place, I have tried to show that the generalization of this model is illusory and dangerous. It is first of all illusory because our so-called scientist-professionals, with the exception of a deluxe minority, are in reality either scientists who do not practice their profession or practitioners who do no research and who, by their own admission are not even in a fit state to exercise their profession well. It is also dangerous, because the scientist-professional model cannot satisfy the multitude of psychological services rightly demanded by the public, and because this model is a source of confusion and in fact deprives professional psychology of the very identity the model was supposed to give it. In the third place, I have proposed the institution of two different courses of psychological training, an academic course and a professional course specifying that these programs must both be at the doctoral level and must demand comparable requirements and be at the same time distinct and complementary. (Pinard, 1967, pp 144–145).

In his talk, Pinard expressed some common concerns of his time. Following recommendations of the Boulder Conference (Raimy, 1950), scientist-practitioner programs for educating professional psychologists were located in academic departments. Everyone who applauded that decision believed that the academic environment would provide the culture of scholarship required for a newly formed profession. Few foresaw, however, the extent to which research would come to dominate American universities in the years following World War II. When I was in graduate school at the University of Minnesota, the chair of the department was Richard M. Elliott, a scholar of great wisdom who deepened the knowledge and extended the vision of every student he touched. Elliott published practically nothing except a book called *The Sunny Side of*

Reprinted from American Psychologist, *40*(4), 441–451.

Asia, which he wrote after a walking tour of China. Today I cannot imagine a person with Elliott's qualifications receiving a faculty appointment at any rank in any major university. Shortly after I came to the University of Illinois, the director of our psychological clinic, a man who had done a great deal to organize services and was the chief practicum supervisor in the clinic but had published only two articles in his life, was promoted from associate to full professor. He would not stand a chance for promotion today.

The shifts in values that required productive scholarship of every professor were well advanced by 1964. As the emphasis on research grew stronger and stronger, the appreciation of mere reflective scholarship, good teaching, and humane public service declined. No longer could faculty in the most ambitious departments devote long hours to teaching or clinical supervision, to the neglect of research, and hope for promotion. No longer could students declare interest solely in practice and hope for admission to the best graduate programs. Yet most students who completed scientist-practitioner programs published no research. And few felt well prepared for the professional work they would spend their lives doing.

The titles of the following journal articles revealed the tensions of the time: "The Case of Clinical Psychology: A Search for Identity" (Kahn & Santostefano, 1962); "Psychology in Flux: The Academic-Professional Bipolarity" (Tryon, 1963); "The Crisis in Clinical Psychology Training" (Blank & David, 1963). In 1964, the American Psychological Association's (APA) ad hoc Committee on the Scientific and Professional Aims of Psychology, with Kenneth E. Clark as chair, was concluding its deliberations. The committee recommended a two-track system of education, one for researchers and one for practitioners (APA, 1967). The Chicago Conference, remembered today mainly for its reaffirmation of the scientist-practitioner model of professional education, was only a year away, and preconference materials had already been distributed to participants (Hoch, Ross, & Winder, 1966). In Canada, similar activities were in progress. The address by Pinard (quoted in the beginning of this article) was one of the position papers for the Couchiching Conference on Professional Psychology. There, in 1965, most of the same issues that preoccupied the Chicago Conference were addressed, and most of the same conclusions were reached (Webster, 1967). Although the academicians who dominated both conferences were willing to consider minor modulations of program philosophy, they did not agree that any fundamental change was needed. Instead, they congratulated themselves for doing what they had been doing and went back to continue business as before.

But neither articles, committees, nor conferences could solve the basic problems of the time. Many scientist-practitioner programs emphasized science so strongly that practice was not only neglected but disparaged. Most programs were tiny. In California, for example, at a time when the general population was increasing rapidly, when California society was in crisis over rural and urban problems alike, and mental health systems were expanding to proportions never seen before in this country, all the California universities combined were turning out fewer than 20 clinical psychologists per year. The public demand for competent practitioners was strong. The demand from students for access to the profession was growing strident. Demands from practioners, who faced hopelessly unmanageable case loads, who were dissatisfied with their own training, and who saw no help available from the universities, grew more militant and better organized. University faculties, sure in their commitments to science and fundamentally preoccupied with their own concerns, did not respond to the pressures. The dam was bound to break.

The early stages of the practitioner movement in psychology have been chronicled elsewhere (Caddy & LaPointe, 1984; Dörken & Cummings, 1977; Peterson, 1982). Only a bare summary is needed here. In 1964, only one program in the country was devoted mainly to the education of practitioners in psychology. That was the program at Adelphi University. In 1965, the Fuller Graduate School of Psychology was established. The Illinois Doctor of Psychology (PsyD) program began in 1968. In 1969, the California School of Professional Psychology accepted its first class of students. Since then, the number of practitioner programs has risen sharply. By 1982, 44 practitioner programs were in operation, with 4,992 students enrolled (Caddy & LaPointe, 1984). Of the 44 programs, 20 are in universities, and 24 are in freestanding professional schools. Twenty-seven programs lead to the PsyD degree, and 17 to the PhD.

The growth curve shown in Figure 1 appears to be rising relentlessly, but there is reason to suppose that the increase in new programs will soon taper off. Unaccredited freestanding schools do not attract students as they once did, and the job market for graduates seems weaker than it was a few years ago. As any dean of an independent school of professional psychology will attest, development of a new school requires tremendous effort. It seems likely that most of the people interested in forming new schools have either already done so or given up. Some growth of PsyD programs will probably take place in small psychology departments in the years ahead, but the period of rapid increase in practitioner programs appears to be ending. Over the past 20 years, the professional school and the professional doctorate have become established in American psychology. What have we learned from the experience?

1. Major research universities will not establish practitioner programs in psychology. The Doctor of Psychology program at the University of Illinois failed. By now, the main reasons are clear. To the Illinois faculty, education for practice was never considered less demanding than education for research. It was always seen as equally demanding and in some ways more so. Specialization is justifiable and necessary for research. A practitioner facing problems as they come from the public must be comprehensively trained. Preparing students not only for individual assessment and psychotherapy but also for a wide range of other skills, from neuropsychology to community intervention,

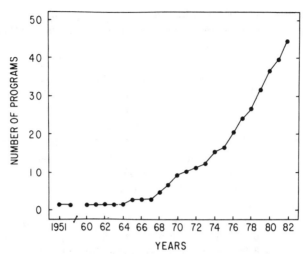

Figure 1   Increase in Practitioner Programs From 1960 to 1982. *From "The Training of Professional Psychologists: Historical Developments and Present Trends" by G. R. Caddy and L. L. LaPointe in* Professional Practice of Psychology *by G. S. Tryon (Ed.), 1984. Copyright 1982 by Ablex Publishing Company Reprinted by permission.*

requires an enormous investment of training resources. In the Illinois conception, especially as it developed after I left, professional psychologists were expected to contribute scholarly knowledge, if not scientific facts, to the discipline. The projects chosen by PsyD students were often more difficult than those elected by PhD students, but demands for thoroughness and all possible rigor were not relaxed. By 1980, when the PsyD program was discontinued, the median time to completion was 7.4 years. Despite efforts by the Illinois faculty to describe the program accurately, many students entered dreaming of careers in the private practice of individual psychotherapy. They were annoyed by requirements that did not serve their personal goals and unsettled by faculty attitudes that attached little value to direct service through long-term individual treatment. They were not stupid. Why should they spend 7.4 years learning things they did not want to learn to obtain a PsyD when they could spend 5 years learning some other things they did not want to learn and get a PhD?

For faculty, the burdens of the program became too heavy to bear. Supervisory help from the local professional community did not materialize as expected. The task of clinical supervision fell mainly to full-time faculty, but in the research culture of the university time devoted to clinical supervision yielded few rewards. Many of the faculty had believed all along that a scientist-professional model of education, flexibly managed, could serve the aims of research and practice alike. Over the course of many discussions, that was the model to which they returned.

Despite the encouragement of practitioner programs by the Vail Conference (Korman, 1976) few were attempted in research universities, and those that were proposed have rarely been sustained. An interfaculty program in clinical psychology and public practice ran for several years at Harvard but was put into moratorium when some of the administrators involved found it too expensive and too heavily ridden with conflict to merit continuation. The current program in counseling and consulting psychology at Harvard is housed in the Graduate School of Education. The Yale faculty endorsed the idea of explicit professional programs and the Doctor of Psychology degree, but neither the money nor the faculty commitment required to develop a professional program are in prospect, and the program in effect there is still a PhD program in clinical and community psychology. Twenty years ago, Paul Meehl returned from the meetings of the Clark committee (APA, 1967) and presented the argument for outright professional education to Minnesota psychologists, but only a few of the other University of Minnesota faculty members supported the idea, and Meehl saw no point in pressing it. Later, a PsyD program in health psychology was formally proposed by clinical psychologists in the medical school, but conflicts with a new administration in the Department of Psychiatry precluded attention to any new developments in psychology. At this time, the proposal is dormant and not likely to be revived.

At New York University (NYU), a PsyD program in clinical psychology was proposed informally as early as 1957. In the 1970s, a formal proposal was approved by the Psychology Department, the Graduate School of Arts and Sciences, the University Committee of Deans, and the Board of Trustees. At the last moment, the proposal was defeated by the clinical faculty, most of whom objected to the central role adjunct faculty were to have in the professional program. A PsyD program in school psychology was later established at NYU, but prospects for a parallel program in clinical psychology are remote.

These are anecdotes but others could be told. Together they form a consistent pattern. The fact is that only three of the 44 practitioner programs in the country are in major *research universities,* as that term is defined by the Carnegie Council on Policy Studies in Higher Education (1976). These are at Rutgers, Yeshiva University, and NYU. The other universities with professional programs, such as Adelphi, Baylor, Wright State, and Denver, are not considered major research universities by the standards of the Carnegie Council, whatever the faculties may think about their reputations. The Carnegie rating system further divides research universities into Class I and Class II. Harvard, Stanford, Yale, the University of Michigan, and the University of California at Berkeley, along with other universities all would recognize, appear in the top group. A large share of the Class I research universities do not even have scientist-professional programs in psychology, let alone programs for training practitioners. There is a very good reason for this. The primary mission of the first class research university is research, not so much education and service, and the faculty in those institutions cannot afford to spend their time supervising practitioners in a minor profession.

For the most part, the major research universities of America have retained small, research-oriented scientist-professional programs in psychology. With only three exceptions, efforts to develop practitioner programs in research universities have failed. Given the incentives that govern faculty behavior, there is no reason to expect these conditions to change.

2. Education of most practitioners in psychology will take place in professional schools and small departments. Although graduates of scientist-professional programs in research universities are usually qualified to practice, the emphasis in those programs is on research, and the programs are very small. At this time, the number of students enrolled in university-based scientist-practitioner programs and the number enrolled in professional schools appear to be about equal. As the new professional schools produce more graduates and as more practitioner programs are established in small departments, the numerical balance in the production of professional psychologists will clearly shift to practitioner programs.

Incentives for developing professional programs in small departments are substantial. Many departments already have master's programs in operation, but graduates of those programs face an uncertain job market. Faculties generally prefer doctoral programs to master's programs for the gain in intellectual stimulation and prestige doctoral programs provide. Universities in which the departments are located often have no doctoral programs in any field, and so administrators are likely to support efforts to elevate their institutions into the class of universities that grant doctoral degrees. Doctor of Psychology programs in universities attract students, graduates gain employment, and all the university-based PsyD programs that have applied for APA accreditation so far have been approved. These conditions are likely to favor development of more PsyD programs in small departments in the years ahead.

This worries me. Programs in professional psychology are not only not developing in the first rank of American universities, they are not developing in the second rank either. Professional programs are not seen at the University of Michigan but at Central Michigan University, not at Florida State University but at Nova, not at Columbia but at Pace University, not at Indiana University but at Indiana State University, not at the University of Kentucky but at Spalding College, not at the State University of Pennsylvania but at Indiana University of Pennsylvania, not at the University of Virginia but at George Mason University.

The Conference Board of Associated Research Councils (CBARC) recently published a report on the scholarly reputations of universities (CBARC, 1983). If ratings of "faculty quality" in that survey are distributed and the positions of practitioner programs in psychology are noted, some interesting facts stand out. The first, already mentioned above, is that professional training in psychology has been abandoned entirely by many of the most prestigious universities. The psychology departments at Stanford, Harvard, Chicago, Princeton, and Northwestern Universities, all of which appear in the top quartile of the CBARC ratings, do not offer training for practice at all. The second fact is that those institutions that do offer direct education for practice do not fare well by the usual standards of faculty scholarship. Among 29 members, associates, and affiliates of the National Council of Schools of Professional Psychology (NCSPP), only one appears in the top quartile on the CBARC scale. One other is in the third quartile. Seven are in the bottom quartile. Twenty of the NCSPP members, who are training many if not most of tomorrow's practitioners, are not listed at all as qualified to educate scholars.

Conditions for access to the profession have changed radically since professional schools started to admit large numbers of students. Established professional schools that took part in a recent survey (Callan, Peterson, & Stricker, 1986) enrolled an average of 49 new students per year (Stricker, in press). This is at least five times larger than typical entering classes in academic departmental programs. Not only are the numbers of students enrolling in professional schools larger than our field has known before, but the selection ratios are also different. Scientist-practitioner programs in prestigious universities receive several hundred applications per year. Some receive more; selection ratios of 1:100 are not unknown, and ratios of 1:15 are not uncommon. Standards for admission are still severe in most university-based professional schools, but freestanding schools admit higher proportions of applicants. The 12 independent schools that took part in the Callan et al. survey invited an average of 46% of applicants to enter their programs. Selection ratios ranged from about 1:3 to 2:3.

I have visited many schools of professional psychology and several small departments that are starting practitioner programs. The faculties usually impress me as bright, sincere, energetic people, dedicated to the education of professional psychologists in a scholarly way. Few are famous scientists. What this condition and the others mentioned above will do to our field is difficult to say, but it will not be the same as it was before.

3. The doctoral degree granted upon completion of graduate study depends on the administrative location of the program in which graduate study is done. Arguments about the proper degree for professional psychologists have been running on for many years. Those who support the PhD claim that it offers greater prestige than a professional degree and is more fitting because practitioners in psychology are really scholar-professionals (Derner, 1959; Stricker, 1975; Weins, 1983). Those who support the PsyD claim that it can be controlled by psychology as the PhD cannot and that it can be employed to certify professional competence in psychology as the PhD cannot (Fox, Barclay, & Rogers, 1982; Meehl, 1971; Peterson, 1976b, 1983).

The past 20 years have shown that rational arguments count less than some other conditions in determining which degree students receive at graduation. If the degree granted in each of the 44 practitioner programs identified by Caddy and LaPointe (1984) is related to the administrative location of the program, as in Table 1, it appears that use of the PhD for outright professional programs is mainly a practice of freestanding schools. Only three university-based professional programs (at Adelphi, the Fuller Graduate School, and the University of California at Davis) award the PhD degree. In most universities, the PhD is reserved for programs with research and scholarship as dominant objectives. Strictures, or the lack of strictures, imposed by state educational authorities also figure strongly in determining which degree will be allowed. All 14 of the PhD programs in freestanding professional schools are in California! In fact, with the single exception of Adelphi University, all the professional schools that grant the PhD degree for practitioner training are in California. There, regulations in higher education are unusually liberal, and the precedent established by the California School of Professional Psychology has been employed by other institutions to justify use of the PhD for practitioners.

Is the PsyD a second-class degree? Not yet, according to graduates who reported that the professional doctorate was more often seen as an asset than as a liability in seeking employment in professional psychology (Peterson, Eaton, Levine & Snepp, 1982). Will the PsyD become a second-class degree? I fear it might, as more and more graduates come from single-purpose professional schools and small departments of uncertain reputation. In the race to poor repute, the PsyD will have stiff competition from the PhD. A professional school of humanistic studies run by 10 full-time and 40 part-time faculty, enrolling 794 students working toward PhDs in counseling, marriage and family therapy, and industrial/organizational psychology (Caddy & LaPointe, 1984) will not improve the value of the PhD. Probably our best hope is that the people who use psychological services will not know the difference, and that the distinction between PhD and PsyD will be just as mysterious and just as inconsequential as the difference between the DDS and the DMD in dentistry.

4. Graduates of scientist-professional programs and graduates of practitioner programs in psychology perform about equally well. The null hypothesis expressed in the sentence above has scarcely been proved. Carefully designed research to test the hypothesis has not been conducted. The few data now

Table 1   Relation between Degree Granted and Administrative Location of Program

Degree	Location of program	
	Independent school	University
PsyD	10	17
PhD	14	3

available comparing graduates of practitioner programs with graduates of scientist-professional programs either show small differences or no differences at all.

By now it seems fairly clear that students intending to enter careers of practice are more satisfied with practitioner programs than with traditional scientist-practitioner programs (Marwit, 1983; Peterson et al., 1982). Student satisfaction, however, says nothing about professional competence as measured by other means.

So far, internship supervisors have detected few differences between students from scientist-professional programs and those from practitioner programs (Shemberg & Leventhal, 1981; Snepp, 1983). Fully 50% of the supervisors in Shemberg and Leventhal's study, for example, saw no difference in the performance of PsyD and PhD interns; 25% thought the PsyDs were worse; and 25% thought the PhDs were worse. In Snepp's study, a tendency was observed toward greater "sensitivity" among PsyD students and more "scientific" attitudes among PhD students, but differences were small, and preparation in various skills was considered equally good for both groups.

Findings like these may give some comfort to those who feared that professional programs would do worse than scientist-professional programs in educating students. But professional programs are clearly justified only if they do a better job of preparing people for practice than traditional PhD programs have done. The PhD programs, conversely, should be evaluated with regard to the productive scholarship of graduates and the claims of devotees that students are well prepared for practice by the training they receive. Adequate comparative studies have not been done. The obstacles to sound research on these questions are formidable. The criterion problem (i.e., how to evaluate competence in professional psychology) is particularly difficult. I do not agree, however, that these difficulties preclude systematic evaluative research (cf. Stern, 1984). Psychologists are perfectly ready to assess human performance in other complex occupations and to evaluate educational programs in other fields. As the APA Task Force on Education, Training, and Service has recommended (APA, 1982), we need to turn our alleged skills in program evaluation upon ourselves.

5. Curricula of professional schools and scientist-professional programs are more alike than different. The self-study by the NCSPP cited above (Callan, Peterson, & Stricker, 1986) concerned more than admissions. Methods for evaluating student competence curricula, faculty characteristics, administrative organization, and psychological service centers were also described in detail. From analyses of the various curricula, a typical program in professional psychology was derived (Kopplin, 1986).

Mean credit requirements are shown in Table 2. APA accreditation criteria strongly influence professional school curricula. All the APA content demands in biological, cognitive-emotional, and social bases of behavior; in professional

Table 2   A Typical Professional School Curriculum

Topic	Credits
Professional issues and ethics	3
Statistics and measurement	4
Research design	3
History and systems	2
Biological bases of behavior	4
Cognitive—emoitonal bases of behavior	3
Social bases of behavior I: Social psychology	3
Social bases of behavior II: Community and systems	3
Individual behavior I: Personality	3
Individual behavior II: Developmental psychology	3
Individual behavior III: Psychopathology	3
Individual behavior IV: Unspecified	3
Assessment I: General	3
Assessment II: Cognitive—intellectual	3
Assessment III: Personality	3
Intervention I: Individual psychotherapy	3
Intervention II: Behavior therapy	3
Intervention III: Group and family therapy	3
Intervention IV: Unspecified	3
Practicum	19
Additional required courses	25
Electives	8
Total	110

ethics; and in history and systems of psychology are met in the typical professional school program. Knowledge of personality theory, psychopathology,
and human development is ordinarily required. Strong demands are set for
professional activities of assessment and intervention (21 credits) and for
supervised practicum experience (19 credits). Statistics, measurement, and
research design are all required, and all but one of the professional schools
requires a dissertation or project devoted to the scholarly study of an issue
pertinent to applied psychology. Amounts of credit devoted to dissertation
work are included in the general set of "additional required courses," which
also includes courses in consultation, program evaluation, special projects, and
advanced courses in any of the areas of the core curriculum.

How different is this from the content of most scientist-professional
programs? Although comparable analyses of the curricula of departmental PhD
programs have not been done, I recently attempted an informal study of the
catalogs of 10 highly regarded scientist-professional programs to see what was
being taught in those programs today. When I coupled that information with the
residual of my experience in reviewing programs for APA accreditation, my
conclusion was that practitioner programs and scientist-professional programs

(not as idealized but as typically implemented in this country) do not differ much after all.

Scientist-professional programs also are designed to meet APA criteria, and so they contain the necessary substance for approval. Assessment, intervention, and supervised practica are all included, though emphasis on assessment is typically less than in practitioner programs, and I saw no departmental PhD program that included the 1,900 hours of supervised preinternship practicum experience required at Adelphi and Baylor. Like the professional programs the scientist-practitioner programs routinely require a one-year predoctoral internship. As appropriate for programs designed to educate researchers, the academic PhD programs put a greater emphasis on research design and the conduct of research than any of the practitioner programs. The programs at Vanderbilt and Duke University, for example, not only require the usual courses in statistics and research design but also involve students in research apprenticeships from the beginning of graduate study. To a greater degree than practitioner programs, scientist-professional programs allow electives and encourage specialization. Students at Michigan State University, for example, are required to choose between curricula in child/family and adult clinical psychology, though some crossover is allowed. Students at Yale elect one of three subthemes in clinical psychology, health psychology, community psychology, or more traditional clinical psychodiagnosis and psychotherapy. Specialization in other scientist-professional programs is common, but even in this regard the distinction from practitioner programs is unclear. The Rutgers PsyD program in clinical psychology, for example, requires students to choose between behavioral and psychodynamic tracks, and a third emphasis on organizational psychology, is under development.

In early formulations (APA, 1967; Peterson, 1966), the differences between research programs and practitioner programs were clear cut. The research programs were designed to educate productive investigators by engaging students in active research throughout graduate study. Professional training was not necessarily reduced in quality but was restricted in scope so that the specialized knowledge required for effective inquiry could be obtained. Training for practice, on the other hand, was to be both thorough and comprehensive, to prepare psychologists for the full range of problems they might face in professional work. Practitioners were educated for the intelligent consumption of research, but the early program proposals contained no dissertation requirements at all.

As the professional programs evolved, however, emphasis on active scholarship increased, and some of the intellectual leaders of the professional school movement (e.g., Meltzoff, 1984) proposed no less an emphasis on scholarly inquiry than is found in most scientist-practitioner programs. The scientist-practitioner programs, for their part, no longer neglect training for practice, as they often did in the past. I have a distinct impression that training for professional service in the best scientist-practitioner programs is better today than it has ever been. In the longer history of applied psychology, the main contribution of the professional schools may be that they forced academic departments and organized psychology to take professional training more seriously than before. In the core of common knowledge, in practicum training for assessment and intervention, and in the requirements for internships and dissertations, the programs in professional schools and in academic departments are more alike than different. If one looks only at curricula, both types of programs seem to be educating scholar-professionals after all.

6. The main differences between practitioner programs and scientist-professional programs lie in the attitudes and interests of faculty and students. The mission statements of scientist-professional programs in academic departments are clear about the emphasis on research in their programs.

The 1984 Duke University clinical program description stated,

> We do not conceive of our mission as the training of mental health professionals, but rather the goal is to train scholar-professionals who have the capacity to transform and better our approaches to mental health related phenomena.

According to the mission statement in the 1984 clinical program description of the University of Illinois,

> we expect all of our students to develop competence in, and an understanding of, both the scholarly and applied aspects of the field. . . . Given the above emphasis, the program is not recommended for those who wish to pursue exclusive professional practice careers.

This is different from the acceptance of professional application for its own sake as expressed in the mission statements of professional schools. According to the mission statement in Adelphi University's 1984 catalog, "The professional school. . . accepts unequivocally the career goal of the students, whether it is clinical practice, research, or teaching." Wright State University, in Ohio, stated in its 1984 graduate catalog that "it is the mission of the School of Professional Psychology to. . . educate and train qualified individuals. . . for quality practice in professional psychology."

The two kinds of institutions accomplish their objectives in different ways, including the kind of faculty members they recruit. No first-rank scientist-practitioner program in the country will accept as a full-time faculty member anyone without a record of production in research, and the values attached to faculty performance are predominantly those of scholarly contribution. Professional schools engage scholars too, but complement their ranks with people whose lives are devoted primarily to professional service. In the free-standing schools, practitioners form most of the faculty. In university-based schools, practitioners are usually hired on an adjunct basis. Either way, role models for professional careers are provided to students, and the value of practice is affirmed in its own right.

Faculties create the cultures within which graduate education takes place. Although the curricula of academic departments and professional schools do not differ widely, I propose that there are some important differences between the cultures of the two different kinds of institutions. Gregory Kimble (1984) has recently done some interesting work on the values and beliefs of psychologists, following the line of thought C. P. Snow (1964) articulated in distinguishing between the scientific and humanist cultures in Western society. With apologies to Charles Osgood, Kimble constructed a device he called the Epistemic Differential. The test consists of statements describing differing views on a range of philosophical issues with which psychologists are perennially concerned, such as the predictability of behavior, relations between nomothetic and idiographic laws, and the relative advantages of data and theory in methodological strategy. Factor analysis defined a coherent scientist/humanist dimension, and the scores of members of several APA divisions were compared. Large differences, significant at the .00001 level, were found. Members of Division 3, Experimental Psychology, expressed views sharply on the side of science. Members of Division 32, Humanistic Psychology, fell to the other side. Members of Division 29, Psychotherapy, were nearly as humanistic as the humanists (Kimble, 1984). So far, no one has compared the faculties of professional schools and academic departments using Kimble's measure, but I will be surprised if substantial differences do not appear when the study is done.

The interests and values of students resemble those of faculty. When Roger Knudson and I examined the interests of students in several clinical psychology programs we found two massive factors, one of interest in research and the other of interest in practice. Students preparing for careers of research and those preparing for careers of practice differed widely in the expected direction (Peterson & Knudson, 1979). Some of the differences are so obvious no studies are needed to demonstrate them. Any site visitor who reviews a program for accreditation will sooner or later get to talking with students about their interests. In the academic departments, students discuss the research they are doing. In the professional schools, students talk about the therapies they are learning.

More than attitudes and interests are required to make a culture. A work culture is formed by a group of people laboring together toward common objectives. A research culture is created by a group of investigators who share the values of science, probe into the questions that intrigue them, dig out the facts, frame ideas and findings into coherent conceptions, talk with each other, and work with each other to find out what is going on in the world—all in an environment that encourages inquiry. The departments of physics at Berkeley or Princeton show us what a research culture can be. In psychology, the Harvard group under Murray in the 1930s, the Yale group under Hull in the 1940s and the Stanford group (I hesitate to name a single leader) in more recent times show what I mean by a research culture.

The culture of practice is different. There a group of professionals are doing their best to provide services to the public. They are engaged in working out the puzzles of the individual case, talking these over with colleagues, despairing over their failures, enjoying their successes, exulting now and then when particularly stubborn problems yield to the solutions they have engineered, designing new programs together, working these into the community, and helping people right now with the best professional service they can offer. The Mayo Medical Center shows what the culture of practice can be. In psychology, Albert Ellis's Institute of Rational-Emotive Therapy and the Psychological Center at the Fuller Graduate School are starting to show what can be done to take psychological services to the people.

Many academic departments bring students into the culture of research. Few of them provide comparable socialization in practice, though many provide satisfactory training for professional work. Professional schools bring students into the culture of practice. Few provide comparable socialization in research, though professional schools that maintain active research programs can provide cultures of research as well.

7. Under some conditions, the cultures of science and practice can be blended. The kinds of science and practice prevalent in 1964, when Pinard delivered his diatribe against the scientist-professional model of education, defied integration. At that time, any "scientific" project that was not empirical in substance and experimental in method stood little chance for approval or publication. "Practice" consisted mainly of individual psychotherapy, indeterminately related to individual assessment procedures of questionable value. Most of the research of the time was irrelevant to practice, the practice of the time was invulnerable to research, and each activity went on in isolation from the other. Over the past 20 years, the definition of acceptable scholarly work has been extended. During the same time, the profession has changed in ways that allow scholarly investigation to improve it. These are the conditions required for the blending of science and practice.

The past 20 years have seen a considerable liberalization of methodological constraint in psychological inquiry. Kimble (1984) wrote about an "easy acceptance" of topics for research that would have been out of bounds in earlier times (p. 838). "Mental imagery, the distinction between remembered and imagined, voluntary behavior, self-awareness and self-control, conceptually driven processing, helplessness and coping, risk taking, metaphoric expression, and inferential processing are a few of these topics, all of which are identified by phrases that catch important ideas in the humanist tradition" (Kimble, 1984, p. 838). In the behavioral tradition of professional psychology, the development of single-subject designs and the successful implementation of field studies have allowed systematic inquiry in areas of clear practical importance. Among titles of doctoral proposals listed by Leitenberg (1974) in describing the scientist-professional program at the University of Vermont are "The Prediction of Medical Rehabilitation Outcome," "A Contingency Management and Fading Procedure for the Modification of the Classroom Behavior of Institutionalized Delinquents," "The Generality Issue in a Head-Start Behavior Modification Program," and "Changes in Interaction Patterns in Multiple Family Therapy." Barlow, Hayes, and Nelson (1984) recently completed an analysis of the issues that divide scientists from practitioners in psychology and proposed an integrated model of applied research that includes clinical observation, generation of new intervention procedures, generation of new measurement procedures, single case studies, clinical analogue studies, short- and long-term outcome studies, evaluation of training and dissemination methods, and evaluation of field efficacy. In the view of Barlow, Hayes, and Nelson, responsible practitioners must employ combinations of these procedures to be accountable, and by the systematic accumulation of knowledge through replicated case studies and other means practitioners may contribute to science as well.

Outside the boundaries of science as conventionally conceived lie the disciplines of humanistic inquiry. The interpretive studies of historians, for example, are not usually regarded as science, but they are not intuitive art either. A disciplined historian has strong concern for such issues as the validity of report and the coherent interpretation of scattered fragments of fact. In literature, the writing of biography requires careful attention to accuracy of account, reconciliation of disparate reports, and elaboration of coherent themes that unify the life of the subject. Some of the humanities require discipline as firm as any science. Thoughtfully conceived and carefully executed, inquiries of these kinds can produce an order as compelling as many an experimental series and often more useful for understanding some of the processes a clinician needs to comprehend. The proper base for practice in psychology is not science but disciplined knowledge. The scholarly activity required to build that knowledge may take many forms. Instead of restricting inquiries to suit our methods, we must design methods to suit the problems we face as practitioners.

As science changes, so will practice. Three surveys (Callan, Peterson, & Stricker, 1986; Garfield & Kurtz, 1976; Peterson et al., 1982) show that professional psychologists spend more time doing individual psychotherapy than any other single activity. I regard the practice of psychotherapy as a perfectly honorable and fairly useful way to make a living, but there is no reason to suppose psychologists do better at it than people from several other professions, including some whose services come cheaper than ours. If professional psychology is to serve the public effectively and efficiently, it will help to broaden our scope from individuals to groups and organizations, to shift our orientation to include prevention as well as treatment, and to extend the settings in which we work from mental health centers to the full range of environments in which human dysfunctions may occur and in which psychological knowledge may be applied to improve human function. Assessment remains a critical skill for professional psychologists, but it cannot be restricted to the assessment of individual personality. We also need to study groups and organizations in natural settings to find out how they work, what can go wrong with them, what can be done to improve them, and how to evaluate any improvements we have attempted. A professional psychology conceived in this way—broad enough to accommodate the problems we address, based on disciplined knowledge, and linking conception, assessment, and intervention as systematically as the human condition allows—can be accountable and self-corrective and thereby more useful to society than much professional activity is today.

The argument for extending the scope of professional psychology has been stated most recently by Sarason (1981) and Levy (1984). Many of the ideas Sarason and Levy expressed so well are embodied in the charters of several schools of professional psychology. How much we actually know about the grand range of problems we have staked out is another matter, but a reasonably firm knowledge base for professional psychology has been established (Peterson, 1976a), and a professional psychology linked with the broad-ranging disciplines of inquiry proposed above offers every promise of improving in the future.

Education for practice is not less difficult than education for research. In some regards, it is more difficult. Knowledge of fact and theory must be just as thorough, and the range of knowledge required for practice is greater. Practitioners must not only understand the facts and concepts of psychology, but they must also know how to apply them in helping others. Frank Hawkinshire, of New York University, has drawn my attention to some ideas of his mentor, W. H. Cowley, about the aims of professional education. Cowley (1960) distinguished among three kinds of education, which he called *logocentric, practicentric,* and *democentric.* Logocentric literally means "centered in knowledge." A logocentrist is concerned with advancing the boundaries of knowledge without concern for practical affairs. Practicentric education is concerned with the skills of practice in applying knowledge to solve problems. Democentric education, in Cowley's definition, is concerned with interpreting knowledge for the public at large, but the meaning of the term would not be violated if the *demos* were taken to be students who enter our schools, and the democentric emphasis in education a concern for the personal development of the people we hope to influence.

Education of scientists is dominantly logocentric and probably must remain so if the science is to advance. Education of professionals is dominantly practicentric and probably must be so if the skills of the profession are to be fully taught. I do not know what we can do to advance the personal development of students. Most of them are well formed when they come to us. We can, however, stop quenching their concern for others in a cold objectivity that does not suit our discipline in the first place. We can stop requiring hypocrisy of them, as we do by refusing entry to the profession unless they pretend interests they do not have. If we can create environments in which proper regard is given to disciplined knowledge, the skills of practice are taught and respected, and the integrity of students is not impaired, it may not matter whether we work in professional schools, large departments, or small departments. We will all be giving students all we can.

REFERENCES

American Psychological Association, Committee on the Scientific and Professional Aims of Psychology. (1967). The scientific and professional aims of psychology. *American Psychologist, 22,* 49–76.

American Psychological Association. (1982). *Report of the APA Task Force on Education, Training, and Service in Psychology.* Washington, DC: Author.

Barlow, D. H., Hayes, S. C., & Nelson, R. O. (1984). *The scientist practitioner: Research and accountability in clinical and educational settings.* New York: Pergamon.

Blank, L., & David, H. P. (1963). The crisis in clinical psychology training. *American Psychologist, 18,* 216–219.

Caddy, G. R., & LaPointe, L. L. (1984). The training of professional psychologists: Historical developments and present trends. In G. S. Tryon (Ed.), *Professional practice of psychology.* Norwood, NJ: Ablex.

Callan, J., Peterson, D. R., & Stricker, G. (Eds.). (1986). *Quality in professional psychological training.* National Council of Schools of Professional Psychology: Author.

Carnegie Council on Policy Studies in Higher Education. (1976). *A classification of institutions of higher education.* Berkeley, CA: Author.

Conference Board of Associated Research Councils. (1983, March). Research programs preserve reputations, national survey finds. *APA Monitor,* p. 7.

Cowley, W. H. (1960). *An overview of American colleges and universities.* Unpublished manuscript, Stanford University, Stanford, CA.

Derner, G. F. (1959). The university and clinical psychology training. In M. H. P. Finn & F. Brown (Eds.), *Training for clinical psychology.* New York: International Universities Press.

Dörken, H., & Cummings, N. A. (1977). A school of psychology as innovation in professional education: The California School of Professional Psychology. *Professional Psychology, 8,* 129–148.

Fox, R. E. Barclay, A. G., & Rogers, D. A. (1982). The foundations of professional psychology. *American Psychologist, 37,* 306–312.

Garfield, S. L., & Kurtz, R. (1976). Clinical psychologists in the 1970s. *American Psychologist, 31,* 1–9.

Hoch, E. L., Ross, A. O., & Winder, C. L. (Eds.). (1966). *Professional prepara-*

tion of clinical psychologists. Washington, DC: American Psychological Association.

Kahn, M. W., & Santostefano, S. (1962). The case of clinical psychology: A search for identity. *American Psychologist, 17,* 185–190.

Kimble, G. A. (1984). Psychology's two cultures. *American Psychologist, 39,* 833–839.

Kopplin, D. A. (1986). Curriculum and curriculum review. In J. Callan, D. R. Peterson, & G. Stricker (Eds.), *Quality in professional psychology training.* National Council of Schools of Professional Psychology: Author.

Korman, M. (Ed.). (1976). *Levels and patterns of professional training in psychology.* Washington, DC: American Psychological Association.

Leitenberg, H. (1974). Training clinical researchers in psychology. *Professional Psychology, 5,* 59–69.

Levy, L. H. (1984). The metamorphosis of clinical psychology: Toward a new charter of human services psychology. *American Psychologist, 39,* 486–494.

Marwit, S. J.(1983). Doctoral candidates' attitudes toward models of professional training. *Professional Psychology: Research and Practice, 14,* 105–111.

Meehl, P. E. (1971). A scientific, scholarly nonresearch doctorate for clinical practitioners. In R. Holt (Ed.), *New horizons for psychotherapy: Autonomy as a profession.* New York: International Universities Press.

Meltzoff, J. (1984). Research training for clinical psychologists: Point-counterpoint. *Professional Psychology: Research and Practice, 15,* 203–209.

Peterson, D. R. (1966). Professional program in an academic psychology department. In E. L. Hoch, A. O. Ross, & C. L. Winder (Eds.), *Professional preparation of clinical psychologists.* Washington, DC: American Psychological Association.

Peterson, D. R. (1976a). Is psychology a profession? *American Psychologist, 31,* 792–298.

Peterson, D. R. (1976b). Need for the Doctor of Psychology degree in professional psychology. *American Psychologist, 31,* 792–298.

Peterson, D. R. (1982). Origins and development of the Doctor of Psychology concept. In G. R. Caddy, D. C. Rimm, H. Watson, & J. H. Johnson (Eds.), *Educating professional psychologists* (pp. 19–38). New Brunswick, NJ: Transaction Books.

Peterson, D. R. (1983). The case for the PsyD. In S. Walfish & G. Sumprer (Eds.), *Clinical, counseling, and community psychology.* New York: Irvington.

Peterson, D. R., Eaton, M. M., Levine, A. R., & Snepp, F. P. (1982). Career experiences of Doctors of Psychology. *Professional Psychology, 13,* 268–277.

Peterson, D. R., & Knudson, R. M. (1979). Work preferences of clinical psychologists. *Professional Psychology, 10,* 175–182.

Pinard, R. P. A. (1967). A professional and an academic degree offered in the same department of psychology. In E. C. Webster (Ed.), *The Couchiching Conference on Professional Psychology.* Montreal, Canada: Canadian Psychological Association.

Raimy, V. C. (Ed.). (1950). *Training in clinical psychology*. New York: Prentice-Hall.

Sarason, A. B. (1981). An asocial psychology and a misdirected clinical psychology. *American Psychologist, 36,* 827–836.

Shemberg, K. M., & Leventhal, D. B. (1981). Attitudes of internship directors toward pre-internship training and clinical training models. *Professional Psychology, 12,* 639–646.

Snepp, F. P. (1983). *Attitudes toward training and the efficacy of the scientist-practitioner and professional models of training in clinical psychology.* Unpublished doctoral dissertation, Rutgers University, New Brunswick, NJ.

Snow, C. P. (1964). *The two cultures and a second look.* London: Cambridge University Press.

Stern, S. (1984). Professional training and professional competence: A critique of current thinking. *Professional Psychology: Research and Practice, 15,* 230–243.

Stricker, G. (1975). On professional schools and professional degrees. *American Psychologist, 30,* 1062–1066.

Stricker, G. (1986). Admissions to professional schools. In J. Callan, D. R. Peterson, & G. Stricker (Eds.), *Quality in professional psychology training.* National Council of Schools of Professional Psychology: Author.

Tryon, R. C. (1963). Psychology in flux: The academic-professional bipolarity. *American Psychologist, 18,* 134–143.

Webster, E. C. (Ed.). (1967). *The Couchiching Conference on Professional Psychology.* Montreal, Canada: Canadian Psychological Association.

Weins, A. H. (1983). The case for the PhD. In S. Walfish & G. Sumprer (Eds.), *Clinical, counseling, and community psychology.* New York: Irvington.

Reading 3

Counseling Psychology versus Clinical Psychology: Further Explorations on a Theme or Once More around the "Identity" Maypole with Gusto

C. Edward Watkins, Jr.
The University of Tennessee at Knoxville

Counseling psychology and clinical psychology have long been at odds in the professional-academic community. Much past and present debate has focused upon presumed distinctions and similarities between these specialties. And such debate appears to have arisen partly from counseling psychologists' pressing need to define themselves. Unforunately, we still remain unsettled as to who we are, where we belong, and what we should do (Delworth, 1977; Pallone,

Reprinted from The Counseling Psychologist, *11*(4), 76–92.

1977; Patterson, 1966, 1967, 1969b; Samler, 1964; Spoth, 1981). Thus, the question of *identity* continues to be an ever present issue in the field (Fretz, 1977; Goldschmitt, Tipton, & Wiggins, 1981).

In this paper, I would like to examine anew the convergences, as well as divergences, that seemingly exist between counseling and clinical psychology. Previous investigations of this type primarily have been oriented toward role and functions considerations; however, I would like to take the preceding studies a step farther by including some other relevant professional aspects. More specifically, the subsequent discussion will entail an examination of five particular counseling-clinical areas, these being: (1) the history of clinical and counseling psychology; (2) roles and functions; (3) training conferences and training/internship experiences; (4) work settings; and (5) the future of clinical and counseling psychology. Through such an analysis, it is hoped that the identity of counseling psychology will be more precisely defined and differentiated.

THE HISTORY OF CLINICAL AND COUNSELING PSYCHOLOGY

Clinical Psychology

The history of clinical psychology proves to be of much interest and fascination (Garfield, 1965, 1974, 1982; Korchin, 1976; Louttit, 1939; Reisman, 1976; Rotter, 1963; Watson, 1953). Three of its most prominent themes appear to have derived from a myriad of significant social changes, so common to the years of the 1920s and 1930s. These themes or movements have been identified as: (1) the psychometric trend, (2) the mental health movement, and (3) the psychodynamic orientation.

The Psychometric Trend   The psychometric tradition can be traced back to the early efforts of Francis Galton, who perhaps is best known for his science of phrenology. However, it was Alfred Binet, with his development of an intelligence test for assessing retardates, who provided psychometrics with some credibility. Lewis Terman's revision of Binet's test tended to have far-reaching effects upon American psychology, and clinicians primarily became the "intelligence testers, par excellence." Subsequently, other intelligence tests were added to the clinical psychologist's armamentarium (e.g., the WISC-R, WAIS-R, and WPPSI). Also the projectives came into marked prominence, including the Rorschach, Draw-A-Person, Bender-Gestalt, and TAT, among others (Korchin & Shuldberg, 1981). As a result, these instruments brought a whole new realm of functioning to the clinician's role—as expert in projective diagnostics.

The Mental Health Movement   The primary impetus for the mental health movement was seemingly Clifford Beers' (1908) book, *A Mind That Found*

Itself. It heightened individuals' awareness of those experiencing emotional difficulties and the types of treatment rendered for these difficulties. As a consequence, child guidance centers were developed in hopes of better attending to the needs of children and families. Lightner Witmer, referred to as the founder of clinical psychology, started the first general psychological clinic in 1896; however, it was not until 1909 that the first true child guidance clinic was established—the Juvenile Psychopathic Institute in Chicago (now known as the Institute for Juvenile Research). Following this, the mental health movement continued to manifest itself as other guidance centers were established. Thus, clinical psychology, with the help of Beers, began to move ever closer to the prospect of providing psychotherapeutic treatment.

The Psychodynamic Orientation Freud's psychoanalytic system tended to have a most significant impact upon the development of clinical psychology. The analytic approach brought with it new ways of conceptualizing human problems and interpreting everyday events. Behavior could be understood *in depth,* and psychologists had a means of comprehending the elusive *why* of persons' thoughts, affects, and actions. Despite clinical psychologists' interests in the analytic orientation, most of their efforts were, in the main, as psychometrists during the 1920s and 1930s. Very little psychotherapy was conducted by these professionals, and their primary function was that of psychological examiner. World War II changed this, however; due to a lack of *helping* personnel in the war, clinical psychologists were called upon to expand their services. Consequently, the clinician became not only psychological examiner but psychotherapist as well. And in capsule fashion, such is the current state of affairs for the clinical psychologist.

Counseling Psychology

Several individuals have addressed the history of the counseling specialty (APA, 1956; Aubrey, 1977; Pepinsky, Hill-Frederick, & Epperson, 1978; Scott, 1980; Super, 1955a; Whiteley, 1980), and like the clinical area, counseling psychology seems to have developed from three specific, though somewhat different traditions. These are: (1) the vocational guidance movement; (2) the psychometric trend; and (3) the psychotherapy tradition.

The Vocational Guidance Movement Perhaps if anyone can be credited with founding the vocational guidance movement, it is Frank Parsons. In 1908, Parsons established the Vocation Bureau in Boston. A year after the bureau opened, Parsons' landmark (1909) book, *Choosing a Vocation,* was published. Since Parsons' initial efforts the field of vocational psychology has continued to ever broaden and expand. The intensive study of persons interested has been made possible via new instrumentation, such as the tests of Kuder and Strong (cf. Campbell & Hansen, 1981; Darley, 1941; Holland, 1979; Kuder,

1977; Kuder & Diamon, 1979; Strong, 1943). Also, in the 1950s several noted career development theorists presented their works, including Ginzberg (1952; Ginzberg, Ginsburg, Axelrad, & Herma, 1951), Holland (1958, 1959), Roe (1951a, 1951b, 1952a, 1952b, 1953, 1956, 1957), and Super (1951, 1953, 1954, 1955b, 1956, 1957). With the advent of these theoretical contributions, the field of vocational psychology flourished and has continued to be of much interest and concern to many contemporary counseling psychologists.

The Psychometric Trend The psychometric trend, as it impacts upon counseling psychology, largely emerged from the dismal depression years. The high rates of unemployment, coupled with the lot of human misery and suffering, brought many to act upon the existing circumstances. As such, vocational guidance workers joined forces with psychometricians, in hopes of "getting adult workers back into the labor force" (Super, 1955a, p. 4). Most prominently, psychometrics provided the vocational guidance movement with a substantive, psychological base. Prior to this time, the "movement was largely devoid of philosophical or psychological underpinnings" (Aubrey, 1977, p. 290), and the psychometric tradition was able to correct a rather marked deficit.

The Psychotherapy Tradition While psychoanalysis was a major influence in clinical psychology's development, it was the orientation of a Wisconsin farm boy, Carl Rogers, that turned counseling psychology "on its heels." Rogers presented his non-directive therapy in 1942, and his initial work proved to have a most revolutionary impact upon the helping professions, in general. Vocational guidance workers began to re-evalute their practices, with clients' personalities in toto emerging as the subject matter of counseling. (It was also during 1942 when Super's *The Dynamics of Vocational Development* was introduced; consequently, vocational development came to be viewed as a developmental, life-span phenomenon, instead of a specific, individual event.) Rogers followed up his first book with many others (e.g., Rogers, 1951, 1961, 1980), each of which has exerted a tremendous influence throughout the years. As such, the concepts of empathy, reflection, self-actualization, and the fully-functioning person have come to be the watchwords of many counselors.

As a result of Rogers' immense impact upon vocational guidance, coupled with the psychometric tradition, counseling psychology was to emerge. However, it was perhaps not until 1942 when the real inauguration was to transpire. During this year, the Veterans Administration—following the Northwestern Conference report—coined a new job title—*counseling psychologist*. And thereby the field of counseling psychology was born. The new job title and field designation were both adopted by the American Psychological Association's (APA) Division of Counseling and Guidance in that same year. The Division's name, then, was changed accordingly, and a novel specialty area was thus identified within the APA: Counseling psychology became a substantive reality.

Evaluation

In regard to historical background, counseling and clinical psychology have emerged from some relatively distinct traditions. Clinical psychology, on the other hand, developed out of a strong psychometric trend, oriented primarily toward intellectual assessment. As time passed, this emphasis on intellective evaluation was colored by Freud's analytic system, which brought with it a focus upon psychodynamics and understanding individuals in depth. Such a focus strongly preoccupied clinical psychology, and numerous projective personality instruments were developed as a result. These instruments enabled the clinician to explore the unconscious worlds of clients and make appropriate diagnostic judgments. More specifically, the primary interest of the clinician was to identify psychopathology, so that psychological treatment could be rendered by a physician or psychiatrist. Thus, in the early years, the clinical psychologist was basically a psychological examiner, who administered intelligence and projective tests. And it was not until World War II that psychotherapy became a clinical function.

In contrast, the roots of counseling psychology tend to be quite different in a number of ways. The primary base appears to have derived from the vocational guidance movement, with the guiding motif of the times being the *matching of person and job.* In an effort to most effectively execute this motif, psychometrics was incorporated into vocational guidance work. The main purpose of the psychometric trend, though, was not to assess personality *in depth;* rather the counselor was interested first and foremost in evaluation of interests and aptitudes. An it was to this end that tests were used. As a further note of interest, counseling psychology was most significantly influenced by Rogers, instead of Freud. While the work of Freud was no doubt felt, it tended not to impact with the force of Rogers' endeavors. Consequently, counseling psychology was founded upon a model of client self-responsibility and self-direction as well as a belief in the constructive potentials of the person. Thus, the trend toward vocational and therapeutic counseling was spurred via the work of Carl Rogers, and the guidance worker's functions expanded far beyond that of the initial role—that being as vocational examiner.

ROLES AND FUNCTIONS IN CLINICAL
AND COUNSELING PSYCHOLOGY

Clinical Psychology

The roles and functions of the clinical psychologist have changed over time, causing notable confusion, upheaval, and identity problems in the field (Garfield, 1966). Because of such identity diffusion, clinicians have worked arduously to define "who they are" and "what they do"; and as a result, several prominent themes have been consistently identified as clinical in nature. Shakow

(1975), for example, provides a rather general, ambiguous definition of clinical psychology, focusing upon the skills of diagnosis and therapy. Mill (1959) expands upon the definition of Shakow, indicating that clinical psychologists are involved in a variety of activities. These include not only psychodiagnostics and psychotherapy, but "consultation, training, research, and administration" (p. 708). Garfield (1974) heartily concurs with this view of roles and functions and provides a nice elaboration on Mill (see pp. 1-2). In an interesting and somewhat different vein, Korchin (1976) states that "what best distinguishes the clinician from fellow psychologists. . . is more a way of thinking—the clinical attitude—than emphasis on particular subject matters or techniques" (p. 22).

In considering the four brief definitions, each (excepting that of Korchin) emphasizes the functions of psychodiagnostics and psychotherapy rather prominently. While these delineations prove helpful, perhaps the best roles/ functions definition of the clinical psychologist is that of the APA. In the "Specialty Guidelines for the Delivery of Services by Clinical Psychologists" (APA, 1981a), the following statement—presented here in abbreviated form— is made: *Clinical psychological services* refer to the application of principles, methods, and procedures for understanding, predicting, and alleviating intellectual, emotional, psychological, and behavioral disability and discomfort. . . . Clinical psychological services include the following:

> A. Assessment directed toward diagnosing the nature and causes, and predicting the effects, of subjective distress; of personal, social, and work dysfunction; and of the psychological and emotional factors involved in and consequent to, physical disease and disability. . . .
> B. Interventions directed at identifying and correcting the emotional conflicts, personality disturbances, and skill deficits underlying a person's distress and/or dysfunction (p. 642).

Further identified functions of the clinical psychologist are (1) consultation, (2) program development, (3) supervision, and (4) evaluation of services.

The definition of the APA offers a most concrete and comprehensive definition of clinical psychology. Though numerous other definitions could be proferred, those of Garfield, Korchin, Mill, and Shakow seem quite representative of individual efforts; and the APA's delineation appears the most inclusive in scope, as well as the most unequivocal in presentation.

Counseling Psychology

Like the clinical area, counseling psychology has been defined numerous times. While definitions may have sometimes varied, there does appear to be a marked consistency in how counseling psychologists view themselves. For example, in 1952, the Committee on Counselor Training of the Division of Counseling and Guidance indicated that "the professional goal of the counseling psychologist is to foster the psychological development of the individual. This includes all people on the adjustment continuum. . . . Counseling psychologists will spend the bulk of their time with individuals within the normal range. . . . Counseling stresses the positive and preventative" (APA, 1952b, p. 175; cf. APA, 1956; Hahn, 1955). Thus, at this time the distinction between normal-abnormal seemed to arise as a prime dividing line between counseling and clinical psychology.

Such a distinction has more recently been emphasized by Nelson-Jones (1982). He states that counseling psychology's "clientele tend to be not very seriously disturbed people in non-medical settings. Its concerns are those of the whole person in all areas of human psychological functioning, such as feeling and thinking, personal, marital and sexual relations, and work and recreational activity" (p. 5). Along more of a developmental line, Oetting (1967) indicates that "*Counseling psychology* is the study of the mental health of individuals engaged in developmental processes" (p. 382). He continues, "The counseling psychologist is concerned with identifying the developmental inadequacies and locating or providing experiences that remedy the environmental deficiency" (p. 383).

To obtain a broader perspective on counseling psychology, one last delineation seems appropriate: that of the APA (1981b; cf. Fretz, 1982). The following statement is indicated in the "Specialty Guidelines for the Delivery of Services by Counseling Psychologists":

> *Counseling psychological services* refers to services provided by counseling psychologists that apply principles, methods, and procedures for facilitating effective functioning during the life-span developmental process. In providing such services, counseling psychologists approach practice with a significant emphasis on positive aspects of growth and adjustment and with a developmental orientation (p. 654).

Subsequent to this definition, counseling psychological services are identified as consisting of: (1) assessment, evaluation, and diagnosis, (2) interventions, (3) consultation, (4) program development, (5) supervision, and (6) evaluation. Assessments are viewed as involving the evaluations of educational achievement, academic skills, aptitudes, interests, and other such aspects. Interventions include individual and group counseling, focusing upon career concerns, and personal problems primarily.

The APA's definition of counseling psychology represents a bold effort to delimit this specialty area; and as Kirk (1982) indicates, the Specialty Guidelines "define fairly specifically who is a counseling psychologist, how he or she becomes one, and what he or she does" (p. 55). Thus, while varied attempts have been made to define counseling psychology, the preceding effort appears to be one of the more, if not the most, explicit and comprehensive delineations yet executed.

Evaluation

From this consideration of definitions of roles and functions, several relatively consistent themes—some old, some new—seem to emerge. Each of these so-called "themes" appears to exist on a continuum of sorts. Unfortunately, these continua do not enable absolute or precise demarcations; they do, however, offer a means of conceptualizing seeming differences between counseling and clinical psychology from a relativistic standpoint. The subsequent continua can be divided into three types: (1) population characteristics, (2) assessment, and (3) intervention.

The first continuum presented is that of ego maturity versus ego immaturity. In regard to these terms, counseling psychology seems largely based upon an ego maturity model. That is, the clientele of the counseling psychologist is often viewed as: (1) functioning adequately, (2) competent and capable, or having the ability to be so, (3) productive, or having the potential to be productive, (4) active, rather than passive, and (5) fairly independent, rather than dependent. Conversely, the clientele of the clinician is defined from the perspective of ego immaturity, as: (1) functioning inadequately, (2) incompetent, (3) unproductive, (4) passive, and (5) dependent. The clinical psychologist, then, is more apt to be involved with rather severe psychopathological clients, whereas the counseling psychologist is more prone to assist individuals adjusting to developmental concerns (e.g., career decisions, adapting to college life, and relationship problems).

The second continuum—self-control versus lack of self-control—tends to be an extension of the previous one. Here again, the clients of the counseling psychologist are seen as possessing self-control; those of the clinician lean more toward episodic control or an absence of such control. It is perhaps because of a self-management assumption that self-control procedures have become so popular in counseling psychology (cf. Deffenbacher & Michaels, 1981; Greiner & Karoly, 1976; Heffernan & Richards, 1981; Perri, Richards, & Schultheis, 1977; Richards & Perri, 1978; Thoresen & Ewart, 1976; Thoresen & Mahoney, 1974). However, the popularity of such methods among clinicians must also be recognized (e.g., see Mahoney & Arnkoff, 1978, 1979).

The assessment continuum involves two basic dimensions: objective versus projective. The instrumentation of counseling and clinical psychology derives seemingly from their respective models of the person. Therefore, the counseling psychologist tends more toward objective assessment (e.g., SCII, SDS, Firo-B, CPI, 16PF), because the client's condition usually does not demand an "unconscious evaluation." On the other hand, the "deep, inner mental life" of individuals would fall more to the clinician, whose projective devices are designed to ferret out such aspects for analysis. In essence, within counseling psychology, the conscious and unconscious realms are considered to function in concert; thus, clients' self-reports are viewed as accurate and undistorted representations of the client's internal world. Within clinical psychology, however, conscious and unconscious experiences may be split off from one another, causing various inner confusions and personal upheavals. As a result, self-reports would be more subject to distortion and, therefore, inappropriate for study; projectives, then, become the preferred assessment device.

The fourth continuum relates to interventive roles, these being defined as educational/developmental versus remedial. The work of the clinical psychologist has traditionally been remedial in nature, oriented toward those individuals with disturbing and interfering psychopathology. However, counseling psychologists, while performing their share of remedial work, function more in an educational/facilitative capacity (cf. Authier, Gustafson, Guerney, & Kasdorf, 1975; Ivey, 1974, 1976, 1979; Jordaan, Myers, & Layton, 1968; Thompson & Super, 1964). Such a role includes a variety of activities, some being the leading of structured group experiences (Drum & Knott, 1977) and direct psychological education (Mosher & Sprinthall, 1971), among others. This type of role, then, is foremost for the counseling psychologist. As Ivey (1976) states, "the educational/developmental role of the counseling psychologist must now be considered primary with the preventive role serving as secondary function. The traditional remedial role and rehabilitative role is not discarded, but becomes subsumed under a clarified and enlarged definition of counseling psychology" (p. 72).

Consistent with the preceding point, counseling and clinical psychology appear to differ along a continuum of prevention levels. Caplan (1964) has identified three specific levels of prevention: primary, secondary, and tertiary. Primary prevention, what could be viewed as paramount in the role of counseling psychology, refers to "the creation of an environment which prevents an individual from developing psychological disorders. It is an attempt to change communities for the better" (Nathan & Harris, 1975, p. 52). Nathan and Harris (1975) indicate that secondary prevention is oriented toward "individuals who have exhibited the preliminary indicators of some form of psychologically deviant behavior" (p. 52), whereas tertiary prevention "is given to the individual who has developed a psychological disturbance" (p. 53). It would seem that, while counseling psychology is fundamentally focused upon primary prevention, both specialty areas overlap in regard to secondary prevention. And last, the level of tertiary intervention would appear the basic domain of the clinician— with the counseling psychologist providing some, but not extensive, psychotherapeutic treatment on this level.

In concluding, it must be pointed out that continua of this sort are first and foremost relative constructions. As such, they defy absolute definitions or explanations and offer only the hope of conceptualizing in probablistic fashion. And so is the case with the five continua presented here. Nevertheless, it does seem that the previously indicated dimensions, in large part, typify some of the distinct characteristics of the roles and functions of the counseling psychologist. Further, these dimensions appear also to highlight some of the differences, as well as possible overlap and similarities, existing between counseling and clinical psychology.

TRAINING IN CLINICAL AND COUNSELING PSYCHOLOGY

Clinical Psychology

The training of clinical psychologists has long been a concern to those individuals composing Division 12 (Clinical Psychology), as well as to members of the APA in general (e.g., see AAAP, 1943; Alexander & Baskowitz, 1965; Hoch, Ross, & Winder, 1965, 1966; Kubie, 1947; Lloyd & Newbrough, 1965; Pumroy, 1964). One of the most significant statements on training in clinical psychology was offered in 1947. At that time, the Committee on Training in Clinical Psychology of the APA indicated a basic graduate core for the training of clinicians. This core included a working knowledge of six areas: (1) general psychology; (2) psychodynamics of behavior; (3) diagnostic methods; (4) therapy; (5) research methods; and (6) related disciplines.

Two years following the Committee's report, the first conference on training in clinical psychology was held. The Boulder Conference, as such, was called so that 15 specific issues might be addressed, some of these being (1) the core curriculum in clinical psychology; (2) training for psychotherapy; (3) accreditation of training universities; and (4) licensing and certification (Lloyd & Newbrough, 1965). After this diversity of issues was considered, a rather strong support for a new training model emerged: the scientist-practitioner approach. The clinical psychologist was to be regarded as both a scientist in the field of psychology and an applied practitioner as well. The training model, then, was not either/or in nature, but represented a synthesis of two crucial streams—each of which involved essential skills and ideologies for the clinician.

In 1955 the Stanford Conference was convened so that the issue of training could be further considered. While a number of ideas were presented and reflected upon, there was one item that again gained a forceful consensual endorsement: clinical psychology's basic training model. That is, most conference participants viewed the scientist-practitioner model as a quite valid and viable foundation for clinical training and much in need of support and retention. The third training conference to impact upon clinical psychology— the Miami Beach Conference—was held in December of 1958. From the various areas reviewed by the participants, several future directions for training were strongly indicated: that there was a common core for all psychology specialties, the unique characteristic of the doctoral psychologist was research training, and accreditation was needed for psychology programs.

Following the Miami Beach Conference came the Conference on the Professional Preparation of the Clinical Psychologist which was held in Chicago during 1965. Interestingly, it was at the Chicago Conference that alternative models for training clinicians were first proposed, e.g., psychologist as researcher or professional psychologist (see Cook, Bibace, Garfield, Kelly, & Wexler, 1965, for an explanation of the latter term). In addition, the Doctor of Psychology (Psy.D.) was also presented as a new type of psychology degree. Nevertheless, despite the training models that were considered, the individuals at the Chicago Conference voiced their continuing support for the scientist-practitioner model as being fundamental and essential to the training of clinical psychologists.

The most recent conference to affect clinical psychology was the National Conference on Levels and Patterns of Professional Training in Psychology. This conference referred to as the Vail Conference, was held in Vail, Colorado during 1973. At Vail, conferees again considered and reviewed the professional model, this time agreeing to accept the training approach as both legitimate and viable for the training of clinical psychologists. Thus, while the scientist-practitioner model continues to have strong backing and support (Thelen & Ewing, 1970), the Psy.D. appears also to have gained the favor of many (cf. Peterson, 1969, 1971, 1976; Peterson & Baron, 1975; Peterson, Eaton, Levine, & Snepp, 1980, 1981).

Having reviewed the various conferences on training in clinical psychology, it would perhaps be of interest to examine briefly clinical psychologists' current opinions about their training programs and careers. To better determine such attitudes, a number of survey investigations have been undertaken (Garfield & Kurtz, 1975a; Kelly & Goldberg, 1959; Norcross & Prochaska, 1982c). For example, in a random survey of Division 12 members, Garfield and Kurtz (1976t) found that, "over 59%. . . were 'very satisfied' with clinical psychology as a career and slightly over 30% were "quite satisfied," (p. 5). They continue, "In response to a 6-item rating scale on graduate training, ranging from 'very satisfied' to 'very dissatisfied,' only 22.8%. . . chose the three ratings indicative of dissatisfaction, compared with over 77% who indicated some degree of satisfaction with the training they had received" (p. 5). The most recent survey of this type, proving quite consistent with that of Garfield and Kurtz, was performed by Norcross and Prochaska (1982a, 1982b, 1982c). Concerning graduate training, Norcross and Prochaska (1982c) reported that "over 60% of the participants indicated they were either quite or very satisfied with their graduate training" (p. 2). In regard to career satisfaction, they stated that "almost 90% of the sample are satisfied to some extent with their career" (p. 4). Thus, it would seem that, while some clinicians may have very acrid words for their training programs and careers (cf. Garfield & Kurtz, 1975a, 1976; Norcross & Prochaska, 1982c), the majority feel positively toward them.

Counseling Psychology

There have been two primary conferences related to training in counseling psychology: The Northwestern Conference, which was held in August of 1951, and the Greyston Conference, which took place in January of 1964. Though other more general conferences had an impact upon counseling psychology

(APA, undated), none had such effects as these two in plotting and charting the fundamental directions of the counseling specialty area. The Northwestern Conference was convened to define and review the functions of the counseling psychologist. At the meeting, the role of the counseling psychologist as *developmental facilitator* was indicated and the importance of prevention was accented (APA, 1952b). In addition, a graduate curriculum was outlined by the committee participants. This program of study included coursework in: (1) personality organization and development, (2) knowledge of social environment, (3) appraisal of the individual, (4) counseling, (5) professional orientation, (6) practicum, and (7) research. Further, the issue of practicum training was taken into account (APA, 1952a). Of the many items taken under study, the definition of the counseling psychologist's roles and the delineation of a program outline are perhaps the most significant.

The Greyston Conference (Thompson & Super, 1964) was called to further consider training in counseling psychology and make appropriate recommendations for improvement. Though a diversity of issues was presented, Thompson and Super (1964) indicate that these various concerns can be classed into four broad categories: (1) the roles of counseling psychologists, (2) the content of professional preparation, (3) organizational aspects of training, and (4) unity and diversity. Many of the conclusions that were drawn, as well as the recommendations that were made, tended to reinforce those statements indicated at the Northwestern Conference. The conferees reaffirmed the previously defined roles/functions of the counseling psychologist and the goals that had been identified for counseling psychology. Among the new ideas proposed, the need to emphasize the following curricular areas was indicated: (1) developmental psychology, (2) individual differences, (3) personality theory, (4) sociology, (5) world of work, and (6) education. Also, the conference participants did not voice special objections to the *professional degree* provided that sound, substantive training was offered for students in these programs.

Since 1964, the concerns discussed at the Greyston Conference have continued to be primary considerations for counseling psychologists (e.g., Carkhuff, 1966; Chin, 1967; Gross,1968; Oetting, 1967, Osipow, 1977; Patterson, 1969; Zytowski & Rosen, 1982). As such, academic and internship training has been of special concern to those in Division 17 (Hamilton, 1977; Myers, 1982; Prince & Randolph, 1981). Some useful information on these aspects has been provided by Bankiotes (1975, 1977, 1980), in his three surveys of counseling psychology programs. In his 1977 study, directors of counseling programs were asked to rate counseling courses, as to how likely students would be to take particular classes. Several courses emerged as being frequently taken, whereas others were taken little at all. Some of these most likely to be engaged in were: (1) practicum, (2) counseling theories, (3) group process, (4) quantitative methods, (5) experimental design, (6) tests and measurements, (7) research seminars, (8) psychological assessment, (9) internship, and (10) vocational development.

Bankiotes has also provided some interesting data on internship placements for counseling psychology students. In comparing his 1979 survey with previous such investigations, he states, "Although still serving as the largest setting for internship placements, counseling centers are currently providing a smaller proportion of internship placements for counseling psychology students than they did in the 1973–1975 period. VA hospitals also account for a reduced proportion of placements, while community mental health centers have an increased proportion of internships. Although still a very small proportion of internship placements (4%), the private practice setting appears to be emerging as an additional internship category possibility" (1980, p. 73). Therefore, based upon the results of these surveys, a shift away from the traditional settings of the counseling psychologist has begun. The implications of this shift will most probably have far-reaching effects upon the future training in counseling psychology; some of these implications will be considered in a subsequent section.

Evaluation

The material on training proves to be of particular interest, considering that it is supposedly the training/internship that largely separates counseling and clinical psychology. Conferences dealing with training issues have been prominent in the history of both specialty areas. Interestingly enough, the basic core curriculum identified for clinicans (APA, 1947) and counseling students (APA, 1952b) tended to not be that different. In the two areas, the following coursework was considered important: (1) psychodynamics of behavior (clinical) or personality organization and development (counseling), (2) diagnostic methods (clinical) or appraisal of the individual (counseling), (3) therapy (clinical) or counseling and practicum (counseling), (4) research (clinical) or research (counseling), and (5) related disciplines (clinical) or knowledge of social environment (counseling). The primary distinction between the described curricula lay in clinical psychology's emphasis on general psychology, whereas such fundamental courses were not explicitly delineated in the counseling core. In 1964, however, this facet was modified somewhat at the Greyston Conference. Developmental psychology and individual differences, among other coursework, were suggested, thereby providing a substantive psychological foundation for counseling psychology programs. Also, as a distinctive feature, the "world of work" and vocational psychology were heavily accented in counselor training, thus being viewed as not only essential, but vital to the knowledge-base of the professional counseling psychologist.

As can be discerned, then, counseling and clinical psychology have not appeared to differ markedly in regard to core areas. And such seems to be the fact in contemporary programs as Bankiotes' (1977) survey tends to indicate. Despite fundamental similarities, however, counseling and clinical training appear to diverge more in their foci than the type of courses offered. That is, clinical curricula are, for the most part, oriented toward psychopathology, psychodiagnostics, and therapeutic interventions with the emotionally maladjusted. Conversely, counseling programs emphasize coursework in mental health, vocational and objective personality assessment, and therapeutic interventions for relatively ego mature individuals. Therefore, variations in training derive essentially from the specialty definitions and designated roles/functions identified early on (APA, 1947, 1952b). Consequently, the clinical and counseling programs of today appear to have remained quite consistent with the original missions of Divisions 12 and 17.

One of the seeming convergences of counseling and clinical education lies in psychology's basic training model. The scientist-practitioner approach has long been viewed as a distinct, unique feature in both areas. Further, in the majority of conferences on training, this model has been continually and overwhelmingly supported. Only at the most recent of conferences have alternative training models been consensually endorsed.

While these considerations on training appear most prominent, some other general findings were also related in this section. For instance, the recent surveys of Bankiotes indicate that counseling psychology students are seeking internships in more varied settings. Specifically, an increasing number of individuals are interning at mental health centers, with a smaller proportion opting for counseling center experiences and VA placements. And finally, in regard to surveys of clinical psychologists, these professionals tend to have rather positive feelings toward their training experiences. Unfortunately, no such investigations have been reported for counseling psychologists; therefore, comparisons could not be made across groups on this variable.

THE WORK SETTINGS OF CLINICAL AND COUNSELING PSYCHOLOGISTS

Clinical Psychology

The work settings of clinical psychologists tend to be many and varied. Several surveys have been undertaken to more accurately identify where clinicians work and what they do. Chief among these studies has been the work of Bonneau (1968), Cates (1970), Cates and Dawson (1971), Garfield and Kurtz (1974, 1976), Kelly (1961), Manning and Cates (1972), and Norcross and Prochaska (1982b). Each survey has yielded a number of rather interesting findings, some of which have proven to be relatively consistent over time.

Cates (1970) and Cates and Dawson (1971), for example, found clinical psychologists' employment to be as follows: (1) public/private hospitals/clinics and medical schools—27%; (2) governmental agencies—27%; (3) private practice—17%; (4) colleges/universities—18%; and (5) junior/community colleges—0.4%. The surveys of Garfield and Kurtz (1974, 1976) provided a somewhat similar picture, though increases were reported across several settings.

They indicated that the primary contingent of clinicians is employed either in institutional clinical settings (35%), university settings (29%), or private practice (23%). These three work places, when combined, constituted 86% of the employment settings of clinical psychologists. The most recent surveys of this type were those conducted by Norcross and Prochaska (1982a, 1982b, 1982c). They found that among their participants "roughly one-third of the sample was located in private practice, and another one-third was employed in institutional clinical settings, such as general or psychiatric hospitals, medical schools or clinics" (1982b, p. 1). Approximately 22% were employed in a university job of some kind. As can be discerned, then, while employment in institutional clinical settings has not changed significantly since 1974, more clinicians have gravitated toward private practice and fewer have remained in or moved into university positions.

In regard to the activities performed by clinical psychologists, the surveys of Garfield and Kurtz (1974, 1976) and Norcross and Prochaska (1982a) once again provide some useful information. Garfield and Kurtz, in their 1974 study, indicated that "approximately 25% of [clinicians'] professional time is spent in individual psychotherapy. The next most important activities are teaching and administration, with over 13% of total professional time each" (p. 9). The findings of Norcross and Prochaska (1982a) tend not to be that different from those of Garfield and Kurtz. Norcross and Prochaska report that "psychotherapy is the most frequent activity and takes approximately 35% of the professionals' time. The next three most important activities are administration, diagnosis/ assessment and teaching, with 12% or more of the total professional time attributed to each" (p. 6). In accordance with these results, circa 1981, Norcross and Prochaska were able to conclude that "present... American clinicians appear to be engaged in slightly more psychotherapy and diagnosis/assessment" (p. 6) than was the case in the 1970s. And when the data of Garfield and Kurtz (1974) and Norcross and Prochaska (1982a) are combined, it appears that the most prominent activities of the contemporary clinical psychologist are: (1) individual psychotherapy, (2) administration, (3) diagnosis and assessment, and (4) teaching.

Counseling Psychology

In the area of counseling psychology, a number of attempts have been made to determine where counseling psychologists are employed (Bankiotes, 1977, 1980; Cates, 1970; Cates & Dawson, 1971; Krauskopf, Thoreson, & McAleer, 1973; Yamamoto, 1963). Yamamoto (1963), for example, surveyed 1,016 Division 17 members during the early sixties. He reported that "more than half of Division 17 members are holding their jobs at colleges and universities" (pp. 215-216). These results tend to concur with those of Cates (1970) and Cates and Dawson (1971), who indicated that over 65% of counseling psychologists are employed in some type of educational setting. Further, in the 1973 study of Krauskopf, Thoreson, and McAleer (1973), it was found that "among the individuals sampled, 70% listed their main job location as a university, whereas in descending order, smaller percentages worked in institutional settings, public schools, boards of education, private schools, private educational corporations, industry, and private practice" (p. 373). Thus, as in previous investigations, the educational setting emerged as the primary work place of counseling psychologists.

The more recent reports of Bankiotes (1977, 1980) tend to contrast, however, with earlier studies. In 1976, Bankiotes noted the following trends in counseling psychologists' employment: (1) academic job—17.7%; (2) counseling position—12.5%; (3) mental health center—13.6%; and (4) private practice—4.5%. Based upon these findings, Bankiotes (1977) concluded, "Fewer counseling psychologists are finding their way into positions in higher education" (p. 26). In congruence with this seeming shift, Bankiotes' (1980) survey of 1979 serves to reinforce the previous findings. He reported new graduates' employment to be: (1) academic jobs—17.2%; (2) counseling center positions—12.5%; (3) mental health centers—18.2%; and (4) private practice—7.8%. As a result of these data, Bankiotes stated that "an increasing proportion of counseling psychology students are obtaining... initial job placements in community mental health centers. Private practice settings are also providing an increasing proportion of... employment placements" (p. 74). Therefore, counseling psychologists circa 1979 are continuing to increasingly diversify their work settings; and the trend away from higher education employment seems firmly set in motion.

While there have been several surveys indicating the activities of clinical psychologists, such investigations have not been undertaken often on counseling psychologists. Currently, there appear to be two studies of this type, those of Krauskopf et al. (1973) and Fee, Elkins, and Boyd (1982). However, considering the recent changes in work environments of counselors, the findings of Krauskopf and his associates perhaps are dated. With this cautionary note in mind, the results of their study are indicated briefly. Specifically, the researchers reported that "among the individuals sampled..., 40% worked in primarily administrative positions, 32% in teaching, and 24% reported counseling as their major function. Only 1% of the sample was engaged primarily in research" (p. 373). Unfortunately, a more specific breakdown of psychologists' activities was not provided in the research report. Complementing this study is the recent effort advanced by Fee et al. (1982). In their investigation, they randomly surveyed 500 members of Division 17 and found counseling psychologists' professional time to be divided as follows: (1) counseling/psychotherapy—31.78%; (2) teaching—28.57%; (3) administration—19.96%; and research—7.82%. Thus, the contemporary counseling psychologist's work activities seem to be fairly equivalently split between counseling/psychotherapy and teaching, with administrative and research duties occupying much less time.

Evaluation

The work places and activities of counseling and clinical psychologists seemingly bear some strong similarities and dissimilarities. Primary differences across these variables, however, appear to exist more in degree than in kind, as the described studies have tended to indicate. For instance, it seems that clinical psychologists' chief work settings have been and continue to be: (1) hospitals and clinics, (2) private practice, and (3) colleges and universities. Counseling psychologists have found employment in educational environments, particularly higher education, with the greatest frequency. Other job placements, though with less magnitude, have been in VA hospitals and community mental health centers. Only recently have counseling psychologists had a noticeable represenation among private practitioners.

While these settings appear to be typical work sites for counselors and clinicians, the "new wave" or "new generation" appears to be having an impact on where psychologists work and what they do (cf. Tanney, 1982). More clinical psychologists have moved into private practice than ever before. Those employed in institutional clinical settings have remained fairly stable, whereas the university is a less likely employer of clinicians. In comparison, counseling psychologists are less frequently employed in educational settings and are now accepting more positions with the community mental health center or going into private work (also see May, 1977; Resnick, 1982). Thus, as these data highlight, the trend for both counseling and clinical psychologists is the provision of direct therapeutic services, with teaching in higher education settings becoming a more improbable occupation. The reasons for such shifts are multiple; Foreman (1977) seems to have said it best, though, when he indicated that "higher education as a major source of employment is a dead horse" (p. 47). The current changes, then, seem to have a strong economic-survival factor involved, as well as issues of age and redefinition of professional roles (Tanney, 1982; Zimet, 1982).

Consistent with the move toward more direct service delivery, the functions of the clinical and counseling psychologist will most probably undergo modification. The survey of Norcross and Prochaska (1982a) appears to bear testament for this contention. In their 1981 study, they found that 35% of the sampled clinicians' time was spent in psychotherapy; eight years earlier, Garfield and Kurtz reported the figure of only 25% for the same variable. Other activities performed by clinical psychologists—particularly teaching, administration, and assessment—have remained prominent and consistent over time. And for counseling psychologists, it would also seem quite likely that they will increase their amount of individual and group psychotherapy activity. This appears especially so as counseling psychologists' employment increases in mental health centers and private practices. Therefore, the findings of Krauskopf et al. (1973)—that 40% of counseling psychologists administrate, 32% teach, 24% counsel, and 1% researches—would most likely be an inaccurate representation of the contemporary counselor's activities. Conversely, Fee et al.'s (1982) study would seemingly provide a more realistic picture of the current state. Certainly times have changed since the work of Krauskopf and his associates and, accordingly, counseling and clinical psychology have changed in kind.

The implications of these job shifts can be many and varied for the two specialty areas. As these data indicate, counselors and clinicians are providing services in increasingly similar settings and are, perhaps, offering increasingly similar services. Consequently, it seems very likely that counseling psychology is altering its original model of identity. Rather than focusing upon those unique aspects specified at the Northwestern and Greyston Conferences, counseling psychology may indeed be moving more toward the model of clinical psychology. One result of this move is that the primary role of the counseling psychologist becomes remedial, rather than educational/developmental or preventive. The ramifications of this issue, among others, will be more thoroughly discussed in the subsequent section.

THE FUTURE OF CLINICAL AND COUNSELING PSYCHOLOGY

Clinical Psychology

The future of clinical psychology will probably be characterized by continuing change and diversity. New clinical roles and functions have recently emerged, and psychologists seem to be increasingly expanding their areas of interest and expertise. While traditional roles will undoubtedly receive the ongoing affirmation of clinicians, a strong focus on community psychology and consultative procedures has begun to blossom (Garfield, 1974). Also, health psychology or behavioral medicine has come to be an ever growing and preoccupying domain of the clinical psychologist (e.g., Millon, Green & Meagher, 1982; and Stone, Cohen, & Adler, 1979). For instance, Zimet (1982) firmly indicated this point in his talk at the 1981 APA Convention: "The application of clinical psychology to the general field of health was practically unheard of only a few years ago; it is now a burgeoning area. Both in the areas of prevention and in the areas of psychological aspects of disease and illness, psychology has been gaining a very active role" (p. 13).

While many have noted clinical psychology's possible move toward a preventive stance, still others have addressed the issue of clinical training and education (e.g., Garfield, 1976; Wildman & Wildman, 1974). Walker (1974) indicated that the main roles of the future psychologists will be: (1) research for test development purposes; (2) supervision of psychometricians; (3) test interpretation; and (4) treatment planning. In addition, he believes that the psychologist of tomorrow will largely turn therapeutic duties over to a "new type of psychological professional" and, second, that the day of training general practitioners will draw to a close. From Walker's perspective, then, the future will involve more specialized and specific training in clinical psychology. Korchin (1976) also concurs with this view.

Rotter (1973), in his 1971 Presidential Address to Division 12, offered further possible directions for clinical training. In a vein similar to Walker, he states, "the central function of the clinical psychologist at some future time will be... that of diagnostician and evaluator" (p. 317). Adding to this, he sees a second function of the clinician as that of trainer and supervisor to subdoctoral professionals—those who will provide the actual psychotherapeutic services to clients. Thus, he offered the following statement: "The future clinical psychologist should be, in order of importance: diagnostician, evaluator, trainer, supervisor, and therapist" (pp. 317–318).

In conjunction with a focus on prevention, as well as increased diagnostic and training roles, several individuals have indicated a need to re-establish and fortify the "scientist" in clinical psychologists' training (Garfield, 1966, 1974, 1976; Wildman & Wildman, 1974). To correct the dichotomizing of the scientist-practitioner model, proposals for altering future training have been made on varied occasions. In 1966, Garfield suggested "a setting whereby research and practice are intimately related and tied together" (p. 362). Rotter (1973) said, "what is needed... is... a problem-solving internship" (p. 319). During such an internship, "the intern is placed on a team... [wherein] problem solving involves diagnosis of the nature of the problem, development of measuring instruments, intervention to solve the problem, and evaluation of the results of the intervention" (p. 319). While the ideas of Rotter and Garfield have been recognized, a certain confounding factor—the professional school— has emerged to "muddy the waters." Professional schools of psychology have sprung up quite rapidly across the country. Some have received program approval by the APA, and others are now in the process of doing so. The effects this will have upon restoring or inhibiting the scientist-practitioner model are uncertain at present.

As a final comment on the future of clinical psychology, a few words on approaches to psychotherapy seem in order. Specifically, one of the more recent developments in clinical psychology has been a pronounced trend toward eclecticism (Garfield & Kurtz, 1974, 1977; Prochaska & Norcross, 1982; Smith, 1982). It appears that many clinicians no longer consistently identify themselves with a particular orientation. The probability of such a continuing trend seems rather high, especially in light of Prochaska and Norcross's (1982; see Norcross & Prochaska, 1982b for a contrasting view) and Smith's (1982) recent studies. Thus, as Patterson (1974) stated some eight years ago, "the days of 'schools' in counseling and psychotherapy are drawing to a close" (p. ix). These words seem quite accurate not only for today's clinical psychologist, but for the clinician of tomorrow as well.

Counseling Psychology

The future of counseling psychology appears equally as indefinite as that of clinical psychology. Nevertheless, a number of prominent efforts have been made to address the greening of counseling psychology, as the work of Whiteley and Fretz (1980) indicates. In this regard, Osipow (1980) has presented a rather interesting prediction on what can be expected in times to come. Specifically, he states that, "It would not surprise me to see no distinction among the specialty areas of psychology by name, such as clinical, counseling, school, and so on" (p. 18). Others have also supported Osipow's position. Tyler (1980) contends that "during the next 20 years, the boundaries between counseling and the related psychological specialites will become more and more tenuous until they disappear altogether" (pp. 19-20). Hahn (1980) adds further support to this position, stating that "the distinction between clinical and counseling skills is vanishing steadily" (p. 36). Thus, as these assertions indicate, counseling psychology may indeed be a short-lived specialty within the field (also see Cleveland, 1980).

In congruence with these claims, a number of new (and old) roles and functions have come to increasingly preoccupy counseling psychologists. Of special interest has been the developing area of health psychology. Like many clinicians, those in counseling psychology have attempted to incorporate some aspects of behavioral medicine into their practice. This has included, among other facets, focuses upon cardio-vascular fitness, dietary concerns, weight control, and smoking elimination (cf. Danaher & Lichtenstein, 1978; Hendricks & Carlson, 1981; Martin & Martin, 1982; Thoresen, 1980; Thoresen & Mahoney, 1974; Williams & Long, 1983). Another emerging area within counseling has been that of psychoeducation (Authier, Gustafson, Guerney, & Kasdorf, 1975; Guerney, Stollack, & Guerney, 1970; Ivey, 1974, 1976, 1979, 1980; Patterson 1969a, 1971, 1972). Authier et al. (1975) have seemingly provided one of the best descriptions of the psychoeducator model. They state, "Most of the advocates of such an approach agree that the educational model means psychological practitioners seeing their function not in terms of ab-normality (or illness) ⟶ diagnosis ⟶ therapy ⟶ cure; but rather in terms of client dissatisfaction (or ambition) ⟶ goal setting ⟶ skill teaching ⟶ satisfaction or goal achievement. The person being served is seen as analogous to a pupil, rather than a patient" (p. 31). The work of the counseling psychologist, then, "is no longer primarily counseling" (Ivey, 1976, p. 72), as viewed from the psychoeducation vantage. Instead, the roles of education and prevention emerge as dominant, with remediation services "taking a back seat," so to speak.

Patterson (1972) has offered some interesting comments on the psycho-educator model and the future of counseling psychology. In his Presidential Address to Division 17, he indicated the following:

It appears that perhaps the most effective and efficient way of improving human relationships in our society is not by consulting, but by education and training in good human relationships. Counseling psychologists should therefore become involved not only in the education of counselors. . . but in the education of other groups in human relations. These other groups should include teachers and parents especially, since these are perhaps the two most influential groups on human relationships in our society (p. 6).

(Also, see the works of Berenson, Carkhuff, & Myrus, 1966; Carkhuff, 1971; Carkhuff & Banks, 1970; and Carkhuff, Piaget, & Pierce, 1968.)

Despite the emerging role of psychoeducator, it yet remains for counseling psychology to heartily embrace this treatment modality. At present, the contemporary counseling psychologist functions in large part as a psycho-therapist, rendering facilitation to those experiencing personal difficulties of various kinds. Unfortunately, as the therapeutic counseling or psychotherapy role has been enhanced, the domain of vocational psychology has received decreasing emphasis from counseling psychologists. Super (1977, 1980) has lamented the status of vocational counseling; and as it now seems, the vocational often is viewed as "second-class" or "mamby-pamby" work by counseling practitioners and trainers alike. As a result, it currently appears an exodus from the vocational to the psychotherapeutic is well in progress.

In considering this point further, the studies of Osipow, Cohen, Jenkins, and Dostal (1979), Schneider and Gelso (1972, and Yamamoto (1963) prove instructive. Yamamoto, in his survey regarding Division 17 members' character-istics, concluded that those "who work in clinical settings tend to join Division 12 also, while those who work in educational settings do not strongly show such an inclination" (p. 220). Somewhat similarly, Osipow et al. (1979) found that those members who belonged to Division 17 exclusively were often employed in settings where vocational counseling was conducted; in contrast, Division 17 members who also belonged to Divison(s) 12 and/or 29 were employed in settings where psychotherapy and psychodiagnostics were central. These data led Osipow (1977) to express his realistic concern about the future of counseling psychology.

Further reason for concern was perhaps provided by the study of Schneider and Gelso (1972). These researchers asked counseling psychology program directors to indicate their programs' emphasis upon the "personal" or "voca-tional." The results of the survey led to the following conclusions: (1) social-emotional counseling receives particular training emphasis in the curriculum; (2) preparation for such counseling is stronger than for vocational counseling; and (3) the initial practicum's focus is more toward social-emotional counseling than the vocational. While it is difficult to extrapolate from these findings, current opinion would seem consistent with the program directors' views. Consequently, vocational psychology may have a diminishing role in counseling psychology's future.

While a number of other future directions could be indicated, three particular trends seem to merit attention here. First, like clinical psychologists, the future counseling psychologist will probably provide an increasing amount of training and supervision to master's level counselors and paraprofessionals—the service providers of tomorrow (Patterson, 1972; Daniel & Weikel, 1983). Second, consultation will occur more frequently (Magoon, 1980; Tyler, 1980); the extent of this involvement, however, is uncertain, especially considering the concurrent trend toward increased remedial services. Some balance between these two roles may be established; most likely, psychotherapy will have its heyday, and an equalization process will then take place. The third and last point to be mentioned briefly relates to counseling psychologists' increasing eclecticism. Smith's (1982) recent study explicitly emphasizes this trend. More specifically, from his survey of Division 17 and 12 members, Smith concluded that an eclectic approach "is the clear preference of the largest number of psychologists" (p. 808). The watchword, then, appears decidedly that of eclecticism. Therefore, not only will counseling psychologists seemingly provide more psychotherapy in the near future, but their theoretic orientations will tend markedly toward a general eclectic ideology (cf. Daniel & Weikel, 1983; Prochaska & Norcross, 1982).

Evaluation

The futures of counseling and clinical psychology bear some marked convergences as well as divergences. A number of new roles have been suggested for both specialties, and conversely, some traditional functions have been deemphasized for the times that lie ahead. Among these, various professionals have indicated increasing emphasis on consultation to myriad groups and individuals; also, training and supervision of paraprofessionals and master's level graduates are predicted to become primary duties. In regard to the latter point, it appears, then, that counseling and clinical psychology see their future impact on psychotherapy somewhat similarly—as deriving from the provision of effective training to a new "psychotherapy professional." In addition to consultation and training, other areas of convergences have also been identified. These include escalations of the following: (1) specializations within counseling or clinical psychology, as opposed to the general practitioner approach, (2) interest in and the practice of health psychology, and (3) eclecticism as the preferred therapeutic orientation. Thus, as one can discern, several converging trends have been forecasted between counseling and clinical psychology. And some of these seem to be preventatively oriented, whereas others are more remedial in nature.

Yet while some similarities have been predicted, there too are specialty distinctions that emerge and, therefore, merit consideration. The clinical psychologist of tomorrow, for instance, is expected to engage in increasing diagnostic and evaluation functions and a decreasing amount of psychotherapy.

Accordingly, others have highlighted the clinician's role as scientist, as the need for a solid research base is re-emphasized and acted upon. And of further interest, clinical psychologists will perform more work in community psychology. This point was well-stated by Chin (1967) some 12 years ago: "More and more mental health workers, including clinical psychologists, are moving out of their offices into the community where they offer consultative and educational services to all kinds of agencies and institutions" (p. 376). Based upon the observations of Chin, and others who have offered such predictions, it would seem that the future's clinical psychologist will have four basic roles: (1) research-scientist, (2) diagnostic-evaluator, (3) training and supervision, and (4) consultant.

Counseling psychology, on the other hand, gives the impression of having a somewhat ill-defined future, when compared against clinical psychology. At this juncture, some of the distinct characteristics of counseling psychology appear to be: (1) a decreasing focus upon vocational assessment and vocational counseling, (2) an increase in the provision of psychotherapy, and (3) the emergence of a new role—psychoeducator. For now, the first two characteristics cited seem to be the wave of the future. While the psychoeducator model may be adoped at some time, there are no clear indications as to when, or even if, this will happen. As Hansen (1981) has pointed out, counseling psychology, from an historical perspective, has continued to maintain an ambivalence toward and peculiar relationship with primary prevention activities of this type. Specifically, Hansen examined the relationship between Division 17 and the field of primary prevention, and thereby concluded, "If Division 17 does not move to stake out a realistic position in preventive mental health, it may well find that it has lost one of its chief reasons for being, and that its days as a separate specialty are numbered" (p. 59).

Though Hansen's admonition is well taken, counseling psychology is currently "beefing up" its remediation role and, consequently, de-emphasizing the educational, preventive aspects. The reasons for this state of affairs appear to be multiple; of particular significance, however, is the reality that psychotherapy is economically reimbursable by insurance companies and other such funding sources, whereas prevention efforts are not. With counseling psychologists' increasing move into remedially-oriented workplaces (e.g., private practice, mental health centers), they have been called upon to be reimbursable parties. Where such ability has not existed, many practitioners have found their employment possibilities unduly restricted and curtailed. Thus, psychologists' reimbursement potential has affected not only their employability at certain work sites, but also their professional and economic survival in some cases.

Because of the vast implications of third-party payments, the issues of professional licensure and program accreditation have become of critical significance to counseling psychology (Domke, 1982; Fretz & Mills, 1980a, 1980b; King & Seymour, 1982; Levant, 1981; Tanney, 1980). With the psychology license being requisite to reimbursement status, numerous doctoral programs have striven to provide a curriculum that would enhance their graduates' licensability. To accomplish this goal, program accreditation by the APA has been the primary vehicle upon which most programs have depended. As a result the number of full-and provisionally-approved programs has increased markedly in the last decade. Also, many counseling and guidance and counselor education programs have been revamped to a counseling psychology emphasis. This too has added further to the number of programs that are already approved or are in the process of doing so.

Along with these changes, third-party payments have had myriad other effects upon counseling psychology. A primary derivative has been the continuing controversy over who is a "counseling psychologist" and who is a "counselor" (Bennett, 1980; Dorn, 1982; Hurst & Parker, 1977; Shertzer & Issacson, 1977; Weigel, 1977). Such controversy has engendered some measure of divisiveness between Division 17 and the American Personnel and Guidance Association (APGA)—a form of division with which clinical psychology has not had to contend. Due to these difficulties, APGA has established its own accreditation procedures for programs in guidance, counseling, and counselor education. Also several certification bodies have emerged (e.g., the National Academy of Certified Clinical Mental Health Counselors and National Board of Certified Counselors), and counselor licensure has been implemented in approximately six states as of this writing. At present, then, APGA appears to be going its own way, as is Division 17 and its constituents. (Further elaboration on these issues can be found in the recent articles of Domke, 1982; and King & Seymour, 1982.)

While this effect has proven significant, perhaps counseling psychology's greatest modification has been its increasing adoption of the ego immaturity paradigm of clinical psychology. Consequently, numerous counseling psychologists have identified themselves primarily, if not exlusively, as psychotherapists. Also another role to which many are leaning is that of psychodiagnostician. These role adoptions reflect largely the impact of reimbursement and third-party payments. In essence such roles offer remuneration. Conversely, the unique distinctive features of counseling psychology—its educational, preventive, and developmental aspects—currently appear to be economically untenable. Unfortunately, unless some concerted action is taken to change the status quo, this attitude may be relatively permanent and enduring for our specialty.

Interestingly, if the forecasts presented here are accurate, more clinicians will be leaning in the direction of the ego maturity paradigm than has previously been the case. Regarding the continua presented earlier, counselors and clinicians perhaps will converge at the midpoint, rather than being inclined to a particular side of a continuum. Should these movements be realized, counseling and clinical psychology may even cross over one another in some respects, though the extent of this is impossible to predict. More likely, the two specialty areas will settle in similar territory on some functions, such as psychotherapy, training, and consultation. And consequently, specialty distinctions would fade and ultimately disappear. (If such a state does come to pass, it must be recognized that both specialties have engaged in a mutual collusion of sorts. Therefore, neither is the villain and each is to blame.)

SOME CLOSING COMMENTS AND CONCERNS
ABOUT THE FUTURE OF COUNSELING PSYCHOLOGY

In concluding this review, there are several inferences that can be drawn regarding counseling psychology. For instance, as the preceding information indicates, counseling and clinical psychology converge in some aspects on each of the five surveyed areas. In converse fashion, however, myriad divergences appear quite prominent, particularly on the first four variables under study. And when these various divergences (indicated in the "Evaluation" sections) are considered, a unique and vital "counseling psychology identity" seems to emerge. While such a fact yields some possible satisfactions, our identity proves to be a most short-lived construction; current trends render this identity formulation relatively invalid and, at best, transitory in nature. Therefore, due to apparent shifts in counseling psychology's model, an effort to specifically delineate and differentiate the specialty seems virtually impossible now.

As a consequence of "model distantiation" in counseling psychology, the area will probably experience a number of continuing changes in future years. Many of these changes, as one would expect, will perhaps have both positive and negative effects. I fear, however, that our developing "clinical orientation" may entail more negative effects than positive, and could ultimately lead to a superfluous, if not irrelevant, counseling specialty. It does indeed seem, as Osipow (1977) states, that "too many of us [counseling psychologists] . . . aspire to become clinical psychologists" (p. 94), and "in moving more towards clinical psychology and futher from personnel psychology, . . . counseling psychologists . . . have tended to give up their special identity" (Super, 1977, p. 14). In also considering this trend, Nathan (1977) states, "I would view a national effort on the part of counseling psychology to shift from its vocational/personal counseling mission to an intervention mission as an unfortunate mistake. Many other professions seek to provide psychotherapy; no other profession offers counseling on work-related issues" (p. 37). Thus, though offering vocational services, "the counseling psychologist fills a unique role in our society" (p. 37).

As a result of counseling psychology's decreasing interest in vocational psychology, there will undoubtedly be fewer service providers offering vocational assessment and counseling. This seems most unfortunate when one considers that such training is unique to the counseling specialty. Also, consequent to diminishing concern with the vocational, research on vocational psychology will quite likely be stunted. In the past, counseling psychologists have greatly contributed to the knowledge-base in career development. But their contributions may be minimal and sporadic in future years.

If counseling psychology is to remain a viable specialty, a number of difficult, yet quite significant questions will have to be entertained by us all. For instance, some of these queries would seem to include the following:

1 What role, if any, do we want vocational psychology, primary prevention, and developmental interventions to play in counseling psychology's future?

2 Provided any or all of these is accorded a place, how much didactic emphasis would each merit in counseling psychology training?

3 Similarly, how much practicum/internship emphasis should be given to such areas? and,

4 Most importantly, what actions can counseling psychologists take (e.g., on local, state, or national levels; accountability measures, etc.) to convey the salutary effects of the vocational, preventive, and developmental on personal well-being?

While other questions could be posed, these appear to be basic to the tomorrow of counseling psychology. In essence, then, one point seems relatively clear from this discussion: Whether counseling psychology will continue to exist as a specialty is fundamentally up to the myriad of counseling psychologists. The decision of what we will be is ours. We will plot our own course, either through action, inaction, or default. The future is now firmly at our doorstep. What will we decide?

CONCLUSION

In this article, the convergences and divergences between counseling and clinical psychology have been examined. On each of the five surveyed variables— (1) history, (2) roles/functions, (3) training conferences and experiences, (4) work settings, and (5) the future—some differences were noted for the two specialties. And while these differences indicate a "counseling psychology identity" of sorts, such an identity cannot be maintained due to the direction of current trends. As it now appears, both specialty areas are converging in a number of ways and diverging less and less. The implications of this "coming together" are potentially many and varied. For example, counseling psychology seemingly is abandoning its "roots" and unique qualities. And though clinical psychology is also experiencing some changes, it does not appear to be giving up its distinctiveness as markedly. Some implications of these modifications were discussed, particularly in regard to counseling psychology. Perhaps, if there was one pre-eminent message to emerge from this survey, it was that "counseling psychologists must decide for themselves if they want counseling psychology to continue to exist. In its present form, a demise seems possible, if not highly probable. As such, counseling psychology is at a crossroads; and the decisions we make now will not only determine our specialty's future directions, but more basically its very survival."

REFERENCES

Alexander, I. E., & Baskowitz, H. Current clinical training practices: An overview. In E. L. Hoch, A. O. Ross, & C. L. Winder (Eds.), *Professional preparation of clinical psychologists.* Washington, DC: Americal Psychological Association, 1965.

American Association for Applied Psychology, Committee on Training in Clinical (Applied) Psychology. (B. V. Moore, Chairman.) Proposed program of professional training in clinical psychology. *Journal of Consulting Psychology,* 1943, *7,* 23–26.

American Psychological Association, Division of Counseling Psychology. *An analysis of Stanford Conference proceedings.* Mimeographed, undated.

American Psychological Association, Committee on Training Clinical Psychology. Recommended graduate training program in clinical psychology. *American Psychologist,* 1947, *2,* 529–558.

American Psychological Association, Division of Counseling and Guidance, Committee on Counselor Training. The practicum training of counseling psychologists. *American Psychologist,* 1952, *7,* 182–188. (a)

American Psychological Association, Division of Counseling and Guidance, Committee on Counselor Training. Recommended standards for training counseling psychologists at the doctoral level. *American Psychologist,* 1952, *7,* 175–181. (b)

American Psychological Association, Division of Counseling Psychology, Committee on Definition. Counseling psychology as a specialty. *American Psychologist,* 1956, *11,* 282–285.

American Psychological Association, Committee on Standards for Providers of Psychological Services. Specialty guidelines for the delivery of services by clinical psychologists. *American Psychologist,* 1981, *36,* 640–651. (a)

American Psychological Association, Committee on Standards for Providers of Psychological Services. Specialty guidelines for the delivery of services by counseling psychologists. *American Psychologist,* 1981, *36,* 652–663. (b)

Aubrey, R. F. Historical Development of guidance and counseling and implications for the future. *Personnel and Guidance Journal,* 1977, *55,* 288–295.

Authier, J., Gustafson, K., Guerney, B., Jr., & Kasdorf, J. The psychological practitioner as teacher: A theoretical-historical and practical overview. *The Counseling Psychologist,* 1975, *5*(2), 31–50.

Bankiotes, P. G. The status of training in counseling psychology. *The Counseling Psychologist,* 1975, *5*(4), 106–110.

Bankiotes, P. G. The training of counseling psychologists. *The Counseling Psychologist,* 1977, *7*(2), 23–26.

Bankiotes, P. G. Counseling psychology training: Data and perceptions. *The Counseling Psychologist,* 1980, *8*(4), 73–74.

Beers, C. W. *A mind that found itself.* New York: Longmans Green, 1908.

Bennett, V. C. Who is a professional psychologist? *The Counseling Psychologist,* 1980, *9*(1), 28–32.

Berenson, B. G., Carkhuff, R. R., & Myrus, P. The interpersonal functioning and training of college students. *Journal of Counseling Psychology,* 1966, *13,* 441–446.

Bonneau, A. Psychology's manpower: Report on the 1966 National Register of Scientific and Technical Personnel. *American Psychologist,* 1968, *23,* 325–334.

Campbell, D. P., & Hansen, J. C. *Manual for the Strong-Campbell Interest Inventory.* Palo Alto: CA: Stanford University Press, 1981.

Caplan, G. *Principles of preventive psychiatry.* New York: Basic Books, 1964.

Carkhuff, R. R Training in the counseling and therapeutic processes: Requiem or reveille? *Journal of Counseling Psychology,* 1966, *13,* 360–367.

Carkhuff, R. R. Training as a mode of treatment. *Journal of Counseling Psychology,* 1971, *18,* 123–131.

Carkhuff, R. R., & Banks, G. Training as a preferred mode of facilitating relations between races. *Journal of Counseling Psychology,* 1970, *17,* 413–418.

Carkhuff, R. R., Piaget, J., & Pierce, R. The development of skills in interpersonal functioning. *Counselor Education and Supervision,* 1968, *7,* 102–106.

Cates, J. A. Psychology's manpower: Report on the 1968 National Register of Scientific and Technical Personnel. *American Psychologist,* 1970, *25,* 254–263.

Cates, J. A., & Dawson, W. Preliminary report of the 1970 National Register. *American Psychologist,* 1971, *26,* 390–392.

Chin, A. H. New perspectives on the relationship between clinical and counseling psychology. *Journal of Counseling Psychology,* 1967, *14,* 374–381.

Cleveland, S. E. Counseling psychology: An endangered species? *Professional Psychology,* 1980, *11,* 314–323.

Cook, S., Bibace, R., Garfield, S., Kelly, G., & Wexler, M. Issues in the professional training of clinical psychologists. In C. N. Zimet & F. M. Thorne (Eds.), *Preconference materials: Conference on the Professional Preparation of Clinical Psychologists.* Washington, DC: American Psychological Association, 1965.

Danaher, B., & Lichtenstein, E. *Become an ex-smoker.* Englewood Cliffs, NJ: Prentice-Hall, 1978.

Daniel, R. W., & Weiker, W. J. Trends in counseling: A Delphi study. *Personnel and Guidance Journal,* 1983, *61,* 327–331.

Darley, J. G. *Clinical aspects and interpretation of the Strong Vocational Interest Bank.* New York: Psychological Corporation, 1941.

Deffenbacher, J. L., & Michaels, A. C. Anxiety management training and self-control desensitization—fifteen months later. *Journal of Counseling Psychology,* 1981, *28,* 459–462.

Delworth, U. Counseling psychology: A distinct practice specialty. *The Counseling Psychologist,* 1977, *7*(2), 43–45.

Domke, J. A. Current issues in counseling psychology: Entitlement, education, and identity confusion. *Professional Psychology,* 1982, *13,* 859–870.

Dorn, F. J. Who is the real counseling psychologist? *Personnel and Guidance Journal,* 1982, *61,* 68–69.

Drum, D. J., & Knott, J. E. *Structured groups for facilitating development: Acquiring life skills, resolving life themes, and making life transitions.* New York: Human Sciences, Press, 1977.

Fee, A. F., Elkins, G. R., & Boyd, L. Testing and counseling psychologists: Current practices and implications for training. *Journal of Personality Assessment,* 1982, *46,* 116–118.

Foreman, M. E. The changing scene in higher education and the identity of counseling psychology. *The Counseling Psychologist,* 1977, *7*(2), 45–48.

Fretz, B. R. (Ed.). *The Counseling Psychologist,* 1977, *7*(2).

Fretz, B. R. Perspective and definitions. *The Counseling Psychologist,* 1982, *10*(2), 15–19.

Fretz, B. R., & Mills, D. H. *Licensing and certification of psychologists and counselors.* San Francisco, CA: Jossey-Bass, 1980. (a)

Fretz, B. R., & Mills, D. H. Professional certification in counseling psychology. *The Counseling Psychologist,* 1980, *9*(1), 2–17 (b)

Garfield, S. L. Historical introduction. In B. B. Wolman (Ed.), *Handbook of clinical psychology.* New York: McGraw-Hill, 1965.

Garfield, S. L. Clinical psychology and the search for identity. *American Psychologist,* 1966, *21,* 353–362.

Garfield, S. L. *Clinical psychology: The study of personality and behavior.* Chicago: Aldine, 1974.

Garfield, S. L. Current thoughts on future directions: Response to the Distinguished Contributions Award. *The Clinical Psychologist,* 1976, *30*(1), 5.

Garfield, S. L. Editorial: The 75th anniversary of the first issue of The Psychological Clinic. *Journal of Consulting and Clinical Psychology,* 1982, *50,* 167–170.

Garfield, S. L., & Kurtz, R. A survey of clinical psychologists: Characteristics, activities and orientations. *The Clinical Psychologist,* 1974, *28*(1), 7–10.

Garfield, S. L., & Kurtz, R. Clinical psychologists: A survey of selected attitudes and views. *The Clinical Psychologist,* 1975, *28*(3), 4–7). (a)

Garfield, S. L., & Kurtz, R. Training and career satisfaction among clinical psychologists. *The Clinical Psychologist,* 1975, *28*(2), 6–9. (b)

Garfield, S. L., & Kurtz, R. Clinical psychologists in the 1970s. *American Psychologist,* 1976, *31,* 1–9.

Garfield, S. L., & Kurtz, R. A study of eclectic views. *Journal of Consulting and Clinical Psychology,* 1977, *45,* 78–83.

Ginzberg, E. Toward a theory of occupational choice. *Occupations,* 1952, *30,* 491–494.

Ginzberg, E., Ginsburg, S. W., Axelrad, S., & Herma, J. L. *Occupational choice: An approach to a general theory.* New York: Columbia University Press, 1951.

Goldschmidt, M., Tipton, R. M., & Wiggins, R. C. Professional identity of counseling psychologists. *Journal of Counseling Psychology,* 1981, *28,* 158–167.

Greiner, J. M., & Karoly, P. Effects of self-control training on study activity and academic performance: An analysis of self-monitoring, self-reward, and systematic planning components. *Journal of Counseling Psychology,* 1976, *23,* 495–502.

Gross, R. B. Role and responsibilities of the personal counselor in a university student counseling service. *Journal of Counseling Psychology,* 1968, *15,* 351–356.

Guerney, B. G., Stollak, G. E., & Guerney, L. A format for a new mode of psychological practice: Or how to escape a zombie. *The Counseling Psychologist,* 1970, *2*(2), 97–104.

Hahn, M. E. Counseling psychology. *American Psychologist,* 1955, *10,* 279–282.

Hahn, M. E. Counseling psychology—2000 A.D. *The Counseling Psychologist,* 1980, *8*(4), 36–37.

Hamilton, M. K. Graduate training and professional identity. *The Counseling Psychologist,* 1977, *7*(2), 26–28.

Hansen, F. K. Primary prevention and counseling psychology: Rhetoric or reality. *The Counseling Psychologist,* 1981, *9*(2), 57–60.

Heffernan, T., & Richards, C. S. Self-control and study behavior: Identification and evaluation of natural methods. *Journal of Counseling Psychology,* 1981, *28,* 361–364.

Hendricks, G., & Carlson, J. *The centered athlete.* Englewood Cliffs, NJ: Prentice-Hall, 1981.

Hoch, E. L., Ross, A. O., & Winder, C. L. (Eds.). *Professional preparation of clinical psychologists.* Washington, DC: American Psychological Association, 1965.

Hoch, E. L., Ross, A. O., & Winder, C. L. Conference on the professional preparation of clinical psychologists: A summary. *American Psychologist,* 1966, *21,* 42–51.

Holland, J. L. A personality inventory employing occupational titles. *Journal of Applied Psychology,* 1958, *42,* 336–342.

Holland, J. L. A theory of vocational choice. *Journal of Counseling Psychology,* 1959, *6,* 35–45.

Holland, J. L. *Professional manual for the Self-Directed Search.* Palo Alto, CA: Consulting Psychologists Press, 1979.

Hurst, J. C., & Parker, C. A. Counseling psychology: Tyranny of a title. *The Counseling Psychologist,* 1977, *7*(2), 16–19.

Ivey, A. E. The clinican as a teacher of interpersonal skills: Let's give away what we've got. *The Clinical Psychologist,* 1974, *27*(3), 6–9.

Ivey, A. E. Counseling psychology, the psychoeducator model, and the future. *The Counseling Psychologist,* 1976, *6*(3), 72–75.

Ivey, A. E. Counseling psychology—the most broadly-based applied psychology specialty. *The Counseling Psychologist,* 1979, *8*(3), 3–6.

Ivey, A. E. Counseling 2000: Time to take charge. *The Counseling Psychologist,* 1980, *8*(4), 12–16.

Jordaan, J. P., Myers, R. A., Layton, W. L., & Morgan, H. H. (Eds.), *The counseling psychologist.* New York: Teachers College Press, Columbia University, 1968.

Kelly, E. L. Clinical psychology—1960. Report of survey findings. *Newsletter: Division of Clinical Psychology of the American Psychological Association,* 1961, *14,* 1-11.

Kelly, E. L., & Goldberg, L. R. Correlates of later performances and specialization in psychology: A follow-up study of the trainees assessed in the V.A. selection research project. *Psychological Monographs, General and Applied,* 1959, *73*(12).

King, P. T., & Seymour, W. R. Education and training in counseling psychology. *Professional Psychology,* 1982, *13,* 834-842.

Kirk, B. A. The American Psychological Association's definition of counseling psychology. *Personnel and Guidance Journal,* 1982, *61,* 54-55.

Korchin, S. J. *Modern clinical psychology.* New York: Basic Books, 1976.

Korchin, S. J., & Schuldberg, D. The future of clinical assessment. *American Psychologist,* 1981, *36,* 1147-1158.

Krauskopf, C. J., Thoreson, R. W., & McAleer, C. A. Counseling psychology: The who, what, and where of our profession. *Journal of Counseling Psychology,* 1973, *20,* 370-374.

Kubie, L. S. (Chairman). *Training in clinical psychology. Transactions of the First Conference,* March 27-28, 1947. New York, NY.

Kuder, G. F. *Activity interests and occupational choice.* Chicago: Science Research Associates, 1977.

Kuder, G. F., & Diamond, E. E. *General manual, Kuder Occupational Interest Survey* (2nd ed.). Chicago: Science Research Associates, 1979.

Levant, R. F. Counseling psychologists and the National Register of Health Service Providers in Psychology: A transition policy. *The Counseling Psychologist,* 1981, *9*(2), 82-83.

Lloyd, D. N., & Newbrough, J. R. Previous conferences on graduate education in psychology: A summary and review. In E. L. Hoch, A. O. Ross, & C. L. Winder (Eds.), *Professional preparation of clinical psychologists.* Washington, DC: American Psychological Association, 1965.

Louttit, C. M. The nature of clinical psychology. *Psychological Bulletin,* 939, *36,* 361-389.

Magoon, T. M. The eye of a beholder. *The Counseling Psychologist,* 1980, *8*(4), 26-28.

Mahoney, M. J., & Arnkoff, D. B. Cognitive and self-control therapies. In S. L. Garfield & A. E. Bergin (Eds.), *Handbook of psychotherapy and behavior change* (2nd ed.). New York: Wiley, 1978.

Mahoney, M. J., & Arnkoff, D. B. Self-management. In O. F. Pomerleau & J. P. Brady (Eds.), *Behavioral medicine: Theory and practice.* Baltimore, MD: Williams & Wilkins, 1979.

Manning, T. T., & Cates, J. Specialization within psychology. *American Psychologist,* 1972, *27,* 462-467.

Martin, D., & Martin, M. Nutritional counseling: A humanistic approach to psychological and physical health. *Personnel and Guidance Journal,* 1982, *61,* 21-24.

May, E. P. Counseling psychologists in general medical and surgical hospitals. *The Counseling Psychologist,* 1977, *7*(2), 82-85.

Millon, T., Green, C. J., & Meagher, M. E. *Handbook of clinical health psychology.* New York: Praeger, 1982.

Mill, C. R. Toward an understanding of clinical psychology. *Virginia Medical Monthly,* 1959, *86,* 708–710.

Mills, D. H., Wellner, A. M., & Vandenbos, G. R. The National Register survey: The first comprehensive study of all licensed/certified psychologists. In C. A. Kiesler, N. A. Cummings, & G. R. Vandenbos (Eds.), *Psychology and national health insurance: A sourcebook.* Washington, DC: American Psychological Association, 1979.

Mosher, R. L., & Sprinthall, N. A. Psychological education: A means to promote personal development during adolescence. *The Counseling Psychologist,* 1971, *2*(4), 3–82.

Myers, R. A. Education and training—the next decade. *The Counseling Psychologist,* 1982, *10*(2), 39–44.

Nathan, P. E. A clinical psychologist views counseling psychology. *The Counseling Psychologist,* 1977, *7*(2), 36–37.

Nathan, P. E., & Harris, S. L. *Psychopathology and society.* New York: McGraw-Hill, 1975.

Nelson-Jones, R. *The theory and practice of counseling psychology.* London: Holt, Rinehart & Winston, 1982.

Norcross, J. C., & Prochaska, J. O. A national survey of clinical psychologists: Characteristics and activities. *The Clinical Psychologist,* 1982, *35*(2), 1; 5–8. (a)

Norcross, J. C., & Prochaska, J. O. A national survey of clinical psychologists: Affiliations and orientations. *The Clinical Psychologist,* 1982, *35*(3), 1–2; 5–6. (b)

Norcross, J. C., & Prochaska, J. O. A national survey of clinical psychologists: Views on training career choice, and APA. *The Clinical Psychologist,* 1982, *35*(4), 1; 3–6. (c)

Oetting, E. R. Developmental definition of counseling psychology. *Journal of Counseling Psychology,* 1967, *14,* 382–385.

Osipow, S. H. Will the real counseling psychologist please stand up? *The Counseling Psychologist,* 1977, *7*(2) 93–94.

Osipow, Toward counseling psychology in the year 2000. *The Counseling Psychologist,* 1980, *8*(4), 18–19.

Osipow, S. H., Cohen, W., Jenkins, J., & Dostal, J. Clinical versus counseling psychology: Is there a difference? *Professional Psychology,* 1979, *10,* 148–153.

Pallone, N. J. Counseling psychology: Toward an empirical definition. *The Counseling Psychologist,* 1977, *7*(2), 29–32.

Parsons, F. *Choosing a vocation.* Boston: Houghton Mifflin, 1909.

Patterson, C. H. Counseling. *Annual Review of Psychology,* 1966, *17,* 79–110.

Patterson, C. H. Review of A. S. Thompson and D. E. Super (Eds.), "The professional preparation of counseling psychologists." *Contemporary Psychology,* 1967, *12,* 419–420.

Patterson, C. H. Foreword. In R. R. Carkhuff, *Helping and human relations* (Vol. II). New York: Holt, Rinehart & Winston, 1969. (a)

Patterson, C. H. What is counseling psychology? *Journal of Counseling Psychology*, 1969, *16*, 23–29. (b)

Patterson, C. H. Education and training as the preferred mode of treatment. *The Counseling Psychologist*, 1971, *3*(1), 77–79.

Patterson, C. H. Counseling psychology in the 1970s. *The Counseling Psychologist*, 1972, *3*(2), 4–7.

Patterson, C. H. *Relationship counseling and psychotherapy*. New York: Harper & Row, 1974.

Pepinsky, H. B., Hill-Frederick, J., & Epperson, D. L. *Journal of Counseling Psychology* as a matter of policies. *Journal of Counseling Psychology*, 1978, *25*, 438–498.

Perri, M. G., Richards, C. S., & Schultheis, K. Behavioral self-control and smoking reduction: A study of self-initiated attempts to reduce smoking. *Behavior Therapy*, 1977, *8*, 360–365.

Peterson, D. R. Attitudes concerning the Doctor of Psychology program. *Professional Psychology*, 1969, *1*, 44–47.

Peterson, D. R. Status of the Doctor of Psychology program, 1970. *Professional Psychology*, 1971, *2*, 271–275.

Peterson, D. R. Need for the Doctor of Psychology degree in professional psychology. *American Psychologist*, 1976, *31*, 792–798.

Peterson, D. R., & Baron, A., Jr. Status of the University of Illinois Doctor of Psychology, 1974. *Professional Psychology*, 1975, *6*, 88–95.

Peterson, D. R., Eaton, M. M., Levine, A. R., & Snepp, F. P. Development of Doctor of Psychology programs and experiences of graduates through 1980. *Rutgers Professional Psychology Review*, 1980, *2*, 29–39.

Peterson, D. R., Eaton, M. M., Levine, A. R., & Snepp, F. P. Career experiences of Doctors of Psychology. *Professional Psychology*, 1981, *13*, 268–277.

Prince, M. T., & Randolph, D. L. Differentiating roles of clinical and counseling psychology interns. *Journal of Clinical Psychology*, 1981, *37*, 892–896.

Prochaska, J. O., & Norcross, J. C. The future of psychotherapy: A Delphi poll. *Professional Psychology*, 1982, *13*, 620–627.

Pumroy, D. K. *Training in clinical psychology: The matter from several perspectives*. Washington, DC: American Psychological Association, 1964.

Reisman, J. R. *A history of clinical psychology*. New York: Wiley, 1976.

Resnick, H. The counseling psychologist in community mental health centers and health maintenance organizations—do we belong? *The Counseling Psychologist*, 1982, *10*(2), 53–59.

Richards, C. S., & Perri, M. G. Do self-control treatments last? An evaluation of behavioral problem solving and faded counselor contact as treatment maintenance strategies. *Journal of Counseling Psychology*, 1978, *25*, 376–383.

Robinson, F. P. Counseling psychology since the Northwestern Conference. In A. S. Thompson & D. E. Super (Eds.), *The professional preparation of counseling psychologists*. New York: Teachers College, Columbia University, 1964.

Roe, A. A psychological study of eminent biologists. *Psychological Monographs*, 1951, *65*, No. 14 (Whole No. 331). (a)

Roe, A. A psychological study of eminent physical scientists. *Genetic Psychology Monograph*, 1951, *43*, 121–239. (b)

Roe, A. Analysis of group Rorschachs of psychologists and anthropologists. *Journal of Projective Techniques*, 1952, *16*, 212–224. (a)

Roe, A. Group Rorschachs of university faculties. *Journal of Consulting Psychology*, 1952, *16*, 18–22. (b)

Roe, A. A psychological study of eminent psychologists and anthropologists and a comparison with biological and physical scientists. *Psychological Monographs*, 1953, *67*, No. 2 (Whole No. 352).

Roe, A. *The psychology of occupations*. New York: Wiley, 1956.

Roe, A. Early determinants of vocational choice. *Journal of Counseling Psychology*, 1957, *4*, 212–217.

Rogers, C. R. *Counseling and psychotherapy*. Boston: Houghton Mifflin, 1942.

Rogers, C. R. *Client-centered therapy*. Boston: Houghton Mifflin, 1951.

Rogers, C. R. *On becoming a person*. Boston: Houghton Mifflin, 1961.

Rogers. C. R. *A way of being*. Boston: Houghton Mifflin, 1980.

Rotter, J. B. A historical and theoretical analysis of some broad trends in clinical psychology. In S. Koch (Ed.), *Psychology: A study of a science*. New York: McGraw-Hill, 1963.

Rotter, J. B. The future of clinical psychology. *Journal of Consulting and Clinical Psychology*, 1973, *40*, 313–321.

Samler, J. Where do counseling psychologists work? What do they do? What should they do? In A. S. Thompson & D. E. Super (Eds.), *The professional preparation of counseling psychologists*. New York: Teachers College, Columbia University, 1964.

Schneider, L. J., & Gelso, C. J., "Vocational" versus "personal" emphases in counseling psychology training programs. *The Counseling Psychologist*, 1972, *3*(3), 90–92.

Scott, C. W. History of the Division of Counseling Psychology: 1945–1963. In J. M. Whiteley (Ed.), *The history of counseling psychology*. Monterey, CA: Brooks/Cole, 1980.

Shakow, D. What is clinical psychology? *The Clinical Psychologist*, 1975, *29*(1), 6–8.

Shakow, D. What is clinical psychology? *American Psychologist*, 1976, *31*, 553–560.

Shertzer, B., & Isaacson, L. A counselor educator views counseling psychologists: Problems in professional identity. *The Counseling Psychologist*, 1977, *7*(2), 33–35.

Smith, D. Trends in counseling and psychotherapy. *American Psychologist*, 1982, *37*, 802–809.

Spoth, R. Toward a more clearly articulated identity: The counseling psychologist as developmental orchestrator. *The Counseling Psychologist*, 1981, *9*(2), 52–57.

Stone, G. C., Cohen, F., & Adler, N. E. (Eds.), *Health psychology*. San Francisco, CA: Jossey-Bass, 1979.

Strong, E. K., Jr. *Vocational interests of men and women*. Stanford, CA: Stanford University Press, 1943.

Super, D. E. *The dynamics of vocational development.* New York: Harper, 1942.

Super, D. E. Vocational adjustment: Implementing a self-concept. *Occupations,* 1951, *30,* 1-5.

Super, D. E. A theory of vocational development. *American Psychologist,* 1953, *8,* 185-190.

Super, D. E. Career patterns as a basis for vocational counseling. *Journal of Counseling Psychology,* 1954, *1,* 12-20.

Super, D. E. Personality integration through vocational counseling. *Journal of Counseling Psychology,* 1955, *2,* 217-226. (a)

Super, D. E. Transition: From vocational guidance to counseling psychology. *Journal of Counseling Psychology,* 1955, *2,* 3-9. (b)

Super, D. E. Vocational development: The process of compromise or synthesis. *Journal of Counseling Psychology,* 1966, *3,* 249-253.

Super, D. E. *The psychology of careers.* New York: Harper & Row, 1957.

Super, D. E. The identity crises of counseling psychologists. *The Counseling Psychologist,* 1977, *7*(2), 13-15.

Super, D. E. The year 2000 and all that. *The Counseling Psychologist,* 1980, *8*(4), 22-25.

Tanney, F. Counseling psychology and professional certification: On "telling it like it is" (almost). *The Counseling Psychologist,* 1980, *9*(1), 25-27.

Tanney, F. Counseling psychology in the marketplce. *The Counseling Psychologist,* 1982, *10*(2), 21-29.

Thelen, M. H., & Ewing, D. R. Roles, functions, and training in clinical psychology: A survey of academic clinicians. *American Psychologist,* 1970, *25,* 550-554.

Thompson, A. S., & Super, D. E. (Eds.). *The professional preparation of counseling psychologists.* New York: Teachers College, Columbia University, 1964.

Thoresen, C. E. Reflections on chronic health, self-control, and human ethology. *The Counseling Psychologist,* 1980, *8*(4), 48-58.

Thoresen, C. E., & Ewart, C. K. Behavioral self-control and career development. *The Counseling Psychologist,* 1976, *63,* 29-43.

Thoresen, C. E., & Mahoney, M. J. *Behavioral self-control.* New York: Holt, Rinehart & Winston, 1976.

Tyler, L. E. The next twenty years. *The Counseling Psychologist,* 1980, *8*(4), 19-21.

Walker, C. E. Training in clinical psychology: The future. *The Clinical Psychologist,* 1974, *27*(2), 12-13.

Watson, R. I. A brief history of clinical psychology. *Psychological Bulletin,* 1953, *50,* 321-346.

Weigel, R. I have seen the enemy and they is us—and everyone else. *The Counseling Psychologist,* 1977, *7*(2), 50-53.

Whiteley, J. M. The historical development of counseling psychology: An introduction. In J. M. Whiteley (Ed.), *The history of counseling psychology.* Monterey, CA: Brooks/Cole, 1980.

Wildman, R. W., & Wildman, R. W., II. The uncertain present and future of clinical psychology: A review and comments. *The Clinical Psychologist,* 1974, *27*(4), 19–22.

Williams, R. L., & Long, J. D. *Toward a self-managed life style* (3rd ed.). Boston: Houghton Mifflin, 1983.

Yamamoto, K. Counseling psychologists—who are they? *Journal of Counseling Psychology,* 1963, *10,* 211–221.

Zimet, C. N. The clinical psychologist in the 1980's: Entitled or untitled. *The Clinical Psychologist,* 1982, *35*(2), 12–14.

Zytowski, D. G., & Rosen, D. A.The grand tour: 30 years of counseling psychology in the *Annual Review of Psychology. The Counseling Psychologist,* 1982, *10*(1), 69–81.

Reading 4
School Psychology:
A Historical Perspective

Elizabeth A. Abramowitz
PSI Associates, Inc., Washington, D.C.

Some major historical events are described in this paper to indicate briefly where school psychology has been as a profession in order to suggest where it may be going. From surveys of recent literature and interviews with school psychologists, it is clear that, as a discipline, school psychology is still in its infancy. For example, *The Annual Review of Psychology* does not include school psychology (the closest topical heading is "Instructional Psychology"); it is not included in the major annotated histories of psychology; and in *Education Index,* the cross-references for school psychology are special education topics.

When I interviewed Dr. Howard Cameron, Chairperson of the doctoral program in School Psychology at Howard University, for this paper, he said, "School psychologists need to develop an identity different from that of special educators or clinical psychologists." His observation provides a theme for looking at the recent history of school psychology in the United States, and indeed, at the not-so-recent history as well.

Since Henry James's famous series of talks to teachers in 1892, psychologists have felt the need to define who they are and what exactly they are offering teachers (James, 1958).

For each age, with each new wave of social thought, applied psychologists in the schools have had to define who they are. To Maher (1979), the solution was for school psychologists to evaluate special education programs. If, however,

Reprinted from School Psychology Review, *10*(2), 121–126.

Hughes's (1979) work was indicative, most school psychologists in public schools spent three out of every four hours on the job making assessments.

According to the National Center for Education Statistics, in the 1975–76 school year 10,002 school psychologists were working in elementary and secondary schools, and an additional 2,000 in colleges and universities. Unlike other areas of education, except special education, school psychology at that time was experiencing a chronic manpower shortage; the most severe shortages were in bilingual and minority group practitioners. According to Dr. Cameron, fewer than two dozen blacks and even fewer Hispanics held doctorates in school psychology.

The National Association of School Psychologists (NASP) in 1977, listed 289 programs in school psychology: 77 at the master's level, 147 post-master's, and 65 doctoral. Unquestionably, the small number of doctoral programs all but guarantees an undersupply of school psychologists in the short-term.

The growth of the field of school psychology paralleled increased demands for psychoeducational diagnosticians, as part of implementation of federal and judicial mandates. Ironically school psychology was perhaps the fastest growing and least visible discipline in psychology. Although its growth was closely tied to federal education policy, its presence in federal policy making was relatively invisible.

The historical milestones of school psychology are discussed in this paper. The history reflects efforts to strengthen professional recognition and control over critical aspects of training and practice of school psychology.

HISTORICAL IMPACT OF PROFESSIONAL ASSOCIATIONS

Historically, the role of professional associations has been three-fold: (a) to limit access to the profession; (b) to influence the conditions of work; and (c) to control training and advancement in a field. Since their organization, the two major associations to which school psychologists belong have been trying to fulfill this role as they respond to the specific needs of their members at different periods of time.

As part of the general reorganization of the American Psychological Association in 1945, Division 16 was created. The general purpose of the Division was stated as the application of psychological knowledge in the schools. By 1979, membership had reached 2,500; the members were mostly psychologists who had been trained in doctoral programs and were attached to universities or other institutions of higher education. Their interests, consequently, were focused on research, theory and the training of practitioners.

It was 20 years before a new association, the National Association of School Psychologists (NASP), was organized. The purpose of NASP is similar to that of Division 16, but the membership, currently about 4,000, differs. NASP members primarily have been trained in master's level programs. They work as psychologists and administrators of psychological services in public schools and state departments of education. They are responsive to the practical and political dictates of the school system and state governments for which they work.

Throughout the history of school psychology, there has been a conflict of interests between theoreticians/basic researchers and practitioners which is reflected to some extent in the memberships and policies of both Division 16 and NASP. Both associations have sought to influence different aspects of the practice of school psychology.

Certification/Licensure

The NASP permanent committee on certification published *The Handbook of Certification/Licensure Requirements for School Psychologists* in 1976, to propose certification standards which state departments of education should be encouraged to adopt. The *Handbook* was the first major attempt to set national professional requirements for school psychologists in public schools. Because the supply of school psychologists is low, state departments of education that wish to adopt NASP guidelines have had to make exceptions to meet manpower needs and demands for service.

Licensure as well as certification governs access to the practice of school psychology. The standards for licensure proposed by APA-Division 16 and NASP reflect the interests and training of their respective memberships. For example, APA consistently proposed to state legislatures that the minimum requirements for licensure include doctoral training, whereas NASP sought to change licensure standards to include experienced school psychologists trained at the master's level.

The prize is important—the opportunity to engage in private practice. Thus the struggle over licensure was more intense than that over any other policy difference between NASP and Division 16. To date, the majority of the states issuing general psychology licenses require training at the doctoral level and experience in the field. In several states, special licenses are issued to clinical psychologists who must hold doctorates and have had appropriate internships and experience in the field.

The effect of the current licensure policies has been to limit private practice to school psychologists who hold doctorates.

Accreditation

The third major area of professional association influence was the accreditation of school psychologists. APA accredits school psychology programs administratively located in psychology departments. The National Council of Accreditation of Teacher Education (NCATE) performs the same function for school psychology programs located in schools of education. This bifurcated division of responsibility for accreditation of school psychology was one of the first issues NASP addressed. For almost ten years, NASP opposed the use of non-school psychologists in NCATE accreditation of school psychology programs. Recently, NCATE accepted NASP as a participant in the school psychology accreditation process.

Salary Schedules

NASP and Division 16, at best, had marginal impact on pay schedules for school psychologists. As part of its efforts to influence certification and change state funding formulae for school psychology staff positions, NASP, in particular, addressed this issue, although indirectly. In some states, school psychologists had the same pay schedule and job category as teachers. In other states, job categories for school psychologists were separate and unique. Given the interests and effectiveness of some NASP state chapters, attempts were made over the years to achieve the separate job category with unique job functions for school psychologists.

HISTORIC CONFERENCES

Three conferences addressed the problem of the professional definition of psychology and the needs of the branches. They were held at Boulder, Colorado; the University of Chicago (the Kikert Conference); and Vail, Colorado.

The Boulder Conference, which was called about 20 years ago, was a significant attempt by psychologists to define the boundaries of the discipline. Like the Kikert Conference, which followed it in 1967, the major concern was the split between practitioner and scientific psychologists. Both conferences attempted to resolve differences and to stimulate communication between scientists and practitioners.

During the Vail Conference, in 1969, the conflict between the branches of psychology had intensified rather than diminished. The question raised in the small conference in Boulder became the central topic for the large conference at Vail.

The Vail Conference, which was planned by APA with financing from the National Institute of Mental Health, was attended by about 300 persons. Unlike the previous conferences which were limited in size, scope, and representation, the Vail Conference included various branches of psychology, civil rights groups, and interested consumer groups.

At times, the participants in the Vail Conference appeared to be attempting no less than the comprehensive reform of psychology. They tried to resolve the increasing splits in practitioner groups (e.g. clinicians, community mental health workers and school psychologists); to bridge the widening gap between experimental psychology, the foundation of the disipline, and the newer applied fields; and to address the problems of minority representation in APA and in the different fields.

The voluminous report that came out of the five-day conference reflected the amount of ground which had been covered and the intense interest of the participants. Several of the Vail Conference recommendations, such as endorsement of a Doctor of Psychology degree for practitioners, gradually found support on a number of university campuses.

The Vail Conference was the last major attempt of psychologists to come together across disciplines and to define their training and professional needs and responsibilities.

LEGISLATIVE IMPACT ON SCHOOL PSYCHOLOGY

The expansion of school psychology was directly related to the expansion of the federal role in education. The increased federal mandates, especially that of the Elementary and Secondary Education Act and that of the Education for All Handicapped Children Act of 1975 (Public Law 94-142), increased the demand for the services of school psychologists.

In 1965, passage of the Elementary and Secondary Education Act (ESEA) significantly raised federal aid to education. (Between 1958 and 1965, curriculum improvements and college student aid were funded through the National Defense Education Act.) The by-product of support services for disadvantaged students (Title I) and improvements in local school practices (Title IV) were new demands for school psychologists.

With enactment of Public Law 94-142, the demand for school psychologists again increased dramatically. During the period, however, the number of students entering college with careers in education as goals decreased just as dramatically. The result was the chronic undersupply of school psychologists and the increased assessment backlogs in the schools which we see today.

The impact of these two major federal laws has been both positive and negative, from the perspective of historical needs of school psychology to define itself. On the positive side, the laws increased the visibility of the school psychologist in the schools, provided needed funds for new staff positions and staff development for current personnel, and helped to differentiate school psychologists from classroom teachers and school counselors.

On the negative side, the federal mandates forced school psychologists to spend most if not all their time doing assessments. In 1965, school psychologists were critical members of child-study teams identifying disadvantaged students for compensatory education programs; 15 years later, school psychologists are critical members of child-study teams identifying handicapped students.

The federal mandate of Public Law 94-142 forced a definition of school psychologists which they would not have imposed on themselves. The national conferences, NASP *Standards for the Provision of School Psychological Services,* and studies, such as Hughes (1979), all indicate that school psychologists wanted to reduce the amount of time they spent on assessments and to increase the amount of time spent on mental health consultations and prevention of student learning problems. This desired change in role was not shared by persons outside the school psychology profession (Hughes, 1979), as the decisions of federal and state officials clearly indicate.

Rather than resolving the historical problem of role definition, the new federal mandates created a new identity problem. Until the enactment of Public Law 94-142, associations of school psychologists sought to separate their field from that of clinical psychology; subsequently, school psychologists sought to separate their field from that of special education.

EFFECTS OF LITIGATION

The results of the work of school psychologists can be seen in the major education cases since *Brown v. The Board of Education* (1954). In general, the United States courts always have played a dominant role in education. Public attention and concern with the role taken by the courts reached a peak in relation to school desegregation and nonpublic education cases.

From about 1967 to the present, an increasing number of court cases dealt with the issue of standardized tests of intelligence. There was a direct correlation between the increased number of court cases and the increased demand for special education assessments (Lupiani, 1978). In May 1980, the National Institute of Education and the Bureau of Education for the Handicapped co-sponsored a one-day invitational conference to discuss issues which were related to court decisions on testing and services to handicapped students. The theme underlying the conference was the need for improved school psychological services to meet the needs of disadvantaged and bilingual handicapped students.

Cases, such as *Diana v. California State Department of Education* (1970), *Larry P. v. Riles* (1972), *Pennsylvania Association for Retarded Citizens v. Commonwealth* (1972), *Peter Mills v. Board of Education* (1972), and *Lora v. Board of Education of the City of New York* (1978) illustrate the parental dissatisfaction with the tasks school psychologists were required to perform.

The impact on the profession of these cases has been to increase the demands for "new" school psychologists and "new" testing instruments. The role of school psychologists was changed again by the litigation—this time to members of interdisciplinary child-study teams meeting the needs of handicapped children. Emphasis in the court orders was on the use of culture-fair and linguistically appropriate tests, and on the use of nonstandardized tests as assessment tools. For school psychologists who can operate without a test kit, the advantage may lie in their ability to use mental health consultation and related skills in their work. The climate created by the courts, in fact, may encourage fuller utilization of the skills of school psychologists.

The two major professional associations in school psychology have incorporated the implications of the recent court cases only in part. The NASP publication, *Standards for Practice,* in fact anticipated the types of accountability and range of competencies which school psychologists working under court orders should bring to their jobs. The adoption of these and similar standards was the result of external factors, that is, of litigation and federal legislation discussed earlier rather than of internal factors, such as the demands for reform by staff school psychologists.

POLITICAL CONTEXT OF SCHOOL PSYCHOLOGY

The political context of school psychology includes visible participation in shaping public issues and education policy decisions. The context can be analyzed at the federal, state or local levels. At each, the public record contains testimony submitted by interested educational groups, as well as the highlights of hearings, which indicate the dominant issues.

The review of the debates on federal education policies indicate the lack of visible participation by school psychologists either through the two major professional associations or as individuals. The Ninety-Fifth Congress, for example, spent two years considering Amendments to the Elementary and Secondary Education Act. ESEA is the omnibus education bill that controls about one-half of the federal education budget.

The Education Amendments of 1978 authorized federal involvement in elementary and secondary education through the financing of such programs as Compensatory Education, Gifted and Talented, Bilingual Education, Indian Education, Basic Skills, Educational Technology and local school improvements. Yet, a reviw of the public testimony taken over the two-year period reveals no direct participation by school psychologists in shaping these crucial education policies. Their absence was in sharp contrast to the highly visible participation of other professional education groups, notably, the National Education Association and the American Federation of Teachers.

A similar absence can be found when examining the record of the most hotly contested educational issue other than school busing, namely, tuition tax credits. In surveying the list of the hundreds of professional associations on both sides of the issue, the absence of school psychologist associations was readily apparent. They were also not present at the discussion of the creation of a cabinet-level department of education, the federal education budget cuts in the early 1970s, and the education budget proposals for 1981.

With the exception of the vested interest issues, such as licensure and certification standards, school psychologists did not participate in general education policy debates at either state or local levels. In such states as California and

Ohio, the degree of political involvement at state and local levels appeared to be inversely related to general community interest in the issue.

Although NASP, over the years, had adopted broad resolutions that were indeed applicable to education policy, these resolutions were not refelcted in the thinking of policy makers on the major issues of the last few years.

The U.S. Congress and the Carter administration have begun examining Public Law 94-142, which expires in 1982. Surveys of the policy makers in Congress and the Administration, appear to indicate that the historic political inerta is intact. In a separate survey of selected large education associations actively involved in recommending changes in Public Law 94-142, it also appeared that they neither communicated about or understood the issues in the law that were of concern to school psychologists.

Historically, school psychology seemed to stand outside the political context which, in fact, controlled it. Indeed, as a discipline, school psychology seemed to be invisible in the wider arena where education policies are shaped.

SOCIAL CONTEXT OF SCHOOL PSYCHOLOGY

Atkinson (1977) cautioned against confusing the role of psychologist with that of protagonist. He stressed the importance of maintaining scientific objectivity as part of the discipline. Without taking issue with Atkinson's warning, it is important to note that, with the exception of the Vail Conference, school psychology appeared at first to exist out of context. The social climate of the time does not appear to have had a significant influence on the preoccupation of the field, as evidenced by annotated histories of psychology (Hernstein and Boring, 1965).

It is almost impossible to tell if there were recessions, riots in the streets, taxpayer revolts, declines in pupil populations, parental distrust of educators and dissatisfaction with public education in general, increased racial polarization, and declining test scores from the reality that is pictured in the school psychology journals. Public concerns, for the most part, are not incorporated into the professional concerns of school psychologists.

This historic trend may have had its roots in the desire of psychologists to be objective and scientific. Objectivity may have been actualized as aloofness, and to nonpsychologists, the aloofness may have been interpreted as indifference. Regardless of its origins, the historical consequence was the treatment of school psychology as something outside its social context. Thus, the field has contributed little to the application of psychology to resolving rather than describing the critical recurring problems in education in recent years.

SUMMARY

School psychology is rooted in psychology and education: in scientific psychology through the mental measurement movement, in applied psychology through the mental health movement, and in education through the pupil personnel services movement, and, more recently, through special education. Because school psychologists are part of a dynamic social institution—public education—the role demands and role expectations have shifted over time. In each decade, the task for school psychologists, history seemed to say, was to take time out and redefine what the discipline was at that period, and what its practitioners should be doing.

If past is indeed prologue, then the future concerns of school psychologists will be internal professional interests to the exclusion of the larger concerns. If, however, the past merely serves as a warning, it offers the chance to overcome provincialism in favor of more interactions with educators, consumers of school psychology services, and education policy makers at all levels of government.

REFERENCES

Atkinson, R. C. Reflections of psychology's past and concerns about its future. *American Psychologist,* 1977, *32*(3), 205–10.

Diana v. California State Department of Education. No. C-70-37 (N.D. Cal. 1970).

Hernstein, R. J. and Boring, E G. *A source book in the history of psychology.* Cambridge: Harvard University Press, 1965.

Hughes, J. N. Consistency of administrators' and psychologists' actual and ideal perceptions of school psychologists' activities. *Psychology in the Schools,* 1979, *16*(2), 234–39.

James, W. *Talks to teachers on psychology: and to students on some of life's ideals.* New York: Norton, 1958. (Originally published, 1899.)

Larry P. v. Riles, 343 F. Supp. 1306 (N.D. Cal. 1972).

Lora v. Board of Education of the City of New York, 456 F. Supp. 1211 (1978).

Lupiani, D. A. The practice of defensive school psychology. *Psychology in the Schools,* 1978, *15*(2), 246–51.

Maher, C. A. School psychologists and special education program evaluations: Contributions and considerations. *Psychology in the Schools,* 1979, *16*(2), 240–45.

National Association of School Psychologists. *The handbook of certification/ licensure requirements for school psychologists.* Washington, D.C.: NASP Committee, 1976.

National Association of School Psychologists, *Standards for provision of school psychological services.* Washington, D.C.: NASP Committee, 1977.

Pennsylvania Association for Retarded Citizens v. Commonwealth, 343 F. Supp.
    279 (E.D. Pa. 1972).
Peter Mills v. Board of Education, 343 F. Supp. 855 (D.D.C. 1972).

Reading 5
The Foundations of Professional Psychology

Ronald E. Fox and Allan G. Barclay
Wright State University, Dayton, Ohio

David A. Rodgers
Cleveland Clinic, Cleveland, Ohio

The major gains made by psychology over the past 35 years have highlighted
three problems that constitute significant impediments to the further growth
and development of the profession. These problems are (a) the lack of a single
agreed upon or widely accepted definition of the profession and its scope;
(b) the lack of a uniform general education process for new professionals that
allows the public to develop dependable expectations about the scope and
competency of the profession; and (c) the lack of a credential by which the
practitioner can be unambiguously identified. Psychology has now many
definitions of itself as a profession, causing public confusion; a plethora of educational settings and experiences serve as accepted entry points to professional
practice; and practitioners may possess any of several degrees as acceptable
credentials for entry into practice, most of which can also ambiguously identify
non-practitioner as well as practitioner education.

THE DEFINITION PROBLEM

Ambiguity over the definition of professional psychology lies at the heart of
many of the dilemmas and confusions that confront the profession. Instead of
one definition, there are several. Policy positions of the American Psychological
Association, reflected in its standards for providers of services and in its
credentialing requirements for training programs (APA, 1979), define practitioner specialties rather than the practitioner field generally. There are definitions for clinical psychology, counseling psychology, school psychology, and
industrial psychology, but there are no generic definitions of the profession
that encompass all of the applied areas. *Clinical psychology* and *professional
psychology* are often used interchangeably, to the chagrin of psychologists
in other specialites. *Health care psychology* has been suggested as a term to

Reprinted from American Psychologist, *37*(3), 306–312.

substitute for practitioner psychology, but this ignores the fields of industrial psychology and school psychology, both of which have practitioner dimensions. Indeed, recent APA Council debates concerning "program designation" and revision of the grossly out-of-date APA model psychology licensing legislation (APA, 1967) reveal a distressing lack of agreement and lack of clarity concerning the definitional issues.

The lack of conceptual clarity is revealed, for example, in the APA accreditation process. Accreditation criteria were originally developed for clinical psychology programs as an applied arm of what was basically an academic discipline. Subsequently, school and counseling programs were added to the list. The consequence of this piecemeal process is that, instead of accrediting professional psychology programs, APA accredits specialty programs or subfields of psychology. A single department of psychology with programs in clinical, counseling, and school psychology is required to undergo three separate review processes under the current system. The fact that psychology licensing laws in the United States (like those of the other major professions) are, with very few exceptions, generic while the accreditation procedures are for specialties, adds to general confusion both in the public mind and among psychologists. If medicine were operating as psychology is now dong, a medical school would be required to seek accreditation separately for each medical specialty but would not be required to be accredited as a medical school per se.

This accreditation confusion is further reflected in even the meaning attributed to schools of professional psychology. Although most professional training is currently still in academic departments, where specialization prior to the degree is at least consistent with academic specialization, increasing numbers of professionals are being trained in professional schools, which could be expected to be comprehensive in their professional training as medical schools and law schools are comprehensive in their respective fields. However, many "schools" are nothing more than traditional clinical psychology programs, often not strikingly different from the clinical psychology track in a conventional academic department. Other schools, which are closer to the concept of a true professional school, have separate departments devoted to specialty areas such as school psychology, clinical psychology, and so on. In these schools, the subspecialties are structurally distinct from each other, and again, the concept of a generically trained professional is not approached in practice. It is the exception rather than the rule that a few schools, such as the School of Professional Psychology at Wright State University, are conceptually oriented toward first providing a base of generic training that is comprehensive across subspecialties and then assuming that specialization will occur beyond such a generic base. The focus on subspecialty training, even within professional schools that should be organizationally compatible with a generic base, is of course fostered by the APA accreditation demand and further adds to the confusion of both the profession and the public concerning the definition of professional psychology.

Our profession has grown by the development of its parts, without having a definition of the core profession itself. This would be somewhat analogous to having pediatricians, surgeons, and obstetricians but no physicians. To be sure, clinical psychologists, counseling psychologists, community psychologists, industrial psychologists, and forensic psychologists are all psychologists; but so too are learning psychologists, perception psychologists, physiological psychologists, humanistic psychologists, psychoanalytic psychologists, social psychologists, and many other subgroups that mix theoretical approach, knowledge base, and common interests into the definitional problem. The basic question is how or whether the profession of psychology can represent an identifiable field to the consuming public that can be meaningfully regulated to the benefit of the public under a single professional label, but this question has been left unanswered.

We suggest that the profession of psychology should be identified as dealing with the area of human need, which the underlying science of psychology attempts to understand and elucidate. Since the science of psychology is concerned with understanding the problems of human behavior (especially of purposive, motivated behavior), we suggest that the profession of psychology is concerned with those human problems arising out of or associated with purposive behavior which might potentially be understandable and solvable through adequate scientific knowledge in psychology. We propose the following definition:

> Professional psychology is that profession which is concerned with enhancing the effectiveness of human functioning. Therefore, a professional psychologist is one who has expertise in the development and application of quality services to the public in a controlled, organized, ethical manner; based upon psychological knowledge, attitudes, and skills, in order to enhance the effectiveness of human functioning.[1]

Essentially this same definition has been proposed elsewhere (Dörken & Rodgers, 1976; Rodgers, 1980; Rodgers 1981), and it is not strikingly different from that of Peterson (1976b): "A fully useful professional psychology is the discipline concerned with the assessment and improvement of the psychological functioning of human beings as individuals, in groups, and in social organizations" (p. 793). We suggest our definition for the professional field of practitioner psychology—for the kinds of activities that would require public regulation in the same sense that professions such as law and medicine are regulated. It would not apply to other activities, such as the profession of teaching psychology or the profession of research psychology, which from certain perspectives, could be called "professional psychology." These distinctions have been argued elsewhere and will not be elaborated here (see for example, Rodgers, 1981).

---

[1] This definition was written and adopted by the faculty of the School of Professional Psychology at Wright State University in 1981.

A primary concept of this definition is that all practitioner professions are identified by the field of need which they serve, not by the technology or the defined knowledge base in terms of which they function. The clearest example would be medicine, which is concerned with all human problems of illness, whether or not there is an adequate knowledge base to understand or the technology to effectively treat such illnesses. Bubonic plague was considered a medical problem before there was scientific knowledge as to what caused it. Cancer is considered a medical problem, even though we still do not understand in any comprehensive sense the nature of the cancerous process. Similarly, we suggest that professional psychology should be defined as the profession dealing with the problems of human coping effectiveness, even though we may not understand the disruptions of many patterns of behavior or the effective change processes that would correct such disruptions.

One may object that the proposed definition is too broad and impinges on the legitimate work of other disciplines and professions. Social work, the ministry, medicine, and law, for example, are all involved at times in attempts to improve the effectiveness of human behavior. We suggest two defenses of this definition against such charges. First, it is not intended to be a monopolistic definition, any more than medicine can claim to be the *only* profession that deals with problems of illness. Psychology certainly deals with illness, as do the law at times, social work, and many other professions. Second, however, we do suggest that psychology is the *only* profession that *consistently* focuses its efforts on solving problems through alterations in patterns of behavioral coping. Social work, for example, depends heavily on establishing social structures or placing persons in social structures that will "solve" their problems of poverty, coping incapacity, or the like. The ministry will often focus on spiritual values that may pose more challenges to coping skills than solutions (e.g., when concerning issues of contraception or monogamy). The law, clearly, is not predominantly concerned about the processes of coping effectiveness. We suggest, however, that there is consistency across all practitioner psychology to attempt to solve problems by helping people become effective in their behavioral coping capacities. We help schizophrenics learn how to manage tensions and hallucinations and interpersonal relationships, rather than injecting drugs that alter metabolic pathways. We help executives learn how to be more sensitive to those around them in order to be more effective in an executive capacity. We help the docile learn how to be more assertive. We help persons with migraine headaches learn how to be more relaxed. We help students in the school setting to match their abilities with challenges that the educational process offers. We help people manage their behavior to cope with their environment more effectively.

The Boulder model and the scientist-practitioner conception of the profession have tended to emphasize the validated technology that the professional uses rather than the field of need that the professional psychologist serves. This has been one of the most confusing stumbling blocks to the evolution of a workable definition of the practitioner profession of psychology. Paradoxically, it is ignorance that calls most for a profession, rather than knowledge. To the extent that a field is well understood scientifically, its application to the public's need can be handled appropriately by technicians who are well versed in that technology. For example, one does not need a lawyer to draw up a standard will or to draft a simple contract. A physician is not required to collect blood samples or to provide genetic counseling when the counseling concerns matters that are well established and obtainable from major textbooks. Since these issues have been argued elsewhere (e.g., Rodgers 1980, 1981), further elaboration will not be provided here. To repeat the main argument: the ultimate concern of the professional psychologist is all problems involving human coping skills and human coping effectiveness. Subdomains of practice, which are defined by the type of client complaint (e.g., emotional problems), by the techniques utilized (e.g., behavioral modification therapy), or by the organizational settings in which the service is delivered (e.g., clinic or industry), constitute specific elements or specialties of professional practice and should neither be confused with professional practice in general nor used as the primary definition of professional practice.

PROBLEMS RELATED TO THE EDUCATIONAL PROCESS

The present educational process through which practitioners are trained has several characteristics that contribute to the confusion of the public and of the profession concerning who and what is a professional psychologist. Three features of this system are especially troublesome: First, the organizational settings in which training takes place are basically uncontrolled and so variable as to guarantee nonuniformity of training and confusion as to professional identity. Second, the practicum experiences of students preparing for professional roles are predominantly in service delivery systems controlled by professions other than psychology, so students are not exposed to professional role models of psychologists functioning in psychological settings. Third, both the educational experience and the degree credentialing of practitioner psychologists are frequently blurred with and undifferentiated from the preparation of nonpractitioner psychologists, so the unique responsibilities and attitudes appropriate for the practitioner are neither learned by the future professionals nor clarified for the consuming public. Together, these three dimensions reflect the lack of appropriate and systematic attention to the educational preparation of practitioners in the field of psychology.

Organizational Setting

Currently, professional psychology training programs are housed in a variety of university departments, schools, or colleges (e.g., psychology departments, human development departments, schools of education, medical schools, business schools, etc.). Beginning with the establishment of the California School of Professional Psychology in 1969 (Watson, Caddy, Johnson, & Rimm, 1981), a number of psychology programs have come into existence that are separate educational institutions not affiliated with an established university. Such variability is perhaps not surprising in light of the language of APA's present official policy statement concerning legislative guidelines for regulating the practice of psychology (APA, 1967). This document states that

> Legislation regulating the practice of psychology should be restricted to one level, requiring the doctoral degree in a program that is primarily psychological, and not less than two years of supervised experience, one of which is subsequent to the granting of the doctoral degree. This level should be designated by the title of "psychologist." (p. 1099)

These guidelines do not require a degree in psychology or one from a psychology department or one that is any more precise with regard to content than that the program be "primarily psychological." Most states have followed essentially these guidelines in adopting legal statutes governing the profession. It is therefore little wonder that many organizational settings claim to prepare their students for psychological licensure by having a "primarily psychological" degree program in ministerial training, business training, educational training, human development training, or the like.

Such variety in the organizational settings of psychology training programs contributes to much confusion concerning who is a psychologist and what preparation actually qualifies a person to enter professional practice. When multiple access routes to professional practice are extant, it is difficult for a profession to establish or maintain its integrity as a distinct entity.

We suggest that the variety of institutional structures through which professional training is funneled inevitably leads to confusing and undesirable heterogeneity. We further suggest that certain educational structures better lend themselves to professional training than others do. Other major professions have tended, for cogent reasons, to consolidate their training settings into separate schools or colleges within an established university. Indeed, accreditation criteria for dentistry, medicine, law, and numerous other professions explicitly specify that the organizational structure for approved programs must be a school headed by a Dean or a person of equivalent rank. Such a school or college structure has several advantages for professional training. It is explicitly devoted to the primary goal of training effective professionals. It has far more control of budgetary and curricular matters than do departments or interdepartmental programs. There is greater autonomy for defining faculty standards. Finally, access to both external funding resources and the total university governance system is enhanced. Although other professions have discovered these facts of academic life, professional training in psychology still is housed primarily in traditional academic university departments, which historically have been designed for the acquisition of basic knowledge, not for producing practitioners.

The accreditation standards for law, medicine, dentistry, and optometry specify that their approved professional schools also be part of accredited universities. When provisions are made for so-called "free standing" schools autonomous from university structures, these professions typically require that the school be organized as a nonprofit institution governed by a board whose members have no financial interest in the operation of the school. It is accepted by these professions that the university environment provides optimum conditions for the encouragement of high educational standards and that university traditions have established relatively workable accountability, control, and quality-assurance procedures. In free standing proprietary schools in which the management has a vested financial interest, expensive quality-assurance procedures may suffer—to the detriment of the students, the public, and the profession. We would suggest, therefore, that professional training in psychology not have lower standards than training in other professions. This would mean that the training should be in professional schools with a full-time faculty and administratively headed by a Dean or person of equivalent administrative rank. Ideally the school should be university affiliated, or at least located in a non-profit structure managed by a public board with special obligations to demonstrate academic standards and accountability controls comparable to or exceeding those of schools with university affiliation.

Practicum Training

We regard much practicum training, as it is now constituted, to be generally unsatisfactory. Practicum training is a means by which students are socialized into a profession. For this socialization to occur effectively, students must be able to observe exemplary role models functioning within professional systems that are controlled by the profession and optimally designed to transmit the competencies of that profession to the consumer. *For adequate student practicum training, a profession must control a service delivery system of its own and demonstrate to the students within that delivery system appropriate professional ethics, professional organization, professional competencies, and professional conceptualizations. The delivery system should encompass a wide range of clients and practice settings and provide access to populations diverse enough to ensure student exposure to the broad array of problems with which the profession is concerned.* In professional psychology training programs, more often than not service agencies not within the direct purview of the faculty are given primary, sometimes exclusive, responsibility for student training. Such training often is in professional delivery systems controlled by another profession (such as medicine, education, business, or social work), and the range of psychological problems to which the students are exposed is often extremely restricted and nonrepresentative of the broad base of psychological practice for which the students should be trained. It is impossible to adequately socialize students of one independent profession exclusively in delivery systems designed and controlled by another profession. When the socialization occurs in a hierarchical setting not under the control of the profession, the psychologist learns subordination and therefore does not acquire competence in the independent delivery of responsible, psychologically based, professional services to the public.

Unfortunately, independent psychology delivery systems, except for the relatively narrow range of services provided by the autonomous private practitioner, are virtually nonexistent. Nevertheless, we suggest that to be effective professional psychology training programs *must* develop truly independent psychology practice settings with a relatively comprehensive range of experiences. There are three options that, even under current cultural patterns, could serve this purpose.

First, a university-based professional school is in the proper organizational position to develop a comprehensive psychological service center. Such a center would be our profession's equivalent of a university "teaching hospital," as a vehicle for both the training of students and the professional practice of the faculty. The expense of building such a center would be high but probably feasible in some instances at certain universities.

A second, less costly, option for programs that control their own delivery systems is the establishment of formalized affiliations with community agencies and institutions, one aspect of the affiliation agreement being the authority for the school faculty to control the psychological portion of the program. Such affiliations should be accomplished through specific agreements at the highest organizational levels within the respective institutions—the board of trustees of the university and the ultimate governing authority at the training site—and should commit the two institutions *as institutions* to establishing and managing a psychology training program. The agreements should specify a mutual sharing of resources (space, expenses, materials, and professional staffing), the fixing of responsibility for various aspects of the agreement, and the procedures by which agreements may be modified or terminated. Such agreements can enable significant control of the psychological services in the agency, through specified participation in the joint programming of the faculty, specification of the types of professional activities to be provided, provision for shared financing of various aspects of the total program (such as student support), and joint appointment of supervisors who meet the criteria for academic appointment in the university as well as professional appointment within the agency. Such formalized agreements should not be confused with the common practice of simply obtaining agreement from an institution to allow some students to receive training in its facilities under its supervision.

If they are to be effective, such agreements must go well beyond the usual informal arrangements by which psychology programs are allowed to place students. Under the kind of formal arrangement proposed here, the agency actually becomes an affiliated arm of the university's professional program, subject to the quality control standards of the university itself, and in turn creating professional responsibilities and liabilities (as well as opportunities) for the professional program faculty.

A third option, which might be considered the first step toward a comprehensive service delivery system, is the use of an organized faculty group practice plan as a focus for student training. A professional school can require that all faculty engaged in the teaching of professional services also be involved in the delivery of professional services, through an organized faculty group modeling for the students and to reduce conflict of interest problems that could arise between the private practice of the faculty and the school interests. A properly designed and incorporated faculty group practice plan can: (a) ensure that the faculty is professionally involved in delivering those services that are being taught; (b) prevent inappropriate exploitation of school resources for private gain, as is often a risk in "geographic full-time" arrangements; (c) systematically generate funds to supplement academic salaries, which ordinarily are too limited to recruit outstanding practitioners; (d) add to the breadth of professional practice and professional competency of the faculty; and (e) provide a setting in which students can be integrated into the delivery of psychological services, as appropriate, under direct tutelage of the practicing faculty. With a managed group practice, it is not only possible to deliver, and apprentice students in the delivery of, a wide range of psychological procedures (such as computerized assessment services and the use of psychological technicians as extenders), but also to demonstrate to students the advantages of cooperative group delivery systems using cost and service accountability procedures.

DIFFERENTIATING PRACTITIONER PSYCHOLOGY FROM OTHER PSYCHOLOGICAL EDUCATION

One of the greatest sources of confusion to both the profession and the public is the lack of differentiation between academic and professional training in psychology. These issues have been extensively argued in the literature (Fox, 1980; Meehl, 1971; Perry, 1979; Peterson, 1976a, 1976b; Peterson & Baron, 1975; Rodgers, 1964, 1981; Shoben, 1980; Stricker, 1975). Although we are tempted, we will not enter that particular debate again in this article except to assert our strong preference that the PhD be reserved as the academic or research-oriented degree and that the PsyD be reserved as the practitioner degree. A practice-oriented degree does not, of course, eliminate the possibility of either training or competence in research, as witnessed by the number of physicians in university settings who in fact do competent research, but it does recognize that the primary thrust of the training program is toward professional competence in delivering services to the public rather than toward research competence in furthering the frontiers of basic, as opposed to applied, knowledge.

Adding to urgency of the debate over the PsyD as the degree for the professional practitioner is the multiplicity of present degrees that currently qualify for licensure, a multiplicity that is inevitably confusing to the public and fragmenting to the profession. The PhD, EdD, and PsyD are only three of the most common degrees held by professional psychologists. When the National Registry of Health Service Providers was initiated, 35 different degrees were submitted as professional credentials by psychologists, all of whom were licensed in one or more states (Wellner, 1978). Furthermore, academicians who have never seen patients have obtained licensure as psychological practitioners, and practitioners who have not set foot in a laboratory since they left their degree programs sometimes flaunt their PhDs in ways that irritate their academic colleagues. A standardized degree that is clearly identified with the practitioner field and that is rigorously controlled regarding the nature of qualifying training would at least tend to put in place the potential social instruments for training, identifying, and regulating professional practitioner psychology. Ultimately, both the public and the profession would benefit.

CONCLUSION

It seems almost self-evident to us that the continued growth and development of psychology as a profession will ultimately hinge on our ability to define outselves as a comprehensive discipline that is grounded in psychology but which also includes applied knowledge from other sciences that study human behavior and human coping skills. A profession should define itself in the broadest possible terms, casting as wide a net as possible. We have proposed that professional psychology concern itself with the enhancement of human coping behaviors.

In keeping with a comprehensively defined and broadly based profession, psychologists should be trained in large and complex teaching, research, and service systems administered by a school within a university setting. They should not be trained in small outpatient clinics maintained by academic departments. As a comprehensive profession with its own centers of excellence in practice and research, psychology should have a unique and singular degree as the appropriate credential for its practitioners.

Ours is scarcely a new dream. In the first article of the first volume of the *Journal of Consulting Psychology,* James McKeen Cattell (1937) affirmed that "There will not... be a profession of psychology until we have professional schools and professional standards." He then quoted excerpts from his address to the International Congress of Arts and Science in 1904:

> The present function of a physician, a lawyer, a clergyman, a teacher or a man of business is to a considerable extent that of an amateur psychologist. In the inevitable specialization of modern society, there will become increasing need of those who can be paid for expert psychological advice. We may have experts who will be trained in schools as large and well-equipped as our present schools of medicine, and their profession may become as useful and as honorable. Such a profession clearly offers an opportunity to the charlatan, but it is not the only profession open to him. For the present the psychological expert should doubtless be a member of one of the recognized professions who has the natural endowments, special training and definite knowledge of the conditions that will make his advice and assistance of value. But in the end, there will be not only a science but also a profession of psychology. (p. 3)

REFERENCES

American Psychological Association. Model for state legislation affecting the practice of psychology. *American Psychologist,* 1967, *22,* 1095–1103.

American Psychological Association. *Criteria for accreditation of doctoral training programs and internships in professional psychology.* Washington, D.C.: Author, 1979.

Cattell, J. McK. Retrospect: Psychology as a profession. *Journal of Consulting Psychology,* 1937, *1,* 1–3.

Dörken, H., & Rodgers, D. A. Issues facing professional psychologists. In H. Dörken et al. (Eds.), *The professional psychologist today.* San Francisco: Jossey-Bass, 1976.

Fox, R. E. On reasoning from predicates: The PhD is not a professional degree. *Professional Psychology,* 1980, *11,* 887–891.

Meehl, Paul. A scientific, scholarly, nonresearch doctorate for clinical practitioners: Arguments pro and con. In R. Holt (Ed.), *New horizons for psychotherapy.* New York: International Universities Press, 1971.

Perry, N., Jr. Why clinical psychology does not need alternative training models. *American Psychologist,* 1979, *34,* 603–611.

Peterson, D. R. Is psychology a profession? *American Psychologist,* 1976, *31,* 572–581. (a)

Peterson, D. R. Need for the doctor of psychology degree in professional psychology. *American Psychologist,* 1976, *31,* 792–798. (b)

Peterson, D. R., & Baron, A., Jr. Status of the University of Illinois Doctor of Psychology program, 1974. *Professional Psychology,* 1975, *6,* 88–95.

Rodgers, D. A. In favor of separation of academic and professional training. *American Psychologist,* 1964, *19,* 675–680.

Rodgers, D. A. The status of psychology in hospitals: Technicians or professionals. *The Clinical Psychologist,* 1980, *23,* 5–7.

Rodgers, D. A. A proposed model psychology licensing law. *Professional Practice of Psychology*, 1981, *2*, 47–71.

Shoben, E. J. The PhD is a professional degree. *Professional Psychology*, 1980, *11*, 880–886.

Stricker, G. On professional schools and professional degrees. *American Psychologist*, 1975, *30*, 1062–1066.

Watson, N., Caddy, G., Johnson, J., & Rimm, D. Standards in the education of professional psychologists: The resolutions of the conference at Virginia Beach. *American Psychologist*, 1981, *36*, 514–519.

Wellner, A. (Ed.). *Education and credentialing in psychology*. Washington, D.C.: American Psychological Association, 1978.

Reading 6

The Metamorphosis of Clinical Psychology:
Toward a New Charter as Human Services Psychology

Leon H. Levy
University of Maryland, Baltimore County

One expects professions to grow and change over time as new knowledge and changes in the social structure lead to new models of practice. The contrast between the content and practice of medicine in the Middle Ages and at present is an obvious illustration of this point. And since professions provide the matrix in which specializations develop, consequent changes may also be expected in the emergence of new specializations, in their content and practice, and in their relations to each other. Thus, it seems reasonable that a point may be reached at which a major realignment and reconceptualization of the specializations within a profession, if not of the profession itself, may be called for. Although this point may not have been reached for all professional psychology, I argue in this article that there is good reason to believe that it has been reached for clinical psychology—its largest specialty area—and for a number of related specialties. Because of its size and historic precedence, clinical psychology is the focus of this article; as will become apparent, however, many of the issues raised apply with equal force to other specialites as well.

Over a decade ago, Albee (1970) warned of the possible extinction of clinical psychology. Although unforeseen political and economic events radically altered some of the premises upon which he based his warning—for example, "the *impending shortage of academicians* in psychology that will lure clinical

I wish to thank Sandra M. Levy and Slobodan Petrovich for their helpful comments on a previous draft of this article.

Reprinted from American Psychologist, *39*(5), 486–494.

PhDs into teaching," thereby limiting "the number... available for clinical work" (p. 1080)—the warning itself may not have been so far short of the mark. The contents of clinical psychology training programs and the professional practices and concerns either engaged in or advocated in the name of clinical psychology (Albee, 1970; Fox, 1982; NIMH, 1979; Sarason, 1981)—for example, dealing with racism, delinquency, the prevention and management of general health problems, and primary prevention of mental illness—have become so diverse and extensive that the term *clinical psychology* may be losing its denominative value. As one observer recently put it, "the 'modern' clinical psychologist is everywhere and does everything!" (Des Lauriers, 1977, p. 169).

At the same time, many of the activities, such as treatment of depression, management of stress, and smoking control, that were once fully acepted as falling within the purview of clinical psychology are now either being shared with other specialties within psychology or with other professions or have entered the public domain. Thus, if clinical psychology is not in danger of extinction, its countours have become so blurred and its boundaries so permeable that, while the name remains, the coherence and distinctiveness that once inhered in that name have largely disappeared. After further considering the bases for this assertion, I offer several proposals concerning the opportunities I believe this circumstance affords us. These proposals center on the reconceptualization of clinical psychology as a professional specialty and on the organization of professional psychology training programs and their accreditation.

CLINICAL PSYCHOLOGY'S UNCERTAIN IDENTITY

The identity of a specialty rests upon a specifiable body of knowledge and a set of skills based upon that knowledge (APA, 1981). At perhaps the grossest level, signs of clinical psychology's uncertain identity may be found in the absence of any definition of its essential content and skills in either of the most recent criteria for the accreditation of professional psychology programs (APA, 1973; 1979) that would distinguish it from either counseling or school psychology. Instead, these criteria require programs to define their own models and goals of training and to be evaluated in terms of them. If one turns to these criteria to find out how the profession conceives of clinical psychology—what it believes every clinical psychologist should know, for example—one does not find much enlightenment. This stands in marked contrast to the pioneering report of the Committee on Training in Clinical Psychology, the Shakow Report (APA, 1947), which spelled out in some detail the kinds of knowledge and skills a clinical psychologist should possess. Although, from our present vantage point, one might take issue with the Committee on any number of its recommendations, its report provides a very clear idea of how clinical psychology was conceptualized in 1947. What has happened since then?

One answer may be that the nature of clinical psychology has become so diffuse that a consensus on substantive criteria for the evaluation of training programs would be impossible to achieve. We have, however, failed to confront this possibility because the more recent accreditation criteria were presented as "a single statement of accreditation criteria which would be broadly applicable" (APA, 1973, p. 11) to the three major specialty areas of professional psychology (clinical, counseling, and school psychology). An alternative, perhaps more positive, explanation is that clinical psychology is currently in a period of transition and that the framers of these recent criteria wisely recognized the dangers of foreclosing possibilities for growth and change posed by any more definitively stated criteria. In either case, of course, clinical psychology's identity remains uncertain. But in the latter case it may be seen as an opportunity to explore the "universe of alternatives" that Sarason (1981) suggests we failed to consider in the shaping of clinical psychology following World War II.

The problems encountered in attempts at formally defining clinical psychology provide further evidence of its uncertain identity. Korchin (1976) states that "Clinical psychology is most distinctly defined by the *clinical attitude,* that is, a concern with understanding and helping individuals in psychological distress," and he elaborates further in the same paragraph, "Clinical psychology is concerned with generating and utilizing knowledge about the structure and functioning of human personality. But in his most distinctive role, the clinican works within a *personological* framework" (p. 40). Although consistent with the view of it found in the Shakow Report (APA, 1947) this portrayal of clinical psychology places beyond the pale the substantial number of behaviorally oriented clinical psychology training programs and practicing clinical psychologists (Norcross & Prochaska, 1982) for whom the concept of personality (or personology) plays little or no part. The increasing number of training programs that are identifying themselves as *clinical-community* programs, many of which include courses on systems intervention, are also poorly served by Korchin's definition. And, finally, the definition fails to encompass the growing concern with primary prevention among clinical psychologists (Murphy & Frank, 1979), most often within a social psychological rather than a personological framework. Perhaps it is not surprising that another major text in clinical psychology (Sundberg, Tyler, & Taplin, 1973) contains no formal definition of it at all; in looking to clinical psychology's future, Sundberg et al. conceive of it as "increasingly a *pluralistic* profession [in which] individual psychologists rather than the professional group as a whole. . . make choices about how energies and resources are to be deployed" (p. 536). This view is in agreement with my own, except that I propose that there may be a point beyond which this pluralism may call into question the utility of the continued designation of the profession as clinical psychology.

It seems clear enough from these considerations that clinical psychology has changed in many ways over the last 25 years, and there is no reason to believe that this change will not continue. Thus, it is reasonable to consider whether the point may not have been reached where this change has given way to metamorphosis, where the ways in which we have thought about clinical psychology—with respect to both training and practice—may no longer be the most appropriate or serviceable. Before addressing this possibility, however, it will be helpful to examine some of the forces that have been contributing to this change. They may also suggest directions in which our thinking about clinical psychology's future might profitably turn.

FORCES OF CHANGE

These forces exist at a number of levels and have various sources. For expository purposes, I will distinguish between forces that are internal to clinical psychology and the profession at large and those that are external.

Internal Forces

The Decline of Orthodoxy While the dominant theoretical orientation in 1947, as reflected in the Shakow Report (APA, 1974), was a psychodynamic one, recent surveys of clinical psychologists (Norcross & Prochaska, 1982; Smith, 1982) show this orientation being edged out by eclecticism and being followed at varying distances by behavioral, cognitive-behavioral, person-centered or Rogerian, and systems orientations, each of which claims a substantial number of adherents. With respect to intervention, Goldfried (1980) notes the existence of over 130 different therapeutic approaches, Corsini (1981) lists almost 250, and CHAMPUS (Civilian Health and Medical Program of the Uniformed Services; APA, 1980) includes 43 treatment procedures on its approved list for reimbursement. Thus, orthodoxy has all but disappeared, providing fertile ground for changes of all kinds.

The Emergence of Functional Analytically Based Intervention One consequence of the growth in popularity of behavioral and cognitive perspectives in clinical psychology has been the view that psychological disorders and problems can be dealt with either through the functional analysis of behavior, along operant lines, or through their analysis in terms of a limited number of functional (frequently cognitive) components. A second consequence has been the view of competence assessment and competence building as key issues in the treatment and prevention of psychological disorders (Bloom 1979; Sundberg, Snowden, & Reynolds, 1978). These views have led to the development of training programs for assertiveness, fear reduction, stress management, parent effectiveness, and the acquisition of various social and coping skills, among others. Although originally conducted by professonals, many of these programs are now "packaged" in the form of workshops, are usually not regarded as therapy by participants, and are most frequently not administered by professionals.

Although their effectiveness has not been adequately assessed, these programs have become enormously popular, and they are likely to have a profound effect on how the public views the services of professional psychotherapists as well as many of the problems heretofore thought to require their attention. In particular, it seems probable that these approaches will reduce the range of problems seen by the public as requiring a professional psychotherapist and that this, in turn, will erode the central position that psychotherapy currently occupies in the clinical psychologist's identity, making room for a variety of additional proficiencies and activities.

The Growth of Community Psychology The fact that community psychology was founded largely by clinical psychologists (Anderson, Cooper, Hassol, Klein, Rosenblum, & Bennet, 1966) and that they continue to make up a substantial proportion of the membership of the Division of Community Psychology suggests that many of the values, concerns, and concepts that form the core of community psychology are also shared by a substantial number of clinical psychologists. Moreover, it seems reasonable to assume that those clinical psychologists who have affiliated with community psychology have done so because they saw it as complementing and broadening their knowledge and skills as clinicians. To the extent that this is true, we may expect community psychology to be a major force in shaping the future of clinical psychology.

The Development of New Fields of Psychology The relatively recent establishment of such APA divisions as Rehabilitation Psychology, Health Psychology, and Clinical Neuropsychology reflects the growth of new knowledge and skills in areas once regarded as falling at least in part within the province of clinical psychology. These developments are likely to have several effects on clinical psychology. To the extent that they are accepted as representing new professional specialties (APA, 1981), they can be expected to constrict the province of clinical psychology. As specialties, they may also be expected to compete with clinical psychology for students, for educational and training resources, and for clients. It may also be expected, however, that some clinical psychologists and clinical psychology programs will attempt—in fact, a number have—to assimilate these specialties, treating them as special proficiencies within clinical psychology. Since none of these specialties is concerned with mental health as a primary problem, to the extent that this role is taken, it will require a rethinking of the nature of clinical psychology, especially in relation to other professional specialties.

External Forces

Sociopolitical Forces These are complex and difficult to characterize in any brief and simple way, and I will discuss only two. The first, which might be called *neopopulism,* is characterized by an erosion of respect for authority and tradition, combined with elements of distrust of science and technology. Neopopulism received its major impetus during the 1960s. To it, I would credit the growth in popularity of peer counseling, self-help groups, and alternative forms of mental and general health care. It has also contributed to the view of psychotherapy as a political instrument of indoctrination and maintenance of the status quo (e.g., Halleck, 1971; Hurvitz, 1973). I believe that this force could also be shown to have contributed to the new ethic of accountability and to demands for greater participation by patients in their own treatment. More generally, it has led to a secularization of mental health care: Mental health problems are no longer seen as the exclusive proprietary concern of mental health professionals, nor is their solution believed to depend only on the arcane knowledge possessed by these professionals.

The growth in political power of ethnic and racial minority groups, the poor, and the elderly, calling for equity and redress, represents the second force. It is being manifested in almost every segment of our society. In the area of mental health, its impact may be seen most immediately in those recommendations of the President's Commission on Mental Health (1978) concerning training of minority mental health professionals and the needs of underserved populations and in a proposal currently under consideration in California that psychologists applying for licensure must have taken a certain number of course hours in minority mental health. Combined with the growing influence of minority psychologists within the APA, this force has contributed to the growing recognition of the contribution of social conditions such as discrimination and poverty to psychological distress and to a consequent realization of the limitations of psychotherapy in dealing with this distress. More generally, this force has led to an increasing awareness that if clinical psychologists are to be maximally effective (not only with minority groups), they must develop a better understanding of the impact of cultural variables and the social structure on behavior (Bernal & Padilla, 1982) and also learn how to join their efforts with those of other human services professionals on a fully collaborative basis.

Federal Support The role of federal funding in the development of clinical psychology after World War II has been so well detailed (Miller, 1946; Sarason, 1981) that it only remains to be acknowledged that its influence is continuing to shape clinical psychology, despite recent declines in its level and availability. Most recently, this influence may be seen in the changes that occurred in clinical training programs in response to the 1979 guidelines for applications for clinical psychology training grants issued by the National Institute of Mental Health

(NIMH, 1979). These guidelines stated that support would be provided only for programs that addressed one or more NIMH-listed priorities, which included preparing psychologists "to provide mental health services for the unserved or underserved," "developing strategies for primary prevention," and "preparing psychologists to work more effectively in the general health care field" (pp. 2-4). To address these priorities, training programs have begun to include new bodies of knowledge and new skills not traditionally associated with clinical psychology. Although federal funding for clinical training is currently in jeopardy, much of the conceptual and structural apparatus it has helped erect seems likely to remain.

Federal support for services and research has also been contributing in clinical psychology. To the extent that clinical psychology is responsive to such recent service mandates as deinstitutionalization, substance abuse treatment, crisis intervention, consultation and education, and program evaluation, it must necessarily redraw its borders to include bodies of knowledge and skills not previously thought to reside within them. The recent emergence of behavioral medicine and health psychology as a new focus for research, practice, and training within psychology provides eloquent testimony to the influence of the availability of research funding as well as to the substantive importance of the area itself (Hamburg, Elliott, & Parron, 1982; Matarazzo, 1980). A recent survey of clinical psychology programs (Nelson, 1982) found that of the 25 programs reporting a change in their priorities, the largest number (7) reported an increased emphasis in general health psychology.[1] Other, informal observations suggest that this shift is likely to continue. To the extent that it does, it will mean that increasing numbers of clinical psychologists will be acquiring knowledge in such new (for them) areas as cardiology, endocrinology, immunology, nutrition, and oncology, and their concerns will be extending well beyond the field of mental health.

Because clinical psychology has always been regarded as a mental health specialty, and because of the emphasis that has always been placed upon differentiating it from other psychological specialties, we have failed to either explore or exploit the various dimensions of continuity between it and other specialties. While this failure may have been an understandable consequence of clinical psychology's youth and its search for identity, the potential benefits to be realized by remedying this failure argue strongly that we now move on to integration. This is not to say that distinctions between specialties should not be drawn. Rather, by recognizing the generic similarities between specialties as well as their differences, we may be able to develop a coherent framework within which psychologists can approach problems of research, service, and professional training in a more comprehensive, integrated, and cost-efficient fashion than heretofore.

[1] This change may also have been fostered by the 1979 NIMH training grant application guidelines noted above.

What is called for is a new charter for clinical psychology—one that reflects the transformation that has been taking place in it and one that also provides a conceptual framework in which to locate it in relation to other psychological specialty areas. As a means of initiating this undertaking, I present several proposals. They are phrased in the imperative mood only to enhance their stimulus value; I am fully aware of the heroic nature of these changes and do not presume to offer more than points of departure for the broad-ranging consideration of clinical psychology's future that I believe is called for.

TOWARD A NEW CHARTER FOR CLINICAL PSYCHOLOGY

Given the vast broadening in the range of perspectives, problems, bodies of knowledge, skills, and activities now found in clinical psychology, one is tempted to ask whether it is still clinical psychology. Such a question might be particularly salient to community psychologists, health psychologists, counseling psychologists, and others whose specialties' boundaries with clinical psychology are particularly fuzzy. But the question itself accords too much reality to labels and betrays a tendency toward categorical thinking where it should be functional or dimensional. From an evolutionary perspective, this blurring of boundaries may be seen as the natural consequence of advances in knowledge and understanding in the areas of health and human behavior; they reveal the continuity that exists between clinical psychology and these other professional areas. Thus, I offer the following proposals:

1. *Within professional psychology, a sector identified as human services psychology should be defined so as to include all professional psychology specialties concerned with the promotion of human well-being through the acquisition and application of psychological knowledge concerned with the treatment and prevention of psychological and physical disorders.* Human services psychology would thus include clinical psychology, school psychology, counseling psychology, community psychology, health psychology, and any other psychological specialties to which this definition might apply. At the same time, it would distinguish these specialties from such other professional specialties as consumer psychology, engineering psychology, and industrial and organizational psychology, which generally provide corporate services, thereby providing a rationale for the resolution of a number of the education and credentialing issues (Fox, Barclay, & Rodgers, 1982; Wellner, 1978) involving these various specialties.

Reflecting efforts in recent years to improve the coordination of community health and social welfare services, and conceived of in systems theoretical terms (Baker, 1974; Schulberg, 1972; Thomas & Garrison, 1975), the concept of human services has been used to emphasize the generic nature of the problems addressed by these services and their means of dealing with them. The concept can serve a similar function in psychology. Identifying clinical psychology as a human services psychology specialty would free it from its previously exclusive identification with mental health—itself a troublesome concept—and would also acknowledge the communality of its interests and activities with those of other human services psychology specialties, some of which, such as community psychology, extend beyond health services in their activities. More generally, the concept of human services psychology, when fully elaborated, may go a long way toward combating the overspecialization and fragmentation that have afflicted psychology in recent years (Bevan, 1982; Sanford, 1982).

2. *Research, training, and practice in human services psychology should be based upon a biopsychosocial model of human behavior* (Korchin, 1976; Sundberg et al., 1973). A similar view with respect to medicine was proposed by Engel (1977) and appears to be gaining acceptance (Rosen, Kleinman, & Katon, 1982). Based, in part, upon such a model, it is possible to define in a more functionally precise way the various human services psychology specialties and their interrelations in terms of their relative emphases upon particular bodies of knowledge and sets of skills. These can be represented by the cells of a three-dimensional matrix that I will refer to as the *human services psychology matrix* (see Figure 1).

In barest detail, one dimension of the matrix represents different bio-psychosocial levels of intervention or systems perspectives, of which three are identified—biopsychological, psychobehavioral, and community-social. The second dimension represents modes of intervention or service delivery, which I believe may be adequately characterized as either direct program development and evaluation, or consultation and education. The particular form that these modes take would, of course, vary with the level of intervention involved.

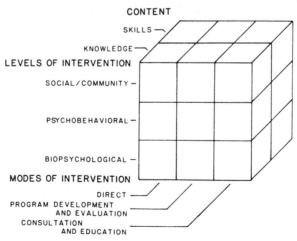

Figure 1 The Human Services Psychology Matrix

The content of human services psychology is represented by the third dimension in which a distinction is drawn between knowledge and skills. For the sake of simplicity, I am including paradigms such as clinical versus public health perspective and the various conceptions of personality under knowledge. Paralleling this distinction, this dimension can also serve to distinguish between science and practice and between education and training. It is possible, of course, that some of the cells of this matrix may be empty. It is also more than likely that other, or finer, distinctions could be drawn with respect to its first two dimensions (Sundberg et al., 1973; Taplin, 1980). Certainly, additional dimensions, such as populations served, could also be added. But since the matrix is intended as a heuristic to aid in our search for a better way of conceptualizing clinical psychology, especially in relation to other specialties, I expect that with use it will undergo modification. Its value is in the structure it provides for our thinking about problems of education and training and practice and the inventory of knowledge and skills upon which they draw.

3. *The identification and development of separate training programs for each defined specialty should be abandoned in favor of generic professional (or scientist/professional) programs, identified as human services psychology training programs, which are distinguished from each other in terms of their particular patterns of focus within the human services psychology matrix and the specialties for which these patterns provide training.* This would have two immediate consequences, both of which I believe would be salutary: It would direct our attention to questions of precisely what kind of training is necessary for the practice of each specialty, and it would allow any single program to offer training in more than one specialty if it had the resources to do so.

The current practice of nominal isomorphism, in which new specialty-defined programs are established to parallel the identification of each new specialty, fails to recognize (and exploit) the generic core of knowledge and skills upon which each of these specialties draws. Instead, it focuses on the differences between specialties and fosters marginal differentiation between programs in which increasingly scarce resources are being wasted through the elaboration of specialty curricula that may be only minimally different from each other. The human services psychology matrix may be expected to counteract this: In making salient the communality in the skills and knowledge required by various specialties, it should lead to increased cost-effectiveness as many programs become aware that with little additional effort and resources they can provide training for more than one specialty, and it may also suggest new patterns of emphasis in training, ones that might draw upon the unique combination of resources available to particular programs. Additionally, because the human services psychology matrix highlights the systems character of the problems with which professional psychology is concerned, it should also foster greater versatility by practitioners in dealing with them: They should become aware of the full range of levels and modes of intervention that might be brought to bear upon these problems, possibly in collaboration with other professionals. Finally nominal isomorphism has obscured the wide diversity that exists among programs within the same nominal specialty; the human services psychology matrix provides a means by which these programs can be more accurately—and functionally—described.

4. *Accreditation at the doctoral level should be functionally rather than categorically based and program-wide rather than specialty-specific.* Rather than the current practice of limiting eligibility for accreditation to programs that identify themselves as either clinical, counseling, or school psychology programs, all programs that provide training within the human services psychology framework should be eligible for accreditation. Whether programs identify themselves as human services psychology programs or by more traditional designations is less important. Rather, the important point is that programs should be required to identify the specialties for which they provide training and those cells within the human services psychology matrix upon which they focus, and they should be evaluated in terms of how well they accomplish their goals. Correspondingly, listings of approved programs should indicate their training foci as well as the specialty training they offer. In this way, accreditation would be open to a wider array of programs, and more precise information would be provided about the bases upon which these programs were evaluated.

Although this and the preceding proposal represent a radical departure from current trends in professional psychology, they are consistent with recent suggestions that have been made, both in and out of psychology, for changes in the accreditation process (Brodie & Heaney, 1978; Fox et al., 1982). Concerned about the costs entailed by the proliferation of program accreditation in the health professions and the failure of single-program accreditation to evaluate the interprofessional components of education in these professions, Brodie and Heaney (1978) proposed a model for multiple program accrediting by multiprofessional teams. They see such a change as consistent with education in the health professions historically "passing from the era of a categorical approach to one that... will be broadly multi- and interprofessional in nature" and with health care practice following a parallel path in becoming "first and foremost patient-oriented, comprehensive in nature, and derived from a conceptual base of shared responsibilities for patient care, where and when indicated" (Brodie & Heaney, 1978, p. 592). From a somewhat different perspective, Fox et al. (1982) question the wisdom of APA's practice of accrediting separate specialty-defined programs and propose instead accreditation of the broader psychology programs in which these programs are housed.

Clearly, psychology has a responsibility to insure sound specialty training. But whether this is best accomplished through separate specialty accreditation is considerably less clear, at least given the current diversity and overlap in training among programs in the traditionally defined specialties of clinical, counseling, and school psychology. In fact, a close reading of the draft criteria for the recognition of specialties in psychology (APA, 1981) suggests that programs in any one of these traditional specialties could provide training in several more narrowly defined specialties. If anything, the foregoing proposals could aid in identifying those specialties for which any given human services psychology program was capable of providing training. Thus, they hold the promise of contributing to both integration and differentiation in the growth of professional psychology.

AFTERWORD

The ideas presented in this article are the distillation of close to three years of effort that went into the development of a newly established PhD program at the University of Maryland Baltimore County (UMBC) in what we have chosen to call, perhaps not surprisingly, *human services psychology*. Included in this effort were analyses of existing professional psychology programs, analyses of the roles and functions of professional psychologists in a variety of work settings, reviews of the literature concerned with professional issues and emerging trends in service delivery (Kiesler, 1980; Matarazzo, 1980; Miller, Mazade, Muller, & Andrulis, 1978), and an inventory of the resources—instructional, clinical, and scientific—that could be drawn upon by any program that we might develop. Also taken into consideration were the political climate in Maryland vis-à-vis higher education and the particular mental health needs of the Baltimore metropolitan area. Centered in our own department, but including selected courses in a graduate policy sciences program on our campus and in several departments in our medical school and social work school, the resulting UMBC human services psychology program allows students to prepare for a number of different specializations, ranging from behavioral medicine, through clinical psychology, to community psychology and mental health policy development and administration. Although components of this program may be found in one or more existing clinical psychology programs, we believe that the program is unique in its attempt to integrate all of these components, conceptually as well as programmatically, and in the range of options it provides students in preparing for their professional careers.

The most common concerns expressed by those who reviewed the proposal for this program or to whom it was described were with its name and with what graduates of the program would call themselves. Another question occasionally asked concerned how graduates of human services psychology programs would differ from those coming out of current (conventionally identified) professional programs. These concerns have undoubtedly occurred to many who have read this article as well. I will therefore address each of them briefly.

In every case where concerns were expressed over our use of *human services* it was in terms of the problems prospective students would have in knowing what the program entailed and whether this would affect the program's eligibility for accreditation. I have attempted to address both of these issues in the body of this article. There may, however, be one additional cause for concern about the use of the term in the minds of some clinical psychologists. Although it might be granted that *human services* is the most appropriate term to encompass all of the activities in which contemporary clinical (as well as community, counseling, and school) psychologists are engaged, because of its common use in referring to social work and welfare services, it may be feared that its use could jeopardize clinical psychogy's status as a health care profession and the eligibility of its practitioners for third-party payments. While it is impossible to say that such fears are groundless, given clinical psychology's experiences in this arena and the current political climate, it can be asserted that any attack on its eligibility that was based on clinical psychology being identified as a human services profession can easily be shown to be without logical foundation: The provision of health care—general, as well as mental—is a fundamental human service; the fact that the treatment of psychological disorders may be only one of a number of human services clinical psychologists are trained to provide makes it no less a health care activity.

The question of what graduates of a human services psychology program would call themselves illustrates the nominal isomorphism that has characterized our thinking about the realtionship between the names of specialties and training programs discussed earlier. We have traditionally called graduates of clinical psychology programs "clinical psychologists," graduates of school psychology programs "school psychologists," and so on. We can understand how this developed historically. But, in fact, it is possible today to find graduates of school psychology programs who are identified as clinical psychologists, and vice versa, and more than a few graduates of counseling psychology programs who are identified as clinical psychologists—some even receiving American Board of Professional Psychology diplomas in clinical psychology. There is no necessary tie between the title of programs and the professional/occupational titles of their graduates. Moreover, uncoupling professional/occupational titles from training program titles, generally, would have the salutary effect of placing greater emphasis on specifying and assessing competencies in the definition and use of both program names and professional/occupational titles. Thus, the answer to the question is that graduates of a human services psychology program would be called by whatever professional/occupational titles for which their training qualifies them.

Finally, although the focus of this article has been on training, it is reasonable to ask whether human services psychology graduates will be more effective in addressing the problems confronting professional psychology than will graduates of conventional professional psychology programs. This is, obviously, an empirical question, but there are several reasons to believe that the answer will be in the affirmative. By virtue of the structure of the program's curriculum and its guiding systems orientation, we should expect its graduates to be more aware of the linkages and continuities between the different specializations in professional psychology and the particular targets of their concern. This should lead to practitioners who are at once more comprehensive in their view of the problems with which they are dealing and more versatile in their approaches to them. Additionally, because of the intrinsically multidisciplinary nature of the human services concept, we should also expect human services psychology graduates to find it easier to develop working relationships with allied human services disciplines. Whether human services psychology graduates will be better able to confront racism, sexism, delinquency, the effects of poverty, and other social ills may be less certain. This will depend, in part, on where in the human services psychology matrix their training was focused. But they should be more ready to recognize the role that these social ills play in human health and psychological well-being; they should be less prone to the "psychocentrism" that has characterized much of professional psychology's thought and practice up to the present. I have no doubt that these expectations also serve as the goals of many current professional psychology programs. My contention is, however, that the approach outlined in this article is a more effective and cost-efficient way of achieving them.

REFERENCES

Albee, G. W. (1970). The uncertain future of clinical psychology. *American Psychologist, 25,* 1071–1080.

American Psychological Association. (1947). Recommended gradaute training program in clinical psychology. *American Psychologist, 2,* 539–558.

American Psychological Association. (1973). *Accreditation: Procedures and criteria.* Washington, DC: Author.

American Psychological Association. (1979). *Criteria for accreditation of doctoral training programs in professional psychology.* Washington, DC: Author.

American Psychological Association. (1980). *APA/CHAMPUS out-patient psychological provider manual.* Washington, DC: Author.

American Psychological Association. Subcommittee on Specialty Criteria. (1981, December). *Manual for the identification and continued recognition of specialties in psychology* (Draft). Washington, DC: Author.

Anderson, l. S., Cooper, S., Hassol, L., Klein, D. C., Rosenblum, G., & Bennett, C. C. (1966). *Community psychology: A report of the Boston conference on the education of psychologists for community mental health.* Boston: Boston University and the South Shore Mental Health Center.

Baker, F. (1974). From community mental health to human service ideology. *American Journal of Public Health, 64,* 576–581.

Bernal, M. F., & Padilla, A. M. (1982). Status of minority curricula and training in clinical psychology. *American Psychologist,* 780–787.

Bevan, W. (1982). A sermon of sorts in three plus parts. *American Psychologist, 37,* 1303–1322.

Bloom, B. L. (1979). Prevention of mental disorders: Recent advances in theory and practice. *Community Mental Health Journal, 15,* 179–191.

Brodie, D. C., & Heaney, R. P. (1978). Need for reform in health professions accrediting. *Science, 201,* 589–593.

Corsini, R. J. (Ed.). (1981). *Handbook of innovative psychotherapies.* New York: Wiley.

Des Lauriers, A. M. (1977). The greatness and misery of clinical psychology. [Review of *modern clinical psychology: Principles of intervention in the clinic and community*]. *Contemporary Psychology, 22,* 169–170.

Engel, G. L. (1977). The need for a new medical model: A challenge for biomedicine. *Science, 196,* 129–136.

Fox, R. E. (1982). The need for a reorientation of clinical psychology. *American Psychologist, 37,* 1051–1057.

Fox, R. E., Barclay, A. G., & Rodgers, D. A. (1982). The foundations of professional psychology. *American Psychologist, 37,* 306–312.

Goldfried, M. R. (1980). Toward the delineation of therapeutic change principles. *American Psychologist, 35,* 991–999.

Halleck, S. L. (1971). *The politics of therapy.* New York: Science House.

Hamburg, D. A., Elliott, G. R., & Parron, D. L. (Eds.). (1982). *Health and behavior: Frontiers of research in the biobehavioral sciences.* Washington, DC: National Academy Press.

Hurvitz, N. (1973). Psychotherapy as a means of social control. *Journal of Consulting and Clinical Psychology,* 232–249.

Kiesler, C. A. (1980). Mental health policy as a field of inquiry for psychology. *American Psychologist, 35,* 1066–1080.

Korchin, S. J. (1976). *Modern clinical psychology: Principles of intervention in the clinic and community.* New York: Basic Books.

Matarazzo, J. D. (1980). Behavioral health and behavioral medicine: Frontiers for a new health psychology. *American Psychologist, 35,* 807–817.

Miller, J. G. (1946). Clinical psychology in the Veterans Administration. *American Psychologist, 1,* 181–189.

Miller, F. T., Mazade, N. A., Muller, S., & Andrulis, D. (1978). Trends in community mental health programming. *American Journal of Community Psychology, 6,* 191–198.

Murphy, L. B., & Frank, C. (1979). Prevention: The clinical psychologist. *Annual Review of Psychology, 30,* 173–207.

National Institute of Mental Health, Division of Manpower and Training Programs, Psychology Education Branch. (1979, July). *Guidelines: Clinical/services program.* Rockville, MD: Author.

Nelson, R. (1982). *Council of University Directors of Clinical Psychology: Summary of second annual questionnaire.* Unpublished manuscript.

Norcross, J. C., & Prochaska, J. O. (1982). A national survey of clinical psychologists: Affiliations and orientation. *The Clinical Psychologist, 35,* 1–6.

President's Commission on Mental Health. (1978). *Report to the President from the President's Commission on Mental Health.* Washington, DC: U.S. Government Printing Office.

Rosen, G., Kleinman, A., & Katon, W. (1982). Somatization in family practice: A biopsychosocial approach. *The Journal of Family Practice, 14,* 493–502.

Sanford, N. (1982). Social psychology: Its place in personology. *American Psychologist, 36,* 827–836.

Sarason, S. B. (1981). An asocial psychology and a misdirected clinical psychology. *American Psychologist, 36,* 827–836.

Schulberg, H. C. (1972). Challenge of human service programs for psychologists. *American Psychologist, 27,* 566–573.

Smith, D. (1982). Trends in counseling and psychotherapy. *American Psychologist, 37,* 802–809.

Sundberg, N. D., Snowden, L. R., & Reynolds, W. M. (1978). Toward assessment of personal competence and incompetence in life situations. *Annual Review of Psychology, 29,* 179–221.

Sundberg, N. D., Tyler, L. E., & Taplin, J. R. (1973). *Clinical psychology: Expanding horizons* (2nd ed.). New York: Appleton-Century-Crofts.

Taplin, J. R. (1980). Implications of general systems theory for assessment and intervention. *Professional Psychology, 11,* 722–727.

Thomas. C. D., & Garrison, V. (1975). A general systems view of community mental health. In L. Bellak & H. H. Barten (Eds.), *Progress in community mental health* (Vol. 3). New York: Bruner/Mazel.

Wellner, A. (Ed.). (1978). *Education and credentialing in psychology.* Washington, DC: American Psychological Association.

Chapter 3

Selection

Over 1,700 graduate students in professional psychology find internships in 400 internship settings in the United States and Canada every year (See APIC Directory for listing). There are no cost estimates available for this procedure which is governed by the policies adopted by the membership of the American Association of Psychology Internship Center (APIC, 1983) and the ethics of the American Psychological Association. The procedure occupies considerable time for graduate students, faculty, and internship centers staff for several months starting in the fall and lasting until February, when on the second Monday of the month and the following one-half day internship offers are tendered and accepted/rejected.

In the following section, the question of what internship centers look for in applicants is addressed in the articles by Sturgis, Verstegen, Randolph, and Garvin (1980); Drummond, Rodolfa, and Smith (1981); Petzel and Berndt (1980); and Tedesco (1979). In a survey of 167 listed programs (43% response rate), Sturgis and colleagues found that internships received anywhere from a handful to 300 applicants. Furthermore, the study reported that the specialty label of the student's program (e.g., clinical) and its approved status increased the probability of receiving an offer. These internship director respondents indicated that clinical skills, including previous relevant experience and perceived quality and quantity of practica, were of primary importance in the selection criteria. Academic credentials were of secondary importance, followed by recommendations, including status of writer and content of letter. Compatibility of student-setting goals, personality characteristics, and approval status of program were also important. Deficiencies in preparation were noted, especially assessment skills and diagnosis of psycho-pathology.

Petzel and Berndt (1980) examined the relative importance of academic and clinical preparation by survey of approved internship programs (75% return rate). Selection committees look for 1000 plus hours of total experience although APA criteria require a minimum of only 400 hours. Moreover, the mean number of expected courses in psychodiagnostics or treatment is approximately 3 in each area. Letters of recommendation, supervised therapy, and diagnostic experience were the most important academic criteria while publications, grade-point averages, and prestige of institutions were the least important.

To punctuate this assertion, the reader needs to look at the Drummond et al. study (1981). The response rate in this sample was 86%, approximately proportionate between approved and nonapproved programs, and closer to the Sturgis sample in representativeness but almost 50 percent greater in number of responses. The Drummond study also reported internships favoring applicants from APA-approved programs, including the provision of higher average stipends for such students. The central importance of letters of recommendation, particularly in APA-approved programs was corroborated. Practicum experience was also found to be highly valued by both approved and nonapproved internships but significantly more so in approved programs. Clinical course work, structured assessment knowledge, and personal and professional goals also ranked high as criteria. APA-approved internship programs were reported to devote significantly more time to supervision and seminars.

The other side of the coin is what prospective interns look for in an internship. Tedesco (1979) surveyed 99 APA-approved internships program directors as well as 170 intern applicants. The students averaged 13 plus applications while the internships received twice that number for every available position. The students desired a standard application deadline. The interns ranked approval status, geographical location, emphasis on adult clinical work, theoretical orientation of faculty, multi-disciplinary setting, mixture of adult, child, and community experiences, and reputation as the seven most important (of 22) factors for choosing to apply to a given internship. The largest number of applicants went to programs in urban centers—New York, Chicago, Los Angeles. The number of applications correlated significantly with number of internship positions, adult-child-community emphasis in the program, faculty research expectations, and supervisory staff. Internship responses—training program characteristics when matched with students' needs—suggest that the desired program is APA-approved, large, emphasizes adult-clinical work, has a variety of experiences available, and is housed in a multidisciplinary setting. Pleasant surroundings and compatible theoretical orientation of the staff make a program ideal for a prospective intern.

Most of the above findings are replicated in a recent study by Burstein, Schoenfeld, Loucks, Stedman, and Costello (1981). Following up 26 "highly desirable" applicants in one program who had chosen other internships, these authors found that interns ranked geography, diversity of program, theoretical orientation, type of facility, reputation, faculty, amount of supervision (and seven other important factors) with decreasing saliency.

Three articles address the process of application and offer different approaches for minimizing the stress and anxiety of this experience. Belar and Orgel (1980) provide a step-by-step cookbook for the graduate student applicant thus contributing to uniformity in the process, perhaps second only to the APIC guidelines. It is noteworthy that this article emphasized ethical aspects of the process. Site visits to a prospective internship setting are quite common, even required at some sites. These visits often clarify for both, intern applicant and program, their mutual suitability.

Hersh and Poey (1984) provide information concerning questions an internship director might ask during a site visit interview and information which the intern applicant should ask (or not ask) internship program personnel. However, it is doubtful whether the staff interviewer could cover all these proposed areas of inquiry. How one graduate program (Georgia State University) has developed a strategy of application for internship that enabled 17 of 20 students to obtain their first choice of internship is spelled out in an article by Georgia State Students—Brill, Wolkin, and McKeel (1983). Their strategy of juxtaposing personal goals and available settings is consistent with Belar and Orgel's suggestions, but provides a flavor of their graduate program as well.

Reading 7

Professional Psychology Internships

Daniel K. Sturgis
Northern Nebraska Mental Health Center, Norfolk, Nebraska

J. Penelope Verstegen
University of Southern Mississippi and Lakeshore Mental Health Institute,
Knoxville, Tennessee

Daniel L. Randolph and Royce B. Garvin
University of Southern Mississippi

In recent years, the employment market for psychologists has changed from chiefly educational settings to primarily mental health delivery agencies (Albee, 1977; Bankiotes, 1978; Woods, 1976) and health care (Asken, 1979; Lubin et al., 1979). This trend has underscored the importance of psychologists obtaining certain skills, competencies, and other credentials requisite to employment in such settings. Further since licensure and supervised internship training experience have become necessary for the psychologist to be included in the National Register of Health Service Providers and consequently to collect third-party payments, the importance of trainees obtaining a predoctoral internship in a recognized community agency appears to have increased.

A series of professional conferences, including the Boulder conference, 1949 (Raimy, 1950), the Greystone conference, 1964 (Thompson & Super, 1964), the Chicago conference, 1965 (Hoch, Ross, & Winder, 1966), and the Vail conference, 1973 (Korman, 1973), have affirmed the importance of the internship experience as an integral part of doctoral training for the psychologist, but there have been only limited attempts to review the availability and nature of internships. Those questions that were unanswered in the literature and became the basis for the study's organization were as follows: From the published list of professional psychology internships, which agencies will accept psychology interns of which academic background? and What skills and competencies are most critical for doctoral students who wish to be accepted for internship training?

METHOD

A one-page questionnaire was designed to elicit demographic information pertaining to the agency as well as information related to the research questions under investigation. Questionnaires were sent to directors of internship training programs that were listed in three sources: *APA-Approved Predoctoral Internships for Doctoral Training in Clinical and Counseling Psychology: 1977* (APA,

Reprinted from Professional Psychology, *11*(4), 567–573.

1977); the *Directory of Internship Programs in Clinical Psychology*[1] (Orgel, 1976); and *Community-oriented Internships and Field Placement Opportunities* (APA, Division 27, Note 1). Only predoctoral internshps located in the United States were inlcuded in the population to be studied. A total of 388 question-naires was sent.

RESULTS

Of the 202 questionnaires returned to the investigators, 35 were only partially complete, leaving 167, or 43 percent of the original population, as the final sample. In addition, a number of agencies returned letters indicating that they either no longer provided internship training or provided only a clerk-ship training experience for master's degree candidates. No follow-up was attempted.

Sample Characteristics

Of the 167 usable questionnaires, 75 were received from APA-approved and 92 were from non-APA-approved internship training programs. APA-approved internships were most frequently located in medical centers and other facilities directly affiliated with universities (64%) or in community mental health centers (31%). Nonapproved internships were most frequently located in community mental health centers (47%) or in medical centers and other university-affiliated facilities (27%). The average number of doctoral level staff at APA-approved settings was 15 $(SD = 10.8)$, and the number at nonapproved settings was 9 $(SD = 10.4)$.

The approved internship settings also had a larger number of interns $(M = 6.3, SD = 3.5)$ compared to the nonapproved ones $(M = 3.5, SD = 3.2)$. Furthermore, the approved centers reported a larger number of applicants $(M = 100.2, SD = 57.1)$ compared to nonapproved centers $(M = 37.9, SD = 37.9)$. Consequently, it is estimated that approved internships accepted 6 percent of all applicants, whereas the nonapproved centers accepted 9 percent of all applicants.

Types of Applicants Considered

One item in the questionnaire sought to determine whether the internship center would accept interns from either APA-approved or nonapproved doctoral training programs in each of the following specialties: clinical, counseling and school psychology, or other. The data clearly indicated that the most desired academic background for interns was an APA-approved program in clinical

[1] The title of this publication has since been changed to *Directory of Internship Programs in Professional Psychology.*

psychology, with virtually all directors (99%) indicating they would consider accepting such applicants. Nonapproved clinical and APA-approved counseling applicants were each indicated acceptable to 67% of the internship directors. Less than half of the respondents (40% for both APA and non-APA centers) indicated a willingness to consider accepting students from nonapproved counseling psychology training programs. Even applications from APA-approved school psychology training programs were considered only in about 20% of the centers. Finally, directors of APA-approved and nonapproved internships did not appear to differ greatly with respect to their willingness to accept interns from a given type of doctoral training program.

Background of Applicants Accepted

Respondents were also asked to indicate the actual number of interns from each specialty program approval status currently on the intern staff. Whereas 96 percent of the APA-approved internships reported having at least one clinical intern from an APA-approved academic program, only 23% reported having a counseling intern from an approved program. Similarly, 35 percent of the nonapproved centers reported accepting nonapproved clinical interns as compared to only 15 percent that accepted a nonapproved counseling intern.

Several differences appeared between approved and nonapproved internship programs. Only about two thirds (71.7%) of the nonapproved internship programs had APA-approved clinical interns, whereas practically all the approved centers had at least one such intern. Also, approved internship programs were more inclined to accept counseling psychology interns who were from APA-approved programs than those from nonapproved programs (23% vs. 15%), whereas nonapproved internship settings were equally likely to have counseling psychology interns from approved and nonapproved training programs (18% vs. 16%).

Intern Selection Criteria

The respondents were asked to list, in order of importance, criteria used in selection of interns. Responses were grouped or clustered into 28 categories, based on agreement of the authors. Arbitrary weights were assigned to the criteria as follows: A criterion ranked first was assigned a weight of three, one ranked second was assigned a two, and one ranked third was assigned a one.

For both approved and nonapproved internships, the most frequently mentioned cluster of criteria for selection of interns was clinical skills, including responses related to previous clinical experience and perceived quality and quantity of practical training in the doctoral program. The second-ranked cluster of responses was academic credentials, including responses related to type of course work, grades, and so forth. The third-ranked cluster was recommendations, including status of the writers of letters of reference as well as the contents of such letters. Other clusters of responses that also ranked high were compatibility of student goals with those of the agency, personality factors, and APA approval of doctoral training program.

Academic Training Deficiencies

Since internship training directors had the unique opportunity to observe a number of interns from diverse training backgrounds, the investigators were interested in the directors' perceptions of any deficiencies seen in the academic training of the interns. This information could be valuable both to academic departments in planning curriculum changes and to individuals having to make applications to internship training centers.

A total of 264 deficiencies were listed. These deficiencies were grouped into 15 response clusters by the investigators. The two clusters that were most often indicated were those dealing with assessment/testing skills, including projective testing (mentioned 74 times), and with diagnosis of psychopathology (mentioned 64 times). The third-ranked cluster, lack of general clinical experience, was mentioned 24 times by directors of approved internship programs, whereas those of nonapproved programs listed it only 6 times. A total of 22 responses reflected the concern of directors for a lack of openness to different ideas and alternative theoretical views on the part of interns. Apparently, directors perceived that some interns learned a single theoretical point of view and were unwilling to consider others. Other deficiencies that were listed less than 10 times were interview skills (9), psychotherapy skills (9), report writing (6), family therapy (4), ethics (4), community experience (3), consultation (2), vocational counseling (3), and psychopharmacology (2).

DISCUSSION

The survey of agencies offering internship training revealed the attitudes of intern directors toward those whom they select as interns, those whom they are willing to consider, the selection process, and the deficits of the interns. These publicized internships apparently are not equally available to all students seeking training. Although the estimated 11,000 applications for the 845 internship positions may give a distorted picture of the actual difficulty in obtaining an internship due to multiple student applications and so forth, clearly, some internships are more difficult to obtain than others, and students with certain backgrounds in training have an advantage. For example, the nonapproved internship programs received on the average only 38% of the number of applications received by the approved programs. Some prestigious training centers reported up to 300 applications; others received only a handful. Considerable variability existed across programs, as evidenced by the large standard deviations reported for numbers of applications. This unequal distribution of applicants suggests that psychology has a rather inefficient system of matching applicants with training centers. Perhaps centers should more precisely and openly state their biases regarding whom they will consider and what specialized training experiences they offer. Furthermore, academic departments should identify training centers where their students are likely to be accepted; this practice could reduce the number of applications that are currently unsuccessful.

The fact that fewer counseling psychology students were accepted for internship training programs than clinical psychology students (672 to 111) may have several possible explanations. First, apparently many internship training program directors are only willing to accept clinical students, whereas others may favor clinical over counseling students in a hierarchical preference order. In addition, fewer students in counseling psychology may have applied for internship training to the centers included in the survey, preferring instead to complete internship requirements in internal or "captive" programs associated with their academic programs. Possibly these students obtain on-campus experiences in such areas as counselor education and supervision and college student personnel services. Although such captive internships may have sufficed when a large majority of counseling psychologists found employment within these settings, they may not provide optimum training for the increasing percentage of counseling psychologists seeking employment in community agencies.

In the same manner, the low receptivity accorded school psychology trainees may relate to the perception that these psychologists are trained for a specific setting (schools) and would therefore have limited interests and skills applicable to a community mental health setting. The comparatively low number of school psychology training programs, particularly those that are APA-approved, would also seem to limit the experience of intern directors with such doctoral students and consequently their willingness to consider them.

The top ranking of clinical skills in the hierarchy of criteria used by internship programs in selecting students concurs with the finding of a previous investigation of community mental health center directors' preferences of doctoral level employee skills (Randolph, 1978). This finding may be viewed as providing support for the inclusion of an off-campus practicum or clinic experience as part of preinternship doctoral training or the requirement of post-master's work experience prior to admission in the doctoral training program.

The rank of the clusters of assessment/testing skills and psychodiagnosis as the most important deficiencies of interns seems to support the need to require courses in these areas as part of the doctoral programs for those students anticipating employment in a community agency. The emphasis on projectives was expected, as this has been found in other surveys (Piotrowski & Keller,

1978; Wade & Baker, 1977). That the directors saw the lack of good assessment skills in general as a serious deficit could have been predicted because of the lower importance currently given to traditional assessment devices in academia (Thelan, Varble, & Johnson, 1968) and the continued debate over their theoretical and practical value (Hogan, DeSoto, & Solano, 1977; Mischel, 1977). Practicing clinicians, such as those providing internship training, are probably less concerned with the research characteristics of assessment devices than academic psychologists and are more concerned with their perceived utility in the study of an individual client (Holt, 1971; Karon, 1978). Consequently, the perception that there are many deficiencies in assessment training may reflect differing emphases between academic departments and internship training settings.

Several additional factors may have influenced the results of the survey. First, less than half of the original population returned completed questionnaires. There was a proportionally greater return from APA-approved programs, although APA approval did not appear to produce much of a difference in response patterns to the questions asked. The similarity of findings to those of earlier studies of APA internships (Lane & Janoka, 1976; Matthews, Matthews, & Maxwell, 1976) seems to indicate that at least this segment of the sample was representative. Further, there is no way of knowing how many doctoral students of a given academic background actually applied to these agencies; thus the rate at which they were accepted cannot be determined. Finally, data regarding the academic backgrounds of the internship training directors were not collected. If those providing internship training are more likely to accept students from backgrounds and training similar to their own, the lack of internship settings in the sample that are traditionally staffed by counseling or school psychologists may account for the relatively low receptivity afforded those professional specialties.

The results of the survey indicate that the specialty label of a training program and its approval status are of considerable importance in determining the likelihood of a student obtaining a professional psychology internship. This seems particularly true if the trainee's program is not APA approved. Since the internship is a transitional experience leading from academia to employment as a professional psychologist, our findings may indicate poor employment possibilities in community agencies for specialties other than clinical psychology. Academic programs that purport to train psychologists for community agencies should make students aware of the possible pitfalls that they may face due to the academic label of their program or its approval status. The study also provides implications for important course work needed by the psychology trainee seeking an internship.

Although the current study provides information about the preferences of internship directors, there is a need for a more extensive questionnaire that might reveal the basis for and flexibility of these attitudes. There is also a need to look at the professional psychology internship from points of view other than that of the internship directors. The views both of psychology trainees in the various specialties and of the directors of academic programs could provide a more comprehensive picture.

REFERENCE NOTE

1 American Psychological Association, Division 27. *Community-oriented internships and field placement opportunities.* Unpublished manuscript, 1976.

REFERENCES

Albee, G. W. The uncertain future of the MA clinical psychologist. *Professional Psychology*, 1977, *8*, 122–124.

American Psychological Association. APA-approved predoctoral internships for doctoral training in clinical and counseling psychology: 1977. *American Psychologist*, 1977, *32*, 1089–1091.

Asken, M. J. Medical Psychology: Toward definition, clarification, and organization. *Professional Psychology*, 1979, *10*, 66–73.

Banikiotes, P. G. The training of counseling psychologists. *Counseling Psychologist*, 1978, *7*, 23–26.

Hoch, E. L., Ross, A. O., & Winder, C. L. (Eds.). *Professional preparation of clinical psychologists.* Washington, D.C.: American Psychological Association, 1966.

Hogan, R., DeSoto, C. B., & Solano, C. Traits, tests, and personality research. *American Psychologist*, 1977, *32*, 255–264.

Holt, R. R. *Assessing personality.* New York: Harcourt Brace Jovanovich, 1971.

Karon, B. P. Projective tests are valid. *American Psychologist*, 1978, *33*, 764–765.

Korman, M. (Ed.). *Levels and patterns of professsional training in psychology.* Washington, D.C.: American Psychological Association, 1973.

Lane, J., & Janoka, C. APA internships available to non-APA counseling applicants. *Counseling Psychologist*, 1976, *6*, 69–70.

Lubin, B., et al. A symposium on psychologists in schools of medicine in 1977. *Professional Psychology*, 1979, *10*, 94–117.

Matthews, J. R., Matthews, L. H., & Maxwell, W. A. A survey of APA-approved internship facilities. *Professional Psychology*, 1976, *7*, 209–213.

Mischel, W. On the future of personality measurement. *American Psychologist*, 1977, *32*, 246–254.

Orgel, S. A., (Ed.). *Directory of internship programs in clinical psychology* (5th ed.). Syracuse, N.Y.: Association of Psychology Internship Centers, 1976.

Piotrowski, C., & Keller, J. W. Psychological test usage in southeastern outpatient mental health facilities in 1975. *Professional Psychology*, 1978, *9*, 63–67.

Raimy, V. C. *Training in clinical psychology.* New York: Prentice-Hall, 1950.

Randolph, D. L. The counseling-community psychologists in the CMHC: Employer perceptions. *Counselor Education and Supervision,* 1978, *17,* 244–253.

Thelan, M. H., Varble, D. L., & Johnson, J. Attitudes of academic clinical psychologists toward projective techniques. *American Psychologist,* 1968, *23,* 517–521.

Thompson, A. S., & Super, D. E. (Eds.). *The professional preparation of counseling psychologists: Report of the 1964 Greystone Conference.* New York: Columbia University, Teachers College, Bureau of Publications, 1964.

Wade, T. C., & Baker, T. B. Opinions and use of psychological tests: A survey of clinical psychologists. *American Psychologist,* 1977, *32,* 974–882.

Woods, P. J. *Career opportunities for psychologists.* Washington, D.C.: American Psychological Association, 1976.

Reading 8

APA Internship Selection Criteria: Relative Importance of Academic and Clinical Preparation

Thomas P. Petzel
Loyola University of Chicago

David J. Berndt
Loyola University of Chicago and Michael Reese Hospital's
Psychiatric and Psychosomatic Institute

By revising the accreditation criteria for doctoral training in clinical psychology, the American Psychological Association (APA; 1979) recognizes that the practitioner model endorsed by the 1973 Vail Conference (Korman, 1973) and scientist-professional model endorsed by the 1949 Boulder Conference (Raimy, 1950) are both acceptable training models. These criteria reaffirm both APA's commitment to training in comprehensive psychological science and requirement that curricula include research methodology, statistics, and history and systems. The criteria also require students to demonstrate competence in each of the following areas: biological, cognitive-affective, and social bases of behavior and individual behavior. Whether or not a program grants a PhD or a PsyD degree, programs in clinical psychology are still expected to provide a broad and thorough training in the domain of the science of psychology.

In contrast to this reaffirmation of the importance of training in basic psychological science, internship training centers have become increasingly dissatisfied with the preparation interns receive in doctoral programs (Dana,

Reprinted from Professional Psychology, *11*(5), 792–796.

Gilliam, & Dana, 1976; Lovitt, 1974; Shemberg & Keeley, 1974). These surveys point not only to a pervasively low evaluation of quality of preparation of intern applicants but single out training in basic skills as a particular weakness.

As internship placements in clinical psychology become increasingly competitive each year, doctoral programs are confronted with the dilemma between the ideal and criteria of the scientist-professional model and the practical demands of providing their students with more practical experience to keep them competitive for quality internship placements. For example, Spitzform and Hamilton (1976) found that clinical practica were given sub- stantially more weight by internship admissions committees than were research, publications, and academic work. However, this survey did not provide data on the kinds and amount of clinical experience internships look for in selecting applicants.

The present study surveyed directors of training in APA-approved internship placements to assess the importance of various criteria to internship selection committees and to determine how much clinical experience is desired to make an applicant competitive. This survey also assessed the number of courses and amount of hours of supervised experience in both diagnostics and treatment that internships look for in their preferred applicants.

METHOD

To evaluate the adequacy of the questionnaire, a questionnaire with a cover letter was mailed as a pilot study to 20 training centers that did not have APA approval. Following feedback from these institutions, the questionnaire with a cover letter was mailed to the directors of training of the 120 APA-approved internships listed in *Directory: Internship Programs in Professional Psychology* (Orgel, 1977). There was a response rate of 55 percent on the first mailing, which was sufficient to warrant a follow-up mailing. The result was a final response rate of 75 percent, or 90 of the 120 internships.

The questionnaire was brief to ensure a high return rate. The one-page questionnaire consisted of the following items: (a) Please rank order the follow- ing nine criteria for their relative importance in your program's intern selection process (personal interview, graduate grade-point average, supervised therapy experience, supervised diagnostic experience, letters of recommendation, prestige of academic institution, personal statement of biography, professional publications and presentations, and academic course work). Give the most important criterion a rank of 1 and the least important a rank of 9. Try to avoid ties, if possible. (b) How many courses in treatment or psychotherapy do you expect your top applicants to have taken? (c) How many courses in psycho- diagnostics should a competitive applicant have? (d) How many hours (in hundreds) of practical clerkship or externship experience in *treatment* do you prefer? (e) How many hours of practical *diagnostic experience* do you look for?

(f) Suggest three courses that you would particularly like to see on an applicant's transcript.

The cover letter and the questionnaire contained words like *top* and *competitive* applicant so as to avoid responses indicating minimum requirements. The survey was looking for the criteria internships use for the interns they actually select.

RESULTS

Not every respondent answered each question in quantifiable manner, so the *n*'s vary somewhat. Respondents were asked to rank order nine criteria for their relative importance in choosing interns. These criteria and their mean rankings are given in Table 1. Similar to the findings of Spitzform and Hamilton (1976), letters of recommendation are the most important data used by internship selection committees. Because of the importance of letters of recommendation demonstrated by two surveys using different methods several years apart, it would be informative in future research to study letters of recommendation in detail. It appears imperative that doctoral program directors of clinical training put a great deal of emphasis and care into writing letters when their students apply for internships. Information about the characteristics and contents of letters of recommendation that are useful to internship selection committees would be helpful to the academic directors of training and would enhance communication between academic departments and internship selection committees.

Inspection of Table 1 also reveals that clinical training experiences and personal data on applicants are considered more important by selection committees than academic and scientific accomplishments. This result confirms that the preference of clinical over academic preparation, as found in the data of Spitzform and Hamilton (1976), is a continuing trend.

Table 1   Mean Ranks of Criteria Used in Intern Selection

Criteria	M	SD	Rank
Letters of recommendation	3.01	2.06	1
Supervised therapy experience	3.25	1.71	2
Supervised diagnostic experience	3.97	2.07	3
Personal interview	4.41	2.89	4
Personal statement of biography	5.21	2.35	5
Academic course work	5.82	4.67	6
Prestige of academic institution	6.26	2.18	7
Graduate grade-point average	7.02	6.88	8
Professional publications and presentations	7.95	8.25	9

Note. $N = 90$.

Table 2   Course Work and Supervised Experience of Competitive Applicants

Course work and supervised experience	M	SD	n
Courses in treatment	3.07	1.59	79
Courses in psychodiagnostics	2.75	1.08	80
Hours of experience in treatment	666.68	461.63	74
Hours of diagnostic experience	420.80	335.40	63

Note. *n*s vary because some responses were not codable.

Table 2 contains data on responses to questions about the amount of course work and supervised experience that internships want in competitive applicants. The accreditation criteria (APA, 1979) require a minimum of 400 hours of practicum experience; yet selection committees look for over 1,000 hours of total experience, according to these results.

This emphasis on the clinical over the academic preparation is further supported by the responses to the question asking which three courses internships would particularly like to see on an applicant's transcript. The most commonly suggested courses were those in which some form of psychodiagnostic assessment was mentioned—the total number being 77. Therapy courses were also stressed—68 in all. Ten courses each were suggested for both behavior modification and for psychoanalytic or egoanalytic theory. Ten suggested courses dealt with either the assessment or treatment of childhood psychopathology, whereas seven preferences for developmental courses were indicated. Parenthetically, only one of the internships stressed life-span developmental psychology. Abnormal psychology or psychopathology (29) and personality theory (12) were two clinically relevant academic courses often suggested by the internships. A small assortment of other categories also was reported. Neurological or physiological psychology was emphasized in nine suggestions, whereas three internships indicated a preference for applicants to have course work in psychopharmachology. Community psychology was mentioned five times, ethics and professional issues were noted four times, and consultation twice. Research methodology, design, or statistics was included by only seven internships, whereas four programs specified psychotherapy research course work, and two listed program evaluation.

Internship centers seem to be asking academic programs to "beef up" training in diagnosis and treatment; yet the profession as a whole, as expressed in the APA-accreditation criteria, endorses quality training in both science and practice. The problem for academic programs is to achieve this goal within the constraints of graduate training. Apparently, many academic programs may have to increase skills training to keep their students competitive for quality internships.

Nevertheless, we feel it is equally important for clinical psychology to maintain its professional identity by teaching a broad understanding of the scientific domain unique to our profession. Clinical psychology doctoral programs must strive to provide both adequate clinical preparation and a corpus of knowledge that will separate clinical psychology from other clinically oriented disciplines.

REFERENCES

American Psychological Association. Accreditation criteria. *APA Monitor,* 1979, *10,* 14–17.

Dana, R. H., Gilliam, M., & Dana, J. M. Adequacy of academic-clinical preparation for internships. *Professional Psychology,* 1976, *7,*112–116.

Korman, M. (Ed.). *Levels and patterns of professional training in psychology* (Vail Conference). Washington, D.C.: American Psychological Association, 1973.

Lovitt, R. Deficits in skill development of clinical psychologists. *Professional Psychology,* 1974, *5,* 415–420.

Orgel, S. A. (Ed.). *Directory: Internship programs in professional psychology.* San Antonio, Tex.: Association of Psychology Internship Centers, 1977.

Raimy, V. C. (Ed.). *Training in clinical psychology* (Boulder Conference). New York: Prentice-Hall, 1950.

Shemberg, K., & Keeley, S. Internship training: Training practices and satisfactions with preinternship preparation. *Professional Psychology,* 1974, *5,* 98–105.

Spitzform, M., & Hamilton, S. A survey of directors from APA-approved internship programs on intern selection. *Professional Psychology,* 1976, *7,* 406–410.

Reading 9

A Survey of APA- and Non-APA-Approved Internship Programs

Fred E. Drummond, Emil Rodolfa, and Darrell Smith
Texas A & M University

The application procedure for students seeking internships and the selection process undertaken by directors of professional psychology internship programs are both difficult, demanding tasks for the respective parties. The entire process

Reprinted from American Psychologist, *36*(4), 411–414. This article was supported in part by funds from the Mini-Grant Program of the Office of University Research at Texas A & M University.

of internship placement has been described as a tense and anxiety-producing experience (Spitzform & Hamilton, 1976; Suran, Crivolio, & Kupst, 1977).

The availability of versus the demand for internships appears to be largely responsible for the difficulties experienced in this application and selection procedure. Clearly, there exists a widening gap between supply and demand with respect to professional psychology internship programs. Tuma and Cerny (1976) determined from a survey of professional psychology graduate programs and predoctoral clinical internship settings that over a five-year period (1971-1972 through 1975-1976), more graduates were seeking internships than there were sites available for them. They predicted a 14% nonplacement rate for 1978-1979.

Another factor which further adds to the arduousness of the selection process is that many equally qualified applicants seek the same internship. Suran et al. (1977) developed an objective rating scale to assess intern selection. The rating scale was composed of five factors: previous clinical experience, academic record, scholarly productivity, letters of recommendation, and "intangibles." All factors except the letters of recommendation were rated on a 0-5 scale. Each of the candidate's three letters was rated on a 1-3 scale. The authors concluded that other internship programs would do well to adopt a similar procedure "for eliminating much of the confusion and guesswork that is involved in candidate evaluations" (p. 595).

Spitzform and Hamilton (1976) surveyed 116 APA-approved internship programs to obtain information on the criteria surrounding intern selection. They noted that their intent was to provide data that would allow intern selection committees to compare their procedures with those of others and that would aid graduates in the application process. The present survey was conducted to update and expand on the study done by Spitzform and Hamilton.

METHOD

Instrument

A one-page questionnaire including 18 possible selection criteria was developed, with space for the directors to list and weight any other criteria that they were currently using. The directors were asked to indicate whether each criterion was used or not and, if used, to weight the importance of the criterion on a scale ranging from 1 (little importance) to 10 (very important). Some of the selection criteria were obtained from Spitzform and Hamilton (1976), and others were developed by the present authors. The questionnaire also asked the directors to indicate the percentage of time the intern devoted to numerous duties, including psychological assessment, research, psychotherapy, intake, and supervision. Additional questions concerned the total number of internship positions available, including funded positions, comparison of salaries for interns from APA- versus non-APA-approved doctoral programs, and APA membership of the selection committee.

Procedure

The questionnaire with return postage was mailed to the directors of 294 APA- and non-APA-approved internship sites, 132 and 162, respectively, in clinical and counseling psychology. The addresses of the sites were obtained from either the *Directory: Internship Programs in Professional Psychology* (Orgel, 1978) or the Association of Psychology Internship Centers clearinghouse. Approximately one month later, a follow-up letter and duplicate questionnaire with return postage were mailed to those programs from which no response had been received.

RESULTS

Questionnaires were returned by 114 (86%) of the APA-approved internship programs and 133 (82%) of the non-APA-approved programs, for a total response rate of 84 percent. Of the 114 APA-approved internship programs responding to the questionnaire, 79 (69%) indicated that they would accept interns from non-APA-approved programs.

A multivariate analysis indicated that a significant difference existed between the approved and the nonapproved internship locations, $F(38, 208)$ $= 4.015$, $p < .0001$. Separate univariate F tests revealed significant differences between the two groups (APA and non-APA) on 13 of the 38 variables under consideration.

The means and standard deviations of selected descriptive characteristics of APA- and non-APA-approved internship settings are presented in Table 1. The APA-approved internship sites offered significantly more internships annually than did the non-APA-approved sites, $F(1, 245) = 45.61, p < .0001$, as well as more funded internship positions, $F(1, 245) = 39.34$, $p < .0001$. Interns from APA-approved institutions received a higher salary at APA-approved internship sites than at non-APA-approved sites, $F(1, 245) = 6.78$, $p < .01$. Interns from APA-approved institutions also received a higher salary than interns from non-APA-approved institutions working at the same APA-approved internship site, $t(113) = 7.36$, $p < .001$, as well as at the same non-APA-approved site, $t(131) = 2.30$, $p < .05$. APA-approved internship programs included a significantly larger number of APA members on their selection committees than did non-APA-approved programs, $F(1, 245) = 35.62$, $p < .0001$.

The means and standard deviations of the weights assigned to the 18 selection criteria by both the APA and the non-APA internship programs are displayed in Table 2. There were significant differences between the two groups

Table 1 Descriptive Characteristics of APA- and Non-APA-Approved Internship Sites

Descriptive characteristic	Internship sites			
	APA		Non-APA	
	M	SD	M	SD
No. internships offered annually	6.69**	3.65	3.72	3.26
No. funded internship positions	5.99**	3.47	3.29	3.30
Mean salary for APA interns	7180.97*	2667.36	5748.01	5330.92
Mean salary for non-APA interns	3775.29	4156.34	4376.83	4298.50
No. APA members comprising internship selection committee	7.32**	5.79	3.99	2.61
No. males on internship selection committee	4.55**	3.65	2.78	2.02
No. females on internship selection committee	2.35**	2.79	1.11	1.31

*p < .01.
**p < .001.

Table 2 Weighting of Selection Criteria by APA- and Non-APA-Approved
Internship Programs

	Internship sites			
	APA		Non-APA	
Selection criterion	M	SD	M	SD
Graduate grade point average	2.96	2.99	3.01	3.12
Graduate Record Exam scores	.28	1.14	.41	1.38
Letters of recommendation	8.25***	2.14	6.79	3.22
Departmental support	6.38*	3.78	5.22	3.99
Publications and presentations	4.23**	2.76	3.15	2.64
Practicum experience	8.04*	1.98	7.28	3.39
Prior work experience	6.47	2.21	6.28	2.99
Personal interview	6.28	4.00	6.07	4.45
APA-approved course work	6.42	2.90	5.53	6.12
Dissertation completed	1.55	2.49	1.42	2.54
Counseling course work	3.26	3.66	4.61**	4.02
Clinical course work	6.91	2.86	6.31	3.45
Completed course work	4.36	3.72	5.50	7.65
Structured assessment knowledge	6.62	2.79	6.79	7.22
Projective assessment knowledge	6.02	3.16	5.55	7.49
Personal and professional goals	7.10	2.49	6.75	7.07
Professional memberships	1.30	2.23	1.39	2.12
Theoretical orientation	3.70	3.29	3.23	3.31

*$p < .05$.
**$p < .01$.
***$p < .001$.

on 5 of the 18 selection criteria. The following criteria were weighted as more important by the APA-approved internship sites than by the non-APA-approved sites: letters of recommendation, $F(1, 245) = 17.10$, $p < .001$; departmental support for application, $F(1, 245) = 5.43$, $p < .05$; publications and presentations, $F(1, 245) = 9.81$, $p < .01$; and practicum experience, $F(1, 245) = 4.39$, $p < .05$. Only one of the selection criteria was weighted as more important by the non-APA-approved internship programs than by the APA-approved programs, namely, course work in a counseling training program, $F(1, 245) = 7.48$, $p < .01$. Ninety-four percent of the total sample reported that there was general agreement among committtee members as to the weighting of the selection criteria.

Table 3 presents the means and standard deviations of the percentages of time devoted by an intern to several work-related areas. It should be noted that this table does not include the results of an "other" category which was made available to directors to indicate any additional areas of work not covered by the survey. This deletion accounts for the differences in the total mean percentage-of-time estimates for the APA and non-APA groups. There were significant differences between the APA-approved and non-APA-approved internship sites on only 2 of the 11 work areas. The APA-approved programs noted that their interns devoted a higher pecentage of their time to seminar attendance, $F(1, 245) = 29.79$, $p < .001$, and to supervision, $F(1, 245) = 6.60$, $p < .05$, than did the interns at non-APA-approved sites.

Table 3   Percentages of Time Devoted to Various Areas of Work by Interns at APA and Non-APA Internship Sites

Area of work	APA		Non-APA	
	M	SD	M	SD
Psychological assessment	12.64	8.69	13.31	10.55
Group psychotherapy	8.82	7.36	8.46	6.52
Individual psychotherapy	22.88	10.88	23.41	14.59
Research	4.76	5.99	4.95	7.98
Seminar attendance	11.50**	5.85	7.45	5.78
Consultation	6.67	5.69	5.47	5.73
Intake	4.53	5.01	4.20	5.45
Case disposition	3.04	4.17	3.32	3.78
Team functions	6.53	10.23	6.22	6.05
Administration	2.04	3.38	1.78	2.69
Supervision	10.53*	7.52	8.20	6.74

*$p < .05$.
**$p < .0001$.

DISCUSSION

Not surprisingly, the results indicate that interns from APA-approved graduate programs have the advantage over non-APA interns in the internship marketplace. In fact, of the 133 non-APA-approved internship programs responding to the questionnaire, 12 noted that they did not consider interns from non-APA graduate programs, and 39 others stated that although they would accept non-APA interns, they provided no funding for them.

The three most important selection criteria (in descending order of weight) for the APA-approved sites are letters of recommendation, practicum experience, and personal and professional goals. The three most important selection criteria (in descending order of weight) for the non-APA-approved internship sites are practicum experience, letters of recommendation and knowledge of structured assessment procedures (those two criteria were equally weighted), and personal and professional goals. The least important of the selection criteria for both groups is Graduate Record Examination scores. APA-approved sites place significantly more emphasis on departmental support for application and publications and/or presentations than do non-APA-approved sites, although neither of these criteria ranked any higher than eighth among the 18 for either group. Non-APA-approved internship programs did weight course work in a counseling training program as significantly more important than did APA-approved programs, but both groups appeared to weight course work in a clinical training program as more important than course work in a counseling training program.

APA-approved internships provide a significantly larger number of internship positions annually, larger number of funded internship positions, and higher salary for APA interns than do non-APA-approved internships. APA interns are funded at higher rates than are non-APA interns at both APA- and non-APA-approved internship sites. In terms of salary, non-APA interns appear to fare better at non-APA-approved sites than at APA-approved locations, although the differences are not significant.

APA-approved internship sites tend to allot significantly more time to the intern for seminar attendance and supervision than do non-APA-approved sites. These differences would appear to favor the former in terms of quality of training experiences. However, it should be pointed out that the findings displayed in Table 3 are of a quantitative nature and do not lend themselves well to comparisons concerning quality of training experiences available to APA- and non-APA-approved sites. Furthermore, it is not suggested that these are the only differences existing between the two groups concerning intern training experiences. Therefore, it is necessary to exercise caution in interpreting these results.

CONCLUSION

Students from APA-approved training programs, as compared with those from non-APA-approved programs, certainly are in a more advantageous and competitive position regarding the limited number of internships available, number of funded internships, average salary, and internship training experiences. The recently approved *Criteria for Accreditation of Doctoral Training Programs and Internships in Professional Psychology* (APA Council of Representatives, 1979) establish this fact in clear terms: "Efforts should be made to select students from APA-approved doctoral programs in the relevant area of professional psychology" (p. 21).

However, the situation for students from non-APA-approved programs appears to be less grim than suggested approximately five years ago (Lane & Janoka, 1976). The results of the present study and informal contact with numerous currently active interns indicate that APA-approved internship opportunities do exist for students from non-APA-approved training programs.

Finally, the findings of this study and the new criteria for accreditation indicate that the odds are distinctly against students from non-APA programs. We believe nevertheless that well-trained students from nonapproved programs may be realistically encouraged to apply and compete for APA internships. Enough positive evidence exists to make the application process a worthwhile risk for these students.

REFERENCES

APA Council of Representatives. *Criteria for accreditation of doctoral training programs and internships in professional psychology.* Washington, D.C.: American Psychological Association, 1979.

Lane, J., & Janoka, C. APA internships available to non-APA counseling applicants. *Counseling Psychologist,* 1976, *6*(3), 69–70.

Orgel, S. A. (Ed.). *Directory: Internship programs in professional psychology* (7th ed.). Syracuse, N.Y.: Association for Psychology Internship Centers, 1978.

Spitzform, M., & Hamilton, S. A survey of directors from APA-approved internship programs on intern selection. *Professional Psychology,* 1976, *7,* 406–410.

Suran, B. G., Crivolio, A. J., & Kupst, M. J. A rating scale for the selection of internship applicants. *Journal of Clinical Psychology,* 1977, *33,* 591–596.

Tuma, J. M., & Cerny, J. A. The internship marketplace: The new depression? *American Psychologist,* 1976, *31,* 664–670.

Reading 10

Factors Involved in the Selection of Doctoral Internships in Clinical Psychology

John F. Tedesco
Des Moines Child Guidance Center, Iowa

The purposes of the present study are to provide a starting point for exploration and clarification of the process of applying for an internship in clinical psychogy and to assist the profession in making better matches between trainees' needs and available training opportunities. Very little information is available either on the factors that influence a potential intern's decision to apply to a particular training facility or on the outcome of those application procedures. Each year doctoral students apply and are accepted or rejected for numerous internship positions. The number of students who require an internship varies from year to year as does the number of available, approved positions. Most students do not know the probability of their being accepted or rejected at a given training site because of the paucity of information available on the number of applications received each year. Should a student spend a good deal of time, energy, and money in applying to many places—the "shotgun" approach? What are the chances of being selected at a particular training facility? How many internship positions are not filled by American Psychological Association (APA)-approved students each year? How many students from APA-approved programs are unable to find an internship at an APA-approved training facility? In sum, very little is known about a very important aspect of training in clinical psychology.

PROCEDURE

A letter was sent to the coordinator of clinical training at each of the 100 fully approved APA doctoral programs in clinical psychology (APA, 1976b). The letter asked each training coordinator to randomly distribute a second letter and a rating scale to three students currently applying to internship training facilities for the 1977–1978 training year. The letter to the students asked them to rate the enclosed list of 22 factors as to how important they were in the student's decision to apply for an internship at a particular institution. The students were requested to return this material prior to the second Monday in February. The material was originally mailed on January 20, 1977, and stamped, self-addressed envelopes were provided for return of the material.

Reprinted from *Professional Psychology,* December, 1979, 852-858. The author wishes to thank Robert and Carole Strahan for their assistance in data analysis.

The factors were derived by discussion over the previous 3 years with local interns, practicum students, and graduate students. It was assumed that the factor "Brochure description of program" would include such variables as diagnostic versus therapy emphasis, seminar offerings, and other program variables.

Approximately 2 weeks after the second Monday in February, a letter and a questionnaire were sent to each of the internship training directors at the 119 fully approved APA internship training facilities for doctoral training in clinical and counseling psychology (APA, 1976a). The letter instructed the internship directors to answer 18 brief corresponding questions regarding the nature of their internship and asked for the number and type of applications received. The purpose was to learn if students actually did what they reported. That is, did they apply to training programs that ranked high on important factors. A second purpose was to learn something in general about how student needs matched available training opportunities. Again, a stamped, self-addressed envelope was provided for return of the material.

RESULTS

Student Responses

The percentage of return on the student questionnaires was unobtainable because the exact number of potential interns at each institution was unknown. Several clinical training coordinators replied that there were no students applying for the 1977-1978 training year. Conversely, several programs had many more than three students applying.

Table 1 shows the rank order of importance of factors rated by internship applicants. The rating scale consisted of the numbers 1 through 7, with 1 labeled "not at all important" and 7 labeled "very important." The midpoint was labeled "of moderate importance."

Trainer Responses

Of the 119 fully approved internship training sites contacted, 99 returned the trainer questionnaire for a return rate of 83.19 percent. In the final calculations the two training sites that indicated they were for Armed Services personnel were excluded. In addition to the 19 questions on the trainer questionnaire, an additional variable was created by calculating the percentage of women/minority available for internship supervision. Table 2 shows the means and standard deviations for the six questions requiring numerical answers.

Table 3 summarizes the responses to questions answered yes or no by trainers. Question 17 was excluded, since it was concerned with whether or not respondents wished to have results of the study returned to them. Question 11, also excluded, dealt with the internship application deadline; of 93 responses

Table 1 Rank Order of Importance of Factors

Factor	N	M	SD
APA approval	170	5.58	1.65
Geographic location	169	5.54	1.57
Emphasis on adult-clinical work	170	5.41	1.56
Theoretical orientation of faculty	170	5.31	1.46
Multidisciplinary setting	169	5.31	1.52
Mixture of child, adult, and community emphasis	170	5.13	1.75
Reputation	170	4.95	1.39
Stipend	170	4.83	1.61
Brochure description of program	169	4.72	1.54
Faculty credentials	169	4.18	1.47
Community psychology emphasis	170	4.00	1.76
University affiliation	168	3.86	1.82
Emphasis on research among faculty	170	3.28	1.72
Personal interview required	166	3.13	2.01
Emphasis on child-clinical work	169	3.08	1.91
Personal contacts at training facility	169	3.05	1.97
Ease of application procedure	169	2.99	1.62
Previous graduate school/training facility relationships	168	2.92	1.83
Dissertation research time	170	2.62	1.65
Number of women/minority groups among faculty	170	2.50	1.78
Distance from graduate school	169	2.19	1.68
Application deadline	170	1.98	1.47

received, the months from November through March were mentioned. The numbers of facilities having deadlines in those months were 2, 9, 67, 14, and 1, respectively.

To examine geographic location, ranked second in importance by the students, the United States and Canada were grouped into regions based on listings in *The World Book Encyclopedia.* The Middle Atlantic region, which has twice as many internship as academic programs, contains three institutions that received 24 (-1 SD) or fewer applications. The Pacific Coast region, with

Table 2 Means, Standard Deviations, and Variance of Trainer Responses

Question	Variable	N	M	SD	Student ranking
1	Number of applicants	98	77.25	53.33	—
2	Number of positions	98	5.67	2.60	—
7	Stipends	96	$6,472.88	$2,593.84	4.83
18	Number of staff	99	16.05	11.90	—
19	Number of women/minority	98	4.98	4.21	2.50
20	Percent of women/minority	98	36.76	38.81	—

Table 3 Summary of Trainer Responses to Yes/No Questions

Question	Variable	N	% yes	Student ranking
3	Emphasis on child-clinical work	99	47.47	3.08
4	University affiliation	98	44.89	3.86
5	Dissertation research time	99	56.56	2.62
6	Ease of application procedure	96	63.54	2.99
8	Emphasis on adult-clinical work	99	63.63	5.41
9	Multidisciplinary setting	99	97.97	5.31
10	Community psychology emphasis	99	38.38	4.00
12	Required interview	98	22.44	3.13
13	Multiple emphases	99	44.44	5.13
14	Specific theoretical orientation	98	23.46	5.31
15	Staff research emphasis	97	42.26	3.28
16	Descriptive brochure mailings	99	58.58	4.72

more than twice the number of internship as academic programs, contains four programs that received 130 (+1 SD) or more applications. The remainder of the regions were relatively well balanced. As might be expected, except for one training site located in New England, those programs that received 183 (+2 SD) applications were located in or near the nation's largest cities—New York, Chicago, and Los Angeles.

The number of applications received correlated positively with the number of internship positions ($r = .28$, $P < .006$); adult, child, and community emphases ($r = .23$, $p < .02$); faculty research expectations ($r = .39$, $p < .0002$); and number of supervisory staff ($r = .41$, $p < .0001$). The same item correlated negatively with the emphasis on child-clinical psychology ($r = -.26$, $p < .01$).

DISCUSSION

The data from the student questionnaire do not indicate in which direction an item is important, so the discussion will formulate hypotheses regarding directionality. In some cases further research may be needed to learn more about directionality. From the students' point of view, the ideal internship would be APA-approved, located in pleasant surroundings, emphasize adult-clinical work, contain a wide variety of training experiences in a multidisciplinary setting, and have a compatible theoretical orientation. The emphasis on a broad, balanced program suggests students were interested in avoiding specialization early in their careers. It was not clear whether this reflects a lack of career goals or a feeling that broad training will increase one's marketability.

When applying to internships, students do not seem too concerned about factors such as personal contacts at the training facility, ease of the application procedure, availability of previous graduate school/training facility relationships, distance of the training site from academic residence, or the application deadline. Characteristics of the internship deemed unimportant were an emphasis on child-clinical work, dissertation research time, and the number of women/minority groups among the faculty. A minority of the students were specifically interested in child-clinical training. Although small, this group is apparently large enough to support a minimum of 16 child-oriented facilities. It would be interesting to learn if the interest in child-clinical training has decreased or increased in recent years, particularly in light of the interest among APA members for a Division of Children and Youth.

By examining Tables 2 and 3, it may be concluded that the typical APA-approved internship meets student needs in that it is large (5.67 internship positions and 16.05 supervisors), emphasizes adult-clinical work (63.63%), has a wide variety of experiences available (44.44% multiple emphases), and is housed in a multidisciplinary setting (97.97%). While it seems unlikely that an intern could obtain an "emphasis" on child, adult, and community psychology all in 1 year, the larger internships apparently allow the intern some opportunity to choose among emphases. It may also be concluded that students' needs and available training opportunities do not match well in the areas of dissertation research time and specific theoretical orientation (i.e. Freudian, Rogerian, behavioral) of the supervisors. Dissertation research time was provided by over 56 percent of internship facilities, yet achieved an average ranking by students of only 2.62. The specific theoretical orientation category achieved an average rank of 5.31, yet was provided by less than 24 percent of the training facilities.

It was impossible to determine the exact number of students applying for an internship during the 1977–1978 training year. However, 7,570 applications were received for a total of 566 positions, averaging 13.62 applications per student and resulting in wasted time, effort, and money on the part of both the students and the trainers. This waste is further complicated by the fact that among those internship programs receiving at least 1 SD above the mean number of applications, the number of applications per internship position was 26.13, with an average of 6.67 available positions. This compares with 2.93 applications per position among those training sites receiving fewer than 24 applications, in spite of the fact that this group averages 5.11 available positions. If students are unfortunate enough to have the majority of their applications going to those particular programs with high numbers of applications, they are in something of a precarious position.

From the students' viewpoint, adoption of a standard application deadline would make the application procedure more efficient and would avoid the confusion that arises from submitting numerous applications between November and March. Additionally, the number of applications for each internship site, along with student ratings of the internship, should be publicized. This would allow students to size up their chances when applying to a particular facility. It would also potentially help students see which of the smaller programs might best suit their needs while increasing their chances of acceptance. Finally, some guidelines for brochure descriptions of training programs could be set forth as to form, length, and accuracy. Standard descriptions, like those published in the Association of Psychology Internship Center (APIC) *Directory* (1976–1977), would help ensure equal advertising opportunities for "rich" and "poor" internship programs alike. Site visitors to APA-approved internship programs could also focus on up-to-date accuracy.

To make things run more smoothly for the internship centers themselves, it is recommended that the "Clearinghouse" project conducted by APIC be continued and expanded. On February 14, 1976 there were 106 unfilled internship positions and 31 unplaced candidates. On March 14, 1976 there were 59 vacant internship positions, 24 of which were APA-approved (APIC Newsletter, 1977). The Clearinghouse was probably not well known or understood by potential consumers. More aggressive publicity would be helpful. It is also recommended that data on how many APA students accepted unapproved internships and vice versa should be collected and provided to the Committee on Accreditation. Under current guidelines an APA-approved internship is automatically put on probation if none of its positions are filled by APA-approved students. This is apparently done to fill all of the APA-approved training positions. This is potentially very detrimental to those small programs of high quality located in a seemingly undesirable region of the country. Finally, it is recommended that the Committee on Accreditation reexamine the wisdom of that practice.

The possibility of a nationwide computer-based matching system, similar to the National Intern and Residency Matching Program, has been investigated by the APIC Committee on Intern Notification Process and found to be too expensive (Mensch & Orgel, 1978). It was suggested that trainers and trainees would be unwilling to incur additional expense. It is recommended that more detailed studies of such a matching system be made and data be gathered on the willingness of potential participants to pay for a system that would ensure maximum use of APA internships by APA students and eliminate at least some of the stress the present procedure involves. While the present study was only concerned with clinical students, a shared computer-based system could benefit school and counseling psychology as well. This would perhaps reduce the costs previously estimated. Such a system would also eliminate much of the alleged abuse associated with notification of acceptance, a separate but related issue.

It is unfortunate that the profession knows and has done so little about such an important step in training. More attention is needed in order to further clarify and streamline internship application procedures.

REFERENCES

American Psychological Association. APA-approved internships for doctoral training in clinical and counseling psychology: 1976. *American Psychologist,* 1976, *31,* 876–878. (a)

American Psychological Association. APA-approved doctoral programs in clinical, counseling, and school psychology: 1976. *American Psychologist,* 1976, *31,* 879–880. (b)

Association of Psychology Internship Centers Executive Committee. *Directory: Internship Programs in Clinical Psychology* (5th ed.). 1976–1977.

Association of Psychology Internship Centers. The APIC Clearinghouse pilot: A review. *APIC Newsletter,* 1977, 14–17.

Mensch, I. N., & Orgel, S. A. National intern and resident matching program. *APIC Newsletter,* 1978, 10–11.

Reading 11

Selection of Internship Site: Basis of Choice by Desirable Candidates

Alvin G. Burstein and Lawrence S. Schoenfeld
The University of Texas Health Science Center at San Antonio
(UTHSCSA)

Sandra Loucks
Trinity University, San Antonio

James M. Stedman
UTHSCSA and Community Guidance Center, San Antonio

Raymond M. Costello
UTHSCSA and Audie Murphy Veterans Hospital, San Antonio

Each year approximately 1,500 graduate students in professional psychology migrate from their campus to internship settings, but little is known about the reasons for their choices. Data compiled by the Association for Psychology Internship Centers (APIC) indicate that approximately 10% of the intern positions were unfilled for the 1980–1981 year and that for the past 3 years, the number of unfilled internship positions has been two to five times greater than the number of unplaced interns. Therefore, intern candidates rather than sites seem to make the choice and the competition for desirable, prospective interns is increasing.

Each year the University of Texas Health Science Center at San Antonio receives approximately 150 completed applications for internship training. These applications are reviewed by a psychology faculty committee, and the applicants are ranked on the basis of a procedure reported elsewhere (Stedman et al., 1981). Of those applying for 1980–1981, 9 were selected out of 38 who were considered highly desirable. After the remaining 29 had chosen

Reprinted from Professional Psychology, *12*(5), 596–598.

their internship sites, they were asked to respond to a survey about their selection process. (The nine candidates who chose to come to our setting were excluded from the survey because they might feel constrained to be overly tactful.) The survey requested the individuals to rank the relative influence that 14 potential factors played in their internship site selection. Twenty-six of the 29 individuals responded—an extremely high return rate.

A Wilcoxon rank-order correlation was computed, comparing the ranks assigned to each factor by each applicant. The calculation indicated a highly significant statistical difference ($\rho = p < .0001$) in the relative rank assigned to the various factors. Table 1 presents, in decreasing importance, the factors in order of the mean rank assigned.

The results are illuminating. First, the desirable nature of this group of applicants is documented by the fact that almost all of them received multiple offers and therefore assigned a very low ranking to the absence of an offer from our facility as a reason for deciding to go elsewhere. Equally interesting is the salience given to geographical location in choosing a site. Program variables, such as diversity of program, theoretical orientation, and so forth, were important but no more so than variable of location. Surprisingly, reputation and the amount of supervision available do not appear to be striking factors, and work load and the stipend level also appear relatively unimportant. Although the real variation in work load is difficult to determine objectively, the senior author's experience is that it varies widely, ranging from agencies that emphasize the 40-hour model to those that have a 50–60 hr/wk workload. The variation in stipends is easier to document. Nationally,

Table 1 Factors in Selection of Internship Sites

Factor	Average rank
Location	4.6
Diversity of program	4.7
Theoretical orientation	4.8
Type facility	5.5
Reputation	5.6
Training facility	5.9
Amount of supervision	6.3
Specificity of program	7.4
Work load	8.3
Interview	8.3
Money	8.5
Time for research	9.5
No UTHSC offer	11.8
Only offer	13.5

Note. Number of respondents = 26. UTHSC = University of Texas Health Science Center.

APIC figures indicate a range from unfunded positions to stipends in excess of $15,000/yr.

Clearly the salience of the location factor may be an artifact of our studying the population of desirable applicants who chose to apply to a training center in the sunny Southwest. Comparison with a relevant group applying to northeastern facilities would shed some light on this hypothesis. The low salience of work load, stipend level, and research may suggest that the intern's primary focus is on what he or she will learn about applied practice. In any case a specified theoretical orientation and program diversity are certainly important factors; therefore, luring students with light work loads, high stipends, and research time does not seem to be an effective procedure.

REFERENCE

Stedman, J. M., Costello, R. M., Gaines, T., Schoenfeld, L. S., Loucks, S., & Burstein, A. G. How clinical psychology interns are selected: A study of decision-making processes. *Professional Psychology* 1981, *12*, 4154–419.

Reading 12
Survival Guide for Intern Applicants

Cynthia D. Belar
University of Florida, Gainesville
Sidney A. Orgel
Upstate Medical Center, New York

For the past 7 years, the Association of Psychology Internship Centers (APIC) has published a *Directory of Internship Programs in Professional Psychology* (1978). The *Directory* is intended to guide students in identifying more easily those programs that are likely to meet their particular training needs. However, it has become increasingly apparent that myths and misinformation abound about the very process of internship application. To provide a pragmatic, step-by-step instructional framework, this survival guide for intern applicants is presented.

OBTAIN INFORMATION

Write the program director indicating your interest in obtaining a descriptive brochure.

Reprinted from Professional Psychology, *11*(4), 672–675.

1. Internship programs are listed and described briefly in the APIC *Directory of Internship Programs in Professional Psychology*. It is a wise idea to consult this first to identify programs that may be of interest to you. American Psychological Association (APA)-approved programs are also listed yearly in the *American Psychologist* (1978), although this latter listing does not indicate the chief psychologist nor does it provide a description of the internship.

2. When requesting information, make sure your inquiry is addressed accurately. Be sure to name the program and the location. For example, inquiries addressed to Internship Program frequently get lost in major medical centers. Such centers typically have 15 or more such internship programs.

REVIEW AND EVALUATE INFORMATION

Review brochures, consult with faculty and your director of training, and make decisions as to where to apply.

1 Gather additional information when necessary.
    a Speak with intern directors.
- Do your homework first; ask specific questions based on your reading of the brochures; do not ask for a "general description" of the program.
- Ask for the names of current or former interns with whom you might communicate (be suspicious if the program is not willing to provide their names).

    b Evaluate interview policies.
- Determine the program's policy concerning interviewing. Some programs wish only to interview those whom they invite. Some programs negatively evaluate "drop-in" visitors.
- Determine the program's use of interviewing in the evaluation process.
- Consult with your supervisor concerning your own interview stimulus value.
- Enact "dry run" interviews, using a fellow student as the interviewer.

COORDINATE THE APPLICATION

Coordinate your application with those of others from your program.

1. Some programs have a limit on the number of applications they will review from each predoctoral program.

2. Your chances for acceptance may be diminished if you compete against 4 or 5 fellow students from your own program at all the places you apply, especially if your class standing is average. (The internship director may call the director of training to request rank ordering of applicants, when there are

several from the same program. This information is not always furnished to the internship center, however.)

SUBMIT APPLICATIONS

1. Comply with application procedures described by the program. Determine program policy about submitting nonrequested materials.

2. If you are requested to submit clinical samples, make sure all identifying information has been removed *and* that informed consent *for such use* has been provided by the patient (American Psychological Association, 1977).

3. Make sure you provide enough time for reference letter writers and transcript offices to process your requests and still meet program deadlines. It is your responsibility to ascertain that your application is complete. (Some programs will request that you forward a stamped self-addressed postcard for this purpose.)

4. Be sure to include a telephone number where you will be available on notification day. Also, many programs need your Social Security number.

5. Sloppily completed applications detract from your candidacy.

WAITING IT OUT

This period can be used for further refinement of your decision making. You should be able to approximate a rank ordering of your preferences during this period. Waiting until the notification date to request further information about the program to which you have applied is irritating to many program directors.

An internship program that indicates that a commitment of acceptance from you is necessary before they will make an offer is not abiding by APIC guidelines. Speak with your director of training. A suggested response to the program is that your program is abiding by APIC guidelines concerning acceptance procedures.

NOTIFICATION DAY (SECOND MONDAY IN FEBRUARY, 8:00 A.M. CST)

1. Be easily accessible by phone.

2. Make plans for consultation with the significant others in your decision (e.g., family, faculty), although good preplanning should reduce the need for last-minute decision making.

3. Remember you have until Tuesday, 12:00 m. CST, to respond to an offer. An internship program that indicates that they will make you an offer only if you will immediately accept is violating APIC guidelines.

4. If you are an alternate, the time you have before your decision is to be

made is negotiated with the internship director, but it should not be before Tuesday, 12:00 m. CST.

5. Release programs from their commitment to you if you have received an offer from one you ranked higher.

6. If you have not been contacted, telephone the programs ranked higher than those from whom you received acceptances to determine your alternate status.

7. When you make your decision, it is courteous to inform those programs that are still considering you as an alternate that you are removing yourself rom consideration.

8. *Second thoughts:* If you have already made a commitment, you must not accept another offer without first discussing this with your director of training and obtaining a realease from your accepted internship site. This should be an eventuality in only the most extreme of circumstances. It is unethical, if not illegal, to renege on a commitment.

CONTACT THE CLEARING HOUSE

If you have not been selected by any internship program that you would choose, contact the APIC Clearing House through Robert J. Silver, Department of Psychology, Austin State Hospital, 4110 Guadalupe, Austin, Texas 78751.

REFERENCES

American Psychological Association, Committee on Scientific and Professional Ethics and Conduct. *Ethical standards of psychologists.* Washington, D.C.: Author, 1977.

APA-approved predoctoral internships for doctoral training in clinical and counseling psychology: 1978. *American Psychologist,* 1978, *33,* 1124–1126.

Association of Psychology Internship Centers. *Directory of internship programs in professional psychology* (7th ed.). Syracuse, N.Y.: Author, 1978.

Reading 13

A Proposed Interviewing Guide for Intern Applicants

Jeffrey B. Hersh and Kent Poey
University of Massachusetts, Amherst

Many internship centers either require or strongly encourage an on-site interview. Some may consider a phone interview. Most will only offer an interview to those applicants who have passed through an initial selection process based on completed written application materials. From our observation the interview is a critical part of selecting intern candidates. Yet many intern applicants appear unprepared to answer rather standard questions. In the interest of clarifying our expectations and hopefully those of other internship centers, we have outlined a series of questions that interns should consider asking intern directors, because such questions typically indicate initiative and interest. There are, however, some questions that are heard in the context of the interview with mixed reactions by intern directors and that may place the intern's evaluation in some negative light. Generally speaking, the best questions are those that reflect motivation to learn and take part in many work activities rather than questions that promote a speculation that the intern may be demanding or complaining.

The listing below is probably more inclusive than encountered in any particular setting. It should be used as a general guide. It is important that the intern applicant prepare himself or herself for the special emphasis of each internship site by anticipating more quesitons in certain categories than others. For instance, a long discussion of inpatient treatment is unlikely to develop in a training site that primarily provides outpatient services. Our hope is that these lists will be an aid for intern applicants in their preparation for interviews and will be used in conjunction with the published *Survival Guide for Intern Applicants* (Belar & Orgel, 1980). Obviously, preparing for an interview involves more than rehearsing answers to several anticipated questions. We hope the intern candidate will take the opportunity to reflect on his or her learning needs, clinical strengths, and future directions. This contemplative process is invaluable to growth and meaningful challenge in general and will aid the intern candidate in setting his or her priorities for the next year specifically. The intern candidate is also advised to meet with the director of clinical training and other intern applicants for support and feedback.

COMMON QUESTIONS ASKED BY INTERNSHIP DIRECTORS

1 General:
What interests you in this internship program?

Reprinted from Professional Psychology: Research and Practice, *15*, 3–5.

Have you worked with client populations similar to those we see here?

What are some books or articles that you have recently read?

What are some of your specialized skills?

2 Individual Adult Therapy:

What kinds of client problems have you worked with and in what modalities?

What experiences have you had doing emergency work and crisis therapy?

What kinds of cases do you work well with and what kinds of cases present particular problems?

What is your therapeutic orientation? How would you describe your therapeutic style?

Describe your conceptualization and treatment of a recent or current case?

What are your strengths as a therapist and what areas need improvement?

3 Group Therapy:

Have you led groups? What kinds—therapeutic, educational?

Have you had cotherapy experience with groups?

What in the cotherapy relationship was helpful or difficult?

4 Child/Family/Couples Therapy:

What is your experience with child therapy? Family? Couples? Describe the kinds of cases you have worked with, including your theoretical orientation.

What have your cotherapy experiences in family and couples work been like?

5 Inpatient:

Have you had inpatient experiences? Acute care? Long-term care? Milieu therapy?

What are your strengths in this area and what areas do you need to improve?

6 Psychological Testing:

What is your background in testing?

What tests are you familiar with?

In what specific areas do you want/need further training?

7 Consultation and Education:

What is your background in consultation and education?

Have you collaborated with other professional groups including teachers, lawyers, physicians, and nurses?

Describe your experiences in conducting workshops?

8 Supervision:

What styles of supervision best facilitate your learning?

What styles of supervision tend to inhibit your learning?

What theoretical orientations would you be most comfortable with in supervision?

Describe a rewarding supervision experience?

9 Work With Special Populations:

Have you worked with people with physical complaints?

Have you worked with clients that present handicapped, gay, minority, or cross-culture concerns?

10 Closing:

What areas of your interest are not addressed by this internship?

What areas are especially attractive?

What are your future plans and goals?

SUGGESTED QUESTIONS TO ASK INTERNSHIP DIRECTORS

1 How are supervisors assigned? What are their theoretical orientations?
2 How much opportunity is there for me to pursue special learning interests?
3 What kind of activities will I be involved in each week?
4 What is the diversity of the client population?
5 What is the relationship between disciplines and working relationships among the staff and interns?
6 Are there any changes in the stipends, vacations, or medical benefits from what is published in the brochure;
7 What office arrangements are provided for an intern, and what clinical support is available?
8 Is it possible to speak with a current intern?
9 Have past interns found jobs available in this area after the internship?
10 How many people are you interviewing? For how many positions? What is the process by which the selection decision is made? (If there are nonfunded intern positions, ask how decisions are made between funded and non-funded slots.)
11 What are the strengths and limits of this program?

EXAMPLES OF QUESTIONS TO AVOID ASKING INTERNSHIP DIRECTORS

1 How long does an intern work each week?
2 I want to complete my dissertation during my internship year. Could I have time off to do this?
3 Are there any opportunities to earn extra money in private practice during the internship year?
4 Persistent or antagonistic questions and comments showing a lot of interest in a work area that the internship program only minimally provides.
5 Questions and comments indicating a resistance to learning the major theoretical orientation presented by the internship center.

In conclusion, the interview and selection process is highly charged for intern applicants and internship directors. Both want to be evaluated positively. Unfortunately sometimes the pressure is handled by trying to make arrangements contrary to the Association of Psychology Internship Centers guidelines (APIC, 1982). An intern should discuss any procedural or ethical concerns with his or her university director of training. An area that is clearly unethical is encountered when the possibility of "early" acceptance is raised either by the intern applicant or the internship director. An example of a potentially problematic area is when an intern is asked to rank the internship among his or her potential choices. We hope this question is asked in a flexible and nondemanding way. Our suggestion is for the intern to respond either by saying that more time is needed to sort out his or her priorities or to answer by placing the internship within a range unless is is definitely and unalterably the first choice. Finally, because our remarks reflect our experiences in one internship site, a survey of internship directors regarding their philosophy of interviewing and the questions asked may add substantial support to our remarks or significantly extend them in important ways. We will conduct such a survey that we hope will benefit both intern applicants and internship settings by clarifying priorities and expectations and by opening the interviewing process to inspection.

REFERENCES

Belar, C., & Orgel, S. (1980). Survival guide for intern applicants. *Professional Psychology, 11,* 672–675.

Association of Psychology Internship Centers. (1982). *Directory of internship programs in professional psychology* (11th ed.). Iowa: Author.

Reading 14
Strategies for Selecting and Securing the Predoctoral Clinical Internship of Choice

Robin Brill, Joan Wolkin, and Nancy McKeel
Georgia State University

Clinical internship is a significant step in the training of clinical psychologists and represents a transition for students to enter the professional ranks. While a number of articles have focused on the criteria used by both applicants and the sites in internship selection, relatively little information is available to guide students through the arduous task of selecting and securing an internship placement. Two exceptions to this are the articles by Belar and Orgel (1980) and

Reprinted from Professional Psychology: Research and Practice, *16,* 3–6.

Craddick, Cole, Dane, Brill, and Wilson (1980). Belar and Orgel (1980) provide a
step-by-step skeletal outline of instructions for applicants, while Craddick
et al. (1980) describe the development by one clinical program of an effective system for internship preparation. The present paper, based on an in-
depth presentation of strategies (Wolkin, Brill, & McKeel, 1982) developed
by Georgia State University's program, is a how-to-guide that has proven
highly effective for the students at that university. Included are tips and
exercises to help the student formulate personal and professional goals
with which compatible sites can then be matched, ideas for presenting application materials, considerations for the interviewing process, suggestions
for handling phone calls on acceptance day, and attention to the changes
required by the student as the transition to internship occurs.

Applying for internship is a time-consuming, demanding, anxiety-
provoking, and expensive endeavor. All of these costs can be reduced through
the development of clear strategies. Last year, 17 of the 20 students applying
obtained their first choice. Many were accepted by *all* of the sites to which
they applied, and all received placements.

DEFINING GOALS

In the '82–83 APIC Directory, over 300 internship training sites were
listed. How does one choose? Clarifying personal and professional preferences is important. A first step is consideration of short-term and long-
term goals. One approach to this task is presented through the following
imagery exercise which you may either want to do yourself or with a
friend. Reserve approximately 20 uninterrupted minutes to spend in a relaxing
place.

> Make yourself comfortable and focus for a few minutes on your breath-
> ing, using relaxation techniques that work for you. Now, imagine
> yourself 30 years from now, pleased with how you have lived your
> life. As you look back over your lifetime, focus on giving answers to
> these questions. How did you spend the bulk of your working time?
> What did you do? What was most important and satisfying to you?
>
> Now, consider where you are currently in the process of obtaining
> some of these experiences. What kind of training do you require to
> facilitate moving toward your goals? Consider the internship experience.
> What might a training site provide that meets the next few steps in the
> process of meeting your goals. Jot down three of these. Follow the same
> route for finding three of your most significant *personal* considerations.
> Family/relationships, geography, climate, cost of living, stipend, and job
> prospects may be important factors. Reviewing these two lists, again
> consider prospective sites. To what extent do they correspond with your
> priorities?

CHOOSING SITES

Once you have clarified your goals, consulting the directory with clearly defined personal and professional requirements gives direction to the task of choosing prospective sites. A year to a year and a half is not too early to begin this search.

At Georgia State, the Director of Internship and a Student Internship Committee compile and update internship resources. All students have access to a library that contains directories, files of current brochures and applications for centers across the United States and Canada, and a booklet of questionnaires completed by previous interns who have evaluated their internship sites.

Students choose six desirable sites. In consultation with the Internship Director, the selection is narrowed to four programs. Since positive experiences with previous interns from a university heighten the possibility of future selection of students from that program, one site that has accepted Georgia State students previously is included as one of the four choices. Although limiting the selection to four sites may seem risky, the advantages of this approach seem to far outweigh the disadvantages for students, faculty, and internship site directors. Time, energy, and money are saved for the student, faculty, and training sites by limiting the number of applications. Since the student has carefully considered each site and clarified her/his goals, the student can place greater emphasis on each application, communicating how the training sought is compatible with the training offered. The faculty and administrative staff have fewer letters of recommendation to prepare, and materials processed by the internship centers are reduced, thereby expediting selection and reducing the problem of multiple offers.

In addition to a limitation of the number of sites to which a particular student is allowed to apply, only one student from the Georgia State program is permitted to apply to any one site. This guideline reduces competition and fosters cooperation among students in approaching the taxing application process. Sharing information, tips, vitae, and preparing for interviews together is common. Furthermore, this restriction maximizes the possibility of diversified training through the interchange of interns with varying perspectives and educational orientations.

APPLYING TO THE SITES

November seems to be the ideal time to send in applications. The Christmas rush is avoided. Faculty and supervisors are generally more accessible prior to the holidays. Plenty of processing time is available before deadline dates and there is time to obtain additional information about the sites through perhaps contacting faculty familar with the programs, previous inerns at the sites, and current interns.

Included in every internship application are a vita, cover letter, transcripts, letters of recommendation, and any additional information requested by each site. The vita should contain pertinent professional experience, including volunteer work, employment, practica, clinical coursework, supervision, publications and presentations, honors and awards, workshops, and membership in professional organizations. Present the information in a succinct, well-organized, clearly communicated style. Use underlining, headings, and sections to highlight material. Reviewing other students' vitae may prove helpful in composing your own.

The cover letter provides a professional presentation and gives an opportunity to make more direct and personal contact with the internship director. Include reasons for choosing the program, how training offered fits with your goals, assets that make you particularly attractive to them, any additional information not included elsewhere, as well as the names of individuals serving as references.

It is important that letters of recommendation be provided only by those faculty and supervisors who are very familiar with your qualifications and who can speak highly of you without reservation.

Finally, if a site is your first choice, this information can be communicated in the cover letter and confirmed by the Director of Internship Training through her/his contact with the site. It is important that this commitment be honored by accepting an offer if it is made. If a site is not a first choice, leave doors open by communicating a positive tone in the cover letter. It may be helpful to have a friend or faculty member review completed application materials, thereby lending a different perspective and an opportunity for final revision before mailing.

INTERVIEWING

Even though APIC guidelines state that sites cannot make interviews mandatory, in practice many sites only make offers to students who have been interviewed. In other cases, interviews are discouraged or phone interviews are acceptable alternatives to an in-person visit. Information about each site's preference should be obtained so that one is competing on an equal basis wth other applicants. Careful consideration tailored to each site's unique preference is suggested.

Solid preparation for an interview is important. Dress professionally and present yourself confidently and competently without appearing arrogant. Prepare questions and think of what may make you stand out and be remembered. Interviewers see many candidates in a short period of time and may have difficulty differentiating them later. Carefully review the materials about the site. Phrase questions in such a way that familiarity with the program is communicated. Questions may include quantity, quality, and type of supervision, educational opportunities, nature of the client population, relationship between psychiatry and psychology, time allotments for various activities, types and numbers of therapy clients and assessments, strengths and weaknesses of the program, and potential interaction among interns.

Questions that may be asked by the interviewer include: Why did you choose to apply to this site? What are your strengths and weaknesses as a candidate for this program, as a therapist, or as a clinician? What is your therapeutic orientation? Or perhaps they may ask you to trace a successful and unsuccessful therapy case and explain the reasons for each. If possible, review letters of recommendation prior to the interview. Often, questions can be anticipated.

A site visit or phone interview are important for other reasons. They give the applicant additional information about the program, which can help her/him to further clarify their site preference. Finally, assuming that an interview was successful, the student may wish to reinforce the interest through a letter or phone call. Negotiations take place prior to the acceptance day and additional communication may prove critical.

ACCEPTANCE DAY

Be sure that the sites have the appropriate phone number where you can be reached. Calls are made to the home number unless the site is informed otherwise. Remain by the phone. When an offer is made, accept it if it's your first choice. When unsure of a response, thank the caller, inform them that the offer will be considered, and assure them that the call will be returned as soon as a decision has been reached. Once an offer is accepted, call the other sites immediately. Other students are waiting for the positions being held. If the first choice has not called by the end of the first day, it is possible to hold the second choice until almost the deadline the next day. Prompt responses are considerate of your peers as well as the sites. If more than one offer is received, make a decision and release other offers.

PREPARING FOR THE CHANGE

What are the personal and professional meanings that underlie this move from student to intern? Often the change involves a geographic move, leaving the familiar people and places and entering another. This move represents a major disruption in the life of the newly accepted intern, yet there is almost no attention in the literature to this adjustment. The lack of attention to the goodbyes and hellos coincides with the historical denial of death in the psychological literature and culture at large. Few structures are oriented toward recognition of and support for dealing with loss and change.

Following is an imagery exercise that can be used by the student-intern prior to the beginning of internship to prepare her/himself for the upcoming change (L. Maholick, personal communication). It can be read by a friend or recorded on tape. Three dots are used to indicate pauses during which the directive can be followed.

Choose a quiet, private setting, in which you are free of interruptions. Sit comfortably. Let yourself relax. Close your eyes. Breathe deeply. And with each exhale, relax more and more beginning at the top of your head and on down. . . Now choose a special place, your special place, a place that is safe. It may be the ocean or a place in the mountains, somewhere that is not a part of what you'll be leaving when you go on internship. Go to that place now. Breathe the air, look around, hear the sounds, feel the light. Take it all in. . . Now choose a place to sit or lie down. Where you will be comfortable. From this position, you can see across time and space. . . Picture yourself at your school. Take a couple of minutes to walk around visiting those places and people that are important to you knowing that you will be leaving soon. . . Now see yourself with a person who is special to you. Maybe a favorite professor, another student, a friend, or someone in your family. Meet at a place agreeable to the two of you. Go there now. Spend a couple of minutes talking with this person. Let yourself be aware of all of your thoughts and feelings about leaving school, the you of this time of your life, telling about your significant experiences while there, and how you feel about what you're doing. Spend a couple of minutes doing that. . . Now it's time to move on. Go home, to your own apartment or house. Stand in the front. Look at it. Walk around. Now go inside. Take in all you home has meant to you. Go through room by room remembering experiences, the joy, the pain, all parts, and saying goodbye. Take a minute or so to do that. . . With all the feelings of leaving, go to the airport or get in the car, whatever way you are traveling. Let yourself feel all that is there, knowing that this time and place and these people have *been* in your life. And allow yourself to let go of that part of your personal and professional experience. Know that you are moving on into a new dimension. Your wisdom and learning is inside of you as you move on. See yourself coming into the new city, the new place that will be your home. Say hello as you enter this place. Take a minute to locate your new home. Know that it is there waiting for you. Allow yourself to discover it now. . . Now go to the place where you're going to intern. Before you go inside, take a look at it. This strange new place will be central to your life for the next year. Feel the air. Hear the sounds. Take in this new environment. Go inside. Experience this new place. Walk around. Let in the new. Now meet with your supervisor or director of the program or meet another intern. Take two minutes for saying hello and for discovering what you're getting into. You might consider what will help you feel more at home . . . With all of your thoughts and feelings, return to you new home. Take a minute to do something special in your new place. Prepare a meal, perform some ritual to claim you new space. . . Now when you're ready, return to where you began. The meadow or ocean, the place you chose initially. Breathe the air. Feel the sunlight. Look around. Listen to the sounds of this special place. Let all of your experience be with you, all the feelings and thoughts, and in your own time, slowly open your eyes and be present.

CLOSING COMMENTS

Success in the internship application process and the training experience depends on a number of factors. Careful consideration and preparation by the student in both academic and personal realms is essential. The time between acceptance day and entry as an intern is a period of transition, and delineation of the factors that aid the student in making a successful move will likely maximize the intern's performance as well as the site's satisfaction.

REFERENCES

Association of Psychology Internship Centers. *Directory of internship programs in professional psychology.*

Belar, C. D., & Orgel, S. A. (1980). Survival guide for intern applicants. *Professional Psychology,* 1980, *11*(4), 672–675.

Craddick, R. A., Cole, M. A., Dane, J., Brill, R., & Wilson, J. A. (1980). The process of selecting predoctoral internship training sites. *Professional Psychology, 11*(4), 548–549.

Foster, L. M. (1976). Truth in advertising psychology internship programs. *Professional Psychology, 7,* 120–124.

Lamb, D. H., Baker, J. M., Jennings, M. L., & Yarris, E. (1982). Passages of an internship in professional psychology. *Professional Psychology, 13*(5), 661–669.

Wolkin, J. R., Brill, R., & McKeel, N. (1982). Selecting and securing the internship of choice. Symposium presented at the South Eastern Psychological Convention, New Orleans, Louisiana.

Chapter 4

Internship Training

GENERAL: READINGS 15 TO 26

This section (pp. 233–328), which focuses on general topics of training, begins with the Kurz, Fuchs, Dabek, Kurtz, and Helfrich (1982) study of the 1979 APIC Directory, which contained 272 internship entries. Their findings document wide variations along a number of parameters in the listed predoctoral internship programs. Medical settings have historically provided the largest single number of internship settings. Burstein, Barnes, and Quesada (1976) delineate training advantages and risks involved in psychiatric affiliations within medical settings. As health psychology becomes a more popular and viable arena of clinical activities, internships will expand into other health care components of medical settings beyond psychiatry. Swan, Piccione, and Anderson (1980) present their model of developing behavioral medicine competencies in a clinical psychology internship that is housed in a large VA Medical Center.

One of the areas of health psychology activities of recent vintage is neuropsychology. Goldberg and McNamara (1984) in their survey of APA-approved clinical and counseling internships conclude that although neuropsychology training was reported as available in over half of the responding internships centers, the apparent variability in quality of training makes that number suspect. Predoctoral internship training does not result in competent specialization in neuropsychology.

Siegler, Gentry, and Edwards (1979) surveyed both graduate programs and internships in gerontology. Their data was collected in 1975–76, and it is likely that significant changes have taken place since then in the relatively low gerontology interest, knowledge of the area, and contact with geriatric patients.

The Veterans Administration has been in the forefront of training recently by providing special slots for internships with a geriatric focus as a result of its aging patient population. The rest of the internships training world cannot be far behind as the general population of the aged continues to increase.

Gold, Meltzer, and Sherr (1982) point out that physical rehabilitation settings offer unique learning opportunities for clinical and counseling psychology doctoral students. Among these opportunities are functioning as a consultant, working on multidisciplinary health care teams, and learning psychological assessment procedures, as well as report-writing skills, which vary considerably from the more typical mental health delivery system requirements.

Community Mental Health Centers (CMHC's) have been an important component of internship opportunities for professional psychologists during the last decade. In a survey of CMHC Directors (79% return of sample), Zolik, Bogat, and Jason (1983) found that about half had their own training program, while the other half were part of a larger training arrangement. The CMHC's consider their outstanding teaching contribution to be in the traditional clinical areas, although the presence of consultation activities may bode well for the possibility of a more preventive CMHC's service delivery orientation.

Crisis intervention experiences for interns in hospitals are exemplified in the article by Barlow (1974). Types of experiences, clinical problems, and richness of clinical and personal learning in this front-line professional activity are reported.

As professional psychology moves in various new directions, it may be anticipated that internship training will be variable and inconsistent. Such was the case in forensic psychology training according to recent survey findings by Lawlor, Siskind, and Brooks (1981). They advocate a relatively minor set of experiences in legal/forensic issues during predoctoral internship, and suggest postdoctoral training for a specialization in the area.

Group treatment has become a more common service modality, perhaps above and beyond its share of clinical or research-based decisions for utilization as demand and cost-effectiveness issues play greater roles in the delivery of mental health services. Carmody and Zohn (1980), surveying internship group treatment training opportunities, found an interest and emphasis on group methods. However, these authors feel that an increasing emphasis in this area is required. This may already be happening as exemplified in the survey findings four years later by Drummond et al. (1981), that, on the average, almost 9 percent of the internship time was devoted to group therapy.

Professional psychologists are assuming greater administrative responsibilities in a variety of clinical program settings. Edwards and Wyrick (1977) describe one internship program in which a specific administrative role—chief intern—has been developed. The authors noted that their survey findings suggest that many internships do provide some administrative experience, although these experiences may be fragmentary and not representative of typical professional job responsibilities.

Lastly, in this section, the article by Monti, Wallander, and Delancey (1983) on their survey findings in seminar training concludes that internships have incorporated some of the didactic training missing in graduate programs by means of internship seminars. These seminars focus on assessment, neuropsychology, psychopharmacology, and psychotherapy. The authors suggest better communication between parent graduate professional education institutions and internship centers concerning gaps and overlap in training experiences of students.

SUPERVISION: READINGS 27 TO 34

The supervision literature (pp. 328–418) begins with a survey of internship training practices. Three papers which describe models are followed by a growth exposition, cotherapy issues, an essay on supervisor integrity and maturity, and supervision of diagnostic testing.

Hess and Hess (1983) surveyed 151 APA-approved predoctoral internship programs. A ratio of one hour of individual supervision to three hours of psychotherapy was typical with interns receiving 4.25 supervision hours per week. Supervisory staff are providing 3.76 hours of supervision per week but these staff members have not had specific training in psychotherapy supervision. Assessment of supervision quality has not been attempted. However, one-third of programs provide some training in supervision for interns and the time required for this training tends to dilute their ongoing supervision. Programs that accepted both psychology and nonpsychology graduate students were more likely to have doctoral interns and others supervising although they also had more doctoral level and Diplomate status persons as faculty. Programs that viewed supervision as important also used seminars, vertical teams, audiotapes, cotherapy, case conferences, and one-way observations.

Supervision from a systems aegis allows each of the component parts to be considered in relation to desired outcomes. Curtis and Yager (1981) have identified one set of components that includes initial supervisor goals, assessing supervisee skill level, establishing learning needs by negotiation, determining supervisory focus, stating desired learning goals, implementing supervisory interventions, evaluating supervisee progress leading to decisions for continuation or termination of supervisory process, and evaluation of supervisory skills. This model provides for collaborative development of expectations within a time perspective with carefully specified stages for progress. Both interpersonal dynamics and environmental settings can be used as reference points for monitoring the supervisee. While this particular systems analysis is presented as a framework for supervision of school psychologists, it is applicable to all professional psychology interns.

A professional model for psychotherapy supervision (McElfresh, 1983) deals with the interactions between supervisory roles, student needs, and the area of concern. The supervisory roles include teacher-student, therapist-patient, consultant, and administrator. Student needs are for conceptualization (knowledge), process (skills), and personalization (attitudes). The content areas are client activities, therapeutic relationship, and learning relationship. McElfresh recommends that student needs be the primary axis. Application of this model is made using a student psychotherapy skills checklist of clinical experiences in order to develop an individualized training plan. In addition, a contract between student and supervisor outlines needs, learning objectives, and proposed training strategies. This contract is used not only for goal setting by the student but for evaluation after a 90-day period, with contract renegotiation whenever necessary.

Grater (1985) presents four stages of supervisory focus that are uniquely applicable to psychotherapy supervision. These stages include learning of basic skills, an expansion of the range of skills, identification of habitual client patterns coupled with selection of appropriate intervention technique, and learning to use oneself. These latter two stages—selection of interventions and use of self—are considered to be an essential focus of learning and supervision. The intern learns to avoid previously-elicited reaction patterns to habitual client behaviors and provides instead a corrective emotional experience for the client. This stage is exciting and threatening as well as rewarding. The final stage provides an opportunity to develop skills and sensitivity in the use of self as a powerful assessment and intervention vehicle. By this stage the trainee is typically in the last half of the internship year and is encouraged to develop new responses to interpersonal threats as they occur in therapy. Supervision encourages the intern to focus on intervention that is based on the interaction between herself/himself, the client, a particular issue, and possible types of interventions. Complete mastery of all stages is not to be expected by the end of the internship.

Friedlander, Dye, Costello, and Kobos (1984) describe the complexity of supervision that stems from divided commitment to supervisee and client, communication about a relationship with another person, processes that parallel psychotherapy, and extreme individual differences among supervisees. The control and examination of anxiety in the supervisee relates to unresolved authority problems of both participants. Case management versus therapist self-examination is balanced in favor of therapy process unless therapist idiosyncracies/psychopathology are providing interferences. Supervision includes preparation, augmentation of therapist knowledge of participating patients, and working through therapist feelings that represent unresolved conflicts. Therapist growth is stimulated by crises including confrontation with personal limits, therapy as communication, and a goodness of fit between intervention models and patient needs. The impact of supervision is contained in modeling problem-solving behaviors and management of growth crises rather than in facts, models, or techniques.

Berkman and Berkman (1984) provide a unique discussion of the supervision of cotherapy. The relationship between cotherapists must be one of deep involvement with "affective honesty" to enable each to help the other express and resolve feelings that inhibit movement in therapy. In family therapy, the family learns about interpersonal relationships from cotherapists. Cotherapist distress may mimic the dynamics of the family in treatment (symmetrical) or be contained in behavior that is opposite or contrasting from the treatment family (complementarity). Supervision of cotherapy is focused on the use of self-awareness to achieve differentiation from the patient and increased understanding. Cotherapist difficulties arise from their emotional interplay with one another, individual dynamics and transferences, and countertransference reactions to the family. Since cotherapy is like marriage, in effect, one family system is treating another family system. To the extent that the cotherapists do not function as a unit, there will be supervisory issues. Supervision initially deals with the cotherapists' relationships and ultimately with the therapists as a family unit.

Rozsnafszky (1979) believes that effective treatment or supervision results from maturity and integrity coupled with therapeutic power derived from a consistent approach. She describes three particular male therapists who were progenitors of her own trust and growth. However, without these by-products of self-knowledge and awareness—integrity and maturity—therapists or supervisors may become "psychonoxious" and harmful to patients and/or interns. Five types of male immaturity are described. The Teddy Bear uses supervision as a harmless opportunity for flirtation. Macho Mouth uses verbal lewdness as a vehicle for sexual innuendos. The Fox is glib, ostensibly supportive of women's issues but uses supervision to weaken their defenses for his own ultimate sexual purposes. The Dale Carnegie Toucher masks a hands-on approach with warmth and good will. Sexual warmth and pseudo-intimacy substitute for supervision. Super-Guru uses charisma as a basis for sexual exploitation.

Rozsnafszky describes four types of female immaturity. Women supervisors or therapists may need to prove attractiveness to male interns or patients, ignore sexual implications of appearance/behavior, or focus on either sexual or maternal conquest. Daisy Miller uses innocent yet seductive flirtation. Beauty Unaware does not flirt but uses her appearance to gain protection/attention. Big Mother forces improvement to document her own power. Seductive Mother is selectively tough and tender, needing reassurance of attractiveness and power.

Smith and Harty (1981) describe issues in supervision of diagnostic testing. Educational supervision which is the fostering of student skills is distinguished from administrative supervision or quality control and performance evaluation. The supervisory relationship is a learning alliance which may focus on the inference process, theory versus data, defensive organization, ego functions, symptomatology, treatment responsiveness, diagnostic questions and test data, and communication issues. Special emphasis should be placed on administration and scoring, the inference process, and communication of findings. Supervision techniques are related to student skill level and begin with review of referral questions with regard to choice of instruments, communication with other professionals, and patient resistances. Test data should be examined collaboratively in order to exemplify techniques for using data. Once skills are adequately developed, the supervision may focus on the report. These authors are reluctant to omit careful examination of data by the supervisor as the basis for focus on the report, although supervisors could deal exclusively with the report since report content and style provides data on adequacy of assessment.

GENERAL

Reading 15

Characteristics of Predoctoral Internships in Professional Psychology

Ronald B. Kurz, Marilyn Fuchs, Ruth F. Dabek, Steven M. S. Kurtz and W. Thomas Helfrich
Children's Hospital National Medical Center, Washington, D.C.

The organized internship experience has served a major function in training professional psychologists for more than 30 years. Each year, approximately 1,500 students enter internship training, consume some $10 million in stipend support, soak up staff time and agency resources, and in the process become socialized into scientifically based professional psychology (Burstein, 1980). Despite its importance to the development of the various fields of professional psychology and to prospective interns and their faculty advisors, there is relatively little systematic knowledge about the characteristics of different types of internship programs and settings. Drummond, Rodolfa, and Smith (1981) conducted a mailed survey of APA-approved and non-APA-approved internships, from which they were able to describe differences between the two types of programs on such variables as number of internship slots, number of funded positions, average intern stipends, and composition of internship selection committees. Their data provide useful information about the differences between approved and nonapproved programs and, in the process, lend credence to the accreditation enterprise. However, internships vary on other important variables aside from accreditation status. Indeed, when graduate students decide on programs for internship training, both APA approval and type of program or agency setting are weighed heavily (Tedesco, 1979). The purpose of the present investigation, therefore, was to describe the characteristics of internships in different settings and to point up training differences among agency types.

The Association of Psychology Internship Centers (APIC) has published a directory of internship training opportunities yearly since 1972. This directory provides useful information about internship training, including data on APA approval, size of staff and intern class, stipends, amounts of time interns spend in various training activities, theoretical orientation of the program, and the types of doctoral programs from which the internship will accept students. The eighth edition of this directory (Kurz, 1979) provided the basic data for the present study. There are 272 internship entries in the directory. Each internship was classified according to whether it was APA approved ($n = 134$) or not ($n = 138$)[1] and also according to type of agency setting. There were 12

---

[1] The directory listed 93% of APA approved internship programs. Although the proportion of non-APA-approved internship programs cannot be determined, the directory is believed to include the majority of functional programs.

Reprinted from American Psychologist, *37*(11), 1213-1220.

clearly discernible types of setting: children's facility (children's clinic, child and family service agency, child guidance clinic, etc.; $n = 29$), children's hospital (pediatric general hospital; $n = 8$), community mental health center ($n = 41$), consortium (combination of two or more autonomous agencies jointly offering a training program; $n = 4$), prison system ($n = 2$), general hospital ($n = 11$), medical center (comprehensive general medical facility associated with a medical school, but not including pediatric medical centers or VA medical centers; $n = 55$), military service ($n = 4$), private psychiatric hospital ($n = 11$), state mental hospital ($n = 28$), university counseling center ($n = 27$), and Veterans Administration hospital ($n = 52$). In almost all instances the type of setting was readily apparent from the name of the agency. Where the name was ambiguous or otherwise did not identify the setting, the agency was telephoned to determine setting type.

In recording the data for each internship entry in the directory, it was noted that some agencies gave ranges rather than a single number. In those instances, the lower number was used. For example, if the stipend was given as $5,000–$8,000, the item was recorded as $5,000. In a few instances where more than one theoretical orientation of the program was listed, only the first theoretical orientation was recorded. Regarding the item on major theoretical views represented by staff, most programs listed all or most of the major categories of clinical psychological theory; therefore, rather than recording all of the listed viewpoints, only the first was recorded. This procedure was used on the assumption that the first mentioned was likely to be the dominant viewpoint. Agencies used a wide variety of terms for their orientations and the major views of the staff members. In this analysis these were classified into the modal types of *eclectic, psychodynamic,* and *behavioral/cognitive.* Orientations and views that clearly did not fit these categories were classified as *other.* Typical entries in the category included family systems, humanistic, biochemical, nondirective, and Gestalt.

The characteristics of the 272 internship programs in the directory are found in Tables 1 through 4. Table 1 gives the number of full-time staff members available to supervise interns, the number of interns, the number of funded interns, and the stipend. For each variable, the n on which the data are based is given. These ns are less than the total (272), because in some instances the directory entries did not have complete information on each item. This is true of all the tables in this report. Of particular interest in Table 1 are the great range, variation, and substantial differences that exist among internship programs with respect to these basic demographic characteristics.

Table 2 gives the mean percentage of time interns spend in the various training activities. The directory does not define these activities; it rather assumes some common understanding of what is involved in *assessment, therapy, consultation,* and so forth. Considering the high degree of variation among programs in the demographic variables noted in Table 1, it may be that the

Table 1   Staff Intern and Stipend Characteristics of Internship Programs

Variable	n	M	SD	Mdn	Range
Number of staff[a]	182	11.34	8.27	9.4	2–50
Number of interns	269	5.10	3.08	4.5	0–19
Number of interns funded	267	4.63	2.94	4.0	0–17
Stipend ($)	251	7,041.38	2,555.94	6,790.36	0–18,000

[a]Number of full-time staff available to supervise interns. This was the first year this item appeared in the directory, therefore there are more missing entries for this item than for the others.

various programs define these activities in very different ways. Nevertheless, it is of interest here that therapy, however defined, is by far the predominant activity of internship training and that, the Boulder model notwithstanding, research occupies a rather small amount of time in internship training.

Information on theoretical orientation is found in Table 3, which shows that internship programs tend to describe themselves as eclectic, probably because they have staffs with diverse views. When they list the major theoretical views of their staffs, they tend to list some form of psychodynamic theory first. If it can be assumed that the first listed view is the strongest or most frequently represented view on the staff, then these data suggest that more than half of the internships are heavily invested in psychodynamic theory and that almost a fifth of the programs have at least one staff member who is inclined toward behavioral and cognitive psychology. Whereas the largest proportion of programs describe themselves as eclectic, less than 10% of the programs have staff members who consider themselves eclectic.

Table 4 shows the percentage of internship programs that accept students from the various types of APA-approved and non-APA-approved doctoral programs. Students from APA-approved doctoral training programs in clinical psychology are the much-preferred interns. For the agencies listed in the directory, which lean heavily toward service and training in clinical psychology,

Table 2   Percentage of Time Interns Spend in Various Training Activities

Activity	N	M %	SD
Assessment	258	18.71	9.79
Therapy	258	40.01	11.91
Research	221	7.31	5.20
Seminar attendance	259	13.66	6.92
Consultation	242	11.93	7.23
Other	182	10.68	13.31

Table 3 Theoretical Orientation of Internship and Major Theoretical Views of Staff

Variable	n	Eclectic	Psychodynamic	Behavioral/ cognitive	Other
Theoretical orientation of program	228	56.6	28.1	3.5	12.0
Major views of staff	261	8.0	50.6	18.4	22.2

Note. Values are in percentages.

it is more difficult for students from non-APA-approved counseling programs and from all school psychology programs (regardless of accreditation status of the school psychology programs) to gain acceptance.

To discern whether there are any differences in internship characteristics associated with accreditation status and the type of agency setting of the program, the data were cast in a series of 2×12 tables and examined for patterns and trends. These data are presented in Tables 5–14. Concerning the number of full-time staff members availabe to supervise, both accreditation status and type of setting have an effect (see Table 5). In almost every type of setting, the APA-approved programs have larger full-time supervisory staffs than. the non-APA-approved programs. In some cases, notably the medical centers, the difference in favor of the APA-approved settings is striking. Agency settings with relatively larger staffs are consortia, general hospitals, medical centers, and state hospitals. The single prison system, a statewide program, reporting on this variable also has a large staff.

Table 6 reveals a clear trend for APA-accredited internship programs to have more interns than non-APA-accredited programs. Except for the consortia, there are few differences among settings in the number of interns. Because

Table 4 Percentage of Internship Programs Accepting Students from APA-Approved and Non-APA-Approved Doctoral Programs

Program type	APA-approved		Non-APA-approved	
	%	n[a]	%	n[a]
Clinical	99.6	242	69.8	222
Counseling	66.4	226	41.1	214
School	24.1	212	14.2	204
Other[b]	68.4	76	—	—

[a]Blank directory entries were not tabulated.

[b]Includes such listings as experimental, developmental PhD retraining programs, and other areas for which accreditation is not available.

Table 5 Number of Full-Time Staff Members Available to Supervise Interns by Internship Setting and Accreditation Status

Setting	APA-approved			Non-APA-approved		
	n	M	SD	n	M	SD
Children's facility	9	7.33	3.64	11	5.36	3.72
Children's medical center	3	9.00	5.00	2	7.00	4.24
Community mental health center	13	12.07	7.17	15	10.47	7.88
Consortium	3	26.00	7.81	0	—	—
General hospital	3	18.33	10.21	3	9.33	9.24
Medical center	23	19.44	11.50	12	6.67	3.63
Military service	1	6.00	—	0	—	—
Prison system	1	18.00	—	0	—	—
Private psychiatric hospital	3	6.33	1.53	4	6.75	2.50
State hospital	13	16.69	11.63	9	10.22	4.06
University counseling center	6	7.00	3.03	14	8.50	6.15
VA facility	16	10.56	4.01	18	9.73	6.27

Note. n = number of programs in each category. This number varies from table to table because not all programs listed in the directory responded to every item.

Table 6 Number of Interns by Internship Setting and Accreditation Status

Setting	APA-approved			Non-APA-approved		
	n	M	SD	n	M	SD
Children's facility	14	5.36	2.85	15	2.93	1.62
Children's medical center	5	4.80	2.17	3	4.67	1.53
Community mental health center	17	5.29	2.17	24	3.38	1.93
Consortium	3	10.00	5.00	0	—	—
General hospital	3	6.00	1.00	4	3.25	1.50
Medical center	39	7.05	2.84	20	4.55	2.67
Military service	3	6.33	4.93	0	—	—
Prison system	1	3.00	—	1	13.00	—
Private psychiatric hospital	4	5.50	3.10	7	4.43	2.64
State hospital	17	5.77	2.20	11	4.00	2.19
University counseling center	9	6.78	5.33	18	3.67	3.09
VA facility	21	7.29	3.94	29	3.52	1.71

Note. n = number of programs in each category. This number varies from table to table because not all programs listed in the directory responded to every item.

consortium programs are structured out of several agencies, they are naturally quite large compared to other programs.

Table 7 shows the number of funded interns. The APA-approved programs tend to have a larger number of funded interns than the non-APA-approved programs. Among the various settings, the consortia, medical centers, university counseling centers, and VA facilities tend to have more funded interns. The single non-APA-accredited prison system program with an unusually large number of funded interns is a nationwide program with interns in several institutions around the country.

APA approval does not appear to be related to the size of the stipend, as can be noted in Table 8, but there are large differences associated with agency setting. The military services and the prison systems have strikingly high stipends, and the state hospitals are strong in this area as well.

Turning to the way interns spend their time in training, both accreditation status and agency setting make a difference in the amount of training in assessment (see Table 9). In practically every setting the accredited programs require less assessment. Among the settings, the children's facilities, children's medical centers, medical centers, and the VA facilities tend to offer more training in assessment. The two prison systems in the directory also require relatively more assessment. University counseling centers and community mental health centers are noticeably low in amount of time spent in assessment training. As can be seen in Table 10, there is very little variation, either by accreditation status or by setting, in the amount of time devoted to therapy. Examination of the time spent in research training (Table 11) does not reveal consistent differences related to accreditation status, but some of the settings stand out for their devotion to this area of training: medical centers, prison systems, state hospitals, and VA facilities. Table 12 shows the time devoted to seminars. Although there is a fair amount of variation among settings, either accredited or not, there does not appear to be any consistent trend relating seminar time to accreditation status or setting. Concerning consultation training time (Table 13), the four accredited military service settings and the two prison systems are clearly ahead of the others in this area. Overall, accreditation status does not appear to make a difference in consultation training. The "other" category of training activity was selected in a large number of entries. These data are displayed in Table 14, which shows considerable difference among the programs that utilized this entry. Content analyses of these entries indicated that the most common special areas mentioned were experience and training in administration, supervision and supervision training, and community outreach. Community mental health centers frequently mentioned community outreach training in this category, whereas university counseling centers often listed training in supervision.

The findings of this study attest to the great amount of variation that exists among predoctoral psychology internship training programs. Staff sizes

Table 7 Number of Funded Interns by Internship Setting and Accreditation Status

Setting	APA-approved			Non-APA-approved		
	n	M	SD	n	M	SD
Children's facility	14	4.86	2.66	14	2.50	1.40
Children's medical center	5	3.80	1.30	3	4.33	1.53
Community mental health center	17	4.65	1.32	24	2.83	1.61
Consortium	4	7.76	4.57	0	–	–
General hospital	3	5.67	0.58	4	2.50	1.00
Medical center	39	6.74	2.54	19	4.16	2.95
Military service	4	6.75	4.11	0	–	–
Prison system	1	3.00	–	1	13.00	–
Private psychiatric hospital	4	5.50	3.11	7	3.33	2.93
State hospital	17	5.06	2.41	10	3.40	1.90
University counseling center	9	6.67	5.43	18	3.17	3.09
VA facility	21	6.38	3.10	29	3.31	1.73

Note. n = number of programs in each category. This number varies from table to table because not all programs listed in the directory responded to every item.

Table 8 Stipend by Internship Setting and Accreditation Status

Setting	APA-approved			Non-APA-approved		
	n	M ($)	SD ($)	n	M ($)	SD ($)
Children's facility	13	5,923	923	15	5,540	2,689
Children's medical center	5	5,440	245	3	6,540	2,346
Community mental health center	15	6,772	1,745	22	6,632	2,123
Consortium	4	7,982	2,030	0	—	—
General hospital	3	5,948	821	4	7,862	848
Medical hospital	38	6,370	1,553	18	6,069	3,337
Military service	4	13,100	2,146	0	—	—
Prison system	1	14,440	—	1	16,000	—
Private psychiatric hospital	4	7,886	2,646	6	6,421	3,178
State hospital	15	9,633	2,548	9	8,268	1,592
University counseling center	9	7,474	2,043	18	7,005	2,527
VA facility	21	7,143	982	23	7,198	1,953

Note. n = number of programs in each category. This number varies from table to table because not all programs listed in the directory responded to every item.

Table 9 Percentage of Time Devoted to Assessment by Internship Setting and Accreditation Status

Setting	APA-approved			Non-APA-approved		
	n	M	SD	n	M	SD
Children's facility	14	16.64	7.55	15	24.67	14.94
Children's medical center	5	21.00	6.52	2	27.50	3.54
Community mental health center	17	13.59	5.03	23	16.09	6.56
Consortium	4	18.75	7.50	0	—	—
General hospital	3	12.67	2.52	4	25.75	9.43
Medical center	35	19.83	7.05	20	25.00	14.69
Military service	4	17.50	5.00	0	—	—
Prison system	1	25.00	—	1	20.00	—
Private psychiatric hospital	4	22.50	6.46	7	15.00	9.57
State hospital	14	13.57	5.50	11	22.55	9.91
University counseling center	9	13.90	19.33	17	11.00	5.87
VA facility	19	18.52	6.09	29	22.07	7.80

Note. n = number of programs in each category. This number varies from table to table because not all programs listed in the directory responded to every item.

Table 10 Percentage of Time Devoted to Therapy by Internship Setting and Accreditation Status

Setting	APA-approved			Non-APA-approved		
	n	M	SD	n	M	SD
Children's facility	14	40.93	11.53	15	38.00	12.93
Children's medical center	5	40.00	11.73	2	37.50	10.61
Community mental health center	16	39.56	9.89	23	46.26	10.66
Consortium	4	40.00	10.80	0	—	—
General hospital	3	38.33	12.58	4	45.00	5.77
Medical center	35	39.66	9.50	20	36.00	11.43
Military service	4	32.50	9.57	0	—	—
Prison system	1	40.00	—	1	40.00	—
Private psychiatric hospital	4	38.75	10.31	7	44.29	17.18
State hospital	14	37.93	13.79	11	34.55	9.34
University counseling center	9	34.44	13.33	18	42.72	16.27
VA facility	19	41.74	12.42	29	40.79	11.09

Note. n = number of programs in each category. This number varies from table to table because not all programs listed in the directory responded to every item.

243

Table 11 Percentage of Time Devoted to Research by Internship Setting and Accreditation Status

Setting	APA-approved			Non-APA-approved		
	n	M	SD	n	M	SD
Children's facility	13	6.92	5.60	10	5.30	5.14
Children's medical center	4	5.50	3.32	2	7.50	3.54
Community mental health center	15	6.07	4.23	21	4.05	5.84
Consortium	4	6.25	2.50	0	—	—
General hospital	3	3.33	2.89	4	7.75	3.30
Medical center	28	8.14	5.98	15	8.20	5.86
Military service	4	7.75	5.00	0	—	—
Prison system	1	10.00	—	1	10.00	—
Private psychiatric hospital	3	4.33	1.16	5	7.00	5.70
State hospital	12	8.00	5.92	9	6.67	3.84
University counseling center	9	5.90	4.43	15	7.60	5.45
VA facility	16	9.00	4.08	27	10.30	4.86

Note. n = number of programs in each category. This number varies from table to table because not all programs listed in the directory responded to every item.

Table 12 Percentage of Time Devoted to Seminars by Internship Setting and Accreditation Status

Setting	APA-approved			Non-APA-approved		
	n	M	SD	n	M	SD
Children's facility	14	16.07	5.26	15	13.20	7.22
Children's medical center	5	16.40	5.60	2	17.50	3.54
Community mental health center	17	14.77	8.04	23	11.04	5.97
Consortium	4	12.50	2.89	0	—	—
General hospital	3	16.67	7.64	4	10.75	5.38
Medical center	35	15.31	6.39	20	14.15	4.84
Military service	4	12.50	5.00	0	—	—
Prison system	1	20.00	—	1	10.00	—
Private psychiatric hospital	4	13.75	2.50	7	13.86	10.04
State hospital	15	15.27	5.24	11	18.00	11.75
University counseling center	9	13.11	5.78	18	10.78	9.93
VA facility	19	11.84	4.13	28	11.93	7.47

Note. n = number of programs in each category. This number varies from table to table because not all programs listed in the directory responded to every item.

Table 13 Percentage of Time Devoted to Consultation by Internship Setting and Accreditation Status

Setting	APA-approved			Non-APA-approved		
	n	M	SD	n	M	SD
Children's facility	14	15.00	7.34	14	14.29	8.52
Children's medical center	4	12.75	5.19	2	10.00	7.07
Community mental health center	15	12.53	8.97	22	12.32	8.12
Consortium	4	15.75	5.38	0	—	—
General hospital	2	10.00	7.07	4	7.00	4.76
Medical center	31	12.94	6.75	18	10.56	6.16
Military service	4	21.25	12.50	0	—	—
Prison system	1	20.00	—	1	20.00	—
Private psychiatric hospital	4	8.75	6.29	6	9.17	6.65
State hospital	14	10.29	6.91	11	9.18	5.53
University counseling center	9	7.89	2.80	18	11.44	5.74
VA facility	18	13.33	8.68	26	10.27	6.73

Note. n = number of programs in each category. This number varies from table to table because not all programs listed in the directory responded to every item.

Table 14 Percentage of Time Devoted to Other Activities by Internship Setting and Accreditation Status

Setting	APA-approved			Non-APA-approved		
	n	M	SD	n	M	SD
Children's facility	10	8.50	14.15	12	7.67	13.78
Children's medical center	3	4.33	7.51	2	0.00	–
Community mental health center	11	19.36	10.02	16	12.44	13.52
Consortium	3	10.00	8.66	0	–	–
General hospital	3	22.33	13.65	2	0.00	–
Medical center	24	8.29	10.27	16	9.69	11.76
Military service	3	1.67	2.89	0	–	–
Prison system	0	–	–	1	0.00	–
Private psychiatric hospital	3	15.00	13.23	3	8.00	13.86
State hospital	11	17.55	17.00	8	5.00	7.56
University counseling center	7	23.71	16.63	12	18.92	22.87
VA facility	13	4.92	8.07	18	7.00	7.28

Note. n = number of programs in each category. This number varies from table to table because not all programs listed in the directory responded to every item.

vary tremendously, and stipends range from zero to the level of a starting salary for a new PhD staff member in many recently advertised positions. The size of programs varies from no interns at all (indicating that some advertised internships are actually nonfunctional) to intern classes that surpass the size of the faculty in many major training institutions. Although training in psychotherapy receives major commitment in most internship programs, there is much variation in training efforts devoted to such areas as assessment and research.

As noted in the survey reported by Drummond et al. (1981), APA-approved internships were found in the present study to differ from non-APA-approved programs in a number of important characteristics. Both sets of data indicate that the approved programs are larger and offer more funded slots. In addition, our study demonstrated that the APA-approved internships have larger full-time supervisory staffs and devote less time to training in assessment than non-APA-approved programs. It should be noted that our data apparently failed to replicate Drummond et al.'s finding that approved programs offer more time in seminar training. Perhaps the reason for this difference is that the Drummond et al. instrument listed many more activities of interns, so that sharper differentiations could be made than those found in the APIC directory.

Apart from important differences relating to APA approval, this investigation clearly indicated that there are differences in programs related to the type of agency setting. Interns can select programs to meet a wide variety of special needs and interests. If a large, full-time supervisory staff is deemed a virtue, then the medical centers, state hospitals, and consortia are the places to go. For a better chance at getting a funded position, interns should seek primarily the consortium, medical center, university counseling center, and VA internships. For some interns, the size of the stipend is very important, in which case the programs offered by the state hospitals, the military, and the prison systems would be most attractive, and the children's facilities and children's medical centers would be least so.

Considering the amounts of time devoted to various training activities, there are no clear differences related to setting in training in psychotherapy, consultation, and seminar attendance. Certainly, there are large individual differences in these areas across all 272 programs listed in the APIC directory; however, these were not systematically related to agency type. It is not surprising, however, that children's facilities and children's hospitals, where assessment issues are frequently of great import in day-to-day clinical activity, offer the most training in that endeavor. For opposite reasons, university counseling centers offer the least assessment training. If an intern wishes research experience during an internship, the choice should generally be either the VA settings, which frequently have specific funds earmarked for research, or the medical centers, which are likely to have large, grant-funded research programs and whose faculties must satisfy the usual scholarly publication requirements for promotion and tenure. Although their number is small, prison system training programs offer a relatively large amount of time for research. The prisons and the military services are strong in consultation training. Finally, the data suggest that the university counseling centers are the programs to choose for training supervision and that the community mental health centers are strong on training in outreach activities.

There was a broad array of theoretical orientations and major viewpoints of staff members, including some inventive and seemingly unique theories, but these were not systematically related to either APA approval or type of setting. Despite the variety, the predominant orientation of internship training tends to be some version of psychodynamic theory.

Drummond et al. (1981) noted that although students from APA-approved programs have the edge on admissions to internships of all types, internship training positions may still be found for students from non-APA-approved doctoral programs. Our data support this conclusion. Certainly students from the approved clinical programs are the much-preferred internship candidates; however, even the least preferred, the non-APA-approved school psychology students, still have a variety of agencies that will consider them should they wish to apply to the primarily clinically oriented programs in the directory. It should be noted that the overall acceptance situation is currently clouded with uncertainty. Several years ago Tuma and Cerny (1976) predicted a shortage of internship opportunities. More recently there was evidence of a growing oversupply of internship slots (Burstein, 1981; Silver, Miller, MacDonald, & Lee, 1981), but with the imminent loss of funding from the National Institute of Mental Health and other support for training, it is likely that internship programs will contract and that the Tuma and Cerny predictions will be belatedly upheld.

REFERENCES

Burstein, A. G. Remarks from the chair. *APIC Newsletter*, 1980, *5*, 1–2.

Burstein, A. G. Remarks from the chair. *APIC Newsletter*, 1981, *6*, 1–2.

Drummond, F. E., Rodolfa, E., & Smith, D. A survey of APA- and non-APA-approved internship programs. *American Psychologist*, 1981, *36*, 411–414.

Kurz, R. B. (Ed.). *Directory: Internship programs in professional psychology* (8th Ed.). Washington, D.C.: Association of Psychology Internship Centers, 1979.

Silver, R. J., Miller, D. R., MacDonald, J., & Lee, R. A. A review and evaluation of 1980 APIC Clearinghouse operations. *APIC Newsletter*, 1981, *6*, 10–13.

Tedesco, J. F. Factors involved in the selection of doctoral internships in clinical psychology. *Professional Psychology*, 1979, *10*, 852–858.

Tuma, J. M., & Cerny, J. A. The internship marketplace: The new depression. *American Psychologist*, 1976, *31*, 664–670.

Reading 16

Training Clinical Psychologists in Medical Settings: Ideological and Practical Considerations

Alvin G. Burstein
University of Texas Health Science Center in San Antonio

Robert H. Barnes
St. Luke's Hospital Medical Center in Phoenix, Arizona

Gustavo M. Quesada
Texas Tech University Complex in Lubbock

A delusion, cultivated by some segments of American medicine, is that psychotherapy is an exclusively medical province. This delusion, like all delusions, has the intrapsychic function of reducing anxiety, but at the expense of reality testing. Because psychology training in a medical setting usually involves obtaining sanction from the psychiatric staff and because our ability to correct a misperception depends on understanding its origins and functions, this article explores the sources that contribute to the perpetuation of the belief in question and examines some general questions about interdisciplinary training.

IDEOLOGICAL SOURCES

Membership in any profession involves the sharing of an ideology or a set of unexamined beliefs and values. The ideology of medicine includes three elements that imply that the practice of psychotherapy is a particular province of physicians: (a) the psychosomatic concept, (b) the concept of treating the whole person, and (c) the concept of patient care and medical responsibility.

The Psychosomatic Concept

Many models have been proposed to conceptualize the relationship between physical and mental phenomena. One set can be regarded as real, the other as epiphenomenal; both can be regarded as double aspects of a single underlying reality, or they can be regarded as basically independent but coincidentally related. The conventional modern assumption is reductionistic: It is assumed that mental phenomena can be reduced to "simple," more "basic," and more "real" biological factors. For psychiatry, the reductionist assumption has been reinforced by contemporary interest in hallucinogenic drugs and by the apparent recent success of several somatotherapies, including the major tranquilizers.

Nevertheless, the merits of the reductionist assumption are not totally persuasive. An alternative to reductionism is the doctrine of emergent qualities

Reprinted from Professional Psychology, *7*, 396–402.

positing that as systems become more complex, new qualities emerge, and that theories appropriate to the various levels of complexity are not mutually translatable. From this point of view, the contents of consciousness cannot possibly be stated as a set of biochemical equations. This position does not imply that the mind-body systems are totally unrelated but that they are not *totally* reducible to one another's terms.

To many physicians and biologists, reductionism also implies that the somatic impact on the psyche is more real, or profound than the reverse. Again, this assumption can be questioned. Current work on bioconditioning, the hypnotic induction of profound physiological events, the efficacy of psycho-prophylaxis in childbirth, and the psychoeducational treatment of frigidity and impotence all suggest that the system can be entered, sometimes with better effect, from the psychic end.

If the psychosomatic concept in its reductionist form is abandoned, the question arises as to whether psychic and somatic treatment techniques are identical, overlapping, or distinct; the answer to that question requires a review of the remaining two concepts.

Treating the Whole Person

Medicine has always struggled to reconcile its altruism and materialism, its scientific and humane sides. The trend toward specialization and briefer, more limited patient contacts has been counterbalanced by an effort to reemphasize humane values in medical practice. The student is reminded, "You are not treating a broken leg, you are treating a *whole* person."

Realistically, however, treatment has become increasingly complex, to the point that no single individual can master the full range of clinical knowledge and techniques. Hence, the need for specialization and hence the correlated need for the professional to acknowledge, unburdened by the distortions of neurotic shame, the limits of competence, and his or her need to tap the skills of fellow professionals. Recognition that one is treating a whole person need not imply that no others are involved.

We come, therefore, to a partial answer to the question raised in the previous section: Even if therapeutic skills are relatively homogeneous or overlapping in theory, the complexity of modern therapeutics makes it impossible for any one person to treat every aspect of a "whole" person.

Even if treatment of medical problems is a specialty, the notion that psychotherapy is the prerogative of *medical* specialists remains and is considered as follows in relation to the concept of patient care.

Patient Care and Medical Responsibility

All expert-client relationships assume that the expert is a better judge of what actions are required of him or her in the helping relationship than is the client.

This asymmetry tends to evoke automatically emotional attitudes (transference and countertransference) in the helper and the person helped that are derivative of parent-child roles played in the past.

The asymmetry of the doctor-patient relationship is reinforced by many factors: the highly specialized knowledge possessed by the physician, the life and death stakes at times involved, or the patient's inability to control the situation when he or she is a child, or unconscious, or too frightened. In fact a psychosocial definition of illness should have at its core the patient's reduced ability to deal with the biological process with his or her personal resources. Illness, requiring exogenous expertise, becomes thus distinguished from "natural" processes like hunger.

In part because the patient may be objectively helpless and in part because of transference-countertransference attitudes, the doctor feels a quasi-religious need to be selfless, omniscient, and omnipotent. This need can create difficulties when the physician develops inappropriate shame about normal materialistic self-interest or about recognizing the limits of professional competence. On the other hand, the ability to act quickly and decisively in life or death situations may require some blunting of the capacity to experience anxiety or self-doubt. The question remains, however, as to whether medical responsibility for patient care, in the sense of the good shepherd's categorical imperative to protect the patient from all harm, facilitates every aspect of psychiatric treatment.

If one defines persons with behavioral and emotional difficulties as mentally ill in the psychosocial sense described above, then psychiatry becomes the practice of dealing with patients not competent to handle their own problems. That the care of such patients is a significant issue is made manifest by the social sanctions (e.g., commitment) that have been developed in connection with them. The treatment of these patients may well require a pastoral attitude in their physician.

With respect to other emotionally troubled patients, however, the situation is quite different. A central goal of the specific technique of insight-oriented psychotherapy is to reveal the irrational nature of transference feelings and to disencumber the "patient" of their erosive impact on reality testing, thus contradicting a pastoral attitude.

Therefore, with respect to patient care attitudes occurring in psychiatric practice, a distinction should be made between psychotherapy, practiced without the patient's adult collaboration and other practice, therapeutic to the psyche, which *requires* the adult collaboration of the patient. With respect to this latter form of practice, some aspects of medical ideology are quite possibly a hindrance.

ECONOMIC ISSUES

Economic considerations also powerfully contribute to the view that psychotherapy is an exclusively medical province. While psychotherapy has historical origins in religion, education, and psychology, as well as in medicine, the private practice of psychotherapy has clearly a medical origin. Therapeutic entrepreneurs, working on a fee-for-service basis, developed directly from the office practice of medicine. The pay for such practice has generally been greater than for institutional psychiatry, and therefore the private practitioner has come to enjoy higher status.

A second factor has been the tendency of the nonmedical practitioner to seize on the terms *therapy* and *treatment* (as opposed to *counseling* or *teaching*) to characterize his or her efforts. This mimicry, an attempt to claim the prestige of the higher status physician role, has been strongly reinforced by the commercial motive of attaining reimbursement via health insurance coverage.

The nonmedical practitioner is an economic threat to psychiatrists committed to the entrepreneurial model in two ways. As a lower status practitioner, he or she tends to prefer the protection of institutional practice and hence helps to propagate a socialized or community model that competes with the entrepreneurial one. Second, when in private practice, his or her rates tend to be lower. Although some private purchasers of therapeutic services may be willing to purchase status, third-party purchasers (e.g., insurance companies) may be attracted by lower fees. If the economic picture becomes more bleak, physician practitioners will be motivated by self-interest to encourage guild-type restraints upon the practice of psychotherapy. This economic struggle is already being played out on the national legislative level by the psychiatric and psychologist lobbyists engaged over the pending health insurance legislation.

Whatever the outcome of the political struggles, and however the mythology of medicine is structured, it is clear that psychotherapy, defined as the collaborative exploration of one's feelings and thoughts, and psychotherapeutic success, defined as the feeling of psychic liberation that may be induced by that activity, does not and will not occur solely in physician's offices. Perhaps, more important, if behavioral science becomes more responsive to current social needs, the outlook and funtion of both psychology and psychiatry will change. The prospect of those changes raises the following questions: (a) How can the ideological socialization be examined for their utility to professional function? (b) What particular efforts require a professional with medical skills and sanctions? What professional efforts do *not* require medical skills and sanctions? Can and should such a division be made? (c) What should be the relationship between the physician and the nonmedical, applied behavioral scientist? (d) Depending on answers to the above, how should their graduate education and practical experience (e.g., residencies) be coordinated?

FOSTERING THE EXAMINATION OF IDEOLOGICAL STEREOTYPES

Central is a clarification of the psychiatrist's conceptualization of his or her role function in caring for patients, particularly his or her function vis-à-vis other mental health professionals and paraprofessionals. We focus on the psychiatrist, because in the medical school or hospital setting, his or her accommodation to the training of psychologists means the giving up of exclusivist views about patient care, and the sharing of power and status. It is the students, intern and resident, whose professional identities are sufficiently fluid as to permit them albeit painfully, to examine such core assumptions and role definitions and to try out alternatives. For that reason, it is unfortunate if training is used as an opportunity to confirm the old clichés; rather, it should be the occasion for stimulating the most radical questioning about professional identity. The faculty has the responsibility to provide a climate in which such questions can be addressed. Interdisciplinary training programs are of value because the incompatibility of various professional mythologies becomes blatant and the presumptive nature of core values is revealed. Therefore, interdisciplinary team involvement at all points in practical training is the most important mechanism by which to rid the psychiatrists and psychologists of unrealistic ideological stereotypes as to what their functioning may be.

An important training goal is the preparation of the trainee for the future of his profession. The cottage industry day of the solo practitioner, isolated in his or her own office, is clearly on the wane. Whether the health care world becomes one great health maintenance organization after the format of the Kaiser Permanente model or a diverse set of differing models, it seems that professional collaboration in the sense of a close working together under one roof, physical or administrative, will be the dominant format for care giving.

If team functioning is limited to inpatient units, then the only model seen may be one in which the psychiatrist is captain. In addition to inpatient work, the trainees should have considerable experience in day care (partial hospitalization) and in outpatient clinic team activity, where a clinical psychologist or a social worker may be a team leader, as well as working in outreach programs characterized by paraprofessional leadership.

In addition to varied, team-oriented applied experiences, trainees should participate in seminars dealing with the development and functioning of care-giving professions and care systems; issues of legal and moral responsibility; and the sociology and dynamics of administration and management of care-giving systems. Thus a broader view of the impact of public responsibility on medicine, education, and other areas would be developed.

ASSESSING MEDICAL VERSUS NONMEDICAL CONTRIBUTIONS

There are clinical activities that only a licensed physician can perform legally. The medical (including neurological) evaluation of emotionally disturbed individuals requiring such examinations is such an activity; in addition subsequent somatic therapies must be his or her responsibility, including psychoactive drugs, electroshock treatment, etc., aimed at influencing behavioral function as well as broader somatic therapies aimed at correcting physical defects or deficiencies adversely affecting behavior.

Second, there are clinical situations in which direct review, supervision, or participation by the medical trained specialist is indicated. The care of committed psychotic or suicidal patients, generally on in inpatient or day-care-type service, generally requires medical participation in a team effort involving psychologists, nurses, social workers, and/or paraprofessionals. Here rational— not ritual—working relationships in which the nonphysician decides and acts in certain areas and the psychiatrist decides and acts in others must be established. Thus, on an inpatient or day-care service, the nonphysician professional might have responsibility for verbal psychotherapy, whereas the psychiatrist might be responsible for the psychoactive medication, with both activities being interrelated through direct and continuing consultation. Decisions such as discharge would be made jointly, with the realization on both sides that the physician has, as our laws are *currently* interpreted, the prime medical/legal responsibility for the consequence of such decisions. In practical terms, this has meant that if damages for malpractice are awarded, the physician and the institution, not the medical team members, are liable. This convention is eroding, and the courts are beginning to hold other professionals liable as well.

Third, there are activities that the nonphysician might well carry on independently, and be responsible for, with optional consultation that carries with it no medical/legal responsibility for the consultant. Examples are such activities as group or individual psychotherapy, remedial rehabilitative and emotional reeducation programs, and other types of intervention. Consultation on such activities is more a matter of teaching than of assuming medical/legal responsibility. The circumstance that the physician is often the best educator member of the team, and hence involved in such teaching, has combined with the mystique of medical responsibility to produce an unfortunate confusion of the ability to teach with medical/legal responsibility.

Clearly, distinctions between medical and nonmedical functions can feasibly be made. Further, it is economically indefensible to involve the high cost of medical education as a prerequisite for activities that do not require medical skills.

DEFINING RECIPROCAL ROLES OF PHYSICIANS AND NONPHYSICIANS

The foregoing considerations clarify the relationship between medical and nonmedical applied behavioral scientists. Basically, job roles should be defined on the basis of professional training, both academic and practicum, with the medically trained individual having responsibility for evaluation and treatment of organic/physiological parameters.

A major difficulty in defining professional interrelationships springs from the fact that both physicians and nonphysicians are trained in the diffuse area called psychotherapy. As the earlier argument showed, a medical degree does not bestow any exclusive facility or privilege to do psychotherapy, except in situations in which somatotherapies are concurrently involved. In such situations, there may be a considerable advantage to the psychotherapist if he or she is also responsible for the somatic agents. At other times, this may not be necessary. Much would depend on the willingness of the physician to administer the "medicine," while someone else takes the responsibility for the patient's education. The medical/legal issues raised by such arrangements have not been fully clarified. Legal changes will generally follow and reflect changing patterns of relationships in the broader society between physicians, nonphysicians, and their clients, but will sometimes lead the way to change.

In general, as long as we suffer from a severe shortage of physicians, it is unwise to encourage physicians to do the same things that nonphysicians can be trained to do, particularly when the latter are less expensively trained and are more readily available.

COORDINATION OF GRADUATE TRAINING

In light of the viewpoints expressed above, some of the graduate education and almost all of the practicum experience of doctoral-level applied behavioral scientists should be supplied in the same programs. Medical students interested in becoming psychiatrists should be equipped during medical school with the basic behavioral science knowledge via graduate-level courses in social psychology, personality theory, statistics, testing and measurement, etc. Practicum experience for both psychiatric and clinical psychology trainees is best provided in the same training program, and concurrently with emphasis on ways in which their particular roles vary. Obviously, both groups need role models with whom to identify, and this means that the interdisciplinary faculty must perform in properly differentiated roles on clinical services. This means, of course, that faculties must achieve an intellectual and emotional consensus as the differing roles of psychiatrists and psychologists.

Another issue should be broached, the question of whether both the needs of our society and the individual needs of practitioners might be served by merging the training of psychiatrists and clinical psychologists into one integrated medical school-graduate school program. As an experimental approach to the production of theory builders and teachers (as opposed to practitioners), such a program has much to recommend it. While full-time practitioners of psychiatry and non-medical psychotherapists can be and should be produced without such elaborate training, a relatively small number of MD-PhD products, competent to practice in and to research the broadest range of human problems, might serve as the vanguard of conceptualizers for a psychological science less tied to historical accident and professional rivalry.

Reading 17
Internship Training in Behavioral Medicine: Program Description, Issues, and Guidelines

Gary E. Swan
Stanford University and SRI International, California

Anthony Piccione
Community Hospital of Indianapolis

David C. Anderson
Loma Linda Veterans Administration Medical Center, California

The field of behavioral medicine is a robust and growing area of professional endeavor. Evidence of its increasing emergence is provided by the publication of a new broadbased journal entitled *Journal of Behavioral Medicine;* the organization of Division 38, Health Psychology, of the American Psychological Association; and the formation of the Academy of Behavioral Medicine Research, the Society for Behavioral Medicine, and several special interest groups.

Developing concomitantly with this activity is an awareness that many new opportunities exist for the practicing psychologist, both within and outside the confines of a medical setting. Accordingly, it seems reasonable to predict that as the scope and depth of activity in the field increase, more and more professionals will desire training in both application and research.

A recent survey of medical and educational centers revealed only a handful

Reprinted from Professional Psychology, *11*(2), 339–346. Special thanks are due *Harold Dickman and Donald Lim* for their advice, support, and encouragement during the developmental phase of the training program.

of formal programs providing training in the field (Weiss, 1978), including the medical schools of Harvard, Johns Hopkins, University of Mississippi, University of Pennsylvania, Stanford, and Yale. As one might expect, the emphasis in these programs is primarily on research. But training is also necessary in the clinical application of research findings. For clinical psychologists, such a training opportunity can be provided during their internship year. However, no formal guidelines exist that indicate what training is necessary and sufficient for psychologists to gain professional competency in behavioral medicine.

The present article shares the knowledge gained from an experimental internship training program in behavioral medicine conducted at the Palo Alto Veterans Administration (VA) Medical Center. Because such training for clinical psychology interns is rare, it was felt that the efforts and perceptions of the clinical psychologists involved could contribute to the development of other behavioral medicine programs for *psychologists*. Our goal is not to define a model training program, but rather to raise some issues for discussion and offer some general guidelines based on our collective experience. Thus, the present article outlines our strategy for a sequence of training experiences leading to the development of the skills required for competent research in and practice of behavioral medicine.

CHARACTERISTICS OF THE PALO ALTO TRAINING PROGRAM

The Palo Alto VA hospital is a large medical and surgical facility affiliated with the Stanford University Medical School. The two medical complexes combine to provide a variety of specific settings for experience in behavioral medicine (see Figure 1).

Psychology Services at the Palo Alto VA hospital has 35 psychologists on staff, working primarily in traditional inpatient and outpatient psychiatric settings. The hospital has had a VA-approved clinical psychology internship program since 1946. In 1977 the program was given full American Psychological Association (APA) accreditation for 5 years. Because no formal training program in behavioral medicine was included, the authors, in coordination with the director of training, developed a training rotation in behavioral medicine during the internship year 1977–1978.

The interns who chose to participate in the behavioral medicine training sequence shared common attributes. All had come from clinical psychology programs with a strong emphasis on the scientist-practitioner model of training; and all had extensive training in the more traditional aspects of human service, including individual, group, and family therapy, as well as a shared emphasis on behavior therapy techniques.

A didactic foundation for the participating interns was provided in a series of behavioral medicine seminars led by experts in various subspecialties (e.g., smoking, hypertension, pain control, sleep disorders). These seminars led directly to the development of a broad perspective necessary to the field of behavioral medicine. Interns were thus able to target areas of interest to them in which research evidence showed a clear promise of clinical effectiveness. Concomitantly, patient populations were also targeted, and resources in the community were identified.

The matrix of intern interests, areas of data-based procedures, and hospital/community needs and resources combined to form a broad-based and highly flexible training program. An organizational diagram of the program is presented in Figure 1.

EXPERIENCES AND TRAINING IN BEHAVIORAL MEDICINE

We have chosen to describe our experiences and training in behavioral medicine in two broad categories: clinical and research. Thus, the training program can be viewed as a direct descendant of the scientist-practitioner model of training initiated in graduate school.

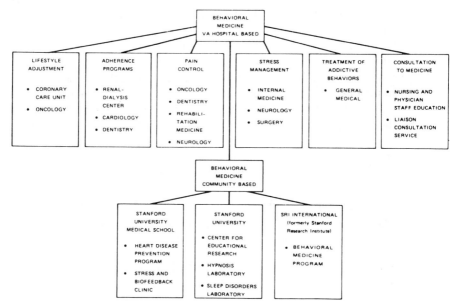

Figure 1 Matrix of settings and interventions relevant to the behavioral medicine training program at the Palo Alto Veterans Administration Medical Center.

Clinical Activities

Stress and Pain Management An ongoing caseload of 6 to 12 male and female pain patients, 22-62 years of age, was maintained throughout the training period. Referral sources included the general medical wards, oncology and nerve block units, surgery and spinal cord injury wards, neurology department, and self-referrals. Treatment approaches included the use of cognitive/behavioral treatment strategies (see Davidson, 1976); tension reduction techniques included progressive relaxation training (Bernstein & Borkovec, 1973), electromyographic and/or peripheral temperature biofeedback (Fuller, 1977), modified autogenic training, breathing exercises, and meditation (see Benson, 1975).

Several patients were seen on a regular basis at the ear, eye, nose, and throat oncology ward. These people were facing a number of serious problems: life-threatening and painful cancer and surgery, stressful and painful postsurgical facial disfigurement, and life-style readjustment. In addition to stress and pain reduction interventions, supportive counseling and family involvement were used to help facilitate the adjustment and comfort of the cancer patient.

Adherence to Therapeutic Regimens The nonadherent medical patient poses an acute problem for medical personnel; in some cases nonadherence can be life threatening (Gutch & Stoner, 1975). The psychologist trained in behavioral assessment may successfully apply a functional analysis to this situation.

Adherence counseling was provided to several patients undergoing hemodialysis in the artificial kidney center. The regimen usually prescribed for patients on a dialysis machine involves a low-salt diet and controlled fluid intake. Adherence, then, is often hindered by the complexity of the regimen, as well as by interpersonal factors in the patient-practitioner relationship (Marston, 1970). In the case of one renal dialysis patient, it was determined by functional analysis that the patient's nonadherent behavior was being maintained by that patient's primary nurse. Once this information was obtained, it was possible to approach the problem with a different focus, including staff training in behavioral principles and more constructive methods of communication.

Other Applications and Involvement Other patients were seen in the coronary care unit; most were recovering from a myocardial infarction. Involvement with these patients consisted of postmyocardial infarction counseling, crisis intervention, and adherence counseling. Discussion of life-style often suggested ways in which the patient could alter his or her coronary-prone behaviors (see Jenkins, 1978).

Research Activities

While at the Palo Alto VA hospital, the present authors wrote several research proposals in connection with this training program. One proposal viewed pain caused by cancer as a stressor that could be managed with the aid of various cognitive strategies contained in the larger structure of Meichenbaum's stress inoculation (see Davidson, 1976). This study is currently being implemented by members of the oncology nursing staff at the VA hospital.

A behavioral dentistry research and treatment team was also developed (see Kleinknecht, Klepac, & Bernstein, 1976). Adherence and prediction of adherence to oral health regimens were pinpointed as central problems in dentistry. Consequently, a research proposal on a self-management approach to oral health care was written under the joint sponsorship of the Dentistry and Psychology Services.

A research study was designed to investigate the effectiveness of a behavioral approach for reducing the frequency and intensity of nocturnal bruxism. The procedure combined the use of biofeedback with all-night sleep recordings, and results are currently being analyzed.

In conjunction with the Health Services Research Group at SRI International, training was obtained in the design and implementation of a 3-year study to assess the psychophysiological components of the coronary-prone or Type A behavior pattern.

TRAINING ISSUES IN BEHAVIORAL MEDICINE

As a direct result of our applied and research experience in behavioral medicine at the settings indicated in Figure 1, we have formulated the following issues that one should consider before becoming involved in or implementing such a training program.

The Definition of Behavioral Medicine

One's definition of behavioral medicine will determine the character and content of the design of the training program. As yet, there is no generally accepted definition of the field. However, a variety of definitions have been proposed.

After much discussion, participants at the recent Yale Conference on Behavioral Medicine finally decided on a definition that emphasizes the interdisciplinary nature of the field (Schwartz & Weiss, 1978). The Yale Conference definition has been challenged, however, for not placing adequate emphasis on the experimental analysis of behavior as the source of much of the current activity in the field. Consequently, Pomerleau (1978) proposed a revised definition emphasizing the application of behavioral principles to the treatment and prevention of medical problems.

In agreement with Pomerleau's emphasis on the contribution and use of behavior modification and behavior therapy (including biofeedback), we believe that the training program should reflect a primary emphasis on data-based behavioral approaches to physical disorders and health maintenance.

The Role of Self-Management

It seems clear that part of behavioral medicine involves the application of specific behavioral procedures to preexisting physical ailments. In this sense, the traditional approach of providing a treatment for a diagnosed "illness" is maintained.

It is our belief, however, that behavioral medicine makes its greatest contribution not in its occasional use in the traditional medical approach but, rather, in teaching self-control techniques (Stuart, 1977) to clients to *maintain* their health. Consistent with progressive current thought regarding the role of self-responsibility for general health care (see Knowles, 1977), through appropriate guidance the individual may acquire the skills for active participation in the maintenance of his/her own health. Therefore, training at the intern level should focus on the theory and application of self-management strategies as a particularly relevant subset of general behavior therapy interventions.

Behavioral Medicine Interns

Eligibility for internship training in behavioral medicine may be the most sensitive of all the issues. We believe that doctoral level interns in clinical or counseling psychology are the logical candidates. We would also emphasize that psychologists trained under the scientist-practitioner model in graduate school appear to be the most appropriate candidates for admission to a behavioral medicine training program. Furthermore, the psychology interns should be trained along with medical residents in the same program. Such integration at the earliest stage would help to increase the communication between the disciplines necessary for effective therapeutic behavior.

Behavioral Medicine Trainers

We believe strongly that a behavioral medicine training program should be codirected by a behaviorally based clinical psychologist and a physician with specific skills and experience in relevant content areas. Such codirection would give the program more than just a passing emphasis on the collaborative and integrative nature of behavioral medicine. The psychology intern would acquire clinical acumen from the MD, and the medical resident would acquire research skills and a behavioral orientation from the PhD.

Furthermore, we believe that effective use can be made of allied professionals (e.g., dentists, speech therapists, physical therapists). Often these people have specific experience for approaching and working with medical patients that most psychology interns lack.

The Behavioral Medicine Training Setting

Based on the broad range of working environments encompassed by our experiences, we advise flexibility when organizing a behavioral medicine program. Because the practice of behavioral medicine is ultimately a *clinical* human service, the internship setting in a medical facility is the logical choice for this type of training. In contrast to such facilities as community mental health clinics, academic psychology departments, and university-based counseling centers, the medical setting provides for daily "hands-on" experience with real medical disorders. Additionally, the intern can develop his/her skills at generating and promoting referrals from physicians who might not consider sending a patient to the psychology service for treatment. We believe that the experience gained in this setting forms a core from which the intern can effectively operate.

The Elements of Training

Our views assume that the trainee comes from an applied psychology doctoral program and thus has already acquired at least the beginnings of clinical skill, as well as an adequate base of scientifically derived knowledge of human behavior. Included should be a working knowledge of behavioral assessment procedures and basic treatment interventions (e.g., progressive relaxation, operant procedures, systematic desensitization).

Beyond the above prerequisites, we propose training in behavioral medicine to include the following modules not ordinarily available in graduate training programs:

1 Epidemiology—methods of data collection and the prevalence, incidence, and high-risk target groups for various physical disorders.

2 Anatomy, physiology, and psychophysiology of the autonomic and somatic response systems.

3 Pharmacology—drug-related methods of pain and stress management for cardiovascular and nervous system disorders.

4 Cardiology—risk factors for coronary artery disease.

5 Medical/surgical interventions—current treatments of choice for various disorders.

6 Instrumentation—basic operating knowledge of psychophysiological recording equipment (including biofeedback equipment) and psychophysiological assessment techniques.

7 Specialized treatment approaches—biofeedback, hypnosis, autogenics/meditation, imagery, and so forth.

8 General clinical issues related to approaching and treating medical patients from a sociobehavioral perspective.

One other element of training deserves special mention because of its potential importance. Although neuropsychology is not exclusively in the domain of behavioral medicine, we believe such training is critical when working in this field. Neuropsychological assessment bears directly on questions concerning a patient's ability to adhere to regimens as well as on differential diagnosis of physical symptoms that may or may not be stress related (e.g., migraine headaches vs. closed head injury). Therefore, there is a need for increased sensitivity to the possibility of concomitant cerebral dysfunction, the behavioral signs of which may go unnoticed by hospital staff.

Accreditation of the Behavioral Medicine Training Program

The training program outlined here was undertaken *in the context* of an internship program already accredited by APA. Assuming that administrative and staffing issues could be resolved, we believe that a behavioral medicine training program, standing by itself, would be eligible for APA internship accreditation. The participating intern would have contact with a diversity of settings, experiences, professionals, and disciplines. Moreover, the emphasis on service would be retained by the necessity for crisis intervention, brief family therapy, and psychological assessment in addition to individual therapy for stress and pain management and group therapy for addictive habit management. Settings in which these services could be provided include inpatient medical and surgical wards, intensive and coronary care units, emergency room service, and outpatient clinics.

The primary difference between the present training program and a more traditional internship is the shift of focus from the assessment and treatment of psychopathology to the assessment and treatment of the interface between behavior and general health. APA internship accreditation guidelines are broad enough to allow for the inclusion of training experiences in this interface (APA, 1973).

Employment in Behavioral Medicine

A critical issue in choosing to obtain training in any field of endeavor is the potential for improved employment opportunities. Although relevant statistics are not yet available for behavioral medicine, there appear to be a growing number of possibilities. Lubin, Nathan, and Matarazzo (1978) recently reported on the increasing number of psychologists involved in behavioral science education in university medical settings. Similar opportunities are becoming increasingly available in family medicine residency programs in community hospitals (Asken & Sheinvold, 1978). Research positions are available in university-based psychophysiology laboratories and in health-related research centers. Many possibilities also exist in applied settings, including hospital-based departments of medical psychology or behavioral medicine, pain and rehabilitation centers, and biofeedback and stress management clinics. These employment opportunities, spanning the spectrum of education, research, and applied aspects of health psychology, are likely to increase as the field develops.

From our perspective as consumers of training in behavioral medicine, these are the major issues associated with the training of professionals in the new field of behavioral medicine. We expect and welcome other opinions as to what constitutes the necessary and sufficient training experiences leading to competence. It is important for psychologists to continue this discussion in order to preserve the integrity of psychology's contribution to this burgeoning field.

REFERENCES

American Psychological Association. *Accreditation procedures and criteria.* Washington, D.C.: Author, 1973.

Asken, M. J., & Sheinvold, A. T. Psychologists in medical education. *American Psychologist,* 1978, *33,* 1147.

Benson, H. *The relaxation response.* New York: Avon Books, 1975.

Bernstein, D. A., & Borkovec, T. D. *Progressive relaxation training: A manual for helping professions.* Champaign, Ill.: Research Press, 1973.

Davidson, P. O. (Ed.). *The behavioral management of anxiety, depression, and pain.* New York: Brunner/Mazel, 1976.

Fuller, G. D. *Biofeedback: Methods and procedures in clinical practice.* San Francisco: Biofeedback Press, 1977.

Gutch, C. F., & Stoner, M. H. *Review of hemodialysis for nurses and dialysis personnel* (2nd ed.). St. Louis, Mo.: Mosby, 1975.

Jenkins, C. D. Behavioral risk factors in coronary artery disease. *Annual Review of Medicine,* 1978, *29,* 543–562.

Kleinknecht, R. A., Klepac, R. K., & Bernstein, D. A. Psychology and dentistry: Potential benefits from a health care liaison. *Professional Psychology,* 1976, *7,* 585–592.

Knowles, J. H. (Ed.). *Doing better and feeling worse: Health in the United States.* New York: Norton, 1977.

Lubin, B., Nathan, R. G., & Matarazzo, J. D. Psychologists in medical education. *American Psychologist,* 1978, *33,* 339–343.

Marston, W. V. Compliance with medical regimens: A review of the literature. *Nursing Research,* 1970, *19,* 312–323.

Pomerleau, O. F. On behaviorism in behavioral medicine. *Behavioral Medicine Newsletter,* 1978, *1,* 2.

Schwartz, G. E., & Weiss, S. M. Yale conference on behavioral medicine: A proposed definition and statement of goals. *Journal of Behavioral Medicine,* 1978, *1,* 3–12.

Stuart, R. B. (Ed.). *Behavioral self-management: Strategies, techniques and outcomes.* New York: Brunner/Mazel, 1977.

Weiss, S. M. News and developments in behavioral medicine. *Journal of Behavioral Medicine,* 1978, *1,* 135–139.

Reading 18

Internship Training in Clinical Neuropsychology

Alan L. Goldberg
Charlotte Rehabilitation Hospital, North Carolina

Kathleen M. McNamara
Wright State University, Dayton, Ohio

In recent years, there has been explosive growth in the field of clinical neuropsychology. Evidence of this growth is widespread. Membership has swelled in professional organizations devoted to neuropsychology. Articles addressing topics in
neuropsychology are appearing in greater numbers in psychology journals. In
addition, numerous books of particular interest to practicing neuropsychologists
have been penned (Goldberg & McNamara, 1983). Increased interest in neuropsychology is likewise reflected in the number of graduate programs offering
training in this field (Golden & Kuperman, 1980a; Noonberg & Page, 1982; Sheer
& Lubin, 1980). As the field has matured, increasing attention to training models
and credentialing has occurred (Meier, 1981). Literature concerning training has
most often stressed theory, research, and above all, academic requirements. Opportunities for development, application, and/or refinement of practical neuropsychology skills have been addressed infrequently. Noonberg and Page (1982),
in their findings on this issue, reveal that, of those academic departments offering neuropsychology training, several devote no time to practical training,
whereas only 38% of the programs offer practica or traineeships. The only article
directly addressing internship training in neuropsychology (Golden & Kuperman,
1980b) is based on survey data collected almost 5 years ago. Since that time the
number of American Psychological Association (APA)-approved internships has
increased precipitously, and with the rapid growth and expansion in the field of
clinical neuropsychology, another survey of available training on internships
seems warranted.

This article provides a basic assessment of neuropsychology training experiences currently available in APA-approved predoctoral clinical and counseling
psychology internship programs. Such information is not only helpful to professionals practicing in the field, but to programs that might be considering the inclusion of neuropsychology training and to students seeking some way to critically evaluate an internship site that claims to offer training in this specialty area.

METHOD

To gather information on training, a survey was sent to the directors of all
internship sites listed as fully approved by the APA in the December 1982
American Psychologist. Training directors were requested to forward the surveys

Reprinted from Professional Psychology: Research and Practice, *15*(4), 509–514.

to the individual(s) directly responsible for neuropsychology training. Self-addressed, stamped envelopes were enclosed to facilitate responses.

The survey included forced-choice questions relating to areas such as length of rotation, assessment techniques used, area of neuropsychology service emphasized, minimum requirements for assessment skills, types of populations and referral issues, didactic training available, and judged competency upon completion of the programs. Space was provided for additional comments. A copy of the full survey instrument is available, on request, from the second author.

RESULTS

Of the 205 surveys sent, 136 were returned, which yielded a 67% return rate. This is in comparison to the 77% return rate reported by Golden et al. (1980b) in the previous study of this issue. At least 82% of the sites (111) indicated that there was some exposure to neuropsychology, although only 57% have a formalized part-time or full-time rotation (see Table 1). Availability of full or partial rotations and expected time commitments for each are presented in Table 2. Three respondents indicated that neuropsychology rotations would be in place for trainees commencing internships in September, 1983. Nine of the sites offered a full-time, 12-month rotation, whereas the majority of sites with a full-time rotation required a 3-4 month commitment.

Populations seen by interns taking neuropsychology rotations include patients of all ages. Of responding agencies, 87% work with adults, 46% work with adolescents, and 44% work with children. Although many sites offer nearly exclusive work with adults, interns who work with adolescents and children typically gain exposure to adult patients as well.

Patients who are seen for neuropsychological evaluation are referred by, in descending order, psychiatrists, neurologists, psychologists, neurosurgeons, and pediatricians. The percentage of sites endorsing any one referral source ranges from 12%-63%. In addition, 33% of respondents indicate "other" referral sources (e.g., educators, family practitioners, internists). Referral questions are likewise diverse and include evaluation of psychiatric disorders, vascular disorders, head trauma, seizure disorders, learning disabilities and attention

Table 1   Types of Rotations Offered

Rotation	%
Full rotation only	21
Full or partial rotation	13
Partial rotation only	22
No rotation	43

Table 2 Availability of Rotations in Neuropsychology

Characteristic	Full major rotation	Partial rotation	None
% of sites offering	35%	35%	43%
Mean no. of months	5.6	5.3	
Range of months	2–12	1–12	
Mean no. of hours	640	265	
Range of hours	20–3,000	10–1,200	

deficit disorders, toxic and metabolic disturbances, space occupying lesions, and vocational capabilities. A more comprehensive discussion of referral sources and referral issues at internship sites is available (McNamara, Goldberg, & Munger, 1983).

The focus of training and the type of assessment instruments utilized are also highly variable. Training sites were queried as to their emphasis on test administration, test interpretation, or cognitive rehabilitation. Table 3 presents the summary data for this information. Assessment is clearly the focus of neuropsychology training at this time. Assesment instruments range from the Halstead-Reitan Battery and the Luria-Nebraska Battery to a variety of tasks and instruments assembled into nonstandardized batteries chosen for more in-depth analysis of specific skills/deficits. The Halstead-Reitan Battery is clearly the battery of choice, although a focus on a qualitative assessment, not limited to any standard battery, continues to be the most prevalent approach. Table 4 lists assessment instruments used.

Comments indicate that although hands-on experience in neuropsychology is available in many internship settings, the pattern is for only a fraction of the total intern pool to elect such training. Seminars specifically devoted to neuropsychology are made available to interns in 61% of the programs in this sample. This allows a larger group to gain familiarity with neuropsychology and learn about screening and referral.

The assortment of available experiences already described makes direct comparison of rotation requirements from program to program unfeasible. Comments indicate that requirements are highly individualized, depending on level of preinternship training and the intern's commitment to specialization.

Table 3 Training Emphasis

Emphasis	% of respondents endorsing
Interpretation of tests	82
Test administration	65
Cognitive rehabilitation	19

Table 4 Assessment Instruments Used

Type of battery	% of respondents endorsing
Nonstandardized (emphasis on qualitative assessment)	78
Halstead-Reitan	63
Luria-Nebraska	35

Respondents' views on the ability of interns completing their rotations to practice as neuropsychologists were assessed. The vast majority of respondents (74%) state that they encourage interns to use neuropsychology knowledge and skills as a part of general assessment practice. For most interns completing rotations and expressing further interest in neuropsychology, postdoctoral training is recommended. Of respondents offering full major neuropsychology rotations, 14% rated their interns competent to practice as neuropsychologists upon completion of a rotation and internship. A chi-square analysis indicates that this is a greater positive response rate than would be expected by chance ($p < .05$). When the total sample of respondents is considered, 15% indicate that a small proportion of their interns are urged to be adequately prepared to secure full-time employment as neuropsychologists. Comments indicate that this adequacy is largely based on preinternship preparation and experience supplemented by internship experiences. Golden et al.'s (1980b) comments on this issue of the adequacy of training are relevant here, and the reader is encouraged to review that discussion.

Neuropsychology specialization among respondents varies widely in spite of the fact that they are identified as responsible for neuropsychology training in their respective agencies. The average time that individuals completing the survey spend in the practice of neuropsychology is 48%, with a range of 0%–100%. Half of the respondents practice neuropsychology at least 50% of the time (M = 15% time).

Because the degree of commitment to practice, as reflected in the afore-mentioned percentages, may influence the setting in which an intern is trained, data were reanalyzed using a chi-square analysis to look at differences in respondents who spend the majority of their time (50% or more) in neuropsychology and those who spend less time in neuropsychology practice. As expected, the presence of rotations is significantly greater in setting where respondents practice neuropsychology a majority of the time ($p < .001$). Those who practice neuropsychology more than 50% of the time are likely to use qualitative assessment ($p < .001$), to emphasize test administration ($p < .05$), to stress test interpretation ($p < .001$), to be involved in cognitive rehabilitation ($p < .05$), to consult with other health care professionals on neuropsychology cases ($p < .001$), and to offer neuropsychology seminars ($p < .02$).

DISCUSSION

Results demonstrate that practical neuropsychology training is available in more than half (57%) of the APA-approved internship training centers in the sample. In addition a few programs anticipate adding such training in the coming year. This 57% reflects a significant decrease from the percentage of programs reported to offer neuropsychology training in the Golden and Kuperman (1980b) sample. They may reflect the fact that many recently approved programs are in community clinical health centers and settings other than major medical centers.

The mere fact that an intern has completed a neuropsychology rotation is not valuable data in and of itself. Rotations are too variable in hour requirements and experiences for this to be the case. More useful basic information might be obtained by prospective employers who inquire about the number of supervised hours of neuropsychology experience. Similarly, data concerning type of training activity (test administration, test interpretation, and/or cognitive rehabilitation) and diversity of patient population (age, reason for referral) with which a candidate has experience would prove beneficial. The variability in rotations reflected in our sample is similar to that seen in the Golden and Kuperman (1980b) samples where rotation length, patient population, and number of cases seen varied widely.

Although there has been debate in the literature and at scientific meetings concerning the use of standardized versus nonstandardized batteries and the composure of such batteries, results of this study suggest that neuropsychologists are in agreement on the importance of qualitative analysis of performance. A full 78% of respondents indicate that interns learn about neuropsychological assessment through qualitative assessment using a variety of instruments. These respondents include both those who teach the Halstead-Reitan Battery and those who teach the Luria-Nebraska Battery as well as those using nonstandardized approaches. Responses indicate that the Luria-Nebraska Battery has gained a significant following since Golden and Kuperman's (1980b) study. Thirty-five percent of the current sample endorsed its use.

The issue of quality in practical neuropsychology training is raised by this study. Those responsible for internship neuropsychology training vary widely in their time commitments to neuropsychology practice. Presumably the depth of their specialty training in this field may be variable as well. Analyses indicate significant differences in the type of training available when those spending the bulk of their time in neuropsychology are compared with respondents spending less time in this specialty area. This has implications for the degree of competence interns can achieve in neuropsychology practice in these settings.

Data on perceived competency of trainees to later practice neuropsychology raises questions concerning reliance on postdoctoral training to ensure such competency. Students are likely to have difficulty gaining competency with the range of referral problems and patients seen by those in full-time neuropsychology practice during an internship year when the development of other general competencies are required. Yet, students may be able to arrange for sufficient neuropsychology experience through a combination of extensive preinternship and internship experiences, because as many as 88% of clinical psychology programs offer preinternship training in neuropsychology (Noonberg & Page, 1982). Specialized neuropsychology internships do exist, some of these being formally structured, whereas others are designed by supervisors and students working conjointly to meet perceived training needs. Those who complete such rigorous training may be able to function semiautonomously as neuropsychologists, with less supervision than would be expected in a postdoctoral training program. Economic considerations, such as cutbacks in funding for educational programs, concomitant reduction in the availability of postdoctoral training programs, and potential income loss suffered by postdoctoral trainees, all speak for a closer look at the quality of predoctoral training in neuropsychology. Members of the American Board of Professional Neuropsychologists and the American Board of Clinical Psychology/American Board of Professional Psychology are considering the credentialing of neuropsychologists. Perhaps, psychologists who are "board certified" neuropsychologists can be viewed as acceptable supervisors of beginning neuropsychologists who have completed one of the aforementioned specialty internships.

A number of questions have been raised by this study, yet the interpretation of results must be done with caution. Although the response rate to this survey is commensurate with that found in aforementioned training surveys, a full third of internship sites did not respond to the present survey. The results of this survey might be dramatically different depending on whether these sites offer neuropsychology training. Additional comments to this lengthy survey reflected an intensive involvement by respondents in neuropsychology training, suggesting that most sites offering neuropsychology training may have responded. It is alarming to note that although interest in the field of clinical neuropsychology has increased greatly over the past 5 years, internship sites offering practical training in the field have not increased to match this interest. Clearly, further investigation and quality control of neuropsychology internship and preinternship training is necessary.

REFERENCES

American Psychological Association. (1982). Approved predoctoral internships for doctoral training in clinical and counseling psychology. *American Psychologist, 37,* 1369–1373.

Goldberg, A., & McNamara, K. M. (1983). *Recommended readings in clinical neuropsychology: The practitioner's view.* Manuscript submitted for publication.

Golden, C. J., & Kuperman, S. K. (1980a). Graduate training in clinical neuropsychology. *Professional Psychology, 11,* 55–63.
Golden, C. J., & Kuperman, S. K. (1980b). Training opportunities in neuropsychology at APA-approved internship settings. *Professional Psychology,
11,* 907–918.
McNamara, K. M., Goldberg, A. L., & Munger, M. P. (1983). *Referral sources
and referral issues encountered in neuropsychology rotations: Implications
for training.* Manuscript submitted for publication.
Meier, M. J. (1981). Education for competency assurance in human neuropsy-
chology: Antecedents, models, and directions. In S. B. Filskov & T. J. Boll
(Eds.), *Handbook of clinical neuropsychology* (pp. 754–781). New York:
Wiley-Interscience.
Noonberg, A. R., & Page, H. A. (1982). Graduate neuropsychology training:
A later look. *Professional Psychology, 13,* 252–257.
Sheer, D. E., & Lubin, B. (1980). Survey of training programs in clinical
neuropsychology. *Journal of Clinical Psychology, 36,* 1035–1040.

Reading 19

Training in Geropsychology:
A Survey of Graduate and Internship Training
Programs

Ilene C. Siegler and W. Doyle Gentry
Duke University Medical Center

C. Drew Edwards
Commonwealth Psychiatric Center in Richmond, Virginia

Lawton and Gottesman (Gottesman, 1977; Lawton, 1970; Lawton & Gottesman, 1974) discussed the deficit of professional interest and expertise among
clinical psychologists regarding psychological services to the elderly. For
example, Gottesman (1977) noted that at least 700 clinicians with a primary
interest in aging would be needed if each one of the 174,000 geriatric patients
currently residing in mental institutions in the United States were to receive
psychological services on a 1-day-a-year basis.

Although only 5% of the elderly are in institutions, a large proportion of
the residents in mental hospitals and nursing homes are old. Butler (1975)
reported that up to 50% of nursing home patients are mentally impaired, but the
mental health needs of nursing home patients are often overlooked. For the

Reprinted from Professional Psychology, *10*(3), 390–395. This research was supported
in part by National Institutes of Health Grant AG00364 to the Center for the Study of
Aging and Human Development.

majority of older people who reside in the community, the need for mental health services is probably similar to that of the adult population. Older people respond to treatment as well as adults do, as evidenced by the fact that studies in private mental hospitals report as many as 75% of the older patients improve and return to their homes within 2 months (Butler, 1975). The need for "gero-psychologists" is obvious.

Yet, Lawton and Gottesman (1974) found that (a) the gerontological content in psychological journals likely to be read by clinicians is essentially nil, (b) only a small number of clinical psychologists have expressed definite interest in problems of the aged by joining the Division of Adult Development and Aging (Division 20) of the American Psychological Association, (c) typically, the clinician who does provide services to the elderly "learns as he practices" in a very informal manner, and (d) it is still difficult to find separate, formal courses in graduate programs of most universities that deal specifically with clinical psychology and aging. In short, they conclude that "the deficit lies in the training of psychologists" (p. 692).

However, detailed information describing formal and informal didactic and clinical training opportunities for psychology graduate students interested in working with the elderly is currently unavailable. The present study sought to provide such information by surveying APA-approved programs in graduate departments and internship training sites throughout the country. In addition to asking specific questions about training opportunities available to students and interns, the survey inquired about the availability of faculty with special interest or expertise in geropsychology; the perceived importance of training in geropsychology, as viewed by persons administratively responsible for such training programs; and the degree of interest in geropsychology thought to be present among trainees in the respective programs.

METHOD

Separate questionnaires designed to assess available training opportunities for graduate students and interns regarding the psychology of aging were sent to all of the training directors of the 101 APA-approved doctoral programs in clinical psychology and the directors of the 118 APA-approved predoctoral internship programs in clinical and counseling psychology listed in the November 1975 issue of the *American Psychologist*. The questionnaires, which contained a cover letter briefly explaining the purpose of the survey, were mailed early in December 1975, and a second follow-up questionnaire was sent in March 1976 to those programs not responding initially. As the results are discussed question by question, the questionnaires are not reproduced here.[1]

---

[1] Detailed responses to the questionnaire broken down by institution and copies of the questionnaire are available from the first author.

RESULTS

University Programs

Training directors from 76 (75%) of the 101 programs returned the completed questionnaire. Of those programs responding, only 25 (33%) offered at least one formal course devoted specifically to the psychology of aging. Included were courses entitled "behavioral problems of older adults," "development in adult years," "adult development and aging," "psychopathology of aging," "aging and maturity," "cognition and aging," and "death and aging." Only 4 programs (5%) had two such courses in their clinical curriculum. With one exception, these courses were elective, and the majority (79%) were classified as nonclinical in orientation.

A total of only 21 programs (28%) noted one or more courses that included some aspect of geropsychology as a significant part of the subject content. For the most part, these included courses in developmental psychology, neuropsychology, psychological assessment, and behavior modification of adult disorders. In all, 10 of the 21 programs required students to take such courses; the remaining 11 programs offered them as electives. In only 38% of these courses was the orientation clearly identified as clinical.

A total of 34 programs (45%) listed one or more practicum facilities available to students which involved work with elderly clients. For the most part, these facilities were outside the confines of the university and included VA domicilaries, nursing homes, state hospitals, and community mental health centers. In 86% of the programs, experience in the practicum facilities involving work with aged clients was elective rather than required.

Only one program, at the University of Southern California, has a formal program or subspecialty in the clinical psychology of aging. This represents 1% of the programs responding.[2]

In all, 38 of the university programs (50%) acknowledged having faculty with special interests and/or clinical expertise in geropsychology.

The majority of the programs (63%) did not have or know of other programs in nearby departments, divisions, or centers that might offer training in geropsychology for their students. Those who did list other available programs cited the following as examples: various types of aging centers, programs in medical and nursing schools, and experiences offered by university departments of sociology and social work.

A total of 73 training directors indicated both the degree of importance they attached to training in geropsychology for clinical students and what they perceived to be the degree of interest in such training opportunities among their trainees. The mean level of importance assigned to geropsychology training

[2] After completion of the survey, a second program, with a specialty in aging, was started at Northwestern Medical School.

was 3.02 on a 5-point scale, with a normal distribution of ratings from 1 to 5. The mean level of interest in this area thought to characterize clinical students was 2.17, with a skewed distribution of ratings, which indicated a low level of interest in the majority of cases. In fact, only five training directors (7%) indicated more than moderate interest in clinical psychology of aging among their students. The directors' ratings were significantly different on the two survey items, $t(72) = 7.73$, $p < .0005$, suggesting that the training directors felt this type of training was more important in the students' career development than the students felt it was.

Only 53 of the training directors indicated numerically the percentage of students they thought were interested in such training, either at the clinical or nonclinical level. The mean response was 13%, and almost all of the directors indicated that 1/3 or less of their trainees would have such an interest.

Internship Programs

Directors from 97 (82%) of the 118 internship programs returned the completed questionnaire. Of those programs responding, only 22 (23%) indicated that they offered some formal, programmatic experience for interns in working with elderly clients.[3] They generally mentioned the following types of experience: specific rotations in geriatric wards, formal didactic seminars and courses in gerontology, access to older clients through rotations in psychosomatic medicine and outpatient psychiatry, and work with the elderly in nursing homes and on wards for terminally ill patients. In all cases, such experiences were available within the internship institution; in 9 programs (41%) they were required, whereas in the remaining 13, they were elective.

The geropsychology experiences available to interns in these programs included psychological assessment of intellectual functioning (91%) and organicity (91%), individual therapy (73%), group therapy (59%), and various other activities, such as ward administrator and consultation with mental health agencies regarding psychological services to the aged.

An additional 42 programs (43%) noted that interns occasionally came in contact with older clients as part of their diagnostic and therapeutic services to adult patients. Such contact was, however, informal, infrequent, and not systematically aimed at providing the intern with clinical expertise in geropsychology.

A total of 31 (32%) of the responding intern programs claimed to have faculty with special interests and/or clinical expertise in geropsychology. However, most of these individuals were concentrated in those programs offering a formal experience in the clinical psychology of aging. A total of 19 (86%) of the latter 22 programs identified such individuals, as compared with only

[3]After completion of the survey, an internship program specializing in aging was started at Hutchings Psychiatric Center in Syracuse, New York.

12 (16%) of the remaining 75 programs. Virtually none of the responding programs cited other, nearby facilities that were known to offer geropsychology experiences and might be available to their interns.

In all, 81 directors rated both the degree of importance they attached to training in geropsychology and the degree of interest they perceived their interns had in such training opportunities. The mean level of importance assigned to this type of training experience was 2.83 for all directors, 3.25 for directors of programs with formal geropsychology experiences, and 2.69 for programs without such training opportunities. The difference between ratings by directors of programs with formal experiences and those by directors of programs without formal experiences was significant beyond the .05 level, $t(59) = 2.00$.

The mean level of interest assigned to interns for training in geropsychology was 1.91 by all directors, 2.20 by directors of programs with formal experience, and 1.79 by directors of programs without formal experience. The difference between ratings by directors with and without formal geropsychology training was significant beyond the .02 level, $t(59) = 2.41$.

It was also noted that training directors tended to view geropsychology training as more important than did interns (at least as the directors viewed their level of interest) both in programs with and without formal, programmatic exposure to clinical psychology and aging.

DISCUSSION

The results of this survey offer a mixed picture. Compared with 1970, there has been a tremendous increase in the number of aging centers on university campuses, and most respondents indicated that there were resource people on their campuses knowledgeable about aging. What is distressing is that the increased interest on campus and in psychology departments does not appear to be having much of an impact on clinical programs. The findings indicate that the chances of a psychology trainee getting any experience in dealing with issues of aging and/or working with elderly clients are only about 1 in 4 (25%). This is true even when one considers the range of didactic/practicum experiences offered in internship training programs.

This rather limited exposure to geropsychology is further diluted by several factors. First, the majority of courses and practica in graduate programs dealing with aging and the aged are elective in nature and have a nonclinical orientation. Given the fact that the perceived interest of most students in this areas of study is not high, it seems very unlikely that they will in fact elect such experiences. Second, the clinical experiences in internship programs involving work with the aged are limited to traditional clinical roles, such as psychological assessment and psychotherapy, and do not include the types of services suggested by Lawton and Gottesman (1974), which might be most useful to the elderly living in the community. Third, most faculty in both the graduate and internship training programs are described as having no special interest or expertise in geropsychology. This factor alone raises serious questions about (a) whether training in geropsychology is characterized as a situation in which, at least presently, "the blind are leading the blind," that is, the faculty know little or no more about normal and abnormal aging than the students they teach and (b) whether one can realistically expect any measurable rate of growth, either in terms of the degree of importance that is assigned to training in geropsychology or in terms of the actual amount of exposure provided for trainees on this topic. Fourth, there seem to be few resources available outside of graduate and internship programs for students interested in learning more about geropsychology. For better or worse, this puts the total burden for training on these programs, which, as we have described here, are ill equipped for such a mission.

There has been a growth of interest in aging on the national scene, as evidenced by the creation of the National Institute on Aging as one of the 11 institutes of the National Institutes of Health in 1974 and the creation of the Center for Studies of the Mental Health of the Aging within the National Institute of Mental Health in August of 1975.

The field of psychology has much to offer in providing personnel to help meet the mental health needs of the elderly. Clinical training programs and internships could provide the most comprehensive type of training. However, if these programs choose *not* to offer training in these areas, the mental health needs of the elderly will continue to be met by psychiatrists and social workers. Our survey revealed only two such programs. We do not suggest that every program should offer a subspecialty in geropsychology, but it seems that more than two programs are required to meet this growing need.

REFERENCES

Butler, R. N. *Why survive?* New York: Harper & Row, 1975.

Gottesman, L. E. Clinical psychology and aging: A role model. In W. D. Gentry (Ed.), *Geropsychology: A model of training and clinical service.* Cambridge, Mass.: Ballinger, 1977.

Lawton, M. P. Gerontology in clinical psychology, and vice-versa. *Agin g and Human Development*, 1979, *1*, 147–159.

Lawton, M. P., & Gottesman, L. E. Psychological services to the elderly. *American Psychologist*, 1974, *29*, 689–693.

Reading 20
Professional Transition:
Psychology Internships in Rehabilitation Settings

Judy R. Gold
New York University and St. Vincent's Hospital, New York

Robin Hirtz Meltzer
New York University and St. Peter's College in New Jersey

Rose Lynn Sherr
New York University Medical Center

Issues regarding both the experiential and training components of clinical and counseling internships have been recognized in the literature (Dana, Gilliam, & Dana, 1976; Rosenkrantz & Holmes, 1974; Sturgis, Verstegen, Randolph, & Garvin, 1980; Comings, Note 1) and are reflected in the training practices of internship programs. Internships that occur in specialized training sites pose unique challenges to interns, but those issues have been only minimally explored.

There has been an absence of published material concerning the issues of training clinical and counseling psychology interns in physical rehabilitation settings. The lack is especially striking since the psychological tasks of clients/patients in rehabilitation settings are different from those in psychiatric and other facilities (Shontz & Wright, 1980) and since the structure of the service delivery system in rehabilitation differs from that in other settings. Consequently, the role of psychologists in rehabilitation is modified (Sherr, 1975), and hence interns must learn new professional role behaviors in order to function effectively in the rehabilitation setting.

Despite the unique professional role demands placed on interns in physical rehabilitation settings, all too often the training offered in these sites does not focus on acquiring appropriate skills to deal with these distinctive skills, with only cursory recognition of the unique aspects of the setting.

This limited approach to training restricts the ability of students schooled in traditional clinical and counseling psychology doctoral programs to obtain maximal benefits from their experience and provide effective services to their clients in the rehabilitation setting. To develop training approaches more congruent with the characteristics and needs of the site, it is necessary to analyze the distinctive aspects of role functioning of the psychologist-clinician in rehabilitation facilities and to explore appropriate augmentation and modification of intern training procedures. The present article addresses this task.

Reprinted from Professional Psychology, *13*(3), 397–403.

TRANSITIONAL PROCESSES IN ALL INTERNSHIP SETTINGS

Certain transitional aspects of the internship experience occur in both specialized and more usual training settings. The internship marks the relinquishing of the student role appropriate in the classroom and demands the gradually increasing assumption of behaviors that characterize independent professional functioning.

For most interns the internship is a transitional point that marks the end of course work, affords the opportunity of applying theoretical knowledge and sharpening recently acquired clinical skills, and offers possibilities for new research endeavors. This transition takes place under conditions that Lewin (1938) termed "conflicting and overlapping situations"; that is, interns must function in multiple roles, some of which are antagonistic to others. More specifically, while being supervisees and students, interns must also function as competent diagnosticians, therapists, and consultants to colleagues (Shows, 1976; Comings, Note 1). Such roles require behaviors that are still new. Thus, as supervisees, interns' professional behavior is monitored constantly, and they undergo a thorough analysis of their lack of expertise and areas of weakness. Despite the ongoing supervision and the conflicting demands, the interns must attain a sense of themselves as competent professionals.

THE PHYSICAL REHABILITATION SETTING

The unique nature of the psychological tasks in the physical rehabilitation setting adds to the transitional demands experienced by interns. The distinctive characteristics and needs of the patient population, the particular goals of rehabilitation, and the composition and organization of the professional staff in the setting increase the uncertainty about the appropriate application of previously learned professional behaviors.

One of the most obvious differences between a physical rehabilitation center and a psychiatric or counseling facility is the rehabilitation center's population, which consists of people who have suffered dramatic and catastrophic violation of their physical integrity. Patients usually view their primary problem as a physical one and enter the rehabilitation institution hoping for full recovery. During the course of the process, they begin to acknowledge the demanding emotional tasks of rehabilitation and may start to focus on psychological issues. Still, they do not anticipate working with psychologists, since prior to their disability and hospitalization they often would not have considered psychological treatment nor have been referred to it.

The predominant psychological issues for this population are feelings of depression, isolation, and loneliness that are frequently unrelated to preexisting intrapsychic problems; rather, they may be related to situational or environmental factors, such as loss of premorbid independent status, lack of mobility, devaluative social attitudes, and inaccessible living conditions (Dembo, Diller, Gordon, Leviton, & Sherr, 1973; Thoben, 1975). Thus, the psychological task they face is the mobilization of personal and environmental assets.

Psychological interventions are molded both by the nature of these issues and by the orientation of the patients and staff toward the real-life demands involved in the attainment of maximal functioning. The psychologist's work is geared toward increasing the patient's sense of control and facilitating the achievement of rehabilitation goals. Consequently, psychological interventions must address daily considerations and priorities that may override or differ from treatment dictated by theoretical issues of psychotherapeutic practice.

In the rehabilitation setting the psychologist functions as part of an interdisciplinary team. The work of the team is directed toward specific, concrete, observable results, and the tasks are parceled and assigned to the various disciplines, with an implicit demand for accountability. The activities of the psychologist are expected to mesh with those of such disciplines as physical therapy, vocational counseling, and speech therapy, and goals are established by ongoing interaction with the diverse disciplines. This is in contrast to the psychiatric or mental health facility, where the primary goal of the entire, relatively homogeneous staff is to promote the psychological health of patients.

UNIQUE TRANSITIONAL PROCESSES IN THE REHABILITATION INTERNSHIP

Most psychology interns in rehabilitation centers do not come from rehabilitation psychology doctoral programs and have had no prior preparation for meeting the demands of the rehabilitation setting. Their difficulty in adjusting to the internshp experience is compounded by the necessity of acquiring a large body of new information, reexamining certain aspects of their own personal values, and modifying their concept of professional functioning.

The professional task is made more complex by the physical conditions of the patient population, which can place personal stress on the intern. Working with persons with disabilities tends to heighten the interns' feelings of physical vulnerability. It may be the first time they have confronted their own vulnerability and the sense of potential for bodily trauma in their own lives. In addition, to function effectively, interns are forced to confront their emotional responses to disability and their preexisting positive and negative prejudices.

The physical conditions represented in the patient population raise other, more circumscribed, professional issues for interns. For example, the traditional psychotherapeutic prohibitions against physical contact with patients must be ignored, because in rehabilitation settings it is sometimes necessary to push wheelchairs and/or assist patients in transfers from their wheelchair or bed. Another issue pertains to the actual content of the therapy sessions for which the intern has had little or no previous experience. Discussing such topics as bowel and bladder incontinence, permanent alterations of sexual functioning, or intellectual impairments resulting from brain damage is initially anxiety producing and, undoubtedly, awkward.

The interns must also develop an appropriate orientation for effective participation on the multidisciplinary rehabilitation team. Joining in the team's development of goals and acquiring its confidence while protecting their patients' interest and confidentiality is a demanding task, especially for those interns whose graduate programs emphasized the one-to-one nature of the psychotherapist-patient relationship.

Howard Rusk, a pioneer in the development of physical rehabilitation, has noted the communal nature of effective rehabilitation:

> One of the major developments in rehabilitation. . . has been the utilization of the team approach in various disciplines. . . brought together through the medium of a group of professionally trained persons who focus their skills and abilities on the individual as a whole in terms of his total environment and his total problems.
>
> There is probably no better example of Gestaltism than in the rehabilitation team, for the full force of disciplines on the rehabilitation team can be brought to bear only in their relationships to each other. (Rusk, 1962, pp. v–vi)

It is essential to recognize that like most cohesive groups, the rehabilitation team operates simultaneously on both the instrumental and affective level. On the instrumental level the team establishes rehabilitation goals, follows patient progress, pinpoints problem areas, and monitors each of the members' work to assure that the process goes smoothly. On the affective level the team operates within a status hierarchy between disciplines and within each discipline; the hierarchy determines who speaks to whom, in what fashion, and with how much power. Further, the team serves as a source of emotional support and encouragement for each of its members.

As newcomers to the team, interns must unravel its mores and interact accordingly. Further, they must learn to translate psychological data into terms that are understandable to team members, many of whom have only minimal knowledge of psychological constructs and are interested primarily in concrete results. In addition, interns must reevaluate the concept of patient confidentiality, since it is often in the patient's best interest that team members understand the patient's dynamics and points of view. For interns to be their patients' advocates, they must learn to share with the team and join in its goals yet maintain allegiance to their patients' right to privacy and self-determination.

Another aspect of working with a rehabilitation team is that frequently the course of psychological treatment is influenced by the concerns of the team. For instance, the focus of the treatment might have to be shifted from certain issues of concern to the patient, such as depression, to an issue, such as denial, that is impeding the patient's rehabilitation progress. In conducting psychological interventions, interns must learn to balance the priorities of the patient with the priorities of the team—often a Herculean task.

The team approach also creates a conflict in the traditional concept of the exclusivity of the psychotherapist-patient relationship. In a rehabilitation setting, the psychotherapist may have contact with many significant people in the patient's life (e.g., other therapists, employers, family members) and may acquire information about the patient from outside sources. Such contacts demand reevaluation, modification, and expansion of certain concepts of professional behavior taught in graduate school.

RECOMMENDATIONS FOR TRAINING
IN A REHABILITATION SETTING

The major issues and conflicts engendered by an internship in a physical rehabilitation setting have been presented. Their centrality points to the need for developing specific training vehicles during the internship years. Training that primarily focuses on sharpening clinical skills, without incorporating the unique aspects of the setting, limits the effectiveness of patient care as well as the opportunity for interns to profit maximally from their experience. A second need is to introduce during the initial phase of the internship experience the critical social and psychological issues of persons with disabilities, the larger rehabilitation service delivery structure, essential diagnostic and intervention techniques appropriate for the population, knowledge of the physical and medical aspects of disability, and an understanding of the team approach.

There are many possible means of instruction, depending on the resources of the facility. In addition to lectures, discussions, and experiences simulating physical disability (e.g., Wright, 1975), a compilation of seminal articles could be distributed and reviewed during the orientation period. Since it is known that patients' and professionals' views of the rehabilitation process often differ (Dembo, 1964; Leviton, 1973), a part of the interns' instruction might be presented by current or former rehabilitation clients. In addition, to compensate for the probable lack of prior contact with disabled persons, interns could be provided with opportunities to learn of issues of everyday living as experienced by people with disabilities who are at least a few years past the rehabilitation process.

Although initial orientation is essential to introduce the aforementioned issues, continued training throughout the internship experience is equally important. The data offered in orientation cannot be fully absorbed and integrated due to the generally minimal level of rehabilitation knowledge and heightened feelings of anxiety present in the beginning of training. As the interns become more exposed and sensitized to the psychological aspects of disability, and as the "newness" of the setting diminishes, their ability to utilize the specialized information increases. Furthermore, ongoing training provides a forum in which experiential and theoretical knowledge may be combined. Training must also provide formal opportunities for interns to address the conflicts between previously learned professional guidelines and the needs of the new setting as well as to deal with countertransferential issues related to working with persons with physical disabilities.

In addition to the traditional clinical instruction offered through the year, preparation should be provided in the particular skills and orientation necessary for appropriate psychological assessment of those with physical disabilities who are being treated in the setting. Interns are often not well versed in the specific evaluation techniques appropriate for special populations, nor do they have the skills necessary for developing evaluations that are applicable to rehabilitation questions and goals. The latter ability requires a broadening and a flexibility of previously held views of evaluation and an integrating of them into the orientation of rehabilitation (see, e.g., Wright, 1960). Specific issues that arise in rehabilitation also should be incorporated. Training in the diagnostic testing of brain damage and perceptual-motor functioning, in evaluation of the reality-based depth of mourning reactions, in dealing with issues of independence-dependence, and in adequately determining personal and environmental assets would help in the process. Another aspect of training in appropriate evaluation techniques is teaching the interns to write reports of the evaluation that are useful, oriented toward rehabilitation issues, and understandable to team members while conveying the richness of the person and of the obtained data.

The particular demands of working with a multidisciplinary team should be recognized in the training experience. Although some team meetings may parallel the traditional medical case conference, more often they are ongoing, decision-making forums addressing aspects of patient care and management. Structured social psychological and functional analyses of the team approach during the course of the internship would enable the intern to better utilize group skills and to establish effective channels of communication with the various disciplines. Initially, it is important to aid the intern in learning about the interaction and the hierarchy of disciplines within the team, since the hierarchy is usually implicit in the minds of the staff and not overtly acknowledged. Furthermore, the intern must learn to translate psychological material into a form that is both ethical and useful to the team members, who may be unfamilar with psychological jargon. Because the psychologist functions as a consultant to the other disciplines, sensitive and personal information is acquired from both team members and patients. There is also an exchange of such information between the psychologist and the other members of the team. Consequently, issues of confidentiality need to be addressed throughout the internship experience.

The particular means of incorporating the rehabilitation information into the internship training program can vary. Similarly, emphases on particular aspects of the experience will differ according to the needs, skills, and theoretical biases of each facility. What is most important is that clear recognition be given to the special issues of psychological practice in rehabilitation settings and that the recognition be translated into effective training procedures.

REFERENCE NOTE

1 Comings, M. *Stress in the internship year.* Paper presented at the annual meeting of the American Psychological Association, Montreal, Canada, September 1980.

REFERENCES

Dana, R. H., Gilliam, M., & Dana, J. M. Adequacy of academic-clinical preparation for internship, *Professional Psychology,* 1976, *7,* 112–116.

Dembo, T. Sensitivity of one person to another, *Rehabilitation Literature,* 1964, *25,* 231–235.

Dembo, T., Diller, L., Gordon, W. A., Leviton, G., & Sherr, R. A view of rehabilitation psychology, *American Psychologist,* 1973, *28,* 719–722.

Leviton, G. Professional and client viewpoints on rehabilitation issues. *Rehabilitation Psychology,* 1973, *20,* 1–80.

Lewin, K. *The conceptual representation and the measurement of psychological forces.* Durham, N.C.: Duke University Press, 1938.

Rosenkrantz, A. L., & Holmes, G. R. A pilot study of clinical internship training at the William S. Hall Psychiatric Institute. *Journal of Clinical Psychology,* 1974, *30,* 417–419.

Rusk, H. A. Foreword. In J. Garrett & E. Levine (Eds.), *Psychological practices with the physically disabled.* New York: Columbia University Press, 1962.

Sherr, R. Developing direct psychological services that incorporate the insider's position. *Rehabilitation Psychology,* 1975, *22,* 124–128.

Shontz, F. C., & Wright, B. A. The distinctiveness of rehabilitation psychology. *Professional Psychology,* 1980, *11,* 919–924.

Shows, W. Problems of training psychology interns in medical schools: A case of trying to change the leopard's spots. *Professional Psychology,* 1976, *7,* 205–208.

Sturgis, D. K., Verstegan, J. P., Randolph, D. L., & Garvin, R. B. Professional psychology internships. *Professional Psychology,* 1980, *11,* 567–574.

Thoben, P. J. Civil rights and employment of the severely handicapped. *Rehabilitation Counseling Bulletin,* 1975, *18,* 240–244.

Wright, B. A. *Physical disability—A psychological approach.* New York: Harper, 1960.

Wright, B. A. Sensitizing outsiders to the position of the insider. *Rehabilitation Psychology,* 1975, *22,* 129–135.

Reading 21

Training of Interns and Practicum Students at Community Mental Health Centers

Edwin S. Zolik, G. Anne Bogat, and Leonard A. Jason
DePaul University, Chicago

In the past decade, the ideology of community mental health/community psychology (CMH/CP) has increasingly permeated both academic and applied settings. In support of this thesis, Meyer and Gerrard (1977) reported that the number of masters and doctoral training programs in universities offering a curriculum or major in community mental health and community psychology has expanded exponentially in the past 10 years, increasing from 10 to 62. Barton, Andrulis, Grove, and Aponte (1977) have reported an almost threefold increase in the number of departments reporting courses relating to CMH/CP topics (from 50 to 141 university programs) and a doubling (from 10 to 20) of doctoral departments reporting that they offer a specialized curriculum in community psychology.

Zolik, Sirbu, and Hopkinson (1976) surveyed advanced graduate students in clinical psychology with interests in CMH/CP in terms of their exposure to CMH/CP curricula and training. Results in that comprehensive study indicated that only four areas (primary prevention, ethics of community intervention, program evaluation, and crisis intervention) were reported by more than 50% of the respondents as being covered in academic course work. Similarly, only four types of field experience (crisis intervention, case and consultee-centered consultation to non-mental health organizations, school mental health programs, and alcoholism and drug abuse) were reported as being available by more than 50% of the respondents. The study patently indicated the need for an even greater expansion of CMH/CP-related courses and programs in university settings to more adequately meet student interests.

Several studies have described training, staff orientation, and internships at various CMHC settings (Pinkerton, Miller, & Edgerton, 1972; Weiss, 1975; Taynor, Perry, & Frederick, 1976; Bloom & Parad, 1977a, 1977b). A recent survey of APA-approved training facilities (Matthews, Matthews, & Maxwell, 1976) reported general areas which were covered, as well as training orientations. Barton et al. (1977) in a survey of approved internship programs found that 47 of 60 internship settings responding to the survey reported having some CMH/CP content in their programs. To assist students in screening training

Reprinted from American Journal of Community Psychology, *11* (6), 673–686. Sincere thanks are extended to the 464 CMHC training directors who participated in this survey.

facilities, APA Division 27 (1975) has assembled a manual containing a comprehensive list of CMHC internship placements.

The present study is the first comprehensive assessment of all federally funded CMHCs in regard to training opportunities for interns and practicum students. While the studies cited contribute importantly to our knowledge base, specific information concerning the character of field training and internships available at community mental health centers, where most intensive training in CMH/CP might be available, has still not been adequately surveyed and represents a high priority need for community psychologists.

METHOD

Participants

Directors of training in psychology at each of the 589 federally funded and former-funded CMHCs were mailed a questionnaire under the auspices of the Education and Training Committee of APA Divsion 27. Three months later a second mailing was sent to each center which had not responded. CMHCs developed and funded by state and local agencies which had not received federal funds were excluded because of potential program differences resulting from the inapplicability of federal guidelines to such centers and the difficulties associated with developing a comprehensive national roster of such centers.

Survey Instrument

The questionnaire consisted of two parts. The first section was designed to obtain specific data encompassing the following areas: (a) descriptive information concerning intern and practicum students (e.g., number of students at each center, salaries, time commitments, etc.), (b) staff members' involvement and conceptual orientation toward training, (c) the types of consultation activities and theoretical models available at each CMHC, and (d) the importance of community-related experiences. The second part consisted of an inventory of 35 specific training experiences an intern or practicum student might receive at a CMHC. Directors of psychology training programs were requested to indicate in which areas training experiences were considered to be exceptional.

RESULTS

The initial mailing resulted in 307 completed surveys; the second mailing increased the sample size to 464, for a 70% return rate. From the total sample to 464 CMHCs, 30% ($N = 137$) offered an internship and 52% ($N = 240$) offered practicum training to graduate students. Of the 137 CMHCs offering doctoral training, only 12.4% were APA-approved programs.

Although 137 CMHCs had an internship program, only 122 (89%) of these centers had doctoral level interns in training. These 122 CMHCs reported that they had 377 interns ($M = 3.1$ per CMHC, range $= 1$-12 interns. Of the 240 CMHCs offering practicum experiences, only 207 (86%) actually had practicum students. These centers were accommodating 924 practicum students ($M = 4.5$ per CMHC, range $= 1$-20).

The analyses in the remainder of the study are based, unless otherwise specified, on the 137 CMHCs offering internship training and the 130 CMHCs providing only practicum training. Data concerning practicum training from the 110 CMHCs that offered both intern and practicum training were not obtained as the concern was with the highest level of training offered by a CMHC and to avoid encumbering training directors with a time-consuming task which could have affected the response rate to the survey and the quality of the data.

Stipends and Cooperative Arrangements

Financial support provided to interns ranged from no support to stipends over $10,000. Of the 137 CMHCs, 31% paid no stipend and an additional 5% reported that a stipend was paid by another agency. Of the 87 centers which did offer a stipend, 3% paid between 0-$2,000; 13% between $2,001-$4,000; 45% between $4,001-$6,000; 27% between $6,001-$8,000; 10% between $8,001-$10,000; and 2% paid more than $10,000. Of the 240 practicum training CMHCs, 89% did not pay a stipend; 2% offered a stipend of less than $500, and 2.5% paid between $500 and $999. The remaining 6.5% of centers offered stipends in the $1000 and $3000 range for the academic year.

Interagency collaboration in internship training is dependent on the orientation of a CMHC as well as the availability and interest of other agencies. Directors reported that 52% of the internship programs were based solely within the CMHCs and that 48% involved various cooperative arrangements. In the latter group, 24% were described as cooperative programs with joint funding between the CMHC and the cooperating agencies. Many centers provided training on a rotational basis to interns based in another facility, very often a state or Veterans Administration hospital. However, regardless of whether the internship was based solely within or funded by the CMHC, 66% of the CMHCs indicated that external placements for training in other agencies were available to interns, provided these sites were particularly relevant to community psychology/community mental health.

Among the 130 centers providing only practicum training, 71% reported that the practicum program was based solely within the CMHC, 16% were reported as cooperative programs with funding only from the CMHC, 11% as cooperative programs with funding from CMHC and cooperating agencies, and 2% as cooperative programs with no funding from the CMHC.

Staff Orientation

As exposure to various practices and orientations during the formative years of graduate training has implications for the student's future orientation and activities, inquiry was directed at student involvement in CMH/CP activities and the perceived importance of such activities on the part of the training staff. Involvement in CMH/CP activities was reported as required, as contrasted to optional, by 64% of the internship centers and 52% of the practicum centers. From the viewpoint of the training staff, community-related experiences for interns were considered to be of "great importance" at 36% of the centers, of "considerable importance" at 25%, of "some importance" at 30%, and of "minimal importance" at 9%. For practicum students, community-related experiences were considered by training staff to be of "great importance" at 24% of the practicum training centers, of "considerable importance" at 34%, of "some importance" at 31%, and of "minimal importance" at 11%.

Inquiry also was directed to whether centers made a formal distinction between clinical and community training by offering separate tracks or programs for each. Directors at 20% of the internship centers reported the existence of such a formal distinction at their centers, as contrasted to only 5% of the centers offering practicum training.

"Tailor-Made" Training Options and Traditional Activities

As the number of activities engaged in by mental health professionals has broadened considerably in the last decade, and the interests of students have had a similar diversification, directors were asked whether it was possible for a student to have tailor-made components as part of his training to meet unique interests and needs.

Ninety-seven percent of the internship CMHCs and 96% of the practicum CMHCs indicated that an individual tailor-made component to meet unique needs and interests could be developed, especially if such training adhered to certain training requirements and was compatible with the goals and aims of the center. Centers which reported the possibility of a tailor-made component indicated that an average of 13.6 hours (median = 10.1 hours, range = 2–40 hours) could be allotted to such activities. Tailor-made practicum experiences were reported as being possible on an average of 9.2 hours per week (median = 4.8 hours, range = 2–40 hours).

Full-time interns were reported as involved in traditional clinical diagnostic activities on an average of 7.5 hours per week (range = 0–20 hours), and an average of 15.0 hours (range = 0–34 hours) in traditional psychotherapeutic activities. Practicum students spent an average of 7.6 hours (range = 0–20 hours) in traditional diagnostic and assessment work, and an average of 9.0 hours (range = 0–20 hours) in psychotherapeutic activities.

Supervision

Directors of the 137 internship centers reported that a total of 850 psychologists ($M = 6.2$, median = 3.5) were involved in providing some supervision to interns. Of these staff members, 46% ($M = 4.4$) were involved in supervising interns "almost exclusively" in traditional clinical activities (diagnosis, assessment, psychotherapy), and another 15% ($M = 2.2$) were involved "almost exclusively" in supervising community-oriented activities (consultation, community mental health). Most centers indicated that staff supervised both traditional and community-oriented activities; 83 centers (61%) reported that they did not have any staff whose supervision was "almost exclusively" in community-oriented activities.

In the group of 130 practicum centers there were a total of 412 psychologists ($M = 3.2$) involved in supervising practicum students. Of these psychologists, 35% ($M = 2.7$) were involved in supervising practicum students "almost exclusively" in traditional and 14% ($M = 1.6$) "almost exclusively" in community-oriented activities. Supervision in more practicum training centers than internship centers was characterized by staff providing supervision in both traditional and community areas, as indicated by 94 centers (72%) reporting that no staff supervised community activities "almost exclusively."

Consultation

Of the 137 CMHCs providing training to interns, 10 centers reported that no time was allocated or training in consultation, and another 13 centers reported that time for consultation was by arrangement and varied. The remaining 114 centers (83%) reported a specific number of hours per week available for consultation by interns. The mean number of hours per week was 6.8 hours (range = 1-20 hours). Among the 130 CMHCs providing only practicum training, 48 centers offered no training in consultation, and 16 centers indicated that it was available by arrangement. For the remaining 66 CMHCs (51%) reporting specific hours available for consultation, the mean number of hours per week was 5.1 hours (range = 1-20 hours). However, the median number of hours was 2.8 hours.

Table 1 presents the various settings utilized for consultation training and the percentage of CMHCs reporting consultation in these settings either by arrangement or by specific time allocations. The five major consultation settings in which interns are involved as reported by the largest percentage of CMHCs are schools, courts, welfare agencies, preschool settings, and other mental health agencies. The five settings reported by the largest percentage of CMHCs for training practicum students are schools, welfare agencies, courts, other mental health agencies, and day-care programs. The other category included such settings as city government, legal advocacy groups, housing

Table 1 Consultation Training of Interns and Practicum Students in Various Settings

Consultation setting	% CMHCs reporting training		Mean and range of hours of consultation	
	Intern[a]	Practicum[b]	Intern	Practicum
Preschool	38.6	23.2	1.9 (1– 6)	2.9 (1– 6)
Day care	33.1	25.7	1.5 (1– 4)	2.6 (1– 6)
Medical-surgical hospital	30.7	19.5	2.6 (1–10)	2.3 (1– 8)
Schools	71.6	62.8	2.9 (1–10)	2.7 (1–20)
Industry	5.5	4.9	.0 (0)	2.0 (2)
Clergy	17.3	17.1	1.4 (1– 2)	1.0 (1)
Courts	43.3	31.7	1.5 (1– 5)	2.1 (1– 8)
Prisons	26.8	17.1	1.1 (1– 2)	2.0 (1– 3)
Halfway houses, nursing homes, rehabilitation	28.1	14.7	1.8 (1– 8)	1.5 (1– 2)
Other mental health agencies	37.0	25.6	2.0 (1– 5)	2.3 (1– 8)
Welfare	38.6	32.9	1.7 (1– 5)	1.4 (1– 2)
Public health	22.1	18.3	1.5 (1– 3)	2.0 (1– 3)
Community education/ agencies	9.4	3.6	2.2 (1– 5)	1.0 (1)
Law enforcement, police, probation	7.1	1.2	1.3 (1– 2)	.0 (0)
Other	11.0	12.2	2.3 (1– 4)	1.8 (1– 4)

[a]N = 127 Intern level CMHCs.
[b]N = 82 Practicum level CMHCs.

projects, morticians, and other community groups. The mean number of hours and range of hours per week for interns and practicum students also are presented in Table 1 for those CMHCs reporting the number of hours for the various settings.

In most CMHCs (77%) it was possible for the student to become exposed to more than one approach to consultation. The three major theoretical orientations to consultation reported by intern level CMHCs were behavior modification (60.6%), the Caplanian approach (55.8%), and the group process model (50.4%). Practicum level CMHCs reported the following three: behavior modification (57.3%), the group process approach (50.0%), and the Caplanian model (35.4%). The social action approach was reported by 25% of both types of CMHCs. Other approaches reported by both groups of CMHCs included an ecological approach, eclectic approaches to consultation, the Tavistock model, and the Carkhuff's human resource development model.

Areas of Training

As a result of the variety of services which CMHCs are mandated to provide, they theoretically are in a position to provide students with a greater breadth of experience than are other types of mental health facilities. To obtain information on the types of experience available to interns and practicum students, directors were requested to indicate for 35 areas of possible experience (a) whether trainees were involved in the particular area, and (b) whether trainees typically were not involved, although training in the specific area was available. Usable data were provided by 124 training directors of internship level CMHCs and 110 directors of practicum level CMHCs. Table 2 presents an analysis of the training experiences of both groups of trainees.

The involvement of interns in the 35 experiential areas ranged from 0 to 93.3%. The five areas of involvement at the greatest percent of CMHCs were adult outpatient, adolescent outpatient, child outpatient, crisis intervention, and case consultation to non-mental health agencies. At the other extreme, 15 areas—predominantly related to community psychology—were reported by 25% or fewer of the centers as areas in which interns received training.

Table 2 also lists the percentage of the 110 practicum level CMHCs that provide training in each area. The six areas in which 50% or more of the CMHCs reported practicum student involvement were adult outpatient, adolescent outpatient, child outpatient, crisis intervention, adult day hospital, and case consultation to non-mental health agencies. In 21 of the experiential areas, practicum student involvement was reported by less than 25% of the CMHCs.

For each of the 35 areas, directors of training were asked to rank from 1 to 5 (1 being the highest) the five areas in which available training was exceptional or outstanding. The proportion of centers ranking each of the items 1, 2, 3, 4, and 5 was computed. Each rank was weighted (rank 1 was multiplied by 5, rank 2 by 4, etc.) and summed for each area. The summed weighted proportions for the areas were then rank ordered. In Table 2 the lower ranks represent the outstanding areas of training. The five ranked areas of training considered as outstanding at intern level CMHCs were (a) adult outpatient, (b) child outpatient, (c) crisis intervention, (d) adolescent outpatient, and (e) adult day hospital. The same areas were considered as outstanding at practicum training CMHCs with the exception of the adult inpatient diagnostics and therapy which replaced adult day hospital as the fifth most outstanding area.

DISCUSSION

The present study provides the first comprehensive analysis of training opportunities for interns and practicum students at CMHCs. Among the 464 CMHCs responding to the survey, 30% had training programs at the internship level

Table 2 Percentages of CMHCs Reporting Various Training Experiencies

Experience areas	Trainees involved in activity		Available but trainees typically not involved		Ranking	
	Intern[a]	Practicum[b]	Intern[a]	Practicum[b]	Intern	Practicum
Adult inpatient diagnostics and therapy	54.8	39.1	21.8	21.8	6	5
Child inpatient diagnostics and therapy	21.8	17.3	10.5	17.3	18.5	11
Adolescent inpatient diagnostics and therapy	34.7	26.4	18.6	14.5	14	17
Adult outpatient	93.5	85.5	2.4	7.3	1	1
Adolescent outpatient	90.3	79.1	4.1	8.2	4	3
Child outpatient	85.5	75.5	4.8	9.1	2	2
Adult day hospital	58.9	50.0	25.8	30.0	5	7
Adolescent day hospital	26.6	14.5	14.5	13.6	12.5	24
Child day hospital	25.0	11.8	12.9	6.4	8	13
After-care and follow-up services	56.5	48.2	32.3	29.1	7	8
Alcoholism	40.3	43.6	33.1	25.5	12.5	6
Drug abuse	40.3	35.5	33.1	30.0	20.5	15
Crisis intervention	82.3	61.8	13.7	15.5	3	4
Early screening and identification	46.8	31.8	17.7	20.9	23	10
Primary prevention	53.2	30.9	19.4	17.3	11	16
Prenatal programs (i.e., disadvantaged, etc.)	8.1	2.7	23.4	10.0	34.5	33

Note. See footnote on Page 294.

Postnatal programs (0–3 yrs.) (i.e., developmental disabilities, disadvantaged)	18.6	3.6	29.8	12.7	27	33
Preschool and day-care programs	34.7	17.3	25.0	22.7	24.5	12
School mental health programs	44.4	29.1	24.2	26.4	9	14
Paraprofessional training	45.2	15.5	28.2	30.0	18.5	22.5
Case consultation to non-mental health agencies	67.0	50.0	18.5	25.5	10	9
Consultee-centered consultation to non-mental health agencies	58.9	34.5	21.8	25.5	17	18
Program consultation to mental health agencies	22.5	13.6	33.9	24.5	34.5	33
Program consultation to non-mental health agencies	35.5	23.6	37.1	26.4	22	20.5
Program evaluation and research	27.4	19.1	43.5	30.9	16	19
Epidemiological studies in mental health	4.0	2.7	33.1	17.3	34.5	33
Utilization of social indicators for program development	12.9	10.9	45.2	27.3	29	29
Development and utilization of management information systems	11.3	9.1	37.1	22.7	15	26.5

Table 2 Percentages of CMHCs Reporting Various Training Experiences (Cont.)

Experience areas	Trainees involved in activity		Available but trainees typically not involved		Ranking	
	Intern[a]	Practicum[b]	Intern[a]	Practicum[b]	Intern	Practicum
Measurement and evaluation of consumer and citizen attitudes	14.5	12.7	45.2	27.3	29	26.5
Research on quality of life	.0	2.7	29.0	12.7	34.5	33
Mental health programs planning and development	21.8	12.7	39.5	29.1	26	20.5
Interagency coordination for service delivery	26.6	20.0	38.7	24.5	29	33
Community dynamics, analysis and modification	13.7	6.4	34.7	24.5	32	33
Advocacy and social action	13.7	16.4	28.2	19.1	31	26.5
Citizen participation in mental health, etc., issues	15.3	11.8	44.4	29.1	24.5	26.5
Other	8.1	2.7	2.4	.0	20.5	22.5

[a]N = 124 intern level CMHCs.
[b]N = 110 practicum level CMHCs.

and 52% provided practicum training. A total of 377 interns and 925 practicum students were in training at these centers. The large number of students being trained at CMHCs, the plans reported by many centers to expand the scope of their training, and the plans for developing new training programs at 40 centers, indicate that CMHCs, prime locales for CMH/CP experiences, have become an important component of the training network in the last decade.

This study revealed specific problems related to trainee stipends at CMHCs. Given the part-time nature of the training experience for most practicum students, the fact that most do not receive stipends is understandable. Interns, however, are usually older, more experienced, and more likely to be involved on a full-time basis. The fact that 31% were not provided stipends is disconcerting. The lack of stipends also is related to the fact the 11% of the intern level CMHCs reported vacancies in their training programs. Training directors in universities need to closely monitor this issue to insure that interns are appropriately reimbursed for their services. Factors associated with this deficit may be related to the failure to include trainee stipends as part of staffing grant requests and that most centers were not yet APA-approved training sites. With the planned phasing out of financial support for training in the 1980s and the conversion of funding CMHCs to a block grant program which provides States with greater control over the programs of CMHCs, the viability of most training programs is going to be in jeopardy unless CMHCs and other training facilities develop alternate sources of funding. CMHC directors, for example, might consider developing closer ties with the business community for subsidizing innovative community-based programs or health promotion interventions within industry as some innovative centers have done. As the funding problem affects academic training programs as well, there is a need to attend to the well-known massive gaps in communication between CMHCs as well as other training facilities, and academic training programs. Joint efforts or at least strong support from the academic community are apt to lead to success, especially in crucial situations. Finally, with the increased control of State authorities in allocating funds to CMHCs, it would behoove CMHCs to explore the possibility of obtaining the support of the political action committees of state psychological associations. Their success in changing mental legislation in the areas of licensing and reimbursement, primarily for the private practice sector of clinical psychology, is well documented. Their sophistication and assistance can constitute a valuable resource in maintaining or increasing funding for training.

The requirement, on the part of the majority of CMHCs, of trainee involvement in CMH/CP activities represents a promising development. Restraints on development in this direction stem from several sources. First, there is a lack of articulation and differentiation between clinical and community activities. For example, CMHCs rarely make formal distinctions between clinical and community activities. Furthermor, the small proportion of staff members involved exclusively in supervising community-oriented activities also points to a lack of differentiation in models and constitutes a limitation in developing community training experiences. Finally, the orientation of the training staff, reported by 39% of the CMHCs community-related activities as being of either minimal or only some importance, constitutes another restraint. As the field of CMH/CP becomes better conceptualized, as the distinction between clinical and community activities becomes more pronounced, and as the importance of community-related experiences becomes better appreciated, more personnel and resources hopefully will be exclusively allocated and subsumed within a community perspective.

The tendency of CMHCs to focus on more traditional activities was highlighted by the fact that the areas in which training was considered as exceptional or outstanding were traditional areas such as adult outpatient, child outpatient, adolescent outpatient, adult day hospital, adult inpatient diagnostics and therapy, and crisis intervention. In general, these areas have passive-receptive qualities which have been used to characterize the traditional model. Areas ranked lowest in terms of training being exceptional included those which have been more compatibly subsumed within a community ideology (i.e., community dynamics, organization analyses and modification, research on social indicators of quality of life, epidemiological studies in mental health, program consultation, prenatal care programs, postnatal care programs, inter-agency coordination for service delivery). Examination of areas in Table 2 in which training is available but in which trainees are not involved in many centers indicates that the potential for an expansion of training in community-oriented areas currently exists.

At the present time, training at CMHCs still is largely embedded within the traditional framework. In part, this might be due to overwhelming requests for traditional services which are readily reimbursable, and the failure to accept that only by a significant investment in indirect services (i.e., consultation, prevention, etc.) can the need for traditional services be reduced. Part of this effort has to involve a reeducation of many non-mental health professionals as well as the community. Jason and Glenwick (1979) reported that school personnel rated traditional services as significantly more desirable than community-oriented activities. This traditionally oriented attitude, coupled with the large percentage of CMHCs in this study providing case consultation to schools, supports the need for such reeducation endeavors. Even though there is a pressing demand for traditional services, it is incumbent upon CMHC training facilities to explore the possibilities of an active, preventively oriented community orientation.

Over half of the CMHCs were amenable to tailor-made components in training. This strongly suggests that CMHCs are somewhat responsive to the individual needs of students. Interns and practicum students need to be apprised of the fact that many centers welcome inquiries concerning arranging such experiences. This receptivity among CMHCs can serve as a catalyst for breaking out of the procrustean bed and precipitating innovation in CMHCs. Validating and legitimizing the input of students represents a healthy trend within the CMH/CP movement.

Intern and practicum students were involved most frequently in providing consultation to schools, welfare agencies, courts, mental health agencies, and least frequently in providing consultation to more nontraditional sites (i.e., industry, prisons, clergy, law enforcement, and community education). CMHCs might profit from investing more time in exploring the possibilities of extending mental health consultation services to these nontraditional settings.

Lipsey (1974) has indicated that relevance is the most important issue confronting contemporary psychology. There is an increasing demand to apply psychological research to specific problems. The type of training available in CMHCs is an important factor in determining the extent to which future psychologists will contribute to the solution of widespread social problems.

CONCLUSION

The training of interns and practicum students has become a significant part of the overall program of CMHCs over the last decade. Although many centers provide innovative training in areas consistent with the philosophies of community mental health/community psychology, CMHCs consider the outstanding training which they provide to be in the traditional clinical areas. The fact that the revolution envisaged by the early proponents of the CMH/CP ideology has become transformed into an evolution is not cause for dismay but rather constitutes a study in social change. The planned incorporation of additional CMH/CP components into training programs augurs well for the future. However, the future of training programs is dependent on the extent to which the profession as a whole marshals its resources to not only maintain but increase the financial resources required for maintaining our network of training facilities—CMHCs along with other facilities.

REFERENCES

American Psychological Association, Division of Community Psychology (Division 27). *Interim report of the task force on internships and field placements.* Community-Oriented Internship and Field Placement Opportunities. December 1975. (Mimeograph)

Barton, A., Andrulis, D. P., Grove, W. P., & Aponte, J. F. Training programs in the mid-1970s. In I. Iscoe, B. L. Bloom, & C. D. Spielberger (Eds.), *Community psychology in transition.* Washington, C.C.: Hemisphere, 1977.

Bloom, B. L., & Parad, H. J. Values of community mental health center staff. *Professional Psychology,* 1977, *8,* 33–47. (a)

Bloom, B. L., & Parad, H. J. Professional activities and training needs of community mental health center staff. In I. Iscoe, B. L. Bloom, & C. D.

Spielberger (Eds.), *Community psychology in transition.* Washington, D. C.: Hemisphere, 1977. (b)

Jason, L. A., & Glenwick, D. S. Community psychology and the schools. A comparison of urban and rural perspectives. *Journal of Community Psychology,* 1979, *7,* 50–52.

Lipsey, M. W. Research and relevance. A survey of graduate students and faculty in psychology. *American Psychologist,* 1974, *29,* 541–553.

Matthews, J. R., Matthews, L. H., & Maxwell, W. A. A survey of APA-approved internship facilities. *Professional Psychology,* 1976, *7,* 209–213.

Meyer, M. I., & Gerrard, M. Graduate training in community psychology. *American Journal of Community Psychology,* 1977, *5,* 155–164.

Pinkerton, R. S., Miller, F. T., & Edgerton, W. J. The community mental health center and psychology internship training. *Professional Psychology,* 1972, *3,* 57–62.

Taynor, J., Perry, J., & Frederick, P. A brief program to upgrade the skills of community caregivers. *Community Mental Health Journal,* 1976, *12,* 13–19.

Tuma, J. M., & Cerny, J. A. The internship marketplace: The new depression? *American Psychologist,* 1976, *31,* 664–670.

Weiss, S. L. The clinical psychology intern evaluates the training experience. *Professional Psychology,* 1975, *6,* 435–441.

Zolik, E. S., Sirbu, W., & Hopkinson, D. Perspectives of clinical students on training in community mental health and community psychology. *American Journal of Community Psychology,* 1976, *4,* 339–349.

Reading 22

Psychologists in the Emergency Room

David H. Barlow
University of Mississippi Medical School

A growing diversity of experiences and greatly increased responsibility are two of the most prominent trends in clinical psychology training (Hafner, 1973). Psychologists and psychology interns used to function in rather restricted roles as members of a "health team" on inpatient units, but today full patient responsibility from admission to discharge is common. Similarly, direct patient contact has been abandoned altogether in some settings in favor of consultative roles. As psychologists demonstrate competence in an increasing number of settings and roles, other settings appear that require new skill, and thus role definitions become more diffuse. One new setting at the University of Mississippi Medical Center in Jackson is the emergency room, both in the University

Reprinted from Professional Psychology, *5,* 251–256. The assistance of Dick Eisler, who read an earlier version of this manuscript, is gratefully acknowledged.

Hospital and in the Veterans Administration Hospital on campus. For the past two years psychology interns have been placed in rotation with psychiatric residents on call to the emergency room 24 hours a day including weekends. Placement in the setting has provided the intern with experiences not available elsewhere and has required skills that often must be developed under pressure. These experiences, in turn, have changed the intern's perception of his role and have affected the training program in the Medical Center. The purpose of this article is to outline the intern's functioning in the emergency room and the contribution of this experience to his training.

THE EMERGENCY ROOM

The emergency room is typical of general hospital emergency rooms in urban areas. A variety of people, predominately lower class but increasingly middle class, are seen for the gamut of medical, surgical, and psychological crises ordinarily encountered in an emergency room. The emergency room is permanently staffed by clerical help, nursing personnel, and medical interns. In practice, the clerical staff screens each patient and refers him to the medical intern. If further specialized help is needed the medical intern requests consultation from the appropriate clinical department, for example, surgery, medicine, or psychiatry. Approximately 150 such consultations are requested each month from the emergency room at University Hospital. The emergency room at the VA hospital operates in a similar fashion, but patients are screened initially by an on-duty medical or surgical resident on nights and weekends and by a full-time staff physician during the day.

The placement of clinical psychology interns in the emergency room followed a series of policy changes on the inpatient psychiatry units. These changes resulted in the assumption of full patient responsibility by the psychology intern from admission to discharge. Patients admitted to the unit are randomly assigned to the psychiatric resident or the intern on service. Thus patients assigned to interns range from those with severe neurotic and psychotic disorders to those with chronic brain syndromes. Interns write all nonmedical orders on charts; they consult medical staff when necessary for pharmacologic or organic interventions but retain overall responsibility for the continuity of patient care. The success with nondiscriminatory assignment of patients demonstrated the competency of interns with the full range of behavior disorders and paved the way for the emergency room assignment.

During the spring of 1971 the chief psychiatric resident toured the emergency room facilities with the interns, introduced them to the personnel, and detailed the procedures. After observing the residents managing two or three cases, the interns were put on first call exclusively for two weeks but were backed up each time by a senior resident. That is, the intern would be paged and would arrive at the emergency room first, work up the case, and make recommendations. A senior resident was then called in to check the recommendations and give immediate feedback to the intern on possible errors. At this point interns were placed in rotation with residents.

EMERGENCY ROOM PROCEDURES

Since the Psychiatry Department is responsible for two emergency rooms, one at University Hospital and one at the neighboring VA hospital, a two-person system was devised to cover calls on nights and weekends. In this system the first-call person would answer all calls unless he was already tied up in one emergency room, in which case the second call person would be paged. Since some cases admitted to the respective inpatient units would require immediate psychotropic medication, it was decided to maintain an intern-resident combination on call. Staff members are assigned to a "third" call, backing up interns and residents. During the past year, however, staff was seldom telephoned and was never called to the emergency room.

Frequency of night and weekend call depends, of course, on the number of people available for call. Typically, during the last 12 months there were seven interns and six or seven residents available for call, resulting in one night or weekend on first call and one night or weekend on second call every two weeks. As in most settings, however, the 13 or 14 interns and residents were constantly switching off with each other, resulting in a varying distribution of call nights in a given month. Calls during the day (8:00 a.m. to 5:00 p.m.) were handled in rotation by psychology interns and psychiatric residents on respective University or VA inpatient services.

When on call at night, the intern picks up the pager, which has a range of approximately 10 miles, at 5:00 p.m. and is responsible for calls until 8:00 a.m. the following morning. Weekend call begins at 8:00 a.m. Saturday morning and ends at 8:00 a.m. Monday morning.

If called, the intern proceeds to the emergency room and checks the chart for preliminary information before being briefed by the medical intern. He then interviews the patient, formulates the problem, and makes a disposition. Dispositions vary a great deal in specifics, but the three most common ones are admission to the psychiatric unit, commitment to the State Hospital, or release to go home with a return appointment scheduled in the outpatient clinic. If admission to the hospital is recommended, the intern does such things as checking on bed status, seeing the patient to the unit, and writing initial orders. For admission to the VA unit, however, a physician must sign the admitting order.

FUNCTIONING OF THE INTERN IN THE EMERGENCY
ROOM

Interns averaged approximately two calls a night in the emergency room, with a range of zero to five. Since interns on call to the emergency room are also on call to the inpatient unit, additional calls may come from this source. The amount of time spent in the emergency room varies greatly with the type of case. Occasionally, an intern has spent all night in the emergency room and, in at least one instance, all weekend.

For a period of approximately two months, interns were asked to turn in brief reports each morning on the type of problem encountered and the disposition made. A series of 10 consecutive calls at one point during the two months is representative of an intern's experiences in this setting. A breakdown of these calls by diagnostic categories or presenting complaints and disposition revealed the following pattern:

• Two depressive reactions ranging from moderate to severe. In one case a serious suicidal attempt was made. One patient was admitted to the hospital; one was given an appointment in the outpatient clinic.

• Two alcoholics. One patient was judged to be in impending delerium tremens and was admitted to the hosptial. A second was given an appointment in the outpatient clinic.

• One schizophrenic, a former patient who had stopped taking medication. This patient was readmitted to the hospital.

• One patient with psychosomatic problems involving abdominal pain was given an appointment in the outpatient clinic.

• One adult male reported he had a gun and feared he was going to kill someone. Admission to the State Hospital was arranged.

• One young male was brought in by local police after stealing a car. The patrolman reported that the young man was disoriented and unresponsive. On interview no problem was noted and he was taken to the Youth Detention Center.

• One young female engaging in hysterical fits which were brought under control. After giving appropriate advice to her family on handling fits, the intern gave the girl an outpatient appointment and sent her home.

• One adult female presenting Parkinsonian symptoms after deciding to begin taking phenothiazines once again after a lapse. The psychiatric resident was contacted to prescribe anti-Parkinson medication and an outpatient appointment was given.

Although the range of problems encountered in the emergency room is difficult to classify, this series is reasonably representative of the total experience, with the possible exceptions of alcohol abuse which is somewhat more frequent, particularly in the VA emergency room, and drug abuse which is also more frequent.

Much of the training value of the emergency room, however, is not represented by these "typical" cases, but rather by the more extreme crises not previously encountered by interns, who occasionally have to make life or death decisions instantly. Often the intern must coordinate a variety of groups such as police or clergy and other medical personnel to see that these decisions are implemented.

One such situation encountered by several interns during the last few years has been caused by aggressive police action on alleged drug abuse cases, particularly among teenagers. On these occasions police would enter the emergency room demanding to interview and/or search suspected persons. Interns were required in this instance to assert their responsibility for the case and refuse the requests until proper assessment of the case was made.

A second crisis experience common in the emergency room is the violent and assaultive paranoid schizophrenic, who is occasionally armed. A tendency among new interns is to take the "heroic" approach by entering the room alone to reason with the agitated patient. After one assault, word quickly spreads that a team approach involving emergency room guards is more effective.

VALUE OF TRAINING EXPERIENCE

Typically, interns experience two reactions to emergency room duty. The initial response is moderate to severe anxiety. One intern reported an inability to sleep nights during the first few months on call. A second response, which seems to emerge between the third and sixth month, is an increasing sense of confidence. Toward the end of the year interns reported that they would feel quite comfortable and capable confronting any crisis situation in the course of professional duties. Although we have not attempted to quantify the sense of "mastery," interns report this to be one of the more significant developments during training.

Interns noted three additional advantages of the emergency room experience. First, seeing a variety of people in acute distress broadened their clinical experience. Second, the necessity of making quick and accurate assessments and formulations sharpened interviewing skills. Finally, the interns thought this an invaluable opportunity to apply various intervention procedures under stressful circumstances, necessitating close cooperation with nonpsychiatric physicians, families, community workers, clergy, and police.

Among the disadvantages of emergency room experience, the most frequently noted was the inconvenience of being on call nights and weekends. A second negative aspect cited by some interns was the occasional case in which differentiating physical from psychological problems is difficult, for example, a conversion reaction. Although the medical intern is supposed to rule out physical causes, occasionally this is not done properly. The intern must then call in additional medical consultation, usually from the psychiatric resident on second call. Generally, interns rate the emergency room duties as a valuable training experience.

DISCUSSION

Although there are some similarities, experience in the emergency room differs from experience in a crisis intervention program (Darbonne, 1967). In crisis intervention the case is handled from screening to discharge by the same person or team that is responsible for assembling relevant people, intervening in social systems, and bringing the problem to resolution in one to six sessions. On the other hand, the emergency room requires rapid assessment, mediation with other professionals and agencies, and responsibility for disposition; it does not require "taking the case," which is an essential ingredient in crisis intervention.

An initial concern among staff was that interns would rely too heavily on admission to the hospital as a solution to the problems typically encountered in the emergency room. This possibility was closely watched because over-reliance on admission would indicate that interns were unable or unwilling to implement alternative approaches to problems. In practice this was not an issue. This fact can be best exemplified in the handling of suicidal gestures. As interns gained confidence in their abilities, calls concerning recent suicidal gestures judged to be manipulative were handled by brief family intervention and immediate release of the client to the family, despite occasional doubts by the medical intern.

The competent functioning of psychology interns in the emergency room has also affected the training program in the University and the perception of the psychologist's role by nonpsychiatric physicians. Generally, the medical and psychology interns got along very well. Medical interns reported that psychology interns came promptly to the emergency room and spent adequate time with the patients. Frequently the major criticism of psychologists as professionals is not concerned with competence but rather with responsibility and dedication to clients. Psychologists are often seen as 9:00 to 5:00 people who do not have the experience or training that promotes a sense of patient responsibility. This attitude is prevalent throughout the health care professions and has been used as an argument against freedom-of-choice insurance laws in some states. Psychologists in the emergency room very quickly dispelled this attitude and enhanced the reputation and standing of the training program in the University.

A natural consequence of this situation was a question by staff in other departments, "If psychology students do this, what do psychiatric residents do?" This question is also asked by the residents and interns themselves as they struggle to identify their roles in professions in which role diffusion is becoming the rule rather than the exception. Although it is not the purpose of this article to examine this question, it is clear that there are no easy answers. In any case, the purpose of emergency room service is not to promote role diffusion, although that is one consequence. Nor is its purpose to train interns to work in emergency rooms, since this has not been a function of psychologists to date. The primary training value of the emergency room setting is the experience the intern receives in handling a variety of crises involving behavioral or emotional factors and an awareness of the contribution of physical or medical factors to some of these crises.

The skills and confidence gained in this setting will prove valuable to psychologists who are being asked to deal with crises in an increasing number of settings and will give the psychologist the ability to manage these crises, calling in appropriate consultation when needed. The alternative is continued abdication of these responsibilities to other professions.

REFERENCES

Darbonne, A. Crisis: A review of theory, practice and research. *Psychotherapy: Theory, Research and Practice,* 1967, 4, 371–379.
Hafner, A. J. Innovations in clinical psychology internship training, *Professional Psychology,* 1973, 4, 111–118.

Reading 23
Forensic Training at Internships: Update and Criticism of Current Unspecified Training Models

Richard J. Lawlor
Indiana University School of Medicine

George Siskind and James Brooks
Larue D. Carter Memorial Hospital in Indianapolis and Indiana
University School of Medicine

In the 1970s, an increased interest in the relationship between psychology, law, and corrections produced a common interest in developing formal training in the area of forensic psychology (Fenster, Litwack, & Symonds, 1975; Goldenberg, 1978; Kaslow & Abrams, 1976; McCreary, 1977; Poythress, 1979; Shealy, 1977). The suggestions offered have emphasized course-work-oriented approaches (e.g., Kaslow & Abrams); practicum-oriented approaches (Golden-

Reprinted from Professional Psychology, *12*(3), 400–405. We would like to thank *Eugene E. Levitt, William George McAdoo, and David S. Wachtel* for their critical readings of and helpful comments on preliminary drafts of this article.

berg); and a combined didactic curriculum emphasis with several types of field placements (Poythress).[1] The common denominator of these approaches is an emphasis on both intensive and extensive training at the graduate school level. A specific result of this type of thinking has been the development of joint PhD-JD programs (e.g., Nebraska; Johns Hopkins-University of Maryland; Hahnemann Medical College-Villanova).

Surveying the next step in legal/forensic training—the internship experience—Levine, Wilson, and Sales (1980) thoroughly documented the sites as well as the types of legal/forensic experiences available as of late 1975. Although noting questions still to be answered regarding the quantity and quality of these experiences, the authors seemed favorably disposed to expansion of such training opportunities during internship training. The present report is an update of some of the data obtained by Levine et al., but is basically a report of who (staff and interns) is doing what (legal/forensic evaluations, treatment, teaching, and supervision), with whom (patient populations), and how much of the time. The data are compared wherever possible with the data obtained by Levine, but they are used in the present context primarily as a basis for discussion of current approaches to legal/forensic training and implications for future planning. The data are also used in suggesting some modifications in current trends in this training, particularly at the internship level.

METHOD

An 11-item questionnaire was mailed to the 127 American Psychological Association (APA)-approved internship programs (APA, 1978). Information was requested as to type of legal/forensic activity conducted by both staff and interns, frequency of such activities, populations involved, who carries primary responsibility for instruction and supervision of these activities, and amount of didactic legal/forensic instruction available.

RESULTS

Of 127 questionnaires mailed, 78 (62%) were returned and 76 (61%) were usable. This return is similar to that of Levine et al., who surveyed 120 sites, with a 71% return. Fifty-three (70%) of the sites conducted at least some type of forensic evaluation. At 40 sites (53%), staff conducted civil competency evaluations, whereas interns conducted such evaluations at 29 sites (38%), either regularly or occasionally. Criminal competency examinations were reported by staff at 35 sites (46%) and by interns at 18 sites (24%). Thirty-six

---

[1] In a similar vein, writing with regard to training of lawyers, Hirsch (1979) advocated that specific programs should be developed in law schools to train future attorneys in "forensic medicine."

sites (47%) reported regular or occasional evaluations by staff in conjunction with insanity defenses in the course of criminal trials, and 24 sites (31%) reported these evaluations by interns. Evaluations by staff for "other civil issues," (e.g., child abuse, child custody, probation, workmen's compensation, "liability suits," etc.) were reported by 26 sites (34%) and by interns at 12 sites (16%). The most frequent use of these latter evaluations was child custody (16 sites), with the least frequent being probation, workmen's compensation, and presentencing evaluations (1 site each).

A total of 59 sites (77%) reported at least some treatment activity either in a correctional setting or with court-committed patients. Nineteen sites (25%) reported that staff treated prisoners, whereas 16 sites (21%) reported that interns treated prisoners. Treatment of committed patients by staff was reported at 37 sites (48%) and by interns at 30 sites (39%). Forty-three sites (56%) reported staff treatment of court-referred civil cases, and 34 sites (45%) reported such treatment by interns. On the other hand, an even greater amount of staff treatment with court-referred criminal cases was reported at 47 sites (62%) and also of intern treatment of this population at 41 sites (54%).

Estimates of percentage of total time spent by staff and interns in legal/forensic activities with populations of adults, adolescents, and children indicated that 55 sites had legal/forensic activities with adults and 51 sites with adolescents; children received legal/forensic attention at 40 sites. More precise information based on these data is afforded by the time percentage data that indicated that 43 of 55 adult sites showed that both staff and interns used 50% or more of their legal/forensic time for adults; that 36 of 51 sites showed staff an interns used less than 40% of the legal/forensic time for adolescents; and, finally, that 31 of the 40 sites showed staff and interns used *less than 30%* of the legal/forensic time for children. The data were so similar in fact, for both staff and interns that the curves, when plotted were essentially identical, with the only difference being the lesser quantity of activity by the interns.

No clear pattern of didactic training emerged from our data, with only 25 (32%) sites requiring some form of didactic instruction. The form of this instruction varied from seminars on a wide range of legal/forensic topics to single-lecture offerings regarding a particular state's mental health and psychology licensing laws. Similarly, in regard to clinical experience, few sites required legal/forensic experience by interns. Only 16 sites (21%) required evaluations; 8 sites (11%) required treatment; and only 10 sites (13%) required legal/forensic consultation experience.

Our data also indicated that instruction in and supervision of legal/forensic experiences were provided overwhelmingly by psychologists themselves. Psychiatrists were utilized as supervisors and/or instructors at only four sites (5%). Attorneys were utilized for instruction at only eight sites (about 10%), and other personnel (i.e., police officers, probation officers, etc.) were utilized even less (less than 2% of the sites).

DISCUSSION

Before discussing the implications of our data for both present and future training of practitioners in the legal/forensic areas, it is important to note the trends in amount and type of activity of the last several years. Comparisons of our data with that of Levine et al. (1980) indicate that in the last 4 years, a large increase in legal/forensic activity has occurred. Extracting from Levine's (1980) Table 2 (p. 69), the actual number of sites offering evaluation experiences in 1975 was 29 (34%); this number has now increased to 53 (70%). The earlier number of sites affording treatment experiences, 17 (20%), has increased to 59 (77%). In contrast, didactic instruction has increased from 21 sites (24%) to only 25 sites (32%). Thus, without a corresponding increase in didactic instruction, both evaluaton and treatment experiences have more than doubled, with the greater emphasis on the latter. The pattern of this increase, in conjunction with the striking similarity of staff and intern activity in the legal/forensic area, leads to the conclusion that growth has been haphazard, uncoordinated, and unplanned.

Didactic and Clinical Experience

Serious concerns are warranted then when one considers the matter of specific didactic training at internship sites. Despite the already noted increase between 1975 and 1979 in evaluations (34% to 70% of responding sites) and treatment (20% to 77% of the sites), didactic training sites have only increased 8% (from 21 to 25 sites). Although many sites have limited lectures or seminars on various topics, the discrepancy between the number of sites offering didactic work and actual clinical experience is striking. Similarly, our data show that the strong correspondence, in fact the almost identical curves, between staff and intern experiences with adults, children, and adolescents suggests that training is based almost exclusively on an apprenticeship system, with interns doing what staff do, and little more. This conclusion is further supported by our data that indicate that, other than in those settings dealing with court-committed patients and prisoners, the most common "point of entry" is the child-legal/forensic experience, that is, custody, placement, and so forth. This point of entry typically involves evaluation, which according to our data is receiving less emphasis than treatment or evaluation with adults. There are no data from Levine's study that allow direct comparison with our data on the percentage of legal/forensic time spent with the different age groups. But the most frequently reported legal/forensic experience in our data is in treatment of either court-committed patients or correction inmates, which is similar to Levine's (1980) findings that "those training sites offering and requiring the greatest amount of legal/forensic exposure are large state hospitals servicing a high number of court committed patients" (p. 70). One wonders whether the current almost exclusively adult-oriented emphasis is the one best geared to train psychologists to meet the range of existing and future legal/forensic needs.

Lack of Interdisciplinary Focus

There is also another legitimate criticism of the present state of training in the internship centers. Psychologists in legal/forensic areas are still ignoring the idea that psychology needs to engage in more interdisicplinary training, as has been often noted (Proshansky, 1972). Ignoring the contributions of other disciplines may have serious consequences in addition to the ever present problem of communication difficulties. No matter how experienced psychologists may be in working with various aspects of legal, judicial, and criminal justice systems, they are still not expert in their understanding of these systems. Particularly in relation to law—given the rapidity with which law changes—even the relatively sophisticated psychologist is generally unable to keep up with changes in the law, though the area of law involved is quite small. Thus, training programs offering legal/forensic experiences should arrange interdisciplinary contacts with the fields of law and criminal justice. Furthermore, despite Bazelon's (1974) nine criticisms, psychiatry has a long history of legal/forensic activity. Psychology can learn from the experience of other mental health practitioners in this field.

Premature Specialization

The conclusions suggested by the results of our survey, in comparison with the earlier data, remind us of two minor but salient events of the past 5 years— articles published by Cronbach (1975) and Sarason (1976). Cronbach discussed the reasons for 10 years of unproductive investigation in the laboratory, and Sarason discussed the failure of the movement into the community. In each case, the avoidable failures resulted from a narrow view of the problems and issues. Premature specialization has a high potential for producing a limited, narrow view of problems and issues. Efforts based on the narrow view are generally wasteful; result in greater costs to the public; and produce specialists with a limited perspective on psychology, who are less able to provide comprehensive services to a range of populations and are excessively dependent on other more broadly educated professionals. In addition, ideas and information that can make the difference between failure and success are often ignored or unknown. Frequently, potentially fruitful associations are unconnected when one proceeds from too narrow a base of knowledge and skills. In our view, the best way to avoid the limitations of this narrow view, which results from the developing apprenticeship model of training as it exists, is to emphasize broad, thorough, fundamental education and training of psychologists.

The Joint PhD-JD programs that initially appear to be a solution to this problem in fact may not be. Those programs that require the time and effort for genuine competence in both psychology and law are, of course, not subject to this concern. Realistically, however, these programs are scarce, and they produce few graduates and practitioners. The majority of psychologists functioning in the legal/forensic area will continue to come from PhD programs. Although suggestions have been made to increase the amount of legal/forensic course work within the context of PhD programs, this apparent solution is subject to the criticisms of lengthening programs inordinately and/or decreasing the amount of fundamental course work in psychology. If in doubt about the need for fundamental knowledge and skills in psychology, either as a practitioner or researcher, the recent article by Loftus and Monahan (1980) will help to reaffirm the often ignored idea that we must indeed be psychologists first and legal/forensic specialists second.

If we are not to be expedient, concerned only about current staff interests, or weaken or dilute graduate education and internship training, what is an appropriate model? At the risk of being thought stodgy and ultraconservative, the model we propose would start with a maximum of 3 to 6 hours of legal/forensic course work at the graduate school level. The essential focus of the course work would be a broad introduction to the issues in criminal, civil, and child/juvenile law, as suggested by Poythress (1979), with a caveat that the course work alone is not intended to prepare one to become a legal/forensic expert. In addition, the 6 hours would include actual case presentations that illustrate the ways in which psychological knowledge and skills are relevant to legal issues.

In contrast to Poythress, we do not recommend a more intensive development of topical seminars and skills in the use of law libraries, legal research tools, and so forth. Nor do we recommend field placement or practica in agencies focusing on legal/forensic issues at the expense of more basic clinical or research skills. Such practical experience should come in the next step in the development of competence in the legal/forensic area—the internship. During the internship, in addition to receiving additional didactic instruction, the intern should receive his first experiences in applying more than minimally acceptable clinical skills to legal/forensic issues. This of course means that these experiences must ordinarily come later in the internship period and would involve relatively minor amounts of time. Both of these suggestions are consistent with the requirements that an internship, like graduate training, should be devoted to the development of a broad base of knowledge and skills, not to narrow specialization.

Obviously, genuine working competence is to be gained through continuing education programs and postdoctoral training. This position is consistent with the hope that the new PhD will see the degree as a step in the lifelong process of education and training.

Careful consideration of these recommendations clearly indicates a need to effectively encourage, develop, and implement continuing education and postdoctoral training in both academic and work settings. Psychologists are obviously needed and can be productive in the legal/forensic arena. The logical answer to this need for more effective growth of training programs is the establishment of the Division of Law and Psychology within the APA framework and coordination of the Division's efforts with the already existing American Board of Forensic Psychology. Together the two groups can encourage development of such a program and explore core content and sequence issues of such programs. Between them they can offer a much needed but seldom utilized opportunity for researchers and practitioners to work together to provide programs, stimulation, and guidance in the legal/forensic area and avoid the shortcomings of the apprenticeship model.

REFERENCES

American Psychological Association. APA-approved predoctoral internships for doctoral training in clinical and counseling psychology: 1978. *American Psychologist*, 1978, *33*, 1124–1126.

Bazelon, D. Psychiatrists and the adversary process. *Scientific American*, 1974, *230*, 18–23.

Cronbach, L. J. Beyond the two disciplines of scientific psychology. *American Psychologist*, 1975, *30*, 116–127.

Fenster, C. A., Litwack, T. R., & Symonds, M. The making of a forensic psychologist: Needs and goals for doctoral training. *Professional Psychology*, 1975, *6*, 457–467.

Goldenberg, E. E. Teaching mental health and law: A reply to Shealey. *Professional Psychology*, 1978, *9*, 174–175.

Hirsch, H. L. Why we need courses in forensic medicine. *Case and Comment* (March–April, 1979), 36–40.

Kaslow, F. W., & Abrams, J. C. Forensic psychology and criminal justice: An evolving subspecialty at Hahnemann Medical College. *Professional Psychology*, 1976, *7*, 445–452.

Levine, D., Wilson, K., & Sales, B. D. An exploratory assessment of APA internships with legal/forensic experiences. *Professional Psychology*, 1980, *11*, 64–71.

Loftus, E., & Monahan, J. Trial by data: Psychological research as legal evidence. *American Psychologist*, 1980, *35*, 270–283.

McCreary, C. P. Training psychology and law students to work together, *Professional Psychology*, 1977, *8*, 103–108.

Poythress, N. G. A proposal for training in forensic psychology. *American Psychologist*, 1979, *34*, 612–621.

Proshansky, H. M. For what are we training our graduate students? *American Psychologist*, 1972, *27*, 205–212.

Sarason, S. B. Community psychology networks and Mr. Everyman. *American Psychologist*, 1976, *31*, 317–328.

Shealy, A. E. Teaching forensic psychology, *Professional Psychology*, 1977, *8*, 8–10.

Reading 24

APA-Approved Group Treatment Internship Training Opportunities: Present Status and Future Directions

Timothy Carmody
University of Oregon Health Sciences Center, Portland

Joseph Zohn
Jerry L. Pettis Memorial Veterans Administration Medical Center,
Loma Linda, California

During the past 10 years, there has been considerable growth in the application of group treatment methods in the health care field (Garfield, 1974; Lieberman, 1976; Lubin, 1976; O'Hearne, 1974). Harman (1974) emphasized the expanding utilization of various forms of group intervention such as sensitivity/encounter, behavioral, transactional analysis, and gestalt groups. In describing current issues and trends in psychotherapy, Saccuzzo (1977) noted that the effectiveness of group treatment methods has led to their increased use across a wide variety of client populations and disorders. Group therapy approaches are no longer considered an inferior or substitute form of intervention. Rather, group therapy is often considered the treatment of choice for many adult, child, and adolescent patients (Back, 1974; Greene & Crowder, 1972; Richardson & Meyer, 1972; Rogers, 1968; Vorrath & Brendtro, 1974). Meyer and Smith (1977) contended that group therapy provides clients with a greater range of behavioral and attitudinal models, more realistic feedback, and consensual validation of decisions and future plans.

Since increasing demands for treatment and costs of mental health services have necessitated a greater reliance on group treatment approaches, it seems imperative to examine the training received by students in this area in American Psychological Association (APA)-approved graduate and internship programs. The data from a previous survey (Zohn & Carmdoy, 1978) suggested that many APA-approved doctoral programs have opted to de-emphasize training in group treatment methods. The clinical training directors of APA-approved doctoral programs in clinical psychology reported that, although student interest had increased significantly over the past 5 years, only meager increases in actual program offerings (e.g., course work) had taken place. Considering the student interest and appropriateness of the group modality, it is surprising to the present authors that the current training opportunities in most graduate programs are generally not adequate to prepare students for clinical work as group psycho-therapists. Several clinical directors gave the rationale that interested students could recieve the necessary training during the internship years. Given this

Reprinted from Professional Psychology, *11*(2), 213–219.

explanation, it seemed logical to survey the directors of APA-approved intern-ship centers to examine training opportunities in group treatment methods. It was expected that group forms of intervention would be utilized more exten-sively among internship centers than in the academic settings previously surveyed. It was uncertain, however, whether or not these internship centers would provide more adequate training in group treatment methods than the previously surveyed graduate programs.

The purpose of the present survey was therefore threefold: (1) to investigate training opportunities in group treatment methods in APA-approved internship programs in clinical psychology, (b) to examine similarities and differences between training opportunities provided in this area in APA-approved doctoral programs compared to clinical internship settings, and (c) to provide prospective interns in clinical psychology with information regarding the availability of training in group treatment approaches in specific APA-approved internship programs throughout the nation.

METHOD

A questionnaire designed to assess recent trends in group therapy training opportunities was mailed to the directors of the 110 APA-approved internship programs in clinical psychology, as listed in the November 1974 issue of the *American Psychologist*. A cover letter explaining the purpose of the survey accompanied the questionnaire.

Internship training directors were asked to describe course work in group treatment methods, practicum experiences, amount of type of supervision, opportunities for trainees to become involved as group participants, special funds allocated for such training, and the number of staff involved in this aspect of training both 5 years ago and at the present time. A similar questionnaire was used in the Zohn and Carmody (1978) survey of training opportunities in group treatment methods in APA-approved doctoral programs in clinical psychology.[1]

Approximately 1 month after the initial mailing, an additional questionnaire was sent with a stamped, self-addressed envelope to those directors who had not responded to the first questionnaire.

RESULTS

A total of 87 responses (79.1%) were received from the 110 training programs surveyed. The present findings are based on the information provided on these 87 returned questionnaires.

_____

[1] A copy of the questionnaire used in the present study is available from the first author.

First, the clinical orientation of staff members in the internship center was surveyed. Fifty-six programs (64.4%) reported that the orientation of their staff was eclectic. Twenty-five facilities (29%) reported that their staff was generally analytic in orientation. This is in sharp contrast to doctoral programs that reported analytic orientations in only 7% of the schools surveyed (Zohn & Carmody, 1978).

Clinical directors were also asked to indicate the number of staff involved in training and supervising interns in group treatment methods 5 years ago and at the present time. Over one third (39.1%) of the respondents indicated that either one or two staff members are currently involved in this aspect of training, compared with 34.5% 5 years ago. The number of faculty involved in group therapy training has increased only slightly over the past 5 years. The mean number per program was 1.63 5 years ago and is presently 2.02.

Table 1 summarizes information concerning specific aspects of training in group therapy provided 5 years ago and at the present time. To statistically examine recent trends in group therapy training, the number of affirmative responses in each category was tallied and submitted to a series of chi-square tests, corrected for continuity. Although trends toward increased training opportunities were apparent, the results of the chi-square tests indicated that these trends were significant only for didactic training (Question 4) in group therapy, χ^2 (1) = 4.12, p < .05, corrected. In addition, correlated t tests indicated that reported program emphasis in group therapy training has increased over the past 5 years, $t(86) = 4.56, p < .001$. Reported interest among trainees has also increased significantly over the past years, $t(86) = 5.14, p < .001$.

Further, the number of courses offered in group treatment methods has risen slightly over the past 5 years. The number of courses offered 5 years ago ranged from 0 to 8 ($M = .83$). Presently, the number ranges from 0 to 6 ($M = 1.2$). The percentage of programs offering at least one course in group treatment methods has increased from 34.5% to 43.6%. It is also interesting

Table 1 Recent Trends in Group Treatment Methods Training

	Percentage of affirmative responses	
Aspect of training	5 years ago	Present
Staff involved in traing (Question 3)	65.2	70.7
Didactic training (Question 4)	49.4	71.1
Opportunity for participation (Question 6)	88.6	91.1
Practicum experience (Question 7)	92.0	97.7
Supervision received (Question 8)	91.0	98.8

Note. Number of questionnaires = 87 out of 110.

Table 2   Types of Groups in which Training is Presently
Provided

Type of group	Percentage of programs
Group psychotherapy	95.4
Behavioral	34.5
Sensitivity encounter	27.5
Psychodrama	20.7
Others[a]	25.3

Note. Rows total more than 100% because respondents could
mark more than one response.

[a]This category refers, for example, to gestalt groups, family
therapy, drug addiction groups, self-help programs, anxiety and
weight management, bioenergies, transactional analysis, parent
training, ward government meetings, systems, socialization, multi-
family groups, milieu treatment, and so forth.

to note that 39 programs (44.8%) reported that funds were presently allocated
for training in group treatment methods compared with 37.1% of doctoral
programs (Zohn & Carmody, 1978).

Table 2 lists the types of group approaches in which training is currently
provided. As expected, group psychotherapy is included in almost all internship
programs. Focused behavioral approaches (e.g., weight management, assertion
training) were the next most popular form of group intervention.

Since 71% of those internship programs were characterized as eclectic
(40/56), and 80% of the analytically oriented programs (20/25) were described
as providing some form of group therapy training, it is not possible to rely on
stated theoretical orientation of an internship center as a means of predicting
the likelihood of adequate group therapy training. There were too few programs
described as primarily behavioral or "other" in orientation to interpret the
data. Geographically, some form of group therapy training was reported in all
regions of the country. However, those programs in the Eastern region of the
country that were described as analytic in orientation seemed to provide
relatively fewer opportunities for group therapy training. As far as the type of
training settings is concerned, group therapy training was reported to be available in 6 of 7 state hospitals (86%), 20 of 26 medical schools (77%), 12 of 16
general hospitals (75%), 6 of 8 universities (75%), and 19 of 30 mental health/
child guidance centers (63%). However, it must be kept in mind that the above
statistics merely reflect the existence of some opportunity for group therapy
training rather than the quality or extent of training provided by each type of
institution.

Finally, these findings were compared with the results of our recent survey
of doctoral programs (Zohn & Carmody, 1978). In terms of specific forms
of training provided (e.g., practicum), chi-square tests indicated no significant

differences. However, internship programs reported significantly greater emphasis than doctoral programs both 5 years ago and now $t(173) = 3.74$, $p < .001$, and $t(173) = 2.04$, $p < .05$, respectively. Internship programs also reported significantly greater trainee interest in group treatment methods both 5 years ago and now, $t(173) = 5.23$, $p < .001$, and $t(173) = 5.77$, $p < .001$, respectively.

DISCUSSION

The results of the present survey appear to indicate significant increases in reported trainee interest and program emphasis in group therapy over the past 5 years among APA-approved internship centers. However, concomitant increases in the number of staff and amount of supervised practicums in group treatment were not evident. Although the number of course offerings in group treatment methods was reported to have increased significantly over the past 5 years, most other aspects of group training (e.g., participation as a group member, supervision) have not been concurrently expanded. Comparing internship and doctoral programs, the former reported greater trainee interest and program emphasis. But no significant differences were found between internship and doctoral programs in the mean number of staff, number of practicums, didactic offerings, supervision provided in group treatment approaches, or funds allocated for such training.

In light of the previously mentioned interest in and pragmatic justifications for group psychotherapy training, it is puzzling to the present authors that the APA-approved graduate schools and internship settings have not augmented training to a greater degree in this area. Perhaps the unresponsiveness of many established training programs is indicative of prevailing differences in attitude and orientation among various programs presently vying for the right to train the clinicians of the future (e.g., the APA-approved programs, the professional schools, "growth centers," etc.). It is hoped that APA-approved programs will not become too rigid in their approach to training, clinging steadfastly to the training pattern of the past. Although many programs appear to be attempting to provide an adequate compromise between the scientific and clinical aspects of training, other facilities seem unwilling or incapable of taking this step. As the functions that psychologists serve continue to expand in the future, it will become increasingly imperative that training centers retain the flexibility to prepare their students to capably fill those evolving roles. If our more traditional training facilities remain insensitive to the changes in training needs, it seems inevitable that the highly qualified graduate students of the future will extend their search for programs to obtain the kind of training they desire. A result of this situation may well be that these students will more seriously consider alternative predoctoral and internship centers to meet their training needs. To ensure the high standards of training and professional competence of future clinicians, it seems both reasonable and desirable that our training centers carefully evaluate and implement the needed changes in course offerings as well as other related aspects of training.

A few clinical training directors commented that supervision and didactic presentations in group treatment methods were provided by outside consultants. The question arises as to what extent APA-approved internship programs should be directly involved in such training. In his classic article on group psycho-therapy training, Berman (1975) addressed the question of predoctoral training in group treatment methods. Reviewing various training models, Berman concluded that "the student cannot possibly experience the depth and breadth of the group psychotherapy field within the span of his predoctoral education" (p. 342). Berman further pointed out that such training could only be provided at the postdoctoral level, given the extensive requirements at the predoctoral level in the basic science of psychology and individual therapy. He went on to outline guidelines proposed by the American Group Psychotherapy Association (AGPA) for a 2-year postdoctoral training programs in group therapy. These guidelines recommended a minimum of 90 hours of didactic course work, 180 hours of supervised practicum, and 60 hours of case seminars and participation in group therapy (Berman, 1975).

Predoctoral internship centers appear to be optimal settings to initiate such postdoctoral training. After examining training models in psychology, Wolff (1972) indicated that graduate programs have relied on the internship year to provide intensive training opportunities in clinical work, but those anticipated training experiences did not always occur. The results of the present survey provide corroborative evidence that this may well be the case in the area of group treatment methods. Those training centers interested in enhancing the quality of their group treatment methods training may benefit from examining the standards of a few well-established group therapy training programs. For example, at the University of Texas Counseling Center, trainees attend didactic meetings in group therapy for 12 months, lead six different types of groups, and participate in at least six day-long training/ experimental group sessions. At the University of Rochester School of Medicine, a formal training program in group therapy was developed in 1973. This program includes intensive didactic, experiential, and clinical training oppor-tunities.

Clinical internship training directors throughout the country reported a variety of group treatment methods in hospital and community settings (e.g., problem-oriented community meetings, ward government sessions, self-help groups, and applications of behavioral medicine in group intervention). Target populations have included such diverse groups as adult outpatients, specific vocational groups, schizophrenic adults, the aged, terminally ill patients, alcoholics, widows, cardiac patients, and adolescents. This impressive list of group interventions points out the variety of clinical experiences potentially available to trainees at various internship centers. It also demonstrates the need for more comprehensive training programs in this important area.

Training in group treatment methods was reported to be available in each region of the country. Only among analytically oriented internship programs in the East did there seem to be relatively fewer opportunities for training in group treatment methods. Further, the few APA-approved internship programs housed in state hospitals reported the greatest proportion of training centers with training in group treatment methods. Training programs in medical schools, general hospitals, and universities were similar in this regard, with mental health and child guidance centers reporting a somewhat smaller proportion for group treatment training programs.

Given the increasing demands for service and the rising costs of health care, group forms of intervention are becoming more common both in mental health and medical settings. The cost effectiveness of group treatment methods in behavioral medicine, for example, has been demonstrated with overutilizers of medical services (Olbrisch, 1977). Olbrisch has suggested that the application of group approaches in medical settings will improve the chance of psychology's inclusion in the national health insurance programs currently being considered by budget-conscious government officials.

In summary, the present survey indicated an expanding interest in and emphasis on group treatment methods in internship programs. However, it is also clear that such training opportunities need to be dramatically increased to adequately prepare interns for clinical work in group intervention. The manner in which group training opportunities are further expanded remains to be formulated by individual training programs. For example, internship centers specializing in medical psychology might focus on group approaches in the area of behavioral medicine. The potential applications of group intervention are nearly unlimited. However, the role that established APA-approved doctoral and internship training programs in psychology will play in the development and competent utilization of group treatment methods in the future will be largely determined by the commitment these programs are willing to make toward improving the quality of the training they provide in this area.

REFERENCES

Back, K. Intervention techniques: Small groups. In M. Rosenzweig & L. Porter (Eds.), *Annual review of psychology*. Palo Alto, Calif.: Annual Reviews, 1974.

Berman, A. L. Group psychotherapy training: Issues and models. *Small Group Behavior*, 1975, *6*, 325–344.

Garfield, S. L. *Clinical psychology: The study of personality and behavior*. Chicago: Aldine, 1974.

Greene, R., & Crowder, D. Group psychotherapy with adolescents. *Journal of Contemporary Psychotherapy*, 1972, *5*, 55–61.

Harman, R. L. Techniques of Gestalt therapy. *Professional Psychology*, 1974, *5*, 257–263.

Lieberman, M. A. Change induction in small groups. In M. R. Rosenzweig & L. Porter (Eds.), *Annual review of psychology*. Palo Alto, Calif: Annual Reviews, 1976.

Lubin, B. Group therapy. In I. B. Weiner (Ed.), *Clinical methods in psychology*. New York: Wiley, 1976.

Meyer, R. G., & Smith, S. R. A crisis in group therapy. *American Psychologist*, 1977, *32*, 638–643.

O'Hearne, J. J. Presidential address: We've come a long way—Now what? *International Journal of Group Psychotherapy*, 1974, *24*, 151–158.

Olbrisch, M. E. Psychotherapeutic interventions in physical health: Effectiveness and economic efficiency. *American Psychologist*, 1977, *32*, 761–766.

Richardson, C., & Meyer, R. Techniques in guided group interaction. *Child Welfare*, 1972, *51*, 519–527.

Rogers, C. Interpersonal relationships: Year 2,000. *Journal of Applied Behavioral Science*, 1968, *4*, 265–280.

Saccuzzo, D. P. The practice of psychotherapy in America: Issues and trends. *Professional Psychology*, 1977, *8*, 298–307.

Vorrath, H., & Brendtro, Z. *Positive peer culture*. Chicago: Aldine, 1974.

Wolff, W. M. Training model trends in psychology. *Professional Psychology*, 1972, *4*, 343–350.

Zohn, J. C., & Carmody, T. P. Training opportunities in group treatment methods in APA-approved clinical psychology programs. *Professional Psychology*, 1978, *9*, 50–62.

Reading 25
An Administrative Rotation in the Clinical Psychology Internship: The Chief Intern at Duke Medical Center

Drew Edwards and Linda C. Wyrick
Durham, North Carolina

Today psychologists are increasingly assuming major administrative responsibilities in clinical settings (Feinberg, 1971; Sundberg, Tyler, & Taplin, 1973). Traditionally, psychologists have been administrators within academic departments of psychology and have performed primarily ancillary administrative functions in interdisciplinary clinical settings (e.g., as directors of psychological services in mental health or child guidance clinics). Currently, however, psychologists are becoming increasingly visible in such primary leadership roles

Reprinted from Professional Psychology, *8*, 253–255.

as directorships of mental health clinics and other mental health programs (Dörken, 1970).

Although psychologists are undertaking these major administrative roles, there appears to be little opportunity from them to engage in meaningful administrative functions in their professional graduate school or internship training. In contrast, psychiatric residents are given opportunities to develop administrative skills through chief resident positions in hospitals and clinics.

In a survey of the brochures of 88 predoctoral internship programs in clinical psychology approved by the American Psychological Association (Edwards, Note 1), 12 indicated that interns have an opportunity to engage in some administrative duties, though these were not clearly defined. The brochure of one such program further described opportunities for training in mental health administration and offered a management seminar, though it was not clear whether the intern had leadership or decision-making responsibilities within the context of these experiences. No program was found offering a specific rotation in which the administrative role was clearly defined as the intern's major responsibility.

Recognizing the need for such experiences in preparation for professional careers in clinical psychology, a specific administrative rotation was developed in 1972 as part of the clinical psychology internship program at Duke University Medical Center. This 3-month chief intern rotation, which is available to four trainees each year, originally arose out of both training concerns and practical needs associated with the Psychodiagnostic Laboratory at Duke Medical Center. This laboratory, which has been described elsewhere (Gentry, 1974), serves as a clearinghouse for all requests for psychological consultation in the hospital and functions in a similar fashion to other hospital laboratories (e.g., electroencephalography, radiology, nuclear medicine). The laboratory employs paraprofessional technicians who administer and score psychological tests ordered by interns and faculty. During the first 2 years of the chief intern rotation experience at Duke, most of the administrative duties centered around the functions of the laboratory and included such tasks as clarifying referral and assessment questions, and distributing and handling daily laboratory matters related to efficiency, quality control, billing, and personnel relations among technicians and between technicians and interns. The chief intern also served as the group spokesman for the interns in terms of bringing their problems and suggestions to the director of the laboratory, director of training, or the faculty as a whole.

Since 1974, changes in the Psychodiagnostic Laboratory have resulted in a much needed broadening of the chief intern's role. Because of increasing demand for psychological consultation in the hospital, the time-consuming job of classifying, recording, and distributing consult requests is now handled by an administrative secretary. The chief intern serves as a backup person to respond to professional issues regarding complex consultation requests. He continues as the liaison person between laboratory technicians and interns, and assists in maintaining group cohesion and productive working relations among technicians and between technicians and interns. The chief intern is involved in the selection of technicians, and last year one of the chief interns assumed complete responsibility for designing, coordinating, and executing a 6-week training program for new technicians.

During the past year, chief interns participated in cost analyses of the financial structure of the laboratory. Such analyses included consultation with systems engineers to develop computer simulations of laboratory fucntioning, consultation with the hospital business administration and medical insurance administrators, and preparation of projected budgets based on cost accounting.

Chief interns, working closely with the director of the laboratory, have been exposed to a variety of professional issues to which administrators in a variety of clinical settings must respond. These include the general areas of cost accounting for medical insurance purposes, projected fiscal budgets, growth and expansion plans, maintenance of both efficiency and quality within a paraprofessional setting, and definition of role relations between parapro-fessionals and professionals both within psychology and between psychology and other disciplines (psychiatry, social work, and other medical departments). In short, the chief intern is a major force in the efficient day-to-day operation of the laboratory and gains a broad educational experience from his involvement.

The chief intern remains the official representative of the intern group and now also functions as assistant director of internship training. In this capacity, he serves as a voting member of the internship training committee and is involved in intern selection for the following year. Last year, a chief intern designed an effective orientation manual and program for incoming interns.

A major responsibility of the chief intern related to the internship program is the planning of seminars and workshops for the group. He processes interns' suggestions for seminars, speakers, workshops, and so forth, and delegates where necessary and appropriate responsibility for making such arrangements. Last year, for instance, the chief intern organized a series of seminars on issues in psychological assessment and arranged for speakers for each of these. Chief interns also brought in outside consultants to give workshops in areas related to psychotherapy.

Each week the chief intern meets with his group to discuss administrative matters and to help develop solutions and make recommendations concerning issues that may arise. Every other week, the four individuals who serve as chief intern during the year meet with the director of the Psychodiagnostic Labora-tory and the director of Internship Training to consider general issues related to administration, as well as to talk about special concerns that may be present. In addition, both directors are available to the chief intern at any time for on-the-spot consultation. Although guidance and supervision are readily avail-able, the chief intern is given responsibility and support for his own decisions.

Daily incidents involving financial issues, personnel relations, public relations, and quality patient care arise which demand immediate action and decisions, mature judgment, careful weighing of issues, and consideration of the needs and opinions of others. As such, the rotation provides ongoing daily and realistic education in administration. It involves not only long-range planning and programming but also immediate, reactive decision making.

In addition to his administrative responsibilities, the chief intern engages in psychological assessment, individual psychotherapy, community consultation, and research, as do his colleagues. He also serves as cotherapist for an inpatient psychotherapy group which meets 4 days a week. The chief intern rotation, then, is a very full one. Because the opportunities available to the chief have expanded over the last year, the rotation has also become popular, as witnessed by the fact that five people wished to take it this year. Informal feedback from interns suggests that the experience is useful in giving them a taste of administrative work and in helping them to decide whether they would like to be involved in administration as a part of their professional careers.

REFERENCE NOTE

1 Edwards, D. Unpublished survey, October 1975.

REFERENCES

Dörken, H. Utilization of psychologists in positions of responsibility in public mental health programs: A national survey. *American Psychologist,* 1970, *25,* 953–958.

Feinberg, M. R. The powers and pitfalls of the clinical and industrial psychologist as an administrator. In L. Abt & B. Riess (Eds.), *Progress in clinical psychology* (Vol. 9). New York: Grune & Stratton, 1971.

Gentry, W. D. Three models of training and utilization. *Professional Psychology,* 1974, *5,* 207–213.

Sundberg, N. D., Tyler, L. E., & Taplin, J. R. *Clinical psychology: Expanding horizons* (2nd ed.). Englewood Cliffs, N.J.: Prentice-Hall, 1973.

Reading 26

Seminar Training in APA-Approved Internship Programs:
Is There a Core Curriculum?

Peter M. Monti and Ann L. Delancey
Brown University, Providence, Rhode Island

Jan L. Wallander
University of Southern California, Los Angeles

Clinical psychology internship training can be a bridge between formal academic training and learning that continues throughout one's professional career. As such, the internship is of great importance in the psychology training enterprise. Although once fashioned like an apprenticeship that accommodated the needs of the particular student, internship training at many sites has gradually evolved into a more formal experience with many structured components. In light of this, the question arises; Is there now a universal set of goals and objectives, a body of information and skills, and a minimum competency to be expected of a psychology intern? Merenda (1974), asking similar questions of academic graduate training, found that although there was a core of required courses, this core was variable. It is important also to ask these questions of the internship experience.

To this end the *Accreditation Handbook* of the American Psychological Association (APA, Note 1) might be expected to provide useful information. However, although this document stresses broad principles, it does not include specific goals and objectives for the internship in terms of either knowledge or skills. Moreover, whereas the Association of Psychology Internship Centers has made more specific recommendations (Beutler, 1981) about internship training needing to cover four core areas and five target populations, the status of those recommendations is not clear.

This lack of universal formal structure suggests that the core curriculum of the internship, if indeed there is a core, needs to be investigated through other means. Granted the internship is a complex integration of theory, practice, and research, which may preclude specification. However, the cognitive and theoretical basis of the internship presumably provides the framework in which skills and knowledge both merge and emerge. This integration of skills and knowledge usually occurs in seminars and other didactic experiences. Therefore, it is important to understand this component of the internship curriculum and to determine if there is a core within this component.

Foremost, such an understanding should facilitate coordination of the

Reprinted from Professional Psychology: Research and Practice, *14*(4), 490–496. The authors would like to thank *David B. Abrams* for his helpful comments on an earlier draft of this manuscript.

training of students on the one hand and professionals on the other. A concern presently exists that there is duplication in efforts between formal graduate and internship training that can lead to ineffective training and important gaps in the background of some doctoral-level psychologists (Sturgis, Verstegen, Randolph, & Garvin, 1980). Furthermore, the lack of normative data on didactic training at the internship level makes it difficult for the prospective intern to choose an appropriate training site. In general, knowledge about the cognitive and theoretical emphases at training sites, as communicated through seminars, may provide a better idea of how psychologists at these sites define the role of clinical psychology and how they feel their programs uniquely contribute to the growth and development of professional psychologists.

Thus far, little is known about what internship programs offer regarding seminar experiences. Although usually structured within a particular internship, it is unclear how seminars or other group learning experiences vary across settings. Although we are not arguing for the standardization of all training, differences in cognitive and theoretical emphases deserve documentation for the previously noted reasons. In particular, better communication about the content of internship training programs should lead to better coordination in training efforts and ultimately to a better trained psychologist.

METHOD

A two-page questionnaire was developed to elicit from all directors of APA-approved clinical and counseling psychology internship programs information relevant to the seminar-training component of their programs. Seminar was defined as any structured and regular group learning experience excluding direct clinical supervision and staffings. The questionnaire consisted of checklist items as well as open-ended questions. Although most questions concerned content areas taught, by whom, and for how long, other questions concerned number of interns, philosophy of training, methods of teaching, and evaluation of training experiences.

The questionnaire was mailed to all 175 APA fully approved predoctoral internships listed in the December, 1980, issue of the *American Psychologist* (APA, 1980). The first mailing was sent out at the end of March, 1981, and a second mailing was sent out 6 weeks later. Return postage and a cover letter were provided. By mid-June, 1981, 122 (70%) internship programs had responded.

RESULTS

Sample Information

Data analyses were conducted on those 110 programs that had furnished complete information. These were divided into four groups, according to type of facility: (a) medical school and hospital facilities, including consortia ($n = 40$); (b) VA, military and other federal facilities ($n = 31$); (c) state and private psychiatric residential facilities ($n = 17$); and (d) community, including child guidance and student counseling, facilities ($n = 22$). Further, 13 of the programs were identified as targeting child populations almost exclusively, whereas the remaining were labeled general. The mean number of interns at each site was 6.67 ($SD = 3.33$), with a range from 3 to 16.

Overall Sample

Programs indicated the number of hours interns were required to participate in seminars on various content areas as well as how many hours were totally available (required plus optional hours). Although 18 content areas were specifically listed on the questionnaire, programs were also asked to add others in which they offered seminars. Less than 5% of the responders added seminars, suggesting that those listed on the questionnaire practically exhausted the range, and, therefore, analyses were restricted to these. Descriptive summary statistics for each of the seminar areas are provided in Table 1. Probably the most distinguishing feature of these data is the great variation among programs, making general statements difficult. In all but three content areas, for example, most programs did not require seminars; this created highly skewed distributions. The most common areas, however, were assessment, professional issues, neuropsychology, and psychopharmacology; over 50% of the programs offered formal didactic training in these areas. Also, seminars in some aspect of psychotherapy were highly common, although this is not directly evident from Table 1 due to the breakdown into more specific types of psychotherapy. Disregarding this, about 70% of all programs required a seminar on some aspect of psychotherapy. In contrast, the least common areas for required seminars were personal issues, research, behavioral medicine, and crisis intervention, together with a few specific types of psychotherapy. The mean number of content areas included in the seminar curriculum of each program was 5.95 ($SD = 3.84$, maximum = 15). That is, an intern in the average program would get specific group training in about 6 of the 18 content areas listed.

On close examination, out of an average of 143 required seminar hours per year, interns spent 45% of those hours in the traditional clinical areas of assessment, individual and family psychotherapy, and neuropsychology. The least amount of time was spent on some specific types of psychotherapy, research, crisis intervention, and consultation. Different programs, however, emphasized different areas, as suggested by the information on maximum hours any one program offered in a specific content area. An intern could apparently get extensive (up to 200 hours in some cases) specialized formal training in any of these areas. Some programs reported that they preferred to make seminars optional instead of required; other programs reported that they made more than the required hours available, if desired. As evident in Table 1,

Table 1 Required Seminars in Different Content Areas (Percentage of Programs and Number of Hours)

Content areas	Overall sample			Total[a]		General internship facilities								Child internship facilities	
				Maximum hours		Medical		Federal		Residential		Community			
	%	M	SD		M	%	M	%	M	%	M	%	M	%	M
Psychotherapy[b]	23	9	21	100	11	23	8	19	4	35	18	18	12	8	5
Individual	46	17	25	100	21	38	15	42	14	59	26	59	16	69	18
Couples	17	2	6	48	5	18	2	23	2	6	0	18	4	15	4
Family	39	14	32	200	27	40	16	29	3	47	22	46	20	46	29
Group	36	7	17	100	12	28	6	39	8	59	15	27	2	23	3
Sex	14	1	4	25	5	15	1	19	2	6	0	9	1	8	0
Assessment	65	23	27	100	27	60	21	61	17	77	37	68	23	77	30
Professional issues	55	9	17	100	10	48	8	52	3	53	12	73	16	69	15
Neuropsychology	54	11	22	160	26	50	15	58	8	65	42	46	8	39	14
Psychopharmacology	50	5	15	100	7	55	5	39	2	53	8	55	9	54	5
Interviewing	35	8	20	125	9	38	12	36	3	35	6	27	9	39	13
Behavior therapy	32	7	17	100	13	33	8	42	9	24	8	23	3	31	6
Consultation	29	4	9	50	7	30	5	29	2	29	5	27	3	21	4
Crisis intervention	25	3	15	150	4	28	2	32	2	6	0	23	10	8	2
Psychopathology	25	5	13	60	10	25	6	19	1	29	7	27	5	31	6
Behavioral medicine	23	6	19	150	10	28	6	36	8	6	0	9	7	0	0
Research	19	3	11	100	7	18	5	19	2	18	3	23	2	15	2
Personal issues	11	5	16	100	8	8	3	7	1	24	9	14	10	8	8
Total	100	143	132	497	227	100	143	100	90	100	178	100	158	100	163

[a]Totally available at a program (required plus optional).
[b]Separate from the specific types that follow.

the distribution across content areas of the total number of seminar hours available (required and/or optional) in these programs usually followed the pattern of only required hours, as discussed earlier.

Information also was sought as to what type of professional was teaching each seminar. Although there were numerous individual exceptions, the modal teacher for every seminar, save one, was a PhD psychologist. Predictably, psychopharmacology was usually taught by a physician.

Type of Facility

Descriptive summary statistics were separately calculated for each of the seminar areas for each category (according to type of facility). An inspection of Table 1 shows apparent differences among facilities in their average seminar curricula. Because of likely dependence among the dependent variables, a one-way multivariate analysis of variance was first conducted to test for this difference. Consequently, facility was the class variable, and the vector of the number of hours requried of each seminar was the dependent variable. Unexpectedly, it came out nonsignificant. This may have partly been due to the large variation for each entry in this vector even among programs within each type of facility.

Because of an a priori specific interest, a one-way analysis of variance was conducted on the total number of hours of required seminars in which types of facility again was the class variable. This test was also nonsignificant, as was a similar test on number of content areas covered by the average seminar curriculum of each type of facility. The mean number of content areas was about 6 for each type of facility (range = 5.78-6.29). Further evidence for a lack of differences among facilities was provided by the percentage of programs that offered seminars in specific content areas. In general, with little variation, assessment, professional issues, neuropsychology, and psychotherapy were the most poopular areas for required seminars. Finally, the types of facilities did not differ in terms of what professional directed the various seminars except that in community settings, physicians taught crisis intervention and behavioral medicine more often than other professionals.

Target Populations

The same descriptive statistics were also computed for the group of 13 programs identified as child-clinical. These data are presented in Table 1. Although statistical comparisons were made, the data for the remaining 97 general internships are not presented separately, because they were highly similar to those for the overall sample. When comparing child with general internships, the Hotellings T^2 test between target populations came out nonsignificant for the vector of number of hours required of each seminar. Similarly, the student's t test on total number of hours required seminars was nonsignificant between types of internship, as was the test on number of content areas included in the average curriculum. Child internships stressed the same types of traditional content areas in their required seminars as the overall sample. In contrast to general internships, however, physicians were employed more often than other professionals to teach seminars on interviewing, crisis intervention, and psychotherapy.

DISCUSSION

Although the present results suggest that internships are highly variable regarding their seminar offerings, a core program among many internships included seminars on assessment, professional issues, neuropsychology, psychopharmacology, and psychotherapy. Interestingly, these offerings did not significantly differ across type of internship facilities. Also of interest, and somewhat surprising, is the fact that the average internship required 143 hours of seminars for each of its interns. This amount of time is the equivalent of from three to four graduate courses or seminars. Initially this seems like a good deal of "classroom" time for what is traditionally considered a primarily "applied" experience.

These results are less surprising, however, when viewed in the context of the recent literature on internship training. Several reports have noted dissatisfaction on the part of internship programs regarding the adequacy of preinternship training. Dana, Gilliam, and Dana (1976) and Shemberg and Keeley (1974) point to deficiencies in the areas of assessment and treatment. More recently, Sturgis et al. (1980) found that the clusters of assessment/testing skills and psychodiagnosis emerged as the most important deficiencies of interns. From a somewhat different perspective, Petzel and Berndt (1980) found that when they surveyed internship directors as to which three courses internships would particularly like to see on an applicant's transcript, the most commonly suggested courses were those in which some type of psychodiagnostic assessment or therapy was mentioned. Although many authors (e.g., Sturgis et al., 1980) suggest that their data support the need to require courses in assessment and treatment as part of doctoral programs, out study suggests that internships are providing extensive seminar work in these areas.

The present findings, combined with those of recent surveys in which internship directors voiced dissatisfaction about adequacy of preinternship training, suggest that the internship has acquired some of the traditional didactic training associated with doctoral programs. The core of this training seems to be the content areas of assessment, neuropsychology, psychopharmacology, and psychotherapy. Although the extent of overlap between this core and that currently offered in academic departments of psychology is unknown, the likelihood for duplication of efforts is great. Furthermore, important gaps could be filled in by well-planned seminar trade-offs between academic departments of psychology and internship programs. This state of affairs suggests the need for greater communication among all involved in the graduate-level psychology training experience.

REFERENCE NOTE

1 American Psychological Association, Committee on Accreditation. *Accreditation handbook.* Washington, D.C.: Author, April 1980.

REFERENCES

American Psychological Association. APA-approved predoctoral internships for doctoral training in clinical and counseling psychology: 1980. *American Psychologist,* 1980, *35,* 1111–1115.

Beutler, L. E. Should internships be extended? *APIC Newsletter,* April 1981, 12–14.

Dana, R. H., Gilliam, M., & Dana, J. M. Adequacy of academic clinical preparation for internships. *Professional Psychology,* 1976, *7,* 112–116.

Merenda, P. Current status of graduate education in psychology. *American Psychologist,* 1974, *29,* 627–631.

Petzel, T. P., & Berndt, D. J. APA internship selection criteria: Relative importance of academic and clinical preparation. *Professional Psychology,* 1980, *11,* 792–796.

Shemberg, K., & Keeley, S. Internship training: Training practices and satisfaction with preinternship preparation. *Professional Psychology,* 1974, *5,* 98–105.

Sturgis, D. K., Verstegen, J. P., Randolph, D. L., & Garvin, R. B. Professional psychology internships. *Professional Psychology,* 1980, *11,* 567–573.

SUPERVISION

Reading 27

Psychotherapy Supervision:
A Survey of Internship Training Practices

Allen K. Hess
Auburn University, Alabama

Kathryn A. Hess
East Alabama Mental Health Center

Presently, about 1,500 doctoral clinical students serve an internship each year (Stedman et al., 1981). Although the internship is central to professional training in psychology, little information is available on the extent and nature of psychotherapy supervision provided to interns. Such information would

Reprinted from Professional Psychology: Research and Practice, *14*(4), 504–513. The help of Donna Deleza in conducting the study and the cooperation of the directors of clinical training are sincerely appreciated. An anonymous reviewer provided many excellent suggestions, for which we are grateful.

help administrators and professional staff at internship sites to plan internships. It would also help potential interns in their selection of internship sites.

To provide such data on psychotherapy training during internships, we conducted a survey of the American Psychological Association (APA)-accredited predoctoral internship programs. Specific foci were (a) amount of supervision, (b) types of supervision provided, (c) training level and experiences of supervisors, (d) quality control or monitoring of supervision, and (e) training in supervision per se provided by the internship.

METHOD

A five-page survey[1] was sent to the APA-accredited predoctoral internships listed in the December 1979 *American Psychologist*. The first survey wave was sent in August 1980, the second wave in September 1980, and the third wave in October 1980. The surveys were addressed to the director of clinical training of the psychology department, division, or service of the facility. Franked return envelopes were provided. The waves elicited response rates of 34.44% (52 responses), 24.50% (37 responses), and 5.30% (8 responses), respectively, for a total of 64.24% (97 responses). The geographical distribution of the sites indicates that the returned surveys are representative of internships. Other program descriptors were similar between the present sample and internships generally.

Five returned surveys were incomplete: One included the information in another program directed by the same individual, one no longer had a psychology training program, and three did not "have time" to complete the survey. Hence, the total number of usable surveys was 92 (61%). The number of spontaneous comments made on the survey protocols suggests that the respondents were highly involved in participating in the study.

RESULTS

Amount of Psychotherapy Training Provided

Responses to the question, "Are there rules of thumb about the amount of psychotherapy supervision a trainee receives?" revealed an average of 3 psychotherapy hours the intern delivers to 1 hour of supervision received ($M = 2.98$, $N = 45$, range $= .5$-19.0 psychotherapy hours delivered). In response to the question, "How much supervision per week would you estimate each trainee receives?" the most frequent responses were 4 hours ($n = 13$) per week ($m = 4.25$, $n = 87$, range $= .2$-10.0).

---

[1] Available upon request from the authors.

Types of Supervision

Table 1 presents a variety of supervisory methods and media and a 4-point scale on which the respondent could rate the frequency of use of the type of instruction. The most commonly used method is individual, or one-to-one, supervision, followed by structured seminars, audiotapes, videotapes, group supervision (one supervisor to several supervisees), in vivo observation, assigned readings, films, large groups (several supervisors and several supervisees), and vertical team supervision.

Training of Supervisors

Eighty-nine internships reported an average of 10.9 PhD supervisors ($SD = 7.16$, range = 1-40), with 2.6 holding the American Board of Professional Psychology Diplomate (range = 0-14). Thirteen facilities reported having EdD supervisors on staff (mode = 1), and seven facilities reported have PsyD supervisors on staff. Forty-seven facilities reported using social workers as supervisors; the mean number of social workers was 2.7. Virtually all (45) reported that the social workers had Association of Clinical Social Workers' (ACSW) status ($M = 2.67$). Ten internships reported using counselors ($M = 4.2$). Sixty-nine facilities reporting psychiatrists on the supervisor staff, employed an average of 5.17. In 63 of these facilities, 4.43 were board certified. In addition, a lawyer, a psychiatric nurse, and four master's-level psychologists served on supervisory staffs.

Two hundred twenty-six (34%) supervisors had 0-5 years of clinical experience, 209 (31%) had 6-10 years, 104 (16%) had 11-15 years, 56 (8%) had 16-20 years, and 68 (11%) had 21 or more years ($N = 663$ supervisors). In terms of supervisory experience, 253 (41%) had 0-5 years, 190 (31%) had 6-10 years, 79 (13%) had 11-15 years, 54 (9%) had 16-20 years, and 44 (7%) had 21 or more years. The average supervisor had 9.28 years of clinical experience ($SD = 4.21$, $N = 75$, range = 0-19, mode = 10 years) and 7.59 years of supervising experience ($SD = 4.08$, $N = 71$, range = 1-16, mode = 7 years), according to respondents' estimates. Thirty-six sites (39%) reported some ongoing training for supervisors; the remaining sites either lacked such training (26%, 24 sites) or failed to respond to the item (35%, 32 sites).

Ongoing Supervision Training for Supervisors

Table 2 shows the ongoing education of supervisors in the programs. Informal training seemed to be mostly "curbside consultation" with a colleague (used in 52 programs) when a supervisor was perplexed.

Trainee Feedback Regarding Supervisor Performance

Three feedback procedures are used by facilities to assess the supervisors' performance (see Table 3). The procedures are written evaluations of supervisors

Table 1 Supervisory Methods: Frequency of Use

Rank	Method	N^a	Mean rating	SD	None	Infrequently	Sometimes	Quite often
1	Individual supervision	91	3.95	.35	1 (1.10)	0	2 (2.2)	88 (96.7)
2	Supervision seminar	91	3.47	.97	4 (4.4)	9 (9.9)	22 (23.0)	56 (61.5)
3	Audiotape	88	3.03	.89	4 (4.5)	21 (23.0)	31 (35.2)	32 (36.4)
4	Videotape	90	2.89	.71	2 (2.2)	22 (24.4)	50 (55.6)	16 (17.8)
5	Group supervision	89	2.89	.79	2 (2.3)	27 (30.3)	39 (43.8)	21 (23.6)
6	In vivo supervision	89	2.82	.86	4 (4.5)	27 (30.3)	38 (42.7)	20 (22.5)
7	Readings on supervision	89	2.78	.86	7 (7.9)	20 (22.5)	46 (51.7)	16 (18.0)
8	Films on supervision	89	2.16	.82	17 (19.1)	48 (54.0)	17 (19.1)	7 (7.9)
9	Large supervisory groups	87	1.84	.89	34 (38.9)	35 (40.2)	14 (16.1)	4 (4.6)
	Other^b	14	3.5	.52				

Note. The 1–4 scale is depicted in right most four columns. Figures in parenthesis are percentages.

^{a}Due to respondents answering some items but not others, Ns vary for responses and are noted for each item.

^{b}Due to an N of 14, "other" was not ranked, but it included cotherapy—supervision with intern (5); case conferences (3); quadrads—two senior psychologist with two interns (1); one-way observation (1); observation by faculty (1); unspecified (3).

Table 2 Quality Monitoring of Psychotherapy Supervision: Ongoing Training for Faculty ($N = 86$)

Type	Frequency	%
Formal		
None	41	45
Seminar	21	23
Administrative	16	17
No response to the item	12	13
Collegial consultation	2	2
Informal		
Yes	52	47
No	28	30
No response	12	13

by trainees ($n = 72$); the trainee's evaluation, as conveyed to the director of training or another responsible staff person ($n = 66$); and the trainee's evaluation of the faculty to the faculty ($n = 64$). Surprisingly, monitoring client progress (unreported), listening to tapes of supervision ($n = 9$), and monitoring supervision in person ($n = 7$) were infrequently used. Several facilities reported

Table 3 Quality Monitoring or Feedback Procedures Used

Type	Frequency
Trainee provides written evaluation	72
Trainee informally informs the director	66
Trainee informally informs the faculty	64
Another staff member supervises the supervisor	24
Another staff member monitors supervision	17
Another staff member monitors supervision by tape	9
Another staff member monitors supervision in person	7
None	4
Other[a]	

Note. Since a program might use more than one type of feedback structure, the frequency totals are greater than the number of programs.

[a]Includes biweekly supervisor staff meetings with the director, peer discussion, and review.

peer evaluation by supervisors of supervisors either in a group or via evaluating trainee performance at presentation.

Rewards for Supervision

Table 4 depicts the reward structures for supervision. Collegial esteem was checked by two thirds of the respondents. Salary, promotions, and release time were checked by one fifth of the programs, whereas 14 respondents checked "none," an item not among the response choices on the survey. "Other" responses focused on supervision as part of the job, working for praise, doing an important job, getting to work with interns and residents, and better paid staff being allowed to supervise. Faculty spent 3.76 hours per week ($SD = 2.13$, $N = 87$, range .2-10.0 hours) with modes of 2 ($n = 15$), 2.5 ($n = 10$), and 4 ($n = 17$) hours supervising trainees. This represents 10.83% ($SD = 7.25\%$) of the faculty's time per week. A sense of dedication toward training, acceptance of training as a built-in part of the job, and intrinsic enjoyment of supervising trainees may account for this investment of time in training.

Facilities that reward supervision with salary tend to provide a higher ratio of service hours per supervision hours, or less supervision for interns, $r(17) = .68$, $p = .002$. Spontaneous comments to the question of type of rewards tended to elicit comments that supervision is part of the job and no specific rewards are tied to this activity. In fact, 16 programs said supervision was considered in promotion decisions, 20 related supervision to salary raises, 15 said supervision rated release time from activities, and 61 said supervision garners collegial esteem. Seventeen "other" responses were listed, including "part of job," "able to work with interns and residents," "higher level faculty function"; several directors promised supervisors "love" and "undying gratitude."

Table 4 Kind of Formal and Informal Credit or Reward Structures for Psychotherapy Supervisors

Type	Frequency
Collegial esteem	61
Salary	20
Promotion	16
Release time	15
None	14
Other (part of the job, praise, getting to work with interns and residents)	17

Note. Since a program might use more than one type of reward structure, the frequency totals are greater than the number of programs.

Psychotherapy Supervision Training Provided

Respondents answered the question, "Do you consider it important for the interns to have training in psychotherapy supervision?" On a 5-point scale (1 = not at all important, 3 = somewhat important, and 5 = quite important). The mean rating was 3.32 ($SD = 1.22$, $n = 86$, no response = 6), with 20 ratings of 5, 14 ratings of 4 (a mode of 3, $n = 34$), 10 ratings of 2, and 3 ratings of 1.

Tables 5 and 6 show procedures used by respondents in training interns to supervise and experiences considered important in the development of psychotherapy supervisors. Primary training procedures included individual supervision of supervision, followed by vertical teams and groups of one supervisor and several supervisees. Respondents wrote in various procedures listed under "other." Twenty-eight respondents added "none" and indicated some emphatic positions that this type of activity was inappropriate for interns, as reflected by strong statements added by respondents. Two major types of responses were as follows: (a) "It is inappropriate to train interns in supervision, due to their lack of psychotherapy experience and our lack of time due to the training needs currently existing." "This questionnaire is based on the assumption of a training model incompatible with ours, presumably one that views the interns as not as ready for supervisory tasks." (b) "We had not thought of this area as one in which training need be provided. Indeed it ought to be an integral part of the training experiences."

Descriptive Parameters of Training Programs

The questionnaire data revealed some dimensions along which predoctoral internship programs differed. The dimensions were (a) boundaries, or the degree

Table 5   Teaching Psychotherapy Supervision: Procedures Used in Training Interns in Psychotherapy Supervision

Type	Frequency
1. Individual, one-to-one supervision of supervision	35
2. Vertical teams (e.g., senior supervising postdoctoral fellow who supervises predoctoral intern)	25
3. Group (one supervisor to several supervisees)	21
4. Structured seminar (readings, lectures)	18
5. In vivo observation	16
6. Assigned readings	15
7. Videotapes	12
8. Audiotapes	11
9. Group (several supervisors and several supervisees)	8
10. Films	5
11. None	28
12. Others (includes cotherapy, peer review, modeling)	8

Table 6 Teaching Psychotherapy Supervision: Training Experiences Considered Important in the Development of Psychotherapy Supervisors

Experience	Frequency
1. Supervision of psychotherapy	24
2. Supervision of supervision	19
3. Role model (observation)	17
4. Seminar—course	10
5. Own psychotherapy	8
5. Workshops	8
7. Experience (unspecified)	3
7. Doing psychotherapy	3
7. None	3
10. Teaching experience	2

to which a program is confined to psychology trainees (e.g., social workers) and (b) intensity, or the degree to which a program provides a high level of supervision. Table 7 shows the number of programs training nonpsychology intern personnel. Table 8 shows the correlation between programs considering types of trainees served.

Boundaries Programs that accepted psychology and nonpsychology graduate students for training were called "open"; programs that only accepted psychology students were called "closed." In open programs, virtually all the trainees (97.8%) were supervised by the training faculty, whereas 30.7% were supervised by doctoral interns. Open programs are more likely to have interns supervising graduate students, $r(91) = .18$, $p = .08$, paraprofessionals, $r(91) = .21$, $p = .05$, and ministerial personnel, $r(91) = .31$, $p = .003$. Faculty at open programs tend to have more PhDs and ABPP Diplomates. Large group supervision was used less frequently in open programs, whereas readings, audiotape, individual (one to one), seminars, and videotapes were used more often. Inter-

Table 7 Types of Nonintern Trainees Served (Frequencies)

Trainee	% facilities
Psychiatric residents	65.3
Graduate students	55.4
Social workers	43.5
Paraprofessionals	42.3
Nurses	35.7
Other medical specialties	22.0
Ministers	14.1

Table 8 Types of Trainees Served (Correlations)

Nonintern trainees	1	2	3	4	5	6
1. Paraprofessionals						
2. Nurses	.187 (.075)					
3. Graduate students	.398 (.0001)	.171 (.10)				
4. Social workers	.300 (.005)	.409 (.0001)	.203 (.052)			
5. Psychiatric residents	.089 (ns)	.250 (.081)	.148 (ns)	.249 (.02)		
6. Ministers	.489 (.0001)	.434 (.0001)	.349 (.0007)	.365 (.0003)	.218 (.037)	
7. Other medical specialties	.298 (.004)	.117 (ns)	.221 (.036)	.131 (ns)	.200 (.057)	.194 (.064)

Note. $N = 92$ except for other medical specialites, which has $N = 91$. Probabilities that $r =$ are in parentheses.

estingly, the more an agency used interns to supervise others, the less intensive was their rule-of-thumb ratio of service hours the intern provided to supervisory hours the intern received, $r(85) = .27$, $p = .012$. Programs viewing supervision training as important tended to use seminars, $r(85) = .27$, $p = .013$, vertical teams $r(80) = .20$, $p = .07$, audiotapes, $r(82) = .21$, $p = .055$, and other techniques, $r(14) = .39$, $p = .17$, such as cotherapy, case conferences, and one-way observations.

Programs with counselors on the supervising faculty tended to use vertical teams, $r(8) = .80$, $p = .02$, and not to use interns as supervisors of others, $r(10) = .67$, $p = .03$; the number of respondents with counselors on staff is small enough to warrant caution in the stability of these correlations.

Intensity Programs defined as high on intensity of supervision (a low ratio of hours of service to hours of supervision for interns) used individual supervision more often, $r(82) = .247$, $p = .02$; tended to have faculty supervise nonpsychology trainees, $r(86) = .23$, $p = .05$; and used audio and videotapes, $r(80) = .38$, $p = .005$, and $r(81) = .26$, $p = .02$, and seminars, $r(86) = .22$, $p = .05$, more frequently.

DISCUSSION

It appears that a rule of thumb of 3:1 hours of service hours of supervision is provided, which equals about 4¼ hours of supervision received by trainees and about 3¾ hours, or about 11%, of faculty time. Data concerning satisfaction and efficacy of this level of supervision are beyond the scope of this study, but such data are certainly necessary for better administrative planning and accreditation policymaking in psychology training and education areas.

The supervisors are predominantly PhDs, one fourth of whom earned Diplomates (ABPP). Several hundred psychiatrists, most of whom are board certified, about 100 social workers, almost all of whom have ACSW status, and a few EdD and PsyD supervisors staff the surveyed facilities. Overall, the staffs are composed of psychologists who have earned PhDs or allied professionals who have attained certified or Board status.

Thirty-four percent of supervisors have between 0 and 5 years of clinical experience, and 31% have between 5 and 10 years of clinical experience. Forty-one percent have 0–5 years of supervisory experience, and 31% have 6–10 years of supervisory experience. Thus 65% have 10 or fewer years of clinical experience, and 72% have 10 or fewer years of supervisory experience. This, plus the virtual identity ($r = .987$) between years of clinical experience and supervisory experience, leads to several conclusions: (a) Supervisors are predominantly less experienced (65% are reported to have accumulated 10 or fewer years of clinical experience), and (b) they tend to have fewer years of supervisory experience (72% have 10 or fewer years of supervisory experience).

Perhaps the more experienced clinicians are ensconced in private practice or administration, or there are few experienced clinicians[2] available, given the recent growth of PhD graduates (Korchin, 1976). Since the effect of the experience level of supervisors on the training of the student therapists is unknown, the implications of fewer highly experienced supervisors is unclear and warrants investigation.

Supervisors had 9.3 years of clinical experience and 7.6 years of supervisory experience. Yet they apparently lack training in psychotherapy supervision, given that only one third of the facilities reported training for supervisors. Perhaps the assumption is made that the clinicians were already trained when hired for the position, that they would learn to supervise on the job, that being a therapist is sufficient supervisory training, or that having been supervised imparts supervision training. These assumptions are questionable, since few doctoral programs (Sanchez, Note 1; Stanton, Sanchez, & Klesges, Note 2) or internships offer supervisory training. This lack of supervisory training is problematic, since one third of the facilities have interns supervising others, often without any supervision themselves. This inattention to the emerging field of psychotherapy supervision (Hess, 1980) is paralleled by the lack of contingent reward structures for psychotherapy supervision. The Division of Psychotherapy of the APA (APA, 1971) called for hiring and promotion on the basis of excellence in supervision and requested that time be allowed for supervision as part of the faculty members' teaching load.

Ongoing supervisor training occurs mostly on an ad hoc basis. Basically, feedback is provided by trainees to either the supervisor, or the director of clinical training, or other faculty; it is then relayed to the supervisor. The validity of such ratings is undetermined and may tap various ill-defined and idiosyncratic dimensions. Psychometrically sound supervision rating scales need to be developed. Monitoring tapes of supervision and the therapist's learning of psychotherapy could be two more direct methods of supervisor performance appraisal, which could help supervisors develop their skills.

Although over half of the clinical psychologists supervise others' psychotherapy on their first job (Stanton et al., Note 2), they do not get training in supervision. This reflects the finding that only one out of five directors of training deem it "quite important" to give such training. Some directors were offended at the suggestion that interns were anywhere near ready to receive such training despite the specific recommendations from Division 29 (APA, 1971) that faculty and students have practica and course work in supervision. Paradoxically, the interns denied supervision training will be the staff that the directors are hiring to supervise the next year's class of interns. There is con-

---

[2] The value judgment of what constitutes an appropriate level of experience is the authors' and such judgment calls for a more empirical base than is currently available.

siderable ambivalence as to (a) the importance of training supervision, (b) when supervision training should be done, and (c) who should do it.

In summary, supervisors tend to be well trained, moderately experienced, and professionally committed to supervision, although untrained in supervision specifically. Moreover the modal technique remains individual (one-to-one) supervision. Training interns in supervision is usually not done; when it is, the intern tends to get less supervision of his or her psychotherapy. Instead, both psychotherapy supervision and supervision of the interns' supervision are needed. Typically, training directors feel supervisory training ought to be done elsewhere, where there is both faculty and trainee time for it.

Only 14% of respondents in a study by Stanton et al. (Note 2) said they came from doctoral programs offering supervisory training, whereas 90% of that sample said they would opt for such a course. Psychotherapy supervision is now fifth in terms of time spent on activities by clinical psychologists; it is ahead of such activities as group psychotherapy, behavior modification, and research (Garfield & Kurtz, 1976), all of which are prominently featured in graduate school and internship curricula. Yet little specific attention, a sparse literature, and much anxiety on the part of the new PhD-turned supervisor (cf. Styczynski, 1980) characterize psychotherapy supervision for psychologists. A more focused and central role for psychotherapy supervision is necessary (Hess, 1980). Supervisors must become familiar with more supervisory methods, and supervisees must receive the kind of training that will help them maximize their skills to promote their clients' welfare. Recent attacks against nonmedical psychotherapists and more importantly our trainees, their clients' welfare, and our ethical codes enjoin us in this effort.

REFERENCE NOTES

1 Sanchez, V. C. *Experiences in and satisfaction with clinical supervision: A survey of clinical psychology interns at APA-approved internships.* Paper presented at the meeting of the Western Psychological Association, Honolulu, May 1980.

2 Stanton, A. L., Sanchez, V. C., & Klesges, R. C. *Supervision skills: Do APA-approved clinical programs teach them?* Paper presented at the meeting of the American Psychological Association, Los Angeles, August 1981.

REFERENCES

American Psychological Association, Division of Psychotherapy. Recommended standards for psychotherapy education in psychology doctoral program. *Professional Psychology,* 1971, *2,* 148–154.

Garfield, S. L., & Kurtz, R. Clinical psychologists in the 1970s. *American Psychologist,* 1976, *31,* 1–9.

Hess, A. K. *Psychotherapy supervision: Theory, practice and research.* New York: Wiley-Interscience, 1980.

Korchin, S. J. *Modern clinical psychology: Principles of intervention in the clinic and community.* New York: Basic Books, 1976.

Stedman, J. M., Costello, R. M., Gaines, T., Jr., Schoefeld, L. S., Loucks, S., & Burnstein, A. G. How clinical psychology interns are selected: A study of decision-making processes. *Professional Psychology,* 1981, *12,* 415–419.

Styczynski, L. E. The transition from supervisee to supervisor. In A. K. Hess (Ed.), *Psychotherapy supervision: Theory, research and practice.* New York: Wiley Interscience, 1980.

Reading 28

A Systems Model for the Supervision of School Psychological Services

Michael J. Curtis and Geoffrey G. Yager
University of Cincinnati

The purpose of this paper is to present the application of "systems thinking" to the work of supervision of school psychological services. Considering the space limitations imposed upon any one journal article, our treatment of this topic must be considered introductory and, in many respects, rather cursory. We will introduce some elements of a systems approach to supervision while necessarily ignoring other potential applications.

What is a system? During the past ten to fifteen years, the word "system" has become an everyday part of our vocabulary: "You can't buck the system." "All systems are go!" "She's moving up in the system." Each of these uses of the word "system" carries with it a common notion: a system is the orderly combination of a set of component parts (subsystems) that serves to produce a definable outcome or product. Ideally, the system can be described or illustrated to clarify the interrelationships between the parts and the whole (Horan, 1972; Stewart, Winborn, Johnson, Burks & Engelkes, 1978).

As the subsequent portions of this paper will serve to illustrate, supervision of school psychological services is rather complex. It might be helpful, therefore, to introduce the concept of a system by citing a concrete, well-defined, familiar example found in many of our own homes: the stereo system. A stereo system is made up of a set of components: amplifier, tape deck, AM–FM receiver, turntable, and speakers. These subsystems are combined in an orderly fashion (e.g., the turntable must provide input to the amplifier) such that an auditory product is created. A map of the connections between components could easily

Reprinted from School Psychology Review, *10*(4), 425–433.

be designed. The stereo system may be perceived as a subsystem in a larger system (e.g., the electrical system of a house), or it may be viewed as the supersystem of the amplifier whose component subsystems could be identified and interrelated as in a circuit diagram of the amplifier's wiring.

In examining supervision from a systems perspective, we are forced to view supervisees within the context of the larger systems in which they function, as well as in terms of their own intrapersonal subsystems. Unlike more traditional supervisory models, we cannot focus our exclusive attention during supervision upon the intrapersonal dynamics or the specific behaviors of the supervisee. While we may well need to deal with intrapersonal aspects of supervisee behaviors, we will do so within the context of the supervisory subsystem as a component of larger systems, including the university's training program, the school's educational program, and the support network of the community at large.

If the reader at this point is commenting that, "this is really a complex way of looking at supervision," we readily agree! An alteration in *any* subsystem of a larger system will likely have an effect upon the output of the system itself! Just as a worn needle will reduce the quality of sound resulting from our stereo system, an ineffective supervisory system may result in poorer education for students in the schools.

A BRIEF HISTORY OF THE SYSTEMS APPROACH

Systems analysis was developed to aid progress toward understanding and improving the performance of certain goal-related programs. It is a methodology whereby complex organizational problems can be resolved through a careful analysis of the specific steps which lead from the initial development of ideas to the eventual attainment of the organization's goals. In business, industry, and government, systems analysis and planning have become commonplace since World War II. For example, the design and accomplishment of placing a human being on the moon in 1969 would have been impossible without a system analysis that clarified what needed to be accomplished at each step along the way.

Although military and industrial applications had existed for several years, systems applications to the behavioral sciences were not discussed until the mid 1950's (Miller, 1955). As might well be expected, a systems model for the behavioral sciences must address interrelationships among *living* systems. Living systems, of course, have more degrees of freedom in responding to outside input than do inert systems. For example, the stereo system (inert) will either play very loud music or break when the volume of its amplifier subsystem is turned to maximum. A human being under the stress of scalding a hand may scream, or curse, or cry, or silently bear the pain (several possibilities among many). Additionally, this individual, as a living system, is ordinarily in a position to learn from the accident that led to the scalding and to avoid a similar event in the future. A system with the ability to react to input from the outside environment is called an "open system." All living systems are open systems.

A relevant example of an open system may help to clarify the importance of the "openness" concept. The school system is, of course, a living system which includes a variety of subsystems (e.g., elementary and secondary schools, administrative functions, school psychological services, maintenance, cafeteria services, and many more). Each subsystem interrelates with the others to produce the definable product of educated children and adults. Were the school system unable to react to input from environments outside its direct boundaries, it would readily experience major problems such as passing bond levies and millages. As times change, the needs of the community (the suprasystem in which the school is located) are altered. A variable school system can anticipate these changes by reacting and adjusting as differences are first detected.

The example of the school system also helps raise one additional important point. The developer of a systems model *must* identify the specific *level* of the system to be analyzed and stay *at that level* in the analysis. With a school system, there are numerous levels of systems and subsystems that could well be investigated: the entire system, the individual school, the English department in one school, the school psychological services program in the district, or, the role and functions of one individual teacher or pupil. Each of these levels is definable as a living system. In our systems analysis, we have chosen to focus our attention directly on the supervisor and the roles and functions of that individual.

SYSTEMS SUPERVISION

Supervisory effectiveness is not an attainment that should be presumed to be inherently associated with one whose title is "supervisor." It represents a proficient level of performance that results from the development of a rather specific set of skills. Yet, as with any area of professional functioning, supervision must reflect a philosophical foundation. Rather than engage in what could otherwise be described as haphazard activities (whether or not some of those activities prove successful), the supervisor should purposefully select strategies that are consistent with a conceptual framework for supervision. The systems supervision model provides one such framework.

As with any systems analysis, we have attempted to identify the component parts of supervision and to establish the interrelationships among these parts. Were others to have studied the same system, it is likely that they would have divided the system into different although equally valid, subsystems. Additionally, our combination of the parts of the system (i.e., our synthesis) may well be somewhat unique. Figure 1 illustrates our conceptualization of systems supervision. As might be expected, this model synthesizes ideas from a number

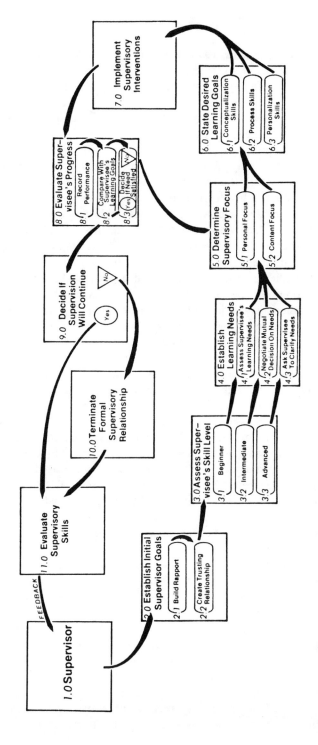

Figure 1 Flowchart of systems supervision.

343

of sources (Bernard, 1979; Boyd, 1978; Littrell, Lee-Borden, & Lorenz, 1979; Stewart et al., 1978).

The systems supervision model displayed in Figure 1 contains the esential elements of all supervisory activities. Since we have designed this model from the perspective of the supervisor, each of the subsystems (boxes) gives an intruction to the supervisor.

Although we do not have the space in the present article to explain the model fully, a very brief "walk through" would prove instructive. We begin with the "supervisor" (Subsystem 1.0). At the start of any supervisory relationship, supervisors will have certain initial goals that they will wish to attain irrespective of the individual supervisee. The establishment of a base of rapport and trust (Subsystem 2.0) will certainly be among these initial goals. Because openness and understanding are needed for optimal learning, the strength of the relationship established here will be crucial to the achievement of all that follows. Among the methods used to attain a good working relationship is the brief clarification of the supervisor's intentions regarding the content and direction of supervision. There is nothing that will tend to destroy a possible trusting relationship more than a supervisor who is directing supervision in a manner that is totally inconsistent with the approach expected by the supervisee.

Since the specific needs of supervisees will be based on their attained level of skills, supervisors next must assess the supervisees' performance level (Subsystem 3.0). As Subsystem 4.0 indicates, beginners' needs are assessed by the supervisor. For example, the professor of the introductory course in psychoeducational assessment does not ask the class what it feels it should learn in that course. On the other hand, intermediate level school psychologists (e.g., internship level students) would more appropriately *consult* with their supervisors in collaboratively identifying their learning needs. At an advanced level (e.g., experienced school psychologists in the field), the supervisor generally is less involved in the formulation of learning needs; advanced level psychologists typically know themselves what they must learn. However, the supervisor's input may be important in helping supervisees recognize the emergence of professional trends and issues.

Once the needs have been established, a supervisory focus will be determined (Subsystem 5.0). A personal focus would involve exploration of the supervisee's feelings and the interconnections between the supervisee's personal dynamics and the dynamics of a "problem" situation. A content focus, on the other hand, would incorporate teaching and information giving as the primary supervisor behavior. In summary, a personal focus would very much resemble a therapeutic supervisory model, while a content focus would be similar to a teaching model of supervision. As with the determination of the supervisee's learning needs, the method of making the supervisory focus decision (i.e., supervisor decision, mutual decision, or supervisee decision) would be largely influenced by the supervisee's capacity for self-evaluation.

After the assessment of needs (Subsystem 4.0) and the determination of focus (Subsystem 5.0) have been completed, the supervisor and supervisee should decide upon and state the desired learning goals for supervision. These goals should be specific and measurable (Subsystem 6.0). Goals may fall within any of three primary areas (Bernard, 1979):

6.1 *Conceptualization skills.* Those skills not directly active but more explanatory and cognitive in nature are conceptualization skills. The skill of conceptualizing a student's needs based upon a multifactored evaluation would fit within this area.

6.2 *Process skills.* These skills include any and all active behaviors related to the process of implementing psychological services in the schools. Counseling, test administration and interpretation, consultation, conducting child-centered groups, and leading in-service programs are all process skills.

6.3 *Personalization skills.* These are skills that relate to the supervisee's own personal issues and interpersonal dynamics. Such skills will be addressed in supervision when a school psychologist knows what needs to be done (conceptualization), has the ability to do it (process), but, for some reason, cannot perform because of some personal difficulty (e.g., anxiety, family problems, lack of commitment).

Consistent with the supervisory focus selected in Subsystem 5.0, a supervisory intervention will be implemented (Subsystem 7.0). As was indicated earlier, a personal focus might lead to "therapy-like" supervision. A content focus might encourage outside readings, academic discussions, lectures, or suggested coursework. The intervention might involve a variety of other methods including, but not limited to model role playing, direct observation and feedback, contingency contracting, or consultation. In many cases, the intervention might be designed and implemented by the supervisee, in effect self-supervision. As in some of the earlier stages, the nature of the intervention would be influenced by the skill level of the supervisee. Some supervisees would require direct supervisor intervention while others would be very capable of carrying out the intervention themselves. After the intervention has been implemented, the supervisee's progress toward attainment of the identified goals should be regularly evaluated (Subsystem 8.0). As certain supervisory needs are satisfied, a decision may be necessary regarding whether or not supervision will continue (Subsystem 9.0). Ideally, supervision is an on-going process. When supervision continues, a reassessment of the supervisee's present level of performance would be appropriate. If it is decided that formal supervision should end, termination occurs (Subsystem 10.0). In either case, there should be a careful review of the supervisor's learning and skills (Subsystem 11.0). The supervisor's new insights on the supervisory process provide feedback to the supervisor subsystem which is the initial step in the model. It must be emphasized that except in the case of a limited, time-specific supervisory relationship, the model requires a cyclical, on-going process of evaluation, intervention and re-evaluation. Furthermore, it reflects a process and is not limited to a specific content focus. In some cases, behavioral interventions will be appropriate while in others a psychotherapeutic process might be in order.

AN ILLUSTRATIVE EXAMPLE

Perhaps the most effective way to clarify the usefulness of the systems supervision model would be to provide an example. Imagine yourself as the supervisor of Sally, a graduate student in school psychology who is beginning her internship in a local school district. You immediately assess her skill level as intermediate (Subsystem 3.2). You and Sally mutually determine her learning needs to include (a) increased practice in and feedback on psychosocial testing and (b) increased poise and confidence in dealing with parents in a variety of school conference situations (Subsystem 4.2).

You have supervised Sally for several weeks when she comes in one afternoon and says: "I am at my wits' end! I just cannot understand what it is about the other school psychologists in my district; they simply don't seem to like me!" Sensing Sally's emotional upset, you feel that is is most appropriate for you to direct attention to Sally's intrapersonal and interpersonal dynamics in her relationships with these other school psychologists. This, of course, is the definition of a personal focus (Subsystem 5.1). Listening empathetically and posing therapeutic questions, you aid Sally in exploring what seems to be happening in her relationship with the other school psychologists.

Through the personal focus, Sally expresses feelings related to all three desired learning goals (Subsystem 6.0): she cannot understand conceptually what is occurring (Subsystem 6.1); she doesn't know how to handle the covert hostility she feels during staff meetings (Subsystem 6.2); and she is depressed and down on herself as a result of these experiences (Subsystem 6.3). Sally explores each of these areas for a period of time and eventually states a learning goal in each area. She wishes to understand what is happening so that she can use certain process skills to change the situation and, thereby, reduce her negative feelings.

Once Sally had clarified her goal, you could have switched to another focus (Subsystem 5.0), but you decided to continue with the self-exploration/ therapeutic type of supervisory intervention (Subsystem 7.0). At the end of the meeting, you ask Sally to give some additional thought to her feelings and reactions in the staff meetings. Sally agrees to write down some of her experiences and bring them to your next session (also Subsystem 7.0).

When Sally returns a week later, you both evaluate where Sally stands in terms of meeting the learning goals she had stated during the last session.

You glance through the notes that Sally had taken during the week and find that she continues to be upset about her interactions with the staff. However, in her notes, Sally has identified certain aspects of the concern that had not been stated earlier: her interpretations of hostile feelings from the staff occur only after Sally has mentioned something she learned in her graduate program (Subsystem 8.0).

Since Sally's learning goals have not been met, you recycle to Subsystem 5.0 again. At this point, you feel more able, however, to give some direct suggestions and advice. Therefore, you choose a content focus (Subsystem 5.2) for this meeting. Taking a teacher-oriented focus, you could offer instruction in any number of possible areas. It happens that you choose to direct your content to conceptualization skills (Subsystem 6.1), and you tell Sally about systems theory. The psychological services staff in the school district is one such system. Sally, being a recent addition to that system, has undoubtedly altered its normal manner of operation. You explain to Sally that it is certainly possible that the other psychologists are not so much responding to her as a person as they are reacting to her as a new, unpredictable subsystem. A systems explanation, of course, is not the only theoretical/content explanation that you might have given. It is only one possibility.

Sally understands this conceptualization and agrees that this certainly could be occurring. Her next question is: "What can I do about it?" Continuing with a content focus, you respond to what is now related to the process learning goal (Subsystem 6.2). You proceed to outline several methods for dealing with the situation and you and Sally role play some possible techniques (Subsystem 7.0). Sally agrees to "tone down" her presentation of new ideas to sound less theoretical and more practical; she will reflect more of the other staff members feelings and ideas during meetings; and she will give the others more direct, verbal reinforcement for their established methods of practice (also Subsystem 7.0).

Sally may or may not arrive at your meeting the following week with her learning goals achieved, but your first order of business will be to check on her progress. The focus may change or it may remain the same. The critical point is that, as the supervisor, you are continually defining what you and the supervisee are intending to accomplish, *and* you are evaluating the progress of supervision.

PERMEABILITY OF SYSTEMS BOUNDARIES

Although the systems supervision model provides us with a valuable map of the supervision process, we feel that several other systems concepts are extremely helpful when applied to supervision. One such concept is the notion of boundaries between systems. Each supervisee's psychological boundaries (separation from other systems) vary in permeability depending upon that individual's learning history. The extent of a supervisee's boundary permeability has direct relevance to the course of supervision.

Figure 2 depicts three supervisees with boundaries of significantly different permeability. Illustration A represents a supervisee with an impermeable boundary. Such an individual provides particularly difficult problems for the supervisor. All external forces or influence, regardless of magnitude, are rejected. Thus, a supervisor's attempt to offer help and advice to this individual is ignored. During a training program, such people are likely to say to their teachers and supervisor, "I already know everything I need to know; I am only in this program to get my credentials!" In other cases, the completion of a masters or doctoral degree will trigger the shutdown of some school psychologists' boundaries: "I have finished my degree, and I know all I need to know!" Inflexibility and stagnation are characteristic of such individuals. They are unable to respond to feedback on their performance. Unfortunately, the impermeable boundary also prevents these same individuals from sharing any personal feelings or thoughts with their supervisors. Thus, even those issues that are identified as troublesome are never addressed and cannot be effectively resolved.

Individual B in Figure 2 is a supervisee without a functional boundary. The boundary represents a fusion of the supervisee with the supervisor in a manner that is clearly unproductive for the development of the supervisee's skills. Individuals without defined boundaries accept all external input regardless of magnitude or importance. They demonstrate a lack of discrimination by reacting equally to every outside influence. In supervision, these "totally open" supervisees lose their identities and attempt to duplicate on the job every wish

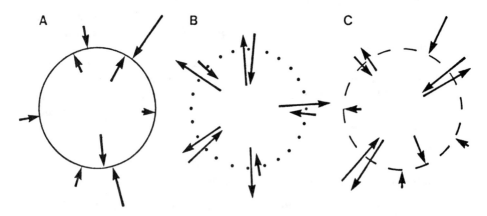

Figure 2   Three systems with differing permeability levels.
    A. Impermeable boundary.
    B. Totally open boundary.
    C. Semipermeable boundary.

of their supervisors or others. Clearly, since every piece of feedback is viewed as equally important, such individuals become easily overwhelmed and worn out. Supervisees need to be able to determine the relative importance of a supervisor's comments. Input regarding the attractiveness of their clothes or their ability to answer questions about a child's psychological assessment should not merit equal attention.

Individual C (Figure 2) is able to maintain autonomy while remaining open to feedback and new learning. This type of individual has a semi-permeable boundary. Under most circumstances, supervisees with such boundaries are operating at the most desirable level of openness. These individuals are able to select and accept certain external forces and reject others. Each force that is accepted is responded to in a manner that is commensurate with the perceived importance of the force. Influences that are of greater importance (longer arrows) are given greater attention in the formulation and execution of responses. The supervisee with a semi-permeable boundary may provide the supervisor with some challenging and growth-producing experiences. After all, some of those external forces which are not accepted may have originated in the supervisor.

In systems terminology, we would say that the individual depicted in Figure 2C is in a state of *dynamic equilibrium*. When input is received, this person is able to use that input constructively and react in such a way as to maintain stability despite system change.

In seeking a state of equilibrium, the school psychologist supervisee must strive for the development of a capacity for self-awareness (internal analysis), as well as for external systems analysis (i.e., an understanding of the environmental context in which s/he functions). While external systems such as the school and the community are readily recognized as influential components in the suprasystem, clients and the supervisor cannot be overlooked as influential sources of input to the individual. In the school setting, the external systems that the supervisee must consider include legislative and judicial bodies, the community-at-large, specific influential community subgroups, professional organizations, parents, school and district administrators, instructional staff, building and support personnel, students as a whole, as well as specific student clients, and the supervisor. It should be remembered that as living systems, all of these influencing agents are in a state of dynamic change. Furthermore, their boundaries often overlap, and a change in one system may stimulate corresponding changes in a number of other systems. Therefore, systems analysis must be viewed as an on-going process during which the individual is continually assessing the interactions between internal and external sources of influence. Even an in-depth systems analysis will not necessarily provide "answers" to all of the questions that will face the individual school psychologist. However, familiarity with systems theory would provide supervisees with a perspective through which they can better understand and interact with other influential systems in the professional setting.

SUPERVISOR INTERVENTIONS

As supervisors, we must recognize that our job is not simply that of reducing supervisees' stresses engendered by realizations of the numerous forces competing to influence their work. Supervisee stress or tension should not automatically elicit our concern for its elimination. All living systems experience stress; it is the level of stress that is most important in determining our strategies for intervention. "Tension reduction and relief of stress are often the focus of our efforts, but sometimes at the price of overlooking the possibility of increasing tension in order to facilitate creativity, innovation, or change" (Chin, 1976, p. 93).

The issue of stress and change in the supervisee is somewhat analogous to the relationship between motivation and human learning. Under conditions of extremely high or extremely low motivation, learning is minimal, while under moderate levels of motivation, the rate of learning reaches its highest point. Similarly, if the supervisee is in a state of extremely high or extremely low stress, learning through supervision will likely be very limited. The objective of the supervisor would be either to decrease or to increase the supervisee's stress to a level of moderation which would be facilitative of learning.

In the case of the individual with the impermeable boundary (Figure 2A), it is important to recognize that no input is accepted by the supervisee, including that of the supervisor. As a first step, it is necessary for the supervisor to establish a relationship of trust in order for the supervisee's boundary to become more permeable, at least to the supervisor. Once the supervisor has gained access to the supervisee, it is then possible to introduce gradually those external messages that have not been accepted by the supervisee.

A supervisee with an impermeable boundary could be in a state of either high stress (many strong, but withheld internal forces), or low stress (few if any internal forces). The supervisee's level of stress will not be discernable, however, until access has been attained. If the supervisee happens to be highly stressed, the input of new information must proceed in as non-threatening a manner as possible. To do otherwise might elicit a supervisee response that would in essence close the boundaries once again. On the other hand, it would be appropriate to increase the stress level of the supervisee who exhibits very little tension.

For supervisees whose boundaries are too permeable (Figure 2B), a different intervention would be necessary. Since these individuals tend to overreact to all external influences, they are always under stress. Supervisors have no difficulty in gaining access to these individuals. Unfortunately, the input of the supervisor merits no more attention than the most insignificant message from any other external source. For the supervisor to have an impact, it is necessary to employ tactics which would markedly reduce the number of external forces before they reach the supervisee. For example, all requests for assistance of certain types could be directed to personnel other than the supervisee for the time being. Or it might be necessary to actually move the supervisee to a different environmental sphere which includes fewer influential forces. As an example of the latter strategy, a supervisee might be removed from a school which is itself in turmoil. Such a setting would constantly place excessive demands upon the supervisee who was personally not functioning well to begin with. Reassignment of this individual to a school where demands were less severe would reduce the level of stress and allow the supervisee to attend more intently to the input of the supervisor. It would then be possible for the supervisor to work with this individual to develop a better understanding of which environmental forces should be accepted, interpreted and responded to in an appropriate manner. In effect, this individual would need to develop a semi-permeable boundary.

The primary goal of the supervisor is to develop in supervisees the skills to seek out and accent constructive feedback (external input) regarding their actions and to incorporate that information in improving the quality of inter-action with the environment (performance). As Chin (1976) suggests, ". . . the single most important improvement the change agent can help a client system achieve is to increase its diagnostic sensitivity to the effects of its own actions upon others" (p. 95).

THE DEVELOPMENTAL ASPECTS OF SYSTEMS SUPERVISION

The systems supervision model represents an extension of the traditional systems model in that it incorporates a number of significant developmental principles. In essence, this expanded model reflects an emphasis on the *collaborative development* of expectations for the supervisee and the means for their attain-ment. Furthermore, it deviates from the "here and now" analysis of the traditional systems model and suggests a time perspective for interactions between the supervisor and the supervisee. Constant change, development, growth and decline are underlying assumptions of the system supervision model. In accordance with this approach, the supervisor and the supervisee collabora-tively develop a *directional focus, stages for progress,* and a *time frame for goal attainment.* The degree of collaboration may be influenced by situational variables such as the supervisee's levels of stress and performance. For example, as was discussed earlier in regard to Subsystem 4.0 (Figure 1), the supervisor should be much more directive in assessing the needs of the entry level trainee than would be necessary with an intern or practitioner under most circum-stances. In the same vein, a supervisee who is operating under extreme stress will in all likelihood not be able to collaborate meaningfully in the supervisory process.

The systems supervision model provides for a consideration of the supervisee's performance from the perspective of both intrapersonal dynamics and the context of the environmental setting. It allows for flexibility on the part of the supervisor in determining the nature and the extent of the intervention that is most appropriate within each supervisory relationship. It is our belief that the systems supervision model offers a viable framework for the supervision of school psychologists during training and in the field.

REFERENCES

Bernard, J. M. Supervisor training: A discriminative model. *Counselor Education and Supervision*, 1979, *19*, 60–68.

Boyd, J. D. *Counselor supervision: Approaches, preparation, practices.* Muncie, IN.: Accelerated Development, Inc., 1978.

Chin, R. The utility of systems models and developmental models for practitioners. In W. G. Bennis, K. D. Benne, R. Chin, & K. F. Corey (Eds.), *The planning of change* (3rd ed.). New York: Holt, Rinehart & Winston, 1976.

Horan, J. J. Behavioral goals in systematic counselor education. *Counselor Education and Supervision*, 1972, *11*, 162–170.

Littrell, J. M., Lee-Borden, N., & Lorenz, J. R. A developmental framework for counseling supervision. *Counselor Education and Supervision*, 1979, *19*, 129–136.

Miller, J. G. Toward a general theory for the behavioral sciences. *American Psychologist*, 1955, *10*, 513–553.

Stewart, N. R., Winborn, B. B., Johnson, R. G., Burks, H. M., Jr., & Engelkes, Jr. R. *Systematic counseling.* Englewood Cliffs, N.J.: Prentice-Hall, Inc., 1978.

Reading 29
The Professional Model of Psychotherapy Supervision

Thomas A. McElfresh
Wright State University, Dayton, Ohio

INTRODUCTION

For psychotherapy supervision to be effective, certain criteria must be met consistently. Supervision without direction, clarity or relevance is rarely productive. Inadequate training is costly to students of psychotherapy and their present and future clients. Supervision thoughtfully planned and skillfully executed is likely to yield productive results, in the same way that skillfully executed psychotherapy yields positive outcomes.

Psychotherapy supervision has been explained through *conceptual* models (Ekstein & Wallerstein, 1958; Hess, 1980; Schmidt, 1979; Yogev, 1982). Many *practical* models have been presented (Bernard, 1979; Hogan, 1964; Levine & Tilker, 1974; Wasik & Fishbein, 1982). Extant models of supervision are frequently unsystematic and lack comprehensiveness. The Professional Model provides a thorough and organized approach to the task of psychotherapy supervision.

The Professional Model addresses trainee needs regardless of theoretical orientation or level of clinical experience. The theoretical constructs of the professional model can be utilized independently of the practical applications. Greater clarity and efficiency in psychotherapy supervision result as the conceptual and practical aspects of the professional model are combined.

THEORETICAL FRAMEWORK

Four basic supervisory roles have been identified in the literature: (1) the teacher-student approach (Walz & Roeber, 1962); (2) the therapist-patient approach (Arbuckle, 1958); (3) the consultant approach (Hackney, 1971); and (4) the administrator approach (Ekstein, 1964; Watson, 1973).

The supervisor as teacher focuses on the didactic aspects of training as in the transmission of information to the student. The supervisor as therapist focuses on the student's personal needs in an attempt to overcome the anxieties and conflicts that inhibit professional development. The supervisor as consultant is available to discuss the methods and dynamics of various clinical activities and clarify or introduce new concepts. The supervisor as administrator plays an important role in the evaluation of student performance, the assignment of cases, the distribution of work, and the policy and polity of clinical training.

Bernard (1979) developed a structured model of supervision by matching trainee needs with various supervisory roles. The areas of student need identified were conceptualization, process, and personalization. These areas correspond to the popular *knowledge, skills,* and *attitudes* paradigm.

Training in conceptualization includes the development of a theoretical perspective and conceptual framework by which the student sees the world. Training in the process aspect of psychotherapy is aimed at the mechanics of the therapeutic process. The area of personalization refers not only to the student's development of a professional identity, but to the personality characteristics and personal behaviors of the student in and out of the therapy hour.

Effective supervision will focus on one of three content areas: (1) the client's intrapsychic and interpersonal activities, (2) the student's therapeutic relationship with the client, or (3) the student's learning relationship with the supervisor.

By focusing on the client's intrapsychic and interpersonal activities, training is directed toward problem identification, assessment and diagnosis, the measurement of treatment effects, and the identification of life themes, self-esteem, and motivation. Viewing the therapist-patient relationship offers the therapist-in-training exposure to psychotherapy process variables of communication, contact and withdrawal, transference and countertransference, and the stimulus value and therapeutic influence of the student. Attention paid to the relationship between the supervisor and supervisee highlights professional role modeling when it occurs. The student gains insights from being the receiver of attention and the self-inspection encouraged in supervision offers the student awarenesses of the client role.

The Professional Model is a three-dimensional model. It is the only known model to integrate the above mentioned supervisory roles and areas of student need, with content areas of focus during supervision. The first dimension (A) includes the primary areas of student need in the establishment of effective clinical skills. The second dimension (B) reflects the various roles supervisors may assume. The final dimension (C) is the focus of attention during supervision. Figure 1 details the Professional Model of psychotherapy supervision schematically.

The Professional Model calls for the supervisor and student to agree as to which axis (A, B, or C) will be primary. Is the supervisor's role and style going to vary dependent upon student need and area of focus? Frequently, regardless of student need, the supervisor's role and style has been one with which the supervisor feels most comfortable. Using this multi-dimensional model, supervisors add to their idiosyncratic strengths and become comfortable with a variety of different roles and use the data at hand to select the most effective role for a supervisory contact.

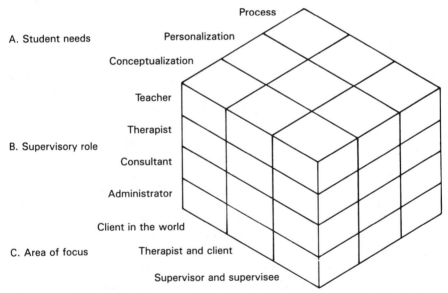

Figure 1 Schematic diagram of the Professional Model of Psychotherapy Supervision.

It is recommended that the primary axis be the student's need (A). Both the supervisor's role (B) and the area of focus (C) vary in order to fully address the student's needs in the most effective way. A supervisor working with a trainee who is deficient in a specified area cannot assume that one role is always the best. If a supervisor sees a specific area of student need as requiring a specific supervisory role at all times, then the supervisor is going to be ineffective at least part of the time. The Professional Model is a need-specific model and there are several choice points for the supervisor to consider.

Table 1 outlines the alternative choices regarding roles that supervisors may consider with respect to student needs. Each cell contains a typical student training need and a possible supervisory response.

Table 2 outlines typical content areas for supervision and training based upon mutual consideration of the area of student need and the area of focus in supervision. This grid is particularly useful in the identification of specific problem areas in the student's training.

Table 3 delineates many supervisory alternatives based on the specific area of focus in supervision.

PRACTICAL APPLICATIONS

The format for the Professional Model is a simple and straightforward one. After the initial introductory meeting where important personal and professional information is mutually shared and the model of supervision is explained to the student, an assessment of the student's strengths and weaknesses is made.

A psychotherapy skills checklist of clinical experiences is completed by the student (see Appendix 1). The information obtained assists the supervisor and the student in identifying strengths, deficits, and interests. An individualized training plan is then developed.

The Professional Model includes a mutually agreed upon training contract for both the student and the supervisor. The Individualized Training Plan (ITP) systematically outlines specific student needs and learning objectives with proposed training strategies for meeting these needs (see Appendix 2). The student is actively involved in the goal-setting process. The ITP also specifies the methods of evaluating student performance.

Minor adjustments are made in the ITP as training and supervision are provided. An Individualized Training Review (ITR) is included to afford both parties the opportunity to evaluate or renegotiate the ITP (see Appendix 3). It is recommended that the ITR be utilized no less than once every 90 days. The ITR details progress made toward the training goals. Both the student and supervisor rate the level of goal attainment.

Depending upon the level of goal attainment, the ITP is continued for another 90 days, renegotiated totally or in part, or terminated. Training recommendations are made by either party concerning the quality of pro-

Table 1 Alternative Choices

Supervisory roles	A. Areas of student need		
	Conceptualization	Process	Personalization
Teacher	The student is missing important information and is not picking up on critical issues presented by the client.	The student wants to use a specific procedure or style with a client but has never learned the method.	The student is unaware of his/her tendency to interpret things for the client and the effect this has on the client.
	The supervisor uses audio and video tapes to show the student where and how important information was given by the client.	The supervisor teaches the student the technique or method of therapy.	The supervisor assigns readings dealing with the role and effect of interpretation in psychotherapy.
Therapist	The student feels lost and is not sure where therapy is going.	The student has difficulty in making an effective intervention with a particular client.	The student is unaware that the client is sexually attracted to him/her.
	The supervisor helps the student relate his/her feelings of confusion and attempts are made to clarify the goals for therapy.	The supervisor attempts to help the student determine the effect of this particular client on him/her which reduces the intervention's effect.	The supervisor attempts to help the student confront his/her own sexuality and resistance to seeing sexual cues from clients.
Consultant	The student feels his/her present theoretical orientation inadequately describes the client.	The student discovers that a client responds especially well to a certain type of intervention and wants to expand on this intervention further with the client.	The student would like to feel more comfortable with disabled clients.

	The supervisor discusses several conceptualization models for the student to consider.	The supervisor works with the student to find different ways of making the same intervention and discusses ways to practice these.	The supervisor and student discuss social values and stereotypes regarding handicapped people.
Administrator	The student wants to pursue a behavioral orientation.	The student has difficulty in functioning in a professional manner.	The student is presenting signs of boredom or burnout.
	The supervisor assigns initial cases where the presenting problem is chiefly behavioral.	The supervisor confronts the student and recommends remediation of skill development courses or dismissal from the training program.	The supervisor increases or decreases the number of cases that are seen by the student. Renegotiation of the ITP.

Note. Adapted from Bernard (1979, p. 65).

Table 2 Typical Content Areas

	A. Areas of student need		
Supervisory roles	Conceptualization	Process	Personalization
Client in the world	The student has questions regarding: What motivates people? Why do people do what they do? Is behavior environ- mentally determined or generated internally? Is there an unconscious? What are common social variables that affecting the client?	The student learns to deal with the client's significant others as helping in the client's adjustment.	Focus upon the student's values and opinions about the client's lifestyle. Barriers to understanding the client are explored.
Therapist and client	Development of a theoretical orientation. The student develops a rationale for doing the interventions that he/she does. The student needs a sense of what is correct and appropriate in terms of doing therapy. The student gains knowledge of ethics.	The student learns to skillfully confront, effectively support, and lead to a successful termination.	The student's anxiety level changes. The student becomes aware of prejudices and countertransferences.
Supervisor and supervisee	By focusing on him/herself, the student gains awareness of the client role. The student sees the image of a competent and professional psychotherapist.	The student learns to be introspective and is able to act sensitively to the immediate process of the moment.	Identification of and dealing with dependencies, avoidance behavior and game-playing.

Table 3 Supervisory Alternatives

Supervisory roles	Client in the world	C. Focus of supervision		
		Therapist and client	Supervisor and supervisee	
Teacher	Training in DSM III. Training in the conduct of a diagnostic interview and and mental status exam.	Instructing the student about clinical methods and procedures.	Description and instruction of the purpose and function of supervision. Explanation of the Professional model of supervision.	
Therapist	The student role-plays the client while the supervisor conducts the interaction.	Focusing on and working through of transference and countertransference issues.	Exploring the student's issues with authority, nurturance, interpersonal style, and professional identity.	
Consultant	Discussion of goal setting, treatment planning, and evaluation of treatment.	Discussion of alternative methods of treatment. Discussion of therapy context variables of fees, frequency of session, and appropriateness of referral or termination.	Discussion of the literature on training and supervision with regard to the student's training and supervision.	
Administrator	Suggestion and/or authorization of resources available for the client.	Assignment of cases. Evaluation of skill development.	Negotiations of the ITP. Discussion of the ITR.	

fessional development of the student, areas for future training, and the supervisory process itself. The student may choose to rate the quality of supervision received, in the recommendations section.

Copies of ITP's and ITR's are retained by the supervisor and supervisee for reference. Within a total training program, a student's professional growth and development may be "charted" over a progressive series of plans and reviews. Final plans and reviews are of value to students in planning postgraduate training and continuing education.

DISCUSSION

Effective supervision calls for a variety of supervisory roles and addresses a range of student needs. The particular student need should be the determining factor in selecting the appropriate supervisory role. In view of these premises, it follows that the supervisor needs (a) a range of role alternatives, (b) a framework in which to fit student needs, (c) a specified area of focus during supervision, and (d) systematic guidelines for determining supervisory goals and approaches.

The unique Professional Model of psychotherapy supervision specifies the manner in which supervision is provided. In those places where supervision is thoughtfully planned and skillfully executed, the Professional Model enhances the quality of supervision by offering an endless number of combinations and options for the supervisor and supervisee to consider. In other places where supervision is not as carefully handled, the Professional Model structures the supervisory process to ensure that all parties —supervisor, supervisee, and client— benefit.

REFERENCES

Arbuckle, D. S. (1958). Five philosophical issues in counseling. *Journal of Counseling Psychology, 5*, 211-215.

Bernard, J. M. (1979). Supervisor training: A discrimination model. *Counselor Education and Supervision, 19*, 60-68.

Ekstein, R. (1964). Supervision of psychotherapy: Is it teaching? Is it administration? Or is it therapy? *Psychotherapy: Theory, Research, and Practice, 1*, 137-138.

Ekstein, R., & Wallerstein, R. S. (1958). *The teaching and learning of psychotherapy*. New York: Basic Books.

Hackney, H. L. (1971). Development of a pre-practicum counseling skills model. *Counselor Education and Supervision, 11*, 102-109.

Hess, A. K. (1980). Training models and the nature of psychotherapy supervision. In A. K. Hess (Ed.), *Psychotherapy supervision: Theory, research, and practice*. New York: Wiley.

Hogan, R. A. (1964). Issues and approaches in supervision. *Psychotherapy: Theory, Research, and Practice, 1*, 139-141.

Levine, F. M., & Tilker, H. A. (1974). A behavior modification approach to supervision in psychotherapy. *Psychotherapy: Theory, Research, and Practice, 11,* 182-188.

Schmidt, J. P. (1979). Psychotherapy supervision: A cognitive-behavioral model. *Professional Psychology, 10,* 278-184.

Walz, C. R., & Roeber, E. C. (1962). Supervisor's reactions to a counseling interview. *Counselor Education and Supervision, 1,* 2-7.

Wasik, B. H., & Fishbein, J. E. (1982). Problem-solving: A model for supervision in professional psychology. *Professional Psychology, 13,* 359-564.

Watson, K. W. (1973). Differential supervision. *Social Work, 80,* 80-88.

Yogev, S. (1982). An eclectic model of supervision: A developmental sequence for beginning psychotherapy students. *Professional Psychology, 13,* 236-246.

APPENDIX 1

Psychotherapy Skills Checklist

Trainee: _____Date: _____
Placement: _____Supervisor: _____

1. Briefly describe your personal theory of behavior and behavior change.

2. Approx. # of clients seen: Approx. # of sessions: % of clients served:
___Children   ___Individual   ___White
___Adolescents   ___Marital, conjoint   ___Minority
___Adults   ___Family   ___In-patient
___Older Adults   ___Group   ___Out-patient

3. Briefly describe your past supervision; with who, how often, what kind, etc.

4. Checklist of psychotherapy activities:

Next to each therapy method is a rating column with three, three point scales. The scales below are (P) proficiency, (E) experience, and (N) need.

Proficiency—In your judgment what is your level of expertise in being able to perform the activity designated. Do not be modest, be as realistic as you can.

Experience—Independent of your estimates of proficiency, your personal estimate of the amount of 'hands-on' experience you have in the method indicated.

Need—An estimate, from your personal and career ideal, of your interest or need for learning in the method designated.

The scale points are: (1) High   (2) Moderate   (3) Minimal

Please select those relevent to your (P) proficiency, (E) experience, and (N) learning needs.

Interview Methods

	P	E	N
Information gathering	1 2 3	1 2 3	1 2 3
Initial, individual screening	1 2 3	1 2 3	1 2 3
Initial, couple/family screening	1 2 2	1 2 3	1 2 3
Initial mental status exam	1 2 3	1 2 3	1 2 3

	P			E			N		
Crisis assessment	1	2	3	1	2	3	1	2	3
Behavioral analysis/description	1	2	3	1	2	3	1	2	3
Individualized treatment planning	1	2	3	1	2	3	1	2	3
Situational observation/rating	1	2	3	1	2	3	1	2	3
Other:	1	2	3	1	2	3	1	2	3

Individual Therapies

	P			E			N		
Behavior Modification	1	2	3	1	2	3	1	2	3
Behavior Therapy	1	2	3	1	2	3	1	2	3
Biofeedback	1	2	3	1	2	3	1	2	3
Client-Centered	1	2	3	1	2	3	1	2	3
Cognitive Therapy	1	2	3	1	2	3	1	2	3
Crisis Intervention	1	2	3	1	2	3	1	2	3
Directive Therapy	1	2	3	1	2	3	1	2	3
Eclectic Therapy	1	2	3	1	2	3	1	2	3
Existential Therapy	1	2	3	1	2	3	1	2	3
Gestalt Therapy	1	2	3	1	2	3	1	2	3
Hypnotherapy	1	2	3	1	2	3	1	2	3
Insight Therapy	1	2	3	1	2	3	1	2	3
Non-Directive Therapy	1	2	3	1	2	3	1	2	3
Psychoanalysis	1	2	3	1	2	3	1	2	3
Rational-Emotive Therapy	1	2	3	1	2	3	1	2	3
Reality Therapy	1	2	2	1	2	3	1	2	3
Relaxation Training	1	2	3	1	2	3	1	2	3
Sex Therapy	1	2	3	1	2	3	1	2	3
Supportive Therapy	1	2	3	1	2	3	1	2	3
Transactional Analysis	1	2	3	1	2	3	1	2	3
Other:	1	2	3	1	2	3	1	2	3

Group Therapies

	P			E			N		
Activity therapy	1	2	3	1	2	3	1	2	3
Behavioral	1	2	3	1	2	3	1	2	3
Directive	1	2	3	1	2	3	1	2	3
Eclectic	1	2	3	1	2	3	1	2	3
Encounter	1	2	3	1	2	3	1	2	3
Existential	1	2	3	1	2	3	1	2	3
Gestalt	1	2	3	1	2	3	1	2	3
Humanistic	1	2	3	1	2	3	1	2	3
Psychoanalysis	1	2	3	1	2	3	1	2	3
Psychodrama	1	2	3	1	2	3	1	2	3

	P			E			N		
RET	1	2	3	1	2	3	1	2	3
Reality therapy	1	2	3	1	2	3	1	2	3
Supportive	1	2	3	1	2	3	1	2	3
TA	1	2	3	1	2	3	1	2	3
Other:	1	2	3	1	2	3	1	2	3

Family Therapies

	P			E			N		
Behavioral	1	2	3	1	2	3	1	2	3
Cognitive	1	2	3	1	2	3	1	2	3
Communications	1	2	3	1	2	3	1	2	3
Conjoint	1	2	3	1	2	3	1	2	3
Marital	1	2	3	1	2	3	1	2	3
Network	1	2	3	1	2	3	1	2	3
Psychoanalysis	1	2	3	1	2	3	1	2	3
Psychodynamic	1	2	3	1	2	3	1	2	3
Sex therapy	1	2	3	1	2	3	1	2	3
Strategic	1	2	3	1	2	3	1	2	3
Structural	1	2	3	1	2	3	1	2	3
Systems theory	1	2	3	1	2	3	1	2	3
Other:	1	2	3	1	2	3	1	2	3

APPENDIX 2

Individualized Training Plan

Trainee: _____ ITP #: _____
Program: _____ Date: _____
Placement: _____ Hours of Supervision proposed: _____
Supervisor: _____ Review Date: _____

Summary of Student Needs:

Objectives (please number)   Training Strategy (procedures)

Methods of Evaluation:

                Student X _____
                Supervisory X _____

APPENDIX 3

Individualized Training Review

Trainee: _____ Review for ITP #: _____
Program: _____ # hours in training: _____
Placement: _____ # hours in supervision: _____
Supervisor(s): _____ Date: _____

Progress Toward Objectives (systematically related to ITP)

	none	minor	major	total
Student Estimate of Goal Attainment	____	____	____	____
Supervisor Estimate of Goal Attainment	____	____	____	____

Recommendation:

Disposition: ____   continue ITP, review date ____
             ____   re-negotiate new ITP
             ____   ITP completed
Student _____
Supervisor _____

Reading 30

Stages in Psychotherapy Supervision:
From Therapy Skills to Skilled Therapist

Harry A. Grater
University of Florida, Gainesville

Interest in psychotherapy supervision has included proposed supervisory stages. Stoltenberg (1981) emphasized increasing levels of supervisee autonomy and indicated that the supervisory relationship should develop accordingly. Loganbill, Hardy, and Delworth (1981), borrowing heavily from Erickson, focused on the supervisee's development through the stages of stagnation, confusion, and integration. Fleming (1953) described the stages of imitative, corrective, and creative learning in supervision. Hogan (1964) and Ard (1973) emphasized the supervisee's increasing autonomy culminating in a collaborative relationship.

A major limitation of the above proposals is that they describe stages that are characteristic of human development in general and as such are not uniquely applicable to psychotherapy supervision. An alternative is to define supervisory stages in terms of the changing and increasingly complex focus of the supervisory sessions. Stages based on such a framework are specifically relevant to the process of psychotherapy supervision.

The proposed stages are based on the conclusions reached by numerous writers (Marmor, 1976; Parloff, 1979; Paul, 1967) that progress in psychotherapy results from an interaction between the client, the presenting problem, the therapy techniques being used, and personal interactions of the therapist. How to use these four factors and their interactions to promote therapeutic progress are the goals of supervision.

The following four stages of supervisory focus are proposed:

1 Developing basic therapy skills and adopting the therapist's role.

2 Expanding the range of therapy skills and roles to match the client's problems and role expectations.

3 Developing the trainee's ability to assess the client's habitual and conflicting behavior patterns, particularly how these patterns are repeated in the therapy sessions, and select effective intervention methods.

4 Helping the trainee learn to use the self in assessment and intervention. Each stage of supervision adds an additional factor to the therapeutic interaction, thus increasing the complexity. In view of this, it is necessary for the supervisee to develop adequate mastery of each stage prior to moving on to the more demanding subsequent stages. It would be unreasonable to expect a trainee who has not learned basic counseling skills nor developed a sense of himself

Reprinted from Professional Psychology: Research and Practice, *16*(5), 605–610.

or herself in the therapist's role to move to Stage 2 where learning new skills and an expanded therapist's role is required.

STAGE 1

An emphasis on skill development characterized this stage, which generally extends from the prepracticum through the first practicum rotation. The new supervisee is introduced to and taught to develop basic attending, listening, and responding skills. Prior to seeing one's first client, extensive role playing is needed, and video or audio recordings to provide feedback is recommended. To a significant extent the trainee learns to replace social patterns of interacting with therapeutic responses.

The difficulties and anxieties experienced by the supervisee have been described by Cohen (1980) and Greenberg (1980), whereas Yogev (1982) described a developmental sequence for the beginning psychotherapy student. They describe the supervisee's fears of failure, concerns with the supervisor's evaluation, and lack of an image of themselves as therapists. It is essential that the supervisor provide information and support during this period. Included should be the assurance that the trainee will be assigned selected clients. Careful selection is the ethical responsibility of the supervisor. Referral options should be discussed in case the new therapist is confronted with an inappropriate client. The expectations of the supervisor should be clarified prior to the first interview. It should be communicated that mistakes are expected as a part of the learning process and may be used as a productive part of the therapeutic interaction. Discussing specific fears is also helpful. These fears often include what to do if the client inquires about the trainee's status and prior experience. It is helpful to tell the supervisee that being anxious is part of learning the therapist's role, an experience that the supervisor remembers well.

Supervision of the first interview should have a skills focus to help the supervisee put into practice the skills developed during the prepracticum experiences. In addition helping the new therapist develop sensitivity to the nuances of client statements, use appropriately expressive language, and establish a pace of responding to clients that is neither too slow nor hurried are examples of skill refinements that should be developed during the first interviews. Often responses to the first client sound as if they come directly from the text, and the trainee needs help developing the capacities to attend to the client and respond in a more natural way.

Preparation for future stages begins during Stage 1. Attending to clients who would profit from different approaches leads directly to the next stage. Drawing attention to the trainees' preferred ways of interacting begins to sensitize them to their own input into the therapy process. Discussing with the supervisee their methods of coping with the anxiety produced by seeing clients is a first step. Some supervisees present themselves as unsure and inexperienced, perhaps hoping to minimize the client's expectations. Others attempt to hide their inexperience by appearing intellectual and in charge. Drawing attention to these reactions helps sensitize trainees to their preferred ways of responding to threat and ultimately, to how their responses influence therapy progress.

STAGE 2

Stage 2 supervision is focal during the remaining practicums and should develop on the basis of Stage 1 experiences. The supervisor focuses on clients who would respond more positively to therapy techniques the trainee has not developed. Although skill development is important, client assessment takes on added significance in order for the trainee to match client and technique. The use of cognitive techniques with depressed clients is an excellent example, as is the use of behavioral techniques with selected sexual difficulties. Working with individuals with sexual problems can be particularly helpful for the supervisee. As Kaplan (1979) indicated, whether the use of behavioral techniques consti- tutes the primary intervention or serves as an adjunct to more extensive psychotherapy depends on a careful assessment of the difficulties. The ex- perience allows the supervisor to observe the interaction between assessment and intervention.

Expanded therapist's role flexibility should also be developed during this stage. Although many writers have discussed client role expectations, a recent article by Richert (1983) provides excellent information. Matching client role expectations with a therapist's role behavior was described and given significant importance as a factor determining therapeutic progress. Increasing role flex- ibility is added to the supervisee's expanding mastery of therapeutic skills to increase the range of clients the new therapist can help.

Increasing the skills and roles places additional demands on the new therapists. Some dislike the fact that they are being placed in the role of expert, whereas others feel liberated by their increasing versaitility. Encouraging them to consider the interactions between themselves and the new roles and skills is a significant step in preparation for the supervisory focus in Stages 3 and 4.

STAGE 3

Stage 3 emphasizes the client's interaction patterns, how these patterns relate to presenting difficulties, and appropriate therapist responses. Mueller and Kell (1972) and Rioch, Coulter, and Weinberger (1976) eloquently described the complexities of supervision at this stage. The goal of supervision is to assure that the process of therapy, the interaction between therapist and client, is, in the words of Alexander and French (1946), a corrective emotional experi- ence. The importance of this variable is recognized by therapists of diverse orientations. Harrison and Beck (1982), although they use a cognitive approach

369

in working with depressed clients, recognize that different therapy relationships are needed for different categories of depressed clients. In cases of autonomy-related depression, they recommend a collaborative relationship, whereas with sociotropic-related depression, they suggest a closer relationship. Kohut and Wolff (1982), using a psychodynamic approach, suggest a different therapist-client relationship for patients based on the nature of the client's self-disturbance. Helping supervisees recognize different client patterns and respond accordingly is the focus of supervision in Stage 3, which usually occupies the first half of the internship.

Recognizing that basic patterns are introduced into the therapy relationship is essential. The therapist is often invited by the client to interact in an established maladaptive pattern: A passive client invites the therapist to be dominant and active, a detached individual emotionally pushes the therapist away, and a victimized client attempts to get the therapist to side with him or her against the oppressor. The supervisee is helped to recognize these patterns and to develop ways of interacting that encourage change rather than reinforce old behaviors. A passive client is helped to develop autonomy; the therapist stays emotionally involved with the detached individual; and the victimized client is encouraged to relinquish the role of the helpless victim. Interventions at Stage 3 are based, to a significant degree, on assessments of the interactions between client, the problems, and the techniques.

Stage 3 is an exciting and demanding one for most trainees. It requires a great degree of sensitivity and the capacity to make flexible, relevant interventions. The process focus adds a new dimension to the potential influence of the therapist. Because the client-therapist interaction is crucial, Stage 3 is often personally threatening as well as exciting. The increased involvement of the therapist as a person leads directly to Stage 4.

STAGE 4

The focus of supervision has progressed from Stage 1, which emphasized skills, to Stage 4, which helps the trainee understand the interactions between client, techniques, presenting problems, and the therapist. The fourth stage helps new therapists learn how to "use themselves" in assessment and therapy. Although the therapist's responses are focal, the goal of Stage 4 is not to encourage therapists to "fly by the seats of their pants." Instead, it is to help them develop skill and sensitivity in using the self as a powerful tool in assessment and intervention. It is the focus of supervision for the advanced intern.

In previous stages, supervisees had been encouraged to focus on their unique ways of responding—particularly to threatening situations. How they responded to their anxiety during the first therapy sessions was suggested as a starting point for this process. In Stage 4, the way the new therapists respond to threats becomes more focal. Responses to threat in the therapy situation vary from becoming quiet and withdrawn to being talkative and overbearing. Therapists in Stage 4 are encouraged to develop a new response to threat, namely to attend to the process or topic that is producing anxiety and to take the steps necessary to allow client exploration.

Developing sensitivity to the ongoing therapy process is critical during this stage. A supervisee entering this stage was discussing a detached client. She felt the therapy hours followed a consistent pattern, starting productively but deteriorating as the hour progressed. It seemed probable that the emotional closeness of the therapist threatened the client, who became more detached to protect himself. Listening to tapes supported this hypothesis. The therapist was able to recall her responses—that is, she was aware of having a sense of emotional involvement, which was quickly followed by a feeling of being "pushed away," and then experiencing increased feelings of detachment and boredom. It was significant that, in this case, the client was discussing his relationships with friends, which followed a similar pattern to that experienced by the therapist. The client felt his friends liked him at first but became disinterested after knowing him for a while. The supervisee learned to respond quickly to the cues of feeling emotionally involved then pushed away. She was able, by using these cues, to stay emotionally involved but maintain enough distance so the client did not become unduly anxious. Gradually she was able to help him reduce his protective detachment, to explore fears of emotional involvement, and to understand how his protective behavior had influenced his relationships with friends.

Stage 4 supervision encourages the supervisee to develop interventions based on interactions between himself or herself, the client, presenting problems, and available techniques. An advanced supervisee was working with a young man of approximately the same age as the therapist. The presenting problems focused on the client's relationship with his father, which had deteriorated during adolescence, conflicts the therapist had experienced and worked through. The client was not deeply disturbed, and a highly collaborative relationship had been established between the client and therapist. Based on these considerations, self-disclosure on the part of the therapist was introduced into the therapy process. The therapy relationship developed at a level similar to what Sullivan (1953) called *chumship,* a close peer relationship where mutual sharing is emphasized. Therapy was intense, relatively brief, and highly effective. By using self-disclosure, the therapist was able to help the client expand awareness of his feelings about his father. Anger and disappointment were followed by strong feelings of loss and grief. The therapy relationship changed during this period, and again, the therapist's feelings were a clue to the change. Instead of a peer relationship, the client needed support while he experienced feelings of loss and grief. During these counseling sessions, a more father-son interaction developed. As the termination of therapy approached, the interaction changed again to a more collaborative pattern. The therapist's capacity to use himself in the therapy was probably the most important factor that helped the client make significant progress.

Supervision at the different stages requires different supervisory skills and talents. The supervisory activities in Stages 1 and 2 fit into what Hart (1982) called the *skill development model*. Interactions are similar to a student-teacher pattern, and to be effective the supervisor must be familiar with therapy skills, client assessment, and teaching techniques. In Stages 3 and 4, client-therapist interactions are focal, an emphasis that Abroms (1977) called *metatherapy*, that is, therapy about therapy. Those involved in effective Stage 3 and 4 supervisions are sensitive to the process of therapy, namely to the client-therapist patterns of interacting, and are able to provide emotional support in an anxiety-producing experience.

Although four different stages of supervision have been described, it should not be assumed that each stage has been fully mastered. Although returning to Stage 1 is rarely needed, even the most experienced therapists learn new techniques. However, the supervisee who has successfully completed the four stages is able to appreciate the interactions between the client, problems, techniques, and the therapist. New techniques are selected and molded with these factors in mind and, at this point, the process of becoming a skilled therapist is well underway.

REFERENCES

Abroms, G. M. (1977). Supervision as metatherapy. In F. W. Kaslow & Associates (Eds.), *Supervision, consultation, and staff training in the helping professions*. San Francisco, CA: Jossey-Bass.

Alexander, F., & French, T. (1946). *Psychoanalytic psychotherapy*. New York: Ronald Press.

Ard, B. N. (1973). Providing clinical supervision for marriage counselors: A model for supervisor and supervisee. *The Family Coordinator, 22*, 91-97.

Cohen, L. (1980). The new supervisee views supervision. In A. K. Hess (Ed.), *Psychotherapy supervision*. New York: Wiley.

Fleming, J. (1953). The role of supervision in psychiatric training. *Bulletin of the Menninger Clinic, 17*, 157-169.

Greenberg, L. (1980). Supervision from the perspective of the supervisee. In A. K. Hess (Ed.), *Psychotherapy Supervision*. New York: Wiley.

Harrison, R. P., & Beck, A. T. (1982). Cognitive therapy for depression: History, concepts and procedures. In P. A. Keller & L. G. Ritt (Eds.), *Innovations in clinical practice* (Vol. 1). Sarasota, FL: Professional Resource Exchange.

Hart, G. M. (1982). *The process of clinical supervision*. Baltimore, MD: Johns Hopkins University Press.

Hogan, R. A. (1964). Issues and approaches in supervision. *Psychotherapy: Theory, Research and Practice, 1*, 139-141.

Kaplan, H. S. (1979). *Disorders of sexual desire*. New York: Brunner/Mazel.

Kohut, H., & Wolff, E. S. (1982). The disorders of the self and their treatment.

In S. Slipp (Ed.), *Curative factors in dynamic psychotherapy*. New York: McGraw-Hill.

Loganbill, C., Hardy, E., & Delworth, U. (1981). Supervision: A conceptual model. *The Counseling Psychologist, 10*(1), 3–42.

Marmor, J. (1976). Common operational factors in diverse approaches to behavior change. In A. Burton (Ed.), *What makes behavior change possible?* New York: Brunner/Mazel.

Mueller, W. J., & Kell, B. L. (1972). *Coping with conflict: Supervising counselors and psychotherapists*. Englewood Cliffs, NJ: Prentice-Hall.

Parloff, M. B. (1979). Can psychotherapy research guide the policymaker? A little knowledge may be a dangerous thing. *American Psychologist, 34,* 296–306.

Paul, G. L. (1967). Strategy of outcome research in psychotherapy. *Journal in Consulting Psychology, 31,* 109–119.

Richert, A. (1983). A differential prescription for psychotherapy on the basis of client role preferences. *Psychotherapy: Theory, Research and Practice, 20,* 321–329.

Rioch, M. J., Coulter, W. R., & Weinberger, D. M. (1976). *Dialogues for therapists*. San Francisco, CA: Jossey-Bass.

Stoltenberg, C. (1981). Approaching supervision from a developmental perspective: The counselor complexity model. *Journal of Counseling Psychology, 28,* 59–65.

Sullivan, H. S. (1953). *The interpersonal theory of psychiatry*. New York: Norton.

Yogev, S. (1982). An eclectic model of supervision: A developmental sequence for the beginning psychotherapy student. *Professional Psychology, 13,* 236–243.

Reading 31

A Developmental Model for Teaching and Learning in Psychotherapy Supervision

Stephen R. Friedlander
University of Tennessee, Knoxville

Neal W. Dye
Helen Ross McNabb Center and University of Tennessee, Knoxville

Raymond M. Costello and Joseph C. Kobos
University of Texas Health Sciences Center at San Antonio

Clinical supervision can be a dynamic, exciting, and challenging experience for its practitioners and recipients; it can also be frustrating, empty, or hurtful in certain circumstances. One might say of clinical supervision what has been said of being a parent—that one learns how to do it on the job. As parent or

Reprinted from Psychotherapy, *21* (2), 189-196.

as supervisor, however, one can make the mistake of assuming that the job is simple and straightforward, when in fact a multitude of hidden complications await the complacent beginner. Problems with the supervisor, if not recognized and responsibly dealt with, can become problems for patients, just as problems encountered by one family member inevitably affect other members of the family. Since explicit training in supervision is not yet common (Hess, 1980), one presumes that the clinical psychologist who is a supervisor-to-be will synthesize an adequate concept of supervisory technique from the experiences of practicing psychotherapy and having received supervision.

The complexity of the task of supervision derives from several sources. One, the supervisor's commitment is divided between two goals which may be in conflict, i.e., facilitating the student's educational development while also evaluating and controlling to an extent the professional practice of the supervisee in order to safeguard the client's welfare. Second, supervision involves communication between two persons about the relationship which one of them has with a third. In fact, the supervisee participates in a social network complicated by even more elements than these, so the potential obstacles to "differentiation of self" (Bowen, 1973, 1978) are many. Third, the supervisory process has many features in common with psychotherapy, so that "parallel processes" arise and must be handled with sensitivity and discernment (Doerhman, 1976; Ekstein & Wallerstein, 1958; Searles, 1955). Finally, supervision must be adapted to the characteristics of supervisees, who have varying degrees of technical preparation and personal readiness to provide psychotherapy. Therefore, supervision must be based on a complex model of role relationships and objectives.

ANXIETY AND GROWTH IN SUPERVISION

One major factor in supervision is the inevitability of anxiety in the student therapist. Supervision, unlike consultation, is generally imposed rather than freely solicited. The recipient of consultation is free to ignore the recommendations of the consultant, but the recipient of supervision does not enjoy this freedom. Such an arrangement is a natural incubator for unresolved problems of authority in both student and supervisor. A prominent faculty member, for instance, was reported to have initiated the supervisory process with a psychiatric resident assigned to him by stating, "Dr. X, the only problem I can foresee in supervision is your forgetting who is the supervisee and who is the supervisor" (personal communication). Although the resident later conveyed a sense that the overall experience had been a positive one, it is easy to imagine that some individuals would have experienced this communication as an assault or a challenge to resist, rather than as an invitation to work together.

This challenge could be met with overt defiance but more commonly elicits passive-aggressive reactions that can sabotage the therapy and the educational process. For instance, the student therapist withdraws from active engagement in reporting the interaction and formulating problems to be understood and resolved. Instead, he/she asks, "Do you want to listen to the tape?" and turns it on with little or no discussion. The supervisor is expected to focus solely on the language of the client and engage in diagnostic exegesis or to focus on the interventions of the therapist and evaluate them as good or bad. The therapist thereafter endeavors to adhere faithfully (and unthinkingly) to the feedback from the supervisor, often making errors in translation. An avoidant approach to supervision such as this is a subtle problem that is difficult to remedy, since the student is ostensibly doing everything that is expected—seeing the client, recording faithfully, and asking for some form of teaching feedback. It is usually necessary at such times to turn off the recording and enter into a more direct dialogue with the student.

Some student-therapists consistently display a very cautious, tentative style of relating to their clients and to their supervisors. They fail to show initiative in educating their clients about the role expectations for themselves or for their clients and wait for the supervisor to offer guidance and direction. Frequently, they claim that they perceive the supervisor as approximating omniscience and sometimes literally tremble at the thought that they will be scrutinized by such an authority. Supervisors can contribute to this problem if they fail to recognize the student's actual tender, vulnerable position (Chessick, 1971; Havens, 1972), since therapists become known to their supervisors almost as intimately as clients become known to their therapists. The student-therapist is on the spot both intellectually, when translating theory into technique, and emotionally, as the work of dynamic psychotherapy requires empathy and neutrality. Tentativeness is a symptom of the distress of being on the spot and also a sign of defensiveness, in the sense of being part of a system of "innocence" utilized by the therapist to protect a fragile sense of competence (Barnett, 1980).

The supervisory solution involves maintaining a balanced perspective about details and wholes and maintaining a perspective about what differentiates supervision from psychotherapy. For example, an iatrogenic problem develops from an excessive emphasis on "microscopic" details, resulting in failure to monitor and evaluate the therapist's general approach to the client. Students become hypervigilant about making mistakes and retreat into the security of silence or low-risk interpretations. Also, a supervisor can be overly concerned with explicating "hidden" features of the therapist's personality.

SUPERVISING THE THERAPIST OR THE CASE

Opinions vary widely on the optimal point of balance between attending strictly to the therapist's management of *the case* and legitimate examination of the therapist's underlying thoughts and feelings (see Chessick, 1971; Ekstein & Wallerstein, 1956; Spiegel & Grunebaum, 1974, for discussion of this issue).

It is our position that the supervisor may detect and point out idiosyncracies of the therapist that indicate a need for psychotherapy, and this occasionally provokes a brief abreaction of feeling. However, detailed exploration of the dynamic origins and significance of these idiosyncracies is deferred unless they seriously constrain the therapist's ability to recognize problems and make appropriate changes. A failure to maintain adequate separation between supervision and psychotherapy generally results in student alienation from faculty and compensatory attempts to maintain a "good front" at the expense of a learning alliance. Further discussions of the concern that students feel about scrutiny by supervisors may be found in Barnat (1973a, b). Cohen (1980), Gaoni & Neumann (1974), Greenberg (1980), and Marshall & Canfer (1980).

Why are supervisees sometimes slow to accept new perspectives based on interpretations or suggestions provided by their supervisors? The facetious answer is that some students are sufficiently mature not to fuse with or cling to their supervisors. A more telling observation is that the individual supervisor is not the single source of information to which students respond. Typically therapists in training carry out their work in an experiential context that includes such significant figures as the student's personal psychotherapist, other past and present supervisors, various academic instructors, and the clinical faculty as an administrative whole (Emch, 1955). The diversity of pushes and pulls within this field complicates the situation of integrating communication from a particular supervisor.

Students sometimes utilize the diversity of professional opinions as an argument for "anything goes," hoping to stymie the supervisor's effort to formulate or validate treatment strategy. An example of this point can be provided. A student who had been conducting individual psychotherapy with a young female patient for a period of nine months was assigned a new supervisor for the case at the start of the next school year. In the initial supervisory session with the new supervisor, the student therapist reported that the treatment relationship had been antagonistic and unproductive until recently but was currently proceeding well. He mentioned in the closing moments of his first supervisory session that he regularly concluded therapy sessions by hugging the patient to provide "support" and "reassurance" that she could count on him. The supervisor told him that this was not a constructive practice and should be discontinued. The student became angry and defensive and suggested that the supervisor did not know enough about the case to appreciate the beneficial effects of this technique. When the therapist eventually conformed to the supervisor's direction not to engage in further hugging, he was surprised to find that the patient quickly "developed" a capacity to discuss her hostility and insecurity directly. Nevertheless, the supervisory relationship was continually strained by the student's insistent claim that the therapist's "humanistic" approach was consistently beneficial to the client despite the supervisor's "rigid" and seemingly doctrinaire disagreement. Throughout their work together, the student stipulated that the supervisor's position wwas derived from a general orientation to psychotherapeutic method that was not universally endorsed, and he argued that many practitioners view "humanistic psychology" as preferable to psychoanalytic technique. Further support of his own position was said to consist of a history of approval by previous and other current clinical supervisors. This student was highly defensive and argumentative at times, provocatively challenging the supervisor and distorting what he communicated about the case. The underlying aim seemed to be to manipulate the supervisor into harsh criticism and autocratic control which the therapist would then feel justified in rejecting.

THE EXPANDING SCOPE OF SUPERVISION

Grotjahn (1955) described three phases in the evolution of effective supervisory relationships. The encounter with the hugging therapist is illustrative of the supervisor's task in the first phase, "the period of preparation" (although the actual outcome was not typical). The basis for a really significant learning relationshp generally develops in this early stage when the student finds technical help readily available in combination with respect and encouragement. The main aim of supervision is to contain and, where possible, prevent the typical mistakes of beginners—giving hasty reassurance and naive support, for instance. Supervision is essentially patient-oriented in contrast to therapist-oriented at this stage.

We think supervisors should generally refrain from directing the therapist to do particular things, although suggestions for action may well be useful. However, a supervisor may at times restrict a therapist from proceeding in a fashion that is either countertherapeutic for the client or countereducational for the therapist. Ordinarily such interventions can be organized as interpretations of the therapy process rather than frank prohibitions. Posing objective questions that require more information about the client also assists the therapist in orienting to important aspects of the work to be done. When a student is not spontaneous and free in reporting the patient's material or in demonstrating his own feelings and reactions toward the patient, movement toward the next stage will be impeded. Therefore, the supervisor attends closely to issues of communication with the supervisee, but only comments directly on them when the problems are severe. An approach based on these principles generally alleviates rather than exacerbates anxieties about autonomy and initiative with respect to the intricate responsibilities of learning to do psychotherapy.

The second phase of supervision described by Grotjahn (1955) is primarily oriented toward elaborating and clarifying the therapist's knowledge of the patient's personality and psychopathology. An example of this phase of supervision of a student therapist who had been treating a young woman in individual therapy for approximately a year, during which period there had been two previous supervisors. The patient was repeatedly observed to speak as little as two or three sentence fragments during the course of a forty-five minute session and spend the remaining time in silence. According to the student, the first supervisor saw the patient as very fragile and arrested at an early stage of development; he encouraged the therapist to accept the silent behavior and make direct interpretations of the feelings which were presumably experienced but unexpressed. The therapist understood the supervisor's intent to be that she respond gently to her patient with sympathetic and supportive messages. The second supervisor, observing videotape recordings of treatment, seeing essentially the same patient behavior, believed that the patient was hostile, manipulative, and resistant to treatment. He recommended direct interpretation of these dynamics and silence otherwise until the patient communicated "honestly" and "meaningfully." The therapist understood this supervisor's intent to be that she respond aggressively to her patient with messages that were skeptical and challenging. The patient's behavior shifted in response to these changes in the therapist's behavior, from passively withdrawn and mildly bizarre communications to a mixture of withdrawn behavior and "hostile" interchanges.

The therapist felt some dismay at the prospect of having a third supervisor. She was quite ambivalent about the patient and the value of the therapy so far. The therapist felt that both previous supervisor's views and recommendations were plausible and helpful, but found continued responsibility for treating this patient aversive. The third supervisor was able to facilitate a significant reversal of the therapist's feelings about the patient over the course of several months by propounding a view of the patient's personality and the dynamics of the treatment relationship which validated significant portions of both previous, seemingly incompatible supervisory viewpoints. The therapist came to enjoy her work with this client, for the most part feeling secure in the belief that the treatment effects were generally positive and feeling encouraged about her own ability to think meaningfully about issues of clinical technique without depending on passive utilization of the supervisor's resources.

Assuming that, under the best of circumstances, the supervisory framework is not contaminated by pathological dynamics, and that the supervisor's style of communication is sensitive to the defensive needs of the therapist, beginning therapists might still have difficulty balancing self-esteem needs with the acquisition of so much new information. The doubt and uncertainty about overall strategy and therapeutic technique which the student with three supervisors felt is commonly encountered in supervision. Her efforts to absorb and employ each supervisor's guidance concerning a baffling patient were colored by passivity and a front of innocence. It could be inferred that there was hidden resistance to supervision, but her response might be better understood as the inevitable utilization of characterological defenses against complex feelings evoked by conflicting instructions from authority figures. While there may have been some elements of distortion in her understanding of the previous supervisors' formulations and proposals for actions, it seems that their recommendations for treatment were truly divergent and contradictory. Our profession has not evolved to a stage where consensus about good treatment exists in each and every case, although at times consensus about bad treatment is within reach. The point to be made is that hereogeneity and theoretical conflict among the authorities contributes in a practical sense to the anxiety of therapists in training. A realistic and moderate degree of dependence on supervisory guidance is felt to be desirable; extremes of influencibility in either direction— too much or too little—pose problems.

It has often been observed that the patient's neurotic conflict can be acted out in the therapist's relationship to the supervisor with similar defenses and resistances. Moreover, the therapist's countertransference tendencies with the patient are at times echoed in the supervisor's response to the therapist. The parallelism of these two processes is mutually reinforcing. Needless to say, there is limited hope for progress on the patient's part until the problem is well understood by the therapist. The therapist, however, faces a barrier to identifying the problem and communicating meaningfully about it when similar defenses against anxiety are operating in the relationship with the supervisor. The revelation of these tendencies, referred to as parallel process (Doehrmann, 1976; Ekstein & Wallerstein, 1958), provided a major advance in understanding the process of supervision. A supervisor who approaches the task strictly in terms of scrutinizing the behavior of patient and therapist is likely to fail to observe or understand how his/her experience and interaction can contribute to forces that maintain particular symptoms and resistances. The prospective liability of parallel process can be turned into an asset, however, by the supervisor who is alert to his/her own potential for countertransference-based response (Langs, 1980). Further discussion of parallel process can be found in Caligor (1980) and Gediman (1980).

Several of us are experimenting informally with a type of role-induction training for students anticipating supervision. At the simplest level, we sometimes share written material about supervision or encourage students to discuss at the outset their personal objectives, self-assessments, and expectations about the supervisor. A portion of an introductory course on psychotherapy is now devoted to supervision, reviewing the rationale for the necessity of supervision, examining the mutual responsibilities of supervisor and supervisee, and freely discussing the issues. Students often need active encouragement to discuss process issues frankly with supervisors when the issues of authority and support are not well defined. The potential benefit to students of explicit teaching about the process of supervision can be seen in the following notes, drawn from a student journal about experiences in supervision:

A pattern that persisted throughout the year involved my reluctance to admit I was getting much out of the supervision. My patient was also slow to acknowledge what he thought I had done for him or his attachment to me. He was much more likely to attack or criticize me and my work.

In the last quarter of the year, I finally articulated for myself an element of the supervisory group process that made me very uncomfortable. That was the feeling that no matter how much discussion of differing perceptions was encouraged, I felt my supervisor looked with much disapproval at anyone who disagreed with him. As a result, I was reluctant to express a differing view or to discuss any instances when I felt I had handled something poorly in therapy. About that same time, I realized I had a very judgmental attitude in relation to several of my patient's behaviors. As accepting and empathic as I was trying to be, I realized I was irritated by his slowness to change those things he claimed he wanted to change.

Despite the possibility of disapproval, as the year wore on, I became more open with my disagreements and difficult movement in therapy [sic]. Typically, the resulting discussions were helpful. One instance that stands out in my memory involved a discussion of my patient criticizing my work. Developing a formulation to understand his behavior enabled me to sit through it the next time without becoming anxious and defensive. As a result, I was better able to interpret for him the pattern of his behavior.

The material also serves to illustrate the third phase of supervision, the period of working through (Grotjahn, 1955). The practice of psychotherapy evokes feelings in the therapist, some of which are likely to be manifestations of unresolved, personal conflicts. Both as therapist and as patient, one learns things about oneself that facilitate using the supervisor as a consultant to monitor and revise therapeutic operations as necessary. Thus, in the third phase, the therapist who has begun systematic and intensive self-exploration in the context of a training analysis or personal psychotherapy is able to gain more understanding of self and patient through the dialectic relationships which emerge between the therapy received, the therapy provided, and the reflective function of supervision. This openness becomes the foundation for the lifelong learning that good psychotherapy demands of its practitioners.

The material discussed so far illustrates some of the requirements of successful supervision. Both supervisor and student need to have a reasonable degree of personal maturity and willingness to learn. The supervisor also needs technical knowledge of psychotherapy, sensitivity to the student therapist's position, and understanding of dynamic aspects such as parallel process that are specific to the supervisory relationship. The student needs some conceptual knowledge of personality theory and psychopathology; some preliminary exposure to psychotherapy through direct observation, role play, or review of transcripts; and a capable supervisor.

Mastery of the complications of supervision requires a clear and appropriate understanding of the task and the responsibilities that go with it. However, therapists at different stages of training have different needs, so the supervisor's model must have sufficient flexibility to define varying functions and goals in relation to the varying needs. In the last section of this paper, we present a model of supervision that is organized along developmental lines. Grotjahn's model of supervisory relationship defined general parameters of the learning process; the developmental model attempts to define specific issues of teaching and learning that pertain to the practice of psychotherapy.

A DEVELOPMENTAL MODEL FOR SUPERVISION

Therapist growth and its facilitation can be defined in terms of a set of developmental crises which reflect stages of learning and maturation in a person attempting to assimilate and integrate the range of knowledge and skills which the role of psychotherapist demands. In the spirit of Erikson (1950), we take the term crisis to indicate that which a) challenges or taxes the competencies of the developing therapist; b) requires a significant shift in the therapist's view of his or her purpose; c) is accompanied by a degree of anxiety; and (d) depends upon new discovery and reintegration of previous learning. We have been anticipated in using the concept of crisis in this context by Chessick (1971), who spoke of supervision in its entirety as a chronically painful process in which the therapist-in-training must "mourn the loss of systematized and controlling. . . styles of relating. . ., must suffer tension and depression, and must struggle to comprehend the unknown inside himself as well as what is around him and his patients" (Chessick, 1971, p. 273). We believe, however, that good supervision evokes excitement in students about the prospects for future activity.

The growth orientation of an Eriksonian outlook, combined with the theory of motivation for competence proposed by White (1960), provides a specific framework for moderation of the therapist's anxiety. Beginning therapists are undertaking major new responsibilities, and they must grow in understanding of their patient's personality dynamics, their psychopathology, conceptual sophistication about interpersonal aspects of the treatment process, and in self-awareness. A student therapist's movement toward growth in all these areas can be facilitated by a supervisor who formulates expectations, directives, and interpretations in terms close to the therapist's capabilities. This supportive approach is preferable, in our opinion, to an approach which emphasizes confronting, undoing, suppressing, or eliminating faults or defects. The supervisor applies the model by relating difficulties faced by the therapist to a developmental issue for the therapist.

The first crisis in learning psychotherapy concerns the demand for wide-ranging tolerance of ambiguity. This demand is difficult to meet, because in the therapeutic relationship the therapist must function as a participant-observer without the usual gratifications associated with previous relationships. The optimal resolution requires personal flexibility and expanded acceptance of diverse values, perceptions, and actions. The supervisory emphasis is on the experience of learning-to-learn, "deutero-learning," as Bateson (1942, 1972) called it. One risk is that the therapist may retreat from ambiguity into the shelter of a constricted facade of authority, knowledgeability, and pseudo-expertise. The result, which can be observed with depressing frequency in fully-trained professionals, is a therapist who cannot relax and who consequently cannot allow the patient to deal with the ambiguity and anxiety that he or she experiences in life and in therapy. In such an event there lies the essential defeat of psychotherapy.

The second crisis is the challenge of recognition and acceptance of the limits on one's capacity to offer therapeutic conditions. Here the student-therapist is faced with the "hard facts of life" about therapeutic process—that understanding does not come easily, that one's attempts to establish rapport and communication are subject to unexpected responses by the patient, and that the tools one brings to organize and explain what is occurring are at best imperfect. At a more personal level, the crisis involves an encounter with the reality of practice as contrasted with theoretical descriptions of therapy. This issue emphasizes human fallibility and imperfection. The rules governing the therapeutic relationship are discovered to be different from those the therapist has internalized to govern other relationships.

During this stage, the therapist encounters guilt along with the discovery that taking responsibility for the quality of a relationship with another human being requires modification of intuitively accepted concepts of caring. A risk here is that the therapist may become too subjective and so lose the participant-observer perspective. Another risk is that the therapist may be overwhelmed by the patient's pathology or neediness and pull away defensively, searching for shortcuts around issues that could be dismissed as not essential to the task. The result of the former alternative is a therapist who never gets around to the main objectives of therapy; of the latter, a therapist who resists individualizing the therapy to fit the needs, strengths, and liabilities of the patient and who dismisses failures of fit by resorting to concepts (resistance, lack of motivation, or untreatability) which are, in this context, more accurately seen as means for shifting blame to the patient. The optimal resolution of this crisis is an appreciation and respect for the person who is the patient as well as for the therapeutic activity.

The third crisis concerns the discovery of therapy as communication in the deepest sense of the word, in contrast to a view of therapy as a sequential or repeated administration of techniques. Successful resolution of this issue allows the therapist to enter not only the patient's reality but also the reality created by the interaction of patient and therapist within the treatment context (Langs,

1978). With time, experience, and confidence, sensitivity to process enriches the therapist's awareness of the patient's distinctiveness as she or he attempts to grasp and hold something meaningful. The timing of interventions improves "naturally" from a sense which no set of techniques can explicitly delineate. Failure to resolve this crisis may reflect inadequate resolution of crises encountered in previous stages—an inability to sustain involvement with patients in the therapeutic relationship that is disguised by manipulation and intellectualization, or is openly characterized by inflexibility and intolerance for ambiguity. Lack of appreciation for therapeutic process as mutual communication restricts a therapist to a world of patient deviance, with a mission to correct the errant and dispense the "truth."

The final crisis promotes the emergence of a conceptual set in which a variety of models of therapeutic intervention are related to the needs of varying patients. Failure at this stage can result in the premature crystallizing and illusory "choice" of one model for all one's interventions or in a superficial eclecticism, in which the effort to attain intellectual integrity and consistency is foregone. We believe that the competent therapist approaches prospective patients with an evaluative interest that eschews repetitive use of the same technique regardless of outcome while striving for relevance based on intellectual discipline. Successful resolution frees the therapist to see therapeutic activity as the selective application of models of understanding and therapy based upon multiple determining factors. The therapist learns that therapeutic models can be tested continually and actively. The willingness to test hypotheses and to evaluate effectiveness of "which treatment for which person and which problem" elevates the therapist beyond a single "truth." Differentiation of the therapist from his models encourages innovation and the capacity for genuine initiative. The optimal resolution of this crisis leads to a therapist who can teach therapy, precisely because the emergence and growth of a conceptual set for therapy is a prerequisite for such teaching.

It must be clearly stated that the stage model that we propose is not to be understood as predicting unidirectional progress through discrete sequential stages. In a general sense, we find that the issues are likely to arise all at once but tend to be susceptible to resolution in the order outlined above: obviously this is not a rigid developmental path in which problems to be confronted are singular or the resolutions achieved more than good approximations of the ideal. The second qualification to be added is that development in some sense depends on moderations; one can fail to resolve each crisis by too much rigidity or too little or by too much independence or too little.

THE LONG-RANGE SIGNIFICANCE OF SUPERVISION

We think that the impact of supervision on the training of therapists transcends facts, models, and techniques, because the growth-facilitating or growth-inhibiting aspects of training have long lasting effects. Too often graduates refuse to continue supervision on an elective basis because of prior experience in which the iatrogenic problems in their training therapy cases were poorly resolved. Conversely, some graduates approach their work in a way that reflects the beneficial impact of supervisors, who encouraged the therapist with his or her process of growth in becoming a therapist. We hold that our behavior in dealing with problems in supervised psychotherapy is the real modeling we provide and this modeling is a crucial aspect of supervision. The emphasis on growth and its crises that characterize our own therapeutic activity could be equally enhancing to the quality of our supervisory practice and the results of our training programs.

REFERENCES

Barnat, M. (1973*a*). Student reactions to supervision: Quests for a contract. *Professional Psychology*, 4(1), 17–22.

Barnat, M. (1973*b*). Student reactions to the first supervisory year: Relationship and resolutions. *Journal of Education for Social Work*, 9(3), 3–8.

Barnett, J. (1980). Interpersonal processes, cognition, and the analysis of character. *Contemporary Psychoanalysis*, 16(3), 397–416.

Bateson, G. (1972). Social planning and the concept of deutero-learning. In *Steps to an Ecology of Mind*. New York: Ballantine.

Bowen, M. (1973/1978). Toward the differentiation of self. *Family Therapy in Clinical Practice*. New York: Jason Aronson.

Caligor, L. (1981). Parallel and reciprocal processes in psychoanalytic supervision. *Contemporary Psychoanalysis*, 17(1), 1–27.

Chessick, R. D. (1971). How the resident and the supervisor disappoint each other. *American Journal of Psychotherapy*, 25, 272–283.

Cohen, L. (1980). The new supervisee views supervision. *In* A. K. Hess (Ed.), *Psychotherapy Supervision: Theory, Research and Practice*. New York: John Wiley, pp. 70–84.

Doehrman, M. (1976). Parallel process in supervision and psychotherapy. *Bulletin of the Menninger Clinic*, 40(1), 9–104.

Ekstein, R. & Wallerstein, R. (1958). *The Teaching and Learning of Psychotherapy*. New York: Basic Books.

Erikson, E. H. (1950). *Childhood and Society*. New York: W. W. Norton.

Emch, M. (1955). The social context of supervision. *International Journal of Psychoanalysis*, 36, 298–306.

Gaoni, B. & Neumann, M. (1974). Supervision from the point of view of the supervisee. *American Journal of Psychotherapy*, 23, 108–114.

Gediman, H. K. & Wolkenfeld, F. (1980). The parallelism phenomenon in psychoanalysis and supervision: Its reconsideration as a triadic system. *Psychoanalytic Quarterly*, 49(2), 243–255.

Greenberg. L. (1980). Supervision from the perspective of the supervisee.

In A. K. Hess (Ed.), *Psychotherapy Supervision: Theory, Research and Practice.* New York: John Wiley, pp. 85-91.

Grotjahn, M. (1955). Problems and techniques of supervision. *Psychiatry,* 18, 9-15.

Havens, L. (1971). Clinical methods in psychiatry. *International Journal of Psychiatry,* 10(2), 7-28.

Hess, A. K. (Ed.) (1980). *Psychotherapy Supervision: Theory, Research and Practice.* New York: John Wiley.

Langs, R. *The Listening Process.* New York: Jason Aronson.

Langs, R. (1980). Supervision and the bipersonal field. *In* A. K. Hess (Ed.), *Psychotherapy Supervision: Theory, Research and Practice.* New York: John Wiley, pp. 103-125.

Marshall, W. R. & Confer, W. N. (1980). Psychotherapy supervision: supervisees' perspective. *In* A. K. Hess (Ed.), *Psychotherapy Supervision: Theory, Research and Practice.* New York: Wiley, pp. 92-100.

Spiegel, D. & Grunebaum, H. Training versus treating the psychiatric resident. *American Journal of Psychotherapy.*

Searles, H. F. The informational value of the supervisor's emotional experiences. *Psychiatry,* 18, 135-146.

White, R. W. (1960). Competence and the psychosexual stages of development. *In* M. R. Jones (Ed.), *Nebraska Symposium on Motivation.* Lincoln: University of Nebraska Press.

Reading 32

The Supervision of Cotherapist Teams in Family Therapy

Arnold S. Berkman and Claire Fleet Berkman
Michigan State University

Co-therapy can be a hell of a mess.
(Napier & Whitaker, 1972)

Among psychotherapeutic endeavors, family therapy is perhaps the most complex and most demanding. The family therapist must observe, synthesize, and conceptualize individual data, family data, and group data which are embedded in the emotionally charged atmosphere of a troubled family. The family therapist must not only experience nondefensively but also must integrate and utilize the wide range of affects which are stimulated. The continual presence of intense affect is one of the few predictable occurrences in the kaleidoscopic prism of family psychotherapy.

Reprinted from Psychotherapy, *21*(2), 197-205.

Most contemporary family therapy approaches, such as Minuchin's (1974) "Structured Family Therapy," which requires that the therapist "join" the family in order to change the family organization, stresses active interacting and encountering. Such therapeutic work is exhausting and stressful. Rubenstein & Wiener (1967) suggest that in-depth therapeutic interaction with a troubled family over a fairly long duration of time can stimulate "more disturbing feelings in the therapist than either individual or group therapy" (p. 209), and that such feelings could be overwhelming for a single therapist to handle alone. Not only do such feelings emerge as a result of the interaction of family members during a therapeutic session but also as a result of the interactions that have occurred in the therapist's own family of origin.

Family therapists are vulnerable to being incorporated into the family's pathological processes. For example, it is not atypical for a couple to use the therapist much as the same couple might use their child, as an intermediary or "messenger" between parents, thus ensuring distance and nonrelating; or for one or the other of the spouses to encourage the therapist to take sides, thus encouraging splitting. In many families such potentially antitherapeutic maneuvers are done with exquisite subtlety. In the context of intense affect such maneuvers can be a seductive trap for a family therapist to enter, particularly since the therapist's response to such maneuvers is often partially a product of the family's stimulation of the therapist's own conflicts. In such instances the presence of a cotherapist can be particularly helpful.

THE DEFINITION AND USE OF COTHERAPY

Cotherapy is the use of two psychotherapists, often, but not always, a male and female working together with a single patient, couple, group, or family. Whitaker *et al.* (1949, 1950) emphasize the importance of cotherapy as a way to facilitate the resolution of therapeutic impasses, since one therapist could help the other therapist express and resolve feelings which might block therapeutic movement. Kell & Burow (1970) also mention the importance of cotherapy as a means to resolve conflicts in dyadic psychotherapy. Furthermore, the presence of a cotherapist makes it possible for one therapist "at a given time to attend more completely to oneself and to see, understand, and utilize what one is really thinking, feeling, fantasizing, and imaging" (Kell & Burow, 1970).

The use of cotherapists in the treatment of disturbed families has been suggested in order to neutralize the effects of transference, countertransference, and engulfment, and also to provide a catalyst for the emergence of dynamic themes and issues which the presence of two cotherapists can stimulate (Belmont & Jasnow, 1961; Boszormenyi-Nagy & Framo, 1965; Rubenstein & Wiener, 1967; Sonne & Lincoln, 1965, 1966). Napier & Whitaker (1972) point out that the presence of a cotherapist enables a therapist to become involved with families at levels which would not be possible if a cotherapist were not present to remain as a "back-up person" who is anchored to reality, and who can intervene if necessary. Cotherapists also offer one another support by being able to be calm in the midst of intense family anxiety, agitation, rage and depression. Boszormenyi-Nagy & Spark (1973) describe cotherapy with families:

> Specifically, one therapist may enter into and remain supportive of the family symbiosis, dependency needs, their seeming helplessness, and their excessive demands on the therapist. If so, the other therapist can remain free in a session to help his co-therapist and the family members emerge from this level of relating. He may 'disrupt' the splitting techniques that the family is attempting to use on the therapy team. One therapist must remain firm and strong for progression, growth, and individuation, while the other therapist may temporarily accept and support the symbiosis. . . . Both therapists are available to the family for sympathetic listening, interest, and for increased self-other understanding. In other sessions, one may respond actively on a verbal level, in which the other is passively alert but listening and noting nonverbal behavior (Boszormenyi-Nagy & Spark, 1973, p. 204).

THE COTHERAPY RELATIONSHIP

The major impact of cotherapy occurs as a result of a number of interacting variables, the most important of which is the very real relationship between the cotherapists. Treppa (1969) points out that in order to be effective, cotherapists must be deeply involved with one another. Such involvement prevents the recapitulation of the patient's earlier pathological relationship. Mullan & Sanguiliano (1964) mention the experiential, authentic, and spontaneous nature of the cotherapy relationship, indicating that "affective honesty" between the cotherapists is essential. Kell & Burow (1970) emphasize the importance of a collaborative relationship between the cotherapists, citing several variables which are crucial to the establishment and maintenance of the collaboration. The cotherapists must be separate and autonomous individuals, yet must also be able to depend upon one another; similarly, the cotherapists must be able to disagree with one another and yet understand one another. According to Kell & Burow, "Mutual respect, awareness and acceptance of differences, owning of one's own competency, freedom to feel and to express feelings, both affectionate ones and those that are less positive, are the primary elements which make up a good [cotherapy] relationship" (p. 223). Boszormenyi-Nagy & Spark (1973) list empathy, compassion, trust, and complementarity as the major components of an effective cotherapy relationship.

THE COTHERAPY RELATIONSHIP IN FAMILY THERAPY

The relationship between cotherapists in family therapy is crucial. Boszormenyi-Nagy & Spark (1973) mention that if the cotherapists like, trust, respect, and are loyal to one another, and if their personalities are complementary, they can model for troubled families effective and satisfying relationships. According to Goldenberg & Goldenberg (1980), "The way the co-therapists live their relationship—degrading or undercutting each other, or supporting and allowing freedom for one another—teaches the family far more about interpersonal relations than what the therapists may say about family relationships" (p. 237).

The literature on the cotherapy relationship has primarily focused upon such variables as the personalities of the therapists (Treppa, 1969), the selection of cotherapy partners (Kamerschen, 1969), satisfaction of cotherapists with one another, and other variables which pertain to the interacting relationship between cotherapists. The literature has given relatively little attention, however, to the triadic interplay among cotherapists and patients. This latter focus is particularly important in understanding the nature of cotherapy with families. The relationship between the cotherapists in family therapy affects and is affected by the complex relationships among family members. Such interactions can either enhance or impede the process of family therapy.

Bienenfeld (personal communication, 1980) labels interactional disturbances between cotherapists as either "symmetrical" or "complementary." In symmetrical interactions, the cotherapy pairs might behave like or mimic the dynamic interaction of the family being treated. In complementary interactions, the cotherapist might behave in an opposite manner to the family being treated. Whether the interaction between the cotherapists is symmetrical or complementary depends upon the dynamics of the cotherapists and of the families. Such interactions impede family therapy.

The success of cotherapy with families is a function of the skill with which the cotherapists can utilize themselves and their relationship in a manner which is therapeutically useful. For example, an intense fight between the cotherapists in front of the family can be productive if it can serve as a model of how two people who care for one another, resolve those difficulties, and grow as a result. Such a fight can be destructive, however, if it is not resolved.

The following example demonstrates not only the vulnerability of the cotherapy relationship to conflicts within the family being treated, but also demonstrates how interactional processes can operate in a dysfunctional manner between the treating cotherapist team and the family in treatment.[1] Mrs. M.

[1] The vignettes described in this paper are not actual cases. They are intended as examples to illustrate the process of cotherapist supervision and are not intended to represent actual data.

sought help because she was concerned that her nine-year-old daughter, Suzie, was overweight, related poorly to her peers, and seemed to be fearful of the world outside her home. Mrs. M. and Suzie were being seen together by a cotherapy team. Mrs. M. was of working-class background, and her daughter was an only child, born when Mrs. M. was in her late thirties. Mr. M. had left the family and had no contact with Mrs. M. or Suzie for the last five years. The cotherapists were a female psychology intern, Miss B., and a senior female faculty psychologist, Dr. J.

The cotherapists indicated that they were working fairly well with the family, although Miss B., the psychology intern, had a vague sense of dissatisfaction with the cotherapy relationship. She described feeling engulfed by her cotherapists, and was annoyed that Dr. J. often said, "*We* think," when Miss B. had not been consulted at all as to how she felt or what she thought. Miss B. felt that Dr. J. was nice but assumed many things about her. It was difficult for Miss B. to put boundaries around herself.

In supervision, Dr. J. was surprised to hear Miss B.'s comments. Dr. J. felt nurturant toward Miss B. and had just wanted to help make the sessions go smoothly. Dr. J. remembered how it was when she had started out doing cotherapy and had always wanted to feel included. Dr. J. did admit, however, to a certain sadness in observing Miss B. as she began her career, since Dr. J. felt herself to be "over the hill." Dr. J. noted that Miss B. seemed so young, so fresh, so vital, and that she herself felt menopausal and dried out. It was as if by taking care of Miss B. that Dr. J. could stifle the competitiveness, resentfulness, and sadness that she felt for her own lost youth. Miss B. indicated that she liked feeling being taken care of, but also resented that care, since it made her feel dependent.

The supervisor remarked that little was said about the family that was being treated. When the dynamics of the family were explored, it became clear that Mrs. M. had a "symbiotic" relationship with Suzie. Clearly, Mrs. M. had been unable to experience the loss she felt when her husband left the family. She denied that loss by her overabundant nurturance of her daughter in order to compensate for her feelings of rejection as a woman. It was somehow easier to retreat to too much nurturance than to compete in the world on her own terms.

Helping Miss B. and Dr. J. to acknowledge and understand the conflictual aspects of their own relationship, and how such conflicts were stimulated by some parallel issues in the relationship between Mrs. M. and Suzie was an important focus of supervision with these cotherapists. The nature of the conflicts experienced by Suzie and Mrs. M. stimulated already existing conflicts experienced by Dr. J. and Miss B. in their cotherapy relationship. Their interaction with one another compounded those conflicts, and initiated a retreat from some central issues in the mother-daughter relationship. The cotherapists were blocked in their own ability to work in nonconflictual ways with each other. Supervision differentiated to cotherapists from one another so that effective therapy could proceed.

THE PROCESS OF SUPERVISION: SOME GENERAL CONCEPTIONS

A useful way to conceptualize psychotherapy supervision is in terms of its goals. According to Mueller & Kell (1972), such goals are inextricably woven into the psychotherapeutic process. In order for people to change, the therapist must use himself or herself as an effective human tool whose effectiveness is a function of the therapist's self-understanding—particularly of those feelings, motives, conflicts, and anxieties that are stimulated in the therapist when particular patient conflicts are approached. Here, the goal of supervision is expanded self-awareness and the use of that enhanced self-awareness to achieve greater differentiation from the patient and increased understanding of the patient. "Learning *what* is therapeutic is an insufficient goal of supervision. . . . A major part of what is therapeutic is the way in which the therapist uses himself" (Mueller & Kell, 1972, p. 5).

Searles (1965) views the goal of supervision as one in which the supervisor helps the therapist achieve "a larger and deeper understanding of what is going on between the patient and himself" (p. 585). A major aspect of Searles' conception of supervision is that the supervisor is at greater psychological distance from the patient's psychopathology than is the therapist. In this sense, the supervisor has a "super vision" of the treatment relationship. It is through the process of supervision that the therapist identifies with the supervisor's distance from the patient's psychopathology.

Ekstein & Wallerstein's (1972) conception of supervision emphasizes the importance of the supervisor-therapist relationship, and how that relationship seems to parallel the therapist-patient relationship. Ekstein & Wallerstein utilize the therapist's experience within the supervisory relationship to expand awareness and increase understanding. According to Ekstein & Wallerstein, the difficulties which exist in the relationship between the supervisor and therapist are related to the difficulties which exist between the therapist and patient. The resolution of the difficulties between supervisor and therapist should enable the therapist less defensively and less constrictedly to achieve greater understanding of himself or herself, the patient, and the therapeutic relationship.

Supervision is traditionally the vehicle which facilitates the emergence into the therapist's awareness of those unconscious forces and behaviors of which therapists must become aware in order for effective therapy to occur. Supervision enables the therapist to expand his or her awareness in such a way that the feelings which emerge in the process of therapy can be differentiated, understood, and utilized as tools which enhance the therapeutic process.

The generalization of these conceptions of supervision of individual therapists into the supervision of cotherapists engaged in family therapy is complex. The few efforts that have been made to look at family therapy supervision give little attention to the dynamic interplay between therapists and family. These efforts typically focus instead upon the teaching of family therapy techniques (Montalvo, 1973; Constantine, 1976).

SOURCES OF COTHERAPIST DIFFICULTY

A convenient way to organize the difficulties which occur between cotherapists on the one hand and between cotherapists and families on the other is to categorize such difficulties in terms of the sources from which they might derive. Such an organization enables the supervisor to become aware of, to focus upon, and to have a structure upon which to conceptualize what it is that is happening between the cotherapists. There are three possible sources of such difficulties: 1) difficulties might derive from sources which are inherent in realistic perceptions, feelings, and interactions between the cotherapists; 2) difficulties might derive from the individual psychodyanmics of the cotherapists and the associated distorted "transferential" perceptions and feelings of the cotherapists concerning one another; and 3) difficulties might derive from distorted or "countertransferential" perceptions and feelings concerning the family.

Any one of the infinite variety of difficulties which can occur between cotherapists can be traced to one of these sources or the interaction of several of these particular sources. Supervision of cotherapists is initially a process which helps the cotherapists become aware of the sources of their difficulties and then helps them explore how such difficulties are products of the complex interaction of such sources. The cotherapists' enhanced differentiation and expanded awareness will enable them to understand, bring under conscious control, and contain the antitherapeutic behaviors which operate in their interaction with one another and with the family.

REALISTIC SOURCES OF COTHERAPIST DIFFICULTY

Reality issues between cotherapists are issues which can be attributed to those reality factors which, by their very being, become factors in the cotherapy relationship. One therapist might be a psychiatrist and the other, a psychologist; one therapist might be a trainee and the other, a trainer; one therapist might be white and the other, black; one therapist might have a strong feminist orientation and the other might be a politically and socially conservative male. Reality issues always exist between cotherapists. No matter how obvious such issues might be, it is imperative that they be acknowledged by the cotherapists. Often the achievement of such acknowledgment requires supervision in order to circumvent the denial or lack of awareness by the cotherapists of the existence of such reality issues.

Dr. Z., an experienced, middle-aged psychiatrist, and Miss P., a graduate student in clinical psychology, 20 years his junior, were cotherapists with the White family. This family was Miss P.'s first experience with family therapy. She had previously worked only with individuals and children. The White family included an architect husband, his draftsman wife, and their three young boys. They were referred by their family physician because of frequent somatic symptoms in two of the children. It quickly became apparent that this family had difficulty in expressing anger directly. It was less risky to get "sick to one's stomach" or "have a headache" than to express anger.

Although Miss P. was somewhat apprehensive about her new work with the family, the initial session with the White family proceeded well. After about five or six sessions, Miss P. found herself withdrawing in the cotherapy relationship. She felt awed by Dr. Z.'s skills and experience. As she became increasingly, more impressed with the high quality of his work, she began to feel increasingly worse about herself. She began to have bouts of diarrhea prior to therapy sessions with the family.

As Dr. Z. and Miss P. began to discuss their experiences with this case, it became clear that a major issue between them was the difference in their experience level and the meaning that this differential experience had for them. Dr. Z. said that he felt protective toward Miss P. and found it difficult to be critical of her since he "didn't want to upset her." Miss P. expressed her fondness and affection toward Dr. Z. as well as her feeling that she learned much simply by being in the same room with him. She also expressed her difficulty in confronting him directly at those times in which she wanted to intervene or perceived the situation differently. It became important for Dr. Z. and Miss P. to be able to acknowledge not only that the difference in their experience with family therapy was realistic, but also to acknowledge that each of them had an obligation to share their individual perceptions and to discuss what was happening in their relationship and between them and the family.

It was not happenstance that Miss P.'s bouts of diarrhea (a relatively infrequent occurrence for her) occurred while treating the White family. Further exploration in supervision revealed that Miss P. identified with Mrs. White, who had been, prior to marriage, Mr. White's draftsman and assistant. In Miss P.'s sensitive and intuitive way, she resonated to Mrs. White's feelings of admiration toward her husband coupled with her inability to assert her own feelings to him. Just as it was easier for his family to absorb or swallow difficult feelings than to process them, so too was it easier for the cotherapists to ignore such feelings. In this particular case, the already existing conflicts between the cotherapists, having their source in reality issues, were intensified by similar conflicts experienced by the family.

Although a reality issue might be a source of cotherapist conflict, such conflict can be intensified as the reality issue interacts with other sources of cotherapist difficulty. In this example it is evident that supervision must enable the cotherapists to recognize how they are interacting, how their feelings about one another are further stimulated and fueled by the family's problems, interaction, and dynamics, and how the cotherapists' own conflicts concerning their professional selves and characteristic ways of dealing with such conflicts operate both with each other and with the family.

INDIVIDUAL PSYCHODYNAMIC AND TRANSFERENTIAL SOURCES OF COTHERAPIST DIFFICULTY

These sources of conflict between cotherapists are inherent in the unique psychodynamics of each cotherapist. Like reality sources, psychodynamic sources already exist prior to the formation of the cotherapy relationship, and can intrude themselves into the relationship in dysfunctional ways. Unlike reality issues, which are attributable to external, fairly well-fixed and readily observable characteristics of the cotherapists, psychodyanmic sources are internal, fairly fluid, and typically operate unconsciously.

Such psychodynamic issues, although seemingly circumscribed, are enormously complex. For example, a cotherapist who has conflicts concerning dependency can be either dependent or perhaps reactively independent with his or her cotherapist, not only in their interaction as cotherapists, but also in management, logistical, and planning endeavors on behalf of the family. Such behavior can stimulate responses by the cotherapy partner which are also a function of the partner's own psychodynamics. Such interactions will intrude themselves into the cotherapy team's work with the family in ways which will cause the family to respond according to the unconscious workings of the cotherapists' conflicts, thus beginning a spiral of malignant interaction between the cotherapists, and between the cotherapists and the family.

Some difficulties between cotherapists that derive from the individual psychodynamics of the cotherapists can be understood, in the broadest sense, in terms similar to transference. Transference, as used here, is a reexperiencing of what was earlier felt toward important figures in an individual's life. Just as a patient's distorted perceptions, fantasies, and behavior toward the therapist are transferentially as well as realistically derived, so too can be the cotherapists' distorted perceptions, fantasies, and behavior toward one another. In this sense, "transference" can occur between cotherapists. The following is an example of psychodynamic and transferential sources of cotherapist difficulty:

Dr. P., a verbal postdoctoral, clinical psychology fellow, and Dr. F., a shy, retiring, first-year psychiatric resident, were cotherapists. Mrs. and Mrs. Smith sought help because they were concerned that their two sons, nine and seven years old, were constantly fighting with one another. Dr. F. requested supervision after four sessions with the Smiths because he was so enraged with Dr. P. that he was seriously considering removing himself from treatment with the family. Dr. F. related that Dr. P. was domineering, intrusive, and "took over the session." Dr. F. was hurt when he noticed that Mrs. Smith addressed all of her comments to Dr. P., turning her chair toward him, never seeming to acknowledge Dr. F.'s presence in the room.

Dr. F. indicated during supervision that it would have been easier for him if he had a female cotherapist. He said that having two men in the room so close in age presented "intrinsic structural difficulties." Dr. F.'s associations to two men being in the same room were to his older brother, and as he continued to talk he became aware of several similarities between Dr. P. and Dr. F.'s own brother, including the fact that both held doctorates in clinical psychology. Dr. F. was able to understand that the intensity of the rage he felt toward Dr. P. had genetic links in his own background. Dr. P., a somewhat grandiose and narcissistic young man, admitted to enjoying the attention that Mrs. Smith was placing on him. He, like Dr. F., noticed that Mrs. Smith seemed to address all of her questions to him, but attributed her behavior to his being "a more sensitive therapist."

It was necessary in supervision for Dr. F. and Dr. P. to untangle their own relationship. Dr. P. was able to see the sense of entitlement he felt in relationship to Dr. F. He acknowledged that being the center of attention was his "due." Sorting through the transferential aspects of Dr. P.'s and Dr. F.'s relationship—Dr. P. representing Dr. F.'s competitive sibling, while Dr. F. seemed to represent the all-giving, adoring mother for Dr. P.—enabled the cotherapists to turn their attention to the family and to understand in greater depth why Mrs. Smith would turn all of her attention to Dr. P. Further supervision indicated that Mrs. Smith had split Dr. P. and Dr. F. Dr. P. was perceived as the caring, loving cotherapist, while Dr. F. was made inconsequential. That Mrs. Smith had also made a similar split between her two sons more easily became apparent to the cotherapists. Supervision facilitated the cotherapists' differentiation from one another, and deepened their affective understanding of some of the dynamic issues underlying the Smith family's difficulties.

Psychodynamic issues and associated transference issues between cotherapists also interact with the other two sources of therapist difficulty—reality issues and countertransference issues—almost to a point where the distinctions between these three different sources of cotherapist difficulty are blurred. It is only when these different sources of conflict are sorted out that it becomes apparent that a particular difficulty between the cotherapists has its genesis in the unique psychodynamics of one or both of the cotherapists.

COUNTERTRANSFERENCE SOURCES OF COTHERAPISTS' DIFFICULTY

Langs (1976), in a comprehensive review, defined countertransference as the therapist's "own inappropriate reactions to the patient based on his own unresolved intrapsychic conflicts and unconscious fantasies" (p. 275). Although the concept of countertransference has its roots in the literature of individual psychoanalysis and psychotherapy, such concepts are applicable to family therapy. The family therapist responds to countertransferential stimulation from particular individuals in the family and also from the family as a whole, interacting as a system.

For example, a senior male cotherapist, quite conscious of his own psychodynamic conflicts concerning control, unconsciously and countertransferentially reacts to the father's need to be in control. Through a process of projective identification with the father he acts out a battle for control with his more junior female cotherapist. The junior female cotherapist might be aware of feeling controlled by her cotherapist, but might respond to this in terms of her own conflicts concerning men in authority. She might—depending on the unique psychodynamics which she brings into the relationship, and her associated transferential feelings to her senior co-therapist—either become reactive and battle her cotherapist for control, or become submissive and allow her cotherapist to dominate her. Such interactions can either stimulate similar battles for control within the family or reinforce a dominance/submission style of interaction within the family.

It is not uncommon for cotherapists to be aware that marital partners in a family are engaged in a battle for control or that a dominance/submission paradigm is occurring. The cotherapists may not, however, be aware that the family's seeming battle for control is really an acting out of the cotherapists' own conflicted relationship. Attempts to help the family resolve their seeming control issues, without the cotherapists resolving their own control issues, will be futile. Other examples of cotherapists difficulties having their source in countertransference issues include adopting of a smug pseudomutual stance of competence and togetherness in order to deny the fear of the inevitability of tragic failure in working with a family enmeshed in intractable pain; scapegoating of a particular family member by the cotherapists; allowing either splitting by the family of the cotherapists or by the cotherapists of family members; and acting out family conflicts by the cotherapists, particularly sexuality, aggression, and dependency.

The following is an example of countertransferential sources of cotherapist difficulties: Ms. L. and Ms. C. were cotherapists. Dr. F., a fifty-year-old professor of English literature at a large state university, and his woman friend, Ms. A., a twenty-nine-year-old instructor in a community college, sought help concerning their relationship with each other and with Dr. F.'s three children.

Dr. F. was separated from his wife of sixteen years, moving in with his woman friend upon the separation. They sought help three weeks after the separation occurred.

The cotherapists related in supervision their strong feelings regarding the manner in which Dr. F. "ought" to be managing the separation. Dr. F. frequently visited the children in their mother's home, in essence babysitting while his estranged wife went out. He agreed with her feeling that the children should not be brought to his apartment which he shared with Ms. A. The cotherapists were sharply divided about this arrangement. Ms. L. felt that Dr. F.'s behavior was inappropriate and reflected his inability to separate psychologically from his estranged wife. She felt that he was being controlled, saying, "There's no reason in the world that the children can't visit him in his apartment." Ms. C., on the other hand, was sympathetic to Dr. F. She felt that he was particularly sensitive to his children's needs and that "this is the way he needs to be at this time."

In supervision, Ms. L. indicated that she was at present "involved" with an older man who had left his wife and two young children in order to live with Ms. L. She was struggling with her lover's attachment to his children. Supervision helped her realize the strength of her identification with the patient, Ms. A. The other cotherapist, Ms. C., indicated that her parents divorced when she was quite young. She and her father enjoyed a loving but intermittent relationship. Ms. C. strongly identified with the children and seemed particularly sensitive to, sympathetic with, and supportive of Dr. F. as a father.

The cotherapists' perceptions of some central issues between Dr. F. and Ms. A. were distorted by their own intense feelings which the patients' situation stimulated. In order for therapy to proceed constructively, it was necessary for Ms. L. to acknowledge and differentiate her own rage and guilt concerning her lover's relationship with his children, from Dr. F.'s attachment not only to his children but to his estranged wife as well. Ms. C., in supervision, was able to confront and explore the painful circumstances of her parents' divorce and her profound sense of loss of her father.

The cotherapists' conflict with one another as they each began to act upon their own countertransferentially stimulated feelings also reflected aspects of the struggle between Dr. F. and Ms. A. Labeling, differentiating, and integrating the countertransferential feelings in which the cotherapists became enmeshed enabled them to focus once again upon the couple with whom they were working.

SUPERVISION OF COTHERAPY WITH FAMILIES: CONCLUDING OBSERVATIONS

The supervision of cotherapists in family therapy is different from the supervision of individual therapists in individual therapy. Napier & Whitaker (1972) compare cotherapy to a marriage, and like a marriage there exists a binding commitment or contract. The use of cotherapists in family therapy creates a situation in which one "family" system is treating another family system. Many difficulties can occur because the cotherapists remain two individual therapists who are working alongside one another rather than working with one another as a unit.

An initial task of supervision is to facilitate the development of a commitment and subsequent contract between the cotherapists: not only will they work with one another, but they will also work on their relationship, encountering conflicts between themselves, acknowledging such conflicts, and achieving sufficient resolutions so that they could use themselves and their relationship in the service of troubled families. Without such a commitment, there cannot be a "marriage," and without such a "marriage" there cannot be the strong alliance between cotherapists which is necessary for any productive therapy to occur. A strong cotherapist "marriage" is the foundation upon which the previously described sources of cotherapist difficulty must be resolved.

Just as it is crucial for a family therapist to maintain a family perspective, in the sense that the patient in treatment is an interacting family unit rather than an individual, it is equally important that the supervisor also maintain a family perspective, in the sense that the supervisee is an interacting cotherapy unit rather than an individual. Both the therapist and the supervisee are the "twosome" (Napier & Whitaker, 1972, p. 498). The cotherapists do indeed have a marriage, and if supervision can be the catalyst for that marriage to flourish, then there is every reason to believe that the cotherapists' shared strength, growth, and creativity will become powerful tools with which to help others.

REFERENCES

Belmont, L. P. & Jasnow, A. (1961). The utilization of cotherapists and of group therapy techniques in a family-oriented approach to a disturbed child. *International Journal of Group Psychotherapy*, 11, 319–328.

Boszormenyi-Nagy, I. & Framo, J. L. (1965). *Intensive Family Therapy: Theoretical and Practical Aspects.* New York: Harper & Row.

Boszormenyi-Nagy, I. & Spark, G. M. (1973). *Invisible Loyalties: Reciprocity in Intergenerational Family Therapy.* New York: Harper & Row.

Constantine, L. (1976). Designed experience: A multiple, good-directed training program in family therapy. *Family Process,* 15, 373–387.

Doehrman, M. J. G. (1976). Parallel process in supervision and psychotherapy. *Bulletin of the Menninger Clinic,* 40, 9–104.

Ekstein, R. & Wallerstein, R. S. (1972). *The Teaching and Learning of Psychotherapy.* New York: International Universities Press.

Goldenberg, I. & Goldenberg, H. (1980). *Family Therapy: An Overview.* Monterey, Calif.: Brooks/Cole.

Kamerschen, K. (1969). Multiple therapy: Variables relative to co-therapist satisfaction. Unpublished doctoral dissertation. Michigan State University.

Kell, B. L. & Burow, J. M. (1970). *Developmental Counseling and Therapy.* Boston: Houghton Mifflin.

Langs, R. (1976). *The Therapeutic Interaction, Vol. II; A Critical Overview and Synthesis.* New York: Jason Aronson.

Minuchin, S. (1974). *Families and Family Therapy.* Cambridge, Mass.: Harvard University Press.

Montalvo, B. (1973). Aspects of live supervision. *Family Process,* 12, 343–359.

Mueller, W. J. & Kell, B. L. (1972). *Coping with Conflict: Supervising Counselors and Psychotherapists.* New York: Appleton-Century-Crofts.

Mullan, H. & Sanguiliano, I. (1964). *The Therapist's Contribution to the Treatment Process.* Springfield, Ill.: Charles C. Thomas.

Napier, A. & Whitaker, C. (1972). A conversation about co-therapy. *In* A. Ferber, M. Mendelsohn and A. Napier (Eds.), *The Book of Family Therapy.* New York.: Science House, pp. 491–499.

Rubenstein, D. & Wiener, O. R. (1967). Co-therapy teamwork relationships in family psychotherapy. *In* G. H. Zuk and I. Boszomenyi-Nagy (Eds.), *Family Therapy and Disturbed Families.* Palo Alto, Calif.: Science and Behavior Books, pp. 206–220.

Searles, H. (1965). Problems of psychoanalytic supervision. *In* H. Searles (Ed.), *Collected Papers on Schizophrenia and Related Subjects.* London: Hogarth, pp. 585, 604.

Sonne, J. C. & Lincoln, G. (1965). Heterosexual co-therapy relationship and its significance for family therapy. *In* A. S. Friedman, I. Boszormenyi-Nagy, J. E. Jungreis, G. Lincoln, H. E. Mitchell, J. C. Sonne, R. V. Speck and G. Spivack (Eds.), *Psychotherapy for the Whole Family.* New York: Springer, pp. 213–227.

Sonne, J. C. & Lincoln, G. (1966). The importance of a heterosexual co-therapy relationship in the construction of a family image. *Psychiatric Research Reports,* 20, 196–205.

Treppa, J. A. (1969). An investigation of some of the dynamics of the interpersonal relationships between pairs of multiple therapists. Unpublished doctoral dissertation. Michigan State University.

Treppa, J. A. (1971). Multiple therapy: Its growth and importance. *American Journal of Psychotherapy,* 25, 447–457.

Whitaker, C. A., Warkentin, J. & Johnson, N. L. (1949). A philosophical basis for brief psychotherapy. *Psychiatric Quarterly,* 23, 439–443.

Whitaker, C. A., Warkentin, J. & Johnson, N. L. (1950). The psychotherapeutic impasse. *American Journal of Orthopsychiatry,* 20, 641–647.

Reading 33

Beyond Schools of Psychotherapy:
Integrity and Maturity in Therapy and Supervision

Jane Rozsnafszky
University of Minnesota Medical School

As a therapist-in-training, I was confronted by numerous schools of psycho-therapy, each claiming superior success and attracting adherents. One of my fond memories of graduate school is the excitement of discovering different therapies and evolving my own theoretical identity as a therapist. Sorting out conflicting claims, I rejected Freud and became a reality-oriented Adlerian, synthesizing Transactional Analysis, Reality Therapy, and Rational-Emotive Therapy (Rozsnafszky, 1974). I have since moved toward an eclectic, psycho-analytic orientation with an emphasis on family systems.

Though theoretical questions of the various schools of therapy interest me, I am more concerned lately with the broader ethical issues underlying the therapeutic interaction than with theoretical position. My experience and observation have convinced me that the most important considerations in therapy and supervision are the integrity and maturity of the therapist. If the therapist has these qualities, coupled with therapeutic power derived from some coherent approach to therapy, she/he is likely to get constructive results. If she/he lacks integrity and maturity, no degree of charisma and intellect can compensate. Indeed, I believe that she/he may become a menace, a "psycho-noxious" therapist whose patients are harmed by therapy (Bergin, 1971, p. 251). Bergin has suggested that certain therapists foster a "deterioration effect" (p. 246), and Strupp (1960) found that nearly a third of the therapists he studied had what he considered anti-therapeutic attitudes.

In this paper, I will attempt to define and illustrate the integrity and maturity necessary for the effective teaching and practice of therapy, and, in contrast, the specific types of immaturity and anti-therapeutic attitudes that produce psychonoxious therapy. Maturity and integrity are achieved, I believe, as the therapist gains self-knowledge and awareness of her/his motives, the knowledge of "the psychopharmacology of his most important drug—himself" (Fromm-Reichmann, 1959, p. 29).

The Freudians have long insisted on a personal analysis for analysts to qualify for the profession. But many of the therapies currently in vogue, such as Transactional Analysis and Rational-Emotive Therapy, do not stress the necessity for the therapist to do her/his own emotional work as a prerequisite to the practice of therapy. Therapists of these and similar schools, who may themselves be lacking in self-awareness and maturity, can hardly foster such

Reprinted from Psychotherapy: Theory, Research and Practice, *16*(2), 190–198.

qualities in their students or deal maturely with their patients. When the therapist has failed to face his/her own unresolved emotional issues, psychonoxious therapy and supervision are, I think, inevitable and dangerous.

This paper will describe the types of immature supervision and therapy I have encountered, illustrating how the therapeutic interaction is conducted for the therapist-supervisor's personal gratification rather than for the patient-student's. Both therapy and supervision are included in the topic of this paper, for, although they differ in important ways, they are similar in that the character of both the therapist and supervisor is of crucial importance in fostering growth and change. Certainly, issues of the transference between student-therapist and supervisor are similar in many respects to those between patient and therapist.

At first, I observed this immature form of therapy and supervision among male therapists with women as victims. As I considered the issue, I concluded that the problem was male sexism. The APA report on sex bias in therapy presents compelling evidence, particularly where sex between female patient and male therapist is involved (Report on the Task Force, etc., 1975). My reading in the literature on feminist therapy provided graphic illustration of male immaturity and resulting exploitation of women. Yet, as I continued to consider the problem I realized that the best model of integrity and maturity I knew was a man and that I had observed women, some of them feminists, whose attitudes and practices seemed anti-therapeutic.

The problem is broader than male sexism. Rather, at the core of psychonoxious therapy and supervision is immaturity in both men and women, resulting primarily from unresolved adolescent issues of affirming one's appeal to the opposite sex. Because of the nature of the therapeutic relationship, these unresolved issues take on crucial importance in the therapy or supervision. (It would be possible to trace the chain of psychological causation further to unresolved issues with the therapists' parents, but the level of adolescent immaturity that is my focus seems sufficient in explanatory power for purposes of this paper and plausible from various theoretical viewpoints.)

My strategy will be to explain my view of the mechanism of immaturity typical for each sex, then give examples of therapists who illustrate each type in their practice of therapy and supervision. I will also describe therapist-supervisors who have achieved maturity and practice with integrity, showing the contrast with the immature. My examples are drawn from some 3000 hours of my own training and professional experience as well as from experiences of friends and colleagues. Some individuals described are composites to protect their identities, but all of the incidents and conversations actually took place. Truth, on this subject, is more powerful than fiction.

MALE IMMATURITY

In immature male therapists, whether they are treating patients or supervising students, a pattern repeats itself with distressing regularity. The therapist's behavior, in therapy and out, is devoted to his need to prove his masculinity by conquest over women. The "hunter-huntee" game is what one candid male calls it; the need to "score," says another man. At parties, where men play this game persistenly, "You can see guys in the corner, "workin'," says a third male informant. The more insecure a man is, the more he needs "notches on his gun," proof of his male power.

This pattern of male domination and need for conquest is older than written history. Despite talk of women's liberation and relaxation of sex roles, many men still seem to need to prove themselves to women. Perhaps in adolescence this behavior is acceptable. Even in adulthood it is understandable when the odds are fair. But in therapy the odds are not fair. The woman who comes to trust her therapist relaxes her defenses and is vulnerable in a way that invites male conquest. If the male therapist needs conquest to ease his insecurity, the woman patient makes a perfect target. This interpretation is perhaps simply one way of conceptualizing typical male countertransferential issues. The point, however, is that the therapy may serve primarily to allow the therapist to prove himself as a man. The patient's welfare becomes a secondary consideration.

Types of Immature Males

The following five types, in order of least to most dangerous, are all variations on this pattern of male insecurity, leading to the need for conquest.

Teddy Bear Teddy Bear seems harmless in his romantic crushes on the female students he supervises. His need for conquest seems satisfied by his successful attempt to supervise attractive women almost exclusively. In individual supervisory sessions with women, Teddy is a gentleman, though he carefully avoids dealing with the powerful transferential issues of therapy that his women students have to face as they treat their male patients.

Teddy Bear comes closes to the actual expression of his adolescent fantasies of conquest in an ongoing training group he sponsors. The group is typically composed of male supervisors and female students (a new crop of naive females enters yearly). Supposedly the group is set up to enable participants to learn new therapeutic techniques and to create trust among students and supervisors. In a typical session, each male chooses a female partner for an exercise, although occasionally, since these are "liberated" men, the women choose partners. A typical exercise found Teddy Bear paired with a new female student. The partners in the exercise were to try to communicate to each other by saying one word at a time, alternately. Teddy Bear began by saying, "Lips," to which his partner answered, "Whose?" "Yours," said Teddy; "Oh," said his partner, acknowledging Teddy's dominance and getting the payoff she wanted in her own game. Later this woman and two others giggled together over Teddy Bear. All of them had wanted him as a partner, since he was "cute."

When confronted two years later by a former group member on the purpose of this training group, Teddy Bear acknowledged the hidden agenda of the group, but said that the flirtatious group games just added "sparkle to life." True, and possibly harmless enough, but learning to do therapy requires more than polishing one's ability to flirt. And Teddy Bear was one of the men who sat and sulked the day the women in the group decided that they wanted to pair up with each other. This rebellion lasted for about a half hour of exercises, when the men regained their authority and the adolescent games continued. Never was the process of the group faced honestly by group members. Usually what happened was that, as the women students caught on to the actual purpose of the group, they dropped out, unless their need for male attention was stronger than their desire to mature as therapists.

Macho Mouth Whether through breeding or timidity, Teddy Bear is a gentleman; Macho Mouth is not. His need to conquer women is typically expressed in his lewd comments. At the end of one supervisory session with a woman student, he told the secretary, who phoned his office with a message for the student: "She'll be out as soon as she gets her clothes back on." To another woman student, he said, "You'll have to start wearing a gunny sack; your figure is distracting." To a third woman, who mentioned to him that she was "waiting for a patient to come," he responded, "Why, Carol, I didn't know you were a sex therapist." When this woman, after tolerating his remarks for several months, finally objected to them, he replied, "What's wrong with you; you must think you're awfully important. Maybe you need a course in human sexuality."

To Macho Mouth's credit, however, he did stop the sexual innuendos to this woman. Furthermore, after the student in the gunny sack incident confronted him over an ethical issue in one of their co-therapy cases, he stopped making remarks to her as well. But it is as though the woman students are the supervisors, training Macho Mouth. What can he teach them about therapy, when his own need to "score" is so overwhelming? Even if he does have something to teach (and he does seem to be a therapist of some competence, at least with males and couples), how can the women develop the trust necessary to allow real supervision to take place?

The Fox At least women know they cannot trust Macho Mouth. What makes the Fox dangerous is that he lies so skillfully that he appears trustworthy. He expresses great support for women's liberation, participating in a candlelight march for the cause, and saying to one woman in a supervisory session, "I know I still have some bias against blacks, because of the way I was reared, but I don't have a problem with the male-female issue. I can really treat women as persons."

Another of his students, needing help on how to deal with her attraction to her co-therapist, trusted him enough to ask him. She knew that he and his former female co-therapist had worked closely together and she asked him how they dealt with the feelings between them. He responded with pretended innocence, saying that this had not been an issue for them. The student later heard rumors about the highly charged relationship between the Fox and his former co-therapist. Instead of doing honest supervision, the Fox seemed to be using supervisory sessions with this woman to weaken her defenses for his own purposes. In a typical session, he told her about an encounter workshop he had recently attended where he had taken off his wedding ring, "so I could just be myself." At this workshop, he said he had begun to overcome his "hangup" about beautiful women, giving a hug to one beautiful woman in his group. He then suggested that what our profession needs is more warmth and touching.

In the course of one conversation with this same student, a serious conversation on abortion, the Fox slipped in the remark: "Oh, I don't know, if my favorite mistress got pregnant, I wouldn't want her to get an abortion." Was he advertising an opening in his harem?

Like Teddy Bear, the Fox also finds groups a good place to carry on supervision. His group specializes in body exercises, and the Fox arranged for an evening meeting at a friend's house, where there was a sauna and pool, so that the group could do water exercises. On the morning of the meeting, the Fox passed out books on massage. That evening, he announced the group's agenda: "I thought we could start with some meditation, then pool exercises, sauna, and massage." The women, the same naive type who attend Teddy Bear's group, weren't *that* naive and said they didn't want to do massage with the men.

The Fox's subtle sexual intent toward his women students is bad enough, destroying the necessary trust in the supervisor-student relationship. What is worse is his refusal to deal honestly with other aspects of supervision, substituting gossip about his students. Yet the Fox seems to be a highly intelligent, effective therapist, at least with male patients. He wrote one student a letter of recommendation that was sensitive and perceptive, truly capturing her strengths, unlike the gossip he had spread behind her back. When this student showed the letter to a friend, she lamented: "You see why I like this man—if only I could trust him." The friend replied, with irony, "Well, Sue, you can't have everything."

Trust, however, the essence of supervision and therapy, *is* everything. Because he cannot be trusted, the Fox's potential strengths as a supervisor are wasted. But word has it that the Fox used to be overweight. Perhaps his former self image keeps him from realizing that he is an attractive man, and instead, drives him toward the conquest of women to prove himself.

The Dale Carnegie Toucher The Fox's opposite is the Toucher, whose "hands-on" approach to student and patients has all the subtlety of a Sherman Tank. Although students unanimously resent the Toucher's invasion of their life space, the Toucher seems to exude warmth, good fellowship, and geniality. His ready smile and talk of "openness and trust" make him seem the epitome of the Dale Carnegie techniques of "how to win friends and influence people." And, lest Toucher be labeled a sexist, it should be noted that he bestows his favors on male and female alike. Perhaps the male students find his intrusive even more offensive than the females do. As one male put it, "I need a back rub from a man like I need a hole in the head." Another man expressed his contempt for the "pseudo-intimacy" that the Toucher's hearty embraces represent.

If the Toucher were merely a more obvious version of Teddy Bear, one might excuse his physical intrusiveness as an insecure man's attempt to make human contact. But the Toucher's physical intrusiveness is surpassed only by his corresponding emotional invasion of his students. One of his students, Janet, who was insecure and naive, timidly told him she was uncomfortable with all of his touching. His response was to giver her a book to read, *Be Glad You're a Neurotic*. Janet, who was insecure but not neurotic, obediently read the book and told the Toucher that it didn't seem relevant to her, whereupon he attempted to label her an "A" personality, prone to heart attacks and basically hostile. In the meantime he continued to caress Janet and wrote an evaluation of her that said that she had been "rigid" at first but had "responded well to supervision." He had observed her with a patient only once, in a co-therapy session with him, after which he described her as "brilliant." Her "rigidity" seems to have been her objection to his incessant touching.

One of the Toucher's primary goals in Janet's supervision seemed to be to increase her insecurity, as though evidence of her feelings of weakness and inadequacy lessened his own. After she had finished a particularly difficult preliminary examination, and was feeling relieved, the Toucher said to her: "Don't you feel now as though the prelim wasn't much of an accomplishment, since *you* did it? That's the way I always feel—if *I* can do it, it must not amount to much." When she dissented, saying that she felt proud and competent, he acted as though he did not believe her. Another time, when Janet expressed some power and desire to assert herself, he said, "You can't pull it off, Janet." Janet's basic strength, despite some insecurity, threatened the Toucher. Dominating her sexually and emotionally was his way of taking personal power and autonomy away from her.

During many of Janet's supervisory sessons with the Toucher, he also told her of his marital problems. His wife, it seemed, was jealous and resented his handling other women, for she lacked "openness." This talk of the Toucher's wife led to a feeling of pseudo-intimacy between Janet and the Toucher, and Janet began to develop feelings of sympathy and affection for the Toucher.

She also started to idealize him as a man of openness, warmth, and perception and to model him as a therapist. The "high" she began to get from their pseudo-intimacy, as well as from his hugs and kisses, seemed to her a model for the therapeutic relationship. The particularly unfortunate impact of the Toucher on Janet was that she began to model his behavior with her own patients, hugging and charming them.

Janet was more naive than most. Another woman student of the Toucher called his bluff, and after hearing his sad stories of marital problems, propositioned him. The Toucher turned her down, regretfully, but he had made the conquest by seducing her into asking. This woman summarizes her view of the Toucher: "That man is sick; but I need a letter of recommendation from him."

Like the Fox, the Toucher cannot deal with the conflict of genuine relationships and needs conquest to make him feel like a man. He cultivates sexual warmth and the pseudo-intimacy of discussing his marital problems as a substitute for honest supervision. The second woman may have been sophisticated enough not to be much affected by the Toucher. Janet, on the other hand, was looking for a model and therapist. His line about "openness and warmth" began to corrupt her, and, as a result of his influence, she was becoming a female version of the Toucher.

Super Guru Super-Guru epitomizes the male need for conquest in that the conquest is explicitly sexual. No matter that sexual contact between therapist and patient is considered by the APA to be unethical. All three Super-Gurus described here have the rationalizations to justify their behavior. They also have the necessary combination of psychopathy and charisma to seduce their patients and still collect their customary fees.

Super-Guru A is a local hero who possesses a charisma that has women swooning in the aisles at his workshops. And they do more than swoon in his office. According to rumors, Super-Guru A has affairs with selected women patients. A woman I know who was his patient was not among that select group, but he did touch her breasts as he supposedly helped her deal with her inhibitions. Only in retrospect, long after the termination of her therapy, did this woman begin to question his techniques and come to recognize that she had been exploited by him.

The reader may wonder if the preponderance of negative examples in this paper represents rampant therapeutic abuses characteristic only of Minnesota. I wondered too, until I went to APA in August of 1977. There, to my amazement, I heard two nationally renowned Super-Gurus admit to an audience, with different degrees of directness, that they have sex with some of their patients. Super-Guru B's response was to say that when a sexual relationship develops between a group therapist and a member, "the important thing is to be honest with the group about it." Super-Guru C, on the same panel, was not quite as direct, but his stance was clear to me, as he made a joke of the question. His point of view became even clearer when, after the panel, a woman therapist approached me, thanked me for raising the issue, and said she practiced in the same California city as Super-Guru C. She said that she was scheduled to serve as an expert witness in a lawsuit of a former patient of his, now a patient of hers, with whom Super-Guru C had had sexual intimacies. It was commonly known, she said, that Super-Guru C "will fuck anything female that walks." Upon my return home, a colleague of mine confirmed this evaluation of Super-Guru C. He told me of his experience in a group led by Super-Guru C, during which Super-Guru C had made advances toward a woman friend of his. A year later, Super-Guru C didn't recognize this woman when they met again. She was hurt by her realization that his overtures had meant nothing to him but an attempt at a casual sexual encounter. At least she had had the sense to say "No."

Super-Guru A is a local character. Super-Gurus B and C, however, are respected by leaders in our field. Several years ago books by B and C inspired me and helped shape my thinking as a therapist. Perhaps I should not be surprised when heroes have feet of clay. But this type of character defect seems to me to invalidate the entire professional identity of a psychotherapist. Evidently such immaturity is not limited to the Midwest. I suspect that therapist-supervisor exploitation of patients and students is an iceberg and that this paper is looking at its tip.

FEMALE IMMATURITY

Nor is this exploitation an exclusively male prerogative. Most supervisors and psychologists are male, but I've looked within and around me and seen female immaturity as well. This immaturity is also adolescent, but it takes particular female forms, often complementary to the male forms. The most typical immature female needs to prove her attractiveness to men and naively thinks that when the male gives her attention, he is overwhelmed by her feminine charm. (Actually he is overwhelmed by his own power and charisma; she is simply the vehicle for his conquest.) As with the male, lack of resolution of this issue in a female therapist or supervisor interferes with the therapeutic process. If a woman is desperately trying to prove her femininity, she can hardly consider the best interests of her male patient or student.

Another variation on the theme of female immaturity is the naive woman who ignores the sexual implications of her appearance and behavior, denying the reality of her role as a sexual stimulus. A third kind of immaturity is the need for power, for conquest, similar to this need in the male, expressed by bending the patient or student to her will, though this conquest may take a "maternal" as well as a sexual form.

Types of Immature Females

The female types are presented, as with the males, in the order of least to most dangerous.

Daisy Miller   Henry James' heroine still lives today, with her innocent yet seductive flirtatiousness. She is a daughter, looking for Daddies and attention, using the power of her sexuality to get what she wants. Although mini-skirts are out of fashion, one Daisy I know still wears hers. She fawns and giggles when men are around, and she once asked a visiting consultant what to do about male patients who whistled and made seductive remarks. When he responded, "Look at your own seductiveness," she turned bright red.

A patient I was seeing in individual therapy had another Daisy for his group therapist. At the start of one of our sessions, he described his most recent encounter with Daisy. She had been struggling to turn on a radiator when he walked in to help her. Making witty comments, he put his arm playfully around her. "I had her rolling on the floor laughing," he said. I asked him if he was telling me that I'd be a lot easier to deal with if he could treat me that way. He looked embarrassed and said, "Yeah, I can't con you." Daisy, though needed to affirm her attractiveness by flirting with the patient (and, having been a Daisy once, I remember the urgency of the need). The patient, however, needed genuine contact with another person, for he is an alcoholic whose charming, shallow ways keep him from any but stereotyped contacts with women, such as the episode with Daisy. Daisy's need interfered with what was therapeutic for the patient.

Beauty Unaware   Unlike Daisy, Beauty is not a flirt, but she is also a daughter, needing male protection and attention. Beauty is, as her name implies, physically beautiful, unspoiled by her beauty, but unaware of its impact. She is naive about her effect on male patients.

A Beauty I knew had the group of males for whom she was co-therapist in a constant state of turmoil for no other reason than her striking physical beauty, unadorned by makeup or overdressing. Her male co-therapist, John, was preoccupied with her too, and she was more emotionally involved with him than she admitted to herself. When John and Beauty began to face up to the unspoken feelings between them, John admitted: "A lot of the time I was more worried about your reactions in group than about the patients." He had been idealizing and romanticizing Beauty. She had played the good daughter and enjoyed his care. As she matured as a therapist and established her personal equality with John, they discovered a year of anger underlying the romantic feelings. They fought through the relationship, arriving at personal respect and friendship, without the unrealistic romance that had interfered with their functioning as therapists.

Big Mother   When Big Mother works with a male patient or student, he either improves, or else. She pours her considerable charm and power into an onslaught on the patient's defenses. She invades his physical space, hugging him, and his emotional space, foisting plans on him before he is ready because *she* needs to see his progress as evidence of her power.

One Mother I know was working with a young schizophrenic. She became involved with him in individual therapy, vocational counseling, group therapy, marital counseling, and she wrote to him after he was transferred to another hospital. She pressured him to make premature plans for school, not realizing in her need for success that the patient was barely holding his own. Her immaturity as a therapist was partly the result of her inexperience with schizophrenics and partly the result of needing to prove her own competence. But, as in all the other immature forms of therapy, her own needs took precedence over the patient's.

Seductive Mother   This mother needs both proof of her attractiveness and of her power over her male patients and students. Her manner can be quietly powerful as she skillfully interviews a male alcoholic, penetrating his defenses and uncovering his games, for his benefit. Or she can be strongly confrontive, as when she turned to a silent group member and yelled: "Hey, you son-of-a-bitch, I'm talking to you," shocking the patient into honesty. She uses her special combination of toughness and tenderness effectively, yet her own uncertainty of her role as a woman limits her in dealing with her patients' sexuality. She broadcasts her supposed sexual liberation, saying, "I know we're getting somewhere in group when the guys say they're getting horny." Yet, when asked if she then took the next step and dealt with their specific feelings for her, she looked shocked and said "No." She needed and enjoyed the adolescent locker room talk about being horny, but was not really at ease with her own sexuality. She would have been threatened by dealing openly with her own sexual appeal, for then she would possibly have to face her seductiveness. She did not want to acknowledge that the patients would prefer sexual fantasies about her to dealing with her as a person who was not sexually available. Several months later she started an affair with a patient, an affair that her co-therapist described as "a dead end for them both."

Another, more sophisticated version of Seductive Mother is the group therapist who told a male group member that he ought to have an affair with her—it would improve his marriage. His distraught wife ended up in therapy after the marriage broke up as a result of this affair. Seductive Mother needed an affair to prove her attractiveness and power. She justified her desire by a convoluted rationalization that she was acting for her client's good—to improve his marriage.

THERAPISTS OF INTEGRITY AND MATURITY

The three male therapists/supervisors of integrity I will describe led their women students toward maturity and integrity. These men are not types. Their integrity and maturity reside in their subtlety and idiosyncratic gifts for fostering growth in their patients and students. Nor are these therapists perfect, but they seem to have a sense of their limitations and a humility that comes from mature self-awareness.

Dr. A. Dr. A was supervising a Daisy Miller who, despite considerable intellectual power and charm, was unsure of her attractiveness as a woman. As a result, her relationships with her patients and colleagues reflected a naive seductiveness because of her need for their approval. Dr. A., without directly confronting Daisy, but in an appropriate context, told her of a woman therapist who was said "to seduce her patients" by her actions, despite the lack of explicit sexual contact. Several other times, Dr. A asked Daisy, "What are you trying to prove?" Months passed before these seeds took root and Daisy began to become aware of her motives.

As she began to change, Daisy found her male colleagues resisting her more mature behavior. She had evidently been less threatening to them as a flirtatious innocent, given their own male need for conquest. As Daisy struggled with her feelings, not wanting to relinquish her view of men as good fathers, Dr. A told her the hard reality for professional women he had observed in his long career: "Women have to give out extra professional signals to be taken seriously as professionals." And Dr. A also explained a common male game to Daisy: "To men, women are either daughters, sisters, or mothers, or they're fair game." Daisy needed this reassurance so that she would not blame herself as she struggled toward mature behavior. Dr. A had the integrity to tell Daisy the necessary truth. He was willing to be "disloyal" to his sex for Daisy's good. Later, having come to terms with her new insights, Daisy teased Dr. A, "Don't you feel guilty betraying your sex?"

Dr. B. Dr. B's integrity is his willingness to tell the truth, particularly the truth the patient or student doesn't want to hear. Sarah became angry in their first supervisory session at his reply to her statement: "I'm afraid that if I really level with patients, they'll get angry with me." Dr. B responded: "Perhaps you should look at your own anger." It took months before Sarah could face her fear of her own anger, a fear of losing approval (particularly male approval) if she expressed her anger. It took even longer for her to see than in this society, where anger is the last obscenity, the anger of both therapist and patient is a clue to unresolved issues.

Dr. B did not lecture Sarah. He usually did not explain his epigrammatic statements, and, as Sarah worked out the implications of his cryptic comments, she began to see the power in therapy of saying little, of making each word count. She learned from Dr. B's example that therapy is not teaching. Over-explaining lessens emotional impact.

As a result of Dr. B's supervision, Sarah also came to terms with her tendencies to behave like a combination of Daisy Miller and Seductive Mother with her male patients. When she told Dr. B how she had felt when she had hugged one of her patients after an intense session, he responded: "How did the patient feel about it?" Such a simple, obvious question, yet one Sarah did not want to ask, since the hug felt good to her. She realized that she didn't know how the patient felt and that if she were doing therapy for the patient's welfare and not just to gratify herself, she had better find out. Dr. B, by the way, did not insist that Sarah talk with the patient. He did not label her "seductive," nor did he make her feel inadequate. But his gentle, pointed question left her with the job of examining her conscience, activating her integrity.

Asking her patient, a young male schizophrenic, how he had felt about her hug, was difficult for Sarah, but the patient was honest and clear about his feelings. He said that the hug made him uncomfortable, that it had reminded him of a minister who used to hug him and who "got a hard-on every time." After that, Sarah respected the patient's space, focused on his needs, not her own, and the case had a highly successful outcome.

Dr. C. Dr. C, in his supervision of Anne, illustrates the personal maturity necessary to deal with the relationship in therapy, in contrast to the immature males described, who sexualize their dealings with women to avoid the reality of a relationship.

Under Dr. C's supervision, Anne in transference developed romantic feelings for Dr. C. Instead of cultivating Anne's hero-worship for his own sense of conquest, Dr. C called the game, asking Anne: "How do I fit in with your other men?" Anne cringed as she parried: "You arrogant so-and-so, why do you have to fit in?", and then caught off balance, admitted: "You're another man I'm attracted to." She also had to deal with Dr. C's accurate perception, implied in the question, that she had a collection of men, men whom she needed to attract and whose approval and admiration were overly important to her.

Later, Dr. C went to the heart of Anne's immaturity when he asked another of his pointed questions: "Anne, could you have a power other than the power of your attractiveness?" After the hurt of this question, as Anne faced the game of using the power of her attractiveness, came the joy in affirming another power she potentially possessed, her power as a person. Dr. C's question to Anne implied that she could move beyond a daughter role to her own autonomy. His role in nudging her toward such a change epitomizes his integrity, an integrity and maturity that required that he consider Anne's need for growth, not his own for conquest. Dr. C knew first hand about Anne's powerful attractiveness; he himself had enjoyed it. Indeed, Anne was probably easier for him to deal with personally as a good daughter. After all, like the immature types, Dr. C too has male ego needs, but he does not gratify them at the expense of his patients or students.

As Anne and Dr. C dealt with their relationship, Dr. C admitted his susceptibility to the powerful sexual-emotional forces activated by therapy. He said to Anne: "When I have a good session, I wonder if I've been seduced." Anne learned from him that it is her job as a therapist to do the seducing, to "hook" the patient, to know when he's hooked, and then to "beat like hell" on his neurotic defenses, not wallow in the positive transference for her own gratification. Integrity requires that the therapist consider the patient's true needs, and avoid the power trip of seeming to offer to fulfill these needs her/himself as Big/Seductive Mother/Father. The therapist needs the maturity to know the limitations of what she/he has to offer. By dealing honestly with the process of therapy, she/he can analyze the transference and lead the patient to a working through of conflicts

CONCLUSION

The therapist and supervisors I've described represent, on one hand, the immature types, male and female, who corrupt psychotherapy to ease their own insecurity, and, on the other hand, those who have the integrity and maturity essential for an effective therapist. The potential dangers of the therapeutic interaction are more crucial than techniques or theoretical allegiance. The emotional power that a therapist/supervisor wields makes integrity and maturity his/her most essential characteristics, regardless of other techniques. I am reminded of Freud's response to the charge that psychoanalysis is potentially dangerous: "If the knife will not cut, neither will it serve the surgeon" (1970, p. 180). The emotional knife in the therapeutic interaction requires humility and respect from the "surgeon." The immature types use the knife arrogantly and immaturely as revealed in their urgent, intrusive need for power and domination, their refusal to face anger and conflict, and their use of sex and naiveté to establish pseudo-intimacy and avoid relationships. The mature therapist illustrates a genuine understanding of students' and patients' needs, a willingness to tell hard truths with respect, the maturity to face the therapeutic relationship without sexualizing it, and a sense of their own limitations.

The immature are blind to their own needs and motives, putting them at the mercy of these needs and preventing them from developing integrity and maturity. They lack integrity because of their ego needs, and they use their patients to gratify their power needs. No one, however, is above this potential for corruption, the intrinsic potential for abuse of the emotional power of the therapeutic interaction. We are all, as W. H. Auden (1954) wrote, "composed of Eros and of dust" (p. 230). Yet, aware of our limitations, we are capable of self-knowledge that can produce integrity and maturity to guide us in therapy and supervision.

REFERENCES

Auden, W. H. September 1, 1939. *The Pocket Book of Modern Verse*. New York: Pocket Books, Inc., 1954.
Bergin, A. The evaluation of therapeutic outcomes. *Handbook of psychotherapy*

and behavior change. In A. Bergin & S. L. Garfield (Eds.). New York: John Wiley & Sons, 1971.

Fromm-Reichmann, F. *Psychoanalysis and psychotherapy: selected papers.* Chicago: University of Chicago Press, 1959.

Freud, S. *A general introduction to psychoanalysis.* New York: Pocket Books, Inc., 1970.

Report on the task force of sex bias and sex role stereotyping in psychotherapeutic practice. *American Psychologist,* 30, 12, 1169–1175.

Rozsnafszky, J. The impact of Alfred Adler on three "free-will" therapies of the 1960's. *Journal of Individual Psychology,* 30, 65–80, 1974.

Strupp, H. H. *Psychotherapists in action: explorations of the therapist's contribution to the treatment process.* New York: Grune & Stratton, 1960.

Reading 34
Issues in the Supervision of Diagnostic Testing

William H. Smith
The Menninger Foundation, Topeka, Kansas

Michael K. Harty
The Menninger Foundation and Menninger Memorial Hospital,
Topeka, Kansas

There is a steadily growing literature dealing with the supervision of psychotherapy (e.g., Langs 1979; Lower 1972; Schlessinger 1966). Concepts and techniques of supervision in medicine and social work are well developed and receive regular attention in professional publications (e.g., Kaslow *et al.* 1977). Why is so much less consideration given to the supervision of psychological testing? Is this lack of attention another instance of the tendency to devalue diagnostic functions relative to treatment functions? Supervised experience in testing is part of virtually all clinical psychology graduate programs and internships, and typically plays a part in the experience required for state licensure or certification, diplomate status from the American Board of Professional Psychology, and inclusion in the National Register of Health Care Providers in Psychology. Among those who speak and write about training in clinical psychology there is general agreement that supervision of psychological testing should be done, that it is a valuable part of a student's training, and that it should be carried out by qualified professionals (Blank & David 1964; Finn & Brown 1959; Raimy 1950). They say little, however, about *how* it is to be done, about techniques and problems in its conduct. Even though these authors recognize the importance of the relationship between supervisor and supervisee

Reprinted from the Bulletin of the Menninger Clinic, *45*(1), 55–61.

and how that relationship affects the learning process, generality is the rule, and detail the exception. Their discussions typically focus on what the outcome of supervision should be, but this approach tells the beginning supervisor little about how to proceed.

Our experience is that the supervision of psychological testing presents both technical difficulties and marvelous opportunities for teaching and learning. In this brief communication, we shall discuss a number of issues regarding the techniques and process of supervision that we consider important. Our hope is that in being explicit we shall stimulate curiosity, interest, perhaps controversy, and that this area may begin to receive the attention it deserves, ultimately becoming the subject of research.

Before going further, however, we should explain that we shall be referring to *educational supervision,* in which the education of the student or trainee is a primary goal, in contrast to strictly *administrative supervision,* in which goals are limited to quality control and performance evaluation. Educational supervision in a clinical setting should, of course, serve the latter functions as well. Patients or clients should not be slighted because of students' inexperience; and from an educational standpoint, the supervisor who fails to model a responsible attitude toward the quality of services provided is conveying a dubious message to trainees. But in supervision of the sort we shall discuss, the *development* of skills is emphasized as much as their application, and evaluation must concern education *progress* as well as level of performance.

THE SUPERVISORY RELATIONSHIP

Just as the importance of the patient-examiner relationship tends to be overlooked as a factor influencing test responses, the relationship between supervisor and supervisee often is underestimated as an influence on the work that is done and the learning that occurs. The realistic asymmetry in the relationship—the fact that the supervisor is supposed to teach and to evaluate, the supervisee to learn and be evaluated—may be experienced and dealt with by the participants in ways that interfere with learning. Constrained by his or her wish to be seen in a good light, the student may not feel free to question or challenge the supervisor's views or to defend his or her own ideas vigorously. Pleasing the supervisor may become the goal rather than absorbing and integrating ideas. The supervisor's position of authority may become the focus for resentful or competitive reactions that impair the student's receptivity. For the supervisor, the temptation to play to an admiring audience or to put an impudent rival in his place may prove more compelling than the need to foster the student's development. Perhaps even worse, supervisor and supervisee may enter into a kind of implicit pact that they will remain friendly at all costs, thus avoiding the sometimes painful task of identifying and correcting problems in the student's work.

In short, just as occurs in psychotherapy and in other types of learning situations as well, anxieties associated with the task at hand can give rise to resistances which are manifested as difficulties in the supervisory relationship. The best safeguard for the work when this situation occurs is a kind of *learning alliance* comparable to the therapeutic alliance that sustains psychotherapy through difficult periods. In order to foster such an alliance, the supervisor must be able to convey acceptance of the student's mistakes and flounderings. The supervisor must function like a "loving superego," setting and upholding standards, but guiding instead of punishing. Of course, the presence of such an alliance does not guarantee that the supervisory relationship will be free of problems. It does mean, however, that when problems do occur they are likely to be identified, overcome, and perhaps under some circumstances even explored for their possible diagnostic contribution via the notion of "parallel processes" (Doehrman 1976). As in psychotherapy, what transpires between patient and clinician may affect the relationship between clinician and supervisor, and vice versa.

WHAT SHOULD BE TAUGHT?

Testing supervision offers a remarkable range of opportunities for teaching about the inference process, about the relationship between theory and test data, about defensive organization and ego functions, about symptom formation and expression, about how patients will likely respond to various treatment interventions, about how the student can participate in formulating diagnostic questions that can be realistically answered by the tests and that do not overlook important issues, about how to communicate test findings, and about how to maximize the student's contribution to a referral source or clinical team. From these possibilities, we believe that there are three areas deserving of special emphasis: test administration and scoring, inference making, and the communication of test findings. These skills are central to the student diagnostician's developing competence and the trainee's later independent functioning.

The importance of *administration and scoring* may be easily overlooked if it is too readily assumed that the standardization of the test stimuli automatically extends to the tester as well. Such an assumption may be tempting in view of a number of pressures, among them the clinical need for rapid findings combined with limited supervision time, the fact that test interpretation is often viewed as a more enjoyable and prestigious activity than test administration and scoring, and the student tester's anxiety about being criticized for elementary mistakes. The supervisor should help the student resist these pressures so that basic techniques can be given their due. "Garbage in, garbage out" is as pertinent an adage for test interpretation as for computers. Without good data, even the most sophisticated analysis is crippled, and correct techniques are essential to the validity of test data. Note that we do not use the term *correct techniques* to mean techniques that are rigid or mechanical. Departures from usual procedures of test administration are sometimes necessary and desirable and do not in themselves invalidate the responses that are obtained. However, the supervisor should try to ensure that the student knows and is able to follow the standard procedures, deviates from them knowingly and for appropriate reasons, and uses the proper caution in interpreting data so obtained. Supervision affords the student tester room for considerable flexibility, even creativity, in using altered techniques of administration, scoring, or inquiry designed to probe the limits of a patient's functioning under different conditions. Especially with advanced students, such variations of technique are a desirable focus for supervision.

When dealing with *inference making*, the supervisor should emphasize explicitness, encouraging the student by word and by example to spell out the chains of reasoning that lead from discrete responses to conclusions at successively higher levels of abstraction. Although the supervisor may be able to draw far-reaching conclusions from data that merely puzzle the student, simply stating these conclusions without tracing the logic involved is likely to contribute more to the student's inhibition and sense of awe than to his or her professional development. In contrast, if the question "How do we know this?" constantly accompanies the supervisory work, *both* participants will benefit from the necessity to clarify and organize their ideas.

The emphasis on explicitness should not be misconstrued as a limitation on the kinds of data that may be considered. In our opinion, supervision should deal not only with formal scores and response content from the tests themselves, but with other categories of data as well: the circumstances of the testing; the patient's attitude toward the examiner and toward the testing experience; the patient's expectations of the outcome of the testing; and changes in the patient's stance toward the examiner during the session or across several sessions. Understanding how all these factors influence the test responses and making the necessary adjustments in how the data are viewed is a critical step in moving from a psychometric stance to that of a clinical diagnostician.

Should the student have knowledge of the patient's history or the findings of other clinicians? The novice tester often has difficulty in trusting fully the data he or she has collected, and information from the history may bias the student's reading of the tests to an alarming degree. With no history of psychotic behavior, how can the evidence of thought disorder be believed? With a previous diagnosis of depressive neurosis, how can the tests contain no signs of depression? Doing test analyses "blind," with no information about the patient's history or presenting complaints is one possible remedy for this dilemma. However, while interesting and informative as an exercise, this approach sacrifices so much with respect to the contextual influences on the testing (including, in addition to the patient's attitudes, such matters as a recent death, drug use, etc.) that other solutions must be found. The student's confidence and convictions eventually build as his or her inferences are supported by subsequent developments in treatment and as he or she heeds the supervisor's reminders to trust the data. In the meantime, supervisor and student must guard against the biasing effects of extratest knowledge of the patient, making the best use of such information for orientation to the clinical issues in the case, yet preserving the independence of the current testing perspective.

Turning to the issue of *communication of test findings,* we call attention to an important difference between the supervision of psychotherapy and of psychological testing. Because the focus of psychotherapy supervision is the student's direct work with the patient, and because the effectiveness of that work depends largely on the development of trust, empathy, and rapport between patient and student therapist, it is generally agreed to be an error, albeit a common one, for the supervisor to try to treat the patient through the student. Testing supervision is different in that the student's work with the patient is only a part of the task; communication with professional colleagues, often through written reports, is equally emphasized. The testing supervisor thus has more of a realistic opportunity to intervene directly, through suggestions before the report is drafted and through editing the student's work. But to what extent should the testing supervisor exercise this opportunity? The overactive supervisor may encourage the student to act passively as a mouthpiece, thus shortchanging the learning process; on the other hand, the supervisor who allows the student to submit an inadequate report is shortchanging both the student and the patient. We can only suggest the compromise that the supervisor must be active enough to ensure that an adequate report is written, for obvious clinical, legal, and ethical reasons, but that the report should as much as possible be the student's own work.

The manner in which test findings should be conveyed is in part a matter of institutional requirements, in part of professional standards, and in part of personal style. We shall not belabor the standards of clarity, inclusiveness, and clinical relevance which have been well set forth by others, especially Mayman (1959). A joint commitment to such standards should characterize the supervision. The supervisor should help the student develop a personal style that is comfortable as well as consistent with external requirements and constraints. Toward this end, the supervisor may at certain points encourage experimentation with a variety of styles (Sargent 1951) or recommend the use of a standard outline (Appelbaum 1972). Of course, the bottom line about communication is its effectiveness, and so the student should be encouraged to monitor the fate of his or her findings. If they are being ignored, misunderstood, distorted, or otherwise not optimally used, an undetected problem may be present in the student's reports.

SUPERVISORY TECHNIQUES

Can we be even more specific about techniques of supervision? What actually should take place between student and teacher in the sessions they have together? Clearly, the techniques employed should be linked to the student's level of skill. After the appropriate classroom instruction about test construction, rationale, administration, and scoring, students should watch tests being administered and should have their own test administration observed and criticized. The student tester will then be ready to proceed increasingly independently. When possible, the supervisor and student should meet prior to the first testing appointment in order to review the referral question, the clinical circumstances, and the diagnostic issues that might emerge. During this session, they can make decisions about the tests to be used, about the need for additional communication with whatever other professionals may be involved, and about how to deal with whatever patient resistances may be anticipated. If the testing is conducted across several sessions, a supervisory meeting at some intermediate point will help focus the remaining testing time. In addition, the supervisor can guide the student in his or her interactions with other professionals that may take place during this evaluation period.

Early in the student's development, the supervisor and student should go through the test data together. Basic considerations of scoring accuracy and adequacy of administration will occupy a relatively greater amount of time at this level. When turning to the interpretation, the supervisor should at times "think out loud" about the material, providing a model for how inferences are made, how hypotheses are generated and either supported or discarded, and how issues are hierarchically arranged and organized with respect to their clinical relevance and degree of certainty. The supervisor may offer a method for "inference mapping" and show the student how to keep track of hypotheses and conclusions as they emerge from study of the test data. For individually administered tests, verbatim recordings of the test responses are, of course, invaluable in making a careful analysis of important qualitative and stylistic elements. Even if the supervisor is an active teacher, the student should do what analysis he or she can before the supervisory session, underlining responses that the student considers especially important and perhaps making notes about inferences drawn and how such inferences relate to one another.

As the student's skills develop, the supervisor may do less in the way of actively formulating ideas and may increasingly rely on the student's description of findings and conclusions. At this level, the supervisor may both respond to the student's questions and ask questions to determine whether the student's conclusions are adequately supported by the data and whether every relevant issue is being addressed. For the supervisor to look over the test data, perhaps prior to the first working session, is probably a good idea for some time, until the student is fully capable of independently maintaining a high level of competence in administration, scoring, and inference making. At the most advanced level, the student may use the supervisor almost as a consultant, bringing in a virtually completed assignment and raising certain key questions for the supervisor's judgment.

Dealing with the test report itself deserves special comment. The student's rough draft may have been preceded by considerable supervisory work, but it is here that the clearest view is obtained of how well the student has grasped the issues. In fact, while far from an ideal, supervision could be based on a test report draft alone, since a contradiction, a failure to address a key issue, or focusing on a bit of vagueness can alert the supervisor to a conceptual unclarity, an oversight, or a gap in the student's knowledge of the phenomenon at hand. Atypical styles of writing and difficulties in writing about certain patients also may signal a sort of diagnostic countertransference toward the patient: the patient's pessimism about the future leads the student to omit consideration of treatment alternatives; the report on a manic patient is twice as long as usual; the obsessional patient is written about with endless equivocation. Such reflections in the writing itself may prove helpful in highlighting patient characteristics and may even be pointed to as interactional patterns predictive of subsequent treatment situations. For example, the student who overemphasizes a patient's assets in the test report may be responding to the patient's tendency toward hypomanic denial. Recognizing this intrapsychic maneuver as it is manifested in the testing relationship and subsequent writing could be invaluable in cautioning future treaters against taking the patient's problems too lightly.

From consideration of the reasons for the testing to the shaping of the final report, then, supervision of psychological testing offers abundant opportunities for rich teaching and learning about personality, psychopathology, treatment interventions, and promoting effective use of diagnostic information. In fact, almost every issue touched upon in this brief overview could be the topic of another paper in itself. Just as Ekstein and Wallerstein (1972) consolidated the existing knowledge about psychotherapy supervision in their classic text, *The Teaching and Learnng of Psychotherapy*, we should be hard at work refining and organizing what we know into a companion volume, *The Teaching and Learning of Psychological Testing.*

REFERENCES

Appelbaum, S. A.: A Method of Reporting Psychological Test Findings. *Bull. Menninger Clin.* 36(5):535–45, 1972.

Blank, Leonard & David, H. P., eds.: *Sourcebook for Training in Clinical Psychology.* New York: Springer, 1964.

Doehrman, M. J. G.: Parallel Processes in Supervision and Psychotherapy. *Bull. Menninger Clin.* 40(1):1–104, 1976.

Ekstein, Rudolf & Wallerstein, R. S.: *The Teaching and Learning of Psychotherapy,* Ed. 2. New York: International Universities Press, 1972.

Finn, M. H. P. & Brown, Fred, eds.: *Training for Clinical Psychology.* New York: International Universities Press, 1959.

Kaslow, F. W., et al.: *Supervision, Consultation, and Staff Training in the Helping Professions.* San Francisco: Jossey-Bass, 1977.

Langs, R. J.: *The Supervisory Experience.* New York: Jason Aronson, 1979.

Lower, R. B.: Countertransference Resistances in the Supervisory Situation. *Am. J. Psychiatry* 129(2):156–60, 1972.

Mayman, Martin: Style, Focus, Language and Content of an Ideal Psychological Test Report. *J. Project. Techn.* 23(4):453–58, 1959.

Raimy, V. C., ed.: *Training in Clinical Psychology.* New York: Prentice-Hall, 1950.

Sargent, H. D.: Psychological Test Reporting: An Experiment in Communication. *Bull. Menninger Clin.* 15(5):175–86, 1951.

Schlessinger, N.: Supervision of Psychotherapy: A Critical Review of the Literature. *Arch. Gen. Psychiatry* 15(2):129–34, 1966.

Chapter 5

Evaluation

How do interns evaluate their internship experiences? How do internships evaluate their interns? What are the internship transition processes? These questions are being examined more seriously as their importance is recognized. Not only are these issues of considerable importance to prospective interns and academic training programs, but to the internship agencies themselves and ultimately to the profession of psychology. While there has been a small number of surveys of former interns, these interns are typically from only one academic training program. For example, Steinhelber and Gaynor (1981) report 1968 and 1977 surveys of former clinical psychology interns from one internship setting. These former 1968 interns were primarily involved with research and psychotherapy while the 1977 interns were primarily involved with psychotherapy. However, in 1977 they were engaged in more supervision and significantly less research and assessment. Examination of their data suggested that it was the younger 1977 psychologists who were doing less research and more supervision. In both surveys there was dissatisfaction with psychological testing responsibility, although the satisfaction levels in both samples were comparable.

Phillips (1981) surveyed those internships that have school psychology interns. These internships require 35% of time for psychotherapy, 26% for assessment, 14% for seminars, 12% for consultation, and 8% for supervision and "other" activities. These training settings typically accepted 2 school psychology interns each year with a selection ratio of 1 to 6 with approximately half of the students coming from non-APA-approved accredited programs. Clear distinctions were made between primary and adjunctive roles for these interns. The primary roles were counseling, psychoeducational assessment, remediation of learning difficulties, input on multiprofessional teams, consultation, and child/family interventions.

Dana and Brookings (1980) reported a time-log program evaluation for the Memphis internship consortium that provides comparative data on time usage and affect during different time/activity periods. A direct service time commitment of 24% plus 30% indirect service is somewhat less than the 61% direct service for psychotherapy and assessment reported by Phillips (1981) for school psychology interns. Seminars and supervision time are comparable while the consultation time of 3% is considerably less for these clinical psychology consortia interns. The positive or negative affect associated with each setting, activity, and person with whom interns interacted indicated a prevailing positive affect for service-related activities, negative affect for paper work/recordkeeping, and a range of affect for contacts with other persons. Since this research permitted separation of settings and interns, feedback of data to both internship and individual intern was feasible over a period of years. The particular affect labels were also used to characterize the quality of each intern's responsiveness to the internship experiences.

Kaslow and Rice (1985) use neoanalytic developmental theory as a framework for understanding the nature of the transition experienced by professional psychology graduate students during their internship year. The article describes the stressors encountered and the coping styles used by interns during this change process as well as supportive actions that are possible by the staff. This crucial year in the training of psychologists is seen as the "professional adolescence" of the future psychologist. Early in the internship year the student experiences separation from the support system of the academic setting and no significant immediate bonding to the internship staff, fellow interns, or others. The first few weeks are confusing to the intern as a result of new routines, learning expectancies, new roles etc. Fostering the development of a "holding environment" which is warm, nurturing, and provides limits can be helpful during this period. During the midphase of the internship years, the trainee becomes less dependent upon internship staff as a greater sense of professional identity develops. Staff members can facilitate this healthy development toward separation by being available and acknowledging the unique identity of each intern. Lastly, the intern develops her/his own professional individuality and functions more autonomously. This stage also provides facilitative opportunities for staff members by increasing involvement of the intern in overall internship activities and more collegial relationships with the training staff.

Solway (1985) describes the potential distress that accompanies the transition from a university setting to an internship facility and the new role of professional service-provider. A positive self-image as student clinician may be jeopardized by having to demonstrate clinical skills to new supervisors and learn new skills in a more complex professional world. There are also moderate to severe personal stresses as a result of separation and development of a social network in an unfamiliar environment. The effects of these stressors on clinical performance may be apparent for several months and immediate pressures for immersion in the internship experience may be counterproductive. Transitional professional and/or social experiences may be provided by the graduate program and the internship may be helpful by providing orientation that includes awareness of these sources of stress.

The perspective of interns from Georgia State University during a 10-year period was described by a survey of 35 internship sites in 15 states (Cole, Kolko, & Craddick, 1981). Average weekly activities were reported. Advantages include variety of training experiences, adequate supervision, and flexible working arrangements. The major deficit was poor supervision—both quality and quantity reported by 13% of the sample. In addition, interns were disheartened by politicization and bureaucratization which interfered with training. Academic preinternship training deficiencies were described as relevant only to the program of origin.

Pleck (1976), in a unique and sensitive paper, examined sex role issues, or the "vulgar sexual economy" of internship. While this material is anecdotal and limited to one internship setting, it does indicate that sex role issues are still not being examined in training—either during academic experiences or on internship.

Reading 35

Attitudes, Satisfaction, and Training Recommendations of Former Clinical Psychology Interns: 1968 and 1977

John Steinhelber
University of California, San Francisco and Langley Porter Psychiatric
Institute, San Francisco

Jessica Gaynor
University of California, San Francisco

Evaluations of clinical psychology training programs through surveys of former trainees have been published, such as the VA Selection Research Project (Kelly & Fiske, 1951), which has the rare attribute of subsequent follow-ups (Kelly & Goldberg, 1959; Kelly, 1961; Kelly, Goldberg, Fiske & Kilkowski, 1978). Such studies have value not only for retrospective evaluation of our field but also for planning future training.

The present evaluation study consisted of two surveys of former clinical psychology interns at the Langley Porter Psychiatric Institute (LPPI), University of California, San Francisco. The first survey, in 1968, elicited information regarding former interns' professional activities. The second survey, in 1977, replicated those questions and also sought information about respondents' internship training.

METHOD

Subjects

The subjects in this study were former clinical psychology internship trainees at the Langley Porter Psychiatric Institute. The internship is a 1-year, full-time predoctoral training program approved by the American Psychological Association (APA) Committee on Accreditation. Eight advanced graduate students are accepted for training each year from clinical psychology doctoral programs approved by the APA. Training emphasizes a breadth of experience (psychotherapy and assessment, outpatient and inpatient, adults and children) within a predominantly psychodynamic framework.

Procedure

The study consisted of two surveys, one conducted in 1968[1] and the other in 1977, mailed to all former clinical psychology trainees at LPPI. The first

Reprinted from Professional Psychology, *12*(2), 253-260. The authors wish to thank *Marijean LeGoullon* for her assistance in the data analysis.

[1] The 1968 survey was conducted by Robert E. Harris and Shirley M. Jahnson.

questionnaire was received by all interns who had completed their training between 1946 and 1967. The survey items asked respondents to specify both how their time was currently being spent on various professional activities and how they would ideally like to see their time distributed among these activities. The major purpose of this first questionnaire was to describe the professional careers of former graduates.

A second survey of former clinical psychology interns was conducted in 1977. This questionnaire was mailed to all trainees who graduated between 1946 and 1976. Respondents were asked not only to indicate how they were spending their professional time and how they ideally would like to be spending it (an exact replication of the 1968 questionnaire), but they were also asked to describe the content of their internship, to give their opinions about how satisfied they were with their training, and to say how they would view an ideal internship for today's trainee.

RESULTS

Demographic Characteristics

The 1968 survey sample consisted of 61% ($n = 82$) of all LPPI clinical psychology trainees, and the 1977 survey sample included 44% ($n = 91$) of all trainees. The demographic characteristics of the two samples were similar: Two thirds of the respondents were male, with a mean age of 45; and 9 out of 10 respondents identified themselves as clinical psychologists.[2] Over half of the trainees received their degrees from schools outside of California; however, at the time of the surveys, about 50% of the respondents were living in California. The median date of internship completion was 1958 for the 1968 sample, whereas the median date for internship completion was 1964 for the 1977 sample.

Analyses were computed comparing the demographic characteristics of respondents and nonrespondents to the 1968 and 1977 surveys. One significant difference was found. The 1968 sample included a greater proportion (63%) of males than is characteristic of the total group (56% males) of pre-1968 interns, $\chi^2(1) = 3.78$, $p < .05$. In addition, analyses examined the differential response rate between the two surveys (61% in 1968 and 44% in 1977) and found it not significantly related to the number of years since training in LPPI. Therefore, in general, the survey respondents seemed fairly representative of their respective group of clinical psychology interns trained at LPPI.

_____

[2] Because such a large percentage of respondents identified themselves as clinical psychologists, the remaining analyses excluded the small number of respondents (in 1968 $n = 11$, and in 1977 $n = 7$) who did not identify themselves as clinical psychologists.

Table 1   Univariate Analyses Comparing Percentage of Time Clinical Psychologists Devoted to Professional Activities in 1968 and 1977

| | Year | | | | |
| Activity | 1968 | | 1977 | | |
	M	SD	M	SD	F
Psychotherapy	23.82	30.06	32.44	25.27	1.50
Psychological testing	12.33	21.15	5.52	11.38	5.71*
Teaching	12.74	19.47	15.82	16.07	.46
Supervision	6.00	9.90	12.70	12.70	11.32**
Research	27.74	28.53	13.89	19.82	5.93*
Administration	13.44	19.65	13.15	20.29	.01
Community mental health	1.33	3.55	2.59	5.26	1.63

Note. $N = 27$ (only those subjects who responded to both surveys). The 1968 and 1977 means total only 97.40 and 96.11, respectively, due to the few miscellaneous "other" responses being excluded.

   *$p < .05$.

   **$p < .01$.

Participation in Professional Activities

Respondents to the 1968 and 1977 surveys who identified themselves as clinical psychologists were asked to report the percentage of their time devoted to various professional activities. Clinical psychologists in 1968 reported spending an equal amount of time doing psychotherapy and research (24% for each activity), with less time spent in teaching and supervision (19%), psychological testing (12%), administration (10%), community mental health activities (3%), and miscellaneous other (8%). For clinical psychologists in 1977, a greater proportion of their time was devoted to psychotherapy (31%), with the remainder of their time divided between teaching and supervision (25%), research (14%), administration (13%), psychological testing (8%), community mental health activities (5%), and other (4%).

To examine changes from 1968 to 1977, the percentage of time for those identifying themselves as clinical psychologists was compared for respondents to *both* the 1968 and 1977 surveys.[3] Multivariate analysis of variance (MANOVA) showed that the distribution of time devoted to various professional activities was significantly different in 1968 compared with 1977 for clinical psychologists, Wilks' $\lambda = .4589$, $F(7, 20) = 3.37, p < .01$. Table 1 presents the univariate

[3] The total sample responding to both the 1968 and 1977 surveys represented 33% ($N = 27$) of all clinical psychology interns trained between 1946 and 1967 at LPPI. Chi-square analyses were computed comparing the demographic characteristics of those who did and did not respond to both surveys. No significant differences were found.

analyses comparing the time devoted to individual activities in 1968 and 1977 for clinical psychologists. In 1977 clinical psychologists were doing significantly more supervision of trainees and less psychological testing and research.

To ascertain whether these changes over time were due to maturational effects in individuals or to shifts in the profession, two additional analyses were computed. First, utilizing a median split procedure, dividing the sample into two equal groups, those trained before and after 1964, the professional activities for these two groups were compared for 1977 respondents identifying themselves as clinical psychologists. No significant differences emerged between how younger and older clinical psychologists were spending their professional time in 1977, suggesting that these effects were not due to maturation. Second, utilizing a median split procedure, dividing the sample into clinical psychologists above and below the age of 40, the distribution of time devoted to various activities for younger clinical psychologists in 1968 was compared to that of younger clinical psychologists in 1977. Similarly, time spent in professional activities for older clinical psychologists in 1968 was compared to that of older clinical psychologists in 1977. The MANOVAs for both of these analyses revealed no overall significant differences. However, the univariate statistics supported the hypothesis of shifts in the profession over time by showing that (a) younger clinical psychologists in 1977 were doing significantly less research ($M = 14.09$, $SD = 20.35$) than younger clinical psychologists in 1968 ($M = 20.19$, $SD = 22.72$), $F(1, 30) = 5.90$, $p < .05$, and (b) younger clinical psychologists in 1977 were doing significantly more supervision of trainees ($M = 17.27$, $SD = 16.94$) than younger clinical psychologists in 1968 ($M = 4.90$, $SD = 5.24$), $F(1, 30) = 5.09$, $p < .05$.

Satisfaction with Professional Activities

To understand how satisfied respondents were with their current level of involvement in professional activities, both the 1968 and 1977 questionnaires also solicited the amount of time that *ideally* would be devoted to various activities. The MANOVA showed that for 1968 respondents identifying themselves as clinical psychologists there was a significant difference between how they reportedly were spending their professional time and how they ideally would like to spend their professional time (Wilks' $\lambda = .6104$), $F(7, 52) = 4.74$, $p < .01$. The univariate analyses comparing how they actually and ideally would like to distribute their professional time showed that in 1968 clinical psychologists would have preferred to spend significantly less time (*actual* percentage of time $M = 12.33$, *ideal* $M = 5.89$) doing psychological testing, $F(1, 59) = 13.79$, $p < .01$, as well as less time (*actual* $M = 13.44$, *ideal* $M = 6.74$) involved with administrative responsiblities, $F(1, 59) = 10.56$, $p < .01$. They would have preferred to spend more time (*actual* $M = 1.33$, *ideal* $M = 4.30$) doing community mental health activities, $F(1, 59) = 7.17$, $p < .01$, although the desired increase in time allocated to this type of activity would represent less than 5% of the total effort for clinical psychologists.

Similarly, for 1977 respondents identifying themselves as clinical psychologists, the MANOVA showed that there was a significant difference between how they reportedly were spending their time and how they ideally would like to spend their professional time (Wilks' $\lambda = .7356$), $F(7, 65)$, 3.34, $p < .01$. The univariate analyses comparing how they actually and ideally would like to devote their time to various activities showed that in 1977 clinical psychologists also would have liked to spend less time (*actual M* = 5.52, *ideal M* = 3.70) doing psychological testing, $F(1, 72) = 3.85, p < .05$, as well as less time (*actual M* = 13.15, *ideal M* = 6.30) with administrative activities, $F(1, 72) = 9.27$, $p < .01$. However, clinical psychologists in 1977 would have preferred to spend more time (*actual M* = 13.89), *ideal M* = 22.04) involved in research, $F(1, 72) = 6.45, p < .05$.

To investigate changes in satisfaction with professional activities, a MANOVA was computed comparing 1968 and 1977 satisfaction levels (actual vs. ideal) for clinical psychologists responding to both surveys. The results indicate no significant difference between the general levels of satisfaction in 1968 and 1977. However, the univariate analyses revealed that clinical psychologists were significantly more satisfied with their (decreased) involvement in psychological testing in 1977 ($M_D = 1.63$; $SD = 5.93$) than in 1968 ($M_D = 5.80, SD = 13.93$).

Internship Satisfaction

Former trainees who responded to the 1977 questionnaire were asked to retrospectively rate specific internship experiences in terms of both the training they actually received (1 = None, to 4 = Extensive) and the type of training they would have liked to have had during their internship (1 = None, to 4 = Would have preferred more). Using a median split procedure, the sample was divided into those trainees completing their internship before and after 1964. The average ratings of internship experiences were ranked for these two groups of respondents. Spearman rank correlation coefficients were computed for each group of trainees. For trainees completing their internship before 1964, there was a significant negative correlation between the types of internship experiences they reportedly received and those in which they would have liked to participate more ($\rho = -.58$, $p < .01$). These trainees reported getting their most extensive experience in psychodiagnostic work with adult inpatients and outpatients. In addition, they received substantial training in long-term psychotherapy with adults. However, this group of graduates would have liked less of an emphasis on assessment and more time devoted to other treatment experiences such as brief, group, and family psychotherapy; crisis intervention; and inpatient psychotherapy with adolescents and children.

For trainees completing their internship after 1964, there was a significant positive correlation between the types of internship experiences they received and those to which they would have preferred more exposure ($p = .34, p < .05$). The most extensive training experiences reported by these graduates consisted of a combination of assessment with both inpatient and outpatient adults and outpatient psychotherapy experiences of both brief and long-term duration. Expressed preferences for more extensive training clustered around various outpatient treatment experiences. Psychological testing was seen as overemphasized.

Ideal Internship for Today's Trainees

Respondents to the 1977 questionnaire were asked to rate specific internship experiences in terms of how important they believed them to be for training clinical psychologists today. Using a median split procedure, the sample was divided into those who completed their internship before and after 1964. There were no major differences between these two groups in terms of training experiences that they ranked as most and least important for today's internship programs. Both groups ranked as most important those experiences that involved working with adult outpatients, such as brief and group psychotherapy, intake interviews, and psychological testing. In addition, they stressed the importance of being able to learn a diversity of psychotherapeutic approaches. Both groups also felt the experiences such as research and program evaluation were least important for internship training.

DISCUSSION

This study of former LPPI clinical psychology interns suggested the following: (a) Over the last decade there has been a shift in the relative amount of time these clinical psychologists devote to various professional activities, with today's recent graduates spending more time supervising trainees and less time engaging in psychological testing and research. These changes appeared due to shifts in the profession rather than to maturational effects in the respondents. (b) Today, as well as 10 years ago, there seems to be some discrepancy between how clinical psychologists actually spend their professional time and how they would like to spend it, with respondents to both surveys wanting to spend less time doing psychological testing and aministrative activities and more time doing community mental health work (1968) or research (1977). (c) Trainees interning before 1964 received extensive training in diagnostic assessment and would have preferred more training in psychotherapy, whereas trainees graduating after 1964 reported similar preferences but more congruence between their actual and ideal internship activities. (d) Though respondents indicated that they thought psychological testing was overemphasized in their training, they nevertheless ranked assessment high in their ratings of the content of an ideal internship.

The shift in clinical activities during the last 10 years away from psychological testing and research and toward teaching is an extension of earlier reports
(Kelly, 1961; Kelly et al., 1978). These changes in how clinical psychologists
spend their professional time may represent a general evolution of the field.
Historically, training in clinical psychology was primarily influenced both by
the success of applied psychology during the World War II era, notably in the
field of psychometrics, and by the Boulder model, which emphasized training
the "scientist-practitioner." Consistent with this history, graduates of "traditional" clinical psychology programs have been expected to develop clinical
skills, including a unique expertise in psychological testing, as well as research
skills through their academic university preparation. The relevance of such a
training model is subject to continued examination in light of findings such as
the decreased amount of time most graduates are devoting to psychological
testing and research. The direction of change observed in this study, as well as
the development of new training modalities (e.g., the establishment of professional schools and alternative clinical degrees), suggests that a "clinician-teacher"
role may be a more accurate description of the activities of many contemporary
clinical psychologists. This is similar to the "scholar-practitioner" model
advanced a few years ago by the president of APA's Division of Clinical
Psychology (Derner, 1976). Although the majority of clinical psychology
graduates appear not to practice what the Boulder model attempts to teach,
it might still be argued that research training usefully shapes the attitudes
and understanding of the future "clinician-teacher" or "scholar-practitioner."

Clinical psychologists expressed a desire to spend less time doing psychological testing and administrative activities in both the 1968 and 1977 surveys.
Consistent with our sample's reported professional changes, psychologists'
preferred clinical role appears to be moving away from psychological testing.
This is further supported by trends in the data suggesting that clinical psychologists were spending more time doing psychotherapy and less time doing
psychological testing in 1977 than in 1968 and that they were more satisfied
with a reduced level of involvement in psychological testing in 1977. Discontent
with the amount of time devoted to administrative activities may be due to the
somewhat unexpected administrative responsibilities that accompany many
positions in mental health and teaching settings. Those who view themselves
as clinician-teachers may be disheartened when they find administrative time
replacing the more desired clinical and training aspects of their work.

The findings that clinical psychologists in 1977 wanted to spend more of
their time doing research might appear inconsistent with the hypothesized
shift from the "science-practitioner" to the "clinician-teacher" role. However,
it should be noted that the overall trend from 1968 to 1977 was a decrease in
both the actual and ideal amount of research time.

The observation that interns graduating before 1964 were dissatisfied
with the perceived emphasis of their training in diagnostic assessment is con-

sistent with the hypothesized shift in clinical activities of the psychologist. The pre-1964 to post-1964 shift from a negative to a positive correlation between actual internship activities and desired changes suggests that the LPPI internship has been responsive to these survey findings. Several relevant internship changes have been made. All trainees now do adult psychotherapy all year. Adult assessment is no longer a major training block but is limited and/or integrated with other training on a clinical service. There now are more accessible options in brief therapy and crisis intervention; a family therapy training program has been developed; and for the first time, a regular elective on the inpatient children's ward is offered.

Former trainees commenting on the ideal internship for today's clinical psychology interns stressed the importance of providing experience with adult outpatients by doing assessment, intake interviews, and brief and group psychotherapy. In part these recommendations reflect the current professional activities of former trainees. However, they also add a practical note regarding the kinds of activities in which trainees can expect to be involved once they complete their training.

Clinical psychology faculty groups need to judge the effectiveness of their training efforts in order to make informed decisions about program directions. This particular evaluation effort focused on former trainees' feedback regarding their past and current activities, their relative levels of professional satisfaction, opinions of their internship experiences, and their ideas for future training. The findings suggest a shift in the clinical psychologist's role over the last decade, and there is evidence to indicate that from the trainee's perspective, in some ways this internship program has been responsive to changes in professional values. Trainee feedback over time is a useful source of data for evaluating training endeavors because it provides a historical understanding of the development and direction of the practice of clinical psychology. Results of such surveys and historical analyses, in conjunction with forecasts of future directions in the profession, provide essential information for the planning and modification of training programs for clinical psychologists.

REFERENCES

Derner, G. F. The education for the profession of clinical psychology and the psychology technician. *The Clinical Psychologist*, 1976, *29*, 1-2.

Kelly, E. L. Clinical psychology—1960: Report of survey findings. *Newsletter Division of Clinical Psychology of the American Psychology Association*, 1961, *14*, 1-11.

Kelly, E. L., & Fiske, D. W. *The prediction of performance in clinical psychology*. Ann Arbor: University of Michigan Press, 1951 (Reprinted by Greenwood Press, 1969).

Kelly, E. L., & Goldberg, L. R. Correlates of later performance and specialization in psychology: A follow-up study of the trainees assessed in the VA

selection research project. *Psychological Monographs,* 1959, *73* 12, Whole
No. 482).

Kelly, E. L., Goldberg, L. R., Fiske, D. S., & Kilkowski, J. M. Twenty-five years
later: A follow-up study of the graduate students in clinical psychology
assessed in the VA selection research project. *American Psychologist,* 1978,
33, 746–755.

Reading 36

Experiences of School Psychology Interns in Psychology Internship Centers

Beeman N. Phillips
The University of Texas at Austin

The most widely recognized definition of the doctoral internship is that found in
the American Psychological Association accreditation standards for internships in
professional psychology (APA, 1979). The National Association of School Psychologists (NASP) has also widely recognized school psychology internship guidelines. Despite this consensus on basic tenets and generally desirable qualities,
there is a question as to what the internship should be at the functional
level. One point of view is that it should be a generalized, non-differentiated
professional experience, which contrasts with another view that the specific
structure and the nature of the experiences of the internship should vary from
one specialty to another. However, whether or not one accepts this differentiated model, there is surprisingly little evidence of what happens to trainees
from different specialty backgrounds who are accepted as interns in the same
psychology internship centers.

As a case in point, many school psychologists are committed to the concept
of the differentiated internship, and the experiences of school psychology
students in psychology internship centers therefore ought to be of considerable
significance. In response to this situation, this study examined a number of
characteristics of internships for school psychology students in psychology
internship centers listed in the Association of Psychology Internship Centers
1979–1980 *Directory* as taking school psychology trainees (APIC, 1979).[1] This

Reprinted from Journal of School Psychology, *19,* 217–221.

[1] In order to be listed in the APIC *Directory,* an internship program must be one year
full-time or two years half-time; must accept only applicants enrolled in a doctoral program
in professional psychology; must be directed by a licensed psychologist; must provide
training in a range of professional activities; must provide current descriptions of its
program; and must be a member in good standing of APIC. In addition, no attempt was
made to evaluate the programs listed therein or to authenticate the descriptive data
provided. APIC also operates an internship placement "clearinghouse" for exchange of
information regarding internship candidates and positions still available after the common
acceptance-rejection period (pp. 3 and 7, 1980–81 *Directory*).

study considers how these internship experiences differ, if at all, from the internships provided to other trainees, and also whether center directors perceive that an emphasis on these differences has been misplaced. The implications of the survey's results for broadening the range of internship options for school psychology students are also discussed.

PROCEDURE

Of the more than 300 centers listed, the 1979-80 APIC *Directory* lists 44 centers that consider school psychology trainees as interns. A questionnaire with an accompanying cover letter was sent early in the spring of 1980 to these 44 centers.[2] Responses were received from 35 (a return rate of 80%); the results reported, using information from the questionnaire and the *Directory,* are based on these 35 centers.

Of the 35 centers, 13 reported that they no longer plan to list in the *Directory* that they take school psychology interns. As explanation for their contemplated action, they advised that: (1) the questionnaire caused them to rethink the appropriateness of their earlier decision to consider school psychology trainees; (2) they had all along considered only those students who were clinically interested and prepared; and (3) the pressures for uniformity of training experiences made differentiation between internships difficult. Only 22 centers were left, therefore, for further analysis, and the remaining results here reported are based on these 22 centers.

RESULTS AND DISCUSSION

Some Characteristics of These 22 Centers

Using the information provided in the APIC *Directory,* the majority of the centers are classifiable as clinics. Eleven are located in the northeast, four in the southeast, four in the midwest, and three in the southwest. In addition, they had a median of five interns and a median of 10 full-time psychology staff available to supervise students.

Looking at the range of experiences provided, there was considerable variation across the centers, as well as between interns within the same center. However, the typical intern devoted 35% of his/her time to psychotherapy, 26% to psychological assessment, 14% to seminar attendance, 12% to consultation, 5% to research, and 8% to supervision and other activities.

[2] This study was made possible by the support of APIC and the Council of Directors of School Psychology Programs (CDSPP). The questionnaire covered a variety of areas, including the numbers of school psychology applicants, and trainees, the accessibility of school psychologists and school system experiences to trainees, expectancies concerning preplacement competencies, the availability of selected roles and activities, problems in meeting the needs of school psychology trainees, and attitudes toward future internship developments. A copy of the questionnaire is available on request from the author.

During 1979–80, 19 of the centers had had a total of approximately 100 applications from school psychology trainees, 15 of which were accepted, including eight from non-APA-accredited doctoral programs. An examination of the distribution indicates that both applications and acceptances were fairly evenly divided, with no center accepting more than two. In addition, in eight centers the specific structure of the internship varied somewhat from one specialty to another. An additional 15 of the centers reported that school psychologists are accessible as role models; 16 of them affirmed that school psychologists are available as supervisors.

Placement Expectancies

Preplacement characteristics and competencies can be classified as generic and specialized, with the latter being specific to the specialty or type of setting in which the student is to be placed. When asked what characteristics and competencies they expected all interns to have, directors mentioned both personal and professional qualities, such as an ability to function in an organizational structure, openness to personal growth, respect for the client, personal stability, ability to take initiative and organize one's own time, and high tolerance for ambiguity.

As to professional skills, the directors especially emphasized experience in diagnostic assessment and at least minimal experience in psychotherapy. They also expected all interns to have a basic knowledge of core psychology areas, with special emphasis on developmental and personality theory, as well as on the theoretical foundations of standard structured tests, projective techniques, and psychotherapy.

Most of the centers also have essentially the same expectations for school psychology interns as they have for other interns, although they admittedly "shade" these requirements a little in some instances. When this is done, the centers seek these additional competencies: (a) an understanding of the culture of schools; (b) a knowledge of school learning and behavior disorders; (c) psycho-educational assessment and intervention techniques; (d) related supervised experience in the schools; and (e) some experience with families.

Roles and Activities of School Psychology Interns

Psychology centers offer a variety of potential roles and activities for interns. When the centers were asked to select from a list which roles and activities they considered to be *primary* for a school psychology intern, those roles and activities most clearly identified and listed in rank order, were:

1 Individual and group counseling
2 Psychoeducational assessment, including learning difficulties and behavior and social problems

3 Intervention to remediate learning difficulties and behavior and social problems

4 Working with staffing, guidance, and other committees in multiprofessional teams

5 Functioning as consultant to teachers, administrators, other school personnel, and other professionals

6 Child and family intervention, including parent consultation and education

In contrast, those roles and activities identified as *adjunctive* roles for a school psychology intern, listed in rank order, were:

1 Engaging in data-oriented problem solving and applied research

2 Supervising of nondoctoral school psychological services and other related pupil services personnel

3 Program development and evaluation

4 Assisting administrative personnel in establishing and implementing goals and behavior objectives for instructional and other intervention programs

Overall, it can be seen that the priorities accorded to different roles and activities by center directors are not particularly out of line with the priorities of many school psychologists. However, when one considers the actual experiences of school psychologists, there is a discrepancy between these priorities and what is available to school psychology interns, since adjunctive roles and activities are often more available than primary roles and activities. Moreover, in view of these responses and other questionnaire data, it appears that only about five of these centers provide school psychology interns with systematic and regular experience in a school system, although about an equal number provide such experience in residential and other special schools or provide some opportunities to consult with schools.

Attitudes Toward Differentiated Experience

Center directors were provided with the statement that many school psychologists believe that experiences *in the schools* with children, teachers, parents et al. are central to competent school psychological practice, and that many school psychology trainers believe that 50% or more of a school psychology intern's time should be spent in school and school-related settings. When asked to comment on this, many center directors disagreed, stating that they were inerested in training competent psychologists and that a well trained clinical psychologist can adapt to a wide variety of settings. Others indicated that their centers function under a network model of training that provides some individualization according to student needs and interests, although school districts are generally not available in such rotations. Overall, the internship of school psychology students in most of these centers has a child-clinical emphasis.

Development of Consortium Arrangements That Include School Systems

An important assumption of this survey was that psychology internship centers are interested in providing quality internship experiences for school psychology students. In this regard, the development of more consortium arrangements that involve one or more school districts in the area was suggested as a future possibility. When asked if they saw this as a way to increase the quality of school psychology internships in psychology internship centers, 11 of 14 who responded agreed, although they had few ideas about what factors would need to be considered in the development of such arrangements.

It was also pointed out that psychology internship centers are multiprofessional and interdisciplinary; the directors were asked whether this produced problems that need to be especially considered in the development of quality placements for school psychology trainees. Typical response was that all interns have such problems and that individualized training experiences help to minimize them. Others pointed out that other professionals typically do not make the kinds of distinctions among psychological specialties that psychologists make. Finally, some noted that all interns are identified as clinical psychology interns, which in itself alleviates some of the problems alluded to.

SUMMARY AND CONCLUSIONS

In summary, training in psychology internship centers at the present time is primarily clinical training, with a child-clinical emphasis available to those interns who want it. School psychology students that apply to such centers, therefore, should have a clinical background and be interested in clinically-oriented experience with little direct experience in the schools. The directors of the psychology internship centers do, however, see certain roles and activities as primary functions of school psychologists. They are also receptive to the idea of individualizing internship experiences and are interested in more diversity in the settings available for training purposes and in the inclusion of school systems in their centers' arrangements, although they were not clear about how to include them.

Proponents of broadening the range of internship options for school psychology students could make a case for this in terms of the wide variety of roles and fucntions ascribed to the school psychologist (Hunter & Lambert, 1974) and also in terms of the provisions of P.L. 94-142—especially recent developments concerning the nature of "related services" (Lombard, 1979; Phillips, in press). But in the long view, the need persists to give more attention to the relative importance of generalized versus specialized training in psychological practice. If, for example, by general training in professional psychology one means a source of applied knowledge and skills that enable the school psychologist to construct with some rigor the specific technological foundations of psychological practice, then in principle general professional training is a prerequisite to specialty training and such training would also be necessary for the interpretation and understanding of psychological practice in general. However, general professional training would not yield the specific rules of practice in the schools which must necessarily be provided by specialty-based training, and, although there is no general or mechanical formula for combining generalized and specialized training, more careful delineation will prove useful to the development of school psychology, and ultimately to the development of professional psychology, as well. As to future research, a similar survey of school systems would be desirable, although a listing of school systems with internship centers for such would be difficult to obtain.

REFERENCES

American Psychological Association. *Criteria for accreditation of doctoral programs and internships.* Washington, D.C.: American Psychological Association, 1979.

Association of Psychology Internship Centers, *Directory, Internship Programs in Professional Psychology* (8th ed., 1979–80), 1979.

Hunter, C. P., & Lambert, N. M. Needs assessment activities in school psychology program development. *Journal of School Psychology*, 1974, *12*, 130–137.

Lombard, T. J. Family-oriented emphasis for school psychologists: A needed orientation for training and professional practice. *Professional Psychology*, 1979, *10*, 687–696.

Phillips, B. N. Education and training. In J. R. Bergan (Ed.), *School psychology in contemporary society.* Columbus: Charles Merrill, in press.

P.L. 94-142. *Education for all handicapped children act,* November 29, 1975. Washington, D.C.: U.S. Congress.

Reading 37
Program Evaluation:
An Evolving Methodology for an Internship

Richard H. Dana
University of Arkansas

Jeff B. Brookings
Wittenberg University, Springfield, Ohio

INTRODUCTION

Program evaluation is an accountability device, a statement of what persons are doing who are delivering services and/or receiving training. While some programs do such research, it is often an in-house activity designed to permit a gradual process of change that is based upon data. General methodology that can be applied to different kinds of programs without violation of the integrity of the organization is rare. This methodology has origins in a human science aegis, or action paradigm (Lewin, 1946; 1947) in which the research process is guided by organization needs and includes both participation and information exchange between organization staff and researchers. A first application used a modified Barker stream of behavior account as well as occupancy counts for description of two university psychology training programs (Dana, 1978a). Since only a one-day portion of the university program was sampled, it was not sufficient for description of the increased complexity of structure and function within human service organizations. Subsequent applications of derivative methodology have included a university counseling center (Davenport, 1978), two county social service agencies (Leatherman, 1978; Amos, 1978), and a clinical psychology internship (Barling, 1978).

While the overall methodology has been described elsewhere (Dana, 1978b), the internship data and present status has not been presented except to the par—ticipant interns. This paper describes the methodology as applied to the Memphis Psychology Internship Consortium over a four year period with illustrative internship data from 1978 and intern data from one 1976-1977 intern.

TIME LOG METHODOLOGY

An application of Leary's time log (1970) was used to gather systematic information from interns. This time log provided an hour by hour format

Special acknowledgment is made to Dr. W. Theodore May, Coordinator, Memphis Psychology Internship Consortium, whose training ideals and practices made this research possible and to four generations of interns who invested their time, acumen, and good will in generating data. Thanks are due to Dr. Phil Barling who graciously permitted the data concerning himself as intern to be included and to Darla Amos, Cindy Cohen, and Maria McArthur who participated in data analysis.

with codes for activity, setting, and direction of affect (positive, negative, neutral) as well as space for entry of descriptive data. For each hour of work-related activity, the intern recorded the activity performed, the setting for that activity, the other person(s) present, and the interns' concurrent feelings about that activity. Prior to each data collection period, the internship specified the setting code which included at least 50 settings occupied by interns at any given time. Setting codes are internship-specific while the codes for activities and persons may be relatively consistent across internships.

At the conclusion of one week, the time logs were collected and the data transferred to computer cards. By generating appropriate frequency tables, the affect balance, or the ratios of positive to negative affects, for particular interns, settings, activities, and persons can be examined. For instance, the affect associated with particular activities (collapsed across interns and persons) can be assessed as a function of the specific settings in which they are performed. Since each observation is identified by hour and day, it becomes possible to look at time-related differences in affect balance. The affect balance scores constitute affect values for the interns themselves as well as for the activities, settings, and persons with whom they are involved.

Time logs were collected during a one-week 1976 pilot study on 13 interns, a second 1976–1977 sample of 13 interns during three one-week time periods, a third 1977–1978 sample of 14 interns during two one-week time periods, and a fourth 1978 sample of 12 interns during a one-week time period. Feedback was provided to interns and the internship staff immediately after each data collection period. This feedback also enabled revisions in the time log format and data analysis capabilities for use in subsequent data collection periods.

The Internship

The APA-approved Memphis Internship Consortium consists of the Division of Clinical Psychology in the University of Tennessee Medical School, including four component facilities, as well as the Memphis Veterans Administration Hospital, the Child Development Center, and the Psychological Services Division of the Memphis Board of Education. Interns are encouraged to create individualized, flexible programs that utilize settings available within the community in addition to consortium settings.

Internships are training components of service delivery settings. However, there are no norms for the balance between service and training. Table 1 presents illustrative data for the 1978 interns' affect values and time allocations for activities, settings, and persons. Consortium experience includes more service (56%) than training time (21%) and more indirect (31%) than direct service (25%) while research is deemphasized (3%). Services to clients are varied and include consultation and client advocacy as well as direct contact, staff meetings, and record keeping. The training time is diversified and includes a heavy em-

Table 1 Affect Values and Time Allocations (%) for Activities, Settings, and Persons from 1978 Memphis Consortium Data

Activity	Affect value	Setting	Affect value	Person	Affect value
Direct service (25)	4.8	Medical center (24)	4.3	Alone (32)	1.9
Consultation (4)	17.0	VA hospital (23)	7.4	Client (25)	3.8
Staff meeting (5)	2.0	Mental health centers (13)	2.7	Supervisor (10)	7.0
Supervision (9)	6.0	Public schools (8)	7.7	Staff (17)	5.1
Seminar (11)	4.2	Mental health institute (10)	4.2	Intern (14)	9.3
Paper work (21)	1.7	Miscellaneous (22)	2.6	Other (2)	14.0
Research (3)	11.0				
Indirect service (1)	6.0				
Training/reading (8)	6.8				
Informal (4)	11.5				
Training others (1)	1.0				
Miscellaneous (9)	4.5				

phasis on skills training and experiential process as well as formal supervision and provision of time for relevant reading. While settings are not equally utilized by all interns, a large number of settings are available predominantly in the medical center hospital complex, the Veterans Administration Hospital, and community mental health centers.

Over the years direct services, consultation, supervision, and research have remained constant while there has been an increase in training time at the expense of informal interaction. The mean affect value for interns was 4.3 (Range = 2.3-8.3), reflecting a consistent yearly increase from 3.0 (1977-1978) and 2.8 (1976-1977).

Interns have clear and different feelings regarding their activities. For example, some interns barely tolerate direct service while others find it to be positive and rewarding. A similar range of regard for other professional activities is evident, although interns share a predominantly negative affect for the indirect service of paper work.

Interns have their characteristic affect values which suggest not only relative satisfaction with the program, but may reflect their life-style emotional orientations toward experience. Activities, settings, and persons have their own affect values which suggest the consensual affective response to them by interns. The affect values reveal something of the relative desirability of activities, settings, and persons for these interns.

An Intern

The data in Table 2 can be used to describe the internship experience for one intern during 1976-1977. By comparison with other interns, he works about the same number of hours. He spends increasingly more service hours across the time periods as is typical of all interns, but he began with 32% less than the

Table 2 Summary of Time Usage, Number of Settings, and Affect for an Intern During Three Time Periods, 1976-1977

Settings	Time period			
	I	II	III	Total
Hours				
Total	45	50	48	143
Service	17	24	26	67
Training	17	14	15	46
Research	3	2	0	5
Direct/Indirect service	20/18	28/20	31/23	79/61
Primary/Secondary setting	25/18	22/28	16/32	63/78
N Different settings	9	11	8	14
Affect balance	1.87	3.80	3.00	2.76

usual mean time devoted to service. His training time conforms to that of other interns and decreases slightly over time. His research time is small and disappears with the completion of a dissertation. Typically, interns initially spend three hours in indirect service for every two hours of direct service and thereafter continue to experience a similar but declining imbalance. He consistently spends less time with indirect service than do other interns. During the last time period, he spent more time in secondary settings than did other interns, a reflection of his community interests. Whereas other interns averaged 18 settings across the time periods, he engages with a total of 28 settings, including 14 different settings.

His positive affect is high initially and peaks during the second time period. His overall affect balance was the highest of all interns for that year. An index for typicality of affect was obtained by summing the frequencies of those affect labels whose average occurrence was approximately once during each time period for each intern. His index included 9 of the 13 typical affects. He had more different affect labels (52) than any other intern and his index for individuality—the number of rare affect labels—is exceeded by one other intern.

Individuality is also expressed by the content of the positive, negative, and neutral affect labels. The intern may be described as being primarily involved in an exciting growth experience (i.e., best feeling, camaraderie, centered, closure, collegial, fluid, fun, great, happy, intrigued, in touch, movement, peaceful, quiet, resolved, and self-aware) in which he finds satisfaction and feelings of competence (i.e., accomplished, comfortable, concerned, helpful, informed, insightful, relieved, satisfied, and understood) as well as frustration and fatigue (i.e., ambivalent, anger, confusion, disinterest, dissatisfaction, drained, empty, harried, hurried, puzzled, sad, sleepy, struggling, uncertain, uneasy, unsure, and unfocused). In touch, satisfied, and comfortable occurred seven, six, and four times, respectively, suggesting a balance between sensitive awareness and complacency.

DISCUSSION

Several features of the methodology reported in this paper recommend it as a useful adjunct to traditional program evaluation procedures. In the first place, the use of intern self-observation as *the* data source explicitly recognizes the interface between person and environment. By focusing on the quality of the internship experience, the time-log methodology generates data which are complementary to the program outcome emphasis of standard methodologies.

A second important feature of this evaluation method is the provision of immediate feedback to participating interns and programs. This feedback ensures continuous communication between researchers and institution staff and guarantees a research process that is responsive to both program and staff.

In addition, immediate feedback may promote organization use of research findings by avoiding the ad hoc flavor of outcome-oriented evaluation.

A third aspect of the methodology outlined here is its economy and efficiency in data-gathering. Since the information is recorded and coded by the participants themselves in the course of their everyday activities, the time investment required of interns is negligible. Also, the data can be generated in tabular form on computer output so that the time and expense involved in organizing the data for feedback sessions are minimized.

Fourth, the research process is essentially owned by the agency rather than by outside researchers. Continuous change and refinement of the process thus comes from within the program where the usefulness of data can be readily ascertained. Agency awareness that their monitoring and evaluation of results will be incorporated provides incentive for sustained involvement. In addition, there is abundant potential for relationships based upon good will, information exchange, and mutual respect between researchers and agency staff that develops as a consequence of agency ownership.

Finally, this evaluation method is applicable to a wide variety of programs because the research process is guided by organizational and staff needs. In contrast to fixed, standardized evaluation instrument (e.g., symptom checklists), the time log approach is easily adapted to practically any type of training or service program.

The approach outlined in this paper approximates a "contingency-design" model that includes a systems analytic perspective, a theory-generating methodology, and strategies for collaboration and data utilization (Ketterer & Perkins, 1977). The systems analysis perspective emerges from the study of organization processes, particularly the relationships between internal dynamics and environmental context. The internship process is examined through the eyes of the interns and attempts to make a human distinction between individuals and environmental features, or between intern and internship by means of affect allocation.

A theory-generating methodology identifies a range of relevant variables, uses multiple methods, and comparisons of real or data-created groups. Initial major dimensions of an intern's world are isolated which are then amenable to refinement and change. The provision of activity categories from the internship's history of time and work commitments was articulated on the basis of extensive interviews with interns and staff members long before the design was formulated. While data-created group comparisons have not been accomplished as yet, the vehicle is there in affect values for subsettings that permit features of structures and occupants to be dove-tailed in an exploration of qualitative dimensions of settings.

The collaboration of outside researchers and institution staff has been an experience in continuity of relationships over a four year period that has been the strongest ingredient in the process character of the research. Information exchange has been continuous using formal as well as informal channels. The utilization of research findings has been via data feedback to interns and to the internship. Ted May (1978) has described the enduring values of the research process for the internship and for the interns. The internship now has a follow up study of interns, an ongoing committee to develop standards for a competency based evaluation, and data-based feedback of strength and weakness to administrators as well as for funding agencies and site visit teams. Interns have received some desensitization for their own self-evaluations, some data for mutual feedback in evaluation with internship staff, and some benchmarks for relating their own experience to competencies and affect states regarding a cafeteria array of service and training engagements.

REFERENCES

Amos, S. (1978, August). *Functional and dysfunctional operations in similar social services agencies: Client perspective.* Presented in the symposium on Shoestring Adventures in Program Evaluation at the meeting of the American Psychological Association, Toronto.

Barling, P. (1978, August). *From the inside looking out: Program participants evaluate program evaluation.* Presented in the symposium on Shoestring Adventures in Program Evaluation at the meeting of the American Psychological Association, Toronto.

Dana, R. H. (1978a). Comparisons of competence training in two successful clinical programs. *Psychological Reports, 42,* 919–926.

Dana, R. H. (1978b). *Shoestring adentures in program evaluation: A model, methods, data, and applications.* Fayetteville, AK: University of Arkansas. (ERIC Document Reproduction Service No. ED 167 935)

Davenport, M. P. (1978, August). *A happy interface for evaluation of counseling center in-service training.* Presented in the symposium on Shoestring Adventures in Program Evaluation at the meeting of the American Psychological Association, Toronto.

Ketterer, R. F., & Perkins, D. N. T. (1977, May). *A design for evaluating consultation and education programs in community mental health centers.* Paper presented at the meeting of the Midwestern Psychological Association, Chicago.

Leary, T. (1970). The diagnosis of behavior and the diagnosis of experience. In A. Mahrer (Ed.), *New approaches to personality classifications.* New York: Columbia University Press.

Leatherman, M. (1978, August). *Functional and dysfunctional operation of two similar social service agencies: Agency perspective.* Presented in the symposium on Shoestring Adventures in Program Evaluation at the meeting of the American Psychological Association, Toronto.

Lewin, K. (1946). Action research and minority problems. *Journal of Social Issues, 2*(4), 34–36.

Lewin, K. (1947). Frontiers in group dynamics: Part II. Social planning and action research. *Human Relations, 1,* 143–153.

May, W. T. (1978, August). *Discussion.* Presented in the symposium on Shoestring Adventures in Program Evaluation at the meeting of the American
Psychological Association., Toronto.

Reading 38
Developmental Stresses of Psychology
Internship Training:
What Training Staff Can Do to Help

Nadine J. Kaslow
Yale University School of Medicine

David G. Rice
University of Wisconsin Medical School

Although there is a wealth of information in psychology about emotional
(Mahler, Pine, & Bergman, 1975), social (Erikson, 1968), cognitive (Piaget,
1952), and moral (Kohlberg, 1969) development, only recently has attention
been paid to one's development as a professional (Hess, 1980; Lewis, 1978;
Schuster, Sandt, & Thaler, 1972). During the internship year—a major stage
in the professional life cycle of a clinical psychologist—a sequence of conflicts
typically emerges. Viewing psychology interns from a development perspective
helps the training staff to better understand the intern's experience and to
suggest ways in which the staff can respond effectively. Just as parents need
to be attuned to their children's developmental needs, supervisors, in general
(Friedman & Kaslow, in press), and internship staff members, in particular,
can offer more meaningful relationships when they are aware of their interns'
professional and personal stages of development.

Erikson (1968), in detailing the stages of the life cycle, described adolescence as the time in the individual's life when the crisis of identity is central.
For many psychologists, graduate school represents the prolongation of their
personal adolescence, and the internship year often is perceived as a transition
period from professional adolescence to professional adulthood. One's internship, as with other facets of one's adolescence, is often accompanied by feelings
of "sturm und drung" (Hall, 1905), It is perhaps surprising that the internship
year, typically only one fifth of a graduate student's training, holds such
significance for the intern. For example, applying for an internship is viewed
as such a time of stress that the "Survival Guide for Intern Applicants (Belar

Reprinted from Professional Psychology: Research and Practice, *16*(2), 253-261.
We would like to thank *Sari Gilman,* who provided helpful comments with regard to the
manuscript.

& Orgel, 1980) has been written. Just as adolescence encompasses that transition from childhood to adulthood, the internship year, for many, is a time of transition from being a student to being a professional. Interns are still in training, yet on most internships they have a good deal of professional responsibility. "Am I just a student or am I a competent professional who can function independently?" is a question interns frequently struggle with. Developmentally, adolescence is also a time when there are so many different demands that the adolescent feels torn in a variety of directions and feels overwhelmed. Similarly, the internship year is often like a juggling act in which the balls to be juggled include internship responsibilities, one's dissertation, looking for jobs, and one's personal life. It is like having three or four time-consuming jobs and getting paid very little for them (Solway, 1985).

INTERN DEVELOPMENTAL PHASES

Much individual development and change occurs during adolescence. One model that may be useful in providing a framework for conceptualizing the developmental phases through which interns pass is that proposed by Mahler and her colleagues (Mahler et al., 1975). They detail the phases of development through which individuals progress as they mature. One is faced with the issues connected to each of these stages during many periods of one's life. The internship year is no exception. Just as infants passing through the stages of development need different things from their parents, interns, as they pass through the major stages of separation-individuation, need different things from their internship training staff. The following section discusses the psychology intern as he or she progresses through the separation-individuation process, the tasks of each stage, what interns may need from the internship staff, and some suggestions for what the staff can do to facilitate healthy separation and individuation. The present authors view this model as the appropriate model for internship training, although they realize that there are limitations of a developmental stage model (e.g., Emmerich, 1964) and that other theories, such as behavioral theory (Skinner, 1953), trait theory (e.g., Allport, 1961; Cattell, 1965; Eysenck, 1967), and phenomenological theory (e.g., Kelly, 1955; Rogers, 1951), can also explain adaptation to stress and change in one's life.

DEVELOPMENTAL ISSUES EARLY IN THE INTERNSHIP YEAR

At the beginning of the internship year interns are not so regressed that they actually "fuse" with their intern director or other staff members, as in the case in early child development vis-à-vis a parent. However, for many trainees, the beginning of the internship year is extremely stressful, and most interns are still in the process of developing a sense of themselves professionally; thus they may depend on training staff feedback for developing their personal and professional identities (Yogev, 1982).

There are a number of factors that contribute to making the initial period of the internship difficult. First, the internship application and selection process can be such a difficult experience (Barnes, 1982; Belar & Orgel, 1980; Burstein, Schoenfeld, Loucks, Stedman, & Costello, 1981; Craddick, Cole, Dane, Brill, & Wilson, 1980; Foster, 1976; Petzel & Berndt, 1980; Stedman, Costello, Gaines, Schoenfeld, Loucks, & Burstein, 1981; Tedesco, 1979) that new interns may anticipate the whole internship experience to be problematic. A bond may begin to form between the newly accepted intern and the training staff on internship selection day, because both sides survived the stress and realize they will spend the next year together. This may be the start of positive bonding if each party truly wanted the other. Or the bond may be tenuous, particularly if there has been minimal interaction between the intern and the agency. Finally, the bond may be somewhat negative if the match was a disappointing accommodation on the part of one or both participants.

A large percentage of interns relocate to attend their internship, and this can be stressful. These individuals usually are leaving behind a support system that can include family, friends, trusted graduate school faculty and practica supervisors, patients, and often a therapist (Wachowiak, Bauer, & Simono, 1979). After pulling up their roots in the location where, typically, they have lived for at least 4 years, it is difficult to adjust to a new environment (Goplerud, 1980). Most people have difficulties with terminations and endings and often feel lost and lonely upon leaving (Lamb, Baker, Jennings, & Yarris, 1982).

During the initial weeks of the internship, interns are likely to feel some confusion about what they should do. This concern often takes the form of "Which form do I fill out, when, and how do I fill it out correctly?" One intern labeled his response as a defensive one at this point, because he was obsessed with particulars in an attempt to contain more diffuse anxiety. In addition, many beginning interns feel apprehensive about their ability to handle clinical responsibilities. Most interns have never seen so many patients (or is it clients?) before, and in all likelihood they have never done some of the clinical activities required of them (Shemberg & Leventhal, 1981). Typical areas that frighten, confuse, or overwhelm interns are working with children, families, groups, and inpatients; having supervision with a supervisor watching (Loewenstein, Reder, & Clark, 1982); and doing psychodynamic psychotherapy and psychodiagnostic assessment (Shemberg & Keely, 1974).

Many interns have had a well-established position in their graduate school programs. People knew them and respected them. Once they come to their internship program, they have to prove themselves all over again and in a short period of time. Interns are aware of being formally and/or informally evaluated from early on. For most individuals this is an added stress (Cohen,

1980; Glenwick & Stevens, 1980). It is particularly difficult to be evaluated at a time when one feels so vulnerable. Add to these changes any political strains at the internship, personality conflicts with fellow interns or internship training staff, dissatisfactions with the internship program, as well as one's personal issues, and it is no wonder that many new interns feel anxious and depressed (Goplerud, 1980). Lamb and his colleagues (1982), in discussing the passages of an internship in professional psychology, refer to this initial period as the "early intern syndrome."

How can internship faculty members be helpful during this period? Winnicott's (1965) notion of a "holding environment" seems applicable. A good "hold" is one in which there is a nurturant and warm environment, with appropriate limits set. This fosters the development of trusting relationships and a sense of safety, security, respect, and acceptance for the individual. The following are some suggestions of ways internship staff members can be "good-enough" professional "parents" (Winnicott, 1965) for the interns. Depending on the internship program, different approaches may be more practical, effective, or consistent with the milieu. The staff can be aware of and sensitive to the various professional and personal stresses the intern faces and can make themselves available to provide support for the intern. It is important to be neither neglectful nor overly intrusive. Although interns may be struggling with some early developmental issues, they are not children and usually can handle much of their anxiety on their own. However, it is often helpful to have orientation meetings, information packets, get-togethers, and small-group familiarization meetings. During this "sizing-up" period (Lamb et al., 1982), the faculty can give information about the program, answer questions, and validate perceptions.

In many families, younger children turn to their older siblings for support and guidance. This is the case in graduate school as first- and second-year students frequently ask upper-level students for advice and support. This is more difficult on the internship because it is typically a 1-year program, and often the last group of interns has left or is leaving when the new interns arrive. Whenever possible, a get-together with old and new interns can be helpful. A few programs have a system in which current and future interns correspond prior to the new group beginning their internship. Such peer support has been shown to be critical in the development of professionals (Heiss, 1970).

Often the intern's skills are assessed in the early part of the year. Although this appears in many ways to be the logical time for such an evaluation, many new interns feel anxiety over the need to appear competent in the eyes of their supervisors (Cohen & DeBetz, 1977), may be reluctant to self-disclose about their own ignorance (Arbuckle, 1963), and may have difficulties performing their best at this time. For example, the last intake one did in graduate school is often clinically better than the first intake one does during the internship. Staff members need to give trainees a few weeks to get adjusted before a formal assessment of their skills is made. Throughout the year, constructive feedback from supervisors to interns and from interns to supervisors is important. Evaluations can be done sensitively so that the process does not become another major stress of the internship year.

One sentiment expressed frequently by interns is that they feel so busy and inundated with new information and experiences that they do not have the time to integrate what they are learning. This confusion results in a further professional identity crisis and the intern may be plagued by such questions as "Who should supervise me?", "How can I learn the most?", and "What is my theoretical orientation?"

To summarize, during the initial period, interns feel insecure and generally want supportive "parenting" and caretaking during this time. In addition, early in the year interns tend to want more specific information and guidance (Gybers & Johnston, 1965). The training staff can be most helpful if they are available for the interns but not overly involved or protective. Internships have been rated more favorably by interns who feel that their internships provide a great deal of support (Cole, Kolko, & Craddick, 1981).

DEVELOPMENTAL ISSUES DURING THE MIDPHASE
OF THE INTERNSHIP

After the infant passes through the first phases of development, which are labeled *autistic* and *symbiotic* by Mahler, the separation-individuation process begins and includes differentiation, practicing, and rapprochement subphases (Mahler, 1958). During a comparable period of the internship, the trainee begins to grow away from his or her dependence on the training staff. Interns' attention is focused in a more outward direction, with frequent "check-backs" with the staff as a point of orientation. During this time, a better sense of self as a semi-autonomous professional is developing, along with a greater sense of one's own identity within the internship setting. As the trainee increasingly becomes aware of separateness from the training staff, he or she often wishes to share new experiences with the staff and feel support in return. More collegial staff-trainee relationships are desired. In addition, it is not uncommon for interns to express wishes to choose certain rotations rather than to just do what is required. The above changes usually occur in each intern throughout the course of the internship but may also occur in a condensed fashion during different rotations.

What are the issues and conflicts for psychology interns during these subphases of separation and individuation, or what Lamb et al. (1982) refer to as the "intern identity stage?" Although most interns try to appear as competent as possible early on in their internships, they often feel a lot of self-doubt about themselves as professionals. It is not uncommon for interns to question their basic professional identity as clinical psychology trainees (Lamb et al., 1982).

After all, most interns were trained in an academic psychology department that emphasized some version of the scientist-practitioner model. Although most intern directors are committed to this model (Shemberg & Leventhal, 1981), the model rarely prevails in internship settings. Rather, psychology interns often feel some pressure to leave academic psychology behind and become full-time clinicians. They typically wonder about their unique contribution as psychologists among other mental health professionals. Is there anything that separates them as clinicians from nonpsychologists aside from doing psychodiagnostic assessments? Such identity issues are particularly accentuated in that doing psychological testing is one of the internship chores that is most often complained about. Trainees report that they would like less time to be devoted to psychodiagnostic assessment (Steinhelber & Gaynor, 1981). In medical settings, psychology interns often feel "one-down" to the psychiatry residents, who may have less psychological knowledge but more perceived power, prestige, and higher stipends. The bureaucratic and political disputes between psychology and psychiatry have been found to affect interns negatively, and the training staff needs to help with the effective management of these concerns (Cole et al., 1981). On the other hand, psychologists trained with psychiatry residents, in a setting where the relationships between the two disciplines are basically good, can learn a great deal from the psychiatry trainees and vice versa (Sternbach, Abroms, & Rice, 1969).

On the whole, most people appear to enjoy their internship (Cole et al., 1981) and feel like they learn a tremendous amount. The opportunities to experiment with new ways of doing psychotherapy, to work with a diversity of patient groups, and to learn from stimulating supervisors and teachers is exciting for most interns. Many trainees really enjoy their clinical work and want to develop into more competent and well-rounded clinicians. Initially, they may want a lot of didactic supervision. As the year proceeds, the intern may feel he or she would like a different kind of supervision, more collaborative and fostering a greater degree of supervisee autonomy and independence, which the training staff may or may not be willing to grant. As the intern progresses through the year, he or she feels more able to accurately assess personal strengths and weaknesses and may become less dependent on the training staff feedback.

There are a number of ways staff members can facilitate healthy trainee development during the separation phase of the internship. If the interns feel from the start that they are in a secure environment and can trust the training staff, they will be better able to venture into the agency and will be likely to adjust more easily. As the interns become more involved in their work, the staff needs to emphasize, in words and behavior, their continued emotional availability. Staff members can help each intern feel successful in the program through the acknowledgment of the intern's unique identity and by facilitating the development of more individualized programs. Staff members need to receive information about each intern's background and training, his or her strengths and weaknesses, what the intern wants from the internship, and his or her career goals.

As the staff gets to know each individual better, they can help the intern better juggle his or her various responsibilities. The process can be emotionally draining and time-consuming for both staff and intern, not only because of all the work involved by also because each of these tasks is likely to require the trainee to be in a different stage of development. In addition, the staff, by serving as role models, can help interns integrate academic psychology and clinical work, enabling the intern to feel a more complete identity as a scientist/ professional psychologist. Support, understanding, and guidance offered from internship staff members is immensely appreciated and much needed during this period.

When an intern encounters major personal or professional stress beyond what is typical, his or her development as an intern may be greatly altered. In this regard, a staff member may initiate discussion or be asked by the intern to discuss issues regarding the need for personal psychotherapy (Kaslow & Friedman, 1984). Such matters often require a careful balancing of mutual trust and professional judgment. Attending to such needs sensitively and providing help with arranging a good therapist-intern match can be much appreciated by the intern at such stressful times. It is important that the individuals who seek pesonal therapy during the internship year not be stigmatized by the training staff members or other interns.

THE INDIVIDUATION PHASE

There are two main tasks to be accomplished in individuation, the fourth phase of the separation-individuation process: (a) the achievement of one's own individuality, and (b) the attainment of a certain amount of object constancy. During this period, interns emerge as professionals and begin to function more independently. Within the internship settings, trainees often begin to take more leading roles, to intervene more actively and directly with their patients, and to challenge and disagree with their supervisors (Lamb et al., 1982). Trainees develop more collegial relationships with the training staff. This may take the form of doing co-therapy with faculty members, occasionally asking for consultation rather than supervision, and being more self-disclosing vis-à-vis countertransference issues.

The individuation phase is the time when many interns begin to make plans for the following year. This can be a time of turmoil and confusion as one questions what to do professionally. Some interns avoid this identity crisis, at least for awhile, by returning to their graduate departments to complete a dissertation. Others may prolong their professional "adolescence" by doing a postdoctoral fellowship or pursuing some nonprofessional interests such as traveling. The third group of interns venture out into the job market.

There are some specific ways in which the staff can be helpful to trainees at this point. They can encourage interns to take more initiative, reinforce them for becoming involved in the overall activities of the training center, and be willing to develop more collegial working relationships. Further, the training facility could have a file of postdoctoral fellowships and job listings for the upcoming year, with both faculty and interns contributing information. A systematic form of communication about such opportunities could greatly facilitate interns in settling their immediate professional futures. In addition, the training staff as professional role models may be different from graduate school faculty. Greater familiarity with the range of professional possibilities in psychology is frequently appreciated by interns.

As with so many other life experiences, the intern's individuation process is cut short. So soon after becoming acclimated and, hopefully, cathected to the internship program, he or she needs to think about leaving and the termination of clinical contacts. Discussion about the termination process in psychotherapy can be quite valuable at this point. Mishandling of this stage of the process can be traumatic for the patient and the therapist. Of course, interns also have to say farewell to fellow interns and the training staff. There is a general consensus that a farewell dinner and/or party is a meaningful and needed occasion. Some programs also find that a group retreat to discuss the year can be beneficial.

The consensus that has emerged from interviews with psychology trainees is that they want their internship to provide them with a good general program in which they see a diverse range of pathology, learn a variety of therapeutic techniques, and get good supervision (Cole et al., 1981; Steinhelber & Gaynor, 1981). Most interns prefer a flexible program that can be tailored to their individual needs. Although initially interns may wish to develop a nurturing, supportive bond with their training staff, as the year progresses, they are likely to want more autonomy and opportunities to establish their own personal and professional identity. As interns develop a more positive, stable view of themselves, they usually wish to develop more collegial relationships and/or friendships with the training staff.

REFERENCES

Allport, G. W. (1961). *Pattern and growth in personality*. New York: Holt, Rinehart & Winston.

Arbuckel, D. S. (1963). The learning of counseling: Process not product. *Journal of Counseling Psychology, 10*, 163–168.

Barnes, B. (1982). Do intern applicants really need a survival guide? *Professional Psychology, 13*, 342–344.

Belar, C. E., & Orgel, S. A. (1980). Survival guide for intern applicants. *Professional Psychology, 11*, 672–675.

Burstein, A. G., Schoenfeld, L. S., Loucks, S., Stedman, J. M., & Costello, R. M.

(1981). Selection of internship site: Basis of choice by desirable candidates. *Professional Psychology, 12,* 596–598.

Cattell, R. B. (1965). *The scientific analysis of personality.* Baltimore, MD: Penguin Books.

Cohen, L. (1980). The new supervisor views supervision. In K. A. Hess (Ed.), *Psychotherapy supervision: Theory, practice and research* (pp. 78–84). New York: Wiley-Interscience.

Cohen, R. J., & DeBetz, R. (1977). Responsive supervision of the psychiatric resident and clinical psychology intern. *American Journal of Psychoanalysis, 37,* 51–64.

Cole, M. A., Kolko, D. G., & Craddick, R. A. (1981). The quality and process of the internship experience. *Professional Psychology, 12,* 570–577.

Craddick, R. A., Cole, M. A., Dane, J., Brill, R., & Wilson, J. A. (1980). The process of selecting predoctoral internship training sites. *Professional Psychology, 11,* 548–549.

Emmerich, W. (1964). Continuity and stability in early social development. *Child Development, 35,* 311–332.

Erikson, E. H. (1968). *Identity: Youth and crisis.* New York: Norton.

Eysenck, H. J. (1967). *The biological basis of personality.* Springfield, IL: Charles C Thomas.

Foster, L. M. (1976). Truth in advertising psychology internship programs. *Professional Psychology, 7,* 120–124.

Friedman, D., & Kaslow, N. (in press). The development of professional identity in psychotherapists. In F. W. Kaslow (Ed.), *Supervision.* New York: Haworth Press.

Glenwick, S. D., & Stevens, E. (1980). Vertical supervision: In K. A. Hess (Ed.), *Psychotherapy supervision: Theory, research and practice* (pp. 226–241). New York: Wiley-Interscience.

Goplerud, E. N. (1980). Social support and stress during the first year of graduate school. *Professional Psychology, 11,* 283–290.

Gybers, N. G., & Johnston, J. (1965). Expectations of a practicum supervisor's role. *Counselor Education and Supervision, 4,* 68–74.

Hall, G. S. (1905). *Adolescence.* New York: Appleton.

Heiss, A. M. (1970). *Challenges to graduate schools.* San Francisco, CA: Jossey-Bass.

Hess, A. K. (1980). *Psychotherapy supervision: Theory, practice and research.* New York: Wiley-Interscience.

Kaslow, N. J., & Friedman, D. (1984). Interface of personal treatment and clinical training for psychotherapist trainees. In F. W. Kaslow (Ed.), *Psychotherapy for psychotherapists* (pp. 33–57). New York: Haworth Press.

Kelly, G. A. (1955). *The psychology of personal constructs* (Vols. 1 and 2). New York: Norton.

Kohlberg, L. (1969). *Stages in the development of moral thought and action.* New York: Holt.

Lamb, D. H., Baker, J. M., Jennings, M. L., & Yarris, E. (1982). Passages of an internship in professional psychology. *Professional Psychology, 13,* 661–669.

Levinson, D. (1974). *The psychological development of men in early adulthood and the mid-life transition.* Minneapolis: University of Minnesota Press.

Lewis, J. M. (1978). *To be a therapist: The reaching and learning.* New York: Brunner/Mazel.

Loewenstein, S. F., Reder, P., & Clark, A. (1982). The consumer's response: Trainees discussion of the experience of live supervision. In R. Whiffen & J. Byng-Hall (Eds.), *Family therapy supervision: Recent developments in practice* (pp. 115–129). New York: Grune & Stratton.

Mahler, M. (1958). On two crucial phases of integration of the sense of identity: Separation-individuation and bisexual identity. *Journal of the American Psychoanalytic Association, 6,* 136–139.

Mahler, M., Pine, F., & Bergman, A. (1975). *The psychological birth of the human infant.* New York: Basic Books.

Petzel, T. P., & Berndt, D. J. (1980). APA internship selection criteria: Relative importance and clinical preparation. *Professional Psychology, 11,* 792–796.

Piaget, J. (1952). *The origins of intelligence in children.* New York: International Universities Press.

Rogers, C. R. (1951). *Client-centered therapy: Its current practice, implications and theory.* Boston: Houghton Mifflin.

Schuster, D. B., Sandt, J. J., & Thaler, O. F. (1972). *Clinical supervision of the psychiatric resident.* New York: Brunner/Mazel.

Shemberg, K. M., & Keeley, S. M. (1974). Training practice and satisfaction with preinternship preparation. *Professional Psychology, 5,* 98–105.

Shemberg, K. M., & Leventhal, D. B. (1981). Attitudes of internship directors toward preinternship training and clinical training models. *Professional Psychology, 12,* 639–646.

Skinner, B. F. (1953). *Science and human behavior.* New York: MacMillan.

Solway, K. (1985). Transition from graduate school to internship: A potential crisis. *Professional Psychology, 16,* 50–54.

Stedman, J. M., Costello, R. M., Gaines, T., Schoenfeld, L. S., Loucks, S., & Burstein, A. G. (1981). How clinical psychology interns are selected. A study of decision-making processes. *Professional Psychology, 12,* 415–419.

Steinhelber, J., & Gaynor, J. (1981). Attitudes, satisfaction, and training recommendations for former clinical psychology interns: 1968 and 1977. *Professional Psychology, 12,* 253–260.

Sternbach, R. A., Abroms, G. M., & Rice, D. G. (1969). Clinical responsibility and the psychologist. *Psychiatry, 32,* 165–173.

Tedesco, J. F. (1979). Factors involved in the selection of doctoral internships in clinical psychology. *Professional Psychology, 10,* 852–858.

Wachowiak, D., Bauer, G., & Simono, R. (1979). Passages: Career ladders for college counseling center psychologists. *Professional Psychology, 10,* 723–731.

Winnicott, D. (1958). *Collected papers: Through pediatrics to psychoanalysis.* London: Tavistock.

Winnicott, D. W. (1965). *The maturational processes and the facilitating environment.* New York: International Universities Press.

Yogev, S. (1982). An electric model of supervision: A development sequence for beginning psychotherapy students. *Professional Psychology*, *13*, 236–243.

Reading 39
Transition From Graduate School to Internship: A Potential Crisis

Kenneth S. Solway
Texas Research Institute of Mental Sciences, Houston; Baylor College of Medicine; and University of Houston

According to traditional theory, an emotional crisis is viewed as a disruption in habitual modes of adjustment manifested by cognitive uncertainty, psychosomatic symptoms, and emotional distress (Hirschowitz, 1973). A crisis occurs when usual ways of coping are ineffective in an emotionally hazardous situation (Caplan, 1964). Caplan defined an emotionally hazardous situation as one that arises when a shift or change in an individual's psychosocial environment alters relationships with others or expectations of the self in ways perceived to be negative. However, it seems clear that the shift or change can be perceived or at least anticipated to be positive and can still lead to a crisis. This is often the case with events such as childbirth, marriage, and job promotion. And such is frequently the case for many graduate students when they make the transition from graduate school to their clinical internships.

It is the thesis of this article that the transition between graduate school and professional internship leads to interpersonal and professional changes that are emotionally hazardous. Moreover, the upheavals of the period have not been fully articulated or addressed. The psychology training literature is largely concerned with content and structure; the process of professional and academic training is rarely discussed. Only recently has anyone conceptualized and written about the internshp in terms of the now otherwise popular construct of "passages" (Lamb, Baker, Jennings, & Yarris, 1982) or the equally popular "developmental framework" (Silver, 1982). The remainder of this article, then, deals with the specific stresses associated with the transition between graduate school and professional internship, and I discuss some important implications and recommendations that derive from these stresses.

Reprinted from Professional Psychology: Research and Practice, *16*(1), 50–54. I would like to thank *Randy E. Phelps* who helped significantly in the development of this article, as did scores of former TRIMS interns.

CLINICAL (SUPERVISION) STRESSES

The clearest source of tension experienced by a new intern comes from having to adopt the role of the professional, which is in sharp contrast to the previous university-based role of being an academician and student (Gold, Meltzer, & Sherr, 1982; Shows, 1976). Interns are supervised with considerable intensity; their developing clinical skills are exposed and scrutinized. Often interns are assigned to or choose 6 to 10 supervisors who vary in their clinical-theoretical approach as well as in their styles of supervision. Much like university researchers who sometimes compete for graduate students who will conduct their research, clinical supervisors may compete to recruit interns who will adopt their theoretical and clinical models. This is often reflected in rigid boundaries set by rotation supervisors and by the tension created when an intern wants to spend an hour or two a week outside the assigned rotation.

Most interns enter their internships with a positive and healthy image of themselves as clinicians based on 3 years of work with university- or community-based clinics. When they leave their parent university, they are often at the top of their class, and in many cases they are the most sophisticated student-clinicians around and the expressed source of great pride for their mentors and teachers. If the internship takes place in a setting away from their original school, interns will experience a need to prove themselves again in a new context (i.e., an internship setting). Here they are often perceived as being unseasoned and relatively unskilled (Rosencrantz & Holmes, 1974). Thus new interns are less confident and more sensitive about their skills, and they experience this at a time when supervisors are undergoing their own transition. The supervisors have lost the gratitude and praise bestowed on them by last year's interns, which culminated, perhaps, at an intern banquet or similar function, and they must demonstrate their expertise to a fresh group of trainees. New interns are subjected therein to still another possible source of tension, namely, having to deal with the needs of supervisors who are adjusting to their own losses. One way supervisors may express their grief is by attempting to impress interns with clinical wisdom while overlooking new interns' skills and their needs for support.

Some other sources of anxiety inherent in the clinical activities of an intern include learning new psychotherapy and psychodiagnostic techniques, using different clinical skills consecutively during a work day, regularly confronting forensic and psychopharmacological issues, responding to different supervisors and different styles of supervision (e.g., audiotapes, videotapes, 'bug' in the ear), choosing internship tracks or electives, sensing and coping with competitiveness from other interns and trainees (e.g., psychiatric residents), and, finally, integrating the conflicting needs to develop professional autonomy while accepting the status of being a trainee and supervisee.

INSTITUTIONAL STRESSES

This section emphasizes the problems encountered by interns in relation to the context or background in which training occurs. The transition from university to clinical setting is a challenge when one considers the types of colleagues encountered, the goals of the organizations, and the sources of authority within each institution. The relatively unambiguous student and consumer role is replaced by the relatively unclear status of being a service-provider and professional. Interns must learn a great deal about the day-to-day red tape and administrative responsibilities encountered in service-delivery settings: What are appropriate intake procedures, what kinds of treatment are offered by the institution, how do progress notes and psychological reports get typed, how do various disciplines relate to one another, who are key managers? Less important, but still nagging, issues—such as the availability of office space (or the lack of it), medical and professional insurance, parking, office supplies, and other matters—emerge as one begins work in a new setting. In general, the atmosphere created by an organization devoted to providing service and concerned with cost-effectiveness is quite different from the atmosphere in an institution committed to learning and research.

PERSONAL STRESSES

Before we can find a new something we must deal with a time of nothing. And that prospect awakens old fears and all the old fantasies about death and abandonment. (Bridges, 1980, p. 104)

Personal stresses involve geographical, social, and psychological factors only indirectly associated with the internship, but which are associated with leaving the university setting for the internship site. Indeed, personal stresses often prove to be the most important contributors to how interns adjust to their new settings. It is questionable whether all students expect and prepare for the separation and loss. Usually, graduate students are emersed in completing graduate school course work or dissertation requirements before leaving for their internships, at which point they immediately begin their new work (which most likely entails 50-60 hr weeks). Although many graduate students may have moments of concern or awareness of impending losses, little time is available for the necessary grieving and reintegration process. Also, this transition is perceived to be a personal/professional milestone about which one should be pleased. It is only in the course or action of transition that the mourning is fully experienced. The deceptiveness, and the surprise of these feelings, serves to create and intensify the personal upheaval.

Specific personal stressors include moving to a new and frequently larger city, developing new social networks, changing one's residence, and of course, earning little money. Each of these realities in itself presents its own set of challenges, such as learning the geography of a new environment, developing new friendships, adapting to a new apartment and possibly to roommates, finding inexpensive service providers (e.g., doctors, lawyers, banks), and so on. The intensity of these psychosocial stressors is moderate to severe (4 to 5) when rated on Axis IV as found in the *Diagnostic and Statistical Manual of Mental Disorders,* 3rd ed. (EDM-III; Webb, DiClemente, Johnstone, Sanders, & Perley, 1981).

IMPLICATIONS AND RECOMMENDATIONS

If one accepts the premise that beginning interns experience significant, albeit, variable stress, one must wonder about its effect on their clinical performance. The belief that an intern's clinical work early in the internship year can be used as a base to measure future performance is questionable. One might speculate that interns will have functioned with greater efficiency and resource-fulness while completing their final graduate school practicums than they do early in an internship year. It may be that an intern will only begin to function at full potential during the third or fourth month of the internship or after the first intern evaluation, if feedback is positive and accepting. Although some degree of anxiety is thought to be important for learning, the excesses that can be generated by the transition should make supervisors wary of determining an intern's base rate of development early in the internship year (R. Phelps, personal communication, September 10, 1982).

The idea that interns should be put to work as quickly as possible with little or no orientation is questionable. The opportunity to "break bread" with other interns and faculty in a relatively relaxed atmosphere and to learn about the settings in which work will be done can provide some assistance to the intern in transition. In the process of adapting to new work environments, most employers will allow new employees a reasonable adjustment period. Because supervisors are aware of the abbreviated nature of the internship, they have often felt compelled to get interns busy too quickly.

Directors of clinical graduate programs can assist greatly in providing outgoing students with information regarding the tribulations of transition to internship. This can be accomplished in one or two group meetings during which personal and professional issues are discussed and at which time students can be sensitized to pertinent issues. A more radical suggestion would be for graduate programs to require prospective interns to enroll in a course or participate in forums in which such topics as psychopharmacology, forensics, supervision, the professional standards of the Joint Commission on the Accreditation of Hospitals and of the American Psychological Association, and consultation with members of other disciplines can be explored in some detail.

An annual social function to say goodbye to exiting students may be a useful ritual and may remind students of their impending losses.

Internship centers also might consider various means of assisting incoming interns. In this respect, different centers evolve different strategies depending on internship structure and institutional background. The use of faculty advisors, growth groups, carefully planned orientations and city and internship information packets comes to mind readily. Incoming interns also profit from spending a significant amount of time with outgoing interns. The latter students typically provide the most useful and objective information of anyone, particularly as this information pertains to the availability of extracurricular activities on a limited budget. Clinical supervisors must, for sure, consider the unique and combined stresses of each new intern in supervision. The intensity and kind of countertransference issues will, in part, be dictated by the personal experiences of the intern in transition. It has not been uncommon in my experience to encounter an intern undergoing a delayed grief reaction after the initial excitement of beginning the internship has passed. Internship directors also may observe an inordinate amount of physical illness in interns early in the internship year.

It is not the purpose of this article to alleviate anxieties or grief that interns may experience but, rather, to allay them. For the prospective clinician, the transition from graduate school to a professional internship is, in the vernacular, part of living. I hope, however, that this article demonstrates that this transition is uniquely stressful and that perhaps this stress has not been adequately recognized. Awareness of the factors involved may itself foster productive actions by all concerned. Finally, it is my hope that this article will stimulate reflection and writing that concerns the process of training, for this seems to be a largely neglected area of study.

REFERENCES

Bridges, W. (1980). *Transitions*. Reading, MA: Addison-Wesley.

Caplan, G. (1964). *Principles of preventive psychiatry*. New York: Basic Books.

Gold, J. R., Meltzer, B. H., & Sherr, R. L. (1982). Professional transition: Psychology internships in rehabilitation settings. *Professional Psychology, 13*, 397–403.

Hirschowitz, R. G. (1973). Crisis theory: A formulation. *Psychiatric Annals, 12*, 36–47.

Lamb, D. H., Baker, J. M., Jennings, M. L., & Yarris, E. (1982). Passages of an internship in professional psychology. *Professional Psychology, 13*, 661–669.

Rosencrantz, A. L., & Holmes, G. R. (1974). A pilot of clinical internship training in the William S. Hall Psychiatric Institute. *Southern Journal of Clinical Psychology, 30*, 417–419.

Shows, W. D. (1976). Problems of training psychology interns in medical schools: A case of trying to change the leopard's spots. *Professional Psychology, 7,* 205–208.

Silver, R. (1982). *The internship as a developmental process.* Paper presented at the meeting of the Texas Psychological Association, Dallas.

Webb, L. J., DiClemente, C. C., Johnstone, E. E., Sanders, J. L., & Perley, R. A. (1981). *DSM-III Training Guide.* New York: Bruner/Mazel.

Reading 40

The Quality And Process of the Internship Experience

Michael A. Cole, David J. Kolko, and Ray A. Craddick
Georgia State University.

Investigations into the internship process have typically surveyed internship directors (Dana, Gilliam, & Dana, 1976; Spitzform & Hamilton, 1976; Sturgis, Verategen, Randolph, & Garvin, 1980), whereas very little recent research has focused on the opinions of the consumer—the intern (Khol, Mately, & Turner, 1972). This state of affairs is analogous to conducting clinical research on psychotherapy and assessing only the concerns of the therapist. Furthermore, a growing problem described by some as a "dearth of communication and cooperative endeavor between academic settings and real-world internships," reflects the lack of awareness most interns and academic psychologists have pertaining to the internship process (Dana et al., 1976, p. 116).

In a recent article, Craddick, Cole, Dane, Brill, and Wilson (1980) described a rationale and set of procedures for selecting sites for predoctoral clinical internships. One component of this sytem was the establishment of an annual survey of interns through the use of a deliberately open-ended questionnaire, which was developed to fulfill a number of objectives.

First, the results of the questionnaire would provide pertinent, factual information for students embarking on internships. For example, information was obtained on the favored selection of rotations as well as the most important factors contributing to the former intern's acceptance. Second, the survey would establish a forum for the former and current interns to voice opinions and ideas regarding relevant internship experiences and issues. As such, the intern's opinions were solicited on issues such as the relationship between psychiatrists and psychologists, unmet expectations, emotional climate, and overall advantages and disadvantages. Third, the findings provided a data source to evaluate the intern's actual activities and opportunities as compared to those advertised

Reprinted from Professional Psychology, *12*(5), 570–577.

in the internship's brochure. As Foster (1976) highlighted in her report on the truth-in-advertising internship programs, there is a need for data regarding the often-encountered misrepresentation of internships in their publications. Finally, to provide a unique and valuable source of data for the evaluation of the university's (Georgia State University) courses, practica, and supervision, additional information was gathered from past interns on those aspects of their clinical/academic program that best and least prepared them for internship and clinical practice. As indicated by Shemberg and Keeley (1974) and Sturgis et al. (1980), preinternship training is often deficient in providing students with the necessary assessment, diagnostic, and treatment skills.

METHOD

Fourteen open-ended questions and four 5-point Likert-type items, assessing the quality of various aspects of the internship, constituted the questionnaire. The questionnaire was mailed with a return envelope and a cover letter, which specified its purpose and proposed utilization. The survey was mailed to 79 former interns, who at the time of this inquiry were all in clinical practice, and 12 current interns who had been at their settings for at least 9 months. (All had done their graduate work at Georgia State University.) Follow-up letters were sent to individuals who did not respond within 60 days to the initial inquiry. Ninety-one questionnaires were sent to present and past interns of the clinical program. Sixty inventories (66%) were returned and used in the analysis.

RESULTS

Internship Site Characteristics

The respondents who were surveyed completed their internships between the years 1969–1979, with a skewed distribution toward the later years. Thirty-five internship sites across 15 sites were described. The majority of the sample (53%) attended sites in Georgia. Interns chose cities that were evenly distributed across the country, the majority of which were American Psychological Association (APA) approved (81%). However, none of the internship sites in Georgia were APA approved.

Each intern identified the primary theoretical orientation of the internship site. The majority of the sample attended eclectic (57.3%) or humanistic (27.7%) sites. The remaining 15% attended sites with the following orientations: behavioral (6.6%), psychoanalytic (3.3%), family (1.7%), or other (3.4%).

The total number of interns reported at each internship site ranged from 0–29, with an average of 6. Annual salaries ranged from zero to $16,000, with a mean salary of $7,049. Interestingly, however, there was a significant trend indicating that the average salary has declined across the previous decade ($r = -.23$,

$p < .03$). However, this trend reflects the recent increase in the number of interns accepting positions in programs that offer no stipend.

Interns reported considerable range in the number of different rotations offered at the sites. The average number of rotations was three. Sites varied to a lesser extent in the number of their special populations. Most provided experience with psychiatric inpatients, adult outpatients, and college students. Rotations were also reported in clinical-neuropsychological, psychosomatic, and child-community specialties.

A breakdown of the interns' average weekly work activities is shown in Table 1. As indicated in the table, the interns spent the greatest proportion of their hours in individual therapy (26.6). Diagnostic evaluation was the second most time-consuming activity (14.5). In addition, the interns reported spending an equivalent amount of time (12.8) in miscellaneous activities such as meetings, staffings, seminars, and intakes. The figures in Table 1 are based on the total sample; since many interns did not engage in some activities, the figures may be deflated as a result. For example, family therapy was engaged in on an average of 7.4 hours per week by the nine interns who reported practicing family therapy.

Advantages/Disadvantages of Internship Sites

Forty-three percent of the sample indicated that the major advantage of their site was the diverse range of pathology. The variety of learning and training experiences offered by the setting was considered an important advantage by 36.7% of the sample. Adequate supervision and a flexible working arrangement were also listed by the sample as advantageous (26.0% and 23.6%, respectively).

Table 1 Intern Time Expenditure: Mean Hours and Percentage of Time per Activity

Daily activity	M hr/wk	% of time	% of sample engaging in activity
Therapy (individual)	10.1	26.6	98
Diagnostic evaluations	5.5	14.5	87
Miscellaneous duties	4.8	12.8	65
Therapy (group)	3.8	10.1	88
Supervision	3.5	9.3	95
Psychological testing	3.4	9.0	80
Research	2.7	7.2	43
Administrative duties	1.6	4.4	50
Progress notes	1.3	3.4	38
Family therapy	1.1	3.0	15

Note. Number of respondents = 60.

The major deficit indicated was poor quality and inadequate quantity of supervision. Narrowness of both training scope and patient population was also considered a disadvantage. Interns also related disadvantages imposed by the domination of psychology by psychiatry and the bureaucracy (politics) associated with the internship site.

Intern's Expectations

Each intern listed any expectations that were not met by the internship site. This information would have been valuable prior to accepting the offer to intern at a particular site. Forty-one percent of the sample reported having all expectations met. Thirteen percent indicated that their expectation for adequate supervision was not met. Interns also seemed to be insufficiently apprised of the magnitude of the bureaucracy found in the setting and the limited range of opportunities for additional training. Other unmet expectations concerned the narrowness of patient populations, inadequate pay, limited individual therapy opportunities, overstressful experiences, a nonsupportive emotional climate, and few research opportunities.

Internship Preparation

Aspects of Georgia State University training that the interns felt had facilitated the internship experience were described. One fourth (25%) of the sample indicated that the most significant component of their training was therapy experience. Individual supervision and courses in testing were also highly regarded. Somewhat fewer interns considered practicum experience, exposure to divergent theoretical and therapeutic models, diagnostic training, and behavior therapy course work to be of major importance.

Interns also listed those aspects of their training that were recognized as deficiencies in meeting the professional requirements of their internship sites. The most common deficiency involved insufficient familiarity with the medical model. Related to this deficiency, interns felt inadequately prepared in the areas of diagnostics, psychopharmacology, and testing. Some difficulties were reported in dealing effectively with low-functioning patient populations (e.g., psychotics). In addition, interns indicated having an inadequate understanding of bureaucratic issues and neuropsychological assessment techniques.

Factors Influencing Internship Acceptance

Of those factors that the interns listed as contributing to internship acceptance, a good recommendation from a faculty member was considered most significant. An on-site interview with the director of clinical training was also considered important. A large number of interns could not point to any specific factor that they felt facilitated their acceptance.

Interestingly, some factors presumed important and desirable for gaining internship acceptance were mentioned by only a few interns. Practicum and work experience and publications were considered of minor significance. Publications were deemed important only by those interns who specialized in behavior therapy.

APA Versus Non-APA Distinction

Table 2 indicates that APA internship sites were given higher overall ratings than non-APA sites. Twice as many excellent quality ratings were given for APA-approved sites. In addition, in APA internships the quality of therapy and diagnostic supervision was rated much higher, and the relationship between psychiatrists and psychologists was rated better overall.

Along the same lines, greater faculty support and a better emotional climate were found in APA-approved sites. Specifically, non-APA sites received almost four times as many "very poor" ratings, whereas a much greater percentage of interns from APA sites characterized their emotional climate as excellent.

As a further means of assessing the quality of internship experience, the psychologists were asked whether they would accept the same internship again. Of those interns attending APA sites, 83% stated that they would unequivocally accept the same internship as compared to only 45% of those from non-APA sites. Conversely, 4% and 30% of the psychologists from APA and non-APA sites, respectively, stated that they would definitely not take the same internship again.

The general dissatisfaction expressed by interns from non-APA sites was examined in greater detail by analyzing the specific disadvantages found in accredited and nonaccredited sites. Forty-three percent of non-APA interns versus only 5% of APA interns were dissatisfied with the quality and quantity of supervision offered by the site. The training scope was considered narrow by 26% of the non-APA and only 6% of the APA interns. Comparable percentages were found regarding the sites' range of patient populations.

Fewer significant disadvantages were indicated by interns from APA sites. The only substantive criticisms centered on the overly stressful experience of the internship and the disputes between the psychiatrists and the psychologists. These two disadvantages alone accounted for 50% of the weaknesses attributed to APA programs in comparison to a mere 14% for non-APA programs. No differences between APA and non-APA sites were found in the remaining 10 disadvantages expressed by the interns.

Finally, contrary to expectation, the average salary for interns from non-APA sites was comparable to those for interns from APA sites ($6,974 and $7,169, respectively).

TABLE 2 Ratings of Five Aspects of Internship Experiences at APA and Non-APA-Approved Sites

Quality rating	Diagnostic supervision		Therapy supervision		Psychiatry/ psychology relationship		Overall quality		Psychological climate	
	APA	Non-APA	APA	Non-APA	APA	Non-APA	APA	Non-APA	APA	Non-APA
Very poor	8.6	32.5	4.3	8.1	13.0	54.1	0	10.9	4.3	13.8
Average	13.0	27.0	26.0	46.0	26.1	24.3	4.3	43.2	56.6	75.1
Excellent	78.4	40.5	69.7	45.9	60.9	21.6	95.7	45.9	39.1	8.1

Note. Number of respondents = 60.

Quality of Internship Experience

Several factors were found to influence variables regarding the overall quality of the interns' experience. One such factor concerned the emotional climate and faculty support characteristic of each internship site. Internships that were considered highly supportive were rated highest in terms of overall quality ($r = .60$, $p < .001$). Furthermore, interns attending these sites not only were more inclined to accept the same internship again but also were more likely to promote the internship to fellow students ($r = .50$, $p < .001$). The interns' inclinication to promote the site was, not surprisingly, related to their ratings of the quality of the site, and such internship sites were also distinguished by a greater number of interns ($r = .34$, $p < .004$).

DISCUSSION

The survey of clinical psychology interns who went through the Georgia State University program during the past 10 years resulted in some intriguing findings of particular significance to internships. For example, average salaries earned by interns tended to decrease over the last decade. Although this trend may be due to more students accepting internships without stipend, the mean salary of $7,049 found in this sample is comparable to the $6,235 figure found in a 1976 sample of 95 APA-approved sites (Matthews, Matthews, Maxwell, 1976). This finding lends credence to Landsbaum's (1970) contention that interns select sites for their quality rather than for financial or geographic reasons.

The respondents reported individual psychotherapy and diagnostic evaluations as their major duties during internship. The major work activities reported appear to be consistent with the often-mentioned internship selection criteria of clinical and testing skills proficiency (Dana et al., 1976; Sturgis et al., 1980). Interns are apparently very concerned with the range of training experience they receive. A wide range of pathology and a variety of experiences were seen as advantageous; a narrow training scope was viewed as a major disadvantage; and a wide range of training opportunities was often an unmet expectation held by the interns.

The major deficit across internships was inadequate supervision for therapy and evaluation. Therefore, poor supervision may lead interns to be dissatisfied with the entire training experience more quickly than any other factor, possibly leading them to dissuade potential applicants. Since the quality, quantity, and variety of supervision are usually controlled by the setting's training director, he/she may wish to monitor more closely the supervision available to interns.

Another major deficiency seen by interns was the prevalence of bureaucratic and political disputes, especially between psychologists and psychiatrists. Since most interns were surprised by the extent of these political issues that detracted from their daily training, they expressed a need to be trained in the effective management of such bureaucratic and political concerns.

Inconsistent with some previous surveys of training directors, the interns identified good recommendations and a successful interview as the most important factors contributing to their acceptance, whereas practicum and work experience were de-emphasized. Although recommendations were also previously noted as important by Spitzform and Hamilton (1976), testing skills, general clinical skills, and practicum experience were found to be significant intern assets by Dana et al. (1976), Sturgis et al. (1980), and Spitzform and Hamilton (1976), respectively.

Compared to internships without APA approval, APA sites were given significantly higher ratings across five quality dimensions. Furthermore, many more interns from approved settings said that they would seek the same internship again. These findings are consistent with the intern survey performed by Khol et al. in 1972. Interestingly, students who choose approved internships may have to pay for the comparatively higher quality of their training by working in a more stressful environment and by tolerating more political squabbles between psychology and psychiatry.

SUMMARY

The findings reported in this study offer professionals responsible for the training of psychologists a uniqe feedback source from the intern's perspective. Specifically, the interns provided evaluative information regarding the quality of both their academic and internship training programs. Each intern described assets and liabilities of the internship site, personal expectations (met or unmet) of the internship, the comprehensiveness of their academic and clinical preparation, factors influencing acceptance, and advice to prospective interns. In addition, a comprehensive profile of each site was developed that spanned the interns' predoctoral careers. (This profile originated primarily at Georgia State University.)

Although the findings reflect only one academic program, 34 internship programs across the country were represented in the analysis. The preponderance of non-APA sites came from Georgia, and as such, the findings pertinent to non-APA approved training settings may not necessarily reflect such training across the country. Furthermore, the survey sample of only 60 respondents may limit the extent to which these results can be generalized to other interns. It must be noted, however, that one of the major objectives of this survey was to provide an appraisal of the interns' entire training program for the faculty of this institution. The survey may be of most value in providing one model of a clinical program's method of assessing its graduate students.

Along with the presentation of the findings in this article, the internship survey data were used in three separate in-house efforts to enhance the internship application process for students in Georgia State University's clinical psychology program. First, a copy of each completed questionnaire was placed in the file folder of that internship site for the examination of individual students interested in that setting. Second, the data were accumulated, condensed, and presented in meetings of students planning to intern the following year. Third, after compilation of the data pertaining to the intern's view of the assets and deficits of the university's clinical program, a synopsis of the results was presented to the faculty. Finally, the internship committee plans an annual survey of each year's interns in a continuing effort to evaluate the quality of their academic and internship training. In this manner, our clinical program will remain responsive to the needs of mental health service delivery systems as well as to the future professionals who plan to fulfill these needs.

REFERENCES

Craddick, R. A., Cole, M. A., Dane, J., Brill, R., & Wilson, J. A. The process of selecting predoctoral internship training sites. *Professional Psychology,* 1980, *11,* 548–549.

Dana, R. H., Gilliam, M., & Dana, J. M. Adequacy of academic-clinical preparation for internship. Professional Psychology, 1976, 7, 112–116.

Foster, L. M. Truth-in-advertising psychology internship programs. *Professional Psychology,* 1976, *7,* 120–124.

Khol, T., Mately, R., & Turner, J. Evaluation of APA internship programs: A survey of clinical psychology interns. *Journal of Clinical Psychology,* 1972, *28,* 562–569.

Landsbaum, J. B., & Powell, B. J. Financial provisions in APA-approved clinical internships. *American Psychologist,* 1970, *25,* 1101–1102.

Matthews, J. R., Matthews, L. H., & Maxwell, W. A. A survey of APA-approved internship facilities. *Professional Psychology,* 1976, *7,* 209–213.

Shemberg, K., & Keeley, S. Training practices and satisfaction with preinternship preparation. *Professional Psychology,* 1974, *5,* 98–105.

Spitzform, M., & Hamilton, S. A survey of directors from APA-approved internship programs on intern selection. *Professional Psychology,* 1976, *7,* 406–410.

Sturgis, D., Verstegen, P., Randolph, P., & Garvin, R. Professional psychology internships. *Professional Psychology,* 1980, *11,* 567–573.

Reading 41

Sex Role Issues in Clinical Training

Joseph H. Pleck
University of Michigan, Ann Arbor

I did my internship as a clinical psychologist at a psychiatric teaching hospital in Boston in 1970-71. The psychology service was unique in the hospital in having an almost exactly equal number of men and women, both in the interns and in the staff. Every other group in the hospital was either nearly all-male (like the psychiatric residents and the attendants) or all-female (like the nurses and social workers). At the beginning of the year, the chief psychologist told us that in years past the women and men interns had had rather different experiences on the inpatient services, specifically, that the male psychology interns competed with and struggled to be accepted as equals of the male first-year psychiatric residents, while the female psychology interns usually fit in comfortably with the female nursing staff. After being thus wrapped in these figurative pink and blue blankets, we began our year in the hospital. For whatever reason, this past experience wasn't too far off as a predictor of the future. When I think back on it, this seems to me to be a remarkable example of how gender determines the careers and experiences that people have in institutions even though they enter the institution with identical training and are assigned identical institutional roles.

There were many issues around sex roles in the hospital that year. The hospital had begun admitting women to the psychiatric residency program the previous year; and this year, too, each inpatient service had its exact quota of one female resident. (You might know the study by Wolman & Frank about the unusual stresses experienced by "solo" women in professional groups.) One of the big issues that year was whether women on the nursing staff could wear pantsuits; after a long struggle, they were accepted—white ones, of course. On one of the other inpatient services, the male chief resident decided to "run" a group for the female staff on the service. Back in those days, a male leading a women's group didn't seem like a contradiction to most people. The analogy to what it would mean for a group of blacks in the hospital to meet at the behest of white authority was not available in people's consciousness at that time—perhaps it's a more obvious analogy now. After a while, the women tried to get him to let them meet by themselves, which he didn't like at all. This remained a constant source of tension.

The hospital had a major weekly lecture series, which began with a series of lectures by the clinical director, a nationally-known psychoanalyst, on psychopathology. In the first lecture of the year, he charmingly worked in the

Reprinted from Psychotherapy: Theory, Research and Practice, *13*(1), 17-19.

observation that "all good women are a little hysterical." It was just around this time, incidentally, that the Brovermans published their famous study showing that clinicians viewed many traits as desirable in women which they rated as showing poor adjustment in men and in persons in general. The clinical director followed this up by saying, with a twinkle in his eye, "that's why we marry them and pay for their therapy." From the nervous laughter this evoked, this was a point of considerable anxiety for many in the room. Later in the year there was a lecture in the same series called "Sexual Politics Revisited," in which a visiting New York analyst triumphantly showed (or so he said) that there were some small errors of quotation or fact in Kate Millett's discussion of Freud in *Sexual Politics,* which he proceeded to "interpret" for us. So much for the arguments of women's liberation.

I also worked in the outpatient service. The first patient I saw there was a woman who had been raped two days earlier, who found herself unable to return to her apartment or to be alone, and who experienced terrifying recurrent images of her ordeal. The psychological needs of rape victims was not something that had been covered in my training up to then—perhaps revealing in itself, considering the frequency of rape—but my supervisor in the walk-in clinic had a strategy: he told me that the reason this woman kept remembering the experience was because some part of her liked it and found it pleasurable and exciting, and that she would never be able to let go and forget about the experience until she could acknowledge the parts of heself that found it gratifying. In 1970, such reasoning sounded plausible and suitably "dynamic," and I'm ashamed to say that I began to work with her based on this formulation. Fortunately for her, she didn't return after one visit.

The residents and supervisiors in the hospital varied greatly. Some were genuinely decent people, while others were not. There were rumors around the hospital about certain residents seducing their young female patients. Young females were generally considered to be great prizes of the individual therapy waiting list. I remember one of my supervisors telling me what a great coup he had accomplished in getting me one. It was really easy to be sucked into this vulgar sexual economy, so reflective of the larger society. Another supervisor of mine, after interviewing a couple I was beginning to see, could only react to how seductive he thought the woman had been toward him. Didn't I think that she had shown him a lot of her thighs? Didn't I think that she "slept around" from the way she had acted? All this seemed pretty unfounded to me. Sometimes sexism came down to the most mundane levels. I remember one day when one of the residents on my service saw me buying a sandwich for lunch in the hospital coffee shop, and came over to ask me why I didn't get my wife to make my lunch every morning. I tried to explain that this wasn't part of our relationship, but he just couldn't understand it.

The hospital's attitude toward homosexualtiy was and still is quite typical of its time. One of the residents on my shift in the walk-in clinic, who specialized in treating male homosexuals, including two outpatient therapy groups, had the most arrogant and contemptuous attitude toward them, his conversation liberally sprinkled with references to "fags" and "queers." I was taken aback one day when one of the distinguished senior analysts who was a consultant on our shift joined in, talking to this resident about a patient we had seen together as spending his time in "fairy bars." I also remember a conversation I had once with the chief resident on my ward during a ward coffee hour, when he somehow got to talking about some pornographic comics he had when he was a kid, one in particular about a ship full of "fags" running into a ship full of "dykes," which he found either amusing or exciting. I always felt totally unable to confront these people in these situations. I did work very hard, though, to let the gay people I saw in the walk-in clinic know what the hospital's attitude was. I was surprised at how much blind faith these gay people had in psychiatry. I left the hospital feeling sad for how limited and narrow the experience of these mental health professionals had been. If you had ever had an adult gay experience, or taken a psychedelic drug, or been in an encounter group, you had had experiences which these men had not, yet they were making the most dogmatic and damning judgments about them.

After my internship I worked part-time at a student health service and at a free clinic. I remember a staff meeting at the student health service where the chief psychologist was talking about the declining number of new female patients in the service—a phenomenon happening more generally, I understand, which may be one sign of the changes going on in women today—and said exuberantly "we should all see more female patients; they're attractive, fun to treat, and they get better!" Once again the sexual economy of the patient pool. I wondered whether he could generate much interest in helping men with *their* problems in living.

The free clinic where I worked showed more influence from the women's movement, but a couple of experiences stood out there. We had a legal consultation service as part of the free clinic, and one day I sat in on part of an interview a law student did with a woman who wanted access to her psychiatric records. After it was over, he asked me if I didn't think she was "mannish." When I asked what he meant, he told me that he had tried to put his arm around her when he was leaving, to help her calm down, he said, and that she had pulled away from him. To him, this interaction showed that she was mannish. There was another lawyer on the staff who liked to do female impersonations at the monthly staff meetings, who I didn't know how to deal with at all. One of the other things he was doing was trying to get rid of a gay woman law student that he felt very uncomfortable with, though her work was very good.

My point in pulling together these different examples and incidents from my clinical training and work is not to paint a black picture of the helping professions. I can't say how typical my experience is. I suspect, though, that anyone in mental health work can remember similar incidents in his or her experience, though they may not have "registered" at the time. These incidents, and the social climate in which they pass unnoticed and seem almost routine, reflect a social reality which is full of barriers to change in sex roles for women and men, both "out there" in the world clients live in and inside our own world.

I think there is a place for the helping professions in a society that is going through the changes in sex roles that our is. What concerns me most is that the mental health professions, rather than being in the forefront of these changes, have been lagging behind them. One might have expected clinicians to be the most sensitive to the cost in frustrated lives and potential exacted by the old sex role norms that said that women must stay in the home and that men must be strong. One might have expected the helping professions to be the first to champion the long-overdue changes which are now allowing greater self-actualization for both women and men.

These changes are presenting many new kinds of issues in clinical work, especially about the politics of male-female relationships. Let me give some examples. One student I know preferred to see individuals rather than couples in his social work placement because he felt he didn't want to just help "shore up" the nuclear family. Another man I know is in marital therapy with a man who divorced his first wife who had a career for a second wife who was much more traditional. My friend described how he was beoming aware of the alliance he has *as a male* with the therapist. This patriarchal alliance is a source of support to him, but it also oppresses him because in order to maintain it he has to live up to the therapist's idea of what he should be as a man. The breaking down of the barriers formerly enclosing women and men is raising many hard questions which our training has not prepared us for. To deal with these questions, we are going to have to start examining our own experiences and needs, and begin sharing with others in new ways.

Chapter 6

Future Issues

It may be a bit foolhardy to anticipate developments in the rapidly changing field of internship training. However, concern for costs, accountability, and better utilization of resources play an increasing role in planning and delivery of health and educational services. It is becoming clear that internship programs should also focus on these areas. The papers in this section address some of these issues.

May (1975) contends that developing two year half-time regional internships at larger centers—consortia—and cooperation with a nearby academic doctoral program would make the professional program more realistic, break down academic and practical training barriers and, by implication, would be cost-effective. Weiskopf and Newman (1982) propose a solution to the threat of increasing numbers of unfunded internships—particularly in the financially troubled community mental health centers. By redesigning the internship along identified variables such as amount of required client contact by interns, supervision to direct service ratio, and stipend level, it would be possible to restructure internships (at least in mental health centers) for cost-efficiency. These authors assert that intern programs could even meet interns' different professional goals by manipulating those variables.

Wiens and Dresdale (1982) as well as Carlin (1982) take positions on the function of stipends in internship training. Wiens and Dresdale assert that the internship setting should simulate the conditions in which the clinician will function professionally. However, maintaining high quality in internship training under increases in financial and service pressures is a major issue in training settings. These writers continue by asserting that psychologists (and thus interns) must become more knowledgeable of finances in health care settings and demonstrate their cost-effectiveness. Further, it is contended that greater specificity of learning goals on campus and internship are required—including the development of national standards. For example, interns in the Oregon Health Sciences University training programs have been shown to be cost-effective and accordingly predoctoral interns receive stipends (and possibly status) commensurate with first-year medical residents in that setting.

Carlin (1982) describes the successful introduction of unfunded interns along with funded ones in a large "confederacy" program. The voluntary unfunded interns are of similar caliber as funded ones, according to the program selection process. The unfunded interns have similar perks but trade-off stipends for free choice (nonobligatory) rotations among 24 such possibilities. The interns and supervisory staff have found the arrangement workable, at least in part, because of the unfunded group wanted to come to the program and/or wished to live in the Seattle area.

Langston (1979) takes issue with the traditional patterns of 3 or 4 month rotations during the internship year. The rotational model assumes that prospective interns do not have the knowledge or experience to choose an internship with more intensity and a limited range of clients, or a nonrotational internship. This type of internship—nonrotational—provides opportunities for responsibility of a larger number of clients, greater participation in long-term therapy, observation-in-depth of clients impulse-defense struggles, confrontation of a broad range of interactions encountered by therapists and, lastly, involvement in administration.

The final article in this section is Albee's "The Uncertain Direction of Clinical Psychology" (1982). Although not immediately focused on internship training as such, this article targets all educational and training segments of clinical psychology. Albee contends that recent clinical psychology practice has become narrowed and subsequently equated with psychotherapy. This, he says, is dangerous for two reasons: a) training a large number of psychologist-psychotherapist practitioners will do little to improve the level of mental health of the public and b) this practice model of one-to-one service reinforces a health-illness model used to explain psychopathology. A growing shortage of psychiatrists and increasing third party psychotherapy reimbursement eligibility for psychologists working with personal problems of the educated middle-class are responsible for this narrowing of practice. This flow of human resources towards psychotherapeutic practice has also encouraged the development of professional schools of psychology.

According to Albee, the future holds professionalism and self-interest guild orientations among practitioners. An individual therapy model will leave unserved those who are most seriously in need. The poor, elderly, minority groups, children, adolescents, and unemployed, may have high rates of emotional distress, but these populations do not generally seek or receive psychotherapy. By accepting a medical model, psychology has identified with a traditional illness model and runs the risk of forgetting or ignoring primary prevention of psychopathology. Albee recognizes that prevention means social change and political action leading to a more suitable and just society. Although presently quite limited in scope and number and not necessarily in agreement with the goals and values of Albee's position, internships with a community/ prevention orientation could offer a future alternative to medical model oriented clinical psychology internshps.

Reading 42

On Regionalizing Clinical Psychology Internships

W. Theodore May
University of Tennessee Center for the Health Sciences

The first quarter of a century of graduate education in the framework of the Boulder model (Raimy, 1950) is over. Although changes in the education of clinical psychologists have gradually taken place, the basic thrust of doctoral programs has remained the scientist-practitioner model within the framework of an academic psychology department. There are now, however, broad sets of internal and external forces operating upon the system of clinical psychology graduate education that make significant changes imminent. Wolff (1972) pointed out that changes in recent years have already occurred more rapidly than in the early years after Boulder. Specifically, he suggested, among other things, "a pragmatically oriented clinician-researcher model" (p. 349). The most recent Vail conference on graduate education in clinical psychology (Korman, 1974) signifies a similar break in the pattern of educational programming for clinical psychology.

WHY REEVALUATE CLINICAL TRAINING?

Let us consider some of the existing forces pushing for an uncomfortable (but probably necessary) reevaluation of clinical psychology training.

- There are more undergraduate students majoring in psychology now than at any other time in the history of psychology as an academic subject area.
- There are probably more students in programs leading to graduate degrees in psychology than at any other time during the last 25 years.
- A higher proportion of graduate students is now to be found in the various applied areas of specialties as opposed to the more basic nonapplied areas of psychology.
- The push of graduate education in areas of psychology will probably continue during the forseeable future as our society continues to move toward a greater emphasis on human service delivery as opposed to the production of goods.
- The usual federal funding of graduate programs for both faculty and students will remain at the present level or continue to decrease (e.g., National Institute of Mental Health, National Science Foundation, Veterans Administration, etc.), while state and local funding, of various kinds, as well as their respective input to programs will increase.

Reprinted from Professional Psychology, *6*, 228-233.

• Graduate departments of psychology will have to shift their funding sources in order to remain viable (e.g., revenue sharing, Law Enforcement Assistance Agency, vocational rehabilitation, specialized federal programs, state departments of mental health, education or corrections, comprehensive social services monies through social security, health maintenance organizations planning and research, etc.) as well as receiving greater shares of support from their own institutions.

• Unless graduate departments do the above, they will have to cut back their admissions at a time when efforts toward proportional representation of minority groups (and possibly women) are developing. It is to be expected that the decrease of support for graduate students will yield a significant application and selection bias toward well-to-do and self-financed (probably mostly white and at least middle-class) applicants.

• Furthermore, the ethnic (and possibly female applicant) may have to settle for a lesser academic degree (e.g., BA or MA) for the time being until the student saves enough money through some work-related earnings in order to continue graduate studies. This would deal a setback to hopes of truly representing the total population in the profession of psychology for the immediate future.

• Graduate school faculty members may develop the understanding that they are all faced with the same dilemma. There are indications that some basic psychology faculty members are becoming aware of their need for applied financial support and application of their research.

• It may well be that various interests in more expensive and/or borderline-financed graduate psychology departments that cannot join together for a common purpose may go out of business.

• Social demands for applied psychological services can be expected to continue during these decades of profound cultural change. The development of professional schools by experienced applied psychologists may be expected to increase, provided fiscal problems are solved, as may the sidedoor applied psychology programs (counseling and guidance, social-community, rehabilitation psychology, behavior modification, etc.). The greatest risk will be the possibility of reappearance of inadequate programs as not all states have licensing laws and "freedom of choice" laws.

• Furthermore, it is possible that psychologists may be directly included in health maintenance organizations in whatever national health insurance legislation is to be passed on the federal level.

• The development of better integrated regional educational program cooperation is very much here (e.g., Southern Regional Education Board and Western Interstate Commission on Higher Education, etc.). Further, higher education will be much better coordinated and related within regions and states, thus maximizing resources and minimizing educational duplication and gaps.

- One thrust of such educational reform will be the development of educational ladders within geographical areas so that an individual can move in and out of the educational arena for different levels of preparation with minimal financial cost (i.e., avoiding moving to another geographical area) and no cost regarding his/her academic or experience credits.
- It is likely that departmental territorialities regarding the training of applied psychologists will disappear to a considerable extent, leading perhaps to degrees and training in human services that can be accomplished through the aegis of several departments in one or more educational institutions in a given geographic area.

If the above observations and projections are correct or even directionally accurate, their impact on education and training in applied psychology would be considerable.

THE INTERNSHIP YEAR TODAY

Traditionally, graduate schools have counted on the internship year to teach and enhance skills in the practical aspects of clinical psychology (Wolff, 1972), while graduate psychology departments concentrate on academics and research. Although theoretically probably convenient, this arrangement has worked in practice to the students' detriment. Two authors (Rice & Gurman, 1973, p. 403) stated that this hoped-for meshing has failed for several reasons: (a) value discrepancies that create dissonance in the student, (b) differing goals and expectations leading to mutual disappointments, and (c) the demand for flexibility in the constantly changing clinical practice that may leave the student frustrated and perhaps even nihilistic.

These authors went on to indicate that these conditions lead to a number of unresolved issues in clinical psychology training. These are: (a) diversified versus specialized internship, (b) the detrimental effects of many graduate schools' failure to teach basic skills, (c) the balance on internship between trainee monitoring and independent functioning, and (d) the preservation of research values and role identification in the face of dramatic shifts in institutional values.

After a recent survey of internship centers concerning the preinternship training and preparation of clinical students, Shemberg and Keely (1974) concluded that either internship settings may be forced to accept more training responsibility in the more traditional model or that reciprocal relationships might develop between the parent university and the internship setting.

It does seem obvious that there is a need for substantial communication between universities and internships on these crucial issues beyond that which occurred at the 1965 APA Conference. . . . (Shemberg & Keely, p. 105)

One step in the direction of responding to these unresolved issues could be the regionalization and deschooling of clinical psychology graduate programs through restructuring of the internship experience by elaborating upon presently existing models. The most relevant patterns are herewith briefly described. The Veterans Administration graduate school training arrangement, when both institutions are in the same geographical area, has long provided the potential of a highly correlated, if not fully integrated, academic-practicum experience for the students. The training effectiveness of this relationship has depended on the training-funding regulations within the Veterans Administration, the usual limits of the available clinical population of the setting as well as the relationship of the Veterans Administration Psychology Service staff and the academic faculty. Going from a national pattern to a state-wide one, the recently developed New Jersey Psychology Junior Fellowship Program provides internships in a large variety and number of service and training facilities (mostly state agencies) on a rotating basis. This program is centrally administered through a director of training and a training committee (Roth, Note 1). The psychology program at the University of Michigan has for some years provided a rather unique combination of classroom and applied learning experiences for its students in clinical psychology. Although admitting some students from other clinical programs for the internship experience, the vast majority of students are their own. There is no sharp break between the classroom and all local field placement experiences. Thus, no 12-month internship year as such exists. Rather, graduate students are required to participate half time in several of the eight or nine cooperating practicum settings for at least three years of their graduate training (Cain, Note 2).

A PROPOSED REGIONAL INTERNSHIP MODEL

The present proposal attempts to utilize some of the features of the above-mentioned patterns in forwarding a regional internship model. The following features are proposed:

1. The development of regional internship centers having the following characteristics is suggested: (a) a broad variety of training opportunities in a variety of willing and cooperative settings that are at least sensitive to training of students and capable of providing meaningful and appropriately supervised by competent clinicians in a given geographical area. Such settings might include health sciences centers. Veterans Administration hospitals, child development centers, school psychological services, rehabilitation services, psychiatric hospitals, community mental health centers, general hospitals, children's hospitals, correctional psychology settings, college counseling centers and clinics, etc. (b) ready access to and cooperation with at least one accredited graduate program in clinical and/or counseling psychology in a given geographical area;

(c) a willingness on the part of parent graduate departments to relinquish some of their power and territoriality over students and their educational experiences; (d) a "catchment area" of cooperating academic institutions ranging from one city to a radius of several hundred miles.

2. The internship would consist of two calendar years of halftime practicum experience and the participation simultaneously in 8-10 academic courses at the same time in the third and fourth year of graduate education.

3. The courses would be taught by appropriate internship setting staff (who would have at least an adjunct academic appointment at the various parent institutions) and/or the graduate faculty of the clinical psychology graduate program faculty (or other appropriate faculty) in the geographic area of the regional internship center. Courses such as personality assessment including screening, psychotherapeutic techniques, consultation, community psychology, psychopharmacology, neuroanatomy, neuropsychology, applied research, dissertation research, and outside departmental courses could constitute the "for academic credit" work on a pass-fail basis. The advantages of in vivo coursework and role modeling should be obvious.

4. A number of options are open concerning the fiscal arrangement of such a program. The following, however, seem most desirable: (a) that the funding could be more readily managed (i.e., two years at halftime) as the financial support will more likely come locally or through state agencies and (b) that the funding for course work during the internship years to appropriate faculty could be on the basis of reimbursement from the "home university" where the student is registered and pays his/her fees.

5. Students from different graduate programs would thus spend much time together in both academic and clinical experiences.

6. A typical regional internship setting (perhaps best described as a "consortium") might be able to accommodate 20-40 interns at any one time.

7. A regional internship training director would be needed to coordinate the students' academic and clinical programs with the parent university, on-the-scene faculty, and supervisors. Responsibility for funding for such a position might most properly belong to the clinical facility that is most capable as operating as the core of the consortium.

POSITIVE IMPLICATIONS

If such a program were implemented, the following are some of the positive implications:

Students would be able to complete their academic requirements, perhaps in less time than presently, while at the same time participating in significant and relevant applied experiences, thus decreasing the gap between theory and practice.

Potential for exchange of clinical faculty at the "parent" universities with field faculty and supervisors would be enhanced.

"Parent" universities' teaching demands would be decreased, thus minimizing needs for raising monies for new full-time faculty but paying part-time clinical faculty instead. It would be cheaper for the home university to have courses taught in this way.

Intensive and extensive exposure to at least one other graduate school faculty and nonparent university clinical instructors would occur.

Intensive and extensive interaction (two years) would increase with graduate students from other graduate programs in a geographic region.

A "real world" daily application of academic learnings would result.

The breakdown of academic and field training institutional barriers would be accomplished.

Better trained students would emerge from a more balanced educational experience in which students could obtain experience in a diversity of settings.

Assurance of a given number of internships in a given year for each co-operating graduate clinical psychology program would minimize the paper work associated with multiple applications for internship.

The development of a regional applied psychology manpower corps as interns tend to accept first positions geographically close to their internships would be a probable outcome.

POSSIBLE OBJECTIONS

Possible objections may come from various quarters. Some of these might be:

Faculties of graduate programs might object as some students would be taken away from the preferred seminar courses in the latter stages of graduate education.

Teaching faculty of the clinical faculty and the regional graduate psychology department who would offer courses might present problems concerning "acceptability" to the parent institution department.

Registrars and bursars of various cooperating universities may object as some administrative, record keeping, and payroll adjustments would have to be made.

The affected students could lose a year's assistantship monies from the parent university if he/she is out on two years of internship away from the parent university. This could include the loss of fee remission.

Financial support may have to readjusted during the internship years to a higher level than the one-half amount of the usual full-time internship year stipend.

Funding agencies would have to change their policies regarding the manner of granting and allocating of internship monies, including the possible allocation of locally derived assistantship monies from the graduate school department in the geographical area to the regional internship training center in the same community for additional financial support for interns.

CONCLUSION

Despite these possible, but not insurmountable, objections, graduate programs in clinical psychology are changing and will continue to do so, probably at a more rapid rate in the foreseeable future. Perhaps it is possible for those responsible in graduate education to anticipate realities and begin to work toward desirable training arrangements forwarded by themselves rather than being consistently buffeted by externally imposed constraints.

REFERENCE NOTES

1 Roth L. Personal communication, July 3, 1974.
2 Cain A. Personal communication, June 20, 1974.

REFERENCES

Korman, M. National Conference on Levels and Patterns of Professional Training in Psychology. *American Psychologist,* 1974, *29,* 441–449.

Raimy, V. C. (Ed.). *Training in clinical psychology.* New York: Prentice-Hall, 1950.

Rice, D. G., & Gurman, A S. Unresolved issues in the clinical psychology internship. *Professional Psychology,* 1973, *4,* 403–408.

Shemberg, V. M., & Keely, S. M. Training practices and satisfaction with preinternship preparation. *Professional Psychology,* 1974, *5,* 98–105.

Wolff, W. M. Training model trends in psychology. *Professional Psychology,* 1972, *4,* 343–350.

Reading 43

Redesigning Internship Training Programs: A Cost-Efficient Point of View

Robert Weiskopf
Quinco Consulting Center, Columbus, Indiana

Joseph P. Newman
The University of Wisconsin-Madison

Future trends in mental health will undoubtedly involve decreased federal and state funding that will affect both service and training. At many agencies whose primary mission is service, training may be seen as a "fringe benefit." Administrators may argue that training cannot be justified, as funding for services is cut.

In a survey of internship settings, Tuma and Cerny (1976) found that "the pattern of financial support reported for total number of interns reflects heavy reliance on federal and state sources." In a more recent survey, Zolik, Bogat, and Jason (Note 1) found that in 137 community mental health centers that offer internship training, 31% paid no stipend. Of the remaining 87 centers that offered a stipend, 61% paid less than $6,000.

The changed political and economic realities of the 1980s will make heavy reliance on federal and state funds for internship training untenable in the near future. A likely development will be an increase in internship sites that pay no stipend or a minimal stipend. Such a development would be unfortunate, since to pay no stipend or a minimum stipend devalues the internship year, which traditionally is a valuable period of transition from graduate student to professional.

Another development will be a decrease in the number of internship sites. In 1976 Tuma and Cerny found more demand than supply of internship positions and predicted a 14% nonplacement rate within 3 years. Although this balance may have recently shifted in the direction of more positions than prospective interns, the cuts in funding will clearly leave a number of graduate students without internship placements in the near future, assuming a constant student supply.

Thus two likely developments are an increase in unpaid internship positions and a decrease in the total number of positions and internship sites. One possible solution to the current economic situation is to make internship training a cost-efficient proposition. Loucks, Burstein, Schoenfeld, and Stedman (1980) found that their internship training program at a large medical setting was economically feasible. This article will examine the cost efficiency of internship training in a community mental health center and, more importantly, will

Reprinted from Professional Psychology, *13*(4), 571–576. The authors would like to thank *Ken Heller, Linda McLean, Maria Nehrt, Tom Orr,* and *Lee Weiskopf* for their contributions to this manuscript.

demonstrate how internships can be redesigned to increase their efficiency, given limited funds.

Although this article is a case study and is specific to one setting, we feel it illustrates a general principle that psychology internship training can be designed in a cost-efficient manner that takes into account the institution's as well as the intern's needs and values. This can be accomplished by changing the parameters of intern stipends, amount of direct service, and ratio of direct service to supervision.

In the text that follows, we present a description of the agency and the training program, a discussion of an equation for computing the cost efficiency of this agency's training programs, and some examples of the equation's use. We also include the results of a survey of what interns value in an internship—a dimension that must be taken into account when redesigning a cost-efficient training program.

THE AGENCY AND THE INTERNSHIP PROGRAM

Quinco Consulting Center is a comprehensive community mental health center (CMHC) serving five counties in south central Indiana. Quinco became a comprehensive center in 1972, aided in its transition from an outpatient clinic to a CMHC by a federal staffing grant. Other sources of funding have been state, local, and client fees. The catchment area population is 150,000 and covers a largely rural area, with a few small population centers, the largest being Columbus, Indiana (population 35,000), which houses the main facility. The center maintains a clinical staff of approximately 60 psychologists, social workers, nurses, aides, and so forth and a support staff of 30.

The psychology internship program began in 1970 while the agency was still The Consulting Center, an outpatient facility. For the first 3 years of the program, there was only one intern per year, after which the program increased to three interns. In 1978 the program began training four interns.

In 1975 the internship program received a National Institute of Mental Health (NIMH) training grant that has been renewed each year since then. Internship training at Quinco involves a broad range of experiences, including service on an inpatient unit, consultation and education, program evaluation, emergency services, and outpatient services. The program received provisional American Psychological Association (APA) accreditation in 1978 and full accreditation in 1981. Internship training has always been highly valued by psychologists and other staff at Quinco and has afforded the center innumerable intangible benefits, including stimulation, an influx of new ideas, and positive self-esteem from teaching.

Although Quinco contributed considerable financial support to the interns, external funding helped defray the cost of the program. With the threat of decreased federal funding for training and decreased state and federal funding for services, the cost of clinical training programs must be reexamined. Although the entire staff of Quinco (including management, line staff, and even clerical staff) is supportive of the internship program, with the inevitability of decreasing funds, subjective feelings of satisfaction cannot justify a costly program at an agency whose primary mission is service delivery.

COST EFFICIENCY FOR THE INTERNSHIP PROGRAM: THE WORKING FORMULA

The equation and the assumptions that follow are specific to Quinco, but the principles apply to any internship setting and can even be applied to practicum settings. First, the assumptions will be presented, then the equation, and then some specific applications of the equation.

The Assumptions

Assumption A: That the client-contact hours absorbed by the interns do not prevent other clinical staff from obtaining enough client hours to work at maximum efficiency.

If interns' clinical work leaves other staff idle, then the program is not cost efficient for the center. As state and federal funding decreases, there will be reductions in service staff and there will be little problem in meeting this assumption.

Assumption B: That the task of supervising interns does not reduce the supervisor's own efficiency. (In the equations that follow, the assumption is made that if a supervisor devotes an hour to supervising an intern on a number of direct-service hours, the supervisor still receives only an hour's direct-service credit toward meeting his/her own quota.)

Currently at Quinco a supervisor applies the credit for the intern's cases toward meeting his or her own production quota of direct service. This has made supervision a highly appealing venture, since for 1 hour of supervision, the supervisor generally receives 2 hours of direct-service credit. (As a rule of thumb, 2 hours of clinical work receive 1 hour of supervision.) To make the program cost efficient, this would have to change, and Assumption B would apply.

Assumption C: That each hour of service performed by an intern or the supervisor results in $16.20 of revenue for the center. This figure was derived by dividing the revenue generated by outpatient service ($308,952) by the number of service hours (19,092).

(Note: Since staff, and interns in particular, provide types of direct service other than outpatient, the use of the $16.20 figure represents a means of *estimating* the value of a service hour.)

Assumption D: That the "overhead" of running the center is not substantially changed by the addition of four interns. Most overhead expenses inolve the use of support staff and materials (e.g., record keeping and such expenses are related to the number of clients seen and not the number of staff seeing them).

(Note: The per capita fringe benefits, which average 17% of salary cost, will be included in the equations below.)

Assumption E: The hours of direct service used in the computations pertain to billable service hours and not necessarily to the number of hours spent with clients. This distinction applies when an intern provides multiple billable hours for each hour of contact, as in group therapy.

The Equation

$$(HDSW \times [1-S/R] \times ARH \times 48) - (FBF \times salary).$$

HDSW equals hours of direct service per week. S/R equals supervision ratio, so that $1-S/R$ removes from the intern's service hours the number of staff hours devoted to supervision, which are hours that the supervisor can no longer devote to direct service. ARH equals average revenue per hour of service. Since the figure is not available for total service hours of this center, the estimated ARH for outpatient service for FY 1980 has been substituted. FBF equals fringe benefit factor. This figure is derived by adding 1 to the fringe benefit percentage. Fringe benefits at Quinco are calculated at 17%. Thus, the cost of an employee at Quinco may be estimated by multiplying his or her salary by 1.17. Forty-eight equals a constant pertaining to the number of weeks worked to obtain a yearly estimate. Quinco interns are entitled to a 2-week vacation and nine holidays.

Redesigning a Training Program Using Various Parameters

To illustrate the use of the equation, we will consider two different possible designs of the training program—designs that emphasize different parameters and thus, implicitly, different values

Table 1 presents four different stipend levels. For each stipend level, the table presents three amounts of direct-service contact by three supervision ratios. For these computations, a figure of $16.20 was used for the average revenue per hour of service (the FY80 figure).

To compute the cost of each intern in Quinco's training program as it now stands, the following figures are used: HDSW = 10, S/R = ½, ARH = $16.20, FBF = 1.17, Stipend = $7,800.

Table 1   Net Gain or Loss per Intern

Hours of direct service per week per intern	Ratio of supervision to direct service	Stipend			
		$4,000	$6,000	$8,000	$10,000
12	1/2	$ 3	−$2,354	−$4,694	−$7,017
	1/3	$1,564	−$ 799	−$3,139	−$5,456
	1/4	$2,344	−$ 22	−$2,362	−$4,676
15	1/2	$1,174	−$1,188	−$3,528	−$5,846
	1/3	$3,125	$ 756	−$1,584	−$3,895
	1/4	$4,100	$1,728	−$ 612	−$2,920
20	1/2	$3,125	$ 756	−$1,584	−$3,895
	1/3	$5,622	$3,338	$1,007	−$1,398
	1/4	$7,027	$4,644	$2,304	$ 7

$$(10[1-\tfrac{1}{2}] \times \$16.20 \times 48)-(1.17 \times \$7,800) = -\$5,238.$$

If one takes into account NIMH support, this figure does not represent as large a loss as first appears but rather approaches zero. However, even without support from external sources, this figure is not such a severe loss when computing the same formula for an average staff member will show a much larger loss.

In any case to redesign the internship program without external support and to be self-supporting (i.e., show no loss), one can decrease the stipend, increase the number of direct service hours, or decrease the supervision ratio. Actually, a combination of changes in these parameters is most realistic.

One redesign might involve a decrease of the stipend level to $6,000, an increase in direct service to 15 hours, and a change in the supervision ratio to 1 hour of supervision per 3 hours of direct service. This would lead to a net profit of $756 per intern (Table 1). Such a program would keep the current values essentially intact—considerable individual supervision with room for electives that do not involve direct service and requirements (such as a program evaluation project) that do not involve direct service.

An alternative design would involve a heavier clinical load emphasizing only direct service (i.e., psychotherapy and assessment). In fact, if we increase the direct-service requirement to 20 hours per week and change the supervision ratio to one quarter (still 5 hours of individual supervision per week), the stipend could be increased to $10,000, and the program would still be self-supporting. In such a program the values would shift away from experiences that do not involve direct service and would eliminate such electives as management and prevention and such requirements as program evaluation. However, for prospective interns who primarily want assessment and psychotherapy experience during their internship year, such a program could be appealing.

Intern Values

To be competitive in the internship marketplace, the redesign of an internship program must clearly take into account more than just cost efficiency—even if cost efficiency motivates the changes. One must also consider the quality of training and be sensitive to what interns value. For APA-accredited programs, quality is addressed by the Criteria for Accreditation of Doctoral Training Programs and Internships in Professional Psychology (APA Council of Representatives, Note 2).

To help assess what interns value in their training, a questionnaire was sent to Quinco's 25 past interns. Of these, 24 responded. Former interns were asked to rate 27 components of their training experience according to their value in postinternship employment. For each area and aspect of training, they were asked to rate the quality of training and helpuflness in postinternship employment.

Rank ordering of their responses indicates the following four to be rated the highest in terms of quality: supervision, individual adult outpatient therapy, child therapy, weekly seminars. Rank ordering of the 27 components of training in terms of helpfulness in postinternship employment yields similar results: Supervision, individual adult outpatient therapy, co-therapy, and weekly seminars received the highest ratings. Of the top four ranked items, three (supervision, weekly seminars, and co-therapy) involve an experienced clinician's teaching, either through supervision, didactic training, or modeling. So, in the reorganization of Quinco's internship program to make it more cost efficient, the learning-teaching aspects must remain a top priority. The values of Quinco's previous interns may not represent the values of other interns, and this question might be addressed in further studies of what interns value.

It is interesting to note that Drummond, Rodolfa, and Smith (1981) found that APA-approved internship sites had interns spending a significantly higher percentage of time in seminar attendance and supervision. Quinco's interns, in evaluating their internship experience, ranked these two aspects of training as among the highest in helpfulness in postinternship employment.

CONCLUSIONS

As service and training funds decrease at both the federal and state level, psychology internship programs do not have to dry up or become nonstipended programs. By changing such parameters as the amount of direct service provided by an intern, the ratio of supervision to direct service, and the stipend level, it is possible to redesign psychology internship programs to make them more cost efficient. At one extreme, one could redesign a program to pay a low stipend and require a low amount of direct service. Such a program would appeal to students whose career aspirations would lead to training in nonservice areas, such as research, management, or program evaluation. At the other extreme, one could redesign a program to pay a large stipend and emphasize direct service only—a program that would appeal to students interested in a more clinical career.

By varying such parameters, an internship site can highlight its values while maintaining a competitive, cost-efficient training program.

REFERENCE NOTES

1 Zolik, E. S., Bogat, G. A., & Jason, L. A. *Community training for interns and practicum students at community mental health centers.* Paper presented at the meeting of the American Psychological Association, Montreal, Canada, September 1980.
2 American Psychological Association, Council of Representatives. *Criteria for accreditation of doctoral training programs and internships in professional psychology.* Washington, D.C.: Author 1979.

REFERENCES

Drummond, F. E., Rodolfa, E., & Smith, D. A survey of APA- and non-APA-approved internship programs. *American Psychologist,* 1981, *36,* 411–414.
Loucks, S., Burstein, A. G., Schoenfeld, S., & Stedman, J. M. The real cost of psychology intern services: Are they a good buy? *Professional Psychology,* 1980, *11,* 898–900.
Tuma, J. M., & Cerny, J. A. The internship marketplace: The new depression? *American Psychologist,* 1976, *31,* 664–670.

Reading 44

Maintaining Quality Internship Training in the Face of Increasing Financial and Services Pressure

Arthur N. Wiens
The Oregon Health Sciences University

Laurence E. Dresdale
Private Practice, Rhinebeck, New York

In many respects the culmination of the long and sometimes arduous preparation for clinical psychological practice is the clinical internship experience. It is during the internship year that the neophyte clinician has the opportunity to test and put into practice the clinical skills developed throughout his or her education. The internship setting serves to function as a somewhat safe environment in which to continue the learning process while at the same time it is a transition from graduate school to "the real world." It is here that the student may first begin to experience the full burden of responsibility of daily clinical practice.

Despite whatever clinical practicum experience the graduate student has had prior to internship, it is unlikely that he or she has had the opportunity to deal with the demands of working with patients or clients on a day to day basis for an extended period of time. In addition to the honing of clinical skills there is the maturing of the individual into the professional role of clinical psychologist. It is the development of this element of professional self-image that is one of the most important aspects of the clinical internship experience. Perhaps for the first time the graduate student recognizes that he or she is being perceived by the person coming for help as "the doctor." There is no longer the security of falling back to being a student when confronted by clinical decision requiring immediate and accurate answers.

It is only by dealing with the daily demands, activities, and responsibilities of the clinical practitioner that the student develops self-confidence and the ability to make relatively rapid, sound judgments. Opportunities must be afforded the intern to be on the firing line. He or she should not be too protected by mentors. Indeed, it likely would be a disservice to the intern not to be exposed to the rigors of clinical practice with the opportunity to make independent judgments; be the judgments sound or poor. For it is while under the guidance and supervision of experienced clinicians that judgments may best be reviewed. This review process provides an avenue through which poor judgments may be discussed and rectified and sound judgments may be reinforced. Accordingly, the intern is provided with opportunities to make judgments and to profit from corrective experiences. Through repeated exposure to the clinical decision making process during the internship year, the intern

Paper presented at the Association of Psychology Internship Centers Annual Meeting, Washington, D.C., August 1982 (Revised).

learns what were the most appropriate and therapeutic choices. Consequently, the internship setting should begin to approximate the conditions that the intern will experience upon entering the realm of professional clinical practice. There is little tolerance for poor judgments after the intern has entered such independent clinical practice.

The observation of other individuals, no matter how adept or experienced they are, is no substitute for the direct experience the intern can receive by routine clinical practice. There is a Chinese proverb that perhaps exemplifies the essence of the clinical internship experience; I hear and I forget, I see and I remember, I do and I understand. Only by getting the feel of being a clinician can the intern become a clinician. Clinical practice is not the predominately intellectual experience it may have been in graduate school. Clinical practice does not require the correct answering of exam questions or proficient writing of term papers; instead it is the breathing of life into academic knowledge as one deals with real people and real problems. Through the clinical internship experience the graduate student can come to understand more of the facets of what it means to be a clinician.

This is not to say that activities reinforced in graduate education have no place in clinical practice. Indeed the ability to think critically, evaluate therapeutic effectiveness, create new treatment programs, coherently present data, and make and evaluate reasonable hypotheses, are all skills necessary to the clinician internship and serve a purpose beyond the level of graduate education and theoretical parlance.

The clinical internship is to prepare the intern in the best possible way for the professional activities that will be engaged in upon graduation. The argument can be strongly made that the best method of preparation is one that provides a maximum amount of positive transfer between training and practice. In essence, the more activities an intern does on internship that will be required later on in practice, the better prepared he or she will be. This model indicated immersion in clinical activities with primary responsibility for conducting such practice residing with the intern.

In sum, we assume that internship training is an important component in the development of a clinical psychologist. Maintaining quality internship training in the face of increasing financial and service pressures, however, is a major issue facing psychologists in the real world. To give some context to our further comments we would like to refer briefly to two significant developments in our communities and in psychology.

LOSS OF FISCAL INNOCENCE

Psychologists have made various efforts on their own behalf in the past several year to try to assure that the funding suppport they have been used to will continue. Al Burstein (1982) outlined a number of these efforts in the April, 1982 Newsletter of the Association of Psychology Internship Centers (APIC).

He noted that psychologists have been able to make concerted efforts to resist reduction in federal funds for education and training. Psychologists are also waging an aggressive attack against them in psychotherapeutic practice. Psychologists are showing increasing sophistication in legislatures, in courtrooms, in class action suits and, in testimony before many different committees. Burstein also noted that psychologists are taking vigorous exception to pay-back requirements for training that was directly funded by tax dollars. A major reason for this exception seems to be the assumption that trainees in other disciplines are escaping the obligation for such pay-back and psychologists do not want to be treated deferentially.

Yet, in the past we may have wanted to be treated in special ways because we have assumed ourselves to be "the good guys" and worthy of public support. Again referring to Burstein, we have essentially suggested that what is good for psychologists is good for society, that the public interest and psychology's interest are co-extensive. But we may have to give up the assumption that psychologists are viewed as good guys and that we are loved and the public wants to support us. Many readers may be aware that significant segment of the public views psychologist activities quite suspiciously, perhaps even as quite leftist. This sizable segment of the general population is being added to what is probably a majority of citizens who want relief from tax burdens. Psychologists will have to think about what they cost the taxpayer; the taxpayer, through legislators and administrators, is asking what psychology costs him or her in taxes and in spiralling health care costs. We have to be able to respond to questions such as: What funds can be saved, or reallocated by elimination of psychology services? What services will be lost by eliminating psychology?

To survive as organizational entities in most health care settings, psychologists will have to become very knowledgeable about their budget costs, both direct and indirect. They will have to be able to demonstrate that their existence is cost effective. They will have to document their contributions in such areas as: patient fee generation, unique services to patients, and, necessary and valued educational contributions to other disciplines.

CHALLENGE TO EDUCATIONAL LAISSEZ-FAIRE

As a discipline, psychology has long abstained from giving direction to educational/training programs purporting to prepare persons for the discipline. The end result of such a stance has been painfully apparent to credentialing bodies and licensing boards as they try to identify psychologists for the general public. A great variety of educational and experience backgrounds are claimed to be psychology, or psychological in nature. The profession has also more generally become aware that there are many persons in society who are called psychologists whose encounters with psychology faculties have been of the briefest kind.

In the absence of clear definitions of graduate education and internship training, our programs remain heterogeneous and amorphous. In the face of this diversity we can not describe the exact nature of educational programs we are trying to defend, nor can we operationalize the specific educational/training activities that we are asking to have supported. An individual program director cannot point to nationally mandated program requirements in an effort to maintain quality training. An exception to this assertion is the standards used by the APA Committee on Accreditation. There are, however, many doctoral studies programs and internship programs that do not qualify or apply for accreditation. And we really cannot document how tax-supported programs differ from home-made programs, let alone how they lead to better-qualified practitioners. Many home-made psychologists have cost the taxpayer relatively little; they are relatively self-educated.

You should know our strong conviction that laissez-faire and smorgasboard internship offerings are not the best that psychologist faculties/staffs can do. We believe that we should define acceptable education/training in psychology and document that it is taking place in the individual program and for the individual student. We need to be more specific about what the graduate student is to learn on campus and in the internship field setting. We believe that such definition and documentation are very important quality control measures.

There have undoubtedly been many times when clinical students have been expected during the inernship year to make up for deficits in their graduate school program. The clinical socialization process for academic graduates is often provided by the internship. Internships also provide very specific skill training, for example, biofeedback, neuropsychological assessment, behavior modification. However, if graduate programs and internships are mutually unaware of the specifics of each others characteristics and goals, deficits may go uncorrected, and skills may be duplicated at the expense of expanding and developing on the framework provided by graduate education.

We could ask that graduate programs document precisely what experiences take place in academic and practicum settings, for example, procedures learned, hours of supervision, and experiences with different kinds of patients. Similarly, regarding the internship, we are often left with only impressions of what clinical psychologists and interns do. For example, if we knew that psychologists were required to do neuropsychological examinations routinely in field settings, this could be a reason to request graduate faculties to teach that background and specific subject matter. If we knew how many neuropsychological examinations an intern did during the course of one year we could make a statement about the training emphasis in that area.

With the development of specialty certification procedures, psychology may eventually develop routine residency-type training beyond the internship level. If such residency-type training becomes more routine it will undoubtedly demand of psychology faculties/staff that they define, in advance, what the graduate of such a residency should be able to do on completion. In order to claim skills in given procedures, such a resident would have to document that the procedures have been taught and practiced during training. This is not unlike various medical residents who record every patient contact; in fact, in the surgical specialties the resident has to provide documentation for having completed a specific number of surgical procedures before the experience will qualify for specialty certification.

A PROGRAM DATA BASE

As such specialty areas as behavioral medicine, clinical health psychology, or medical psychology expand it is important to consider what educational background and skills a psychologist must acquire in order to enter the specialty area as a competent professional. The same point can be made about new developments and expansion in other areas of psychology. It is proposed here that regardless of the area of specialization in which the clinician wishes to practice, there are fundamental skills which apply to and cut across areas of specialization. The foundation of clinical psychology, irrespective of the area of practice, is the empirical assessment and evaluation of the problem requiring therapeutic intervention. No matter what the individual practitioner's theoretical orientation is, some form of "diagnosis" is made. The strength of the psychological approach is that the clinician utilizes validated psychodiagnostic procedures to help reach a decision about the nature of a patient's problem.

One perspective on the type of training the graduate student should receive in order to best prepare for clinical internship is to determine what activities the clinical intern actually will be engaged in during training. To develop some data on this question we examined 250 consecutive case files of adult patients referred to our Medical Psychology Outpatient Clinic. The information obtained from each case file was age, sex, inpatient or outpatient, evaluation or treatment, referral source, physical diagnosis, referral question(s), assessment procedures, diagnosis, and whether or not the patient was followed for therapy. These data were then compiled as a representative sample of the nature of the referrals, methods of evaluation and disposition of patients seen during routine clinical practice at an internship program in a health care setting.

The following is a brief summary of the data obtained in our study which describes what the interns were doing and with whom. Patients ranged in age from 16 to 86 years of age with the modal age group being 21 to 25 years of age. Thirty-six percent of patients referred were males and 64% were females. There were 39 separate sources of referral. The majority of sources (64%) were from departments and clinics on our campus. The most frequent source of referral was Psychiatry and second most frequent source was Neurology. Referrals within the sample had a total of 46 separate physical diagnoses. Headache, seizure disorder, head trauma, physical complaints, and dementia were the top five physical diagnoses. It is, however, interesting to note when reasons for referral were examined, the reasons fell within the province of traditional clinical psychology activities. Intellectual and/or personality assessment as isolated referral questions, or in combination, neuropsychological evaluation, and affective status assessment were the top reasons for referral, and accounted for 68% of the referrals. We are not entirely sure that we know what this referral pattern represents. Do we see these referrals because we have trained referral sources that this is what we do? Or, are these critical referral questions that have to be answered so that the referral source can practice appropriately?

The methods of evaluation used for this population are quite time honored. The five most frequently used psychodiagnostic procedures followed by their frequency of usage were: the Clinical Interview (225), Wechsler Adult Intelligence Scale (173), Minnesota Multiphasic Personality Inventory (159), Hopkins Symptom Check List SCL-90-R (115), and the Wechsler Memory Scale (53). Twenty-two separate assessment procedures were used to evaluate the 250 patients. Standardized assessment procedures were used most often as compared with projective techniques. The variety of assessment procedures suggest the importance of familiarity with traditional methods of psychological assessment.

The patients who were evaluated received a total of 34 psychological diagnoses. The most frequent diagnosis, not surprisingly, was depressive reaction. The finding of a wide variety of psychological diagnoses, including both organic and psychological diagnoses, supports the general research findings in the literature that the majority of patients who present with physical complaints are also experiencing some psychological disturbance. Of the 250 patients seen on referral, 61 were subsequently seen for therapy and 189 were not followed by the department thus indicating the importance of the evaluation procedure alone in psychological practice. These data bolster the argument that psychodiagnostic skills are heavily relied upon in a specialized area such as medical psychology.

In summary, it is important that the clinical psychology internship experience be perceived as a continuous rather than a discontinuous step in the education of the clinical psychologist. The internship setting provides the opportunity for the intern to put into practice during his or her daily activities those skills and abilities he or she has acquired during graduate school. Abstract knowledge is no substitute for experience. Nor can the graduate student develop the sense of professionalism that is required without being afforded the opportunities to behave as a professional. Familiarity and adeptness with traditional psychological procedures can provide the intern with the breadth of knowledge that distinguishes the field from other health disciplines which must rely on psychology for empirical determination of a patient's psychological functioning.

AN INDIVIDUAL INTERN DATA BASE

In our efforts to make it possible for an individual intern to document internship training experiences we have developed a productivity system that has both clinic management and educational usefulness; we will return to its clinic management usefulness a bit later. From an education documentation standpoint, we ask each intern to tabulate weekly, and then we can summarize monthly, quarterly, and yearly, a number of appointments scheduled, kept, canceled, and not kept. The age and sex distribution of patients seen are recorded as are the evaluation/treatment procedures done. A record is made of the primary diagnoses assigned to each patient.

For example, during one internship year Intern A schedules 455 patient appointments. Of this total number, 354 (77.8%) were kept, 58 (12.7%) were canceled, and 43 (9.5%) were not kept. Intern A saw a total of 146 male and 208 female appointments during the year. The most frequent evaluation/treatment procedures were: Individual Therapy (adult), Intellectual-Personality Evaluation, Child Therapy, Consultation Interview, Couples Therapy and Neuropsychological Evaluation (partial). The most frequent diagnoses assigned to Intern A's patients were: Avoidant Personality, Psychogenic Pain (site unspecified), Relationship Problems, Nondependent Use of Drugs, Adjustment Reaction, and Major Depressive Disorder.

IMPLICATIONS FOR MAINTAINING QUALITY INTERNSHIP TRAINING

Some psychologists may assume that internship training is likely to be impaired by increasing financial and service pressures. We want to at least suggest that this is not necessarily so. If we keep in mind that the intern should have some experience doing what he or she will do upon graduation, then the experience of these pressures may be a necessary part of internship training. We certainly assume that patient-care responsibility is something the intern should experience; why not also professional self-care and self-survival training? There are some aspects of practice that probably can be learned only when one is busy and under time pressure. We refer to such important aspects of practice as efficiency in practice functioning and economical time management. It may also be that financial pressures will allow the intern to experience the realization that it takes money for psychologists to exist and that somebody pays for our existence.

A major factor in maintaining quality education is a set of educational standards against which a program can measure itself. If national standards can be adopted, a given internship program director can insist on adherence to them. To be useful, however, such standards should be specific enough so that documentation procedures can be developed for them. Training standards might call for seeing a wide age range and diagnostic distribution of patients of both sexes. They might call for some minimum number of assessment/treatment procedures. Such standards calling for distributed or varied training practice experience could do much to deal with the concern that the quality of internship training will suffer because the intern will do the same procedure over and over. With training standards and with documentation both intern and training director will be motivated to see to it that this does not happen; documentation is as much of a report card for the training program as for the student.

With the financial pinch that many institutions find themselves in there is a strong need to take a candid look at all aspects of institutional functioning and to establish budgetary accountability. Coffman, Slaikeu, and Iscoe (1979) describe an approach to cost accounting offices of universities, using their own concepts and methods. Loucks, Burstein, Schoenfeld, & Stedman (1980) comment that with federal funding for psychology internships becoming increasingly uncertain, finding alternative sources of stipends for these trainees is becoming more important. An obvious potential source for these funds is the service settings that provide the training. By and large, such finding will depend on accurate and plausible documentation of the services provided by the trainees and the cost of those services.

To use our own productivity system as an example, a record is made of the clinic or hospital ward from which each patient came; in this way we can identify patient referral sources and also track trends in referrals. We record the pay status and pay codes for each patient and whether the visit was with a new or established patient; in recording the pay codes we identify the source of third-party reimbursement and can document our experience with these payers. Finally, and importantly, it is possible to calculate the fee generation for each individual intern, and other providers, and for our clinic as a whole. In the situation of Intern A, the total number of Evaluation/Treatment procedures that were done by this intern lead to a gross fee generation for one year of $30,523.

When revenue generation and budgetary allocations balance there is nothing to be saved by eliminating psychology and internship stipends. Of course, it is not quite that simple, as Loucks et al. (1980) point out, because the costs of intern supervision and teaching support that the interns require must also be calculated in trying to balance a budget for internship training. However, in our experience, a Medical Psychology Clinic, even with teaching and stipend costs assigned to it, can operate in the black. Given detailed clinic management information, it is possible to be aware of referral sources and to nurture them and, from the standpoint of quality training, to know the patient care activities of each intern and to distribute patient care experiences. When one has a clinical service/training program that ends up the fiscal year in the black, one is in a reasonably good position to continue such a program.

Even so, it is important for psychologist survival and training purposes to also develop and to offer services that are unique to psychology. In our setting these include psychological testing, neuropsychological evaluation, parenting skills training, stress and pain management with psychotherapy and relaxation/biofeedback procedures, and so.

Finally, just as psychologists want to learn from other disciplines, we need to contribute educational experiences in return. For example, residents in other specialty areas, and some medical students, have chosen to spend some of their elective time in our clinic, training especially in the areas of stress management and psychological assessment procedures.

One further comment: our interns have a full schedule of didactic and practice experiences. They are also paid relatively well. The training stipends are the same for the first year Internal Medicine trainee and the Medical Psychology trainee. We do not want the Medical Psychology interns to feel that they are second-class citizens in a health care setting. We consider them the peers of other trainees. To us it is unthinkable that a psychology intern would not have a reasonable stipend. It is hard for us to imagine a health care setting where intern services do not generate patient fees. Not to return some of these fees as a stipend, or perhaps even to use psychology intern fee generation to pay stipends to trainees in other disciplines, is simply discriminatory.

We expect graduate programs to provide their students with the basic knowledge and skills in psychology that will be utilized in the internship year. We expect interns to begin to learn how to assume clinical responsibilities and to face service demands and fiscal pressures; such issues are part of the real world of psychology. We also expect the real world of the internship program and health care setting to reward the intern appropriately, e.g., with a stipend and status comparable to other trainee clinicians in that setting.

REFERENCES

Burstein, A. G. (1982). Remarks from the chair. *APIC Newsletter, 7,* 1–2.

Coffman, D. A., Slaikeu, K. A., & Iscoe, I. (1979). An approach to cost accounting and cost effectiveness in the delivery of campus mental health services. *Professional Psychology, 10,* 656–665.

Loucks, S., Burstein, A. G., Schoenfeld, L. A., & Stedman, J. M. (1980). The real cost of psychology intern services: Are they a good buy? *Professional Psychology, 11,* 898–900.

Reading 45

Is There A Free Lunch? Experiences With Unfunded Interns

Albert S. Carlin
University of Washington School of Medicine

At this time of shrinking federal support for clinical psychology training programs a great deal of creativity will be required in order to continue to provide meaningful training experiences for predoctoral clinical psychology interns. Not only has training grant support diminished, but educational institutions and clinical facilities are also facing potential financial crisis as state support of education erodes and efforts are made to contain costs of medical care. One possible solution is the unfunded intern. The University of Washington Medical School Rotating Psychology Internship (UWRIP) has had long standing experience with unfunded interns and found it to be a workable alternative.

Before reviewing the experiences of the UWRIP with unfunded interns it will be helpful to describe the program. Housed administratively in the Department of Psychiatry & Behavioral Sciences it is a multidepartmental program that also includes the departments of Family Medicine, Rehabilitation Medicine, Pediatrics, Neurological Surgery, Psychiatry and Behavioral Sciences, a pediatrics educationally oriented child development center, and the university student health center. The program might be considered a confederacy which encompasses three hospitals (University Hospital, Harborview Medical Center, and Children's Orthopedic Hospital). A total of 24 separate rotation sites exist. Each intern, in conference with an assigned preceptor, selects a mix of rotations which best meet his/her training needs and goals. The internship year consists of three four month rotations; thus each intern has experiences on three to five clinical training sites, some of which are full time and some half time. All sites provide training in assessment, consultation, and intervention, but each provides a unique slant to the basic armamentarium of the clinical psychologist.

Initially, the program limited interns to those for whom a funded position was available. Occasionally, an individual requested an internship experience after funds were allocated. Frequently the reason had to do with the need to be in Seattle; a spouse assigned to the area by the military, the desire not to interupt children's education, or child custody matters. At times these individuals could garner support from their home institution, at other times a working spouse provided support, still others were faculty on sabbatical from other institutions. At first the program director and steering committee were uneasy about such arrangements. However, they decided that if the person was

Paper presented at the Association of Psychology Internship Centers Annual Meeting, Washington, DC, August 1982.

qualified and if the training experience was available then precluding the experience for that person because we could not pay him seemed unnecessarily rigid. In the halcyon days when funding was less a concern the problematic aspects of unfunded interns revolved not around issues of professional identity, but whether an unfunded intern would be willing to make the same commitment of time and effort as those who were paid. That is, would interns be willing to do "scut work" and put in the extra required hours to make it a valid and intensive experience. Experience revealed that despite their amateur status they were professionals. They worked hard and bore no grudges; inherent reinforcers proved sufficient. With time the presence of a few unfunded interns mixed in per year became the usual state of affairs.

The method of intern selection may help clarify our situation. Stipends are offered on the basis of the ranked average ratings made by two to four faculty members. Initial offers of stipends are made to a limited number of applicants. The next highest group are informed that they may receive an offer of a stipend within the acceptance period, but if they do not, they will definitely be accepted without one if they are interested. The next group of alternates are told the probabilities are less that a stipend will be available for them, but that if they are interested in coming without a stipend it is likely that we will have room for them. The final group, receiving rankings below the top one-third is not accepted. We discourage applicants from informing us of their interest in joining the program on an unfunded basis until all of the stipends have been distributed, although this process cannot be entirely clear cut since most of the interns who choose to come to this program have been offered positions elsewhere and must clarify their situation during the brief, wild February mating period.

The February offers of stipends are made conservatively, since the next year's financial situation is not completely set by that early date. When additional funds become available, as they do most years, the policy is to divide these funds among the nonfunded interns. This is done on the basis of a policy decision to ignore rankings once interns are aboard. The amounts of additional funds have ranged from token sums to additional stipends. Recently we have had the anomalous situation of acquiring an additional stipend which could not be split, and in that situation it was awarded via a lottery among those unfunded interns willing to accept the payback agreement.

As is clear from the above, once the group is in place no distinctions exist between funded and unfunded interns and initial rankings are ignored. Administrative arrangements are made to ensure that all have appropriate identification, library privileges, and even the rarest of all commodities, parking. One difference does exist. The program has access to two different types of funds: those which are allocated to the internship from a training grant or other general funds and require no *quid pro quo* and those generated by a specific training site which require the presence of an intern. Over the years it is usually the case that interns distribute themselves over most of the sites. On occasion a site may be without sufficient self selected interns to constitute the equivalent of a full time intern. If that site has provided an encumbered stipend then an intern is assigned for one or more rotations. Those accepting stipends are aware of this stipulation and agree to it; those who are unfunded are free from any required assignment. Thus only funded interns may be assigned to fulfill a stipend obligation.

So much for the mechanics of the program. If the process of awarding stipends seems complex, the scheduling of the entire group's rotation choices is an astounding process. The complexity of the administrative tasks is the dark side of the rich and flexible program within which faculty and intern tailor a program to meet each intern's training needs.

Our experience with unfunded interns has been an unqualified success. Over the years those few interns who have failed to meet program standards for completion have not been the unfunded. However, it is important to remember that no one was accepted merely because he/she were willing to come unfunded. Entry criteria must be met before anyone is accepted into the program.

Perhaps as a function of cognitive dissonance and efforts to reduce it, unfunded interns have expressed satisfaction with their experiences. None, and they tend to be an assertive and outspoken group not known for their passivity nor for keeping opinions to themselves, has expressed feelings or beliefs of having been exploited or victimized by unfunded status. No doubt most would prefer to be funded (except for one who thought a stipend would complicate her tax status and another who did not want to obligate herself to the payback provisions now in force), but all also preferred the UWRIP or an opportunity to stay in or come to Seattle. In part, some of the unfunded interns may be contributing the "Mt Rainier tax" which many Seattle residents pay for the privilege of seeing that scenic wonder the three or four days a year it shows itself. That is, it is possible that geographic factors may contribute to the UWRIP's ability to attract unfunded interns.

What are the issues surrounding unfunded interns? In terms of consumer satisfaction both interns and faculty psychologists have found the arrangement eminently workable. In large part the success grows from being able to choose talented and promising people from a large pool. Those who have been chosen are committed to an ideal of professionalism built around both a desire for training and getting the job done in a journeyman fashion. The major issues are the meta-issues surrounding the worth and dignity of psychology as a profession. Does the existence of unfunded interns somehow cheapen or demean psychology as a profession? The UWRIP experience suggests not. In part the role models provided by faculty psychologists serves as a prophylaxis. Psychologists provide an active leadership role in the academic departments and the clinical services to which they are attached. Indeed, a psychologist has been acting chair of the Department of Psychiatry and Behavioral Sciences. Perhaps falsely secure, the UWRIP internship faculty is of the opinion that the dignity of a profession resides in what it does as much, if not more, than in its salary. The payoff to unfunded interns is a commitment to the educational and training process. Both interns and faculty choose intern responsibilities on the basis of educational opportunities, not funding. It may be a greater loss to force those in the learning process to engage in activities because they pay rather than because of inherent interest. For example, training opportunities may exist on a service that is not a "money maker" or interns may benefit from evaluating a patient purely out of academic interest. Limiting contact to fee for service may also limit training opportunities. The introduction of pay-back provisions may make some interns sufficiently uneasy about accepting funds that have such contractual agreements.

Certainly the UWRIP preference is to have stipends for all and the group is constantly working to develop new funding sources and increase fiscal stability. The stipends paid are a pittance in relationship to the professionalism, competence, and experience of our interns. The stipends are not remuneration for services rendered, but monies which enable interns to partake of the educational program we offer. As is usually the case, and will probably in the future be more the case, the capacity to train exceeds the capacity to pay. Internship programs must allow sufficient flexibility in their funding arrangements to allow interns choice. Provision of support in the form of stipends, space, and other support services are a mark of the commitment of and institution commitment to the existence of training program. Without such support there is no training program. However, the existence of unfunded interns allows extension of that support and does so without weakening the program or the profession of psychology.

Reading 46
A Case for the Nonrotational Internship

Robert D. Langston
The University of Texas at Austin

THE ROTATIONAL INTERNSHIP: PROS AND CONS

Historically, the internship in clinical psychology has been of a rotational nature: The intern would spend 3 to 4 months on one service, for example, adult inpatient, and then be rotated to another service. Reasons for a rotating internship included the assumption that the student should be exposed to a number of different clinical populations to obtain experience in working with

Reprinted from Professional Psychology, 10(5), 666-669.

all psychological disorders; the assumption that the intern should not be a victim of premature specialization (the training faculty was to assure that this did not occur); and although never explicitly stated, the understanding that the student interns in major centers could provide coverage where there was insufficient professional staff to meet the service needs of all the facilities. If the student did not have this broad clinical experience prior to the internship, then this arrangement was necessary and productive.

The manner in which the intern gained experience in long-term therapy training varied from setting to setting. Usually, the intern maintained a long-term therapeutic relationship with a limited number of patients across the rotational system, regardless of his or her primary rotation. (These patients were often drawn from the intern's first rotation.) By having a limited number of long-term psychotherapy patients, the intern was assured of not being in a repetitive pattern of "hello-good-bye" psychotherapy, which of necessity typifies psychotherapy training at the practicum level. That is, the intern did not move directly from the initial to the terminal stage of the psychotherapy with no middle, or working-through, stage. Since these cases were often assigned during the first rotation, no attempt was made to match the interests of the intern and the reality of the types of patients available from that service.

One of the objections to having internships that exclusively reflect the rotational model is that the rotational model assumes that the intern does not have the knowledge or experience on which to base a reasoned desire for working with a more restricted range of patients during the year. However, according to the descriptive brochures distributed by university training programs, it appears that students are provided with a substantial array of practicum experiences before the internship and that some effort is exerted by the faculty of these programs to assure that students can select, or be assigned to, a variety of settings. Thus, the student is probably exposed to a fairly sizable number of different service settings and patient populations before the internship year and should be in a position to rationally decide whether specialization would be appropriate at the internship level of training. If this is true, then there must be available alternatives to the rotational internship.

THE SINGLE-SERVICE (NONROTATIONAL) INTERNSHIP

One alternative to the rotational internship is the 1-year, single-service internship. The descriptive brochures should emphasize that this is a nonrotational internship and detail the patient population to be served. The prospective intern may then assess whether that particular setting offers what is being sought. This is very much related to the "truth in packaging" concept endorsed by the American Psychological Association. Because the potential hazard in this type of internship training is premature specialization, the single-service internship must be able to assure the student of the availability of a variety of patients, although the number of patients is not as extensive as in the rotational system.

Certain advantages may be realized with the single-service internship, one of which is the opportunity for the intern to work with and assume responsibility for a larger number of patients, including those in long-term therapy, since the constraints imposed by moving from one service to another are not found in the single-service setting. This exposure to working with a large number of patients on a long-term basis has several benefits. First, the intern can witness, under supervision, the variety of ways in which patients negotiate the middle phase of therapy. In all too many writings on psychotherapy, the middle stage is described as if it were a process that is fairly consistent across patients and across therapists, and through the direct experience of working through conflicts with a fairly large number of patients, the intern may ascertain that there are gross differences in the manner in which this stage is negotiated. Second, the intern can observe across patients the complexity of interaction of impulse and defense and experience the various modes of communication used by numbers of patients. Third, the intern will be forced to confront the variety of reactions experienced by the therapist with different patients. Thus, the issue of countertransference becomes one that must be examined. With a more limited number of long-term cases, this phenomenon is often avoided.

Given these advantages, there must also be assurances that not all aspects of clinical diversity are specialized. For example, if one were to consider two basic considerations to be an adequate age range and an adequate sampling of the range of psychopathology, then only one of these should be limited in terms of availability to the intern. As students begin to narrow their interests in psychology, the clearest distinction they make is associated with the age variable. After a number of practica, most students know whether they feel more comfortable or more proficient working with adults or children. (Since some of the techniques used in working with children are highly specialized, then perhaps interns should not be required to assume responsibility for child intervention if, based on their practical experience with children, they feel uncomfortable or nonproficient.)

Within broad age limitations, probably the most important variable is the range and diversity of pathology. Thus, for example, if the age range is constricted to the adult population, then the intern should have the opportunity to work with individuals who range from acute situational disturbances to the flagrant psychoses. Using the same age constriction, it is very important that the intern have a variety of intervention techniques available, ranging from the intake interview and crisis intervention to long-term therapy. Within the self-selected restricted range of age, the single-service intern's proficiency with this specific population would be greater than that of the rotating intern. In our experience, interns who serve in this nonrotational internship attain sufficient depth of understanding of a single age range and can subsequently generalize these experiences to other, and similar, populations. This makes the concern over premature specialization somewhat less significant.

Psychological assessment is another type of clinical activity that should be included in the single-service internship as an integral part of the training. Although there is still considerable sound and fury over the place of assessment in the training of psychologists, there is probably no quicker way to familiarize the intern with psychodynamic operations. That, of course, assumes that the internship agency values the psychodynamic approach. Interns should have the opportunity to evaluate a sizable number of patients so that they not only receive supervised experience in this clinical activity unique to psychology, but that they also observe the complexities of personality organization and operations.

A final opportunity, which is perhaps best available in the single-service internship, is that of involvement in administration. The intern should be intimately involved in all decisions made at an administrative level and understand not only the facts but also the politics underlying the decision-making process. In the rotational internship the trainee is probably not in any one setting long enough to become sufficiently involved in these activities. Paradoxically, psychologists often assume administrative responsibilities later in their career, although they usually have had little or no exposure to this activity in their training. This exposure should cover all aspects of administrative operations, including personnel practices and budgetary considerations. First-hand experience with administration could provide invaluable learning and perhaps reduce the culture shock of the young psychologist who leaves professional training with only a naive application of these administrative skills.

CONCLUSION

It should be reaffirmed that there is, and should be, ample room for both the rotational and single-service internship. Each of the two models has distinct advantages as well as disadvantages. The critical factor would seem to be, however, that certain students benefit more from one than another along the variable of previous clinical experience. It would certainly seem unwise to assert that the rotational internship is the only model that is acceptable, but clearly the APA in its accreditation statement appears to be dangerously close to that position.

Reading 47
The Uncertain Direction of Clinical Psychology

George W. Albee
University of Vermont

INTRODUCTION

One of the major sources of psychology's strength and viability throughout its history has been its diversity. The diversity in its subject matter has been reflected in the diversity of its students. To become a competent psychologist the field has insisted that its students demonstrate knowledge about many areas including the principles of learning, the operation of the central nervous system, the details of the sensory processes, the laws governing perception, the principles of motivation, the complexities of measurement and statistics, the wide range or social influences on behavior, and the dynamics of psychopathology and behavior change. This sprawling, exciting, vast range of topics offered the fledgling psychologist a whole smorgasbord of specialty areas from which to concentrate.

I am concerned at the dramatic narrowing of options and choices in psychology that has developed in recent years. I have been accused often of opposing the practice of psychotherapy by psychologists. The point I have been trying to make is that psychotherapy has become practically the exclusive preoccupation of a great many psychologists, and its attractions as a way of life have become so visible and so seductive as to lure large numbers of young people into this endeavor as their exclusive activity. I see psychology in grave danger of becoming a profession of psychotherapists. This prospect frightens me for two reasons. First, training large numbers of psychologist-psychotherapist practitioners does very little to improve the mental health of the general populace; and second, an exclusive preoccupation by clinical psychologists with one-to-one service locks us into supporting a health-illness medical model to explain psychopathology, because the money to pay for our therapy is channeled through a medical-model conduit.

There is an ancient wisdom, acquired over the past century by the field of public health, that holds that no mass plague or condition afflicting humankind has ever been brought under control or eliminated by attempts at treating affected individuals or by producing large numbers of practitioners (Bloom, 1977; Gordon, 1957). There are many examples of successful reduction and/or elimination of widespread pathological conditions through effective techniques of prevention, so that we can be encouraged to look to preventive efforts in mental health rather than putting all of our eggs in the treatment basket.

Reprinted from J. R. McNamara and A. G. Barclay (Eds.). (1982). *Critical Issues, developments, and trends in professional psychology* (pp. 295–312). New York: Praeger.

GAPS BETWEEN SUPPLY AND DEMAND

According to several independent estimates (Kiesler, 1980; President's Commission on Mental Health, 1978; Ryan, 1969) there are somewhere between 30 million and 35 million people in the United States seriously afflicted with severe emotional disturbances. Klerman (1980) calls these the "hard-core mentally ill." He uses this term in the traditional psychiatric sense. In any event, these seriously disturbed people include persons addicted to alcohol: those with severe incapacitating anxiety; those subject to handicapping depression; those who are psychotic, mentally-retarded, and disturbed as a result of organic deficits, including a large group of aged people. In addition to this 30-odd million people, there is still a much larger group of persons who each year experience acute stress as a result of the traumas of living and who react with emotional disorganization and disruption. Members of this latter large group may have to deal with the death of a loved one; they may be affected by marital disruption and divorce; many experience injury or acute illness leading to hospitalization, surgery, or the application of other high medical technology; many are unemployed or thrown out of work through no fault of their own. Also included in this vast heterogeneous group are persons subject to a high level of chronic stress from which the spikes of acute stress are often completely disorganizing. Examples of this latter group include members of minority groups who must endure chronic discrimination and injustice, women who are underpaid and subject to sexual and other harassment in the workplace, battered wives, and abused children. Klerman (1980) estimates this population of traumatized people to be something like 55 million!

In the most recent year for which we have data, a grand total of 7 million persons were actually seen for at least one interview or at least one contact by all of the mental health facilities in the country (President's Commission on Mental Health, 1978). These 7 million persons seen include those going to the private offices of psychologists and psychiatrists, to the community mental health centers, state hospitals, private psychiatric facilities, and children's treatment centers. The reader may very well pause to contemplate this gap between the number of distressed people in the population and the number of hours of professional help available. Kiesler (1980) has some interesting statistics on the enormous difference between professional time available and professional help needed.

As a result of this gap (which has not narrowed in two decades and more [Albee, 1959]), most emotionally disturbed people are either not receiving any professional intervention or are being "treated" by physicians not prepared by training or inclination to deal with these problems; so the "backbone of treatment" is the prescription of one of the minor tranquilizers.

There are also many "invisible" groups in our society whose members show high rates of significant pathology. A good example here is the 5 million migrant farmworkers and their families who eke out a precarious existence by following the crops and live under the most abysmally inhumane conditions. Five million is only a rough estimate because, as the President's Commission on Mental Health, Task Panel on Migrant and Seasonal Farmworkers (1978) points out, we spend more money in this country counting migratory birds than we spend counting migratory farmworkers. The amount of professional care of any kind available to these unfortunate people is simply zero. Another largely invisible group, with high rates of physical and mental infirmity, is the aged. It is well to remember that when we talk about elderly people we mean, for the most part, elderly women. Because the life expectancy of females in our society is significantly greater than for males, the older the cohort, the more largely it is female. Poverty-striken elderly women are rarely candidates for mental health services, including especially psychotherapy. Also neglected are multiproblem families, children in need of residential care, disturbed adolescents in trouble with the law, premature parents, and discharged or escaped mental hospital cases (Ryan, 1969).

PSYCHOLOGISTS' DENIAL

The psychologists-psychotherapists sitting in their offices in suburban medical buildings seeing a succession of relatively intelligent and verbal clients, mostly young adults, rarely pause to ask where their activity fits into the broader picture of societal need. These psychologists are usually kind, decent folk who believe in "the American Way." They attend PTA meetings, vote for planned increases in school taxes, shut off lights in rooms not in use, and otherwise exhibit admirable character traits. Their capacity for denial is very large. They do not concern themselves with the social injustices of a state hospital system that exists to provide warehouses for social misfits and other members of the "undesirable element." These unfortunates can be involuntarily committed, often by the most casual set of legal steps. They can be forced to ingest poisonous drugs that produce, in nearly half of the cases, an irreversible organic condition called tardive dyskinesia.

Our growing army of psychologists-psychotherapists has made a startling discovery. They have learned that there is a seemingly boundless demand for their services. In many places around the country practicing psychologists have banded together to create professional schools of psychology that really are professional schools of psychotherapy. This development is probably the most important trendsetter on the current psychological scene. At last count there were 35 professional schools at various stages of development, from full operation to final plans on the drawing borads. Within a decade the professional schools of psychology will be producing as many doctorates as all of the university clinical programs put together. At the present time, some 3,000 doctorates a year are leaving alma mater and entering the field (APA, Committee on Employment and Human Resources, 1980). About half of these new doctorates are in the fields of clinical, counseling, and school psychology. This number is destined to increase rapidly.

The American Psychological Association, long run by persons elected from academia, is in the process of being taken over by the professionals. Back in 1970 I predicted that the time was not far off when there would be an American Scientific Psychological Association and an American Professional Psychological Association (Albee, 1970). The current proposals of the APA Blue Ribbon Commission on Reorganization have been developed as a creative way to forestall the eventuality that I predicted by dividing the council into two sections and having alternating presidents from the scientific and professional wings. But this will work only for a time. There appears to be very little limit to the growth rate of professional psychologists-psychotherapists. Their natural enemies, the psychiatrists, are weak, ideologically confused, and numerically reduced in strength with no prospect for any significant growth in their ranks. The number of medical-school graduates entering psychiatric training has declined dramatically over the past 20 years (Albee, 1979). Fewer than 4% of our current medical graduates enter psychiatry, compared with nearly 10% in 1960. The reasons for this decline are to be explained, in part, as a consequence of the reluctance of medical schools to admit applicants who indicate an interest in psychiatry. Physicians and surgeons often do not have a very high opinion of psychiatry, in spite of the intensive recent efforts of psychiatrists to medicalize their specialty with repeated pledges of fealty to an organic model of mental illness and an ever-widening search for real medicines for the mind. Another reason for the rejection of psychiatry by medical students and recent medical graduates is to be found in the low income of psychiatry as a field. Compared with other specialties, psychiatrists are practically paupers. Any competent heart surgeon can make more in one day in the operating room than a psychiatrist can earn in a month seeing a succession of emotionally disturbed clients. In a field that worships income and status, the secret is out. Status of those specializing in psychiatry cannot compare with most other medical specialties.

So psychology is stepping into the breach. Psychology is a field that historically has been a salaried profession. Until fairly recently a majority of psychologists has been employed in educational settings where they have been paid only modest salaries. After World War II, applied psychology branched into employment settings outside academia, mostly in clinics and hospitals where again they were salaried. So, independent, fee-for-service practice is a markedly upward move in income for psychology, with many of the new doctorates earning more than their professors within a year or two of completing their degrees. With this kind of reinforcement, my exhortations to psychologists asking them to take vows of poverty, to enter the struggle for social justice, are merely an exercise in rhetoric with little prospect for success. And there are plenty of senior clinicians prepared to defend the practice of psychotherapy as a major contribution to human welfare (see discussion by Sue, Sue, & Sue, 1981). It is even possible for false prophets to explain why it is perfectly all right for psychology to accept the medical model of mental illness, to ask to be designated as "physicians," and to support laws governing reimbursement for psychotherapy (Derner, 1977). The result is that psychologists-psychotherapists increasingly can turn in claims for third-party reimbursements for the treatment of sick patients without a twinge of guilt. If only we could shut off third-party payments, we could slow down the pell-mell rush of our neophytes into this activity. Our hope for the future is to convince society that emotionally disturbed people are not sick, should not be called patients, and that psychotherapy should not be covered by health insurance.

THE MODEL DOES NOT FIT THE PROBLEMS

For many years I have been arguing that most of the problems that bring people to the psychotherapist's offices and to mental hospitals are not illnesses (Albee, 1964). Indeed, surveys of clients' problems provide evidence to convince all but the most intransigent that middle class people come for help with problems that are more appropriately described as social or interpersonal. Poor people are locked up for social deviances. In the early days of the century, and to an important extent even today, many of these problems have been generated by anxiety over sexuality and by the stresses of powerlessness. The majority of neurotics seeking psychotherapy were concerned with problems of impotence and frigidity; recently, clinicians have reported the ascendance of existential perplexities. In addition, there is a generous sprinkling of persons seeking help who are plagued with feelings of insecurity, anxiety, low self-esteem, guilt, and depression. A significant majority of clients has been women whose problems have been generated by a sexist culture that has tried to force women into demeaning second-class roles. By now everyone knows about the studies that indict members of the mental health professions for sexist attitudes and for a double standard in their definitions of mental health. In any case, we have felt uncomfortable with the sickness model and have recognized the social and interpersonal origins of disturbance.

In his later years even Sigmund Freud, only partially blinded by his paternalistic and chauvinistic sexism, argued strenuously and vociferously against medical training for persons who aspire to be psychoanalysts. He actually believed that medical training for psychotherapists was a hindrance. In *The Question of Lay Analysis* (Freud, 1926/1959) he was angry and critical of the U.S. insistence on medical training as a prerequisite for psychoanalytic training. Articulate and throughtful psychiatrists—Mariner, Szasz, Leifer, Laing, Cooper, Torrey—and sociologists—Goffman, Scheff, Reisman, Waiksman—have shown with devastating clarity the failure and even the dishonesty of the medical model of interpersonal disturbance. Persons from the socialist and Marxist left—Fromm, Goodman, Reich—have shown the social origins of psychopathology (Albee, 1980).

In the face of all of this criticism and opposition to the sickness (medical, illness, defect) model, to what forces can we attribute the ascendancy of the current sickness explanation of mental and emotional problems? I believe the answer is to be found in the same, basic, blatant ethnocentrism that historically has been part of the widespread ideological justification for slavery, for the jailing of paupers, for the exploitation of women, and for the ghastly treatment of foreign-born "lunatics." The best argument for the inhumanity of slavery and the denial of the rights to women and paupers and the warehousing of lunatics was that these people were constitutionally an inferior species and had no more rights than other subhuman species. It was, and is, self-evident to adherents that members of these groups each possess a personal defect that defines them as inferior.

In recent decades two major streams have mixed with U.S. psychiatry. The sickness or defect explanation for psychosis and the requirement of medical training for the practice of psychoanalysis made natural allies of the organic psychiatrists and the analytic psychiatrists and led to the inevitable medical domination of intervention at both levels of disturbance.

Elsewhere I have written in detail about the great misfortune that befell the field of psychology in 1946 (Albee, 1964). Up to then psychology was concerned with the careful research investigation of human behavior and with a largely environmental approach to the understanding of behavior change. Our history had emphasized developmental processes, classical conditioning, and instrumental conditioning. We had little experience with giving professional service, and we were quite unprepared for the values—power and money seeking—of those who controlled the professional marketplace.

Psychology was asked to send our fresh-faced, young, clinical psychology neophytes into the psychiatric setting for their apprenticeship training. The reinforcement schedules in this alien setting were immediate and direct. Graduate departments were given money to support increasing numbers of clinical graduate students, faculty, and applied-research programs. Perhaps too late, some of us realized that we had fallen into a trap. Together with social work, we provided the troops to staff the clinics and hospitals where psychiatry with its sickness model was firmly entrenched. Their small numbers were more than compensated for by their absolute control over us. Like other slaves we learned to speak their language and to adopt their guiding fictions. We even imitated them.

The National Institute for Mental Health (NIMH) poured the lion's share of its training funds into the support of every warm body that psychiatry departments could lure into residency training. Departments of psychiatry and their captive hospitals had as much money as they wanted. They bought us to do their scut work. Ironically, psychology programs got less training money from NIMH, but found other sources of support because graduate students in psychology were so bright and so much better prepared. In spite of this, we all learned to recite our catechism—"mental illness is an illness like any other"—and to say that we were treating sick patients. Many of us adopted this medical-model language without reflection as part of the natural order of things. Psychologists quietly and docilely did research on electric shock (Is the shape of the wave important? What about habit reversal after shock?) and on lobotomy (Is it amount of tissue removed or location?) without protest, and, just like Milgrim's subjects, we followed orders.

It is time and past time to take a stand. We must argue as vociferously as possible that mental illness is not an illness like any other, that generally no illness is involved. I do not want to see national health insurance cover psychotherapy by anybody. This means excluding psychiatry, too. Congress should not be too hard to convince. By the time national health insurance umbrellas over all U.S. medical and surgical care, the cost may well rival the defense budget. Before then Congress may readily agree that we simply cannot afford to pay for professional therapeutic help for troubled marriages, shaky self-esteem, and existential perplexity. The best guesses suggest that national health insurance will start with coverage for catastrophic illnesses, plus some cost-sharing arrangements for specified serious conditions, plus some more extended coverage for the poor and the elderly. But psychology should not relax its efforts. We should lobby actively against including coverage for problems in living and against office psychotherapy by psychiatrists, psychologists, and anyone else in the therapy field.

In an article in the *American Psychologist* (Albee, 1975), I argued that the best possible solution would be no coverage for either psychiatry or psychology for the simplest of reasons: the people we see are not sick. Changing a person's habits and self-confidence does not belong in the health-illness ballpark. One might argue, to be ridiculous, that tennis and golf lessons should also be covered by national health insurance, because they, too, are aimed at making a person healthier and more self-confident through habit training.

The inevitable response to this heresy is the warning that psychology may be left out if we do not lobby to be included in national health insurance along with psychiatry. The fact is that the number of psychiatrists is so small that they could not begin to handle even a modest fraction of persons knocking on their door if outpatient therapy for everyone was included. The ideal situation for psychiatry would be the 1946 model—where a few psychiatrists had the power and the budgetary control, and where social workers and psychologists did their work under exploitative circumstances. Let us not be exploited again! It may be too late, however. Already many departments of psychiatry are hiring salaried psychologists to generate income through psychotherapy fees collected by the department.

As a consequence of our growing emphasis on one-to-one psychotherapy, we are a long, long way from meeting the identified needs for intervention. Candidates for personal psychotherapy rarely are people with alcoholic addictions, incapacitating neuroses, mental conditions associated with old age, nor the serious forms of functional and organic psychoses. Many individuals being seen in our mental health centers and private offices are people with ordinary problems in living—those undergoing marital disruption, identity problems, and existential concerns that bring them to the therapist's chair or couch. So we are actually seeing far fewer than one in five of the seriously disturbed people.

LA PLUS CA CHANGE...

In spite of 20 years of intensive effort since the report of the Joint Commission on Mental Illness and Health (1960) with many millions of federal dollars poured into the support of federal training, the construction of centers, and the support of research, we are still falling behind.

In some ways I feel like Rip Van Winkle awakening from his 20-year nap. In 1959 I wrote *Mental Health Manpower Trends* (Albee, 1959), which examined the nation's needs and resources in the mental health delivery field. The book concluded with the observation that mental health professionals would continue to be in short supply, with psychiatrists being those with thinnest ranks. The book was one of a series published by the Joint Commission on Mental Illness and Health. The final report of that commission, *Action for Mental Health* (1960), led to a whole new national approach to helping emotionally disturbed people. The commission recommended that no new state hospitals be built, that the population of existing state hospitals be reduced drastically, and that a large number of new community mental health centers be built to make hospitalization unnecessary and to provide early help for people in trouble. A young senator, John F. Kennedy, read the book and soon thereafter was elected president. He sent the first ever presidential message on mental health to Congress with recommendations that the federal government get involved in funding mental health programs. Ultimately, the Congress appropriated funds for staffing the centers. Meanwhile, the National Institute for Mental Health was pouring money into the training of more psychiatrists, psychologists, social workers, and psychiatric nurses. The whole thrust of the Joint Commission report had been its emphasis on early treatment. By intervening early, the reasoning went, prolonged and expensive mental hospitalization might be avoided for large numbers of people. The economic savings would more than compensate for the increased costs of early treatment.

While nearly 800 centers were built between 1965 and the present, the whole mental health centers movement has been hampered by the chronic shortage of funds to pay staff salaries. Especially acute has been the shortage of psychiatrists. Despite the very large amount of money that the NIMH has provided to train psychiatrists, very few of those trained at public expense have been willing to throw in their lot with tax-supported and salaried agencies. Most prefer private office practice, although many are willing to provide a few hours a week to agencies. A kind of curious paradox has been developing. Medicine and psychiatry continue to have political clout and have been able to demand allegiance to the medical model for explaining emotional disturbances as a professional ticket of admission for nonphysicians to the centers. Every client (called patient) coming to a center must have a diagnosis taken from the greatly expanded *Diagnostic and Statistical Manual of Mental Disorders* (American Psychiatric Association, 1980), and everyone must have a treatment plan. This means that every user of a center must be found sick and, therefore, eligible for third-party medical payments. At the same time that the medical model has been placed in the center of the stage, a seriously developing and chronic shortage of psychiatrists has also occurred. Recently I reviewed the human resources situation in psychiatry and compared it with the situation 20 years ago. My analysis, published in *Hospital and Community Psychiatry* (Albee, 1979) finds that the shortage of psychiatrists continues after 20 years and grows worse. More than half of all psychiatrists in the country are to be found in five states: New York, Massachusetts, Illinois, Pennsylvania, and California as well as the District of Columbia. The rural states and the poor states have very few psychiatrists. Very few U.S.-trained psychiatrists take jobs in public hospitals or in public, tax-supported clinics and centers. These places have long depended on foreign-trained physicians to fill in their psychiatric vacancies. Now, with a change in the law controlling the use of foreign-trained physicians, this supply is rapidly drying up. The situation effects other branches of medicine in addition to psychiatry, but because of the vast demand for psychiatrists, the situation is more critical in this field.

As a consequence of the shortage of psychiatrists, mental health centers have been forced to appoint as directors qualified people from other disciplines and to hire people from these other disciplines as their front-line intervention personnel. So we see the strange situation of people who do not believe in the medical-illness model for mental disturbance forced to shelve programs aimed at resocialization, day care, consultation and education, and primary prevention, because none of these is reimbursable under the existing medical model.

ARE THERE ALTERNATIVES?

Is there any real hope? Not if we continue our mental health business as usual. Over and over again, surveys have found that individual psychotherapy and individual treatment represents the backbone of the efforts being made in our centers (see Glasscote, Sanders, & Forstenzer, 1964). As long as we labor on that particular treadmill (individual therapy), the situation will remain hopeless.

Two strategies for resolving our shortfall make sense. The first of these is to find alternatives to the one-to-one intervention by highly trained professionals. We need to develop mutual-aid groups, to encourage and develop self-help programs, to find workers who want to get out into the community and use existing networks and support systems (Silverman, 1978).

The second strategy is to put more and more effort into primary prevention. Here we can either work within the system, or attempt to change society in ways to make life more just and less stressful. No mass mental disorder afflicting large numbers of human beings has ever been controlled or eliminated by attempts at treating each affected individual. This is not only sound public health dogma, but it is as applicable to the field of mental health as to the field of public health.

What stands in our way? Why cannot more group programs be developed, more self-help and mutual-help efforts of the sort that have been demonstrated to be effective be developed, and why cannot we put more energy and effort into primary prevention? The answer is deceptively simple. None of these approaches fit the model that dominates our field. The illness model that stresses diagnosis, treatment, and one-to-one intervention discourages efforts by nonprofessionals and laypersons and has taken to arguing vehemently against primary prevention. The arguments of the illness-model adherents have a sort of boring consistency. These hold that only highly qualified health professionals can be invested with responsibility for treating sick patients. Diagnoses are urgently required for treatment plans. Just around the corner, they promise, new drugs and organic treatment methods will soon make dramatic changes in the number of people seen. Further, these people argue, we really do not know enough about the causes of each specific mental illness to do anything significant about prevention (Albee, 1980; Lamb & Zusman, 1979).

These tired old arguments would not be worth considering were it not for the fact that they are advanced by senior and respected people in the field. Why, we ask ourselves, is the medical model defended with such vehemence? Why is primary prevention so strongly rejected? Why are lay groups not welcome in our centers? The answer is also deceptively simple. Changing models means threatening the status quo. As Marx and Engels (1849/1935) pointed out, the ruling ideas of a society are those that support the ruling class. Primary prevention leads inevitably to a demand for social change through political action (Joffe & Albee, 1981).

SOCIAL JUSTICE IS THE GOAL OF PREVENTION

Even the scientific ideas in a given time in history are those that support the ideology of those in power. Occasionally, however, intellectual breakthroughs occur. One of the most important books on social justice is John Rawls's *A Theory of Justice* (1971). Rawls's view on justice has had a great impact on social philosophy and the law. I have not found many mental health professionals who have read Rawls, yet most of us believe in social justice as a prerequisite to positive mental health. The problem is to translate this belief into active opposition to the many forces that lead to injustice in our society. Reading Rawls helps.

Rawls begins with the hypothesis of "justice as fairness" and, in a complex series of intellectual steps, he arrives at two principles he believes essential to a just society. He argues that these principles would be developed by a group of "parties in the original position" each "with a veil of ignorance" about their own sex, their age, social class, and talents. Under these imaginary conditions, rational people, Rawls argues, could arrive at agreements about conditions epitomizing fairness in the society.

His first principle is that "each person is to have an equal right to the most extensive basic liberty compatible with a similar liberty for others" (p. 83). His second principle is that "social and economic inequalities are to be arranged so that they are both (a) to the greatest benefit of the least advantaged and (b) attached to offices and positions open to all under conditions of fair equality of opportunity" (p. 83).

This formulation of a system of justice, if applied to contemporary society, would guarantee, according to Rawls, "political liberty (the right to vote and to be eligible for public office) together with freedom of speech and assembly; liberty of conscience and freedom of thought; freedom of the person along with the right to hold (personal) property; and freedom from arbitrary arrest and seizure as defined by the concept of the rule of law" (p. 61). These liberties are all required to be equal by the first principle, since citizens of a just society are to have the same basic rights. Rawls's second principle is in opposition to the traditional conservative and liberal conception. The dominant view in present society allows for status and income to be determined by individual abilities and talents. Rawls argues that "there is no more reason to permit the distribution of income and wealth to be settled by the distribution of natural assets than by historical and social fortune" (p. 74). In Rawls's theory of justice, in order to provide real equality of opportunity, society must make every attempt to redress the social inequalities that have led to disadvantage. This means more attention and effort must be paid to those in less favorable social positions. This might roughly be translated into programs we call affirmative action. Clearly women, minorities, and the poor have been denied equal opportunity and basic liberty for centuries. If justice is fairness, as Rawls argues, it demands maximum social efforts to compensate for these historical injustices.

If we want to reduce psychopathology, we cannot simply try to help people adjust to an unjust society. We must make every effort to create a just system using our psychological knowledge in the effort.

Elsewhere there is a growing literature on primary prevention (Albee & Joffe, 1977; Bond & Rosen, 1980; Forgays, 1978; Joffe & Albee, 1981; Kent &

Rolf, 1979) in the field of psychopathology. This new emphasis has been called the fourth mental health revolution. For professional psychology, it is a critical option to preserve the viability of the field.

Primary prevention, aimed at preventing emotional distress or enhancing social competence, has specific definable characteristics. It is proactive not reactive, and it deals with large groups of people not yet affected with the conditions to be prevented. While it may direct its efforts at high-risk groups, these characteristics still hold. Preventive programs do not deal necessarily directly with people who might be at risk; they may be concerned instead with changing mass media, with laws affecting children, with changing fiscal and administrative policies. Prevention may also involve efforts at societal reform through political change (Joffe & Albee, 1981).

Persons involved in primary prevention efforts need not be the traditional mental health professionals. Primary prevention is involved when programs teach children better adaptive skills, when slum dwellings are condemned because of the presence of lead paint, when sex-education courses are taught in the schools, when sexist readers in the early grades are changed to nonsexist ones, when job skills are provided to unemployed teenagers, when mass media are enjoined from showing minorities and women in demeaning and stereotyped roles, when governmental programs to reduce unemployment are introduced, or when tax rates are modified to alter massive inequalities in income.

STRATEGIES FOR PREVENTION

In the report of the President's Commission on Mental Health, Task Panel on Prevention (1978), the following prevention programs were described:

1. *Efforts to reduce stress:* These activities can encompass an enormous range of interventions affecting large groups of people without direct contact with the individuals involved. Providing good day care for children of working mothers; developing outreach programs for the recently widowed; developing employment opportunities for teenagers—there are dozens of possible examples of stress-reduction efforts.

2. *Reducing organic factors contributing to distress:* Again, a wide range of activity—from programs to reduce auto accidents, offering genetic counseling, removing junk food from school lunchrooms, bringing free milk to children, encouraging good physical-exercise programs across the age span—all fit here.

3. *Increasing competence and coping skills:* The development of interpersonal cognitive problem-solving skills in kindergarten and the early grades, Head Start programs, planning and preparation for marriage, child rearing, planning for retirement fit here.

4. *Building support groups:* Again the research supports the argument that good support groups to which the individual can turn under stressful conditions significantly reduces the amount of emotional distress and disturbance.

SELECTED READINGS

5. *Improving self-esteem:* The civil rights movement, women's consciousness-raising groups, programs that enhance children's feelings about themselves all reduce later incidence.

All these strategies will require some redistribution of societal power. After reviewing the literature on primary prevention, Marc Kessler and I (1975) said the following:

> Everywhere we looked, every social research study we examined suggested that major sources of human stress and distress generally involve some form of excessive power. The pollutants of a power-consuming industrial society; the exploitation of the weak by the powerful; the overdependence of the automotive culture on powerful engines—power-consuming symbols of potency; the degradation of the environment with the debris of a comfort-loving impulse-yielding society; the power struggle between the rich consuming nations and the exploited third world; the angry retaliation of the impoverished and the exploited; on a more personal level the exploitation of women by men, of children by adults, of the elderly by a youth-worshiping society—it is enough to suggest the hypothesis that a dramatic reduction and control of power might improve the mental health of people. (pp. 577–578)

SUMMARY

The field of psychology appears to be narrowing its substantive focus. The growing emphasis on training graduate students in psychotherapy reflects the growing shortage of psychiatrists and the increasing demand from the general public, particularly from the educated middle class, for professional help with personal probelms. This growth of psychotherapy as the exclusive preoccupation of large numbers of professional psychologists is encouraging the establishment of new professional schools of psychology. Because of the large number of students being attracted to these new schools and the time-limited structure of these programs for earning a degree, their output of doctorates will soon exceed the number granted by the 200 traditional university programs. All of this is leading to a growing tilt in psychology toward professionalism and toward the self-interest reflected in preoccupation with guild issues.

Clearly the number of persons in our society afflicted with "hard-core mental disorders" and others experiencing intense crises each year adds up to many times the number who can be seen in individual psychotherapy. Further, the persons actually seen in individual psychotherapy are not the ones with the most serious problems. The poor, the elderly, children, adolescents, minority-group members, and the unemployed all have high rates of emotional distress, but few of them seek psychotherapy. Psychologists are lured into one-to-one intervention with middle-class clients because of financial rewards and status and the growing visibility of psychotherapists as the new priestly class.

Psychologists interested in psychotherapeutic practice find that they must accept the medical model of disturbance in order to qualify for third-party payments. The field of medicine, and particularly psychiatry, embraces a model (each disease has a separate cause) that discourages and downplays the importance of efforts at primary prevention until the cause has been discovered. Psychology is in danger of neglecting primary-prevention efforts because of its identification with the traditional illness model.

Hopefully a group of dedicated, hard-core preventionists will continue to do research and to demonstrate the compelling arguments favoring prevention efforts as the only way to ever reduce the enormous number of disturbed people in our society. Prevention inevitably means social change and political action leading to a more just and equitable society along the lines suggested in Rawls (1971) and Joffe and Albee (1981). For the near future, however, it is difficult to see how U.S. psychology can avoid being split into two or more incompatible factions.

REFERENCES

Albee, G. *Mental health manpower trends.* New York: Basic Books, 1959.

Albee, G. A declaration of independence for psychology. *Ohio Psychologist,* June 1964.

Albee, G. The uncertain future of clinical psychology. *American Psychologist,* 1970, *25,* 1071-1080.

Albee, G. To thine own self be true. *American Psychologist,* 1975, *30,* 1156-1158.

Albee, G. Psychiatry's human resources: 20 years later. *Hospital and Community Psychiatry,* 1979, *30,* 783-786.

Albee, G. *Science and social change: The primary prevention of disturbance in youth.* St. Paul: Center for Youth Development and Research, University of Minnesota, 1980.

Albee, G., & Joffe, J. (Eds.). *The issues: An overview of primary prevention.* Primary Prevention of Psychopathology (Vol. 1). Hanover, N.H.: University Press of New England, 1977.

American Psychiatric Association. *Diagnostic and statistical manual of mental disorders* (3rd ed.). Washington, D.C.: Author, 1980.

American Psychological Association, Committee on Employment and Human Resources, 1980, Annual Report, mimeographed. (Available from the American Psychological Association, Washington, D.C.).

Bloom, B. *Community mental health: A general introduction.* Monterey, Calif.: Brooks/Cole, 1977.

Bond, l., & Rosen, J. (Eds.). *Competence and coping during adulthood.* Primary Prevention of Psychopathology (Vol. 4). Hanover, N.H.: University Press of New England, 1980.

Derner, G. Debate with Albee. *The Clinical Psychologist,* 1977, *30,* 3.

Forgays, D. (Ed.). *Environmental influences.* Primary Prevention of Psychopathology (Vol. 2). Hanover, N.H.: University Press of New England, 1978.

Freud, S. *The question of lay analysis.* In standard edition of the complete works of Sigmund Freud. London: Hogarth Press, 1957.

Glasscote, R., Sanders, D., & Forstenzer, H. *The community mental health center: An analysis of existing models.* Washington, D.C.: Joint Information Service, 1964.

Gordon, J. Personal communication, 1957.

Joint Commission on Mental Illness and Health. *Action for mental health.* New York: Basic Books, 1960.

Joffe, J., & Albee, G. *Prevention through political action and social change.* Hanover, N.H.: University Press of New England, 1981.

Kent, M., & Rolf, J. (Eds.). *Promoting social competence in children,* Primary prevention of psychopathology (Vol. 3). Hanover, N.H.: University Press of New England, 1979.

Kessler, M., & Albee, G. Primary prevention. *Annual Review of Psychology,* 1975, *26,* 557–591.

Kiesler, C. Mental health policy as a field of inquiry for psychology. *American Psychologist,* 1980, *35,* 1066–1080.

Klerman, G. *The limits of mental health.* Paper presented at University of Vermont Seminar on Social and Behavioral Origins of Mental Illness, Burlington, March 13, 1980.

Lamb, H. R., & Zusman, J. Primary prevention in perspective. *American Journal of Psychiatry,* 1979, *136,* 12–17.

Marx, K., & Engels, F. Manifesto of the communist party: Section II. In Karl Marx (Ed.), *Selected works* (Vol. 1). New York: International Publishers, 1936.

President's Commission on Mental Health. *Report to the president.* Washington, D. C.: U.S. Government Printing Office, 1978.

President's Commission on Mental Health. Task Panel on Migrant and Seasonal Farmworkers. *Report.* Washington, D.C.: U.S. Government Printing Office, 1978.

President's Commission on Mental Health, Task Panel on Prevention. *Report on Primary Prevention.* Washington, D.C.: U.S. Government Printing Office, 1978.

Rawls, J. *A theory of justice.* Cambridge, Mass.: Harvard University Press, 1971.

Ryan, W. *Distress in the city.* Cleveland, Ohio: Case Western University Press, 1969.

Silverman, P. R. *Mutual help groups: A guide for mental health workers.* DHEW, Pub. No. (ADM) 78-646. Washington, D.C.: National Institute for Mental Health, 1978.

Sue, D., Sue, D. W., & Sue, S. *Understanding abnormal behavior.* Boston: Houghton-Mifflin, 1981.

Index